Lecture Notes in Computer Science   10291

Commenced Publication in 1973
Founding and Former Series Editors:
Gerhard Goos, Juris Hartmanis, and Jan van Leeuwen

More information about this series at http://www.springer.com/series/7409

Norbert Streitz · Panos Markopoulos (Eds.)

Distributed, Ambient and Pervasive Interactions

5th International Conference, DAPI 2017
Held as Part of HCI International 2017
Vancouver, BC, Canada, July 9–14, 2017
Proceedings

 Springer

Editors
Norbert Streitz
Smart Future Initiative
Frankfurt
Germany

Panos Markopoulos
Eindhoven University of Technology
Eindhoven
The Netherlands

ISSN 0302-9743   ISSN 1611-3349   (electronic)
Lecture Notes in Computer Science
ISBN 978-3-319-58696-0   ISBN 978-3-319-58697-7   (eBook)
DOI 10.1007/978-3-319-58697-7

Library of Congress Control Number: 2017940252

LNCS Sublibrary: SL3 – Information Systems and Applications, incl. Internet/Web, and HCI

Printed on acid-free paper

This Springer imprint is published by Springer Nature
The registered company is Springer International Publishing AG
The registered company address is: Gewerbestrasse 11, 6330 Cham, Switzerland

Foreword

The 19th International Conference on Human–Computer Interaction, HCI International 2017, was held in Vancouver, Canada, during July 9–14, 2017. The event incorporated the 15 conferences/thematic areas listed on the following page.

A total of 4,340 individuals from academia, research institutes, industry, and governmental agencies from 70 countries submitted contributions, and 1,228 papers have been included in the proceedings. These papers address the latest research and development efforts and highlight the human aspects of design and use of computing systems. The papers thoroughly cover the entire field of human–computer interaction, addressing major advances in knowledge and effective use of computers in a variety of application areas. The volumes constituting the full set of the conference proceedings are listed on the following pages.

I would like to thank the program board chairs and the members of the program boards of all thematic areas and affiliated conferences for their contribution to the highest scientific quality and the overall success of the HCI International 2017 conference.

This conference would not have been possible without the continuous and unwavering support and advice of the founder, Conference General Chair Emeritus and Conference Scientific Advisor Prof. Gavriel Salvendy. For his outstanding efforts, I would like to express my appreciation to the communications chair and editor of *HCI International News*, Dr. Abbas Moallem.

April 2017   Constantine Stephanidis

HCI International 2017 Thematic Areas and Affiliated Conferences

Thematic areas:

- Human–Computer Interaction (HCI 2017)
- Human Interface and the Management of Information (HIMI 2017)

Affiliated conferences:

- 17th International Conference on Engineering Psychology and Cognitive Ergonomics (EPCE 2017)
- 11th International Conference on Universal Access in Human–Computer Interaction (UAHCI 2017)
- 9th International Conference on Virtual, Augmented and Mixed Reality (VAMR 2017)
- 9th International Conference on Cross-Cultural Design (CCD 2017)
- 9th International Conference on Social Computing and Social Media (SCSM 2017)
- 11th International Conference on Augmented Cognition (AC 2017)
- 8th International Conference on Digital Human Modeling and Applications in Health, Safety, Ergonomics and Risk Management (DHM 2017)
- 6th International Conference on Design, User Experience and Usability (DUXU 2017)
- 5th International Conference on Distributed, Ambient and Pervasive Interactions (DAPI 2017)
- 5th International Conference on Human Aspects of Information Security, Privacy and Trust (HAS 2017)
- 4th International Conference on HCI in Business, Government and Organizations (HCIBGO 2017)
- 4th International Conference on Learning and Collaboration Technologies (LCT 2017)
- Third International Conference on Human Aspects of IT for the Aged Population (ITAP 2017)

Conference Proceedings Volumes Full List

1. LNCS 10271, Human–Computer Interaction: User Interface Design, Development and Multimodality (Part I), edited by Masaaki Kurosu
2. LNCS 10272 Human–Computer Interaction: Interaction Contexts (Part II), edited by Masaaki Kurosu
3. LNCS 10273, Human Interface and the Management of Information: Information, Knowledge and Interaction Design (Part I), edited by Sakae Yamamoto
4. LNCS 10274, Human Interface and the Management of Information: Supporting Learning, Decision-Making and Collaboration (Part II), edited by Sakae Yamamoto
5. LNAI 10275, Engineering Psychology and Cognitive Ergonomics: Performance, Emotion and Situation Awareness (Part I), edited by Don Harris
6. LNAI 10276, Engineering Psychology and Cognitive Ergonomics: Cognition and Design (Part II), edited by Don Harris
7. LNCS 10277, Universal Access in Human–Computer Interaction: Design and Development Approaches and Methods (Part I), edited by Margherita Antona and Constantine Stephanidis
8. LNCS 10278, Universal Access in Human–Computer Interaction: Designing Novel Interactions (Part II), edited by Margherita Antona and Constantine Stephanidis
9. LNCS 10279, Universal Access in Human–Computer Interaction: Human and Technological Environments (Part III), edited by Margherita Antona and Constantine Stephanidis
10. LNCS 10280, Virtual, Augmented and Mixed Reality, edited by Stephanie Lackey and Jessie Y.C. Chen
11. LNCS 10281, Cross-Cultural Design, edited by Pei-Luen Patrick Rau
12. LNCS 10282, Social Computing and Social Media: Human Behavior (Part I), edited by Gabriele Meiselwitz
13. LNCS 10283, Social Computing and Social Media: Applications and Analytics (Part II), edited by Gabriele Meiselwitz
14. LNAI 10284, Augmented Cognition: Neurocognition and Machine Learning (Part I), edited by Dylan D. Schmorrow and Cali M. Fidopiastis
15. LNAI 10285, Augmented Cognition: Enhancing Cognition and Behavior in Complex Human Environments (Part II), edited by Dylan D. Schmorrow and Cali M. Fidopiastis
16. LNCS 10286, Digital Human Modeling and Applications in Health, Safety, Ergonomics and Risk Management: Ergonomics and Design (Part I), edited by Vincent G. Duffy
17. LNCS 10287, Digital Human Modeling and Applications in Health, Safety, Ergonomics and Risk Management: Health and Safety (Part II), edited by Vincent G. Duffy
18. LNCS 10288, Design, User Experience, and Usability: Theory, Methodology and Management (Part I), edited by Aaron Marcus and Wentao Wang

Distributed, Ambient and Pervasive Interactions

Program Board Chair(s): **Norbert Streitz, Germany, and Panos Markopoulos, The Netherlands**

- Andreas Braun, Germany
- Adrian David Cheok, Malaysia
- Richard Chow, USA
- Alois Ferscha, Linz, Austria
- Dimitris Grammenos, Greece
- Nuno Guimarães, Portugal
- Dirk Heylen, The Netherlands
- Pedro Isaias, Portugal
- Achilles Kameas, Greece
- Javed Vassilis Khan, The Netherlands
- Kristian Kloeckl, USA
- Shin'ichi Konomi, Japan
- Ben Kröse, The Netherlands
- Antonio Maña, Spain
- Don Marinelli, USA
- Irene Mavrommati, Greece
- Ingrid Mulder, The Netherlands
- Anton Nijholt, The Netherlands
- Fabio Paternó, Italy
- Victor M.R. Penichet, Spain
- Susa Pop, Germany
- Carsten Röcker, Germany
- Tanya Toft, Denmark
- Reiner Wichert, Germany
- Woontack Woo, South Korea
- Xenophon Zabulis, Greece

The full list with the Program Board Chairs and the members of the Program Boards of all thematic areas and affiliated conferences is available online at:

http://www.hci.international/board-members-2017.php

HCI International 2018

The 20th International Conference on Human–Computer Interaction, HCI International 2018, will be held jointly with the affiliated conferences in Las Vegas, NV, USA, at Caesars Palace, July 15–20, 2018. It will cover a broad spectrum of themes related to human–computer interaction, including theoretical issues, methods, tools, processes, and case studies in HCI design, as well as novel interaction techniques, interfaces, and applications. The proceedings will be published by Springer. More information is available on the conference website: http://2018.hci.international/.

General Chair
Prof. Constantine Stephanidis
University of Crete and ICS-FORTH
Heraklion, Crete, Greece
E-mail: general_chair@hcii2018.org

http://2018.hci.international/

Contents

Natural Interaction

Smart Cities

Art and Cultural Heritage in Smart Environments

Ambient Games and Humour

Designing and Evaluating Distributed, Ambient and Pervasive Interactions

What Changes from Ubiquitous Computing to Internet of Things in Interaction Evaluation?

Rossana M.C. Andrade[1(✉)], Rainara M. Carvalho[1], Italo Linhares de Araújo[1], Káthia M. Oliveira[2], and Marcio E.F. Maia[1]

[1] Group of Computer Networks, Software Engineering and Systems (GREat)
Graduate Program in Computer Science (MDCC),
Federal University of Ceará, Fortaleza, Brazil
{rossana,rainaracarvalho,italoaraujo,marcio}@great.ufc.br
[2] Laboratory of Automatic Control, Mechanics and Computer Science for Industrial and Human-machine Systems (LAMIH), University of Valenciennes and Hainaut-Cambrésis (UVHC), CNRS UMR, 8201 Valenciennes, France
kathia.oliveira@univ-valenciennes.fr

Abstract. Internet of Things (IoT) is a new paradigm that includes a network of smart objects, which are embedded sensors, communicating using the Internet. One of the areas that are leading up to IoT is Ubiquitous Computing (UbiComp). There are thus solutions such as frameworks, middlewares, and other development artifacts that come from the UbiComp community and can be used for IoT applications. On the other hand, the interaction evaluation of the applications can be more complex in IoT than in UbiComp systems, once we have two different perspectives: Human-Thing and Thing-Thing interactions. In this paper, based on the literature, our experience in these two domains, and case studies with Ubicomp and IoT applications, we discuss how we can benefit from the UbiComp move towards IoT, focusing on the main differences and similarities related to interaction evaluation. These differences open a set of questions that are also presented and discussed in this paper.

Keywords: Internet of Things · Ubiquitous computing · Quality characteristics · Software measures · Interaction evaluation

1 Introduction

The Internet of Things (IoT) paradigm has recently emerged, and one of the areas that are leading up to IoT is Ubiquitous Computing (UbiComp) [32,52]. The evolution happened due to the association with other areas, such as Cloud Computing, and the hardware advance, which allowed the improvement of the sensors, actuators and the creation of smaller devices with a network connection [1]. In this paradigm, we have several things communicating between themselves.

R.M.C. Andrade—Researcher Scholarship - DT Level 2, sponsored by CNPq
I.L. de Araújo—PhD Scholarship (MDCC/DC/UFC) sponsored by CAPES.

© Springer International Publishing AG 2017
N. Streitz and P. Markopoulos (Eds.): DAPI 2017, LNCS 10291, pp. 3–21, 2017.
DOI: 10.1007/978-3-319-58697-7_1

A thing is an object/device of our daily routine with sensors, actuators, embedded computing and wirelessly interoperable [36].

Ubiquitous Computing (UbiComp), in turn, was defined in 1991 by Mark Weiser who considers that "the most profound technologies are those that disappear. They weave themselves into the fabric of everyday life until they are indistinguishable from it" [55]. UbiComp makes then the technology present in our daily life able to monitor us and provide services, but we do not perceive that we interact with these technologies.

Although UbiComp has preceded IoT and we could identify commonalities between them, the challenges related to building IoT systems are far more complex. These problems arise mainly because of the number of things that make the IoT systems and the different role they play [18,35].

Nevertheless, the interaction evaluation can be even more complex in IoT than in UbiComp systems once we have two different perspectives to take into account: Human-Thing and Thing-Thing interactions [30]. The first one is the interaction between users and things and has more commonalities with the UbiComp interaction evaluation [31]. The second one is the interaction between things themselves [51], which is both a novelty and a challenge.

In this paper, we investigate the innovations and issues introduced by things, considering the literature, our previous experience with Ubicomp [25,26,39], and case studies. Then, we discuss how we can benefit from the UbiComp move towards IoT, highlighting the main commonalities and differences related to interaction evaluation.

For the case studies on interaction evaluation, we choose three ubiquitous applications and two IoT applications. This evaluation was performed using a set of measures that focused on characteristics for UbiComp, such as context-awareness, mobility, transparency, attention and calmness [8], which are also presented in IoT Systems. The results showed that is possible to apply the same measures in both Ubicomp and IoT applications to evaluate user interaction. However, there are specific restrictions of IoT systems that also need to be considered and prioritized in the evaluation. So, we believe and discuss throughout this paper that Thing-Thing interaction severely impacts on Human-Thing interaction evaluation, for example, the responsiveness of the system changes because things are on the Internet [41] and the answer can take a while.

The remainder of this paper is organized as follows. Section 2 presents the main concepts about Human-Computer Interaction (HCI) Evaluation in UbiComp and a brief overview about IoT. Section 3 presents the case studies with UbiComp and IoT applications. Section 4 presents a discussion about open questions that allow the identification of important research challenges and a brief conclusion is presented in Sect. 5.

2   Background

In this section, we bring a brief overview of the ubiquitous computing concepts highlighting the context-awareness and other characteristics that impact the quality of user interaction in these systems. We also introduce the main concepts and elements of IoT to give a general outline to the reader.

2.1 HCI Evaluation in UbiComp

As we introduced before, the Ubiquitous Computing was coined by Mark Weiser in 1991 and became a well-established research area [55]. The main motivation behind UbiComp is to support the user with daily activities without the user noticing they are interacting with a computing infrastructure. Therefore, the technology should be invisible or cause a minimal distraction to the user, changing completely the way users interact with systems [45].

To achieve Mark Weiser's vision of UbiComp, the system should be capable of understanding user's behavior. This is enabled by context-awareness, which captures relevant information during the interaction between users and applications, and applies it to support users in performing their tasks [11]. Therefore, UbiComp allows that the systems capture various information (*e.g.*, GPS, temperature, accelerometer, and magnetometer) without the user noticing, or by voice, gesture and touch. These new sources of inputs make the interaction with users much more natural [8] and allow the interaction being initiated by the system itself.

Regarding HCI evaluation in Ubicomp, a systematic mapping study that we performed in [8] identifies a set of 27 essential quality characteristics to evaluate ubiquitous systems that run in mobile devices (see Fig. 1).

All characteristics found in the systematic mapping impact, somehow, on the quality of interaction in ubiquitous systems and, therefore, need to be taken into account. However, there are general characteristics for any system (for instance, efficiency and security) and specific characteristics for ubicomp applications (marked in bold in Fig. 1). These particular characteristics are better explained as follows:

- Context-awareness is the system's capability of monitoring contextual information regarding the user, the system, and the environment. With this information, the system dynamically and proactively adapts its functions accordingly [20].
- Mobility in Ubiquitous Computing refers to the continuous or uninterrupted use of the systems while the user moves across several devices [56][1].
- Transparency is the system's ability to hide its computing infrastructure in the environment, so the user does not realize that is interacting with a set of computational devices [48].

---

[1] According to [56], there are several definitions for Mobility and they are highly dependent on the community or area. For example, distributed computing introduced mobility as a process migration into operating systems. Mobile computing brings a notion of mobility by making communication, entertainment, and Internet possible while the user is in motion. Then, mobility in this paper is a superset of several areas. The idea is that no computational or communication gap (*e.g.*, networks) should exist when users move.

Acceptability **Attention**

Calmness Availability Device Capability

Ease of Use   Efficiency **Context-Awareness**

Effectiveness Familiarity Interconnectivity

Privacy Network Capability **Mobility** Predictability

Reliability Reversibility

Robustness Scalability

Security

Simplicity Safety Trust

Transparency Utility

Usability User Satisfaction

Fig. 1. Characteristics for HCI evaluation in ubiquitous systems.

- Attention in ubiquitous environment refers to the system's ability to keep the user's focus on real-world interactions rather than in technology [17].
- Calmness is the system's capability of interacting with the user at the right time and situation, presenting only relevant information, using the periphery and the center of attention only when necessary and being easy and natural to use [38].

As these five characteristics directly impact the quality of interaction in Ubi-Comp applications, they need to be taken into account by an HCI evaluation. One way of evaluating these characteristics is using software measures. Our systematic mapping in [8] found 218 citations of measures associated with these five quality characteristics. Most measures found are defined to evaluate the Context-awareness characteristic (44 measures)[8].

However, most of them are simple definitions with no detail about their measurement functions. Because of that, our group has been working on the definition of software measures for these characteristics [14,15,45]. For instance, Table 1 shows a set of software measures for the *Calmness* characteristic already presented in [6].

Knowing that IoT presents similar characteristics from UbiComp, for example, context-awareness [35,52] and transparency [54], it is feasible to use software measures from this area to evaluate the interactions in IoT, *i.e.*, Human-Thing and Thing-Thing interactions.

Table 1. Software measures for the calmness characteristic. Adapted from [6]

Name	Measurement Function
Adaptation degree	$\frac{\sum_{j=1}^{N}(Aj/Bj)*100}{N}$
	Aj=Number of performed adaptations i
	Bj=Number of requested adaptations i
	N=Number of adaptations
Adaptation correctness	$\frac{\sum_{i=1}^{N}(Ai/Bi)*100}{N}$
	Ai=Number of correctly performed adaptations i
	Bi=Number of performed adaptations i
	N=Number of adaptations
Availability degree	X = B, where B is the the element that appears most often among the following options answered by users (i.e., the mode)
	(1) Very Low, (2) Low, (3) Medium and (4) High
Context-awareness timing degree	X = B is the mode
	(1) Very Low, (2) Low, (3) Medium and (4) High
Relevancy degree	X = B, where B is the mode
	(1) Very Low, (2) Low, (3) Medium and (4) High
Courtesy degree	X = B, where B is the mode
	(1) Very Low, (2) Low, (3) Medium and (4) High

2.2 IoT

According to IEEE [32], Internet of Things is a network of objects, which are embedded devices, connected to the Internet [32]. Considering this, Fuqaha et al. [1] define IoT to be formed by six elementary building blocks (see Fig. 2): (i) identification; (ii) sensing; (iii) communication; (iv) computation; (v) services; and (vi) semantic.

The first element, the identification, allows an object to be accessed over the Internet by other objects, in a Thing-Thing interaction, or by an application

Fig. 2. The IoT elements. Source [1]

controlled by the user, in a Human-Thing interaction. Here, the identification is comprised of two elements: (i) the network address of the thing, and (ii) the description of its functionality (*e.g.*, light or A/C).

The sensing is responsible for capturing the information from the environment or for actuating to change that information. Examples of information that can be collected or controlled are luminosity level and temperature. Finally, information gathered from the environment or changed when the actuation is completed must be available on the Internet to be accessed by others things or applications [1].

The communication element is responsible for connecting a thing using the identification element. In IoT, there are several protocols to facilitate the communication, both at the network layer, such as Bluetooth, Wi-Fi, LTE, or NFC, and at the application layer, such as the Constrained Application Protocol (CoAP)[2] and the Message Queue Telemetry Transport (MQTT)[3]. In the network layer, the characteristics of the communication technologies, like range, energy consumption, reliability or routing protocols, define their applicability according to the characteristics of the things. In the application layer, the functionalities required by the application guide the selection of the most appropriate protocol.

The goal of the computation is to process the information perceived from the environment, and to decide when acting on the environment is required, based on the processed information. The processing is executed both on the things embedded in the environment and on processing units located in the cloud. The decision to process it locally on the thing or on the cloud depends on the processing capabilities of the embedded devices, the load inserted by the processing algorithm and the response time required by the application.

The services are an abstraction used to represent the things, with two main responsibilities: (i) encapsulate the functionality provided by each thing; and (ii) provide a known interface to access that functionality. Services improve the interoperability; they hide details about the things, such as operating system or programming language [1].

And the last element, semantics, allows the knowledge representation of both the information collected by the thing and the information processed either by the thing or by a cloud unit [1].

These elements are present in different domains, like e-health, transportation, agriculture. For example, in healthcare, things (smartwatch, camera, presence sensor, heart rate sensor, among others) monitor an elderly in his/her house and the application sends the collected information to the physician, where he/she can control this information and improve user care. In transportation, for example, users can monitor the status of vehicles and they can send a command to change the behavior if it is necessary. Or yet, to control the growth of the plants in agriculture monitoring the sun rays, humidity, rain, among others.

In all these scenarios, the Thing-Thing interaction is present. The work from [51] calls the Thing-Thing communication as machine to machine (M2M).

---

[2] http://coap.technology/.
[3] http://mqtt.org/.

However, M2M refers to those solutions that allow communication between devices of the same type and a specific application, all via wired or wireless communication networks and does not generally allow for the broad sharing of data or connection of the things directly to the Internet [18]. In contrast, IoT also refers to the connection of such systems and sensors to the broader Internet. Therefore, the Thing-Thing interaction refers to the communication between things over the Internet [18]. Then, we believe that the evaluation for IoT should also take into account characteristics of the Thing-Thing interaction that is a critical part of the IoT environment.

Analyzing the IoT elements and the scenarios they are used, two UbiComp features can be identified in IoT as well: context-awareness and adaptability. Context-awareness captures the information from the user environment to provide a better service to the user. The Adaptability uses context information to make changes in the application behavior. For example, when the mobile application identifies the user location to be nearby his/her house, the application sends this information to the user's home and the air conditioner is turned on[4].

In [36], another important feature influencing the application behavior is presented: spontaneous interaction. Razzaque et al. said that subtle interactions exist when users and things move around, coming in and out of their communication range leading to the spontaneous generation of events. Hence, subtle interactions between things have significant implications in the Human-Thing interaction as well. This characteristic can be compared with the service discovery and the context-aware from UbiComp. This occurs for the sake of the new services that can be provided and adapted based on the new devices in or out of the environment.

3   Applications and Evaluations

The applications that are presented in this paper are an essential part of the research conducted by the Group on Computer Networks, Software Engineering and Systems (GREat) of the Federal University of Ceará (UFC). They are a result of both research projects and undergraduate and graduate students work that were developed over the past ten years.

In this section, first, we present three ubiquitous applications as follows. GREatTour is a product of a Mobile Guide dynamic software product line (DSPL) [28,29] and we have been using this application to evaluate several masters and Ph.D. theses in DSPL [2,27,42–44,47] and HCI quality evaluation [16,40,46]. Both GREatMute and GREatPrint were developed in two different master theses to evaluate their findings [34,46].

Then, we show two IoT applications, which are our first efforts to move from Ubicomp to IoT: GREat Room [10] and Automa GREat. Both applications are

---

[4] In the previous section, we defined context-awareness as one of the five characteristics to be evaluated in Ubicomp applications. Adaptability, in this case, is provided by context-awareness, which is the characteristic applied to evaluate IoT applications in this work.

a result of a graduate course about IoT and they have been used as case studies for our research in IoT [4].

3.1 UbiComp Applications

GREat Tour is a UbiComp application to guide visitors in the GREat laboratory [29]. For each room visited, the application shows texts, images, videos, audios and persons who work there. GREat Tour shows this information according to the visitor's location inside the lab. The application also presents some information according to battery level. For example, if the battery's charge is more than 50%, the application presents all kinds of medias. If the charge is less than 50 and more than 30%, the application blocks the videos to the user. If it is less than 30%, the application does not show images and videos.

GREatMute aims to turn off the device's sound according to the user's appointment in his/her agenda and current location [6]. For example, if the user has an appointment 4 p.m. in an office registered in the calendar, the application will check if the user local is equal to the defined in the agenda in the hour recorded. If the answer is affirmative, the sound is turned off. Moreover, this application allows users to specify for which events they would like the device to be put into silent mode; this is done by monitoring for matches with the keywords registered in the system. When the application finds an event in which the title has one of the recorded keywords, GREatMute extracts the information of the start time and end time of the event, using this information to put the phone into the silent profile during this period.

GREatPrint aims to print documents at the nearest printer from the user, providing a ubiquitous and mobile printing service [7]. The application works as follows: after selecting a file, the user click on the print button of the given document, and the application collects the six Wi-Fi networks previously mapped in the laboratory. Then the application sends the document to the server. Based on the GREatPrint Server response, GREatPrint App notifies the user where the file has been printed or if it was not possible to print the file.

These ubiquitous mobile applications (See Fig. 3) were evaluated regarding the following five quality characteristics presented in Sect. 2.1: context-awareness, mobility, transparency, attention, and calmness. Twenty-four measures were collected to evaluate these characteristics, some examples of such measures are presented in Table 1. More details about these evaluations can be found in [6,7]. However, we present some examples of the results of these evaluations in Table 2.

The collection of these software measures makes possible to evaluate the quality of interaction in the applications. The results are an indication that the measures are capable of evaluating a ubiquitous application according to the selected HCI quality characteristics.

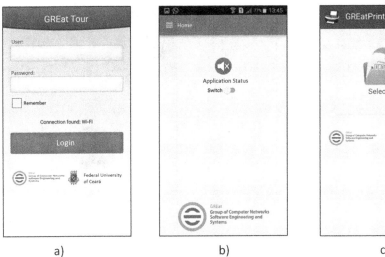

a)   b)   c)

Fig. 3. Screens of (a) GREat Tour, (b) GREat Mute, and (c) GREat print

Table 2. Results for UbiComp applications evaluations. Adapted from [6]

Measure	GREat Tour	GREatMute	GREatPrint
Adaptation degree	72%	92%	79%
Adaptation correctness	100%	27%	52%
Availability degree	Medium	High	Medium
Context-awareness timing degree	Medium	Low	Medium
Relevancy degree	High/Medium	High	High
Courtesy degree	High	High	High

3.2 IoT Applications

Automa GREat is an IoT application developed to control airs conditioners and the lamps of the GREat Lab's seminar room. The users can switch on/off the air conditioners and increase and decrease the temperature. About the lights, the users can turn on/off and set their color and intensity. There are two modes of user interaction with the application: manual and automatic. In the manual mode, the user controls all things, and in the automatic mode, the application uses the motion sensor to turn on/off the things. To manage data from/to devices, the application uses the middleware LoCCAM (Loosely Coupled Context Acquisition Middleware) [23] that is based on [24,25,33,34].

GREat Room provides a way to register the presence of people in a particular room, making possible to see who is in that room at a given time and it can create a report about the presence of the persons. Furthermore, the primary requirement is the creation of the virtual group with these individuals to

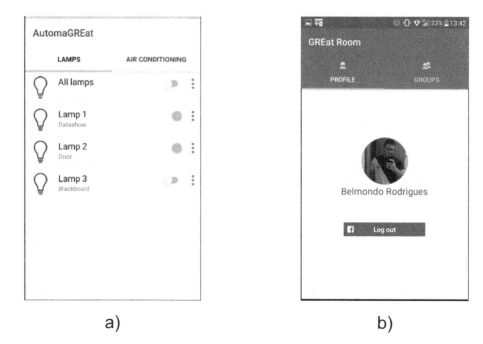

a)   b)

Fig. 4. (a) Screen of the automa GREat, and (b) Screen of the GREat room.

share files. The application uses the information from the beacons to identify new things and persons in the room.

Figure 4 presents the screens of these applications.

These two IoT applications were also evaluated using the software measures for UbiComp applications presented in Sect. 2.1. We present some results of these two evaluations in Table 3. Details of the GREatRoom evaluation can be found in [5].

In general, these measures give us a comprehension into not only whether the app achieves the Human-Thing interaction or not, but also what can be improved

Table 3. Results of IoT applications evaluations. Adapted from [6]

Measure	GREatRoom	AutomaGREat
Adaptation degree	78%	0%
Adaptation correctness	79%	0%
Availability degree	High	Medium
Context-awareness timing degree	High	Medium
Relevancy degree	High	High
Courtesy degree	High	Low

in the application. For example, GREatRoom still needs to be improved regarding the adaptation degree (78%) and adaptation correctness (79%). These measures obtained bad results, because the application presented some problems when the user position is on the border between two environments, where the system cannot be sure which room the user should assign. Moreover, we discover that Automa GREat is not working regarding the context-awareness, which means the application cannot adapt itself when the user enters or leaves a room.

In other measures, we found results that diverge between both applications. For example, we have considerable differences in the "Availability Degree" and "Courtesy Degree". The GREat Room receives the best evaluation, because it reacts correctly and in the better and calm way. Automa GREat, in turn, does not work well in the automatic mode for the sake of the inability of detecting the user presence. This leaves the result "low" in the measure that checks if the behavior changed was the better one. The value "medium" in the "Availability Degree" occurs, because the application does not perform the required functions. Users also consider that the application does not interact at the right moment, what leaves us with the result "medium" in "Context-awareness Timing Degree".

4   Discussion

In this section, based on the applications' evaluations, the literature, and our experience, we discuss how we can benefit from the UbiComp move towards IoT. Also, we detail the main differences between these two kind of applications' evaluations, highlighting what was not detected by the measures from UbiComp applied in the case studies in the previous section. We used the following four open questions to organize our discussion.

What are the commonalities of HCI UbiComp evaluation that can be also used in IoT applications?

The characteristics and measures that come from UbiComp, which are presented in Sect. 2.1, are also useful to evaluate IoT applications and they give us a good insight into what can be improved in IoT applications as presented in Sect. 3. For example, GREatRoom needs to be improved regarding adaptation degree and adaptation correctness degree. Automa GREat, in turn, needs to be improved regarding all measures for the Calmness characteristic. Therefore, these case studies show an example that characteristics and measures for UbiComp are useful to IoT applications. Nevertheless, the evaluations presented in Sect. 3 indicate that:

- The same UbiComp evaluation process can be used to IoT applications. In our work, we used the same process from usability testing with profile questionnaires, observation, and measures collections;
- The necessary data collection for the measures calculation in IoT applications requires the same effort as in UbiComp applications. All IoT applications need to be instrumented like we do in UbiComp applications;

- The questionnaires used to capture the subjective measures from users are relevant and suitable in IoT as well; and
- The results from the measures in IoT can be interpreted following the same analysis procedure as in Ubicomp.

Our answer is that good part of what is used in Human-Things evaluation in UbiComp can be used in IoT. However, several problems arise from the Thing-Thing interaction that needs to be evaluated as pointed out in the next questions.

What interaction problems were not identified in the IoT applications by the UbiComp measures?

Regarding the case studies presented in the previous section, the collected measures were not able to identify several problems that the IoT applications presented. For example, GREatRoom presents problems when multiple mobile devices enter and exit a room, because it generates an inconsistency in the data presented in the application's interface to different users. This is a problem of things being out of sync with the other things.

The other problem is the lack of conflicts handling. Conflicts occur among contrasting goals [37]. Despite being a subject already explored in the field of smart homes and ubiquitous computing, IoT brings greater complexity to this problem, because IoT environments allow remote control by users, automated rules programmed by users and context-aware decisions in the same system. For example, the other application, Automa GREat, has no conflicts handling. If two users send opposing requests, Automa GREat is not able to handle this conflict. Another problem regarding conflicts in IoT, not detected by the evaluations, is when a user may want to turn the lamp on remotely via smartphone, but the application wants to turn it off because no one is at home. Therefore, the measures from UbiComp are not able to evaluate if there are conflicts in Human-Thing and Thing-Thing interactions.

Another issue that was observed during the case study with Automa GREat was a delay when users turned on the air conditioner, which affects the system's responsiveness. Also, the state of things (*i.e.*, air conditioning and lights) were not being displayed properly in the interface, whenever the user changed the tab, the application loses the current state about the things.

In short, the main interaction problems that arise from IoT applications are related to the Thing-Thing interaction, which impact on the Human-Thing interaction. So, to answer this question taking into account the case studies, we should consider the following: synchrony, the lack of conflicts handling and communication delay between things.

What characteristics and measures of Thing-Thing interaction should be evaluated in IoT systems?

Based on the previously questions and literature review, we classify the characteristics that should be evaluated according to two levels: Internet and Thing.

Internet-level is related to intrinsic characteristics of the communication between the things. The only work found, for now, that mentions characteristics for the Thing-Thing interaction is [41], which consider synchronicity, responsiveness, and reliability as significant issues to the interaction quality. These are discussed as follows.

- Synchronicity: The things may be out of sync with other things. In GREat-Room, for example, the time it takes to synchrony the things can not be long because the application can show different information for different users that are in the same context [41]. In Automa GREat, the air conditioner may show a different temperature than what is displayed on the user's device.
- Responsiveness: There are no certainties about how fast it will be for two things to communicate with each other though the Internet. The result is that latency (the time it takes for a message to pass through the network) can be unpredictable, which affects the system responsiveness [41]. In Automa GREat, for example, it is important to measure the time it takes to turn on the air conditioner. This time will affect the user perception of the quality of the interaction.
- Reliability: A command sent through Internet can fail to arrive. It is hard to guarantee that a user command will not get lost. It is not acceptable to have everyday objects failing about their main functions [41]. For example, in Automa GREat, no user would like to use application that fails to turn on lights and air conditioner. Then, it is important to measure, for example, how many failures occur and the time between failures.

Thing-level characteristics are related to components/characteristics that the things may have, and that can be very challenging for Thing-Thing interaction quality and, consequently, to the Human-Thing interaction quality. Battery, context-awareness, interoperability and difficulty of installation are important issues to the Thing-Thing interaction quality.

- Battery: Some things need to be connected all the time, and this requires a lot of energy. It is a big issue manage the trade-off between network and battery. If a thing goes off-line because of battery, the other things will not be synchronized, and then, the synchrony will be affected [41].
- Context-Awareness: The things must have the ability to correctly sensing the environment and the user [35]. If a single thing fails about the context, a chain of failures can happen between things that are connected with it.
- Interoperability: We do not have a real Internet of Things today. In a true IoT, anything can connect to any other thing. However, today, many things are locked in proprietary ecosystems [41,50].
- Difficult of installation: The difficult of installation is about the process of connecting things with other things already existent. This process can be very difficult for a user, since they may use different network technologies [9,19,49].

Therefore, our answer is that software measures should be defined to evaluate the characteristics discussed above: Synchronicity, Responsiveness, Reliability, Battery, Context-Awareness, Interoperability and Difficult of installation.

What are the major challenges to the interaction in IoT applications?

The challenges are related to the increased complexity that an IoT system can have [41,50]. It is possible to add several smart objects in an IoT environment, for example, a smart lock for a door, an intelligent air-conditioning, and a smart coffee. Each one can deliver a service to another. This brings several challenges for the interaction, such as interoperability, consistency of the interactions between several objects and interfaces, detection and resolution of conflicts, and the choice of techniques and methods to evaluate the interaction. These challenges are discussed as follows:

- Interoperability: One of the main challenges of IoT lies into interoperability [41,50,53]. In a true IoT, things can connect with each other, independently of the manufacturer. Today, many IoT devices do not work with all other IoT devices [50]. People are using single IoT systems, for example, Nest[5], Philips lamps[6], Danalock[7], SmartThings[8]. This represents a problem for user interaction because they will depend on the manufacturer. This lack of interoperability between things is important to designers because it creates idealized expectations from IoT that today cannot be achieved [41].
- Consistency of the Interactions: An IoT system can have many interfaces (*e.g.*, mobile phones, tablets, desktops) and many devices [50]. A recent study from [12] states that support for multi-device interactions has fallen behind users' request to leverage the diverse capabilities of the devices that surround them. Thus, there is a difficulty in designing interactions between devices [21], especially in IoT, that one single system will have several components (*e.g.*, mobile interfaces, things, gateways). The lack of tools and methods for testing multi-device user experiences is a research opportunity.
- Verification of Interest Conflicts: an IoT system may have several autonomous rules, many services, many users with different preferences [22]. There is a high risk of users feeling annoyed and overwhelmed by conflicts of interests. Therefore, how to deal with instruction from several users, things and services is a challenge. A research opportunity is to detect or predict if new instructions and actions are in conflict with others.
- Evaluation: There are several possible combinations of things, services, and interfaces that the user could experience, which makes the evaluation a challenge for IoT systems [41,50]. Any combination can generate unexpected behavior and can impact in the user interaction. More research is necessary about how the evaluation has to be performed in such scenarios to efficiently discover user experience problems. Also, it may be necessary to adapt the traditional methods to take into account the Thing-Thing interaction issues

---

[5] https://nest.com/.
[6] http://www.apple.com/br/shop/product/HK9J2BR/A/philips-hue-ambiance-star ter-kit-colorido-10w-a60-220v.
[7] https://danalock.com/.
[8] https://www.smartthings.com/.

previously cited. For example, the existing questionnaires of usability do not consider these issues [3]. Additionally, work from [13] believe that several new heuristics specific to IoT will arise with the spread of the field. We also can cite two more challenges for the evaluation, as follows.

- Data Collection: With our experience in the IoT evaluation, we have also perceived the increase in the complexity of data collection. This occurs for the sake of the various devices presents in the environment. Then, we need to define an interoperable approach capable of accessing these things and capture the data to analyze and evaluate the Thing-Thing interaction.
- Environment Configuration: Moreover, all the situations are important and influence in the data collection such as the environment configuration that contributes and influences in the result of the evaluation. For example, if we consider the infrared sensor embedded in a device in a position inadequate to communicate with another thing, we can have a problem in our data capture and, consequently, in our evaluation.

Therefore, to summarize our answer to the last question, we believe that the main challenges to improve the quality of Human-Thing and Thing-Thing interactions in IoT applications are: Interoperability, Consistency of the Interactions, Verification of Interest Conflicts, and Evaluation.

5   Conclusion

In this paper, we first showed a summary of the HCI quality evaluation in Ubi-Comp and the essential elements of IoT. Then, the interaction evaluation results of three UbiComp applications and two IoT applications are presented. The goal was to identify commonalities and differences between the interaction evaluation of these systems using the same characteristics (i.e., context-awareness, mobility, transparency, attention, and calmness). Next, we discussed IoT and its similarities and differences from Ubicomp using four questions. The evaluations were the foundation for our answers to the open questions together with our experience in these areas and what we found in the literature.

So, we hope to motivate researchers to work on the several challenges that we presented for IoT systems interaction evaluation, especially focusing on the opportunities of the evaluation of Thing-Thing interaction. Moreover, it is important to investigate the commonalities with Ubicomp interaction evaluation and reuse/adapt them to the IoT needs.

References

1. Al-Fuqaha, A., Guizani, M., Mohammadi, M., Aledhari, M., Ayyash, M.: Internet of things: A survey on enabling technologies, protocols, and applications. IEEE Commun. Surv. Tutorials **17**(4), 2347–2376 (2015)
2. Araújo, I.L., Santos, I.S., Filho, J.B.F., Andrade, R.M.C., Neto, P.S.: Generating test cases and procedures from use cases in dynamic software product lines. In: Proceedings of the 32nd ACM SIGApp Symposium On Applied Computing (2017)

3. Assila, A., Ezzedine, H., et al.: Standardized usability questionnaires: Features and quality focus. Electron. J. Comput. Sci. Inf. Technol. eJCIST 6(1) (2016)
4. Carvalho, C.M., Rodrigues, C.A., Aguilar, P.A., de Castro, M.F., Andrade, R.M.C., Boudy, J., Istrate, D.: Adaptive tracking model in the framework of medical nursing home using infrared sensors. In: 2015 IEEE Globecom Workshops (GC Wkshps), pp. 1–6. IEEE (2015)
5. Carvalho, R.M., Andrade, R.M.C., Barbosa, J., Maia, A.M., Junior, B.R., Aguilar, P.A., Bezerra, C.I.M.: Evaluating an IoT application using software measures. In: International Conference on Distributed, Ambient, and Pervasive Interactions. Springer (2017). To be published
6. Carvalho, R.M., Andrade, R.M.C., Oliveira, K.M.: Using the GQM method to evaluate calmness in ubiquitous applications. In: Streitz, N., Markopoulos, P. (eds.) DAPI 2015. LNCS, vol. 9189, pp. 13–24. Springer, Cham (2015). doi:10.1007/978-3-319-20804-6_2
7. Carvalho, R.M., Santos, I.S., Meira, R.G., Aguilar, P.A., Andrade, R.M.C.: Machine learning and location fingerprinting to improve UX in a ubiquitous application. In: Streitz, N., Markopoulos, P. (eds.) DAPI 2016. LNCS, vol. 9749, pp. 168–179. Springer, Cham (2016). doi:10.1007/978-3-319-39862-4_16
8. Carvalho, R.M., de Castro Andrade, R.M., de Oliveira, K.M., de Sousa Santos, I., Bezerra, C.I.M.: Quality characteristics and measures for human–computer interaction evaluation in ubiquitous systems. Softw. Qual. J. 1–53 (2016)
9. Chong, M.K., Mayrhofer, R., Gellersen, H.: A survey of user interaction for spontaneous device association. ACM Comput. Surv. (CSUR) 47(1), 8 (2014)
10. Darin, T.G.R., Barbosa, J., Rodrigues, B., Andrade, R.M.C.: Greatroom: Uma aplicação android basead em proximidade para a criação de salas virtuais inteligentes. Anais do XXII SimpÓsio Brasileiro de Sistemas Multimídia Web, vol. 2, pp. 107–111 (2016). (in Portuguese)
11. Dey, A.K.: Understanding and using context. Pers. Ubiquit. Comput. 5(1), 4–7 (2001)
12. Dong, T., Churchill, E.F., Nichols, J.: Understanding the challenges of designing and developing multi-device experiences. In: Proceedings of the 2016 ACM Conference on Designing Interactive Systems, pp. 62–72. ACM (2016)
13. Fauquex, M., Goyal, S., Evequoz, F., Bocchi, Y.: Creating people-aware IoT applications by combining design thinking and user-centered design methods. In: 2015 IEEE 2nd World Forum on Internet of Things (WF-IoT), pp. 57–62. IEEE (2015)
14. Ferreira, A.B., Braga, R.B., Andrade, R.M.C.: Medidas de qualidade para a avaliação da confiança no funcionamento em sistemas ubíquos. Brazilian Symposium on Software Quality (SBQS) (2016). (in Portuguese)
15. Ferreira, A.B., Piva, L.S., Braga, R.B., Andrade, R.M.: Avaliação da confiança no funcionamento de sistemas de detecção e alerta de quedas. Revista de Informática Aplicada 11(2) (2016)
16. Ferreira, A.B., Braga, R.B., Andrade, R.M.C.: Medidas de qualidade para a avaliação da confiança no funcionamento em sistemas ubíquos. In: Anais do 15° Simpósio Brasileiro de Qualidade de Software (2016). (in Portuguese)
17. Garlan, D., Siewiorek, D.P., Smailagic, A., Steenkiste, P.: Project aura: Toward distraction-free pervasive computing. IEEE Pervasive Comput. 1(2), 22–31 (2002)
18. Holler, J., Tsiatsis, V., Mulligan, C., Avesand, S., Karnouskos, S., Boyle, D.: From Machine-to-machine to the Internet of Things: Introduction to a New Age of Intelligence. Academic Press, Oxford (2014)

19. Jewell, M.O., Costanza, E., Kittley-Davies, J.: Connecting the things to the internet: An evaluation of four configuration strategies for wi-fi devices with minimal user interfaces. In: Proceedings of the 2015 ACM International Joint Conference on Pervasive and Ubiquitous Computing, pp. 767–778. ACM (2015)

20. Kourouthanassis, P.E., Giaglis, G.M., Karaiskos, D.C.: Delineating the degree of 'pervasiveness' in pervasive information systems: An assessment framework and design implications. In: 2008 Panhellenic Conference on Informatics, PCI 2008, pp. 251–255. IEEE (2008)

21. Kray, C., Kortuem, G., Wasinger, R.: Concepts and issues in interfaces for multiple users and multiple devices (2004)

22. Ma, M., Preum, S.M., Tarneberg, W., Ahmed, M., Ruiters, M., Stankovic, J.: Detection of runtime conflicts among services in smart cities. In: 2016 IEEE International Conference on Smart Computing (SMARTCOMP), pp. 1–10. IEEE (2016)

23. Maia, M.E.F., Fonteles, A., Neto, B., Gadelha, R., Viana, W., Andrade, R.M.C.: LOCCAM - loosely coupled context acquisition middleware. In: Proceedings of the 28th Annual ACM Symposium on Applied Computing, SAC 2013, pp. 534–541 (2013). http://doi.acm.org/10.1145/2480362.2480465

24. Maia, M.E.F., Rocha, L.S., Maia, P.H.M., Andrade, R.M.C.: An autonomous middleware model for essential services in distributed mobile applications. In: Venkatasubramanian, N., Getov, V., Steglich, S. (eds.) MOBILWARE 2011. LNICSSITE, vol. 93, pp. 57–70. Springer, Heidelberg (2012). doi:10.1007/978-3-642-30607-5_6

25. Maia, M.E., Andrade, R.M., de Queiroz Filho, C.A., Braga, R.B., Aguiar, S., Mateus, B.G., Nogueira, R., Toorn, F.: Usable-a communication framework for ubiquitous systems. In: 2014 IEEE 28th International Conference on Advanced Information Networking and Applications, pp. 81–88. IEEE (2014)

26. Maia, M.E., Rocha, L.S., Andrade, R.: Requirements and challenges for building service-oriented pervasive middleware. In: Proceedings of the 2009 International Conference on Pervasive Services, pp. 93–102. ACM (2009)

27. Marinho, F.G., Andrade, R.M.C., Werner, C.: A verification mechanism of feature models for mobile and context-aware software product lines. In: 2011 Fifth Brazilian Symposium on Software Components, Architectures and Reuse, pp. 1–10, September 2011

28. Marinho, F.G., Costa, A.L., Lima, F.F.P., Neto, J.B.B., Filho, J.B.F., Rocha, L., Dantas, V.L.L., Andrade, R.M.C., Teixeira, E., Werner, C.: An architecture proposal for nested software product lines in the domain of mobile and context-aware applications. In: 2010 Fourth Brazilian Symposium on Software Components, Architectures and Reuse, pp. 51–60, September 2010

29. Marinho, F.G., Andrade, R.M.C., Werner, C., Viana, W., Maia, M.E.F., Rocha, L.S., Teixeira, E., Filho, J.B.F., Dantas, V.L.L., Lima, F., Aguiar, S.: Mobiline: A nested software product line for the domain of mobile and context-aware applications. Sci. Comput. Program **78**(12), 2381–2398 (2013). http://dx.doi.org/10.1016/j.scico.2012.04.009

30. Mashal, I., Alsaryrah, O., Chung, T.Y., Yang, C.Z., Kuo, W.H., Agrawal, D.P.: Choices for interaction with things on internet and underlying issues. Ad Hoc Netw. **28**, 68–90 (2015)

31. Mayer, S., Tschofen, A., Dey, A.K., Mattern, F.: User interfaces for smart things - a generative approach with semantic interaction descriptions. ACM Trans. Comput. Hum. Interact. **21**(2), 12:1–12:25 (2014)

32. Minerva, R., Biru, A., Rotondi, D.: Towards a definition of the internet of things (IoT). IEEE Internet Initiative, Torino, Italy (2015)

33. Neto, B.J.A., Andrade, R.M.C., Maia, M.E.F., Fonteles, A., Viana, W.: A coordination framework for dynamic adaptation in ubiquitous systems based on distributed tuple space. In: 2013 9th International Wireless Communications and Mobile Computing Conference (IWCMC), pp. 1430–1435, July 2013
34. de Paula Lima, F.F.: SysSU - Um Sistema de Suporte para Computação Ubíqua. Master's thesis, Federal University of Ceará (2011). (in Portuguese)
35. Perera, C., Zaslavsky, A., Christen, P., Georgakopoulos, D.: Context aware computing for the internet of things: A survey. IEEE Commun. Surv. Tutorials **16**(1), 414–454 (2014)
36. Razzaque, M.A., Milojevic-Jevric, M., Palade, A., Clarke, S.: Middleware for internet of things: A survey. IEEE Internet Things J. **3**(1), 70–95 (2016)
37. Reinisch, C., Kofler, M.J., Kastner, W.: Thinkhome: A smart home as digital ecosystem. In: 2010 4th IEEE International Conference on Digital Ecosystems and Technologies (DEST), pp. 256–261. IEEE (2010)
38. Riekki, J., Isomursu, P., Isomursu, M.: Evaluating the calmness of ubiquitous applications. In: Bomarius, F., Iida, H. (eds.) PROFES 2004. LNCS, vol. 3009, pp. 105–119. Springer, Heidelberg (2004). doi:10.1007/978-3-540-24659-6_8
39. Rocha, L.S., Filho, J.B.F., Lima, F.F.P., Maia, M.E.F., Viana, W., de Castro, M.F., Andrade, R.M.C.: Ubiquitous software engineering: Achievements, challenges and beyond. In: 2011 25th Brazilian Symposium on Software Engineering, pp. 132–137, September 2011
40. Rocha, L.C., Andrade, R.M.C., Sampaio, A.L.: Heurísticas para avaliar a usabilidade de aplicações móveis: estudo de caso para aulas de campo em geologia. XIX Congresso Internacional de Informática Educativa (2014). (in Portuguese)
41. Rowland, C., Goodman, E., Charlier, M., Light, A., Lui, A.: Designing Connected Products: UX for the Consumer Internet of Things. O'Reilly Media, Inc., Sebastopol (2015)
42. Santos, I.S., Andrade, R.M.C., Neto, P.A.S.: Um método para geração de cenários de testes para linhas de produtos de software sensíveis ao contexto. VI Simpósio Brasileiro de Computação Ubíqua e Pervasiva (SBCUP) (2014). (in Portuguese)
43. Santos, I.S., Rocha, L.S., Neto, P.A.S., Andrade, R.M.C.: Model verification of dynamic software product lines. In: Proceedings of the 30th Brazilian Symposium on Software Engineering, SBES 2016, pp. 113–122, NY, USA (2016). http://doi. acm.org.ez11.periodicos.capes.gov.br/10.1145/2973839.2973852
44. Santos, I.S.: Um Ambiente para Geração de Cenários de Testes para Linha de Produtos de Software Sensíveis ao Contexto. Master's thesis, Federal University of Ceará (2013). (in Portuguese)
45. Santos, R.M., Oliveira, K.M., Andrade, R.M.C., Santos, I.S., Lima, E.R.: A quality model for human-computer interaction evaluation in ubiquitous systems. In: Collazos, C., Liborio, A., Rusu, C. (eds.) CLIHC 2013. LNCS, vol. 8278, pp. 63–70. Springer, Cham (2013). doi:10.1007/978-3-319-03068-5_13
46. Santos, R.M.: Características e Medidas de Software para Avaliação da Qualidade da Interação Humano-Computador em Sistemas Ubíquos. Master's thesis, Federal University of Ceará (2014). (in Portuguese)
47. Santos, I.S., Andrade, R.M., Santos Neto, P.A.: Templates for textual use cases of software product lines: Results from a systematic mapping study and a controlled experiment. J. Softw. Eng. Res. Dev. **3**(1), 5 (2015). http://dx.doi.org/10.1186/s40411-015-0020-3
48. Satyanarayanan, M.: Pervasive computing: Vision and challenges. IEEE Pers. Commun. **8**(4), 10–17 (2001)

49. Suomalainen, J.: Smartphone assisted security pairings for the internet of things. In: 2014 4th International Conference on Wireless Communications, Vehicular Technology, Information Theory and Aerospace & Electronic Systems (VITAE), pp. 1–5. IEEE (2014)
50. Taivalsaari, A., Mikkonen, T.: A roadmap to the programmable world: Software challenges in the IoT era. IEEE Softw. **34**(1), 72–80 (2017)
51. Tan, L., Wang, N.: Future internet: The internet of things. In: 2010 3rd International Conference on Advanced Computer Theory and Engineering (ICACTE), vol. 5, pp. V5-376–V5-380. IEEE (2010)
52. Vasseur, J.P., Dunkels, A.: Interconnecting smart objects with IP: The next internet. Morgan Kaufmann, San Francisco (2010)
53. Vega-Barbas, M., Casado-Mansilla, D., Valero, M.A., López-de Ipina, D., Bravo, J., Flórez, F.: Smart spaces and smart objects interoperability architecture (S3OiA). In: 2012 Sixth International Conference on Innovative Mobile and Internet Services in Ubiquitous Computing (IMIS), pp. 725–730. IEEE (2012)
54. Weber, R.H.: Internet of things-new security and privacy challenges. Comput. Law Secur. Rev. **26**(1), 23–30 (2010)
55. Weiser, M.: The computer for the 21st century. Sci. Am. **265**(3), 94–104 (1991)
56. Yu, P., Ma, X., Cao, J., Lu, J.: Application mobility in pervasive computing: A survey. Pervasive Mobile Comput. **9**(1), 2–17 (2013)

Evaluating an IoT Application
Using Software Measures

Rainara M. Carvalho[1(✉)], Rossana M.C. Andrade[1], Jefferson Barbosa[1],
Adyson M. Maia[1], Belmondo A. Junior[1], Paulo A. Aguilar[1],
Carla I.M. Bezerra[1], and Káthia M. Oliveira[2]

[1] Group of Computer Networks, Software Engineering and Systems (GREat),
Graduate Program in Computer Science (MDCC),
Federal University of Ceará, Fortaleza, Brazil
{rainaracarvalho,rossana,jeffersonbarbosa,adysonmaia,
belmondorodrigues,pauloaguilar,carlabezerra}@great.ufc.br

[2] Laboratory of Automatic Control, Mechanics and Computer Science for Industrial
and Human-machine Systems (LAMIH), University of Valenciennes
and Hainaut-Cambrésis (UVHC), CNRS UMR, 8201 Valenciennes, France
kathia.oliveira@univ-valenciennes.fr

Abstract. Internet of Things (IoT) allows daily objects, with computing and communication capabilities, to connect to the Internet. In this
scenario, an application called GREatRoom runs in an IoT environment,
which has distributed wireless labels in places and objects, to detect the
presence of nearby users, providing services intuitively and efficiently.
Considering that IoT systems have quality characteristics of human-
computer interaction similar to those of ubiquitous systems, this paper
investigates the applicability of software measures from ubiquitous to IoT
systems and presents the positive results achieved in this evaluation.

Keywords: Internet of Things · HCI quality evaluation · Measures ·
Ubiquitous computing

1 Introduction

Internet of Things (IoT) is a new paradigm that provides a variety of things/
objects capable of interacting and cooperating with each other, using the Internet
[14,15]. IoT technologies have been used to create smart environments such as
smart cities, smart homes, and smart buildings.

Ubiquitous Computing (UbiComp) is one of the areas that are driving IoT
[10,23]. As a consequence, we believe that solutions developed by/for the Ubi-
Comp community can be applied in the IoT systems since both areas have characteristics in common. For instance, the context-awareness feature, which is the

R.M.C. Andrade—Researcher scholarship - DT Level 2, sponsored by CNPq
J. Barbosa—Master Scholarship (MDCC/DC/UFC) sponsored by FUNCAP
A.M. Maia—PhD Scholarship (MDCC/DC/UFC) sponsored by CAPES
B.A. Junior—Master Scholarship (MDCC/DC/UFC) sponsored by CAPES.

N. Streitz and P. Markopoulos (Eds.): DAPI 2017, LNCS 10291, pp. 22–33, 2017.
DOI: 10.1007/978-3-319-58697-7_2

system's capability of monitoring contextual information regarding the user, the system and the environment to provide relevant services, is an important characteristic presented in both areas [6,7,12,13,17,20].

In our research lab, which is called GREat, Group of Computer Network, Software Engineering and Systems[1], IoT applications have been developed to support professors and students in different everyday situations [4]. One of these applications is called GREatRoom [8], which provides a way to register the presence of people in a room, making possible to see who is in the place at a given time. Also, it allows sharing files among individuals in the same room.

GREatRoom uses beacons, Android mobile phones and cloud computing (*i.e.*, Google Cloud) to perform its functionalities. The beacons send broadcast messages using Bluetooth [16], allowing the identification of new objects (smartphones) to a database in a Cloud, which in turn can notify the presence of new objects in a room. The interaction with the user occurs in the Android application, which allows the user to see who is in the room and what files are available to download.

GREatRoom aims to provide an efficient way to register people presence in events such as seminars and workshops, removing the need for manual signatures. However, the risk of users feeling overwhelmed is high, since this IoT application may notify a large number of new objects, such as mobile phones, in a short time. Therefore, we believe that the interaction quality evaluation of IoT applications becomes even more essential in the software development process than in both traditional and ubiquitous computing applications.

This work then aims to use solutions regarding the quality interaction evaluation that come from UbiComp to IoT [5,6]. For that, we apply the work from [5], which defines a set of measures for the interaction quality evaluation of ubiquitous systems, in IoT systems. These measures help to verify if the application does not disturb users unnecessarily and if it supports user activities at the right moment and place, delivering the best service possible. We apply these measures in a case study that allows the identification of problems regarding user interaction. Therefore, a significant contribution of this work is the empirical results about using software measures from UbiComp area in an IoT application. Moreover, we also discuss there are specific characteristics of IoT systems that need to be considered and prioritized when doing such kind of evaluation, for example, the quality of the interaction between things in an IoT environment [14,19].

The rest of this paper is organized as follows: Sect. 2 presents the main concepts about UbiComp, IoT and HCI Quality Evaluation. Section 3 presents the IoT application, GREatRoom. Section 4 presents the evaluation performed in GREatRoom, including results and discussion about the findings. Finally, Sect. 5 presents the conclusions and future work.

---

[1] http://www.great.ufc.br/.

2   Background

2.1   UbiComp and IoT

The idea of UbiComp area is to make computing devices available everywhere, capable of sharing information between people and machines [25]. One of the primary goals of UbiComp is to simplify Human-Computer Interaction (HCI), by making the technology distributed, so that the user does not perceive their presence [11].

Nowadays, we are living a moving towards IoT, and Ubicomp is one of the areas that are leading up to IoT. The term Internet of Things, according to [1], appeared in 1999, where initially the idea was to use the new RFID technology in resource management. Over the past years, new definitions were added to the term to cover a greater number of applications. However, the main idea of having a context-aware technology without human intervention continues until today [9].

There are several IoT definitions in literature, and they have some specificities that differ them from one another. The definition adopted for this work was proposed by [22], which defines IoT as a global, self-configuring network infrastructure where protocols are used to communicate between things. These "things" are represented in both physical and virtual environments, and have identification, physical attributes, virtual personalities, and are seamlessly integrated into a network. In addition to being identifiable, objects/things can have various capabilities, such as processing power, storage, and communication technologies.

Besides, such objects may have ubiquitous computing features, such as context-awareness [9] and transparency [24], making possible to develop smarter applications and, consequently, the possibility of using UbiComp solutions in the IoT environment.

Moreover, Sundmaeker et al. (2010) define "things" as active participants in information where they can interact and communicate with each other and with the environment through the exchange of data and information about the context. Also, they can react autonomously according to the events that trigger actions and create services with or without direct human intervention [22].

UbiComp and IoT areas have also similar descriptions in the part of data sharing between machines to carry out a certain task, in the part of transparency with the end user, among other characteristics.

Therefore, due to these similarities, we believe we can use evaluation techniques and methods from UbiComp to evaluate IoT applications.

2.2   HCI Quality Evaluation

Applications from UbiComp has characteristics that completely change the way users interact with technology, and so impact on usability and user experience [20]. For example, a ubiquitous system has the context-awareness characteristic,

Table 1. Software measures for calmness characteristic. Adapted from [5]

Name	Measurement function
Context correctness	$\frac{\sum_{j=1}^{N}(Ak/Bk)*100}{N}$ Ak = Number of correct context information i Bk = Number of collected context information i N = Number of different context information
Context frequency	Frequency of changing: Low-minutes, Medium-seconds, High-milliseconds
Adaptation time	T = Time taken to adapt
Adaptation degree	$\frac{\sum_{j=1}^{N}(Aj/Bj)*100}{N}$ Aj = Number of performed adaptations i Bj = Number of requested adaptations i N = Number of adaptations
Adaptation correctness	$\frac{\sum_{i=1}^{N}(Ai/Bi)*100}{N}$ Ai = Number of correctly performed adaptations i Bi = Number of performed adaptations i N = Number of adaptations
Availability degree	X = B, where B is the element that appears most often among the following options (*i.e.*, the mode) (1) Very Low, (2) Low, (3) Medium, and (4) High
Context-awareness timing degree	X = B, where B is the mode (1) Very Low, (2) Low, (3) Medium, and (4) High
Number of irrelevant focus changes	X = A, where A = Number of actions that changes user's focus during the application usage
Number of failures	X = N, where N = Total number of failures that has occurred
Relevancy degree	X = B, where B is the mode (1) Very Low, (2) Low, (3) Medium, and (4) High
Courtesy degree	X = B, where B is the mode (1) Very Low, (2) Low, (3) Medium, and (4) High

which means that is capable of collecting contextual data and adapting behavior according to the data [17].

Moreover, these systems can be present in several devices, such as personal computers, smartphones, smart watches and others. Thus, they have the mobility characteristic, what makes it possible for the system to be working everywhere and available at anytime, as a consequence, this creates an increased risk that the user will feel disturbed by the system [18].

The work from [20] proposes a set of measures to evaluate the user interaction with ubiquitous applications regarding context-awareness and the work from [5] proposes a set of software measures (See Table 1) to the calmness characteristic. Calmness is the capability of the system to support user activities at the right time and place, delivering the best service possible [18]. We believe calmness has a great impact on user satisfaction and therefore also on acceptance of the ubiquitous application.

3   GREatRoom

3.1   Main Features

In the GREat research laboratory, there are often several presentations, such as lectures, mini-courses, thesis and dissertations defenses, among others. Such events usually take place in the seminar room and the meeting room. A necessity for such events is to register the presence of people who are attending the events in that room. Nowadays, this registration is done manually, through the collection of signatures. Therefore, in order to improve this activity, GREatRoom application was designed. The main feature of this application is then to provide a way to register the presence of people in a room, making possible to see who is in the room at a given time.

Moreover, there is another need for people who participate in such events as follows. Typically, they present their work use files such as slides, documents, images, videos. After the presentation, they usually share these files with the interested people via email. However, this activity is not always successful, sometimes the presenter forgets to do so or even does not get all emails of the attendees, then people who are interested in the presentation are not always

(a) Without login   (b) With login

Fig. 1. GREatRoom - Initial screens

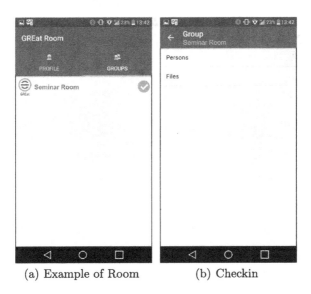

(a) Example of Room   (b) Checkin

Fig. 2. GREatRoom - Room

able to get the file. Thinking about this problem, another feature provided by GREatRoom is allowing the sharing of files among people in the same room. This feature is designed as follows: as soon as a person is registered in the room, he/she can make files available to others who must also be registered in the same room.

The application works as follows: *(i)* The user must log in using a Facebook account (Fig. 1); *(ii)* After performed login, the application automatically detects in which room the user is and then he-she is registered in it. In the example of Fig. 2(a), the user was registered in "Seminar Room"; *(iii)* Then, the application allows the user to access the file options of this room, as well as see the people who are in it (See Fig. 2(b)); and *(iv)* By accessing the persons, the user can visualize that two people besides him/her are in the room (Fig. 3(a)), also he/she can access five files (Fig. 3(b)).

3.2   Overview: Behavior and Technologies

GREatRoom allows the creation of IoT environments through the use of wireless labels (Beacons) distributed in places and objects. In this environment, devices collect user data and adapt their services to create a ubiquitous interactive environment. In this interactive environment, things (objects, places, and users) exchange information, perform processing, and generate information and services.

The interactions with the system are performed by a mobile device with operating system Android and communication Bluetooth. GREatRoom identifies the presence of users in the room and performs a check-in on the attendance list.

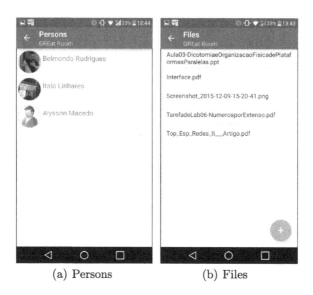

(a) Persons   (b) Files

Fig. 3. GREatRoom - Persons and Files

After the identification, the user may have access to the content and information of a room. The idea is that the user has minimal interaction with the system and some actions are done transparently, ensuring such services are offered in the most natural way possible. However, the system will not perform person management or direct exchange of information between the users.

Figure 4 illustrates the flow of messages of GREatRoom, which uses the Publisher-Subscriber standard [21] to register a user in a room, which is identified by the beacon device that sends broadcast messages. From these messages, it is possible to find new objects in this room. The beacons have a high accuracy of device location, and this is a good point to determine the distance and calculate when a user is present in the room with a higher degree of assertiveness.

The Publisher-Subscriber standard was used to perform event notifications on GREatRoom. This standard uses design principles to minimize the use of

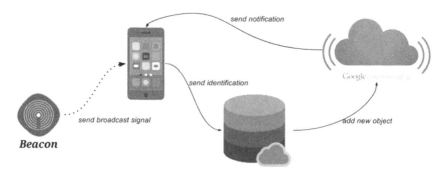

Fig. 4. GREatRoom overview

network bandwidth, to ensure reliability and to guarantee message delivery. These principles are important for the IoT paradigm, because mobile devices have limited resources [2]. In the GREatRoom environment, users have the role of Subscribers who receive notifications that are related to any object present in that room, and the objects are Publishers who will notify all their Subscribers when a change of state occurs.

3.3 Architecture

For the GREatRoom development, the reference architecture proposed by [3] was used. However, only the components for communication, service, and transformation of a physical entity in virtual entity were used. Figure 5 gives an overview of the GREat Room architecture. The description of each component belonging to the system is described as follows:

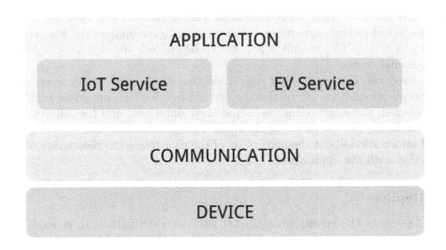

Fig. 5. GREatRoom architecture

Application Layer is responsible for performing part of the data processing sent by the devices and for presenting a user interface.

IoT Service Layer provides a feature to make it accessible to other parts of the IoT system and can be used to obtain information from a feature of a sensor device or a storage resource connected to a network.

Virtual Entity Service Layer is responsible for manipulating entity services and providing access to an entity via operations that enable readings and/or updates of values of its attributes.

Communication Layer is responsible for the transmission of packets between the application and the objects of the environment using addressing and IDs. The arguments for packet transmission can be configured and include unicast/multicast addressing and access control. Another functionality is to obtain a locator from a given ID, which can be done internally based on a lookup table.

Device Layer represents the several devices that can communicate with the Great Room application, such as smartphones, air conditioners and smart lamps.

4 Evaluation

4.1 Planning and Execution

The execution of the evaluation was carried out in parallel with five users in two rooms. Each room had an IOS device with an application installed to simulate signals from a Beacon. At the beginning of the tests, users received training on the purpose of the application and its features. Also, users were instructed to use the system simulating a real situation in which they were in a meeting room.

Initially, each user logged in to use the features. Subsequently, the application allows the visualization of all places near the user and performs the presence of this user in an individual room according to the environment in which he is at the time of the test. After being present in a room the user can view the people and files linked to this same room, being possible to manipulate the files as well as delete a certain file, submit a new file to be shared, and download a file to your personal device.

We used two instruments for data collection in the evaluation: interaction logs and questionnaires. Interaction logs record in a file the contextual information collected, the adaptations made and their durations, and the failures that occurred during the use of the application. The questionnaire allows the collection of information about the perception of the user related to the quality of the interaction with the application.

4.2 Results

Table 2 presents the results from the GREatRoom evaluation. In general, the application showed satisfactory results with the following subjective measures: Availability Degree, Context-Awareness Degree, Relevancy Degree and Courtesy Degree highlights that the application has a good degree of calmness. This is important, because GREatRoom works when users are attending lectures, seminaries and others, then, it requires focus and, thus, it is important not to take the attention away from these activities.

However, the following measures did not present good results: Adaptation Degree, and Adaptation Correctness Degree. It is interesting to highlight that although the application is good in recognizing the context correctly (Context Correctness = 98%) and took little time to adapt (1.28s), the adaptation degree (78%) and adaptation correctness (79%) are below the expected. That happened because the system presented some problems when the user positioned him/herself on the border between two rooms, where the system was not sure which room the user should assign. This result gives an idea of what can be improved about the distance calculation between one beacon and another. One of the solutions is to increase the number of beacons to perform the mapping of the room so that the synchronization between them can be made.

Table 2. Results of the HCI evaluation of GREatRoom

Measure	Results
Context correctness	98%
Context frequency	Low
Adaptation time	1.28s
Adaptation degree	78%
Adaptation correctness Degree	79%
Availability degree	High
Context-awareness Timing Degree	High
Number of focus changes	0 actions
Number of failures	0 failures
Relevancy degree	High
Courtesy degree	High

4.3 Discussion

The measures used to evaluate the application give us an insight into what can be improved in the application. Therefore, this study shows that measures for UbiComp are feasible to be applied in IoT applications. In general, by applying the same measures in ubiquitous [5] and IoT applications we could notice that: *(i)* Collecting the necessary data for the measures calculation requires the same effort; *(ii)* The questionnaires used to capture users' opinion are adequate; and *(iii)* The results from the measures can be interpreted following the same procedures.

However, there are specific characteristics of IoT systems that need to be considered and prioritized when doing such kind of evaluation. This is because a thing in IoT sends data through the Internet to another thing, therefore, the latency, intermittency and reliability are big issues to the quality of the interaction [19]. This indicates that these characteristics should be investigated and also measured. The results of the measures should be analyzed together, considering that the values of one are impacted by the other. Moreover, new quality characteristics specific for IoT applications may also be required.

For example, in GREatRoom, when a new object (*i.e.*, a user) enters the environment, an Internet message is sent to the Cloud, to update the list of people who are in that environment. If the application shows five persons in a room, and then a new user enters in that room, it can take a few minutes for the application be updated. During this time, the application of the users that were initially in the room shows five persons, and the application of the new user shows six persons. Therefore, the time it takes to synchrony the things can not be long, and then it is necessary to measure this synchronicity, characteristic not yet considered in UbiComp applications.

5   Conclusion and Future Work

This paper describes an evaluation of an IoT application using measures of ubiquitous computing systems. Since IoT applications have similar requirements to ubiquitous applications, we apply measures originally defined for ubiquitous systems to an IoT application, called GREatRoom. It was then possible to verify strengths and suggest improvements for this application based on the evaluation, and also raise research perspectives in the area of IoT systems evaluation. We believe that is possible to use good solutions from one area to the other and also discussed that in this paper.

As future work, we plan to distribute several beacons in different types of rooms of GREat to carry out the control of people who attend the different environments of the GREaT laboratory. With this intelligent environment deployed, it is possible to add functionalities to the GREat Room application, allowing the user interact with the objects present in the environment. Another future work is the verification of other quality characteristics from ubiquitous computing [7] and that could have similar aspects with IoT.

Acknowledgments. We thank FCPC (Ceará State Foundation of Research and Culture, Brazil) for making possible the partnership with LG Electronics using the Brazilian Informatics Law (10.176) that give us the financial support. Many thanks to CAPES (Coordination for the Improvement of Higher Education Personnel) as well for partially funding this work.

References

1. Ashton, K.: That internet of things thing. RFiD J. **22**(7), 97–114 (2009)
2. Banks, A., Gupta, R.: MQTT version 3.1.1. OASIS Standard (2014)
3. Bassi, A., Bauer, M., Fiedler, M., Kramp, T., Kranenburg, R., Lange, S., Meissner, S.: Enabling Things to Talk: Designing IoT Solutions with the IoT Architectural Reference Model. Springer, Heidelberg (2013)
4. Carvalho, C.M., Rodrigues, C.A., Aguilar, P.A., de Castro, M.F., Andrade, R.M.C., Boudy, J., Istrate, D.: Adaptive tracking model in the framework of medical nursing home using infrared sensors. In: 2015 IEEE Globecom Workshops (GC Wkshps), pp. 1–6. IEEE (2015)
5. Carvalho, R.M., Andrade, R.M.C., Oliveira, K.M.: Using the GQM method to evaluate calmness in ubiquitous applications. In: Streitz, N., Markopoulos, P. (eds.) DAPI 2015. LNCS, vol. 9189, pp. 13–24. Springer, Cham (2015). doi:10.1007/978-3-319-20804-6_2
6. Carvalho, R.M., Santos, I.S., Meira, R.G., Aguilar, P.A., Andrade, R.M.C.: Machine learning and location fingerprinting to improve UX in a ubiquitous application. In: Streitz, N., Markopoulos, P. (eds.) DAPI 2016. LNCS, vol. 9749, pp. 168–179. Springer, Cham (2016). doi:10.1007/978-3-319-39862-4_16
7. Carvalho, R.M., Andrade, R.M.C., de Oliveira, K.M., de Sousa Santos, I., Bezerra, C.I.M.: Quality characteristics and measures for human-computer interaction evaluation in ubiquitous systems. Softw. Qual. J. **24**(3), 1–53 (2016)

8. Darin, T., Barbosa, J., Rodrigues, B., Andrade, R.M.: Greatroom: Uma aplicação android baseada em proximidade para a criação de salas virtuais inteligentes. Workshop de Ferramentas e Aplicações (WFA). Simpósio Brasileiro de Sistemas Multimídia e Web (2016) (in portuguese)
9. Gubbi, J., Buyya, R., Marusic, S., Palaniswami, M.: Internet of things (IoT): A vision, architectural elements, and future directions. Future Gener. Comput. Syst. **29**(7), 1645–1660 (2013)
10. Holler, J., Tsiatsis, V., Mulligan, C., Avesand, S., Karnouskos, S., Boyle, D.: From Machine-to-machine to the Internet of Things: Introduction to a New Age of Intelligence. Academic Press, Amsterdam (2014)
11. Knappmeyer, M., Kiani, S.L., Reetz, E.S., Baker, N., Tonjes, R.: Survey of context provisioning middleware. IEEE Commun. Surv. Tutorials **15**(3), 1492–1519 (2013)
12. Maia, M.E., Andrade, R.M.C., de Queiroz Filho, C.A., Braga, R.B., Aguiar, S., Mateus, B.G., Nogueira, R., Toorn, F.: Usable-a communication framework for ubiquitous systems. In: 2014 IEEE 28th International Conference on Advanced Information Networking and Applications, pp. 81–88. IEEE (2014)
13. Maia, M.E., Fonteles, A., Neto, B., Gadelha, R., Viana, W., Andrade, R.M.C.: Loccam-loosely coupled context acquisition middleware. In: Proceedings of the 28th Annual ACM Symposium on Applied Computing, pp. 534–541. ACM (2013)
14. Mashal, I., Alsaryrah, O., Chung, T.Y., Yang, C.Z., Kuo, W.H., Agrawal, D.P.: Choices for interaction with things on internet and underlying issues. Ad Hoc Netw. **28**, 68–90 (2015)
15. Miorandi, D., Sicari, S., De Pellegrini, F., Chlamtac, I.: Internet of things: Vision, applications and research challenges. Ad Hoc Netw. **10**(7), 1497–1516 (2012)
16. Newman, N.: Apple ibeacon technology briefing. J. Direct Data Digit. Mark. Pract. **15**(3), 222–225 (2014)
17. Perera, C., Zaslavsky, A., Christen, P., Georgakopoulos, D.: Context aware computing for the internet of things: A survey. IEEE Commun. Surv. Tutorials **16**(1), 414–454 (2014)
18. Riekki, J., Isomursu, P., Isomursu, M.: Evaluating the calmness of ubiquitous applications. In: Bomarius, F., Iida, H. (eds.) PROFES 2004. LNCS, vol. 3009, pp. 105–119. Springer, Heidelberg (2004). doi:10.1007/978-3-540-24659-6_8
19. Rowland, C., Goodman, E., Charlier, M., Light, A., Lui, A.: Designing Connected Products: UX for the Consumer Internet of Things. O'Reilly Media Inc., Sebastopol (2015)
20. Santos, R.M., Oliveira, K.M., Andrade, R.M.C., Santos, I.S., Lima, E.R.: A quality model for human-computer interaction evaluation in ubiquitous systems. In: Collazos, C., Liborio, A., Rusu, C. (eds.) CLIHC 2013. LNCS, vol. 8278, pp. 63–70. Springer, Cham (2013). doi:10.1007/978-3-319-03068-5_13
21. Schmidt, D.C., O'Ryan, C.: Patterns and performance of distributed real-time and embedded publisher/subscriber architectures. J. Syst. Softw. **66**(3), 213–223 (2003)
22. Sundmaeker, H., Guillemin, P., Friess, P., Woelfflé, S.: Vision and challenges for realising the internet of things. Cluster of European Research Projects on the Internet of Things, European Commision (2010)
23. Vasseur, J.P., Dunkels, A.: Interconnecting Smart Objects with Ip: The Next Internet. Morgan Kaufmann, San Francisco (2010)
24. Weber, R.H.: Internet of things-new security and privacy challenges. Comput. Law Secur. Rev. **26**(1), 23–30 (2010)
25. Weiser, M.: The computer for the 21st century. Sci. Am. **265**(3), 94–104 (1991)

Service Design Strategy for Social Internet of Things in China

Jiajia Chen[1,2(✉)]

[1] School of Social and Behavioral Sciences, Nanjing University,
163 Xianlin Avenue, Xixia District, Nanjing 210023, Jiangsu, China
[2] School of Industrial Design, Nanjing University of Arts,
15 Huju North Road, Gulou District, Nanjing 210013, Jiangsu, China
chachachen@126.com

Abstract. Chinese people has experienced fast iteration of lifestyles within 30 years. The Social Network and the Internet of Things seem to invade their lives. And the combination of them will be more evolutionary.

In this paper, firstly, the author explains two typical examples of the Social Network event in China and leads to the three conclusions: Socialization is an inevitable trend for any kind of product on the internet society, China will not be an exception; Any service designed for socialization on the internet in China should be tightly fit to Chinese tradition and culture; Smart phone plays the role of 'smart' intermediator in these scenarios. Secondly, based on the review of the Social Network and the Internet of Things, the author concludes that novel concept of SocialInternet of Things (SIoT) is based on a sort of social relationship among objects, analogously to what happens for humanbeings. It has the advantages of navigability, scalable, trustworthiness and openness. And the core issue of the Social Internet of Things is how to make different objects socialized. In the third part, based on the description of the development of the Social Network and the Internet of Things, the author finds out three strategies for objects to establish the relationship. By the analysis of each strategy, the author finally points out that services designed to achieve symbiosis will be the strategy for the Social Internet of Things.

Keywords: Service design · Social Internet of Things · Design strategy

1 Introduction

Before the eve of Chinese Spring Festival, the most heated topic online is "how to collect the professional blessing card?" Professional blessing card is believed to be the most difficult one to collect in acquiring the 5-blessing card. Professional blessing card, together with another four cards, which are patriotic card, prosperous card, harmonious card and friendly card, can be converted into one card: 5-blessing card. And one 5-blessing card means a free ticket to participate in a carnival of sharing two hundred million RMB together with other 167,966,715 Ali-pay users in one lottery. No matter how little each 5-blessing card holder can have at last, Jack Ma (the actual manipulator of Ali-group) has beautifully beaten Pony Ma(the actual manipulator of Tencent-group)

© Springer International Publishing AG 2017
N. Streitz and P. Markopoulos (Eds.): DAPI 2017, LNCS 10291, pp. 34–44, 2017.
DOI: 10.1007/978-3-319-58697-7_3

in their payment competition among Chinese users this year. Around spring festival in 2014, Pony Ma started to introduce WeChat payment in its social platform. By adopting genius-like brilliant service strategy of handing out red packets among WeChat users, over one hundred million Chinese users has bound their bank accounts to WeChat payment just in two weeks. And WeChat payment has been widely used ever since. Before that, Jack Ma has consumed almost ten years to promote and brand Ali-pay. In the annual meeting of Tencent in 2016, WeChat payment team has won the highest level of internal prize-"The Famous Hall". This prize is established in 2015 by Pony Ma to honor the highest milestone of the development of company in one year. And the number of the prize is one hundred million RMB. It is reported that WeChat Payment has won Ali-pay in off-line payment in 2016 (Fig. 1).

Fig. 1. Steps to collect the 5-blessing card

This story is a typical example of how Chinese internet company use social network to compete in one area. From the story, we can notice that there are not only the service contents that make Chinese people indulge in the social activities, but also the strategy to make what kind of service contents should be paid attention. The service design strategies in the above stories indicate that:

Socialization is an inevitable trend for any kind of product on the internet society, China will not be an exception. There are two kinds of internet product in China: content internet product and function internet product. The former concentrates on helping or encouraging its users to generate communicative information. This product itself can be considered a platform which carry different users as the content providers. The latter is much simpler; the user will have nothing to do with it when its certain function has been used. This product is really worry-saving for its developer. The key point is the maintenance of the technology in order to achieve better user experience, not the maintenance of the content in order to keep its users stay as longer as possible. It can be concluded that the better the content internet product performs, the more abundant flow it will have; on the contrary, the better the function internet product performs, the fast its users will be lost. We can see clearly that Ali-pay has met the dilemma as the function internet product. How to make its users to do something else or how to improve user activity become the key point to solve the dilemma. Socialization, with its sharing purpose, beyond all doubt, becomes the best the solution for Jack Ma. For example, if someone happens to find another person breaks the traffic law, he or she can take the photo and report it through Ali-pay. Then he or she will get paid for this report and share the news with his or her Ali-pay friends to make money together. Not to mention the ethical or social problems here, we can see how hardly Ali-pay is trying to be socialized.

Any service designed for socialization on the internet in China should be tightly fit to Chinese tradition and culture. Why the collection of 5-blessing card and the handing out of WeChat red packets are becoming popular amusement and way of blessing for family members and friends nowadays in China? Because the ideas have been existing for hundreds of years already. Red packet means 'lucky money' in Chinese tradition for Spring Festival. In order to protect the children from being hurt by evils, the elder in the family will use red cord to string the 8 coins and hand out to the children after they pay their respect. When it comes to the Republic of China, people use red envelope to wrap the paper money. That is how red packet come into being. 5-blessing card in Chinese history means five standards for the ultimate happiness of life, which are longevity, wealth, health, love of virtue, and natural death. In modern Chinese society, the standards evolve into the part of the core values of Chinese Socialism, rising from individual perspective to the group points of view. Not to mention the different views on the basic element of society between the west and the east, and different social structure with the context of Chinese culture and other cultures, we can see how advancing Ali-pay is with the environment.

Smart phone plays the role of 'smart' intermediator in these scenarios. On the street of any city in China, you will never find someone scan the character 'Fu' (福) with their laptops or tablets. Undoubtedly, everyone involved in 5-blessing card collection will use its smart phone for many reasons. Among those reasons, there are some quite worthwhile to pay the attention. For example, if some kinds of blessing card you cannot collect by yourself, just ask your families or friends to give you. You can post your needs through WeChat, but you will never have the card unless you also add the one who will give you the card as Ali-pay friend. The good news is you can check all your Ali-pay friends to see how many and what kinds of cards they have already had. Then comes the question: will you trade on Ali-pay or WeChat payment online? Ali-pay will be mostly chosen answer by Chinese people[1]. It is because that Ali-pay rises together with Alibaba and TaoBao users. The long-term user recognition of trustful payment internet product has been established. You can add new friend in both products, but you have to turn off the button of 'see my updates' and tag the stranger on WeChat such as take-out restaurant owner, delivery courier, taxi driver and so on. You do not need to operate more steps in order to keep yourself safe on the internet when doing the same thing on Ali-pay. Then comes the next question: if your families or friends cannot give you the blessing card you need, what will you do? The common way is to buy online. Then Ali-pay, because of its original function, will have more possibilities to add more real 'strangers' than WeChat. When WeChat, QQ, and other forms of social platform become the way to 'add' more people like you nowadays, Ali-pay does return to the initial purpose of social media. What can be next? Smartphone itself can act differently than usual. It can act as a kind of reminder that tells you when to grab the red packets or who is having the card that you need. It also can react automatically if you download and install some magic small APPs to help you realize all of the above scenarios. In some sense, the smart phone becomes really 'smart'. It can connect people by each other and fulfill the task. It is the smart intermediator between people and different tasks. It helps people to perform some established tasks even without people's firsthand operation. So we can deduce a conclusion that social activities online nowadays have the possibility to be completed by smartphones automatically. It infers that social activities online among people actually are the "social activities" among smartphones or other intelligent products.

2   State of the Art

As we can see from the above that if the hardware become socialized among themselves, the object-object interaction and the relationship among them will be inevitably discussed. Will it increase the complexity of object-object interaction? How can it find the other one which provides exactly the service for the benefit of the human beings? How can the relationship among objects be maintained and developed? All these questions lead to the paradigm known as the Social Internet of Things (SIoT). It comes into being when the Social Network meets the Internet of Things[2].

2.1   The Social Network

Starting from the first user of the social network - Justin Hall, student of Swarthmore College, create his 'blog' website in 1994, the history of socialization has been enriched

---

[1] http://www.chyxx.com/industry/201608/439365.html.

[2] In the paper of "The Social Internet of Things (SIoT) – When Social Networks meet the Internet of Things: Concept, Architecture and Network Characterization" (*Computer Network*. 2012), Luigi Atzori and his co-authors have clearly reviewed the brief history of SIoT based on existing studies. In China, there is little research on SIoT, and the existing research on SIoT is no more deep than foreign researchers. So how the Social Networks meets the Internet of Things can be found in the above paper. In this article, the author will not explore any more.

by fast-developing technology. Suddenly, the unplanned rise of social media and self-generated content transformed the internet from a bland information platform into a social network. One of the key words of social network is 'share'. Different from the infant stage - SNS, which aims at providing multiple sections of information, not pays attention to individual consciousness, the Social Network provides a vivid stage for individuals to show themselves. Nowadays, comprehensive social communities, vertical social communities focused on specific areas, and social communities with information flow focus appeared one after another. All in all, the most important things behind all is socialization. Socialization is defined as a kind of communicative and connective behavior in social life. If we enlarge the range of targets for socialization, not only human beings, but also objects can be included.

2.2   The Internet of Things (IoT)

The Internet of Things integrates a large number of heterogeneous and pervasive objects that continuously generate information about the physical world [1], through unique addressing schemes and standard communication protocols, are able to interact with each other and cooperate with their neighbors to reach common goals [2]. If the Social Network can help people interact with each other, the Internet of Things will help to set up intelligent and communicative relationship between human beings and objects and among objects themselves on the internet.

EU [3] has divided the development of The Internet of Things into three stages: the first stage is to be embedded into consumer electronics applications. It can be regarded as build the skin and five senses of The Internet of Things in order to perceive and collect information. Typical 'things' of this stage are two-dimension code tag and reader, RFID tag and reader, cameras, GPS and so on. The second stage is the application of The Internet of Things in vertical industry. In this stage, the nerve center and the brain of The Internet of Things will be build, which means the network including the communication, management and information processing will be formed. We are now in this stage. Unfortunately, the barriers among different hardware platforms, operational systems, data bases and intermediators have not been overcome yet. The barriers lead to different problems such as high cost of the deployment, lack of information share among different systems and industries, and the waste of time and resources. The last stage of The Internet of Things is the final realization of socialization. In this stage, social division of The Internet of Things has been set-up according to the needs of different industries. A wide range of intelligence has been applied not only based on industry expertise, but also help to share the interest. Eventually a new eco-system will be achieved. This new eco-system of The Internet of Things is the Social Internet of Things.

2.3   The Social Internet of Things

As mentioned above, the Social Internet of Things is a new eco-system among intelligent objects. This new eco-system indicates social relationship among objects: every object can look for the desired service using its friendships in a distributed manner. By analysis of the social network structure, which derives from the objects interactions based on the defined social relationships by human beings, things will be associated to the services they can deliver. In this new eco-system, things will be associated to the services they can deliver within a given social network of objects. The advantages of this new eco-system are navigability, scalable, trustworthiness and openness.

Navigability. The Social Internet of Things runs like a human being society. In the system, every object can use its own social relationship to query its friends, the friends of the friends…to find out the most efficient scalable discovery of objects and services.

Scalable. During the process of find out the most efficient choice by using the same principles which human beings react in their social networks, each object will find the result in a distributed manner, which guarantees the scale of search.

Trustworthiness. in another way of explanation, the usefulness of each object's social relationship. Can the friendship between two objects be trusted? It indicates the fact that each object can autonomously learn, storage and adjust the friendship by each interaction with another object. Just like human beings, object will accumulate inter-object experiences to help itself supplement, correct the 'brain' in order to guarantee the efficiency of next interaction - friendship.

Openness. means the system is not closed one, it can be developed by continuous learning of object. In this sense, each object can navigate new object and establish new friendship according to the interest of human beings. What's more, the rules of running the whole system can be the result of participatory design of human beings by using open and shared platform in order to make the system sustainable.

It can be seen that the novel concept of Social Internet of Things (SIoT), based on a sort of social relationship among objects, analogously to what happens for human beings. The Social Internet of Things has the advantages of navigability, scalable, trustworthiness and openness. We also can see that the core issue of the Social Internet of Things is how to make different objects socialized, in another word, how to build the relationship among different objects (Fig. 2).

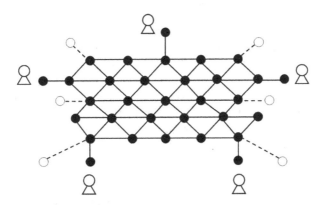

Fig. 2. The visual eco-system of Social Internet of Things

Based on Friske's theory of four elementary relational models[3], [4] has summarized the following relationships that can be derived in the reference system architecture.

Parental Object Relationship. It reflects the homogeneous objects originated in the same period by the same manufacturer.

Co-location Object Relationship. It means the relationship among objects used always in the same place or environment. For example, the popular business idea of smart home or smart city.

Co-work Object Relationship. It is established whenever object collaborate to provide a common IoT application, that is to say, to fulfill the same task.

Ownership Object Relationship. It is established among heterogeneous objects which belong to the same user. For example, a user can own mobile phone, music player, game consoles and other digital appliance at the same time.

Social Object Relationship. It is established among objects when different users' devices and sensors can come into contact with each other for social needs.

2.4   The Development of the Social Network and the Internet of Things in China

The Social Internet of Things has just in its infant stage of China now or even has not come into being.

The development of the Social Network in China has undergone four stages. The earliest stage is the infant stage, evolving from BBS of Web 1.0 era. The first BBS in China is recorded as 'Shu Guang', including the main functions of releasing the information, internet community, real-time message and chatting room. Tianya, Maopu and Xici Alley, which are still popular nowadays, are the typical examples in this stage. In the second stage, the purpose of the social communities is not to collect and release bunch of information, but for entertainment. Not long after Facebook has established in 2004, Ren Ren community (established in 2005) along with Kai Xin community (established in 2008) become the most popular social communities of this stage and embrace the birth of the Social Network in China in Web 2.0 era. In this stage, videos, articles, questions & answers, and even the encyclopedia become the major information which can be shared and found in the community. Due to time consumption in preparation of online information and lack of real-time feedback of the information, in the third stage, the information online can be cut into very short pieces, normally no more than 140 Chinese characters. The quick feedback and interaction between information provider and reader has summoned up mass users in a very short time. Sina Weibo as a typical example in this stage has successfully helped the Social Network in China draw the attention of capital investment. The fourth stage is called vertical social community.

---

[3] A. P. Fiske. The four elementary forms of sociality: framework for aunified theory of social relations. *Psychological review*. Vol. 99, pp.: 689-723. 1992

.

This kind of the Social Network in China is not the end. It aims at small groups of people who share the same interest on a specific area. The basic logic behind this is to enlarge the concept of the micro-group socialization based on the commercial interest of market customization. These four stages show us the fact of development of the Social Network in China: from copy to self-creation for localization purpose. The rising number of users of the Social Network in China also brings the problems such as online water army, zombie fans, false advertisement and so on.

The development of the Internet of Things in China is quite fast. One typical example is the booming of intelligent home appliances in recent years. Before this wave, Chinese government and information integrator has launched the birth of smart earth, smart city, smart transportation, smart government and information construction of industries. The "Internet Plus" strategy made by Chinese government plays an important role for the development of the Internet of Things in China. From the current situation, R&D manufactures such as Haier, Midea, Changhong, HUAWEI, ZET and internet companies such as Baidu, Ali, 360 and Xiaomi will lead the trend of the market. For example, in 2014, Xiaomi has started to plan its market layout of intelligent home appliances and introduce to Chinese markets several home appliances such as smart TV, Xiaomi box, router and air-cleaner. Thanks to its success in smart phone market, in 2015, Xiaomi has introduced several intelligent home appliances sets to market such as multi-functional gateway, sensors for windows and gates, human sensors, and wireless switch.

3 Service Design Strategy

From the review of the basic idea of the Social Network, the Internet of Things, and the Social Internet of Things, we can see that all the foundation of the concepts is the western interpretation of socialization.

From the review of the development of the Social Network and the Internet of Things in China, we can see there are different strategies to establish the social relationship among objects by providing services.

3.1 Assumption 1: Parasitic Strategy

In biology, parasitism is a non-mutual relationship between species, where one species, the parasite, benefits at the expense of the other, the host. In biology, the host will finally be consumed by the parasite. But in the internet society, the parasitic strategy is just to plant objects such as RFID tag to a certain traditional industry for the purpose of information reading. For example, for a shopping mall, traditional products tagged with RFID card will help it to do the storage check and management. By each reading of individual smart phone with RFID reader, the shopping mall can collect the rough data of popularity of each product. This kind of interaction is taken into place within a certain number of objects. But the relationship between each object is not social at all, it is destined. If one of the object in the system fails, other objects will lose their performances. That is to say, all the objects within this strategy cannot make a choice (Fig. 3).

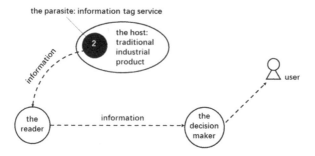

Fig. 3. Parasitic service design strategy

3.2 Assumption 2: Interconnected Strategy

This strategy can be seen from many examples of smart home. For example, the smart doorbell nowadays is become more and more popular in Chinese families. The digital camera acts as the guard to capture and record any movement into images before the door and automatically send it to the smart phone of the house owner. The house owner can even talk to the people at the door even when he or she is not at home through the smart doorbell.

Another example is the object-object interaction between Xiaomi scale and Xiaomi smart bracelet. Will the change in weight directly lead to different standard of exercises through the interaction between these two smart products? The answer is 'No' at present, but 'Yes' in the coming future.

From the first example, we can see how gruffly the data be gathered and sent to the user. The socialization between objects is uncivilized. And the objects remain silent. Even for the smart phone, it is only a tool in this circumstance. And without it, the smart doorbell becomes stupid.

As for the second example, will the scale collect the data of weight and make an analysis? Yes, it is possible. Will the bracelet make the decision for the exercise based on the analysis of the scale? No. It is always the smart phone user who is actually behind all of these objects to make the decisions. The scale and the bracelet only interconnect because of the existence of the smart phone. They cannot make a choice.

But if the big-data model building function can be achieved by the scale or the bracelet through the cloud technology, the objects can understand the user better by better perception and prediction, will the smart phone be replaced? In this sense, the object become really smart to help the users to make some decisions.

3.3 Assumption 3: Symbiosis Strategy

Symbiosis, in Chinese culture, means different people or things can stay with each other in peace. It respects the differentiation, at the same time, emphasizes on the value of concordance among differentiation. It teaches us to look at an object within different systems. These different systems can be seen as the ripple on the water. As shown in Fig. 4, the first level of the object system is family object system. In this system, the original object can have two roles - as equal as other objects in the family or can be the parental object in the family. Within a given rule or standard, the parental role of the object in the family will guide it to find and discover novel resources to implement the services in the family object system. The second level of the object system is co-location object system. In this system, objects can belong to different families. They have to communicate with each other to build up the trustfulness. Co-location means all these objects are performed in one space. The third level of the object system is co-task object system. In this system, objects find each other and connect to fulfill the same task. The efficiency of compatibility with each other will influence a lot on the relationship among the objects. The forth level of the object system is stranger object system. This system is full of uncertainty and risks. The degree of trustfulness is weakest in this level. Many exchanges will happen here in order to establish a relationship. From this picture, we can also infer that symbiosis can be achieved easier in the family system. And through different information exchanges, symbiosis can be achieved from broader level of the object system. The picture also indicates that each object system belongs to a boarder object system. Radical innovation normally happened easily to an object, but gradual innovation should be achieved by the whole system. The real purpose of symbiosis is

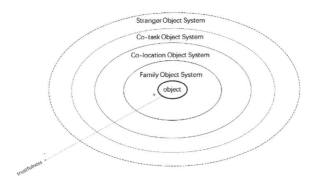

Fig. 4. Symbiosis strategy of an object interpreted by the form of the ripple

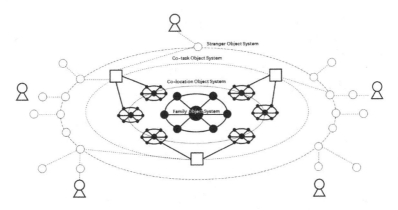

Fig. 5. Symbiosis service design strategy for SIoT

to enhance the value of the whole system by information exchanges among different objects and object systems to build up the relationship. Then the objects within the system become really smart and self-developed, which echoes the nature of the Social Internet of Things (Fig. 5).

4   Conclusion

It is hard to tell whether there is a period in history as bustling as today. Especially in China, Chinese people has experienced fast iteration of lifestyles within 30 years. The Social Network and the Internet of Things seem to invade their lives. And the combination of them will be more evolutionary. It is not a product, or a kind of technology, or a website, or an App to be redesigned. It is actually not the problem of design; it is the birth of a new eco-system which make different objects become socialized.

From Assumption 1-parastic strategy, we can see that it is not the right service design strategy for SIoT. From Assumption 2-interconnected strategy, we can see that the objects in the system are not smart at all and they cannot be socialized with each other without the help of some key technologies such as big data. Neither the former two strategies have considered about the context of SIoT's application. Considering Chinese culture and tradition, the Assumption 3-symbiosis strategy is much closer to what Chinese behave in the Social connection. So the services designed to achieve symbiosis in social connection will be the strategy for the Social Internet of Things in China considering its cultural and traditional context.

References

1. Nitti, M., Atzori, L., Cvijikj, I.P.: Friendship selection in the social internet of things: challenges and possible strategies. IEEE Internet Things J. 2(3), 240–247 (2014)
2. Sarma, S., Brock, D., Ashton, K.: The networked physical world: proposals for the next generation of computing commerce, and automatic identification. AutoID Centre White Paper (1999)
3. Hequan, W.: Things will eventually perceive the society. Machine Design and Manufacturing Engineering (2012)
4. Atzori, L., Iera, A., Morabito, G.: The Social Internet of Things (SIoT)-when social networks meet the internet of things: concept, architecture and network characterization. Comput. Works 56, 3594–3608 (2012)
5. Hu, J.: Social things: design research on social computing. In: Rau, P.-L.P. (ed.) CCD 2016. LNCS, vol. 9741, pp. 79–88. Springer, Cham (2016). doi:10.1007/978-3-319-40093-8_9
6. Atzori, L., Iera, A., Morabito, G.: SIoT: giving a social structure to the internet of things. IEEE Communications Letters (2011)
7. Kranz, M., Roalter, L., Michahelles, F.: Things that twitter: social networks and the internet of things. In: What Can the Internet of Things Do for the Citizen (CIoT) Workshop at the Eighth International Conference Pervasive Computing (2010)
8. Yonghua, L.: 30 years of the social network in china: free connection among people. The Internet Economy (2015)
9. Atzori, L., Iera, A., Morabito, G.: From 'smart objects' to 'social objects': the next evolutionary step of the internet of things. IEEE Internet Things J. 52, 97–105 (2014)

Design for Social Innovation Supported by Social Based Technologies

Teresa Franqueira[✉] and Gonçalo Gomes

Universidade de Aveiro, Aveiro, Portugal
{teresa.franqueira, goncalo}@ua.pt

Abstract. The use and democratisation of new digital technologies have given visibility to groups of people and grassroots organizations that can be considered agents of change in the transition to a more sustainable world. Design plays an important role in the definition of strategies and in the development of innovative solutions to tackle some of the contemporary problems society faces. This paper aims to show several projects developed over the last 5 years in the subject Design for Social Innovation at the Master in Design and the Master in Engineering and Product Design at the University of Aveiro, and its relation to the new social media and technologies. By using Service Design tools to improve Social Innovations and the integration of new digital technologies, we design new and improved solutions to foster sustainable development. The creation of a DESIS Lab has also allowed to develop innovative design solutions within local communities. The methodology used is based on Learning-by-Doing with an important and relevant initial phase using ethnographic methods. The results are showed as academic projects that can be applied and replicated in different contexts.

Keywords: Design · Social innovation · Service design · Social internet of things · DESIS network · ID+ DESIS lab

1 Introduction

The transition from the industrial age to the age of knowledge brought about diverse changes in the way we live, and the progressive meltdown of the welfare state and globalisation have created new problems and, thus, new needs (Beck 2004; Giddens 1999; McLaughlin and Davidson 1985).

The initiatives promoted by groups of citizens and grassroot organizations are a response to everyday problems (like childcare, support of the elderly, healthy food, socialization, amongst others) and to the needs arisen by this new reality, working in a radically different system to the traditional one.

The Web 2.0 phenomenon makes it possible for millions of people to belong to a community, collaborate and share the contents produced in its midst. In virtual communities size is not a problem, in turn it's an opportunity for ever increasing the wealth of contents and broaden its scope of influence and reach. In fact, one of the decisive factors for P2P networks to work is its size: the bigger they are, the bigger the contents produced and shared, and the bigger their attractiveness to a wider audience.

© Springer International Publishing AG 2017
N. Streitz and P. Markopoulos (Eds.): DAPI 2017, LNCS 10291, pp. 45–60, 2017.
DOI: 10.1007/978-3-319-58697-7_4

This "mass-innovation", as Leadbeater (2008) puts it, is the characteristic of the XXI Century: more ideas being shared by more people than ever before, with the help of technology.

When we focus on groups of people that have to collaborate face-to-face, the smaller the better. As they work based in physical peer-to-peer interaction and local collaborative relationships, the bigger they are, the more unmanageable they become as the number of links between people rises much faster than the number of people themselves.

This problem can never be solved, only managed and in modern life the solution has been gathering people together into organizations (Shirky 2008). But the typical organization is hierarchical with members answering to a manager that, in turn must answer to a higher manager and so on. This simplifies communication, by avoiding each member having to communicate with everyone else. And to do this, traditional management needs coordination and needs to simplify it; otherwise the costs of directing the members can be higher than the potential gain from directing them. This is why Shirky (2008) refers that certain activities may have some value but not enough to make them worth pursuing in any organized way.

However, the emergence of new social tools is lowering the costs of coordinating group action. In his book, "Here comes everybody" (Shirky 2008), he argued that we were living in a world where groups of people are coming together to share, work together and take some kind of public action, and that for the first time in history we have the tools that allow it; and that will change society.

8 years later we can see that Internet of Things are shaping society and helping tackling some social and technical problems all around the world.

2   What Is Social Innovation?

Although the Social Innovation topic has been around for 10 years, it has just now reached the political limelight in Europe, be it via EU' s financing policies or via the adoption of social innovation strategies by many governments, especially in countries where the welfare state places a heavy burden on the system.

It is precisely due to a failing welfare state, particularly in Europe, that many citizens have organised themselves to collectively and collaboratively address problems that the Government is unable to tackle (due to an ageing population and declining birth rates, the lack of financial resources made more acute by the 2008 crisis, among other factors).

According to Mulgan (2007) innovation becomes an imperative when problems are getting worse, when systems are not working or when institutions reflect past rather than present problems.

As Saint-Simon[1] phrased it, history consists of a succession of social orders and the movement from one order to the next is triggered by the rise of a new class. Different ideas fit different periods of history. The first of the leading peculiarities of the present age is that it is an age of accelerated transition. Mankind has outgrown old institutions and old doctrines, and has not acquired new ones yet. What we are seeing is that society is trying to acquire new ones, and this is possible through the rise of new ways of doing things.

Among several definitions to explain Social Innovation, we can use the one from Mulgan (2007): new ideas that work to meet pressing unmet needs and improve peoples' lives or the one from DESIS Network[2]: social innovation can be seen as a process of change emerging from the creative re-combination of existing assets (social capital, historical heritage traditional craftsmanship, accessible advanced technology) and aiming at achieving socially recognized goals in new ways. A kind of innovation driven by social demands rather than by the market and/or autonomous techno-scientific research, and generated more by the actors involved than by specialists.

These new ideas have been given birth to new forms of social organization, more innovative and in line with sustainable development and more active civic participation.

Observing contemporary society, cases of social innovation are continuously emerging in the form of new behaviours, new forms of organisation, new ways of living that indicate different and promising developments.

Social entrepreneurs and creative entrepreneurial communities are operating at a micro-level and have the potential to impact on society and profoundly change its character. What they have in common is that they are ordinary people that invent new ways of overcoming everyday problems and of participating in public and social life in an active way. This activity, not so common in a society mostly characterized by passivity, arises from the will to promote change and not to seat back and wait for traditional institutions to solve all everyday problems (Franqueira 2009).

Social innovations are very important because they advance behavioural changes, without which it is not possible to tackle the problems society as a whole faces. It is possible to find technological alternatives to minimise our carbon-foot print, for instances, but if peoples' behaviours are not changed, technology will eventually run out of options.

It can be acknowledged that the best way to manage change is not just through implementing new policies on whole populations but through testing and experiment on a small scale, often involving civil society and social entrepreneurs (Mulgan 2007).

This can be a major opportunity for the intervention of the Design community that is interested in developing innovative sustainable solutions for everyday problems and that wishes to promote, diffuse and eventually replicate those innovative ideas.

---

[1] http://www.britannica.com/EBchecked/topic/518228/Henri-de-Saint-Simon.

[2] http://www.desisnetwork.org/about/.

3 Service Design and Design for Social Innovation

The difficulty to conciliate social wellbeing, as it is understood today, and sustainability concerns converges more and more towards a consensus on the absolute need to implement new policies and strategies based on sustainable development premises, and design cannot be a bystander in the process.

The approach to environmental subjects has been widely developed in the field of eco-design, aiming to minimise the environmental impact by merely redesigning existing products or designing new ones with recycled or eco-materials. However, trying to solve existing problems based on old methods can hardly lead to the implementation of an alternative successful strategy that can assure a truly new beginning. Instead it leads to the reinstatement of an old strategy, only complemented by a new constraint. What are needed are alternative strategies that imply new ways of knowledge and design thinking models, which are able to promote sustainable solutions for a new scenario building. However, the process to reach this aim is far from being simple and obvious, for it implies changes in the socio-economical models built up along the technical history of the post-modern man.

Considering that design has played an instrumental role in the creation of the current system of consumption, shouldn't it be promoting its re-invention, departing from more sustainable principles? That re-invention could be done namely through the empowerment of social innovations and the services created at grassroots level, or by the redesign of top-down initiatives that in its original form have failed to deliver the results needed (Franqueira 2009).

In 1995, Morello (1995) has raised the question of designer's lack of capability to design services, suggesting that the role of the professional designer should be renewed to embrace the new reality and arguing that renewal would entail a deep revisitation of design's conceptions.

Today, social innovation is generating a constellation of small initiatives. Nevertheless, if favourable conditions are created, these small, local social inventions and their working prototypes can spread. They can be scaled-up, consolidated, replicated and integrated with larger programs to generate large-scale sustainable changes. To do that, new strategies able to introduce new ways of thinking in Design are needed, in order to promote sustainable solutions in the formulation of possible scenarios. This is one of the statements underlying the Design debate nowadays, and the role of design must be updated to achieve that goal.

Indeed, social innovation processes require visions, strategies and co-design tools to move from ideas to mature solutions and viable programs. That is, they ask for new design capabilities that, as a whole, can be defined as design for social innovation.

The Design for Social Innovation course has the goal of developing new solutions (or improving existing ones) through Service Design and the incorporation of social innovation bases in the collaboration and participation of all the stakeholders. Even though there is a focus in the exploration of the analogic component that forms social relationships, it's unavoidable to include the new digital platforms and social media as a tool to activate people.

For those working in this field, there has been a debate about the excessive use of Apps and social media platforms by the students as part of the solution to tackle social problems. The power of social networks, Apps, websites, blogs, etc. can't be ignored in defining behaviours, in particular in the new generations and in the organization of bottom-up social initiatives. The intensive use of technologies and technological devices however seems to push them away of the main objective of the problems: the absence of face-to-face relations and how to improve people's lives regarding human relationships.

3.1   Social Innovation and the Internet of Things

The link between Service Design and Design for Social Innovation is inextricable of new technologies and of what its integration allows. The democratisation of access to information through digital platforms allows a growing number of people to use different technologies and media to organise activities and perform tasks.

Groups of people and grassroot organizations find in the social networks and digital technologies the means to reach more people to collaborate, not only in the digital space, but, and more important, in the physical space.

People and objects are part of these solutions where the main and common goal is to create social, economical, environmental and cultural benefits.

These relations between people and things, where people interact with each other and with things, and things interact with people and between it selves, creates a new meaningful "space" - physical and virtual where it seems everything flows to reach a positive impact in our daily lives.

There are many examples on how new technologies are supporting and helping communities, in western countries or in developing regions.

In fact, there are some clusters that benefits from these connections between people, devices, objects and digital and virtual platforms: the health sector, agriculture or education are some of those clusters.

Many elements of the IoT model, such as cheap sensors and wireless technologies, are well suited to conditions in developing countries. Organizations of all kinds are creating and using IoT networks to deliver new solutions that can increase living standards, and they are doing so without the need for large financial investments or the heavy involvement of state bureaucracy (Purdy and Davarzani 2015).

IoT offers us opportunity to be more efficient in how we do things, saving us time, money and often emissions in the process. It allows companies and governments to re-think how they deliver better services to their citizens.

The European Commission and EU member states are committed to developing strategies to support experiments and the deployment of IoT technologies and services.[3] One of the key strategic goals of Europe regarding the IoT is to promote a human-centred IoT where European values empower citizens rather than machines and corporations.

---

[3] www.paneuropeannetworks.com.

Involving citizens in the definition of a better, smarter and collaborative city, is key to have a more participatory and more responsible civil society, where each and everyone can and should contribute, where grassroot organizations can flourish and where governments and corporations have a responsible and ethical approach to welfare and environmental sustainability.

4   ID+ DesisLab and the Course of Design for Social Innovation

Assuming design as an activity of creation - through its interventions, and with social and cultural responsibility, having a strategic role in reducing superfluous consumption in the contemporary society - the course (Design for Social Innovation) now assumes a clear focus on the design of services that promote economic growth through an ethical and responsible approach and an active citizenship through collaboration and co-design practices.

This special focus on the creation of product-service systems allows the bridge between scientific education and the practical extent and points to the need for students to adopt a sensitive approach to the dialogue between design and society, environment and economy. This method aims to provide and develop specific design skills, delivering students essential knowledge about the holistic process of design and the critical analysis of reality, structural to the acquisition of essential knowledge for an innovative design praxis.

This is an approach we develop under the influence of our activity as a DESIS Lab, the only in Portugal and hosted by the Research Institute for Design, Media and Culture [ID+], a multidisciplinary research structure anchored in two institutions: The University of Aveiro (Department of Communication and Art) and the University of Porto (School of Fine Arts).

Named ID+ DESIS Lab and a member of the DESIS Network since 2011, this research lab aims to stimulate design-led sustainable social change initiatives, to map creative communities by gathering case studies of social innovation in Portugal and to promote social innovations and sustainability among the Portuguese design community.

It was within this context, and perceiving that by 2009 courses of "Design for social innovation" in Design Schools, at undergraduate and graduate levels, were almost inexistent in Portugal — and all over the world — that our teaching in this domain began, in this initial phase under the name "Social Ergonomics of Design", an optional course of the Master's Program of Design.

Assuming a role of transition from the well-recognized and established practices, such as product and graphic design, to the emergent reality of service design, the "Social Ergonomics of Design" course allowed us to progressively include the Design for Social Innovation topic on the daily vocabulary of students, colleagues and various stakeholders with whom we established strong collaborations since the beginning of our activity. This condition also promoted an internal debate about the relevance of this new fields of the Design activity and their connection with traditional methods of Design teaching.

The progressive formation of the DESIS Network, with examples of DESIS Labs being created in other universities around the world and projects being developed by other former PhD students, provided positive support in order to overcome local difficulties by indicating that the "Design for Social Innovation" was being constituted as an affirmed field in Design theory and practices. It also worked as an example to be showcased at the University of Aveiro.

DESIS Labs are based in Design Schools and design-oriented universities and can be extensions of already existing entities or new ones. This statement was considered in the constitution of the DESIS Lab in the ID+ Institute. The institute was already established as a research unit in 2011 and included not only social innovation, but also other areas of design theory and practice in its activities. The ID+ DESIS Lab[4] was founded in 2011 as a research group, to operate as part of the +ID Institute. The ID+ DESIS Lab is organized around the following main themes (among others) that are related to social innovation:

service design and strategic design for sustainability;
education for creativity and innovation;
design for the empowerment of local economies and local knowledge.

5 Academic Projects

The last five years showed us that most of the principles previously mentioned were on the foundation of the Design for Social Innovation course, and allowed us to implement new praxis methodologies where students can use, reinterpret and expand most of their traditional design skills acquired during the undergraduate program in Design. The opportunity to work in real contexts and social issues, with people they can interact with, stakeholders eager to collaborate and seeing results having impact in people's life, revealed us that this is a highly rewarded process for students, teachers, stakeholders and the community where the projects are developed and implemented.

The following projects are just some examples of how students tackled selected briefs, in what way they settled strategies to enhance communication between communities and how new technologies are essential in the establishment of these practices.

5.1   Title: Conta" (Tell")

Course edition: 2014/2015
Students: André Silva, Dirce Russo, Jorge Madeira, Luca Gorgoglione, Sara Rizza
Description: A collaboration project with Museu Marítimo de Ílhavo (Maritime Museum of Ílhavo) regarding the preservation of the collective memories of cod fishermen.

---

[4] http://www.idmais.org/desislab/.

Students developed a service where the local community could participate in co-design workshops, based on the storytelling of old fishermen experiences and supported by a network of local institutions, such as schools of Art and Design, schools of Tourism and Hospitality and schools of Performative Arts.

The outcomes of the workshops, might result in gastronomic experiences, exhibitions or performances, among others, could then be enjoyed by the museum's visitors (Figs. 1 and 2).

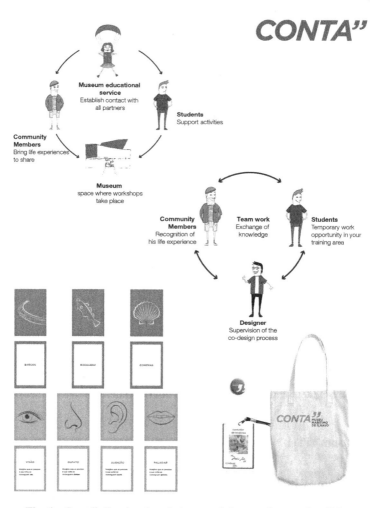

Fig. 1. Conta": Service description, workshop cards, merchandising

Fig. 2. Conta": facebook page and website (homepage, project description, workshop description, calendar)

5.2 Title: Pé Na Ria

Course edition: 2015/2016
Students: Andrea Taverna, Hélder Azevedo, Marta Gonçalves
Description: A tourism service where the heritage, cultural and natural resources of the "Ria" de Aveiro lagoon were enhanced through the connection of memories,

knowledge and traditions from the local community, particularly the fishing activity, and the fishermen themselves. Its main objective was to provide a bigger link between the visitor and the city by proposing a new touristic experience with the guidance of retired professional of several activities associated with the "Ria" de Aveiro lagoon.

Managed through a web platform that allowed the customization of the service, tourists could engage in fishing activities, salt harvesting and gastronomical practices supported by a network of stakeholders that ensured the success of the service (Figs. 3 and 4).

Fig. 3. Pé na Ria: service description, support equipment.

Pé na Ria
Mobile APP and
Website

Fig. 4. Pé na Ria: website (service description, register page, past experiences) and mobile app.

5.3   Title: Avós E Nós (Grandparents and Us/Knots)

Course edition: 2015/2016
Students: Joana Silva, Joana Carvalho, Mónica Carvalho, Tiago Gomes
Description: With the constant average life expectancy increase searching for better practices and solutions that promote wellbeing for elderly people became one of the main issues in modern societies. Raising awareness to ageing among younger

generations was at the core of this service where the challenge stood in achieving intergenerational relations on a "win-win" perspective, simultaneously improving the actual living conditions of elderly and allowing youngers to outlook their own future. The final solution proposed consisted of a web platform — where register members could offer or request specific services — and a "loyalty card" where members might save the total or part of the income from the services provided. This "plafond" could later be used on amenities from nursing homes or health care institutions (Figs. 5 and 6).

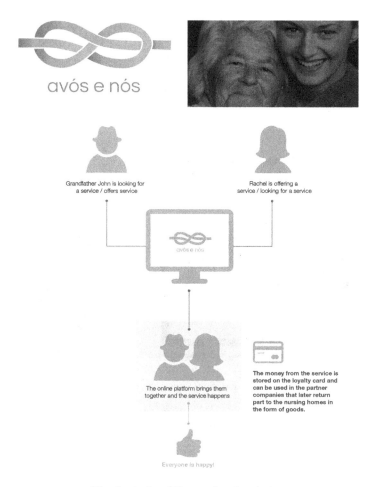

Fig. 5. Avós e Nós: service description

Fig. 6. Avós e Nós: loyalty card, website, advertising

5.4   Title: Cãovida

Course edition: 2013/2014
Students: João Merendeiro, João Jacinto, Carlos Eduardo Pereira, Joana Pires, Cristina Fernandes, José Nogueira
Description: Consisting in the redesign of a pre-existing service, the "Cãovida" project was initially developed with the objective of promoting good health habits in kids by walking a dog. Aimed at younger generations with obesity problems the original service consisted in a kit with a manual, a pedometer, a leash and a scarf.

Identifying several problems, such as the obligation of having a dog, the lack of tracking of the proposed activities and motivational issues, students proposed a "game based" solution where all the tracking activity were registered trough an app with diverse community challenges, where members could compete among themselves. Besides that, dog kennels were included as stakeholders where members could borrow a dog if they don't have their own (Figs. 7 and 8).

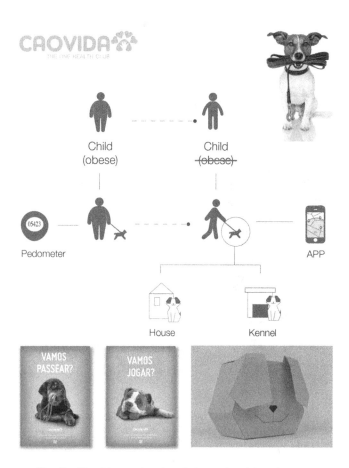

Fig. 7. Cãovida: service description, advertising, kit box.

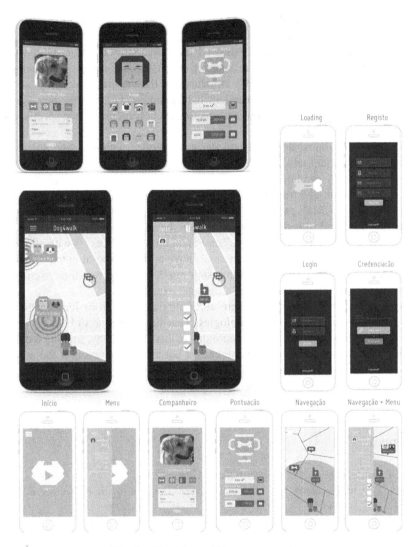

Fig. 8. Cãovida: mobile app screenshots

6   Conclusions

Latest advances in technology, that brought us less expensive ways of mass communication, low-cost hardware, crowdsourcing and internet of things, also provided new ways of (re)envisioning sevices and public services with the potential to have a strong social impact in such different fields as healthcare, environmental sustainability, education, transport, political representation, housing among others. To empower citizens in new ways that, until now, were only accessible to a small minority, with this tools, stimulates dipper level of involvement on their communities and allows them to engage in innovative practices of civic action.

The academic projects presented showed us a diversity of circumstances where distinctive technologies were used to support social actions, either as a back-office infrastructure — when they provide a structure for the service to develop — or as tangible interactive tool that encourages new habits and practices —— as showed on the "Cãovida" where the gamification project was the actual response to one specific social need.

Nowadays it is almost impossible to design a service without using social technologies as an important add-on. All the cases we showed take advantage of some of the most usual tools available for everyone. Digital social networks platforms are currently an important and immediate way of reaching people, as we could see on the "Conta" and "Pé na Ria" examples; dynamic websites are fundamental systems of assuring the flow and speed of communication between providers and users of a service, as presented in the "Avós e Nós" case; and mobile devices — with all the new capabilities that today thousands of individuals have at their disposal in their pocket — also offer new functions like geo tracking, step monitoring and real-time exchange of information, among others, like in the "Cãovida" example.

This is a "brave new world" where technologies learn from humans but also humans have a lot to learn from technologies. Teaching someone to be a twenty first century designer is a task that cannot ignore this reality. In this way, training a designer to develop meaningful social services requires a border interpretation of the notion of social realm, not limited to the social relations between individuals but also between individuals and… things.

References

Beck, U.: La società del rischio. Carocci Editore, Urbino (2004)

Franqueira, T.: Creative places for collaborative cities. Doctoral thesis, Politecnico di Milano (2009)

Giddens, A.: Risk and responsibility. Mod. Law Rev. **62**(1), 1–10 (1999)

Leadbeater, C.: We-Think. Profile Books, London (2008)

McLaughlin, C., Davidson, G.: Builders of the Dawn : Community Lifestyles in a Changing World. Book Publishing Company (1985). 1990

Morello, A.: Discovering design means [Re-]discovering users and projects. In: Discovering Design. The University of Chicago Press, Chicago (1995)

Mulgan, G.: Social Innovation: what is it, why it matters, how it can be accelerated. Basingstoke Press, The Young Foundation Report, The Young Foundation, London (2007)

Purdy, M., Davarzani, L.: The internet of things is now a thing. Stanford Soc. Innov. Rev. **3**(4), 8–10 (2015)

Shirky, C.: Here comes everybody. Penguin Books, London (2008)

Social Impact of Enhanced Gaze Presentation Using Head Mounted Projection

David M. Krum[1], Sin-Hwa Kang[1($\boxtimes$)], Thai Phan[1], Lauren Cairco Dukes[2], and Mark Bolas[1]

[1] USC Institute for Creative Technologies,
12015 Waterfront Drive, Playa Vista, CA 90094, USA
{krum,kang,tphan,bolas}@ict.usc.edu
[2] Clemson University,
101 Calhoun Drive, 105 Sikes Hall, Clemson, SC 29634, USA
lcairco@gmail.com

Abstract. Projected displays can present life-sized imagery of a virtual human character that can be seen by multiple observers. However, typical projected displays can only render that virtual human from a single viewpoint, regardless of whether head tracking is employed. This results in the virtual human being rendered from an incorrect perspective for most individuals in a group of observers. This could result in perceptual miscues, such as the "Mona Lisa" effect, causing the virtual human to appear as if it is simultaneously gazing and pointing at all observers in the room regardless of their location. This may be detrimental to training scenarios in which all trainees must accurately assess where the virtual human is looking or pointing a weapon. In this paper, we discuss our investigations into the presentation of eye gaze using REFLCT, a previously introduced head mounted projective display. REFLCT uses head tracked, head mounted projectors and retroreflective screens to present personalized, perspective correct imagery to multiple users without the occlusion of a traditional head mounted display. We examined how head mounted projection for enhanced presentation of eye gaze might facilitate or otherwise affect social interactions during a multi-person guessing game of "Twenty Questions."

Keywords: Enhanced gaze · Head mounted projection

1 Introduction

Virtual humans are increasingly being researched and developed for applications in which they must engage and interact with real humans. Some of these applications include virtual tour guides for museums [40, 41], adjuncts to therapy [5, 13], support for training [33], and instruments of social science research [38]. While there are many ways to display virtual humans, one important technique for presenting these virtual humans portrays them as life-sized images on large monitors or large projection screens to be viewed by one or more individuals.

© Springer International Publishing AG 2017
N. Streitz and P. Markopoulos (Eds.): DAPI 2017, LNCS 10291, pp. 61–76, 2017.
DOI: 10.1007/978-3-319-58697-7_5

However, such screens have limitations that can hamper important aspects of social interaction.

A large 2D display screen, whether it is large monitor or a large screen for a projector, is typically limited to displaying imagery that is rendered from a single viewpoint at a time. This means that if there are observers who are not standing at the viewpoint location for which the imagery was rendered, then the perspective of that imagery will be incorrect for those observers. The perspective mismatch will occur if there are multiple observers, or if a single observer moves around without providing the rendering system with location updates.

Fig. 1. An over-the-shoulder view of a user interacting with a virtual human, presented with REFLCT, a near axis, head mounted, retro-reflective projection display. The character and wooden wall pattern are projected. The corrugated materials are real props mounted around the retro-reflective screen.

This perspective mismatch can lead to ambiguous social cues when observers try to determine where a virtual human is pointing or looking. The "Mona Lisa" effect is one example of problems that can arise. This effect, named after the painting by Leonardo da Vinci, is a perceptual illusion in which the 2D image of a character appears to be looking or pointing at an observer, regardless of where the observer is standing in relation to the character. There appears to be a human perceptual process that realigns the perceived gaze direction of characters who are depicted as gazing straight out of the image surface. This yields the unsettling effect of characters in paintings who appear to follow observers with their eyes. This perceptual effect and related invariant perception issues have been reported and studied by a number of researchers from the 17th century to current times [12,16,29,34,36]. Some work suggests that the Mona Lisa effect is a consequence of the perceptual system estimating and compensating for the average local slant of the display surface behind the imagery [8,44]. The effect also appears to have a neurological basis [11]. Our research interest is the development of display technologies that help to ameliorate the limitations of displays that yield such mismatched perspective cues, particularly when presenting virtual characters for training.

Some display systems employ multiplexing over time, frequency, or polarization to display more than one viewpoint. For example, a stereoscopic display can alternatively display left and right eye viewpoints for a single individual, using shutter glasses. Agrawala et al. extended this type of time multiplexed stereoscopy to create a head tracked virtual reality display for multiple users, with a trade off in reduced brightness and increasing flickering as users are added, and requiring users to wear shutter glasses and tracking sensors [2]. Leveraging techniques analogous to spatial multiplexing, light field displays, using a single projector and a spinning mirror, or a large array of projectors, can also provide perspective correct imagery to multiple viewers. However, such systems have complex hardware requirements. The spinning mirror approach requires a very high frame rate projector and a rapidly rotating mirror, for example 4,800 frames per second and 1,200 revolutions per minute [20,21]. The projector array approach can require multiple computers driving an array of 216 closely spaced projectors and a anisotropic light shaping diffuser [22].

Another approach to render projected imagery with correct perspective for multiple users led to the development of REFLCT (Retroreflective Environments For Learner-Centered Training), a near axis, head mounted projective display, which utilizes retroreflective screens [10,27]. With REFLCT, each user wears a tracked head mounted projector. Each user can only see the image generated by their own projector, due to the use of retroreflective screens. The retroreflective screens have the property of reflecting the light from each projector straight back to where it came from, and is thus visible only to the wearer of the projector. The system can thus render imagery of a virtual human with perspective correct and consistent gaze for each user. If the virtual character is looking at user A, each and every user will see the character looking at user A.

A unique aspect of the REFLCT system is how it leverages the imperfect performance characteristics of retroreflective materials. Light is not reflected purely on-axis, thus offering substantial energy at slightly off-axis angles. By mounting a pico-projector near a user's eyes, this reflected energy can be seen by the user. Previous head mounted projection systems used earlier projection technologies that provided less light and larger form factors. These systems required the projection to be aligned with the same optical axis as the user's eyes, typically facilitated by employing an optical combiner in front of the user's eyes. Recent pico-projectors offer enough brightness such that this is not an issue.

Retroreflective screen material is placed wherever virtual elements are to be displayed (see Fig. 1). A number of props, such as simulated cinderblock walls, sandbags, and camouflage netting, can be used to create a military themed stage and blend the screens into the environment. Other props could be used for alternative training settings. Retroreflective coatings can also be added to props, in the form of retroreflective cloth, retroreflective tape, or even a coating of fine retroreflective glass beads, allowing an image to be applied to arbitrary surfaces or even a sculpted human form.

In this paper, we discuss our evaluation of REFLCT and its effect on participants performing a multi-party social task.

2 Related Work

Mutual gaze, i.e. looking someone in the eye, is an important social signal for demonstrating interest and attention. Through the use of gaze, conversing parties are able to perform a number of functions to both express and control information flow, such as regulating the flow of conversation, conveying emotions, describing relationships, and constraining the amount of visual information received in order to avoid distraction [3,4,26]. The amount of gaze presented by an individual can influence social perceptions of that individual. Individuals who provided more gaze to an interviewer can receive higher socio-emotional evaluations [15]. Additionally, greater levels of eye contact can be associated with greater perceived dynamism, likability, and believability [9].

Much of the research to examine and enhance the communication of gaze in the human-computer interaction field, has sprung from efforts to improve video conferencing systems or to improve interactions with virtual humans. Some of these systems have included mechanical proxies for conversants and may also employ multiple cameras [31,37]. Other systems have used multi-camera configurations with large displays showing multiple conversants [32] or "video tunnels" [1], which utilize half-silvered mirrors to align cameras and displays and thus the sight lines of video conferencing participants. GAZE-2, developed by Vertegaal et al., is a hybrid approach, using half-silvered mirrors, a small array of cameras, and eye tracking to select and present the video imagery best representing eye contact to other participants in a multi-party video conference [43].

Virtual humans who demonstrate effective gaze can have positive impacts on social interactions. However, gaze may only provide a portion of the social signals needed to facilitate social interactions. Work by Wang et al. demonstrated that a virtual human conveying maximal attention, using continous gaze or staring, was less effective in establishing rapport with human counterparts than virtual humans who combine continuous gaze with postural mimicry and head nods as additional positive social feedback signals [45].

Displays to improve rendering, particularly for presenting individualized and perspective correct imagery for multiple users have followed three main approaches: projector arrays, head-mounted displays (HMDs), and head-mounted projective displays (HMPDs). Projector arrays coupled with asymmetrically diffusing screens [7,22,30] can create individualized perspective-correct views, but are expensive in terms of hardware and calibration effort. They require more projectors than users, with projectors positioned everywhere that a user might be. In most cases, they are configured to offer only horizontal image isolation. Eye-tracked autostereoscopic systems may be used to reduce the number of projectors required, but commercial systems are limited in size and viewing angle [39].

Head mounted displays (HMDs) can provide perspective correct mixed reality imagery for multiple users, using either a video or optical overlay upon a real view of the world. Video overlays mix synthetic imagery with a live camera view of the world using standard opaque head-mounted displays. Video overlays exhibit some artifacts, such as video frame lag (typically 1/30th s) and the downsampling of the world to video resolution. Optical overlays use translucent displays, allowing the real world to be seen through the display. Unfortunately, this often causes the virtual imagery to be translucent. Optical overlays can also make tracker lag and noise more apparent as the virtual imagery is compared to the real world. With either type of overlay, HMDs adds bulky optical elements in front of the user's eyes. These elements make it difficult for trainees to see each others' eyes and facial expressions. They can also interfere with sighting down a weapon.

Head mounted projective displays (HMPDs) can also be used for individualized virtual and augmented reality imagery. The previous generation of HMPDs differs from REFLCT in several ways. Chief among these is the use of projectors that shine onto an optical combiner, a semi-transparent mirror surface, in front of a user's eyes to create a projection path aligned with a user's optical path [14,17–19,35]. The partially reflective surface in front of the eyes can interfere with eye contact and head movements such as sighting down a rifle. The approach of REFLCT can be compared to Karitsuka and Sato [25] in that there is no optical combiner, but instead, REFLCT employs more compact components and a more optimal optical configuration, maintaining a small and fixed distance between the projector and the user's eyes.

3   Method

A user study was employed to examine the ability of the REFLCT system to accurately portray the gaze of a virtual human character in a social situation to multiple viewers at a time. This study engaged participants in a "Twenty Questions" game led by a virtual character. Three individuals asked yes/no questions of the virtual character in order to determine secret objects previously selected by the virtual character. The virtual character was presented using the REFLCT system, which could be used in a normal Head Mounted Projection (HMP) mode, delivering perspective correct imagery to each participant. It could also deliver imagery to each user that was rendered from a single viewpoint, in a Simulated Traditional Projection (STP) mode. Various measures of rapport and social response to the character were recorded using standardized surveys.

3.1   Apparatus

Study participants wore helmets fitted with a REFLCT projection unit (see Fig. 2). Each unit was fashioned out of a high density fiberboard framework, which can support a number of active LED markers for motion capture, a DLP based pico-projector, and an optional USB video camera for monitoring and

Fig. 2. A REFLCT head mounted projector unit incorporates a pico-projector, a mirror, and LED tracking markers onto a helmet. An optional USB video camera shown here can record or convey what the user sees.

recording the user's view. The USB cameras were not used in this study. The pico-projector is vertically mounted and projects down upon a small mirror oriented at 45°, which reflects the light forward. This places the optical axis of the projection closer to the user's eyes. A PhaseSpace Impulse active LED motion capture system determines the position and orientation of each REFLCT projection unit and distributes this information, via VRPN, to a corresponding PC. Each PC then renders the proper perspective view using the Unity game engine. Each REFLCT projector is connected by a DVI cable to the corresponding PC.

The software development environment was centered around the Unity game engine with scripting written in C#. The virtual human character was animated using the Smartbody character animation platform [23,42]. The character's voice consisted of spoken dialogue that was pre-recorded and then processed to determine visemes (mouth movements) and timing for character animation. Most character behaviors were automated, such as head and mouth movements. Specific gaze behaviors could be set according to the needs of the interaction or experimental condition, described later in this paper. Appropriate vocal responses and special gestures, such as affirmative nods, could be triggered by an experimenter operating a Wizard of Oz control panel. This experimenter and the control panel was hidden from the view of the participants during the experiment.

3.2   Design

The experiment used a 2 × 3 factorial between-subjects design with two factors: (i) two different types of projection display: Simulated Traditional Projection display (STP) and Head Mounted Projection display (HMP); and (ii) three different types of eye gaze behavior: extensive gaze, real-life gaze, and random gaze. The HMP condition reflects the true design intent of the REFLCT system. The simulation aspect of the Simulated Traditional Display condition was employed to improve the comparison of display styles with more consistent resolution and brightness than could be achieved by introducing a separate traditional projection display.

Participants. A total of 107 users were recruited via Craigslist and emails to our institute staff mailing list. The users (52% men, 48% women; mean age of 37 years) were randomly assigned to one of the 6 conditions to interact with the virtual character (position was a between subjects condition): HMP with extensive gaze (N = 21), HMP with real-life gaze (N = 17), HMP with random gaze (N = 18), STP with extensive gaze (N = 16), STP with real-life gaze (N = 16), and STP with random gaze (N = 19).

Stimuli. Study participants viewed the virtual character performing one of three gaze conditions. The general qualities of the gaze conditions are listed in this paragraph, and a description of how they were implemented under the two projection display conditions is given in the following paragraphs. The extensive gaze condition presented continuous mutual gaze between the virtual human and each participant throughout an interaction. The real-life gaze condition portrayed the virtual human with a gaze direction that shifted toward the participant who was currently playing his/her turn in the game. The random gaze condition presented the virtual human with a gaze that shifted between random points within the virtual human's visual field, at random intervals between 2 and 10 s.

In the HMP with Extensive gaze condition, each user was presented with full and direct gaze from the virtual human, which would be inconsistent and physically impossible in real life. This is possible in the HMP condition since REFLCT provides each user with a personalized view of the character. In the STP with Extensive gaze condition, users experienced the full gaze of the character as if it was presented on a traditional projection display, which means that the character was rendered from the center position, and thus was constantly staring straight out of the screen. Participants to the left and right positions would experience incorrect perspectives and also the "Mona Lisa" effect.

In the HMP with real-life gaze condition, users experienced consistent and correct perspective rendering of the virtual human's gaze as it shifted between users located at the left, center, and right locations. In the STP with real-life condition, users experienced the same behavior, but with perspective distortion of the character's gaze since the viewpoint was rendered from a single central location. A user at the left or right location would be shown the character rendered as if it was gazing at too great an angle, i.e. turning too sharply and gazing past the user's location.

In the HMP with random gaze condition, each user was presented with consistent and perspective correct rendering of the character shifting gaze between random points at a random interval as previously described. In the STP with random gaze condition, each user was presented with this same gaze behavior, but as rendered from a single central location, introducing perspective distortions.

To evaluate social impact on the participants' experiences, we used existing measurements including Virtual Rapport [24] to measure the users' feelings of being connected and together, as well as PANAS (Positive And Negative Affect Schedule) [46], Person Perception [28], questions concerning the "Twenty Questions" game [6], questions related to virtual human's eye gaze [6], and additional questions concerning the amount of eye contact from the virtual human (i.e. "What percentage of time do you think the virtual character was making eye contact with you?").

3.3 Procedure

Participation required a total of less than 60 min on an individual basis. Upon arrival, study participants were first provided with the informed consent form, which described the study in detail. Participants were asked to read through the document, and were given the opportunity to ask questions about the study.

Participants were then given an online questionnaire to record demographic information, ratings of experiences with video games, prior experience with virtual reality, prior interactions with virtual characters, as well as personality related information.

Participants were then led to the space where the experimental apparatus was located. They were each assigned a position in which to stand. The positions were located approximately 3 meters from the projection screen, and 20 degrees to the left and right of a perpendicular normal vector from the screen's surface. Participants were also joined by confederates, posing as additional participants, to form a group of three game players (1 or 2 participants randomly assigned to the left and/or right positions, and confederates standing in the center and filling any vacant participant positions). As the perspective correct HMP display and the perspective distorted STP display conditions do not differ much when viewed from the center position, only confederates were assigned to that position. The participants and confederates were then assisted in donning of head mounted projection displays and given instructions for the upcoming game play. The participants were then asked to perform one 10 min experimental trial randomly selected out of 6 possible conditions (2 display types × 3 gaze/gesture directions). In each trial, the participants/confederates played guessing games with the virtual character. The games consisted of the virtual character secretly "selecting" a object, such as a frog, tree, or ocean and responding to yes/no questions given by each participant/confederate in turn. The virtual character would respond with a variety of affirmative or negative responses or advise the player's to ask a yes/no question as appropriate. Each game would continue until 20 questions were asked or until the player's correctly guessed the secret object. Additional games would be run until the 10 min trial was completed. The confederates were trained to perform consistent actions throughout all of the interaction sessions and to allow the participants the opportunity to play a significant role in questioning and guessing in the games. Participants completed questionnaires after the experimental trial.

4   Results

We conducted a 2-way ANOVA to investigate the effect of a projection type and a gaze pattern on users' responses to the experience. We also performed a 2-way ANOVA to evaluate the effect of the condition and a gender on users' responses.

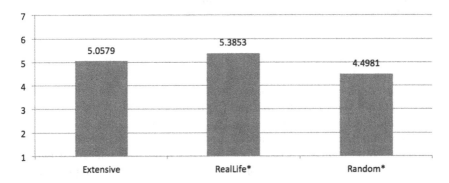

Fig. 3. Difference between user perception of enough and appropriate gaze from the virtual human across 3 gaze conditions (*p < .05).

For users' perceptions of enough and appropriate gaze from the virtual human, the gaze pattern affected the users' perceptions significantly [F(2, 101) = 4.03, p = .021] (see Fig. 3). Users felt they received enough and appropriate levels of gaze when they interacted with a virtual human that displayed the Real-life gaze (M = 5.38), but less so when interacting with a virtual human that presented Extensive gaze (M = 5.06) or Random gaze (M = 4.50). This implies that some users might have felt the extensive gaze to be too much and thus socially inappropriate. A Tukey HSD test shows that there was a statistically significant difference between the Real-life gaze and the Random gaze conditions (p = .018). There was no interaction effect with projection type for appropriate gaze level.

Regarding the users' report of the percentage of eye contact from the virtual human, the results show that there was a statistically significant difference among three gaze patterns [F(2, 101) = 3.97, p = .022] (see Fig. 4). Users reported that they had the greatest amount of eye contact from a virtual human

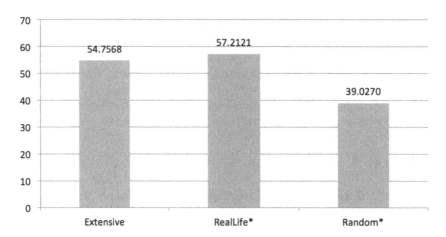

Fig. 4. Differences between user reports concerning the percentage of eye contact from the virtual human across 3 gaze conditions (*p < .05).

that displayed the Real-life gaze (M = 57.21%), compared to interacting with a virtual human that presented Extensive gaze (M = 54.76%) or Random gaze (M = 39.02%). A Tukey HSD test showed that there was a statistically significant difference between the Real-life gaze and the Random gaze (p = .029). There was no interaction effect between projection type and gaze pattern.

A deeper look at the percentage of eye contact from the virtual human, also shows that there is a statistically significant difference when testing the 6 conditions formed by the combination of 2 projection types and 3 gaze patterns [F(5, 93) = 2.86, p = .019] (see Fig. 5). According to the results of a Tukey HSD test, there is no statistically significant difference between any condition as we found no interaction effect between projection type and gaze pattern that is described above. However, there is a trend that users had the greatest eye contact from a virtual human displayed by HMP with extensive gaze (M = 60.14%) and less eye contact when they experienced HMP with real-life gaze (M = 57.65%), STP with real-life (M = 56.75%), or STP with extensive gaze (M = 47.69%).

Users also reported a similar amount of eye contact for the Real Life gaze in both the HMP with real-life gaze (M = 57.65%) and STP with real-life gaze (M = 56.75%) conditions. They also reported much less eye contact for STP with Extensive gaze (M = 47.69%), which is in contrast to the HMP with Extensive gaze condition (M = 60.14%). This is an interesting inconsistency as the extensive gaze condition in the STP projection condition was the worst scoring condition, if we disregard the random gaze conditions that correspond poorly with natural behavior: HMP with random gaze (M = 36.18%) and STP with random gaze (M = 41.63%).

This inconsistency between might be due to some type of interaction between Extensive gaze and the "Mona Lisa" effect, which can realign the apparant gaze direction in the STP projection condition. The "Mona Lisa" effect appears to

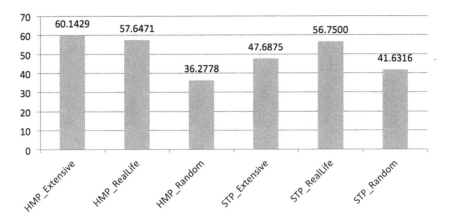

Fig. 5. Differences between user reports concerning the percentage of eye contact from a virtual human across 6 conditions.

break down in this case. Perhaps the Extensive gaze condition magnifies differences between the STP and HMP projection styles, creating increased perception of eye contact for the HMP condition. Perhaps the STP form of Extensive gaze is eventually perceived as slightly off and thus socially inappropriate and not true eye contact.

For users' feelings of rapport, we ran a Factor Analysis and obtained the four sub-scales of rapport scale. The Factor Analysis was a Principal Components Analysis with Varimax rotation (Kaiser-Meyer-Olkin Measure of Sampling Adequacy $= .806$, Bartlett's Test of Sphericity $< .001$). The first factor, Engagement, explains 31.65% of the variance (Cronbach's Alpha $= .91$). The second factor, Attachment, explains 14.21% of the variance (Cronbach's Alpha $= .79$). The third factor, Closeness, explains 6.59% of the variance (Cronbach's Alpha $= .65$). The fourth factor, Connection, explains 6.00% of the variance (Cronbach's Alpha $= .75$). There are low correlations among the sub-scales, thus we ran 2-way ANOVA using the condition and gender as independent variables for each sub-scale separately. The results demonstrate that there is a statistically significant difference among the 6 conditions [$F(5, 93) = 2.64$, p $= .028$] (see Fig. 6) and gender [$F(2, 93) = 7.52$, p $= .001$] for Closeness, but no statistically significant results were seen for the other sub-scales. Post-hoc test shows that HMP with extensive gaze (M $= 3.71$) is significantly higher than HMP with random gaze (2.39). Overall, there is a trend that users had the greatest feeling of closeness to a virtual human in HMP with extensive condition (M $= 3.71$) than HMP with real-life gaze (M $= 3.53$), STP with extensive gaze (M $= 2.94$), or STP with real-life gaze (M $= 2.92$) conditions. This implies that users might have felt more closeness to a virtual human when they had constant mutual gaze from the virtual human via an HMP display although they might have felt extensive gaze as inappropriate gaze as the gaze could be perceived as overwhelming. Users had the least feeling of closeness to a virtual human in the STP with random gaze

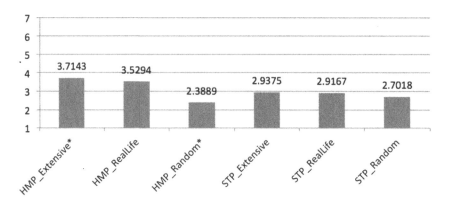

Fig. 6. Differences between users feelings of closeness to the virtual human across 6 conditions ($^*p < .05$).

condition ($M = 2.70$). Male users ($M = 3.24$) reported higher feeling of closeness to the virtual human than female users ($M = 2.69$). There were no other statistically significant results for projection type and gaze pattern nor was there an interaction effect for the two variables.

5   Discussion

With regards to the percentage of gaze perceived by users, the results show an interesting discrepency between extensive gaze in the HMP and STP conditions. The STP with Extensive gaze condition provided a lower level of gaze than the HMP with Extensive gaze condition. The Extensive gaze condition might be magnifying small but perceivable differences in the delivery of gaze between the two projection conditions. The trends in the Closeness subscale of the rapport measure suggest that HMP might facilitate social feelings of closeness, particularly with regards to extensive gaze.

Interestingly, participants appear to overestimate the percentage of eye contact provided to them by the virtual character. In the case of the Real-life gaze condition, the virtual character gazes at each game player in turn. With three players, participants could be expected to respond with estimates near 33%. However, the average estimates were over 50%. The Random gaze estimates were near 40% and should be much lower considering the character's random gaze. However, the participants' seemed to discount the continuous gaze provided in the Extensive gaze condition, responding with over 50% when a reasonable estimation might approach 100%.

The results suggest that behavior of the character is a strong cue for social interactions. For example, the gaze condition was the key factor in users deciding if the character provided the correct and appropriate level of mutual gaze. However, there were some small indications that the HMP condition, when highlighted by extensive gaze, could produce some measurable social effects.

Some participants reported that the character's eyes appeared to move even in the Extensive gaze condition. This may reveal some limitations of the current REFLCT system that reduced the effectiveness of the enhancement of gaze through personalized perspective correct rendering. The human eye can estimate the relative pose of an eyeball by comparing the brightness of the white sclera regions surrounding the iris and framed by the eye socket. If the relative brightness of the left and right regions of sclera varies, the eyeball is perceived as moving left and right. The pico-projectors used in the current REFLCT display take a 640×480 image that is downscaled to 480×320. That low resolution as well as the downscaling approximations could introduce some artifacts. Small movements of the user might shift pixels left and right, substantially changing the small number of pixels available to render the left and right sclera regions and causing variations in brightness and apparent eye motion. The current REFLCT resolution probably caused some uncertainty in judging gaze direction.

6 Conclusion and Future Work

Using a multi-party task involving interactions with a virtual human, this study was able to demonstrate some measurable social effects and trends when using the REFLCT system. The REFLCT system provides personalized perspective correct rendering for multiple users using head worn projectors and retrore-flective screens. This personalized perspective correct imagery can be used to enhance the portrayal of gaze provided by a virtual character. This is preliminary work that identifies future improvements needed in such systems and the subtlety required to measure the social effects involved.

While the gaze behaviors of the virtual character appeared to be strong factors in determining the social response, the projection condition had some influence on social measures. Differences appear to be most apparent with extensive gaze as rendered in REFLCT's head mounted projection display and when compared to a simulated traditional projection display.

Future versions of REFLCT and other head mounted projection systems must provide enough resolution to accurately portray eyes behavior, especially for conveying a steady and direct gaze without movement.

Acknowledgments. The authors would like to thank Joshua Newth and Logan Olson for early contributions to this project. This work was sponsored, in whole or in part, by the U.S. Army Research Laboratory (ARL) under contract number W911F-14-D-0005. Statements, expressed opinions, and content included do not necessarily reflect the position or the policy of the United States Government, and no official endorsement should be inferred.

References

1. Acker, S., Levitt, S.: Designing videoconference facilities for improved eye contact. J. Broadcast. Electron. Media **31**(2), 181–191 (1987)
2. Agrawala, M., Beers, A.C., McDowall, I., Fröhlich, B., Bolas, M., Hanrahan, P.: The two-user responsive workbench: Support for collaboration through individual views of a shared space. In: Proceedings of the 24th Annual Conference on Computer Graphics and Interactive Techniques, SIGGRAPH 1997, pp. 327–332. ACM Press/Addison-Wesley Publishing Co., New York(1997). http://dx.doi.org/10.1145/258734.258875
3. Argyle, M.: The Psychology of Interpersonal Behaviour. Penguin Books, London (1967)
4. Argyle, M., Cook, M.: Gaze and Mutual Gaze. Cambridge University Press, London (1976)
5. Aymerich-Franch, L., Bailenson, J.: The use of doppelgangers in virtual reality to treat public speaking anxiety: a gender comparison. In: Proceedings of the International Society for Presence Research Annual Conference, Vienna, Austria, March 2014
6. Bailenson, J.N., Beall, A.C., Blascovich, J.: Gaze and task performance in shared virtual environments. J. Vis. Comput. Anim. **13**(5), 313–320 (2002)
7. Baker, H., Li, Z.: Camera and projector arrays for immersive 3d video. In: Proceedings of the 2nd International Conference on Immersive Telecommunications, IMMERSCOM 2009, pp. 23:1–23:6. ICST (Institute for Computer Sciences, Social-Informatics and Telecommunications Engineering), ICST, Brussels (2009). http://dl.acm.org/citation.cfm?id=1594108.1594138
8. Banks, M., Rose, H., Vishwanath, D., Girshick, A.: Where should you sit to watch a movie? In: Proceedings of SPIE: Human Vision and Electronic Imaging (2005)
9. Beebe, S.: Effects of eye contact, posture and vocal inflection upon credibility and comprehension. Aust. SCAN J. Hum. Commun. **7**, 57–70 (1980)
10. Bolas, M., Krum, D.M.: Augmented reality applications and user interfaces using head-coupled near-axis personal projectors with novel retroreflective props and surfaces. In: Pervasive 2010 Ubiprojection Workshop, May 2010
11. Boyarskaya, E., Sebastian, A., Bauermann, T., Hecht, H., Tüscher, O.: The Mona Lisa effect: neural correlates of centered and off-centered gaze. Hum Brain Mapp. **36**(2), 619–632 (2015)
12. Brewster, D.: Letters on Natural Magic, Addressed to Sir Walter Scott, BART. John Murray, London (1832)
13. DeVault, D., Artstein, R., Benn, G., Dey, T., Fast, E., Gainer, A., Georgila, K., Gratch, J., Hartholt, A., Lhommet, M., Lucas, G., Marsella, S.C., Fabrizio, M., Nazarian, A., Scherer, S., Stratou, G., Suri, A., Traum, D., Wood, R., Xu, Y., Rizzo, A., Morency, L.P.: SimSensei kiosk: a virtual human interviewer for healthcare decision support. In: Proceedings of the 13th International Conference on Autonomous Agents and Multiagent Systems (AAMAS 2014), pp. 1061–1068. International Foundation for Autonomous Agents and Multiagent Systems, Paris, France, May 2014. http://aamas2014.lip6.fr/proceedings/aamas/p1061.pdf
14. Fergason, J.: Optical system for a head mounted display using a retro-reflector and method of displaying an image. US Patent 5621572 (1997)
15. Goldberg, G.N., Kiesler, C.A., Collins, B.E.: Visual behavior and face-to-face distance during interaction. Sociometry **32**(1), 43–53 (1969)

16. Goldstein, E.: Spatial layout, orientation relative to the observer, and perceived projection in pictures viewed at an angle. J. Exp. Psychol. Hum Percept. Perform. **13**, 256–266 (1987)
17. Hua, H., Gao, C.: A polarized head-mounted projective display. In: ISMAR, pp. 32–35, October 2005
18. Hua, H., Gao, C., Brown, L., Biocca, F., Rolland, J.P.: Design of an ultralight head-mounted projective display (hmpd) and its applications in augmented collaborative environments. In: Proceedings of the SPIE, vol. 4660, pp. 492–497 (2002). http://dx.doi.org/10.1117/12.468067
19. Inami, M., Kawakami, N., Sekiguchi, D., Yanagida, Y., Maeda, T., Tachi, S.: Visuo-haptic display using head-mounted projector. In: Virtual Reality, pp. 233–240 (2000)
20. Jones, A., Lang, M., Fyffe, G., Yu, X., Busch, J., McDowall, I., Bolas, M., Debevec, P.: Achieving eye contact in a one-to-many 3d video teleconferencing system. ACM Trans. Graph. **28**(3), 1–8 (2009). http://doi.acm.org/10.1145/1531326.1531370
21. Jones, A., McDowall, I., Yamada, H., Bolas, M., Debevec, P.: Rendering for an interactive 360 light field display. ACM Trans. Graph. **26**(3), July 2007. http://doi.acm.org/10.1145/1276377.1276427
22. Jones, A., Unger, J., Nagano, K., Busch, J., Yu, X., Peng, H.Y., Alexander, O., Bolas, M., Debevec, P.: An automultiscopic projector array for interactive digital humans. In: SIGGRAPH Emerging Technologies, SIGGRAPH, p. 6:1 (2015). http://doi.acm.org/10.1145/2782782.2792494
23. Kallman, M., Marsella, S.C.: Hierarchical motion controllers for real-time autonomous virtual humans. In: Intelligent Virtual Agents, September 2005
24. Kang, S.H., Gratch, J.: Socially anxious people reveal more personal information with virtual counselors that talk about themselves using intimate human back stories. In: The 17th Annual Review of CyberTherapy and Telemedicine, vol. 181, pp. 202–207 (2012)
25. Karitsuka, T., Sato, K.: A wearable mixed reality with an on-board projector. In: The Second IEEE and ACM International Symposium on Mixed and Augmented Reality, Proceedings, pp. 321–322, October 2003
26. Kendon, A.: Some function of gaze direction in social interaction. Acta Psychol. **32**, 1–25 (1967)
27. Krum, D.M., Suma, E., Bolas, M.: Augmented reality using personal projection and retroflection. Pers. Ubiquit. Comput. **16**(1), 17–26 (2012)
28. Krumhuber, E., Manstead, A., Cosker, D., Marshall, D., Rosin, P.: Effects of dynamic attributes of smiles in human and synthetic faces: a simulated job interview setting. J. Non-Verbal Behav. **33**(1), 1–15 (2009)
29. Maruyama, K., Endo, M., Sakurai, K.: An experimental consideration on "Mona Lisa gaze effect". Tohoku Psychol. Folia **44**, 109–121 (1985)
30. Matusik, W., Pfister, H.: 3D TV: a scalable system for real-time acquisition, transmission, and autostereoscopic display of dynamic scenes. ACM Trans. Graph. **23**(3), 814–824 (2004). http://doi.acm.org/10.1145/1015706.1015805
31. Negroponte, N.: Being Digital. Vintage Books, New York (1995)
32. Okada, K., Maeda, F., Ichikawaa, Y., Matsushita, Y.: Multiparty videoconferencing at virtual social distance: MAJIC design. In: Proceedings of CSCW94. ACM, Chapel Hill (1994)
33. Parsons, T.D., Rizzo, A.: Virtual human patients for training of clinical interview and communication skills. In: Proceedings of the 2008 International Conference on Disability, Virtual Reality and Associated Technology, Maia, Portugal, September 2008

34. Rogers, S., Lunsford, M., Strother, L., Kubovy, M.: The Mona Lisa effect: Perception of gaze direction in real and pictured faces. In: Rogers, S., Effken, J. (eds.) Studies in Perception and Action VII. Lawrence Erlbaum, Oxford (2002)
35. Rolland, J.P., Biocca, F., Hamza-Lup, F., Ha, Y., Martins, R.: Development of head-mounted projection displays for distributed, collaborative, augmented reality applications. Presence **14**(5), 528–549 (2005)
36. Sato, T., Hosokawa, K.: Mona Lisa effect of eyes and face. i-Perception **3**(9), 707 (2012). http://ipe.sagepub.com/content/3/9/707.abstract
37. Sellen, A.: Remote conversations: the effects of mediating talk with technology. Hum. Comput. Interact. **10**(4), 401–444 (1995)
38. Slater, M., Rovira, A., Southern, R., Swapp, D., Zhang, J., Campbell, C.: Bystander responses to a violent incident in an immersive virtual environment. PLoS ONE **8**(1), e52766 (2013)
39. Stolle, H., Olaya, J.C., Buschbeck, S., Sahm, H., Schwerdtner, A.: Technical solutions for a full-resolution autostereoscopic 2d/3d display technology. In: Proceedings of the SPIE, vol. 6803, 68030Q–68030Q-12 (2008). http://dx.doi.org/10.1117/12.766373
40. Swartout, W., Artstein, R., Forbell, E., Foutz, S., Lane, H.C., Lange, B., Morie, J., Noren, D., Rizzo, A., Traum, D.: Virtual humans for learning. AI Mag. Spec. Issue Intell. Learn. Technol. **34**(4), 13–30 (2013)
41. Swartout, W., et al.: Ada and grace: toward realistic and engaging virtual museum guides. In: Allbeck, J., Badler, N., Bickmore, T., Pelachaud, C., Safonova, A. (eds.) IVA 2010. LNCS, vol. 6356, pp. 286–300. Springer, Heidelberg (2010). doi:10.1007/978-3-642-15892-6_30
42. Thiebaux, M., Marshall, A., Marsella, S.C., Kallmann, M.: SmartBody: behavior realization for embodied conversational agents. In: Autonomous Agents and Multiagent Systems (AAMAS), May 2008
43. Vertegaal, R., Weevers, I., Sohn, C., Cheung, C.: Gaze-2: Conveying eye contact in group video conferencing using eye-controlled camera direction. In: Proceedings of the SIGCHI Conference on Human Factors in Computing Systems, CHI 2003, NY, USA, pp. 521–528 (2003). http://doi.acm.org/10.1145/642611.642702
44. Vishwanath, D., Girshick, A., Banks, M.: Why pictures look right when viewed from the wrong place. Nat. Neurosci. **8**(10), 1401–1410 (2005)
45. Wang, N., Gratch, J.: Don't just stare at me!. In: Proceedings of the SIGCHI Conference on Human Factors in Computing Systems, CHI 2010, NY, USA, pp. 1241–1250 (2010). http://doi.acm.org/10.1145/1753326.1753513
46. Watson, D., Clark, L.A., Tellegen, A.: Development and validation of brief measures of positive and negative affect: the panas scales. J. Pers. Soc. Psychol. **54**(6), 1063 (1988)

Individuals' Motivations to Adopt Smart Technologies for Tourism - Discrepancy Between Initial and Post Adoption

Yongda Li[(⊠)]

School of Creative Media, City University of Hong Kong,
Kowloon Tong, Hong Kong
Yongdali2-c@cityu.edu.hk

Abstract. This study examines individuals' motivations to adopt smart technologies for tourism. We employed a case study using a qualitative approach. The results demonstrate that the factors influencing individuals' initial and post adoption differ significantly. For initial use, intrinsic motivation to know was the most important factor. Introjected regulation was the next most influential factor. Capacity-efforts belief was the most powerful amotivational factor hindering initial adoption. For the post adoption of a smart technology, the results indicates that individuals' extrinsic motivation (external regulation) was most influential, followed by intrinsic motivations (i.e., intrinsic motivation to know and intrinsic motivation toward accomplishments), which are also vital in predicting post adoption. The results suggest that users valued pleasure and satisfaction from exploring and learning to use a new technology and users were most concerned about practicality in the prolonged use. This research is a starting point for academia and industry to analyze individuals' diverse motivations regarding smart technology.

Keywords: Smart technology · Hierarchical model of intrinsic and extrinsic motivation · Technology adoption · Intrinsic motivation · Extrinsic motivation

1 Introduction

Along with the construction and development of 'smart city' [72], the term 'smart tourism' has emerged as a significant subsystem of the information network and industrial development of smart cities [1, 80]. Increasing scholarly attention has been devoted to understanding user experiences with smart technology for tourism in the fields of human computer interaction (HCI) and smart tourism. Research has conceptualized the notion of smart tourism [8, 20, 29, 47, 72], built frameworks on smart tourism [36, 58, 65, 74, 80], and explored the roles of main technology applications in smart tourism [18, 39, 78, 80]. However, most previous studies limited their view to improving travelers' experiences in the context of smart tourism. Although researchers have acknowledged that constant evaluation of users' motivations for initial and continued use (post adoption) is necessary [24, 48], little empirical research has systematically examined individuals' motivations for adopting smart technologies for tourism, which limits further development of the theories underlying user experience in

© Springer International Publishing AG 2017
N. Streitz and P. Markopoulos (Eds.): DAPI 2017, LNCS 10291, pp. 77–92, 2017.
DOI: 10.1007/978-3-319-58697-7_6

the context of smart tourism. To fill this gap in understanding, this study addresses the following questions:

(1) What are the factors that influence individuals' initial use of smart technologies for tourism?
(2) What are the factors that influence individuals' continuance intention to use smart technologies for tourism?

To answer these questions, drawing on the Hierarchical Model of Intrinsic and Extrinsic Motivation [71], this study empirically examines an individual's diverse motivations to adopt a smart technology designed for tourism. This study contributes to research on smart tourism by analyzing users' different types of motivations for initial and post adoption of smart technology, and it reveals the significant distinctions between initial- and post-adoption motivations. For industry, this study provides meaningful insights into the design strategies of smart technology, which include an attention-grabbing interface and functions for information and entertainment.

The remainder of this paper is organized as follows. The second section includes five parts: the definition of smartness, smart technology and smart tourism, a brief review of relevant findings on user adoption of smart technology, and the theoretical background for this study. The third section provides a technical overview of the case study of smart technology. The fourth section describes the research methods, which is followed by the interview results in the fifth section. Finally, in the sixth section, we discuss the research implications of this study.

2 Literature Review and Theoretical Background

2.1 The Concept of Smartness

Smartness is a term used to describe innovative and transformative changes driven by new technologies [34]. Smart technologies aim to integrate and share real-time data for communication and collaboration, and they also use complex analytics, modeling, optimization, and visualization to make better operational decisions and implement continuous improvement [25, 32]. Table 1 summarizes the dimensions of smartness. In this study, following Rhiu et al.'s work [53], we define smartness in five dimensions: autonomy, adaptability, multi-functionality, connectivity, and personalization.

2.2 Smart Technology

Smart technology is defined as a technology with a certain degree of smartness that supports new forms of collaboration and value creation, leading to further innovation, entrepreneurship, and competitiveness [21]. As researchers have different views on the concept of smartness, the definitions of smart technology are equivocal, as shown in Table 2.

Table 1. Dimensions of smartness

Dimensions of smartness	Study
Autonomy: a technology operates in an independent and goal-directed way without interference by the user Adaptability: a technology's ability to improve the match between its function and its environment [50] Reactivity: a technology's ability to react to changes in its environment [6] Multi-functionality: a single technology fulfills multiple functions [52] Ability to cooperate: a technology can cooperate with other devices to achieve a common goal Humanlike interaction: a technology communicates and interacts with the user in a natural and human way Personality: a technology's ability to demonstrate the properties of a credible character	[54]
Fitness: a technology speeds up or improves users' routines while avoiding unnecessary work Efficiency: a technology helps users perform tasks faster or better than they can manually	[46]
Autonomy: a technology operates in an independent and goal-directed way without interference by the user Adaptability: a technology's ability to improve the match between its function and its environment [50] Multi-functionality: a single product fulfills multiple functions [52] Connectivity: a technology is connected to individual terminals, mobile devices, data centers, and local area networks based on ICT and IoT Personalization: a technology's ability to demonstrate the properties of a credible character	[53]

Table 2. Definitions of smart technology

Definition	Study
Smart technology is a term to encompass any number of different contexts where a degree of intelligence, however primitive, is embedded within an artifact	[57]
Smart technology is technology with the ability to sense changes in its circumstances and to execute measures enhancing its functionality under the new circumstances, then to offer enormous benefits in performance, efficiency, operation costs and endurance	[76]
Smart technology is not only a multifunctional but also versatile device, because it provides real-time accessibility to anyone, anytime and anything, in addition to timesaving applications	[59]
Smart technology is a self-operative and corrective system that requires little or no human interventions; smart technology has the ability to extract information from its sensors and communicate with its command and control unit or with external devices	[11]
In the context of marketing and economy, smart technology is technology with multi-functionality and high levels of connectivity, which supports new forms of collaboration and value creation that lead to innovation, entrepreneurship and competitiveness	[21]

2.3   Smart Tourism

Smart tourism refers to a platform on which information relating to tourist activities, the consumption of tourism products, and the status of tourism resources can be instantly integrated and then provided to tourists, enterprises and organizations through a variety of end-user devices [28, 80]. Smart tourism applies a new generation of information communication technology (ICT) and applications, and it provides all sorts of tourism information adequately, and in a timely manner. It brings smartness to tourism services, management, and marketing and to tourist experiences [28]. The smart tourism system applies intelligent technologies, which mainly involve the Internet of Things (IoT), cloud computing, mobile communication technology, and artificial intelligence [39, 80].

The definitions, conceptual frameworks, and technological foundations of smart tourism are summarized in Tables 3, 4, and 5, respectively. In this study, smart tourism is defined as tourism supported by the efforts of a destination (such as an airport) to use

Table 3. Definitions of smart tourism

Definition	Study
Smart tourism is a distinct step towards the progression of ICT in tourism sector in that the control and physical dimensions of the tourism are entering the digital platform field and new heights of smartness are attained in the system	[20]
Smart tourism is characterized as human-oriented, green, scientific and technological innovation	[42]
Smart tourism is to employ mobile digital connectivity to create more intelligent, meaningful and sustainable connections between tourists and their destinations, and represents wider efforts to imagine tourism as a form of deep civic engagement, and not just as a simple form of consumption	[47]
Smart tourism is based on a new generation of ICT to meet the needs of individual tourists for high-quality, satisfying services to realize the common sharing and effective use of tourism resources while promoting the integration of social resources	[80]
Smart tourism is a new form of tourism business, facing the future to serve the public, business organizations and government sections	[77]
Smart tourism is the application of networking and intelligent data mining technology applied to tourism experiences, industry development and administrative management through a systematic integration of each, consequently further developing and interacting with tourism and information resources	[64]
Smart tourism means that visitors can also offer values and can create and monitor	[8]
Smart tourism is a new generation communicational technology that combines cloud-computing, networking, the internet with personal mobile terminals (3G technology, personal digital assistant etc.) and artificial intelligence	[58]
To sum up a destination element, smart tourism is a social phenomenon arising from the addition of ICTs with the experience of tourism	[29]
Smart tourism is tourism supported by incorporated hard work at a destination to accumulate and harness the information resulting from the physical infrastructure governmental connections and social sources with the use of advanced technologies to transform the information into onsite experiences and business value-prepositions with a comprehensive focus on sustainability, efficiency and experience fortification	[72]

Table 4. The framework of smart tourism

Framework	Study
Smart tourism has three levels: for tourists, smart tourism provides access to tourism information and promptly arranges travel plans; for managers (such as the government and tourism enterprises), smart tourism is a comprehensive and thorough system incorporating accuracy, convenience, and the ubiquity of tourism information applications by building a tourism service platform that offers visitors catering, transportation, accommodation, traveling, and shopping; from a technical perspective, smart tourism achieves highly systematic and detailed interaction between physical tourism resources and tourism information resources, thereby serving the public, enterprises and the government with a new form of tourism services for the future	[74]
The essential connotation of smart tourism is the application of intelligent technology, including ICT in a tourism industry context	[36]
Smart tourism includes three major layers: a smart information layer that collect data; a smart exchange layer that supports interconnectivity; a smart processing layer responsible for the analysis, visualization, integration, and intelligent use of data	[65]

Table 5. The technological foundation of smart tourism

Technological foundation	Study
The supporting technologies of smart tourism include cloud computing, IoT, high-speed mobile communication technology, geographic information systems, and virtual reality technology	[39]
Smart tourism uses intelligent technology to complete tourism development and management processes and to take advantage of the intelligence and information residing in the entire tourism industry	[74]
Smart tourism is customer-centered, using intelligent technology, computers, mobile devices, and intelligent terminals as the main platforms to provide intelligent service, intelligent business, intelligent management, and intelligent government affairs	[78]
Based on cloud computing technology with smart phones and intelligent terminal equipment, smart tourism can realize the collection, mining analysis, real-time transmission, and automatic induction of tourism information	[18]

advanced technologies to accumulate and harness information and social sources in order to transform this information into onsite experiences and business value prepositions, with a comprehensive focus on sustainability and efficiency [72].

2.4 Previous Findings on User Adoption of Smart Technology

Users are a target group when studying smart technology [27]. Therefore, understanding factors that influence user adoption of smart technology is of interest to both researchers in various fields and the procurers of technology for large organizations

[63]. As user adoption is of great significance to the successful implementation of any new technology [63], previous research notes different system uses, including initial, continuanued (post), and extended (or deep) uses [79]. Initial use is the first-time adoption of a system [73]. Continued use refers to a user's ongoing use of an information system, reflecting a post-adoption behavior beyond initial acceptance [5, 38, 41]. Extended use, or deep use, is the extent to which a user employs different system functionalities to perform various tasks [30, 44]. To realize the benefits of an implemented system, organizations must encourage people to move beyond initial to post-adoption behaviors [38].

2.5 Theoretical Background

Intrinsic Motivation, Extrinsic Motivation and Amotivation
Motivation theorists argue that motivation formulates the mechanism of human behavior and action [81]. A person who feels no impetus to act is unmotivated and someone who is energized to work towards an end is motivated [55]. Motivation is key to understanding users' intentions and expectations regarding system use [41]. It is vital to know the level of motivation and the orientation of the motivation (i.e., what type of motivation) [55]. People's attitudes and goals lie under their actions. A complete analysis of motivation must deal with three important concepts; intrinsic motivation, extrinsic motivation, and amotivation [67]. Intrinsic motivation is at work when someone does an activity in order to obtain pleasure or satisfaction from the activity itself (see [13, 35, 67]). Extrinsic motivation can be seen when someone does something in order to achieve some separable goals, such as receiving a reward or avoiding punishment [13, 14]. Amotivation is the lack of intentionality and thus the relative absence of motivation [14, 33, 67].

Hierarchical Model of Intrinsic and Extrinsic Motivations
The concepts of intrinsic motivation, extrinsic motivation and amotivation need to be interpreted within the full range of motivational processes [68]. Vallerand et al. [69–71] posited three types of intrinsic motivation: Intrinsic Motivation (IM) to know, IM toward accomplishments and IM to experience stimulation. As proposed by Guay et al. [22], extrinsic motivation also includes three types: identified regulation, introjected regulation and external regulation. Deci and Ryan [14], Skinner [60], and Seligman [56], Pelletier et al. [51], and Stewart [62] proposed four types of amotivation: capacity-ability belief, strategy belief, capacity-effort belief, and helplessness belief. Table 6 shows the multidimensional perspective of motivation, which includes 10 motivation subscales [67, 68].

3 Technical Overview of Chigoo Trolley

Chigoo's iFLYMATE is a service platform (Fig. 1a, b) that collects data and provides information to travelers. This platform circles the airport service data center and is based on the IoT and cloud computing. It develops public airport services and

Table 6. Multidimensional motivation subscales

Category	Motivation	Description
Intrinsic motivation (IM)	IM to know	Engaging with the technology for the pleasure/satisfaction that one experiences while learning, exploring, or trying to understand something new (e.g., technological functions for searching travel information and news)
	IM toward accomplishments	Engaging with the technology for pleasure/satisfaction while attempting to reach goals or accomplish or create something new
	IM to experience stimulation	Engaging with the technology to experience pleasure associated mainly with one's senses (e.g., sensory and aesthetic pleasure)
Extrinsic motivation (EM)	External regulation	Behavior is regulated through external means, such as rewards and constraints (e.g., users must use the technology due to constraints related to Wi-Fi usage, phone chargers and airport navigation)
	Introjected regulation	Individuals replace the external source of control (e.g., others' opinions/feelings) with an internal source (user's attitude) and impose pressure on themselves to use a technology for others' sakes
	Identified regulation	Users highly value certain behaviors; they will use the technology even if the process of using the technology is not in itself pleasant
Amotivation	Capacity-ability belief	Users believe that they lack the ability to use the technology (e.g., they are unfamiliar with the new technology)
	Strategy belief	Users believe that the functions of the new technology will not meet their needs
	Capacity-efforts belief	Users believe that using the technology is too demanding, so they do not want to expend the effort necessary to engage with the technology
	Helplessness belief	Users believe that using the technology is inconsequential due to its complexity or poor functionality

value-added advertisements at the airport. CTrolley (Fig. 2), which works based on Chigoo's iFLYMATE platform is a multi-functional smart technology with a high level of connectivity. CTrolley is available to users after they scan their boarding passes on the touch screen, which means that Ctrolley is smart only when the iFLYMATE system adapts itself to users' needs.

CTrolley includes to the five dimensions of smartness: autonomy (cTrolley itself can mine and analyze data after passengers' scanned their boarding passes), adaptability (the setup of cTrolley's wireless access points and power stations can freely upgrade to conform to existing airport infrastructures and are optional if airports have plans for their own wireless internet infrastructure upgrades), multi-functionality

(a)

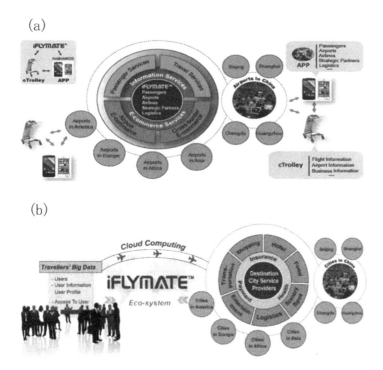

(b)

Fig. 1. Operation process of cTrolley (provided by Chigoo Company) (http://www.chigoo.net/goodsen.html).

(the functions of cTrolley include multiple languages, indoor navigation, real time flight status, boarding guidance and reminders, entertainment, free Wi-Fi hotspots, phone chargers, etc.), connectivity (cTrolley is connected to the airport service data center and is based on the IoT and cloud computing), personalization (cTrolley can automatically log users into their personal accounts after they have scanned their boarding passes and serve travelers based on their previous preferences recorded in its system).

4   Methods

We employed a smart technology case study using a qualitative approach to conduct an exploratory research on user adoption of smart technology for tourism. The threefold methodology included document analysis, in-depth and sequential interview [43] with purposive sampling, and post hoc analysis based on summaries of the interview content. The case study was conducted in Guangzhou Baiyun International Airport. First, documentation of cTrolley's operational process and outlook was examined in order to identify the practical processes underpinning the technological solution and its use [48]. Second, as suggested in sequential interview guidelines [43], we did not set a specific

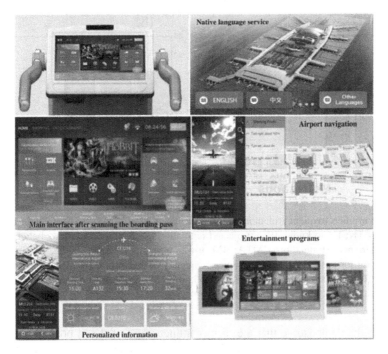

Fig. 2. CTrolley touch screen view (provided by Chigoo Company) (http://www.chigoo.net/goodsen.html).

number of interviewees prior to data collection; instead, we conducted interviews until we reached an information saturation point. The first interview yielded a set of findings and a set of questions that informed the next interviews; when an interview provided little new or surprising information, then saturation had been reached, and we ended the interview process [61]. Third, we examined and analyzed the results based on the content of the interviews and on observation.

5   Results

Our interview questions were semi-structured. We asked interviewees two main questions: "What motivated you to use cTrolley the first time?" and "What motivated you to continue to use cTrolley in the departure lounge?" Different types of motivation were identified based on the interviewees'. Interviews were conducted from 11:00 AM to 5:00 PM for three days, and the interview targets were passengers using cTrolley in the departure lounge. Our information reached saturation with forty-fifth interviewee. We invited 52 people to be interviewed, and 45 agreed to participate. The interviewees included 17 females and 28 males. Fifty-three percent of the interviewees were between the ages of 18 and 30, 22% were aged 30–40, 11% were under 18, and 13% were over 40. Fifty-eight percent of the interviewees were business travelers and 42% were traveling for leisure. Figure 3 shows the frequency of occurrence.

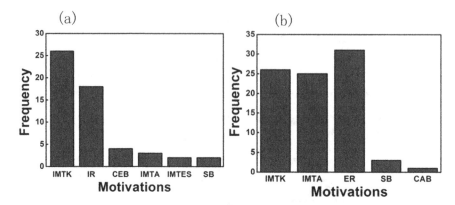

Fig. 3. Occurrence frequency of motivation subscales for initial use. (a) Motivation for initial adoption. IMTK: IM to know, IR: Introjected regulation, CEB: Capacity-efforts belief, IMTES: IM to experience stimulation, IMTA: IM toward accomplishments, SB: Strategy belief. (b) Motivation for post adoption. Occurrence frequency of motivation subscales for continuance intention (ER: External regulation, IMTK: IM to know, IMTA: IM toward accomplishments, SB: Strategy belief, CAB: Capacity-ability belief).

The results demonstrate that the factors influencing initial and post adoption for a smart technology differ significantly. The results show that IM to know was the most important factor for initial adoption, whereas introjected regulation (extrinsic motivation) was found to be the second most-influential factor. The most powerful amotivaitonal factor for initial use was capacity-efforts belief.

> *Interviewee No. 32 said: "I haven't seen a trolley with a touch screen in the airport before, so I think this is a very interesting smart technology. I want to know what functions it has and I want to explore it. So I am using it."*

> *Interviewee No. 10 said: "At first I simply wanted to put my luggage on this trolley, but then I noticed the touch screen on it. I'm curious about this new technology, so I try it."*

> *Interviewee No. 1 said: "My kids are interested in this smart technology. They told me they wanted to play with it, so I took this cTrolley with me."*

> *Interviewee No. 4 said: "I noticed that others are using the cTrolley, so I took one."*

> *Interviewee No. 16 said: "I have never used such a thing before, and I don't want to waste my time and efforts to trying it."*

The results (Fig. 3b) also indicate that individuals' external regulation (extrinsic motivation) might significantly influence individuals' post adoption. The results show that IM to know and IM towards accomplishments (intrinsic motivation) played important roles in explaining continued use. The results suggest that users value pleasure and satisfaction from exploring and accomplishing new things. The most influential amotivational factor for post adoption was found to be strategy belief.

Interviewee No. 40 said: "I keep using it because I need it to charge my phone. I also need the free Wi-Fi"

Interviewee No. 21 said, "I found out that the cTrolley has a navigation function. I always get lost in the airport, so now I always take a cTrolley so I can use the GPS."

Interviewee No. 7 said, "I use the smart trolley to play games and watch movies while I am waiting for my airplane. It is a good way to kill time. And I was happy to find that there are various kinds of games and movies on it. Also, I want to know my departure information, and this trolley can give me a voice reminder of my departure information at any time. That's really practical."

Interviewee No. 19 said, "My phone is totally enough for me. My phone has more functions than this trolley has. And my phone can do everything that this trolley can, so why should I use this technology?"

The results reveal that users are concerned about practicality when adopting a new smart technology, and this factor was the most important one determining long-term use; the smart technology's practical functions include search functions for departure and destination information, news and airport navigation, etc.

6 Discussion

This study investigates factors that influence users' adoption of smart technology for tourism. The study revealed the different types of motivation behind user behaviors based on multidimensional motivation subscales [67]. Our study shows that the motivation subscales differ significantly from initial use to post-adoption. Intrinsic motivation, extrinsic motivation, and amotivation all influence user adoption of the technology.

This study is the first step in analyzing users' different types of motivations for initial use and post-adoption behavior with smart technology. We have specifically examined various dimensions of user motivation. This gives us a better understanding of users' motivations for adopting smart technology. Conceptually, the distinction between initial and post adoption is clarified by analyzing users motivation separately. Aside from IM to know, external regulation has the strongest influence on initial use and post adoption behavior, which indicates the external control or social pressure on user's adoption of smart technology. Furthermore, our study highlight that amotivation should not be ignored when understanding user adoption of smart technology.

We want to pinpoint several design strategies based on our research. First, since IM to know and introjected regulation have the strongest influence on initial use, the initial appearance of smart technology outlook should grab the attention of potential users. External regulation has the strong influence on post-adoption behavior and can even affect users who were amotivated for the first use. Therefore, more steady functions as free Wi-Fi, phone charger should be developed. IM to know and IM toward accomplishments are also very important, so information and entertainment are important functions.

6.1 Limitations

This research has two limitations. First, our data may lack diversity because the interviews were conducted in one location and all interviewees were Chinese. Second, our results only present 8 motivation subscales out of 10 proposed by Vallerand [68]. Identified regulation and helplessness beliefs did not appear in the interviews, indicating future research needs to further examine the diverse individual motivations for adopting a new smart technology in different contexts.

Both practitioners and researchers are increasingly interest in understanding why people adopt smart technologies in order to design and evaluate technology [15]. Future research should better clarify the distinction between the three intrinsic motivation subscales. Amotivation subscales should also be considered when evaluating the factors influencing technology adoption. Furthermore, in order to make full use of the multidimensional perspective of motivation, a more diverse set of subjects should be examined.

Acknowledgement. I truly thank Dr. Ayoung Suh, School of Creative Media, City University of Hong Kong, for her great help and supervision for this research.

References

1. Albino, V., Berardi, U., Dangelico, R.M.: Smart cities: definitions, dimensions, performance, and initiatives. J. Urban Technol. **22**(1), 3–21 (2015). doi:10.1080/10630732.2014.942092
2. Berlyne, D.E.: Aesthetics and Psychobiology, p. 336. Appleton-Century-Crofts, New York (1971)
3. Boes, K., Buhalis, D., Inversini, A.: Conceptualising smart tourism destination dimensions. In: Tussyadiah, I., Inversini, A. (eds.) Information and Communication Technologies in Tourism 2015, pp. 391–403. Springer, Cham (2015). doi:10.1007/978-3-319-14343-9_29
4. Bowen, G.A.: Document analysis as a qualitative research method. Qual. Res. J. **9**(2), 27–40 (2009). doi:10.3316/QRJ0902027
5. Bhattacherjee, A.: Understanding information systems continuance: an expectation confirmation model. MIS Q. **15**(3), 351–370 (2001). doi:10.2307/3250921
6. Bradshaw, J.M.: Software Agents. American Association for Artificial Intelligence, Menlo Park (1997)
7. Brophy, J.: Socializing students' motivation to learn. In: Maher, M.L., Kleiber, D.A. (eds.) Advances in Motivation and Achievements, vol. 5, pp. 181–210. JAI Press, Greenwich (1987)
8. Buhalis, D., Amaranggana, A.: Smart tourism destinations. In: Xiang, Z., Tussyadiah, I. (eds.) Information and Communication Technologies in Tourism 2014, pp. 553–564. Springer, Cham (2013). doi:10.1007/978-3-319-03973-2_40
9. Csikszentmihalyi, M.: Beyond Boredom and Anxiety. Jossey-Bass, San Francisco (1975)
10. Csikszentmihalyi, M.: Intrinsic rewards and emergent motivation. In: Lepper, M.R., Greene, D. (eds.) The Hidden Costs of Reward: New Perspectives on the Psychology of Human Motivation, pp. 205–216. Wiley, New York (1978)
11. Debnath, A., Haque, M., Chin, H., Yuen, B.: Sustainable urban transport: smart technology initiatives in Singapore. Transp. Res. Rec. J. Transp. Res. Board, no. 2243, 38–45 (2011). doi:10.3141/2243-05

12. Deci, E.L., Ryan, R.M.: Intrinsic Motivation. Wiley, New York (1975)
13. Deci, E.L., Ryan, R.M.: The empirical exploration of intrinsic motivational processes. Adv. Exp. Soc. Psychol. **13**, 39–80 (1980). doi:10.1016/S0065-2601(08)60130-6
14. Deci, E.L., Ryan, R.M.: Intrinsic Motivation and Self-determination in Human Behavior. Plenum Press, New York (1985)
15. Dillon, A., Morris, M.: User acceptance of information technology: theories and models. Ann. Rev. Inf. Sci. Technol. **14**(4), 3–32 (1996). Information Today, Medford, NJ
16. Dweck, C.S., Leggett, E.L.: A social-cognitive approach to motivation and personality. Psychol. Rev. **95**(2), 256 (1988). doi:10.1037/0033-295X.95.2.256
17. Emmons, R.A.: Levels and domains in personality: an introduction. J. Pers. **63**(3), 341–364 (1995). doi:10.1111/j.1467-6494.1995.tb00499.x
18. Fu, Y., Zheng, X.: China smart tourism development status and countermeasures. 我国智慧旅游的发展现状及对策研究. Dev. Res., no. 4, 62–65 (2013). doi:10.13483/j.cnki.kfyj.2013.04.034
19. Goddard, N.D.R., Kemp, R.M.J., Lane, R.: An overview of smart technology. Packaging Technol. Sci. **10**(3), 129–143 (1997). doi:10.1002/(SICI)1099-1522(19970501/30)10:3<129:AID-PTS393>3.0.CO;2-C
20. Gretzel, U.: Intelligent systems in tourism: a social science perspective. Ann. Tourism Res. **38**(3), 757–779 (2011). doi:10.1016/j.annals.2011.04.014
21. Gretzel, U., Sigala, M., Xiang, Z., Koo, C.: Smart tourism: foundations and developments. Electron Markets **25**, 179–188 (2015). doi:10.1007/s12525-015-0196-8
22. Guay, F., Blais, M.R., Vallerand, R.J., Pelletier, L.G.: The global motivation scale. Unpublished manuscript. Université duq Uébec aMontréal (1999)
23. Guo, Y., Liu, H., Chai, Y.: The embedding convergence of smart cities and tourism Internet of Things in China: an advance perspective. Adv. Hospitality Tourism Res. (AHTR) **2**(1), 54–69 (2014)
24. Gupta, S., Vajic, M.: The contextual and dialectical nature of experiences. In: Fitzsimmons, J.A., Fitzsimmons, M.J. (eds.) New Service Development: Creating Memorable Experiences, pp. 33–51. Sage, Thousand Oaks (2000)
25. Harrison, C., Eckman, B., Hamilton, R., Hartswick, P., Kalagnanam, J., Paraszczak, J., Williams, P.: Foundations for smarter cities. IBM J. Res. Dev. **54**(4), 1–16 (2010). doi:10.1147/JRD.2010.2048257
26. Harter, S.: A new self-report scale of intrinsic versus extrinsic orientation in the classroom: motivational and informational components. Dev. Psychol. **17**(3), 300 (1981). doi:10.1037/0012-1649.17.3.300
27. Hauttekeete, L., Stragier, J., Haerick, W., De Marez, L.: Smart, smarter, smartest… the consumer meets the smart electrical grid. In: 2010 9th Conference on Telecommunications Internet and Media Techno Economics (CTTE), pp. 1–6. IEEE (2010). doi:10.1109/CTTE.2010.5557717
28. Huang, C., Li, Y.: In the 12th five-year plan, the system research of smarter tourism under the background of smarter cities. "十二五"期间"智慧城市"背景下的"智慧旅游"体系研究. In: Proceedings of Annual Conference of Tourism Tribune, pp. 55–68 (2011)
29. Hunter, W.C., Chung, N., Gretzel, U., Koo, C.: Constructivist research in smart tourism. Asia Pac. J. Inf. Syst. **25**(1), 105–120 (2015)
30. Jasperson, J.S., Carter, P.E., Zmud, R.W.: A comprehensive conceptualization of post-adoptive behaviors associated with information technology enabled work systems. MIS Q. **29**(3), 525–557 (2005)
31. Kagan, J.: Motives and development. J. Pers. Soc. Psychol. **22**(1), 5 (1972)
32. Kitchin, R.: Getting smarter about smart cities: improving data privacy and data security. Data Protection Unit, Department of the Taoiseach, Dublin, Ireland (2016)

33. Koestner, R., Losier, G.F., Vallerand, R.J., Carducci, D.: Identified and introjected forms of political internalization: extending self-determination theory. J. Pers. Soc. Psychol. **70**(5), 1025 (1996). doi:10.1037/0022-3514.70.5.1025

34. Leahy, M., Davis, N., Lewin, C., Charania, A., Nordin, H., Orlic, D., Butler, D., Lopez-Fernandez, O.: Smart partnerships to increase equity in education. Educ. Technol. Soc. **19**(3), 84–98 (2016)

35. Lepper, M.R., Greene, D., Nisbett, R.E.: Undermining children's intrinsic interest with extrinsic reward: a test of the "over justification" hypothesis. J. Pers. Soc. Psychol. **28**(1), 129 (1973). doi:10.1037/h0035519

36. Li, D., Jia, Z., Wang, J., Chen, X.: Smart tourism management and intelligent recommendation technology. 智慧旅游管理与智能推荐技术. China Manage. Informationization **7**, 80–81 (2013)

37. Li, Y., Hu, C., Huang, C., Duan, L.: The concept of mart tourism under the context of tourism information service. 旅游信息服务视阈下的智慧旅游概念探讨. Tourism Tribune **29**(5), 106–107 (2014). doi:10.3969/j.issn.1002-5006.2014.05.0111

38. Limayem, M., Hirt, S.G., Cheung, C.M.K.: How habit limits the predictive power of intention: the case of information systems continuance. MIS Q. **31**(4), 705–737 (2007)

39. Liu, J., Fan, Y.: The form, value and development trend of intelligent tourism. 智慧旅游的构成、价值与发展趋势. Chonqing Soc. Sci. **10**, 121–124 (2011)

40. Lloyd, J., Barenblatt, L.: Intrinsic intellectuality: its relations to social class, intelligence, and achievement. J. Pers. Soc. Psychol. **46**(3), 646 (1984). doi:10.1037/0022-3514.46.3.646

41. Lowry, P.B., Gaskin, J., Moody, G.D.: Proposing the multi-motive information systems continuance model (MISC) to better explain end-user system evaluations and continuance intentions. J. Assoc. Inf. Syst. **16**(7), 515–579 (2015)

42. Ma, Y., Liu, J.: The enormous prospects of the smart tourism applications. 智慧旅游应用前景巨大. China Tourism News, p. 13 (2011)

43. Mack, N., Woodsong, C., MacQueen, K.M., Guest, G., Namey, E.: Qualitative research methods: a data collector's field guide. Family Health International (FHI), North Carolina, USA (2005)

44. Maruping, L.M., Magni, M.: What's the weather like? The effect of team learning climate, empowerment climate, and gender on individuals' technology exploration and use. J. Manage. Inf. Syst. **29**(1), 79–114 (2012). doi:10.2753/MIS0742-1222290103

45. Maslow, A.H., Frager, R., Cox, R.: Motivation and Personality. Fadiman, J., McReynolds, C. (eds.) vol. 2, pp. 1887–1904, Harper & Row, New York (1970)

46. Mennicken, S., Huang, E.M.: Hacking the natural habitat: an in-the-wild study of smart homes, their development, and the people who live in them. In: Kay, J., Lukowicz, P., Tokuda, H., Olivier, P., Krüger, A. (eds.) Pervasive 2012. LNCS, vol. 7319, pp. 143–160. Springer, Heidelberg (2012). doi:10.1007/978-3-642-31205-2_10

47. Molz, J.G.: Travel Connections: Tourism, Technology and Togetherness in a Mobile World, p. 532. Routledge, New York (2012)

48. Neuhofer, B., Buhalis, D., Ladkin, A.: Smart technologies for personalized experiences: a case study in the hospitality domain. Electron Markets **25**, 243–254 (2015). doi:10.1007/s12525-015-0182-1

49. Nicholls, J.G.: Achievement motivation: conceptions of ability, subjective experience, task choice, and performance. Psychol. Rev. **91**, 328–346 (1984). doi:10.1037/0033-295X.91.3.328

50. Nicoll, D.: Taxonomy of information intensive products. The University of Edinburgh Management School, Edinburgh (Working Paper) (1999)

51. Pelletier, L.G., Tuson, K.M., Green-Demers, I., Noels, K., Beaton, A.M.: Why are you doing things for the environment? The motivation toward the environment scale (mtes) 1. J. Appl. Soc. Psychol. **28**(5), 437–468 (1998). doi:10.1111/j.1559-1816.1998.tb01714.x

52. Poole, S., Simon, M.: Technological trends, product design and the environment. Des. Stud. **18**(3), 237–248 (1997). doi:10.1016/S0142-694X(97)00003-3

53. Rhiu, I., Ahn, S.H., Park, D., Kim, W., Yun, M.H.: An analysis of user experience of smartphone based on product smartness utilizing social media data. In: Proceedings of the Human Factors and Ergonomics Society Annual Meeting, vol. 60, no. 1, pp. 1198–1199. SAGE Publications (2016)

54. Rijsdijk, S.A., Hultink, E.J.: How today's consumers perceive tomorrow's smart products. J. Prod. Innov. Manag. **26**(1), 24–42 (2009). doi:10.1111/j.1540-5885.2009.00332.x

55. Ryan, R.M., Deci, E.L.: Intrinsic and extrinsic motivations: classic definitions and new directions. Contemp. Educ. Psychol. **25**(1), 54–67 (2000). doi:10.1006/ceps.1999.1020

56. Seligman, M.E.: Helplessness: On Depression, Development, and Death. W H Freeman/Times Books/Henry Holt and Co, New York (1975)

57. Sheen, M.R., MacBryde, J.C.: The importance of complementary assets in the development of smart technology. Technovation **15**(2), 99–109 (1995). doi:10.1016/0166-4972(95)96613-X

58. Shi, Y.: The next generation of communications technology in the era of economic experience: smart tourism application. 体验经济时代下新一代通信技术在智慧旅游中的应用. Technol. Horiz. **9**, 180–193 (2013)

59. Shim, J.P., Dekleva, S., Guo, C., Mittleman, D.: Twitter, Google, iPhone/iPad, and Facebook (TGIF) and smart technology environments: How well do educators communicate with students via TGIF? Commun. Assoc. Inf. Syst. **29**(35), 657–672 (2011)

60. Skinner, E.A.: Perceived Control, Motivation, and Coping, vol. 8. Sage Publications, Thousand Oaks (1995)

61. Small, M.L.: 'How many cases do I need?': on science and the logic of case selection in field-based research. Ethnography **10**(5), 6–38 (2009)

62. Stewart, D., Greendemers, I., Pelletier, L.G., Tuson, K.: Is helplessness a dimension of environmental amotivation-new developments in the amotivation towards the environment scale. In: Canadian Psychology-psychologie Canadienne, vol. 36, no. 2, p. 115. Canadian Psychol Assoc, Canada (1995)

63. Taherdoost, H., Masrom, M.: An examination of smart card technology acceptance using adoption model. In: Proceedings of the ITI 2009 31st International Conference on Information Technology Interfaces 2009, pp. 329–334. IEEE (2009). doi:10.1109/ITI.2009.5196103

64. Tang, H.: Smart tourism and informationization. "智慧旅游"与信息化. China Tourism News, no. 11 (2012)

65. Tu, Q.H., Liu, A.L.: Framework of smart tourism research and related progress in China. In: International Conference on Management and Engineering (CME 2014), pp. 140–146. DEStech Publications, Inc. (2014)

66. Uskov, V., Lyamin, A., Lisitsyna, L., Sekar, B.: Smart e-Learning as a student-centered biotechnical system. In: Vincenti, G., Bucciero, A., Vaz de Carvalho, C. (eds.) eLEOT 2014. LNICSSITE, vol. 138, pp. 167–175. Springer, Cham (2014). doi:10.1007/978-3-319-13293-8_21

67. Vallerand, R.J.: Toward a hierarchical model of intrinsic and extrinsic motivation. Adv. Exp. Soc. Psychol. **29**, 271–360 (1997). doi:10.1016/S0065-2601(08)60019-2

68. Vallerand, R.J.: Intrinsic and extrinsic motivation in sport and physical activity. In: Handbook of Sport Psychology, vol. 3, pp. 59–83 (2007)

69. Vallerand, R.J., Blais, M.R., Brière, N.M., Pelletier, L.G.: Construction et validation de l'échelle de motivation en éducation (EME). Can. J. Behav. Sci. **21**(3), 323 (1989). doi:10.1037/h0079855

70. Vallerand, R.J., Pelletier, L.G., Blais, M.R., Briere, N.M., Senecal, C., Vallieres, E.F.: The academic motivation scale: a measure of intrinsic, extrinsic, and amotivation in education. Educ. Psychol. Measur. **52**(4), 1003–1017 (1992)

71. Vallerand, R.J., Pelletier, L.G., Blais, M.R., Briere, N.M., Senecal, C., Vallieres, E.F.: On the assessment of intrinsic, extrinsic, and amotivation in education: evidence on the concurrent and construct validity of the academic motivation scale. Educ. Psychol. Measur. **53**(1), 159–172 (1993)

72. Vasavada, M., Padhiyar, Y.J.: "Smart tourism": growth for tomorrow. J. Res. **1**(12), 55–61 (2016)

73. Venkatesh, V., Davis, F.D.: A theoretical extension of the technology acceptance model: four longitudinal field studies. Manage. Sci. **46**(2), 186–204 (2000). doi:10.1287/mnsc.46.2.186.11926

74. Wang, H., Jin, T., Zhou, B., Shui, K.R., Zhou, M.: Smart Tourism. 智慧旅游, pp. 10–12. Tsinghua University Press, Beijing (2012)

75. White, R.W.: Motivation reconsidered. Psychol. Rev. **66**, 297–333 (1959). doi:10.1037/h0040934

76. Worden, K., Bullough, W.A., Haywood, J. (eds.): Smart Technologies. World Scientific, Singapore (2003)

77. Yan, M.: Smart tourism and its development: taking Nanjing as an example. 智慧旅游及其发展—以江苏省南京市为例. Chin. Econ. Bus. Herald **20**, 75–77 (2012)

78. Yao, G.: Analysis of smart tourism construction framework. "智慧旅游"的建设框架探析. Nanjing University of Posts and Telecommunications (The Social Sciences Edition), vol. 14, no. 2, pp. 5–9 (2012)

79. Yen, H.R., Hu, P.J.H., Hsu, S.H.Y., Li, E.Y.: A multilevel approach to examine employees' loyal use of ERP systems in organizations. J. Manage. Inf. Syst. **32**(4), 144–178 (2015). doi:10.1080/07421222.2015.1138373

80. Zhang, L.Y., Li, N., Liu, M.: On the basic concept of smarter tourism and its theoretical system. 智慧旅游的基本概念与理论体系. Tourism Tribune **5**, 66–73 (2012)

81. Zhang, S., Zhao, J., Tan, W.: Extending TAM for online learning systems: an intrinsic motivation perspective. Tsinghua Sci. Technol. **13**(3), 312–317 (2008). doi:10.1016/S1007-0214(08)70050-6

82. Zuckerman, M.: Sensation Seeking: Beyond the Optimal Level of Arousal. L. Erlbaum Associates, Hillsdale (1979)

Usability Evaluation and Redesign of an IoE Portal

Lúcia Satiko Nomiso[(✉)], Eduardo Hideki Tanaka,
and Daniel Augusto Guerra da Costa

Eldorado Research Institute, Campinas, SP, Brazil
{lucia.nomiso,eduardo.tanaka,daniel.costa}@eldorado.org.br

Abstract. A smart building is one of the most typical Internet of Everything (IoE) applications nowadays. Usually, a smart building aims to reduce energy consumption and, consequently, costs, or to enhance the work environment by increasing indoor thermal comfort. In general, building managers and air conditioning system technicians of smart buildings take actions such as increase or decrease the indoor air temperature and ventilation based on the data collected about the rooms (temperature, humidity, overall thermal satisfaction, and others). However, it is not always an easy task to extract useful information from all the data generated from a smart building, given the huge amount of data produced and the particular characteristics of each set of data. Therefore, this paper presents a usability evaluation applied to a Web portal containing charts summarizing both the historical and real-time data collected in a smart building. Taking into account the findings from this usability evaluation, the Web portal was redesigned and re-evaluated, receiving a more positive feedback from users.

Keywords: Internet of Everything · Smart building · Usability evaluation

1 Introduction

One of the common issues of Internet of Everything (IoE) [1] systems is the huge volume of data frequently produced. Additionally, these data are often heterogeneous and must be handled very differently [2] – sensors data should not be handled and presented the same way as user inputs and senses, for instance. Thus, anyone who wants to analyze IoE data and take some action based on them need to easily understand what happened in the past and get an updated status of the whole IoE environment. Moreover, information visualization and architecture are critical areas to consider when designing a system to present overall data about an IoE solution.

One of the areas that are facing those IoE challenges are the smart building environments. Most smart building projects pursue energy efficiency by monitoring and controlling lighting, heating and cooling systems and room occupancy [3, 4]. In fact, energy consumption has become a great concern not only because of costs but also due to the increase of the awareness of climate changes and the regulatory policies adopted in some countries [5]. Other aspects that are noticeable in some smart building projects are comfort and user satisfaction, which consider key variables such as temperature, humidity, ventilating and lighting [6]. More specifically, thermal comfort is directly related to people's productivity in a work environment according to some researches

© Springer International Publishing AG 2017
N. Streitz and P. Markopoulos (Eds.): DAPI 2017, LNCS 10291, pp. 93–104, 2017.
DOI: 10.1007/978-3-319-58697-7_7

[7, 8]. Therefore, and although there are trade-offs, an ideal smart building should take into account both energy efficiency and user satisfaction.

Based on these assumptions about smart buildings, an IoE system was implemented as a proof of concept in an ordinary office building with hundreds of employees in order to make it a smart building, able to monitor temperature, humidity, subjective user thermal comfort and room occupancy. To achieve this, small devices containing sensors were built and installed in several rooms. Additionally, to assist the building managers and the air conditioning system technicians to understand all data gathered by the devices and take appropriate actions if required, a Web portal was also developed to present consolidated information about the building, both historical and real-time. However, this Web portal was initially designed by software engineers without any user-centered design expertise. As a result, users complained about the usability of the Web portal, so that a redesign was required.

Thus, this paper presents the major issues reported by the users and the challenges of redesigning this Web portal. The next sections will present the IoE system, the issues discovered when users explored the Web portal and the major changes applied to the Web portal after a usability review.

2   The IoE System

The IoE environment object of this study is a resource to allow smart offices/buildings in the future, assisting building managers and air conditioning system technicians to reduce energy consumption while keeping the temperature of the rooms adequate for people to work. Then, as a proof of concept, 48 small, low cost devices with temperature and humidity sensors were developed and installed all over the offices of a building. Temperature and humidity are key parameters to estimate thermal comfort, as proposed by ISO 7730 [9]. However, in addition to temperature and humidity, many other factors impact on thermal sensation: people's metabolic rate, age, height, weight, clothing and even cultural and climate differences among countries [10]. Collect all these factors and include them in a model to estimate indoor thermal sensation is very complex and not too easy to apply.

In order to make it as simple as possible, the proposed model didn't collect those additional data to estimate indoor thermal sensation. Instead, it requests that people send their subjective thermal sensation as proposed by the thermal comfort judgement scales of ISO 10551 [11]. Then, and in addition to the temperature and humidity sensors, the developed devices have three voting buttons ("hot", "nice" and "cold") to allow people to express their subjective thermal sensation. Figure 1 shows some photos of the device and highlight the key elements present.

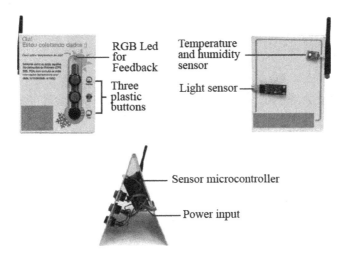

Fig. 1. IoE device.

All data collected through the sensors and the voting buttons of the devices are presented in a Web portal (Figs. 2 and 3), as well as information about the usage of the meeting rooms in the building, especially the scheduled and occupied times, which are not always the same.

Fig. 2. Home page.

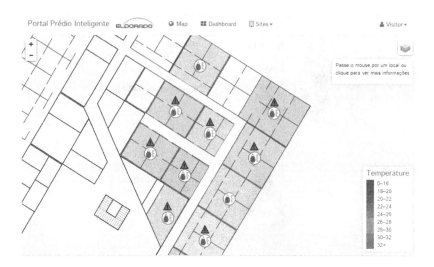

Fig. 3. Temperature and humidity graph of a specified room.

Like many other IoE systems nowadays, the proposed solution does not have a smart, automatic analyzer that can discover and resolve real-time numerical and descriptive sensing and take rational actions based on them [2]. Therefore, a human analysis is still required.

3   Usability Review: Initial Version

As previously mentioned, the proposed IoE system, both the devices and the Web portal, were initially designed and developed by software engineers without any experience with user-centered design. Usability researchers joined the team only after a few months of the first release of the project and, since the first contacts with the devices and with the portal, their feelings were that a redesign would be required.

Given that feelings, usability researchers decided to get a fast feedback from people who had been used the devices and the Web portal. To do so, informal interviews were applied and reinforced that the hypothesis of poor usability may be real. However, a more precise usability study was required to understand the issues and discover potential user demands not yet covered by the device and the Web Portal. Thus, a user survey was performed to evaluate the devices, whose major results were also described on [12], whereas, to evaluate the Web portal, a usability review assisted by the DECIDE framework [13] was done and will be described in the remaining parts of this paper.

Guided by the DECIDE framework, the selected high-level goals of the Web portal evaluation were to discover the major users' concerns and avoid them in a redesigned version of the Web portal. An invitation was sent to workers of the building who had little or no experience with the Web portal and 17 were selected as participants of the usability review. Before proceeding with the usability review, each participant had to fill and sign an agreement form and, also, it was explained that the object of the study was only the usability of the Web portal, not the participant, and that his/her identity and any personal data would be anonymously handled.

Then, each participant was requested to freely explore the Web portal and check key areas of it: Home page, Map and Dashboard. And, at the end, all participants answered a questionnaire with both open and Likert-scale questions to collect their opinions and suggestions. The summarized results for each of the key areas are presented next.

Home page

"What should I find here?", 70.5% of participants mentioned the lack of information on the Home page, having no idea about the purpose of the Web portal.

Map

"What is the meaning of that symbol?", 41.1% of users mentioned that symbols in the map were unrepresentative. Colors in charts did not have enough contrast for 29.5% of the users.

Dashboard

"I understand nothing about this chart", charts were unclear, especially the X axis, for 29.4% of users, who also complained about tight space among columns and about information overhead. Colors in charts and the "ideal temperature average" indicator were also problematic.

Figures 4, 5 and 6 present bar charts with the consolidate data of some of the Likert-scale questions. From these charts, it is possible to notice that most of the participants easily found the information they wanted in the Web portal, the overall look and feel was appealing for less than 50% of the participants and the charts and graphs present on the Web portal were easy to read and understand for a little more than 50% of the participants.

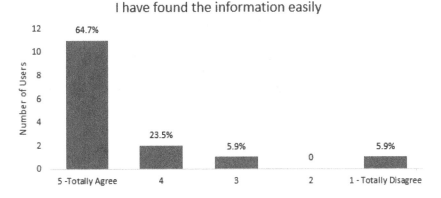

Fig. 4. Ease to find information.

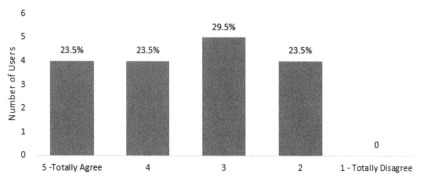

Fig. 5. Overall look and feel evaluation.

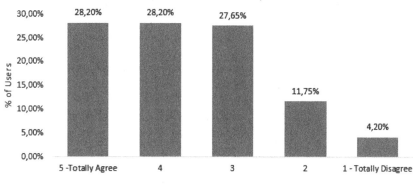

Fig. 6. Charts.

The word cloud present on Fig. 7 shows the most frequent terms present in the answers of the open questions. Most of the words are related to things that users didn't find too easy to do on the Web portal and suggestions to enhance their experience using the Web portal.

Fig. 7. Tag cloud.

4   Proposed Redesign

Taking into account the findings of the usability review, usability specialists proposed a redesigned version of the Web portal, trying to fix the issues reported by the users and fulfill their expectations. Table 1 presents a comparison between the initial version of the key areas of the Web portal (Home Page, Map and Dashboard) and the redesigned version of them.

This redesigned version of Web portal was then implemented, published and re-evaluated using the same procedure as mentioned in the previous section. The details of this usability review are presented in the next section.

Table 1. Before and after comparison.

Before	After
Home Page	
Map	
Dashboard	

5   Usability Review: Redesigned Version

In the usability review of the redesigned version of the Web portal, 15 people volunteered and had to perform the same explorations of the key areas (Home page, Map and Dashboard) as the first usability review and answered a similar survey at the end. The major results for each key area are summarized below.

Home page. "Can I change the language?", the Web portal was written in English, but all the participants (and, in fact, most of the workers of the office building) were Brazilians. Therefore, some participants requested an option to switch from English to Portuguese.

Also, in order to provide more information about the IoE environment and its objectives, an "About" page was created and included inside the Web portal, but it was not accessible through the Home page, which caused some complaints from some participants, who would like to have that kind of information on the first page they accessed. Figure 8 shows this new "About" page.

Fig. 8. New page "About" page.

Also, 20% of the participants complained about the "Smart IoT" logo shown at the top of the Home page, arguing that the logo looks like "SNART" or "SOART", not "SMART". Actually, the idea was to resemble an infinite symbol (∞) in the middle of the logo. Figure 9 shows the new logo.

Fig. 9. New logo for the "Smart IoT Portal".

Map. "Maps are realistic and I found my location quickly", this was a common comment from the participants about the redesigned Map section of the Web Portal. However, a few issues were yet found: 26.7% of the participants reported that mouse hover event was not working properly due to the position of the icons to represent the humidity, as shown on Fig. 10 (the highlighted cactus and the umbrella icons). Thus, the pop up dialog to present detailed information of the rooms was not opening if the mouse was hovering at the top of these icons – but it was working as expected if mouse hovering any other places.

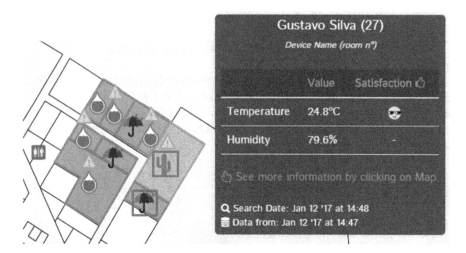

Fig. 10. Humidity indicator icons (cactus and umbrella) conflicted with the mouse hover event. (Color figure online)

Another interesting issue found in the Map section was about the adopted colors to represent nice thermal sensation (green) and hot (orange). One of the participants was color-blind and commented that it was difficult to distinguish these colors.

Dashboard. In Dashboard, participants reported that it was difficult to identify the rooms by their numbers – although this issue had already been there since the previous version, it was only identified in the redesigned version of the Web portal. Another issue that was also present in the previous version but only found in the redesigned version was the lack of a "loading" feedback while the graphs are not yet shown on the page.

Figures 11, 12 and 13 present bar charts with the consolidate data of some of the Likert-scale questions and compare with the previous results. It is interesting to notice

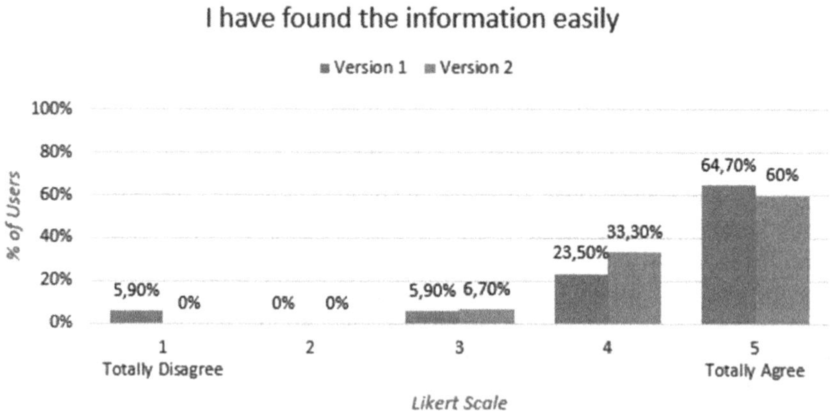

I have found the information easily

■ Version 1   ■ Version 2

Fig. 11. Ease to find information.

that, for the "ease to find", the proportion of "Totally agree" answerers decreased, but the amount of positive answers (4 and 5 in the scale) increased from 88.2% to 93.3%. Additionally, answers for the questions the about overall look and feel and the chars were more positive for the redesigned version of the Web portal.

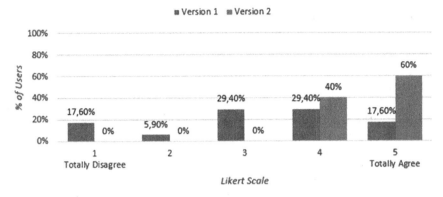

Fig. 12. Overall look and feel evaluation.

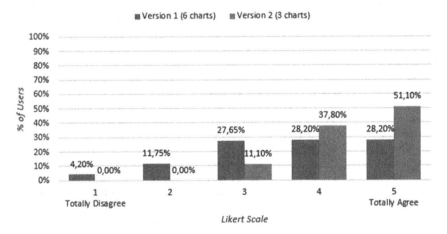

Fig. 13. Charts.

6 Concluding Remarks

The amount of different information on the IoE Web portal was huge and it was difficult to understand the state of each room or of the whole building, like many other IoE systems with poor usability. Thus, the portal was redesigned based on the results of a usability review, fixing the major issues found, and has received a more positive feedback. However, new issues that compromise the user experience were found and require other enhancements and fixes that are planned to be implemented in the next versions of the Web portal.

Another future work that is being analyzed by the usability researchers is how to make the Web portal more appealing to users, so that they will access the Web portal and check the thermal sensation statuses more frequently.

Acknowledgments. The authors would like to thank all participants of the usability reviews and also Janaina Ruas, their manager at Eldorado Research Institute, who encouraged and supported this IoE project.

References

1. Bojanova, I., Hurlburt, G., Voas, J.: Today, the Internet of Things. Tomorrow, the Internet of Everything. Beyond that, perhaps, the Internet of Anything—a radically super-connected ecosystem where questions about security, trust, and control assume entirely new dimensions. Information-development, 04 (2013)
2. Barnaghi, P., Sheth, A., Henson, C.: From data to actionable knowledge: big data challenges in the web of things [Guest Editors' Introduction]. IEEE Intell. Syst. **28**(6), 6–11 (2013)
3. Rocha, P., Siddiquia, A., Stadlerc, M.: Improving energy efficiency via smart building energy management systems: a comparison with policy measures. Energy Build. **88**, 203–213 (2015)
4. Agarwal, Y., Balaji, B., Gupta, R., Lyles, J., Wei, M., Weng, T.: Occupancy-driven energy management for smart building automation. In: Proceedings of the 2nd ACM Workshop on Embedded Sensing Systems for Energy-Efficiency in Building (BuildSys 2010), pp. 1–6. ACM, New York (2010)
5. Buckman, A.H., Mayfield, M., Beck, S.B.M.: What is a smart building? Smart Sustain. Built Environ. **3**(2), 92–109 (2014)
6. Yang, R., Wang, L.: Multi-objective optimization for decision-making of energy and comfort management in building automation and control. Sustain. Cities Soc. **2**(1), 1–7 (2012)
7. Jensen, K.L., Toftum, J., Friis-Hansen, P.: A Bayesian network approach to the evaluation of building design and its consequences for employee performance and operational costs. Build. Environ. **44**, 456–462 (2009)
8. Seppänen, O., Fisk, W.J., Lei, Q.H.: Effect of temperature on task performance in office environment. Ernest Orlando Lawrence Berkeley National Laboratory, Berkeley, CA (2006)
9. ISO: ISO 7730:2005 Ergonomics of the thermal environment – Analytical determination and interpretation of thermal comfort using calculation of the PMV and PPD indices and local thermal com-fort criteria (2005)
10. Li, B., Li, W., Liu, H., Yao, R., Tan, M., Jing, S., Ma, X.: Physiological expression of human thermal comfort to indoor operative temperature in the Non-HVAC environment. Indoor Built Environ. **19**(2), 221–229 (2010)
11. ISO: ISO 10551:2011 Ergonomics of the thermal environment – Assessment of the influence of the thermal environment using subjective judgement scales (2011)
12. Tanaka, E.H., Nomiso, L.S., da Costa, D.A.G.: Usability of thermal sensation voting device. In: Stephanidis, C. (ed.) HCI 2016. CCIS, vol. 618, pp. 541–545. Springer, Cham (2016). doi: 10.1007/978-3-319-40542-1_88
13. Rogers, Y., Sharp, H., Preece, J.: Interaction design: beyond human-computer interaction (2011)

'Wizard of Oz' Study for Controlling Living Room Lighting

Jo Olsen[1]([✉]) and Jeremy Spaulding[2]

[1] OSRAM, Beverly, MA, USA
jo.olsen@osram.com
[2] JMS Innovation and Strategy, Washington DC, USA
jeremy.m.spaulding@gmail.com

Abstract. Solid state lighting is changing the way humans experience artificial lighting and enhancing the possibilities of control over our built environments. The goal for this research study was to provide insight for designing human centered controls for tunable solid state lighting for the familiar residential application of living room lighting using a 'Wizard of Oz' methodology. Eight internal subjects and twenty externally sourced subjects experienced controlling the lighting for common scenarios such as reading, watching TV, having a party, saving a scene and recalling a scene. Three Android based mobile device applications were prepared for voice-only, gesture-only, and voice and gesture combined control. One or more "wizards" were employed to close the control loop between the subject's verbal commands and gestures and the tunable solid state lighting settings. Voice clips and sensor data were recorded on the phone, video and audio were captured via a wall mounted camera, and observed and documented. The subjects were aware of the audio, video, data, and note taking but not the "wizard" control. The data was analyzed to extract the unique ways subjects used to control the lighting, think-out-loud information and interview answers were analyzed to develop the mental models behind their control attempts and their thought processes used to reach their high level task goals. Conclusions drawn from this research help shape design decisions for tunable solid state lighting solutions and next-generational controls.

Keywords: Human computer interface · Wizard of oz · Solid State Lighting · Voice · Gesture

1 Introduction

Solid state lighting (SSL) provides possibilities not readily available from legacy lighting technologies and is disrupting the lighting industry: for example there are now many color temperature controllable, as well as color controllable, lighting products on the market. Lighting products are experienced in ways other appliances like toasters and dishwashers are not and now SSL is providing new lighting experience possibilities. This study was conducted as part of internal research by our Central Innovation application and design department within projects on user-experience and advanced natural user interfaces, with the primary goal of developing natural user interface solutions for

© Springer International Publishing AG 2017
N. Streitz and P. Markopoulos (Eds.): DAPI 2017, LNCS 10291, pp. 105–119, 2017.
DOI: 10.1007/978-3-319-58697-7_8

advanced lighting control. The objectives and benefits of this project specifically were multifold. Systems Engineering and Human-centered design principles were used extensively to envision, re-search, and realize lighting solutions that control complex technology yet are compelling, engaging, easy to understand, and enjoyable for people to use. Such concepts may ultimately anticipate human needs and enhance human experience thereby pushing the boundaries of SSL solutions and applications. Natural language interfaces (NLU), voice control, and natural gesture interfaces now being explored for gaming, automotive, medical, and other applications can also be used in advanced lighting applications. A working prototype using Android-based mobile devices was architected and developed to control advanced lighting systems consisting of color tunable lighting and multiple sources.

The experimentation involved subjects controlling tunable lighting in a natural environment of a living room to set the lighting environment to their liking for common tasks within these applications. They controlled the light level and color of multiple lighting fixtures using voice commands, gestures, and a combination of both voice and gesture. They were intentionally not given instruction on what to say or how to gesture with the phone, but instead asked to just try whatever seemed natural to them. Care was taken not to provide language or example gestures for any of the tasks. To close the control loop, one or more "wizards" were employed to actuate the advanced lighting unbeknownst to the subjects.

Voice data and sensor data was recorded on the phone, video and audio was captured via a wall mounted camera, and observer notes were taken. The data was analyzed to extract the unique ways subjects attempted to control the lighting and reach their high level task goals. For example, natural ranges of acceleration data attempted by the subjects for dimming were statistically analyzed and compared to those attempted for shutting off the lights. The common and unique verbal commands and naming conventions were extracted. Mental models of the subjects were gleaned from think-out-loud methodology, as well as, moderator conducted interviews.

The subjects agreed to being recorded and to not disclose what they experienced outside of the experiment. All subjects were provided non-disclosure (NDA), consent, and release forms in advance. The light intensities and modulation levels were limited to well within the levels of normal lighting experience. No excessive glare or flicker was present. The study was approved by our internal review board.

2   Study Development

The approach taken to study natural ways people use to control lighting was to provide a well known and comfortable environment, to refine the instructional script and answer questions in such a way as to not influence the subjects' behavior, to encourage experimentation by saying "just try it", or asking the subjects to demonstrate how they would control the lighting for a given situation, and by employing expert trained personnel known as "wizards" to provide fast feedback. Internal subjects were used to refine the experimental procedure and to train "wizards", moderators, and observers. It was then extended to external subjects recruited by an outside firm.

We recruited 20 participants to come to our facility to participate in a survey about natural language interfaces, voice control, and natural gesture interfaces used in advanced lighting applications. A broad demographic representation of male, female, 18-65 years old was selected but narrowed to those who would likely have or like to have home automation and use a smart phone regularly. We asked for them to be 1 h appointments Monday through Friday at 9:00, 10:30, 1:00, and 2:30. The participants were provided ahead of time and signed on site an NDA, an Informed Consent Form, and a Photo/Video Release.

During the experiments, the lighting was supervisorially or directly controlled by one or more unknown external operators called "wizards". The knowledge that the lighting was being controlled by another person was not given to the subjects. This technique is called "Wizard of OZ" after the famous scene in the well-known old movie by that title, where the wizard is unknowingly controlling equipment from behind a curtain. This technique is well known in human centered interface design (Jacko 2012) (Salvendy 2006) but is to our knowledge novel to lighting and home automation.

Living Room Study Setup Details

The experiment was conducted in our internal laboratory. The study took place in a simulated living environment that is 12 ft. (3.8 m) by 17 ft. (5.2 m) with a 9 ft. (2.7 m) high open box ceiling designed for flexible lighting placement. It was furnished with two comfortable chairs facing a wall mounted TV. This allowed for left handed and right-handed subjects to have their hand movements captured by a wall mounted video camera and directed toward a table lamp on a small table between the chairs. The camera is barely visible as a blue dot above the TV in the photo (depicted in Fig. 1). There were two wall sconces, one on either side of the TV. There were two fake windows with birch trees and grass to give the feel of a lawn in an open neighborhood. These windows could be back illuminated with an edge-lit panel, or not, in order to represent day time or night. The windows remained illuminated throughout the study and the subjects all participated in the during daylight hours. Mounted in the ceiling were six independently controllable tunable fixtures that could produce a wide gamut of colors and variation in color temperature. A coffee table was placed in reach of the comfortable chairs with magazines for reading and the TV remote control. Some details such as artificial and real plants were added to complete the realistic living room environment shown in Fig. 1.

The wizard control room was positioned behind the living room area behind a wall but the "wizards" could directly observe the subjects if need by peering around the wall while staying out of sight of the subjects but insight in the moderator and observer. The "wizards" could hear the subjects directly but had amplified audio and high resolution video from the wall mounted camera. The moderator conducted the experiment from a podium in the front and slightly to the right of the subjects, who were seated in one of the comfortable chairs. The observer was to the right of the subject and though peripherally, the observer could be seen when the subject turned their head and could on occasion add information, clarify points, or even converse with the subject.

Fig. 1. Photo of living room

Human Factors Experimental Procedure

To discover natural ways people use to control lighting, a procedure was developed whereby the subject was unaware of the control mechanisms and was not steered toward any particular vernacular or gestures. Internal subjects were used to refine the procedure and train the moderator, operators, and "wizards". The moderators paid particular attention to making the script flow and sound natural. The observers listened closely for any moderator accidental prompts that would influence naming of light fixtures, colors, color temperature, or commands (trying not to say "save" or "store" or "setting" when we wanted the subject to save a preset was particularly challenging). The "wizards" were trained to try to quickly respond to the subjects actions. They practiced both doing what the subject wanted and intentionally not doing what the subject wanted in order to study subject response to failures, how they recover, and how it effects user experience. Both the moderators and the observers were trained in interview techniques for delving into thought processes behind the attempted actions and for discovering mental models behind those thought processes. Considerable effort was needed to coax the think-out-loud process to make sure the "wizards" could fully understand the intentions of the subjects. This was also necessary for the data analysis task of determining if the intent was met. Fortuitously natural naming conventions, light level and spectral changing commands, range and characteristics of sensor data and type of gestures, and the mental models employed were discovered, even in this preliminary phase and were verified in the external participant phase.

Each external participant was met in the lobby for briefing, signing and witnessing of forms, and then led to the simulated living room. In the living room the participant met the moderator and the observer (if different from the greeter), and were positioned in one of the comfy chairs according their handedness. The moderator read from a script (see Appendix A) that started with a brief description and introductions. Then again, verbal consent was obtained to start recording and the moderator asked the observer to start the recording even though the "wizards" were actually responsible and the observer pretended to start the recording with a remote control and confirmed it is recording. Part of the procedure was developed to intentionally deceive the subject into believing that there were no "wizards" and that the system was a highly intelligent controller. Then each high level task was introduced and instructions were given on how to proceed. The subjects were interviewed after completing all of the tasks, escorted to the lobby, thanked, and told the agency would pay them for their time.

3   Results

Observations and verbatims showed that most of the subjects were amazed at how well the system performed. Only one subject mentioned they thought that there may have been someone controlling the lighting. There were many commonalities in naming, commands, gestures, and choice of modality. Some common mental models emerged. Unique ways in which subjects did these things were studied in more detail for use in developing natural user interface prototypes.

One common way subjects named lights was by their proximity to other objects. Some examples are "lamp on the table", "lights next to the TV", and "ceiling lights". Another common naming convention was by task, "reading light". A third way is to name where or what the light from the source(s) illuminates. Examples of this are: "the light for the chairs", "wall wash", or commanding "light the room".

Common commands that were intuitive such as "turn on" or just "on" outnumbered more obscure commands. "Make the ceiling blue" was one command that emerged that was not predicted ahead of time. The use of the commands "make" and "turn" was noted but not studied in detail.

Subjects showed dissatisfaction in unique ways. For example, when the lighting was too bright, the subjects would shield their eyes with their hand or arm in more of a dramatic gesture than to actually reduce the light level to their eyes. More common dissatisfaction reactions were saying things like "no, no, no", or "not that" separately or in combination with waving the phone back and forth vigorously.

Nearly the same vertical motion was used to dim as to shut-off a light. The acceleration versus time was different. Figure 2 depicts a typical sequence for shutting off two different lights and dimming a third. The typical shape for both is two peaks one negative

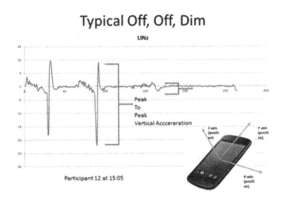

Fig. 2. Vertical accelerometer data stream (Color figure online)

and one positive caused by the slight up and down motion at the ends of a mostly down-ward motion. By analyzing the video feeds that correspond to the accelerometer data and observer notes the subject's intended actions could be categorized. The actions were categorized into three categories: dim, dim to off, and off. A statistically significant difference in peak to peak heights was found between off and the other categories, but not between dim and dim to off. This is graphically illustrated in Fig. 3.

Peak to Peak Vertical Acceleration

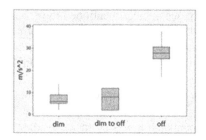

Fig. 3. Statistical analysis of peak to peak vertical accelerometer data

Cognitive models became most obvious when subjects were trying to use gestures to control color. Two major models were gleaned that correspond to peoples experience with color wheels and with color palettes. Some subjects would point the phone around a circle while observing the color change. Those subjects expected the direction or points on the circle to be arranged like color in a rainbow. Those same subjects described it as imagining a color wheel. Similarly some subjects had a color wheel in mind but used a faster circular motion to "spin the wheel" and a stopping or backing up motion to select the color they wanted.

The color pallet models were more complicated since the general understanding of additive and subtractive color space was not generally understood by the external partic-ipants. One subject explained in detail how the front corners of the living room were blue and red, and the rear of the room was yellow. Then by pointing between blue and yellow, green could be produced. Yet during this discussion, there was some confusion about how RGB displays mixed color. In additive color space, blue and yellow will produce white (for example the most typical white LED is made with blue LED light, some of which is converted to yellow using a phosphor). Some of the internal subjects (lighting experts) used the additive model consistently. Some subjects just waved the phone until the color happened to land where they wanted.

4   Conclusions

The results from this study confirm that people interact with lighting in ways that are unique compared to other devices. It is hypothesized that this is due to how central vision contributes to experience and to the nature of light itself in how it travels and reflects off of objects in the immediate world to provide people within this immediate environment with an understanding of how this environment is constructed. The results indicate that systems could be designed with better naming conventions, large vocabulary command sets, and color control based on cognitive color models.

The control system taking advantage of this invention would allow for multiple names and encourage multiple naming by these conventions. By prompting during the configuration phase, sometimes called commissioning, the system could encourage the programmer (commissioner) to consider giving multiple names for the light sources or groups of light sources by what they are next to, by what the light sources are used for, and by where the light source(s) illuminates. In this way, novice users of the system could refer to particular light by the natural naming convention.

When considering how to make a voice controlled system robust, adding more possibilities for commands must be balanced by increased misinterpretations of words from larger vocabularies.

Artificial lighting is critical in nearly every built environment and SSL is making advanced lighting products readily available while providing challenges in the application and control of these solutions (Boyce 2003). Future studies in other applications are under consideration.

Acknowledgments. Support for this work was provided by OSRAM Corporate Innovation through the Applications and Solutions department. Our wizards were all employed by OSRAM and included Travis Miller, Alan Sarkisian, and Charles Brunault. Our moderators included Charles Ring and Ernest Davey. Special thanks to the talents for theatrical design go to Charles Brunault.

Appendix - NUI Script V5.2

Contents
Introduction

Task 1 – Voice – Reading
Task 2 – Voice – Like lighting, think you want to use this later
Task 3 – Voice – TV
Task 4 – Voice – Back to Reading
Task 5 – Gesture – Party
Task 6 – Gesture – Like lighting, think you want to use this later
Task 7 – Gesture – Romance
Task 8 – Gesture – Back to Party
Task 9 – Both – Conversation
Task 10 – Both – Like lighting, think you want to use this later
Task 11 – Both – Cleaning
Task 12 – Both – Back to Conversation
Task 13 – Wrap Up, Interview

Introduction

Mod speaks,

"Welcome to our study on natural interfaces for controlling lighting!

This study will consist of using prototype smart phone applications to control tunable lighting for particular task goals.

The purpose of this activity is to test the robustness of our prototypes. This is intended to help us develop natural interfaces for controlling lighting.

As always, your participation is completely voluntary and you are free to stop at any time during the study for any reason without any penalty and without being asked why. The information you provide is anonymous.

You will be asked to complete a series of exercises involving common residential tasks.

Your voice and gestures will be recorded and analyzed for this experiment. These recordings will be kept anonymous in the reporting of the data and not used for advertising or marketing. If it is OK with you, I am going to start the recording now."

Moderator pretends to start recording, wizard starts recording, Mod says "Experimental run number xx"

Mod speaks,

"You will be asked to use a smart phone application to perform these tasks. This application is very universal and will respond to whatever action or voice command you give.

Before you try to use the smart phone application, we would like you to "think out loud". By this we mean that you should verbalize what you are about to do, or are trying to accomplish and how you plan to do it in detail. The recording of your intentions will be compared to the system response and used to improve the performance of the system.

When your intentions are clear we will ask you to use the smart phone to perform the desired lighting control.

The lighting may not produce the exact color, light level, or effect that you want. The responsiveness and latency may not be consistent. Don't be too concerned about this. We are looking for robustness in our control, and your participation will help us to improve our lighting control. Even if you say something and nothing happens, this is important feedback for the improvement of the system.

If you are ready to continue, please have a seat in the chair and while you get comfortable, spend some time looking around the area and try to imagine you are in your living room.

Mod moves left handed to right chair and right handed to left chair

Wait a minute for the subject to get comfortable

Mod speaks,

"Now I will start a short Demo of the Functionality of the lighting in the room, so you know what you can do with the lights"

Mod pretends to manually start the demo

Wiz runs Demo, - Finish with black-out

Mod pretends to manually reset lights

Wiz - Set lighting to 50% - 3500 K preset, Mod says, "I am resetting the lighting."

Task 1 – Voice – Reading

Start the voice app running. Mod speaks,

"On this smart phone is our prototype voice control application. The voice control will be activated while you press and hold the large button in the center of the screen and will stop after you release the button. While you hold the button, the phone produces a tone to indicate you are in control. You may press and release whenever you want to start and stop controlling.

I will give you a task and then ask you to "think out loud" about what you are going to do. I may ask questions to help clarify what you are planning to do. When we are clear on what you plan to do and how you plan to do it. I will hand you the phone to try to control the lighting.

Do you have any questions? Are you ready?

I am going to ask you to prepare the lighting in the room for reading. I'll give you a minute to sit quietly and think about how you want the room to be for reading."

Pause, give time. Mod speaks,

"OK think out loud now and be explicit about what lights you want to control and how."

Wait for the subject to finish thinking out loud and make sure you are clear on what they want to do and how they want to do it.

Then hand the smart phone to the subject.

Mod speaks,

"Here is the smart phone with the voice control app. Go ahead, press and hold the button on the screen, and speak into the phone to control the lighting."

Subject performs task

Mod - Take the phone from the subject

Task 2 – Voice – Like lighting, think you want to use this later

Mod speaks,

"You like the lighting as is, and you want to save it to be used later.

I'll give you a minute to sit quietly and think about how you want to accomplish the task of saving the lighting using the voice control app."

Pause, give time. Mod speaks,

"OK, think out loud now and be explicit about how you plan to try to do it."

Wait for the subject to finish thinking out loud and make sure you are clear on what they want to do and how they want to do it.

Then hand the smart phone to the subject.

Mod speaks,

"Here is the smart phone with the voice control app. Go ahead, press and hold the button on the screen, and speak into the phone."

Subject performs task

Wiz - Double flashlights – save setting

Mod - Take the phone from the subject

Mod pretends to manually reset lights

Wiz - Set lighting to 50% - 3500 K preset, Mod says, "I am resetting the lighting."

Task 3 – Voice – TV

Mod speaks,

"Next I am going to ask you to prepare the room lighting to watch TV. I'll give you a minute to sit quietly and think about how you want the room lighting to be."

Pause, give time. Mod speaks,

"OK, think out loud now and be explicit about what lights you want to control and how."

Wait for the subject to finish thinking out loud and make sure you are clear on what they want to do and how they want to do it.

Then hand the smart phone to the subject.

Mod speaks,

"Go ahead, press and hold the button on the screen, and use the smart phone voice control app to control the lighting. Release the button when you are finished."

Mod - Take the phone from the subject

Mod pretends to manually reset lights

Wiz - Set lighting to 50% - 3500 K preset, Mod says, "I am resetting the lighting."

Task 4 – Voice – Back to Reading

Mod speaks,

"Now you want to read again.

I'll give you a minute to sit quietly and think about how you want to accomplish the task."

Pause, give time. Mod speaks,

"OK think out loud now and be explicit about how you plan to try to do it."

Wait for the subject to finish thinking out loud and make sure you are clear on what they want to do and how they want to do it.

Then hand the smart phone to the subject.

Mod speaks,

"Here is the smart phone with the voice control app. Go ahead, press and hold the button on the screen, and speak into the phone."

Subject performs task

Wiz – Recall READING preset

Mod - Take the phone from the subject

Mod pretends to manually reset lights

Wiz - Set lighting to 50% - 3500 K preset, Mod says, "I am resetting the lighting."

Task 5 – Gesture – Party

Mod speaks,

"The next application is a gesture control application. Again the phone will be activated when you press and hold the large button in the center of the screen. I will give you a task and ask you to think out loud first. Then when I give the go ahead, press the button and control the lighting by moving the phone with gestures. I will still have you think out loud while you are gesturing to control the lighting.

Do you have any questions? Are you ready?

I am going to ask you to prepare the lighting for a party by changing the overhead lighting to some color. Take a minute to sit quietly and consider how you want to control the lighting. Particularly, consider how you are going to use gestures to get the color you want."

Pause, give EXTRA time. Mod speaks,

"OK, think out loud now and be explicit about what lights you want to control and how."

Wait for the subject to finish thinking out loud and make sure you are clear on what they want to do and how they want to do it.

Then hand the smart phone to the subject.

Mod speaks,

"Here is the phone with the gesture app running. Go ahead, press and hold the button on the screen, and use the smart phone gesture control app to control the lighting. Please verbalize what you are trying to do and how. Do this even though the phone will not respond to voice commands."

Subject performs task

Mod - Take the phone from the subject

Task 6 – Gesture – Like lighting, think you want to use this later

Mod speaks,

"Now I want you to save the lighting as is, to party later.

I'll give you a minute to sit quietly and think about how you want to accomplish the task of saving the lighting using gestures."

Pause, give EXTRA time. Mod speaks,

"OK think out loud now and be explicit about how you plan to try to do it."

Wait for the subject to finish thinking out loud and make sure you are clear on what they want to do and how they want to do it.

Then hand the smart phone to the subject.

Mod speaks,

"Here is the phone with the gesture app running. Go ahead, press and hold the button on the screen, and use the smart phone gesture control app to perform the task. Please verbalize what you are trying to do and how. Do this even though the phone will not respond to voice commands."

Subject performs task

Wiz - Double flashlights – save setting

Mod - Take the phone from the subject

Mod pretends to manually reset lights

Wiz - Set lighting to 50% - 3500 K preset, Mod says, "I am resetting the lighting."

Task 7 – Gesture – Romance

Mod speaks,

"I am going to ask you to prepare the lighting for romance. Take a minute to sit quietly and consider how you want to control the lighting. Particularly, consider how you are going to use gestures to get the lighting you want."

Pause, give EXTRA time. Mod speaks,

"OK, think out loud now and be explicit about what lights you want to control and how."

Wait for the subject to finish thinking out loud and make sure you are clear on what they want to do and how they want to do it.

Then hand the smart phone to the subject.

Mod speaks,

"Here is the phone with the gesture app running. Go ahead, press and hold the button on the screen, and use the smart phone gesture control app to control the lighting. Please verbalize what you are trying to do and how. Do this even though the phone will not respond to voice commands."

Subject performs task

Mod - Take the phone from the subject

Mod pretends to manually reset lights

Wiz - Set lighting to 50% - 3500 K preset, Mod says, "I am resetting the lighting."

Task 8 – Gesture – Back to Party

Mod speaks,

"Now I want you to party again.

I'll give you a minute to sit quietly and think about how you want to accomplish this task using gestures."

Pause, give time. Mod speaks,

"OK think out loud now and be explicit about how you plan to try to do it."

Wait for the subject to finish thinking out loud and make sure you are clear on what they want to do and how they want to do it.

Then hand the smart phone to the subject.

Mod speaks,

"Here is the phone with the gesture app running. Go ahead, press and hold the button on the screen, and use the smart phone gesture control app to perform the task. Please verbalize what you are trying to do and how. Do this even though the phone will not respond to voice commands."

Subject performs task

Wiz – Recall PARTY preset

Mod - Take the phone from the subject

Mod pretends to manually reset lights

Wiz - Set lighting to 50% - 3500 K preset, Mod says, "I am resetting the lighting."

Task 9 – Both – Conversation

Mod speaks,

"The next application responds to both your voice and the gestures you use to move the phone. Again the phone will be activated when you press and hold the large button in the center of the screen. I will give you a task and ask you to think out loud first. Then, when I give the go ahead, please press and hold the button and control the lighting by moving the phone and speaking. I will still ask you to think out loud before and after you are controlling the lighting.

Do you have any questions? Are you ready?

I am going to ask you to prepare the lighting for conversation. Take a minute to sit quietly and consider how you want to control the lighting. Particularly, consider how you are going to use gestures to get the effect you want."

Pause, give time. Mod speaks,

"OK, think out loud now and be explicit about what lights you want to control and how."

Wait for the subject to finish thinking out loud and make sure you are clear on what they want to do and how they want to do it.

Then hand the smart phone to the subject.

Mod speaks,

"Here is the phone with the voice and gesture app running. It may be helpful if you verbalize what you are trying to do and how. Then go ahead, press and hold the button on the screen, and use the smart phone voice and gesture control app to control the lighting.

Subject performs task

Mod - Take the phone from the subject

Task 10 – Both – Like lighting, think you want to use this later

Mod speaks,

"Now I want you to save the lighting as is.

I'll give you a minute to sit quietly and think about how you want to accomplish the task of saving the lighting using both voice and gestures."

Pause, give time. Mod speaks,

"OK think out loud now and be explicit about how you plan to try to do it."

Wait for the subject to finish thinking out loud and make sure you are clear on what they want to do and how they want to do it.

Then hand the smart phone to the subject.

Mod speaks,

"Here is the phone with the both voice and gesture app running. Go ahead, press and hold the button on the screen, and use the smart phone gesture control app to perform the task. Please verbalize what you are trying to do and how."

Subject performs task

Wiz - Double flashlights – save setting

Mod - Take the phone from the subject

Mod pretends to manually reset lights

Wiz - Set lighting to 50% - 3500 K preset, Mod says, "I am resetting the lighting."

Task 11 – Both – Cleaning

Mod speaks,

"Next I am going to ask you to prepare the room for cleaning. I'll give you a minute to sit quietly and think about how you want the room lighting to be."

Pause, give time. Mod speaks,

"OK, think out loud now and be explicit about what lights you want to control and how."

Wait for the subject to finish thinking out loud and make sure you are clear on what they want to do and how they want to do it.

Then hand the smart phone to the subject.

Mod speaks,

"Go ahead, press and hold the button on the screen, and use the smart phone to control the lighting."

Subject performs task

Mod - Take the phone from the subject

Mod pretends to manually reset lights

Wiz - Set lighting to 50% - 3500 K preset, Mod says, "I am resetting the lighting."

Task 12 – Both – Back to Conversation

Mod speaks,

"Now you want to have a conversation again.

I'll give you a minute to sit quietly and think about how you want to accomplish this task using both voice and gestures."

Pause, give time. Mod speaks,

"OK think out loud now and be explicit about how you plan to try to do it."

Wait for the subject to finish thinking out loud and make sure you are clear on what they want to do and how they want to do it.

Then hand the smart phone to the subject.

Mod speaks,

"Here is the phone with the both voice and gesture app running. Go ahead, press and hold the button on the screen, and use the smart phone gesture control app to perform the task."

Subject performs task

Wiz – Recall conversation preset

Mod - Take the phone from the subject

Mod pretends to manually reset lights

Wiz - Set lighting to 50% - 3500 K preset, Mod says, "I am resetting the lighting."

Task 13 – Wrap Up, Interview

Mod speaks,

"Thank you for participating in our study on natural interfaces for controlling lighting! Your participation will certainly help us develop natural interfaces for control-ling lighting. First I would like to ask if you have any comments on your experience. Now I would like to ask you some questions regarding your prior use of lighting controls, or similar controls.

1. Have you used voice or gestures to control lighting?
a. If yes, please describe your experiences.
2. Have you used voice or gestures to control anything else?
a. If yes, please describe your experiences.
3. Specifically have you used the "Magic Wand"?
4. Have you seen the "Magic Wand" used?
5. Was the beep sound, while pressing the button, too loud or disturbing?

Thanks again, please don't share this experience with other colleagues until the end of this study, as we will need to study more volunteers, who are not yet aware of what we are doing. And have a nice day"

Observer's Notes on Participants mood, appearance, engagement ...

References

Boyce, P.R.: Human Factors in Lighting, 2nd edn. Taylor and Francis, London, New York (2003)

Jacko, J.A.: The Human-Computer Interaction Handbook, 3rd edn. CRC Press, Boca Raton (2012)

Salvendy, G.: Handbook of Human Factors and Ergonomics, 3rd edn. Wiley, Hoboken (2006)

Heuristics to Evaluate the Usability of Ubiquitous Systems

Larissa C. Rocha[1]([✉]), Rossana M.C. Andrade[1], Andreia L. Sampaio[2],
and Valéria Lelli[1]

[1] Group of Computer Networks, Software Engineering and Systems (GREat),
Federal University of Ceará (UFC), Fortaleza, Brazil
{larissarocha,rossana,valerialelli}@great.ufc.br
[2] Federal University of Ceará (UFC), Campus Quixadá, Quixadá, Brazil
andreia.ufc@gmail.com

Abstract. While the ubiquitous systems have characteristics that modify the way the user interacts with the systems, Human-Computer Interaction area studies forms of interaction, with usability being one of the main quality criteria. One of the methods used to evaluate usability is Heuristic Evaluation. In the case of ubiquitous systems, that have characteristics such as mobility and context awareness, Nielsen's heuristics, which are widely used in conventional systems, do not focus on these particularities. Therefore, this work proposes specific heuristics to evaluate the usability of ubiquitous systems. Empirical studies and questionnaires were applied with experts in order to evaluate the proposed heuristics. The results point to improvements in both the way of conducting the evaluation and in the heuristics. From these results, the proposed heuristics were refined.

Keywords: Heuristic evaluation · Usability evaluation · Qualitative evaluation · Quality characteristic · Ubiquitous systems

1 Introduction

Ubiquitous systems are design to be present in people's lives, helping users in their daily activities and providing access to information at any time and wherever the user may be (Hansmann et al. 2003).

Nowdays, it is common to see the same user with several devices and several applications interacting with them. However, we have to consider the following question: "Who wants to have hundreds of computers around constantly demanding attention and bombarding us with irrelevant information?" (Riekki et al. 2004). A system that does not efficiently help the users in activities of their daily lives, causing discomfort or insecurity, discourages the user to use it, presenting low usability, according to (Santos 2014).

R.M.C. Andrade—CNPq Productivity Scholarship in Technological Development and Innovative Extension (DT-2).

© Springer International Publishing AG 2017
N. Streitz and P. Markopoulos (Eds.): DAPI 2017, LNCS 10291, pp. 120–141, 2017.
DOI: 10.1007/978-3-319-58697-7_9

Taking then the usability concept that consider usability one of the quality-of-use criteria that respond if the characteristics of the interactions and interface are adequate (Barbosa and Da Silva 2010). Usability is related to how easy it is to use the interface as well as user satisfaction due to the use of the system (Nielsen 1993). So, usability evaluation becomes a priority for ubiquitous systems since ubiquitous computing directly interferes with the user's way of connecting to their systems.

One of the methods to evaluate system usability is the Heuristic Evaluation, an inspection method, created by Jakob Nielsen, where experts are guided by a set of usability principles, known as heuristics, to evaluate the elements of system's interfaces.

To evaluate the usability of specific systems with heuristics, the aspects belonging to the domain of these systems must be considered for more effective results (Moraes and Rosa 2008). In the case of ubiquitous systems, it is necessary to adapt the existing Nielsen's heuristics and to elaborate new heuristics to cover the specific characteristics of these systems, such as context awareness, transparency, attention, calmness and mobility (Santos 2014).

This paper aims to propose heuristics to evaluate the usability of ubiquitous systems, according to the particular characteristics of these systems. At first, a set of 13 heuristics was elaborated using a methodology based on Rusu et al. (2011). This set of heuristics was used in qualitative evaluations: an empirical study, which had the objective of observing the use of these heuristics in a practical evaluation, where experts performed heuristic evaluations; and a questionnaire, where other experts analyzed the heuristics and the process of creating them, reporting total agreement, partial agreement, disagreements and improvements to be applied.

This paper is structured as follows: Sect. 2 provides the theoretical basis: Ubiquitous Systems and Heuristic Evaluation. Section 3 investigates the work related to this research. In Sect. 4, the Ubiquitous Heuristics are elaborated through the execution of the methodology chosen for this purpose. Section 5 presents the questions and structuring of the qualitative evaluations and in Sect. 6 the results of the evaluations are presented and discussed. Finally, Sect. 7 concludes the paper, presenting the final considerations of this work.

2 Background

2.1 Ubiquitous Systems

Weiser (1991) describes his idealization of Ubiquitous Computing as follows: "Ubiquitous computing aims to improve computer use by making many computers available everywhere, but making them effectively invisible to the user." He also says that "The most advanced technologies are those that disappear. In ubiquitous computing, computers will be embedded in the surrounding environment, creating a new paradigm of access and manipulation of information".

Because the ubiquitous systems have differentiated characteristics, the evaluations carried out must take these factors into account. Bezerra et al. (2014) mention three challenges for usability testing in ubiquitous systems: (i) ubiquitous environments have more usability factors that should be evaluated, such as contextual information; (ii) most of the software measures do not consider the factors of ubiquitous applications; (iii) currently, usability testing methods follow the same activities performed in traditional systems.

In Santos (2014) are selected the following characteristics of ubiquitous systems as essential for evaluating the quality of human-computer interaction:

1. *Context Awareness*: corresponds to the ability to collect contextual information and use this information to make adaptations in the systems (Kourouthanassis et al. 2008).
2. *Transparency*: as said by (Satyanarayanan 2001), can be achieved by the proactivity of the system so that the user is minimally distracted.
3. *Attention*: In the ubiquitous environment, computers are hidden and replace user activities, thus enabling the user to focus on the various mental and physical activities such as walking, driving or other real-world interactions (Garlan et al. 2002).
4. *Calmness*: means free of distraction, excitement or disturbance. A quiet application is one that interacts with the user at the right time, only presents relevant information and demand the user's attention only when necessary (Riekki 2004).
5. *Mobility*: in the ubiquitous computing era there is a search for "seamless" mobility that refers to the continuous or uninterrupted use of computing while the user moves through devices (Yu et al. 2013).

These characteristics were selected by Santos (2014) from the main existing definitions of ubiquitous systems to create measures to evaluate the quality of the human-computer interaction of these systems. Once the heuristic evaluation aims to achieve the quality of the human-computer interaction, these characteristics were selected to be part of the scope of the ubiquitous systems of this paper.

2.2   Human-Computer Interaction and Heuristic Evaluation

For Preece et al. (1994), the Human-Computer Interaction (HCI) area concerns the understanding of how people use computer systems to design new systems that better match user's needs.

Usability is one of the main criteria of the quality in use of systems. It is related to the easiness of learning and use of the interface and to the user satisfaction in using it (Nielsen 1993). The ISO/IEC 9126 (2001) regulation was the first standard that defined the term Usability as "A set of attributes related to the effort required to use an interactive system, and related to the individual evaluation of such use by a set of specific users".

To evaluate the usability of systems, methods are proposed to guide the evaluators during the evaluation to maximize the identification of usability defects. One such method is the Heuristic Evaluation.

In 1990, Nielsen and Molich proposed Heuristic Evaluation to find usability issues during the development of interactive systems. This method directs the evaluators to systematically inspect the system interface to identify problems that compromise good usability. The guidance is made by usability guidelines, called "heuristic", which describes recommendations for interfaces and interaction (Barbosa and da Silva 2010). Nielsen's heuristics are widely used to evaluate the usability of any type of systems.

Although the heuristics proposed by Nielsen and Molich are the precursors, Moraes and Rosa (2008) affirm that there are several lists of heuristics in literature, principles or ergonomic criteria that can be used for this type of evaluation. Nevertheless, these lists are generic, so adaptation is necessary to achieve a more effective result.

Barbosa and da Silva (2010) and Preece et al. (2002) recommend the heuristic evaluation in three stages:

1. Preparation: in this first stage are defined and organized the screens to be evaluated and the list of heuristics to be used. In synthesis, the evaluators are told what and how to perform it.
2. Data Collection and Interpretation (evaluation period): each evaluator individually inspects every screen to identify if the guidelines are being followed. If any guideline is violated, then it is considered a potential problem.
3. Consolidation and Report of results: at the end of the inspections, all of the evaluators meet to discuss the results and present a single consolidated report, according to the general consensus.

3   Related Work

In order to identify papers that relate heuristic evaluation to ubiquitous systems, our research was carried out through the ACM, IEEE, Springer, Scopus and BDBComp databases, seeking to answer the following research question: "Which existing papers use Heuristic Evaluation to evaluate the usability of ubiquitous systems?".

The following search string was used: ("heuristic") and ("evaluation" or "assessment") and ("ubiquitous" or "ubiquity" or "pervasive")

As a result, only one paper used Heuristic Evaluation to evaluate a ubiquitous system (Kemp et al. 2008). The authors of this study have developed a framework for the heuristic evaluation of the interface of an e-learning application, which is considered ubiquitous since the authors define the following characteristics for ubiquity: invisibility, usability, universality, and utility. The system evaluated was for desktop and a set of 18 heuristics was generated to evaluate web and ubiquitous systems but adapted to the needs of a distance learning system. They aimed to support learning by minimizing the visibility of the computer so the user could maximize the visibility of teaching content to the student. However, the evaluated system may have compromised issues such as mobility and context awareness, characteristics of the scope of ubiquitous systems of this paper.

As only one paper was selected in our previous research, a new research was conducted to cover other studies that have heuristics to evaluate the usability of mobile and/or context-aware systems. So a new research aimed to answer the following research question: "Which existing works have characteristics or heuristics to evaluate the usability of Ubiquitous systems, mobile or context-awareness systems?".

The search string has been updated to ("heuristic" or "characteristic") and ("evaluation" or "assessment") and ("usability") and ("ubiquitous" or "ubiquity" or "pervasive" or "context" or "mobile").

In total, a new research selected 8 papers, from the reading of their titles and abstracts, to analyze the heuristics and characteristics of the ubiquitous systems. They are presented in Sect. 4.1.

One of these papers (Santos 2014) presents the basis of the characteristics that must be present when evaluating the usability of ubiquitous systems. In this paper, a systematic mapping was carried out to identify the characteristics that influence the quality of HCI in ubiquitous systems. The mapping found 134 characteristics, but there are duplicate characteristics with the same name and meaning and also characteristics with the same meaning, but with different names. In order to obtain the final set of characteristics, an analysis of meanings (semantic analysis) was performed considering what was written in the papers found by the systematic mapping and also in the classical literature of the areas involved. In the end, 26 relevant characteristics for HCI evaluation in ubiquitous systems were identified.

The other seven papers, (Bertini et al. 2006; Kemp et al. 2008; Varsaluoma 2009; Bonifácio 2012; Moraveji and Soesanto 2012; Inostroza et al. 2013; Machado Neto and Pimentel 2013), were analyzed to identify new characteristics not contemplated in Santos (2014). Table 3 shows all 31 characteristics captured using the related works presents in this section.

4   Ubiquitous Heuristics

In this section, we present the methodology used in this work to create the ubiquitous heuristics. Also, we present the initial set of 13 ubiquitous heuristics before the refinement step.

4.1   Methodology

For the creation of the ubiquitous heuristics, a methodology based on Rusu et al. (2011) was followed. Among the reasons for choosing this methodology, it is worth mentioning that is a generic methodology, from which heuristics for specific domains have already been created (e.g., virtual worlds systems, touchscreen-based mobile devices). It is also based on the characteristics of the domain application and indicates Nielsen's Heuristics as the basis for the new heuristics.

One of the steps proposed by Rusu et al. (2011) is the Validation Stage (Step 5), where through heuristic evaluations performed in specific case studies new heuristics against Nielsen's heuristics are compared. However, in this paper, the focus of the evaluation will not be comparing to the proposed heuristics, but to observe their use through an experimental study and to apply a questionnaire to experts, so this stage was adapted as "Evaluation Stage".

The methodology used in this work involves 6 steps, summarized as following and represented in Fig. 1:

- **Step 1: Exploratory Stage** - a bibliographical research is done to collect subjects related to the main topics of the research, such as heuristic evaluation and ubiquitous systems.

- **Step 2: Descriptive Stage** - the most important characteristics of the information collected in Step 1 are highlighted.
- **Step 3: Correlational Stage** - a filter is performed on the information obtained in Step 2 to identify the characteristics that the ubiquitous heuristics should have.
- **Step 4: Explanatory Stage** - formally specifies the initial version of the proposed ubiquitous heuristics, associating the characteristics present in each one and the process used for its creation.
- **Step 5: Evaluation Stage** - observes the use of the proposed heuristics applied in heuristic evaluations performed by experts. In addition, a questionnaire is applied with other experts to evaluate the process of creating the heuristics.
- **Step 6: Refinement Stage** - based on feedback from the evaluation stage (Step 5), the heuristics defined in the Step 4 are refined.

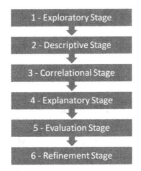

Fig. 1. Methodology used for the creation of Ubiquitous Heuristics, adapted from Rusu et al. (2011)

The following subsections present in detail the execution of steps 1 to 4 of Rusu's methodology. Once the heuristics are defined in Step 4, the Step 5 of the methodology, which we adapted, is carried out by experts through qualitative evaluations (Sect. 5), and the ubiquitous heuristics are refined in Step 6, as we present in Sect. 6.

4.2   Step 1: Exploratory Stage

For the *exploratory stage*, a survey of the bibliography related to the research topics was performed, as presented in Sect. 3.

From the selected papers in the researchs carried out, as presented in Sect. 3, Santos (2014) systematically mapped the characteristics that influence the quality of human-computer interaction in ubiquitous systems. In addition to Santos' work (2014), seven other papers, which include heuristics and characteristics of the ubiquitous systems, were selected: (Bertini et al. 2006; Kemp et al. 2008; Varsaluoma 2009; Bonifácio 2012; Moraveji and Soesanto 2012; Inostroza et al. 2013; Machado Neto and Pimentel 2013).

The selection of these papers, illustrated in Table 1, was carried out according to the reading of their titles and abstracts. After this selection, the full papers were read for content analysis and characteristic identification.

Table 1. Selected papers in the Exploratory Stage and the number of characteristics extracted in the Descriptive Stage.

Paper title	Reference	Amount
"Características e Medidas de Software para Avaliação da Qualidade da Interação Humano-Computador em Sistemas Ubíquos"	(Santos 2014)	26
"Interface Evaluation for Invisibility and Ubiquity – An example from E-learning"	(Kemp et al. 2008)	18
"Usabilidade de Aplicações Web Móvel: Avaliando uma Nova Abordagem de Inspeção através de Estudos Experimentais"	(Bonifácio 2012)	9
Usability Heuristics for Touchscreen-based Mobile Devices: Update	(Inostroza et al. 2013)	7
Heuristics for the Assessment of Interfaces of Mobile Devices	(Neto e Pimentel 2013)	17
Appropriating and Assessing Heuristics for Mobile Computing	(Bertini et al. 2006)	7
Towards Stress-less User Interfaces: 10 Design Heuristics Based on the Psychophysiology of Stress	(Moraveji e Soesanto 2012)	7
Scenarios in the Heuristic Evaluation of Mobile Devices: Emphasizing the Context of Use	(Varsaluoma 2009)	2

4.3   Step 2: Descriptive Stage

The *descriptive stage* highlights the most important characteristics of the information collected earlier. From complete reading of the selected papers from the Exploratory Stage (Table 1), characteristics related to the evaluation of usability in ubiquitous systems were extracted. Such characteristics must be present in the heuristics to be developed in this work.

From the eight selected papers, Kemp (2008) is present in the systematic mapping performed by Santos (2014), where a list of 26 characteristics was extracted to be present in HCI evaluations of ubiquitous systems. This list is called in this paper of "Santos's List".

The characteristics of the "Santos's List" were selected for the elaboration of ubiquitous heuristics. However, the other 6 selected papers (see Table 1) did not enter into the systematic mapping performed by Santos (2014), because they were found due to the bibliographic research being performed with a focus on usability heuristics, which was not the focus of the mapping previously mentioned. Then, Kemp et al. (2008) the others 6 papers were read and 67 characteristics of usability were extracted to be present in ubiquitous systems to identify new characteristic not yet reported in Santos's List.

4.4   Step 3: Correlational Stage

For the *correlational stage*, a filter was performed in the new 67 characteristics identified in the descriptive stage (Subsect. 4.3), since some terms were synonyms or were already present in Santos's List, or were already present in Nielsen's 10 Heuristics, which would be taken as the basis for the creation of the ubiquitous heuristics, proposed in this paper.

Table 2 presents a sample of the analysis performed. In the first column, there is the name of the selected work, in the second column there are the characteristics extracted from that work and in the third column it is said if: the characteristic is already part of Santos's List; the characteristic is present in some Nielsen's Heuristic; or whether it will be added to the final set of characteristics because it has not yet been identified in any of the previous options.

Table 2. Sample of the analysis of identified characteristics[a].

Paper reference	Characteristics	Analysis result
Inostroza (2013)	Mobile Characteristics	Synonym of the Santos's List (device capability)
	Learning Capability	Included
	Flexibility	Included
	Efficiency of use and performance	Synonym of the Santos's List (efficiency)
	Mobile use context	Synonym of the Santos's List (context awareness)
	Screen resolution	Synonym of the Santos's List (device capability)
	Data input for interaction	Included
Neto e Pimentel (2013)	Screen orientation	Synonym of the Santos's List (device capability)
	Interface Consistency	Nielsen's Heuristic
	Interface Standard	Nielsen's Heuristic

[a] The complete table of analysis can be found at: https://github.com/GREatPesquisa/Heuristicas_de_Usabilidade_para_avaliar_Sistemas_Ubiquos

From the analysis, a final set of 31 essential characteristics were identified to be present in the usability evaluation heuristics of ubiquitous systems. A summary of the characteristics is presented in Table 3.

It can be observed that the characteristics adaptation, data entry, flexibility, positioning of components and visualization of information were the new characteristics identified, all others belong to the Santos's List.

Based on the list of 31 characteristics and Nielsen's 10 heuristics, the proposed set of heuristics for the evaluation of the ubiquitous systems was created. This set is called Ubiquitous Heuristics.

To start the creation process, Nielsen's 10 heuristics are taken as a basis, as suggested by Rusu et al. (2011). The description of each one is analyzed to verify whether it remains in the set of Ubiquitous Heuristics. For this analysis, the following processes have been

Table 3. Final set of 31 characteristics identified to be present in the Ubiquitous Heuristics.

Characteristic	Paper reference	Characteristic	Paper reference
1. Acceptability	Santos (2014)	17. Network Capability	Santos (2014)
2. Adaptation	Bertini et al. (2006)	18. Positioning of components	Machado Neto e Pimentel (2013)
3. Attention	Santos (2014)	19. Predictability	Santos (2014)
4. Availability	Santos (2014)	20. Privacy	Santos (2014)
5. Calmness	Santos (2014)	21. Reliability	Santos (2014)
6. Context Awareness	Santos (2014)	22. Robustness	Santos (2014)
7. Data Input	Inostroza et al. (2013)	23. Safety	Santos (2014)
8. Device Capability	Santos (2014)	24. Scalability	Santos (2014)
9. Ease of use	Santos (2014)	25. Security	Santos (2014)
10. Effectiveness	Santos (2014)	26. Simplicity	Santos (2014)
11. Efficiency	Santos (2014)	27. Transparency	Santos (2014)
12. Familiarity	Santos (2014)	28. Trust	Santos (2014)
13. Flexibility	Inostroza et al. (2013)	29. Usability	Santos (2014)
14. Information display	Machado Neto e Pimentel (2013)	30. User Satisfaction	Santos (2014)
15. Interconnectivity	Santos (2014)	31. Utility	Santos (2014)
16. Mobility	Santos (2014)	–	–

defined: (i) Elimination, in which the heuristic is removed because it does not apply to ubiquitous systems; (ii) Junction, in which heuristics are united by addressing the same subject in ubiquitous systems; and (iii) Adaptation, in which heuristics are adapted to suit ubiquitous systems.

During the creation process, we also analysed each characteristic presented in Table 3 to identify which of Nielsen's heuristics could be associated. Thus, each of these heuristics went through one of three processes and had one or more of the 31 characteristics associated with it.

Some of the inherent characteristics of the evaluation of ubiquitous systems were not contemplated by Nielsen's heuristics, and therefore, new heuristics had to be elaborated using the definitions of these characteristics. The initial result is a set of 13 Ubiquitous Heuristics, which are presented in the next subsection.

Table 4 presents the "Ubiquitous Heuristics", their relationship with the Nielsen's heuristics and the process used to define that heuristics, as well as the characteristics present in each one.

Table 4. Relation between the Ubiquitous Heuristics and Nielsen's heuristics, the creation process and the characteristics involved

Nielsen's heuristics	Ubiquitous heuristics	Process	Characteristics
HN1+HN8+HN9	HU1- Calm Communication	Junction	Calmness, Effectiveness, Attention, Utility, Simplicity.
HN2	HU2- Correspondence between the application and the real world	Adaptation	Familiarity, Trust, Information display, Positioning of components.
HN3	HU3 - User Freedom	Adaptation	Calmness, Acceptability, User Satisfaction
HN4	HU4 - Consistency and standards	Adaptation	Ease of Use
HN5	HU5 - Error Prevention	Adaptation	Reliability, Scalability
HN6	–	Elimination	–
HN7	HU6 - Customization	Adaptation	Flexibility
HN10	HU7 - Minimum need of help and documentation	Adaptation	Usability, Ease of use
–	HU8 - Minimal effort	Created	Efficiency, Ease of use, User Satisfaction
–	HU9 - Mobility and mobile devices	Created	Device Capability, Network Capability, Interconnectivity, Mobility
–	HU10 - Privacy and Safety	Created	Privacy, Safety, Security, Availability
–	HU11 - Invisibility and Transparency	Created	Transparency, Predictability
–	HU12 - Context awareness and adaptive interfaces	Created	Context Awareness, Adaptation
–	HU13 - Sensors and data input	Created	Data Input, Robustness

4.5 Step 4: Explanatory Stage

This stage formally specifies the initial version of the set of the proposed heuristics. As illustrated in Table 4, the ubiquitous heuristics from HU1 to HU8 represent the heuristics that were created from the Nielsen's heuristics analysis and the heuristics from HU9 to HU13 were created from characteristics that were not covered by Nielsen's heuristics. The following are the heuristics and the characteristics involved:

- HU1 - *Calm communication*. The system should inform users of what is happening only when needed or when prompted so that it does not disturb the user in their current activity. It should present the exact information that the user needs at the moment, neither more nor less. Communication should be clear, objective and brief, using tone, appropriate emotion, and naturally calm elements. If it is an error message, the problem must be stated accurately and constructively suggesting a solution.

- Characteristic(s): Calmness, Effectiveness, Attention, Utility, Simplicity.
- HU2 - *Correspondence between the application and the real world.* The system must speak the language of the user, with words, phrases, and concepts familiar to the user and in order to inspire trust. The conventions of the real world must be followed, making the information seem logical and natural.
  - Characteristic(s): Familiarity, Trust, Information display, Positioning of components.
- HU3 - *User Freedom.* The user should not feel pressured to perform any task, he has to have the option to interact or not with the application. When the application interacts with the user in a given context, the user should not feel obligated to respond to the interaction and should have the option to ignore it. The user can not feel controlled or overloaded by the application so that the user does not abandon it.
  - Characteristic(s): Calmness, Acceptability, User Satisfaction.
- HU4 - *Consistency and standards.* Application interfaces, ways of interacting or adapting to the context must be consistent and follow a standard to facilitate the user's use of the system.
  - Characteristic(s): Ease of Use.
- HU5 - *Error prevention.* It is necessary to be familiar with the situations that most cause errors and modify the interfaces and interactions so that these errors do not occur. In addition, the application must be able to maintain its functionalities when used in adverse conditions.
  - Characteristic(s): Reliability and Scalability.
- HU6 - *Customization.* The application should give the users the ability to customize configurations according to their needs and experiences.
  - Characteristic(s): Flexibility.
- HU7 - *Minimum need of help and documentation.* Ideally the application should be so easy to use (intuitive) that it does not need help or documentation. If needed, the help should be easily accessible, focused on the user's current activity. The aid guidelines should be objective and not too large.
  - Characteristic(s): Usability and Ease of Use.
- HU8 - *Minimal effort.* The application must easily reach the intended objective. Efficiently using the effort and resources required.
  - Characteristic(s): Efficiency, Ease of Use, User Satisfaction.
- HU9 - *Mobility and Mobile Devices.* Ubiquitous applications should suit the physical displacement of the user and the limitations of mobile devices. Aspects such as, wireless connection, connection between devices, small screen, limited hardware and memory capabilities, and limited power capability are factors that the application needs to circumvent and be natural to the user without causing inconvenience.
  - Characteristic(s): Device capability, network capability, interconnectivity, Mobility.
- HU10 - *Privacy and Safety.* The application must be able to keep the information protected, so that there is no risk of damage in a context of specific use. Information must be transported and stored securely, as well as the application's access controls.

- Characteristic(s): Privacy, Security, Safety, Availability.
- HU11 - *Invisibility and Transparency*. The system must be able to hide computational components so users do not worry about them. Interactions must take place through natural interfaces.
  - Characteristic(s): Transparency, Predictability.
- HU12 - *Context Awareness and Adaptive Interfaces*. The ubiquitous application should react according to the user context, the temporal context, and the context of the device. Interfaces must adapt to this context and bring only relevant information.
  - Characteristic(s): Context Awareness, Adaptation.
- HU13 - *Sensors and data input*. It must be verified whether the data input, whether given by the user or captured by sensors, is being effective and happening in a natural way for the user. The application should work properly in the presence of invalid inputs or stressful environmental conditions.
  - Characteristic(s): Data Input, Robustness.

5 Qualitative Evaluations

Step 5 of the methodology is the *evaluation stage*, which consists of qualitative evaluations of an exploratory nature. Initially, in Sub-sect. 5.1, we present the empirical study carried out using an observation method, in order to explore the use of the proposed heuristics in heuristic evaluations carried out in practice. In Subsect. 5.2, experts answered a questionnaire in what they analyzed the heuristics and the process of creating them, reporting total agreement, partial agreement, disagreements and suggesting improvements to be applied.

5.1 Empirical Study

The empirical study aims to evaluate the use of the proposed heuristics during the heuristic evaluations. In this subsection, we present the research question and how this study was organized.

Research Question. What impressions, doubts, facilities, difficulties, and improvements are identified by experts when using the ubiquitous heuristics in a heuristic evaluation performed in practice?

- Objective: The objective of the study was to explore the ubiquitous heuristics proposed in practical situations of use, in other words, to apply in heuristic evaluations performed by experts, in order to look for new considerations to improve the heuristics and the evaluation method.
- Context: The study was carried out in two days. In the first day three experts participated, and in the second day, four others took part. All participants completed a personal questionnaire and signed a Term of Consent. To perform the evaluations, the following were available: (i) the ubiquitous heuristics for the experts; (ii) a space

to write their considerations; and (iii) a brief presentation of the ubiquitous application to be evaluated. The experts were also asked to verbally express their doubts and impressions during the evaluation so that what was said was recorded and noted.

- Participants: Seven experts participated in the study. Before performing the evaluation, they answered a personal questionnaire with three questions, in which their answers should follow the scale: 1 = Has no experience with the subject; 2 = Knows the concepts, but have had no experience with the subject; 3 = The expert is familiar with the concepts and has had some experiences with the subject; and 4 = Expert in the subject and had several experiences in the area. Table 5 presents the profile of the participants in the study.

Table 5. Profile of the experts of the empirical study.

Experts/Question	What is your experience in the HCI area?	What is your experience with Usability Evaluation Methods?	What is your experience in using Ubiquitous Systems?
Expert 1	3	3	2
Expert 2	3	3	2
Expert 3	4	3	4
Expert 4	3	3	1
Expert 5	3	3	2
Expert 6	2	2	1
Expert 7	3	3	2

We can observe that most of them are familiar with HCI concepts and usability evaluation methods, some a little more experienced and some of them just beginners. However, only one participant is an expert in Ubiquitous Systems. The other participants neither have experiences with ubiquitous systems nor are experts on the topic. Therefore, a training on ubiquitous systems was held to level the participants' knowledge and to help them carry out the evaluation. In addition to the seven participants, there were two observers who acted as facilitators.

- Instrumentation[1]: The instrumentation was done through a printed worksheet with the heuristics delivered to the participants. On the first day of the study, verification items related to the description of each of the heuristics were used. On the second day only the description of the heuristic was. In addition to the spreadsheet, on both days the material was available to report the result of the analysis (and possible problems identified) and smartphones with the GREat Mute[2] application installed. GREat Mute (Carvalho et al. 2015) is an application developed in the Android platform, whose main function is to leave the cell phone in silence according to the events of the user in Google Calendar. For example, whenever there is an event with the

---

[1] The instrumentation models can be found at: https://github.com/GREatPesquisa/Heuristicas_de_Usabilidade_para_avaliar_Sistemas_Ubiquos/tree/master/Avaliacoes_Heuristicas.

[2] Link: https://play.google.com/store/apps/details?id=br.ufc.greatmute4.

words "meeting" or "au-la" in the user's Google Calendar, the mobile is automatically silent if the user is in the location defined in the event, on the day and time. For this, it is enough for the user to register the keywords in GREat Mute.

- Experimental draw: The study was carried out in three stages: 1. pre-evaluation training; 2. execution of heuristic evaluations; and 3. post-evaluation interview (Focus Group). In the *Pre-evaluation training*, the facilitator starts by explaining the purpose of the experiment and the steps to be taken. The experts were invited to complete a personal questionnaire and sign a Consent Term. After this initial stage, the facilitator explains the concepts of ubiquitous systems to level the knowledge of the evaluators in the subject. Next, the application to be evaluated, GREat Mute, is presented on a mobile device. Finally, the evaluation instruments are presented. In the *execution of heuristic evaluations,* the evaluation was carried out based on the spreadsheet provided with the ubiquitous heuristics, which serve as a guide for the experts to evaluate that application. The facilitators ask the experts to note the evaluation time and to state their doubts and thoughts during the evaluation. The results of the heuristic evaluation were reported through the analysis whether or not the application was in agreement with the heuristic. If it did not, the problem was reported in such a way that indicate: the location, the description and the severity of the problem. Throughout the evaluation, two observers remained with the evaluators, observing and noting the interactions, their doubts, and the identified problems. Finally, in the *post-evaluation interview*, the researchers interview the experts to identify their general perceptions about the ubiquitous heuristics and the applied evaluation.

5.2 Questionnaire

A second evaluation was carried out through a questionnaire with experts, aiming to evaluate the process of creating the heuristics and the characteristics associated with them, as well as the process of eliminating the Nielsen's heuristic "Aesthetics and Minimalist Design". In this section, we present the research question and how this study was organized.

Research Question. What are the experts' opinions about the process of creating the ubiquitous heuristics and the characteristics associated with them? What are your considerations?

- Objective. This evaluation aims at the analysis of experts in the process of creating ubiquitous heuristics and of the heuristics themselves.
- Context. A questionnaire was sent by e-mail to 4 experts. They were asked to analyze the process of creating each of the ubiquitous heuristics and give their opinions. After that, the questionnaire was answered and the results were analysed.
- Expert Profile. Table 6 presents the profile of the experts: a doctor, two doctoral students and a master's student, all with more than three years of experience in applying methods to evaluate the usability of systems and with familiarity in the subjects of HCI and ubiquitous computing. Even though expert 4 was not familiar

Table 6. Profile of the experts who participated in the Questionnaire evaluation.

Question/Expert	Expert 1	Expert 2	Expert 3	Expert 4
What is your academic background?	Doctorate (in progress)	Master (in progress)	Doctorate (in progress)	Doctorate
What is your experience in applying methods to evaluate the usability of systems?	More than 3 years	More than 3 years	More than 3 years	More than 3 years
How do you consider your familiarity with the topic of HCI?	Very Familiar	Very Familiar	Very Familiar	Moderately Familiar
How do you consider your familiarity with the topic of Ubiquitous Computing?	Very Familiar	Not Familiar	Moderately Familiar	Moderately Familiar

with ubiquitous computing, he recorded that studied previously the concepts and characteristics of ubiquitous computing to help in the responses of this evaluation.

- Instrumentation[3]. We have used the following instruments: a spreadsheet containing the objective of the evaluation; a set of instructions, which explained the whole process of creating the ubiquitous heuristics (as presented in Sect. 4) and how the experts should complete the questionnaire; the set of 31 characteristics, their definitions and references; a mapping, as shown in Table 4; and of the worksheet for each of the ubiquitous heuristics to be evaluated.
- **Execution.** For each ubiquitous heuristic, there was the corresponding Nielsen's heuristic, the creation process, its definition, and the characteristics present in it. The evaluator had to answer whether (1) he agrees, (2) partially agrees, or (3) disagrees with any of these factors, and write their observations.

6   Results Analysis

This section presents the results obtained in the two qualitative evaluations: empirial study and questionnaire. Based on these results, we have applied the improvements to refine the initial set of ubiquitous heuristics (see Table 4) following Step 6 of the methodology.

6.1   Empirical Study

As the purpose of this study is to explore the heuristics and the stages of heuristic evaluation for ubiquitous systems, the results of the usability problems identified in the GREat Mute application will not be part of the data analysis of this experiment. The factors analyzed are the perceptions obtained by the experts during the heuristic evaluations. It could be observed that:

---

[3] The template for this worksheet can be found at: https://github.com/GREatPesquisa/Heuristicas_de_Usabilidade_para_avaliar_Sistemas_Ubiquos/tree/master/Analise_das_Heuristicas_por_Especialistas.

- The experiment lasted an average of 2 h, each day.
- The expert 2 had doubts about "HU1 - Calm Communication", "*It was not clear to me that this heuristic corresponds to feedback from Nielsen's heuristics*", he said. Still on this heuristic, "*Even though the application is ubiquitous, it is bad that it does not present feedback from time to time*", the expert 3 said.
- The expert 3 questioned the "HU9 - Mobility and Mobile Devices": "*I could not evaluate the HU 9 items here inside the room*", the others also agreed. We observed that the evaluation was happening in a controlled environment and thus it does not give the participants the possibility of mobility, or change their context.
- We have also observed that on the first day experts were not attentive to the heuristic and its definition, just for the check items (the questions), they only read the questions without observing which heuristic they belonged, sometimes leaving the context of the item.
- The expert 1 suggested that users would use the application in their daily lives for a certain period, "*Some heuristics with ubiquitous characteristics can only be perceived with the use in an outside environment, using day-by-day, for a while*". The expert 2 agreed, "*I thought there was not room to evaluate the ubiquitous characteristics.*" The expert 3 believes that to evaluate some heuristics, the Usability Test method is appropriate.
- The experts found the heuristics and steps clear but they could not evaluate all heuristics, for example, the expert 6 said "*I suggest performing the experiment with other applications to look at all the ubiquitous heuristic*". Also the expert 7 suggested setting out examples of what could be a usability problem in each heuristic, to facilitate understanding, differentiating them.
- The experts who participated in the experiment on the second day said that they prefer to evaluate the application by describing the heuristics and not by checking items as a checklists, as reiterated by the expert 4 "*Only the description of the heuristics fit the evaluation, I did not miss a checklist*".
- Although the researchers made it possible for experts to get around during the evaluation, they did not do so because they claimed they would need more time and more sites to perform the tests.
- Facilitators have observed that the ubiquitous heuristics worksheet provided were suitable as a guide.

With these observations, it was concluded that the heuristics worksheet was very efficient to assist the inspector in the inspection that the heuristics were clear and the stages of the evaluation were successful. However, the facilitators of the empirical study observed that not all ubiquitous heuristics could be evaluated. For example, the mobility heuristic, could not be evaluated because the study was done in a controlled environment. In addition, the experiment scenario did not help, ideally, experts should be asked to use the application days before the experiment to assess issues such as mobility and context. It is a lesson learned from this study.

6.2 Questionnaire

The results of the *Questionnaire* evaluation were analyzed. The main considerations of the experts and the improvements made before the analysis are presented as follows:

- The experts did not agree with the junction occurring in "HU1- Calm communication", *"The junction of these three Nielsen's heuristics is inconsistent. This junction resulting in HU1 does not cover the aspects intended by the 3 HNs used and in many aspects is not related to them."*, as can be seen in the expert's speech 3. Therefore, after analyzing all the considerations, we chose the refinement of HU1: for each of the Nielsen's heuristics that had been joined by the junction process, would have a corresponding ubiquitous heuristic. For example, HN8 became HU8 and no longer HU1.
- The heuristic "HN6 - Minimizing user memory overhead" did not have its elimination and justification approved by the experts. The expert 3 said that *"This heuristic should be adapted for use in ubiquitous systems, as the justification for elimination is not adequate. In ubiquitous systems transparency does not necessarily imply the total lack of explicit interaction."*. Expert 4 said that *"This is the heuristic that is more relevant for adapting with ubiquitous systems for preventing exactly this minimization of user load."* Therefore, it was decided that HN6 would be adapted for refinement.
- The heuristic "HU 8-Minimum effort" was created to contemplate the characteristic Efficiency. However, after the experts' comments, for example *"I do not understand why this heuristic was formulated. What need does the ubiquitous system present for such purpose? This heuristic reminds usability as a criterion of quality. I did not understand why."*. This characteristic was allocated in other heuristics, then no longer the there is need for HU8. Therefore, for refinement, "HU 8-Minimum effort" has been eliminated.
- The heuristics "HU7 - Minimum need for help and documentation", "HU11 - Invisibility and Transparency" and "HU 13 - Sensors and data inputs" were accepted in their entirety without any consideration by the experts.
- For the other heuristics, there were minor improvements such as changes in their titles (e.g., "HU6 - Personalization" for "HU7 - Flexibility and Efficiency of use"), in the descriptions and also some characteristics were reallocated.

Based on the presented results, the initial set of heuristics (see Table 4) was refined as will be presented in the next subsection. It is worth mentioning that the results obtained also contributed to improve the way to apply, in future evaluations, the steps of a heuristic evaluation in ubiquitous systems.

6.3 Refinement of Ubiquitous Heuristics

After the evaluations and analysis of the results, it is possible to conduct Step 6 of the methodology, "Refinement Stage". The final version of the Ubiquitous Heuristics proposed in this paper is then presented as follows:

- HU1 - *Visibility of system status.* The system should always provide feedback to the user in response to an interaction performed. This feedback should neither disrupt the user in his current activity nor overwhelm the user with information, but must exist in the form of a noticeable change in some of the interaction modalities of the interface.
  - Characteristics: Calmness, Attention, Information display.
- HU2 - *Correspondence between the system and the real world.* The system must speak the language of the user, with words, symbols, concepts and interactions familiar to the user, instead of being system-oriented. One must follow the conventions of the real world, making the information appear logical and natural and easily reaching the intended goal.
  - Characteristic(s): Familiarity, Information display, Positioning of components, Predictability, Ease of use, Usability.
- HU3 - *User control and freedom.* The user must feel free to interact with the application or not. When the user wishes to interact with the system, must be in control, and at any time can abort a task or undo an operation and return to the previous state. When the application interacts with the user in a given context, the user should not feel obligated to respond to the interaction and should have the option to ignore it in order to keep the focus on their current activity. All of these actions must be clearly marked on the system and their visualization, if any, should maintain the standard throughout the application.
  - Characteristic(s): Calmness, Acceptability, User Satisfaction, Attention.
- HU4 - *Consistency and standards.* Application interfaces, data inputs, ways of interacting or adapting to the context, must be consistent and follow conventions and standards familiar to the user, so that the software can be understood, learned and used.
  - Characteristic(s): Usability, Predictability, Data Input, Familiarity.
- HU5 - *Error prevention.* It is important to know the situations that cause most errors and modify the interfaces and interactions so that users do not make these mistakes when interacting with the application. In addition, the application must be able to keep its services and performance always available when used by one or more users, under specific or adverse conditions.
  - Characteristics(s): Predictability, Flexibility, Reliability, Scalability, Security, Availability.
- HU6 - *Recognition rather than recall.* When there is a dialog or interaction available, the system should minimize the user's memory load, leaving objects, actions, and options available to at least one of the user's senses.
  - Characteristic(s): Information display, Usability, Predictability, Calmness, Attention.
- HU7 - *Flexibility and efficiency of use.* The application should provide shortcuts to accelerate the interaction, in order to reduce the effort required to achieve the intended goal, especially for the advanced user. Completeness of functionality must be maintained when using shortcuts or not. In addition, the system must be flexible, giving the user the ability to customize settings according to their needs and experiences.
  - Characteristic(s): Flexibility, Utility, Efficiency, Effectiveness.

- HU8 - *Aesthetics and Minimalist Design.* Dialogues should contain only relevant and necessary information, neither more nor less. Each extra unit of information in a dialogue competes with relevant units of information. The sequence of interaction and access to components and functionalities should be available depending on the context, in a simple and natural way.
  - Characteristic(s): Simplicity, Calmness, Attention, Positioning of components.
- HU9 - *Help users recognize, diagnose and recover from errors.* Error messages should be simple and expressed in clear language (without codes), accurately indicate the problem and constructively suggest a solution. In addition to texts, messages can be displayed in other formats available on mobile devices, such as image, audio, vibration. Error messages should guide the user with caution, without stress, so that the user does not stop using the system.
  - Characteristic(s): Simplicity, Calmness, Acceptability,
- HU10 - *Help and documentation.* Ideally, the application should be so easy to use (intuitive) that it does not need help or documentation. If necessary, the help should be easily accessible, centered on the user's current activity. Help guidelines should be simple and objective.
  - Characteristic(s): Usability, Ease of use.
- HU11 - *Mobility and Devices.* Ubiquitous applications should maintain their functionality with the physical displacement of the user and on devices with different capacities. Aspects such as wireless networking, device connection, screen size, limited hardware capacity and power capacity are factors what the application needs to take into account to adjust during use without causing inconvenience to the user.
  - Characteristic(s): Device Capability, Network Capability, Interconnectivity, Mobility.
- HU12 - *Privacy and Safety.* The application must be able to keep the information saved and protected, so that there is no risk of damage in a context of specific use. Information must be transported and stored securely, as well as the application's access controls.
  - Characteristic(s): Privacy, Secutity, Safety, Trust.
- HU13 - *Invisibility and Transparency.* The system must be able to hide computational components so users do not worry about them. Interactions must take place through natural interfaces.
  - Characteristic(s): Transparency, Predictability.
- HU14 - *Context Awareness and Adaptive Interfaces.* The ubiquitous application should react according to the context information that the user encounters. Interfaces must adapt to these contexts and bring only relevant information in a way that facilitates the use of the system.
  - Characteristic(s): Context Awareness, Adaptation, Ease of use.
- HU15 - *Sensors and data inputs.* It must be checked whether data input, either by the user or captured from the sensor, is being effective and happening naturally to the user. The application should operate correctly in the presence of invalid inputs or stressful environmental conditions.
  - Characteristic(s): Data Input, Robustness.

The new set of heuristics is summarized in Table 7. The table also shows a new relationship between the ubiquitous heuristics and the Nielsen's heuristics, the process by which the ubiquitous heuristic has been elaborated (e.g., adaption or created) and the characteristics involved in each ubiquitous heuristic.

Table 7. New relation between the ubiquitous heuristics and the Nielsen's heuristics, the creation process and the characteristics involved.

Nielsen	Ubiquitous heuristics	Process	Characteristics
HN1	HU1 - Visibility of system status	Adaptation	Calmness, Attention, Information display
HN2	HU2 - Correspondence between the system and the real world	Adaptation	Familiarity, Information display, Positioning of components, Ease of use, Usability
HN3	HU3 - User control and freedom	Adaptation	Calmness, Acceptability, User Satisfaction, Attention
HN4	HU4 - Consistency and standards	Adaptation	Usability, Predictability, Data Input, Familiarity
HN5	HU5 - Error Prevention	Adaptation	Predictability, Flexibility, Reliability, Scalability, Security, Availability
HN6	HU6 - Recognition rather than recall	Adaptation	Information display, Usability, Predictability, Calmness, Attention
HN7	HU7 - Flexibility and efficiency of use	Adaptation	Flexibility, Utility, Efficiency, Effectiveness
HN8	HU8 - Aesthetic and minimalist design	Adaptation	Simplicity, Calmness, Attention, Positioning of components
HN9	HU9 - Help users recognize, diagnose, and recover from errors	Adaptation	Simplicity, Calmness, Acceptability
HN10	HU10 - Help and documentation	Adaptation	Usability, Ease of Use
–	HU11 - Mobility and Devices	Created	Device Capability, Network Capability, Interconnectivity, Mobility
–	HU12 - Privacy and Safety	Created	Privacy, Security, Safety, Trust
–	HU13 - Invisibility and Transparency	Created	Transparency, Predictability
–	HU14 - Context awareness and Adaptive Interfaces	Created	Context Awareness, Adaptation, Ease of use
–	HU15 - Sensors and Data Input	Created	Data Input and Robustness

7 Conclusion

This paper presented heuristics to evaluate the usability of ubiquitous systems. From a methodology found in the literature to develop heuristics for a given domain, the heuristics for the evaluation of ubiquitous systems were specified. The six-step methodology of Rusu et al. (2011) was taken as a basis and executed. The first four steps were followed and, in the end, a set of heuristics was generated for this purpose.

An empirical study was conducted to observe the use of applied heuristics in heuristic evaluations performed in practice. In addition, expert's analysis through questionnaires were carried out focusing on the evaluation of the creation of heuristics. Several considerations were noted during these evaluations and improvements were applied to better use of the ubiquitous heuristics.

Finally, a final set of 15 ubiquitous heuristics was presented to evaluate the usability of ubiquitous systems, refined from the considerations of the evaluations.

As future work, it is intended to apply the proposed heuristics in an environment, in which it is possible to test the various characteristics contemplated by ubiquitous systems.

Acknowledgements. The authors would like to thank all the experts involved in the heuristic evaluations and their creation analyzes, as well as the GREat team for their support. We also thank the MAxIMUm project - A Measurement-based Approach for the Evaluation of Quality Human-Computer Interaction in Ubiquitous Systems" funded by FUNCAP and CNRS (under grant number INC-0064-00012.01.00/12), and the CAcTUS project - Context-Awareness Testing for Ubiquitous Systems supported by CNPq (MCT/CNPq 14/2013 - Universal) under grant number 484380/2013-3.

References

Barbosa, S.D.J., Da Silva, B.S.: Interação Humano-Computador. Elsevier, Rio de Janeiro, 406 p. (2010). (In Portuguese)

Bertini, E., Gabrielli, S., Kimani, S.: Appropriating and assessing heuristics for mobile computing. In: Conference on Advanced Visual Interfaces (AVI 06), vol. 2, pp. 119–126 (2006)

Bezerra, C.I.M, Oliveira, K.M., Andrade, R.M.C., et al.: Challenges for usability testing in ubiquitous system. In: 1 l'Interaction Homme-Machine (2014)

Bonifácio, B.A., Fernandes, P., Santos F., Oliveira, H.A.B.F, Conte, T.U.: Usabilidade de Aplicações Web Móvel: Avaliando uma Nova Abordagem de Inspeção através de Estudos Experimentais. In: XV Ibero-American Conference on Software Engineering (CIbSE 2012), Buenos Aires. Anais do XV Ibero-American Conference on Software Engineering (CIbSE 2012), vol. 1 (2012). (In Portuguese)

Carvalho, R.M., Andrade, R.M.C., Oliveira, K.M.: Using the GQM method to evaluate calmness in ubiquitous applications. In: Streitz, N., Markopoulos, P. (eds.) Distributed, Ambient, and Pervasive Interactions. DAPI 2015. LNCS, pp. 13–24. Springer, Cham (2015)

Garlan, D., Siewiorek, D.P., Steenkiste, P.: Toward distraction-free pervasive computing. Pervasive Computing, IEEE (2002)

Hansmann, U., Merk, L., Nicklous, M.S., Stober, T.: Pervasive Computing. Springer, Berlin (2003). ISBN 3-540-00218-9

ISO/IEC 9126: Software engineering – Product quality – Part 1 (2001)

Inostroza, R., Rusu, C., Roncagliolo, S., Rusu, V.: Usability heuristics for touchscreen-based mobile devices: update. In: CHI 2013, Chile, pp. 24–29 (2013)

Kemp, E.A., Thompson, A.J., Johnson, R.S.: Interface evaluation for invisibility and ubiquity - an example from e-learning. In: Proceedings of the 9th ACM SIGCHI New Zealand Chapter's International Conference on Human-Computer Interaction: Design Centered HCI (2008)

Kourouthanassis, P.E., Giaglis, G.M., Karaiskos, D.C.: Delineating the degree of "Pervasiveness" in pervasive information systems: an assessment framework and design implications. In: Pan-Hellenic Conference on Informatics, PCI, Proceedings...ago (2008)

Machado Neto, O., Pimentel, M.G.: Heuristics for the assessment of interfaces of mobile devices. In: Proceedings of the 19th Brazilian Symposium on Multimedia and the Web - WebMedia 2013 (2013)

Moraes, A., Rosa, J.G.S.: Avaliação e Projeto no Design de Interfaces. 2ab, Rio de Janeiro, 224 p. (2008). (In Portuguese)

Moraveji, N., Soesanto, C.: Towards stress-less user interfaces: 10 design heuristics based on the psychophysiology of stress. In: Proceedings of the 2012 ACM Annual Conference Extended Abstracts on Human Factors in Computing Systems Extended Abstracts - CHI EA 2012 (2012)

Nielsen, J.: Usability Engineering. Academic Press, New York (1993)

Preece, J., Rogers, Y., Sharp, H., Benyon, D., Holland, S., Carey, T.: Human-Computer Interaction. Addison-Wesley, Reading (1994)

Preece, J., Rogers, Y., Sharp, H.: Interaction Design: Beyond human-computer interaction. Wiley, New York (2002)

Riekki, J., Isomursu, P., Isomursu, M.: Evaluating the calmness of ubiquitous applications. In: Product Focused Software Process Improvement (2004)

Rusu, C., Roncagliolo, S., Rusu, V., Collazos, C.: A methodology to establish usability heuristics. In: Proceedings of the 4th International Conferences on Advances in Computer-Human Interactions (ACHI 2011), IARIA, pp. 59–62 (2011). ISBN: 978-1-61208-003-1

Santos, R.M.: Características e Medidas de Software para Avaliação da Qualidade da Interação Humano-Computador em Sistemas Ubíquos. Dissertação de Mestrado - Mestrado em Ciência da Computação - Universidade Federal do Ceará (UFC), Fortaleza, 2014 (2014). (In Portuguese)

Satyanarayanan, M.: Pervasive computing: vision and challenges. IEEE Pers. Commun. 8(4), 10–17 (2001)

Varsaluoma, J.: Scenarios in the heuristic evaluation of mobile devices: emphasizing the context of use. In: Kurosu, M. (ed.) HCD 2009. LNCS, vol. 5619, pp. 332–341. Springer, Heidelberg (2009). doi:10.1007/978-3-642-02806-9_38

Weiser, M.: The computer for the 21st century. Sci. Am. 265, 94–104 (1991)

Yu, P., Ma, X., Cao, J., Lu, J.: Application mobility in pervasive computing: a survey. Pervasive Mobile Comput. 9(1), 2–17 (2013)

Natural Interaction

Freehand Gesture-Based 3D Manipulation Methods for Interaction with Large Displays

Paulo Dias[1,2(✉)], João Cardoso[1], Beatriz Quintino Ferreira[2],
Carlos Ferreira[2,3], and Beatriz Sousa Santos[1,2]

[1] DETI/UA- Department of Electronics, Telecommunications and Informatics,
University of Aveiro, Campus Universitário de Santiago, 3810-193 Aveiro, Portugal
{paulo.dias,joaocardoso,bss}@ua.pt
[2] IEETA- Institute of Electronics and Informatics Engineering of Aveiro, University of Aveiro,
Campus Universitário de Santiago, 3810-193 Aveiro, Portugal
{mbeatriz,carlosf}@ua.pt
[3] DEGEI/UA- Department of Economics, Management and Industrial Engineering,
University of Aveiro, Campus Universitário de Santiago, 3810-193 Aveiro, Portugal

Abstract. Gesture-based 3D interaction is a research topic with application in numerous scenarios which gained relevance with the recent advances in low-cost tracking systems. Yet, it poses many challenges due to its novelty and consequent lack of systematic development methodologies. Developing easy to use and learn gesture-based 3D interfaces is particularly difficult since the most adequate and intuitive gestures are not always obvious and there is often a variety of different gestures used to perform similar actions. This paper presents the development and evaluation of interaction methods to manipulate 3D virtual objects in a large display set-up using freehand gestures detected by a Kinect depth sensor. We describe the implementation of these methods and the user studies conducted to improve them and assess their usability as manipulation methods. Based on the results of these studies we also propose a method that overcomes the lack of roll movement detection by the Kinect and makes simpler the scaling and rotation in all degrees-of-freedom using hand gestures.

Keywords: 3D user interfaces · Free-hand gesture based interfaces · 3D object manipulation · Large displays · User studies

1   Introduction

The recent developments in low-cost tracking systems such as the Wii Remote, Leap Motion, Microsoft Kinect [1] and the advances in gesture recognition algorithms led to the increasing popularity of gesture-based interfaces given their relevance for a growing number of applications namely in gaming, Virtual and Augmented Reality [2, 3], and in other scenarios [4]. However, the development of gesture interfaces poses several usability and technical issues and challenges related to the lack of universal consensus regarding gesture-function associations, and the need to tackle a variety of environment types and technical limitations as mentioned by Wachs et al. [5] and Norman and Nielsen [6]. 3D user interfaces are seen as the natural choice for large displays contexts as pointed

© Springer International Publishing AG 2017
N. Streitz and P. Markopoulos (Eds.): DAPI 2017, LNCS 10291, pp. 145–158, 2017.
DOI: 10.1007/978-3-319-58697-7_10

out by Bowman [7]. According to these authors the traditional mouse and keyboard setups are difficult to use with public displays also because they are meant to call multiple users to interact. Moreover, users want some freedom of movement in front of the display. Touch screens can solve some of these problems, but not without imposing another set of limitations, e.g. the user must stand at arm's reach from the display limiting the amount of the display that can be seen. Interfaces that do not require the user to wear any additional input devices allowing unconstrained interaction with the user own body through gestures are essential in this public large displays context fostering alternatives in terms of design and interaction [7].

The work presented in this paper was developed as part of a public display interactive system we have installed at the entrance hall of our Department (shown in Fig. 1). The system consists of a large screen and a Kinect sensor, and is meant to provide relevant information concerning our department, and showcase demos or games [8]. Several contents and interaction methods have been developed as part of this interactive system, though most of the content used was 2D based. Besides these existing applications, it was deemed useful to allow virtual walkthroughs as well as the presentation of 3D models of prototypes developed at the department and thus the need to visualize and interact through gestures with the 3D content available on our system appeared. This would allow passing by users to navigate through virtual environments, manipulate 3D models or simply have fun with 3D games. The remaining of this paper describes related work and the design, implementation, and evaluation of suitable methods for the purpose of 3D object manipulation in such a scenario.

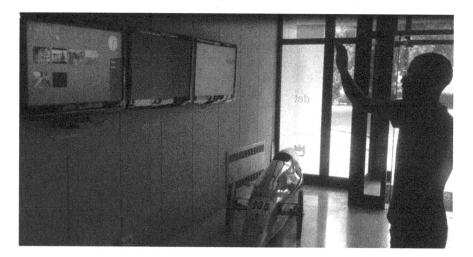

Fig. 1. Public display interactive system installed at the entrance hall of our Department.

2   Related Work

Jankowski and Hachet [9] define three universal interaction tasks commonly used throughout the literature: Navigation – the process of moving around in a virtual environment; Selection and Manipulation – the ability to choose an object and perform translation, rotation and scaling operations; System Control - the communication between user and the system which is not part of the virtual environment. The scope of this paper is only the manipulation task, since the work focuses on the development of gesture-based methods that enable the visualization and manipulation of 3D models. This problem is not new: Bowman and Hodges [10] already mention this capability as a desirable feature in many VR applications that is typically accomplished using a real-world metaphor. Manipulation of 3D virtual objects using hand gestures appeared in the eighties through instrumented gloves [11]. In the following years several other approaches have been used such as the solution of [12] using vision-based gesture tracking, and the ones described in [5, 13, 14]; it is, however, the development of affordable depth cameras that is boosting and encouraging numerous applications since these devices have helped overcome many of the technical challenges of gesture tracking.

Freehand gestures have been used in various situations, as computer aided design, medical systems and assistive technologies, computer supported collaborative work systems, mobile, tangible and wearable computing, as well as in entertainment and human-robot interaction, but virtual reality systems have been a particularly interesting application for spatial freehand gestures, as in [2, 16]. More recently, gestures have also appeared as an attractive alternative in ubiquitous computing or for interaction with large public displays that create the opportunity for passing by users to access and interact with public or private content. These scenarios require at distance interaction and benefit significantly when no input device is needed as in gesture interaction [2, 17].

Real world metaphors are commonly used to accomplish such desirable properties of 3D object visualization and manipulation in interactive systems [15]. In this vein, the work of Song et al. [18] significantly contributed to the development of one of our manipulation methods. They proposed a handle bar metaphor as an effective control between the user's hand gestures and the corresponding virtual object manipulation operations. The main strength of this metaphor is the physical familiarity that is presented to the users, as they mentally map their bi-manual hand gestures to manipulation operations such as translation and rotation in a 3D virtual environment. One of the features that proved to be effective was the visual representation of a virtual handle bar corresponding to the ever-changing positions of the user's hands since it provided a strong sense of control to the user during the interactive visual manipulation.

In our case, previous experience with the system [8], and the literature, namely [18, 19], provided hints on a set of gestures that might be used as a starting point for a refinement process. This process evolved iteratively based on preliminary experiments and the analysis of qualitative and quantitative data collected through the observation of users interacting with the system, logging their interaction, and asking for their opinion and suggestions. The results obtained from this analysis were used as formative evaluation to improve alternative interaction methods until they were usable enough to be integrated in our system. According to [2] the majority of evaluations of freehand gesture systems have been of an exploratory nature used as formative evaluation [20]; however, we deem summative evaluation is important to guarantee the methods are usable enough and thus a final user study was performed to compare the alternatives and select the best fit for the purpose of 3D object manipulation.

3 Proposed Manipulation Methods

According to Bowman et al. [21], the word manipulation means the act of handling physical objects using user's hands. In this paper we consider the manipulation tasks of Rotating and Scaling, which respectively consist in changing the orientation and increasing or decreasing the size of an object. These operations were selected as basic for our system as they will allow the user to view and explore 3D models of prototypes by modifying the zoom and viewpoints.

Two methods for 3D object manipulation dubbed "OneHand" and "HandleBar" were developed. "OneHand" allows the user to rotate the object while grabbing it with the dominant hand (closing hand), while the "HandleBar" method uses the position of the user's hands to determine the rotation angle of the object. A 3D handle-bar model was placed at the center of the object in order to visually map the position of the hands. Both methods also provided scaling operations. While for the "OneHand" we resorted to the GUI, using two additional buttons to increase or decrease the scaling factor of the object, for the "HandleBar" we were inspired by the pinch gesture used to zoom in mobile phones and multi-touch applications but, instead of the fingers, we map the distance between user's hands to the scaling factor.

3.1 OneHand

Our first approach was to manipulate a 3D virtual object with a single hand, using the cursor-based metaphor of grabbing and manipulating it with the hand movement. We implemented the "OneHand" method (Fig. 2) in which the rotation is determined using the offset between the grabbing point (where the grab gesture was first detected) and the position of the moving hand. The Microsoft Kinect SDK provided the grab and release events for the user's dominant hand. The scaling manipulation is implemented using two GUI buttons (Fig. 2 (b)). By continuously pushing either button with the dominant hand it is possible to increase or decrease the scaling factor of the 3D object.

The rotation of the 3D object (Fig. 2 (a)) is calculated for both offsets for axes Y and Z and determined using the 2D coordinates of the hand cursor (screen space), provided by the KinectRegion from SDK controls. Since the rotation of every object on the 3D engine is described by a four-dimensional vector space (Quaternion), we have implemented a function to generate a quaternion from an angle and a direction. The current object rotation is given by the multiplication between the quaternions describing the rotations around Y and Z and the previous accumulated rotations. This accumulated rotation defines all previous transformations and is updated each time a hand release event occurs.

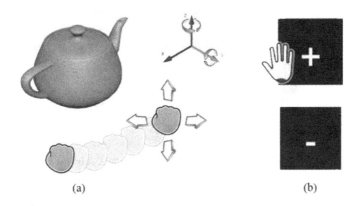

Fig. 2. "OneHand" method (a) Rotation around the Y and Z axes (b) Scaling.

3.2   HandleBar

After preliminary tests it became clear that the "OneHand" method had some limitations due to the cursor-based movement, which implied a mapping of a 2D coordinate space of the cursor into the 3D space of the object. As an additional constraint, the Kinect sensor was not able to detect the wrist orientation which impeded the implementation of all 3 degrees of freedom (DOF) of the rotation. As opposed to "OneHand", in the "HandleBar" method (Fig. 3) manipulation occurs in a 3D space, in which the 3D coordinates of the user's hands are mapped directly for the manipulation of the object. This method implements a handle bar metaphor based upon the experiments of Song et al. [18]. This metaphor consists of a bi-manual interaction to manipulate a single object, using the grab and release gestures. A virtual handle bar is positioned at the center of the 3D object representing the relative orientation of the users' hands, and provides helpful visual feedback. In this method, the KinectRegion provided by the Kinect SDK to obtain the hands position and state was not sufficient. In order to obtain the hands 3D positions it was necessary to access the skeleton data provided by the Kinect SDK. The hands state (close or open) was also provided by the Kinect SDK through the KinectInteraction API.

The rotation and scaling were implemented with 2 DOF as in "OneHand". For each axis, the rotation of the object is based on the relative offset of the handle bar rotation (hands position). When both hands are closed (grab) the current rotation of the object is temporarily stored, and the offset is determined based on the relative position of each hand. Then, similarly to the "OneHand", we generate the quaternion from the angle and direction. In this case, the vectors encoding the direction are different, since the rotation DOF differ from the previous method. Figure 3(a, b) shows the two implemented rotations: to rotate the object around the Z axis, the user must move one of his/her hands forward and the other backwards, we map the angle between the imaginary line between both hands and the X axis of the object to the rotation of the object; to rotate around the X axis, one hand must move up and the other one move down and the rotation angle is the angle between the line defined by the hands and the Y axis of the object. No absolute angular mapping is needed since each time the user opens at least one hand, the rotation

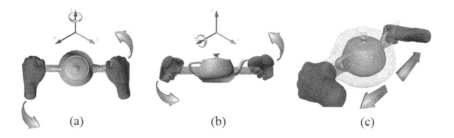

Fig. 3. "HandleBar" method. (a) Top view, rotation around the Z axis. (b) Front view, rotation around the X axis. (c) Scaling. (Color figure online)

is stored and the user may re-initiate a bi-manual grab gesture at a new position and perform a further rotation. This allows the user to make large angular changes to the 3D virtual object with respect to the two axes without getting into an undesirable situation where, for example, the front hand occludes the back hand, making it impossible to determine the rotation angle. The object scaling is computed using the distance between the left hand and the right hand: the farther the hands, the larger the object. Again, we use an accumulation strategy, enabling the user to perform successive scaling operations. When the user reaches his/her maximum arm stretch or both hands are close together, he/she can release the manipulation by opening at least one hand; this event causes the storage of the current scaling, and the user may place their hands in another position and start another manipulation. Also, a color scheme gives feedback to the user when both hands are opened (white) and when both hands are in the grabbing state (green).

3.3 Improved HandleBar

During preliminary evaluation tests, some users proposed an improvement to the "HandleBar" method (Fig. 4). They suggested that we could use both hands movement in the same direction (up or down) to introduce the missing DOF, (rotation around the Y axis). This improvement was implemented first by checking if both hands are in the grab state. Then we analyze if both hands are parallel with each other, i.e. the hands are at the same height. If these two conditions are verified during the interaction, the angle between the Y axis and the imaginary line going from a reference position (the hip center joint) to the middle point between both hands is determined; with this distance we compute the rotation. This implies that the hip center joint position is retrieved from the skeleton data in each frame. Apart from that, the algorithm is similar to the one used in the original "HandleBar" method. This improvement allowed the full rotation DOFs (roll, pitch and yaw). In order to give visual feedback about the different rotations, we added an extra condition to the color scheme of the handle bar (orange) when the new gesture corresponding to a rotation around the Y axis is detected.

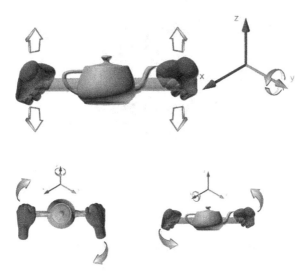

Fig. 4. Improved "HandleBar" method.

4   User Studies

We conducted a preliminary test with 8 students to establish the experimental protocol to be used. Moreover, this test served as testbed to determine which performance measures should be logged in order to evaluate the usability of the methods. This preliminary test also provided a way to improve the "HandleBar" method, as previously mentioned.

In order to evaluate the new version of "HandleBar", comparing it with the "OneHand" method, a second user study was performed with the collaboration of 40 participants. This section presents the protocol used in these studies, as well as the main results.

4.1   Preliminary Test

The first test comprised two tasks meant to assess the usability of "OneHand" and "HandleBar", as well as the accuracy attained by users with both methods while manipulating an object. The first task consisted in manipulating a sphere with a marker (represented by a multi-colored cross) using rotation only (Fig. 5); the goal was to rotate the sphere such that the marker was aligned with respect to the target (represented by a similar but transparent cross), thus matching the colors of both crosses. This task ended when users considered that the pointer best overlapped the target and did not interact with the system for 15 s. During the manipulation several events were automatically logged by the system in order to obtain the solid angular difference between models, elapsed time, and scaling.

Fig. 5. 3D Manipulation – model used in the rotation test.

The second task introduced the scaling manipulation; this task consisted in manipulating a 3D model in order to match it to a target represented by the same model with a degree of transparency and in a different position (Fig. 6). The above mentioned termination condition was also used for this task; however, while the user was performing the task, the scaling value of the model was also recorded in addition to the other performance variables.

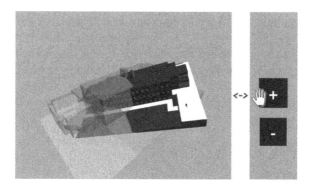

Fig. 6. 3D Manipulation with "OneHand" – model and GUI buttons used in the test with rotation and scaling.

Each participant completed the two tasks using both methods and answered a post-task questionnaire including a few questions regarding the methods.

As mentioned, this preliminary test allowed fine tuning the experimental protocol, namely the variables logged. We observed that the total task time was not the best performance measure, as some users were perfectionists trying to leave the model as aligned as possible with the target and thus taking more time, while others just quickly performed the manipulation leaving the model fairly unaligned. Alternatively, the time users took to achieve an angular distance between the two models below 5° was logged. The underlying idea of measuring this time interval is to evaluate which method allows users to reach faster a small angular difference between models, meaning that it might be better suited for a coarse manipulation.

4.2 Controlled Experiment

The second study was a controlled experiment designed to test the (equality) hypothesis: both methods provide the same level of usability in the given context. The independent (input) variable was the manipulation method with two levels, "OneHand" and "Improved HandleBar". Participants' performance and satisfaction, as well as opinion on the methods were the dependent (output) variables. Performance was assessed through the above mentioned measures: angular distance between the final position of the manipulated object and the target position, scaling factor (a scaling factor of 1 means exactly the same scaling between source and target models) and the time to accomplish various tasks. Participants' satisfaction and preferences were obtained from the post-experiment questionnaire. The questionnaire included ten questions to be answered in a 5 level Likert-type scale, as well as the possibility to leave any comments or suggestions concerning the methods. Questions were used to evaluate intuitiveness, need for training, easiness to obtain the desired position, annoying characteristics, and overall satisfaction.

As a within-subject experimental design was used, we counterbalanced for possible effects of learning or boredom on the results by asking half of the users to start by one method and the other half by the other method. The protocol for the experiment is illustrated in Fig. 7 and included 40 volunteer students (34 male and 6 female), aged between

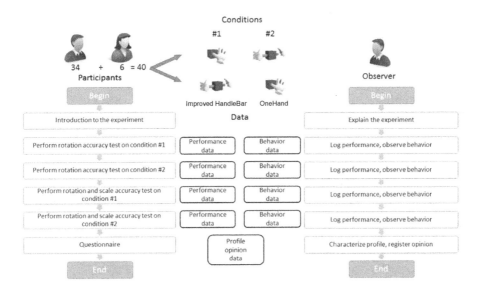

Fig. 7. Experimental protocol: within-group experimental design; input variable (with two levels): manipulation method ("OneHand" and "Improved HandleBar"); output variables: participant's performance, satisfaction and opinion.

20 and 27 years old. Most of the users stated in the questionnaire they did not have significant experience with 3D user interfaces.

5   Results and Discussion

Figure 8 and Table 1 present the main results for the controlled experiment. The average times, and final angular distances in degrees (between source and target models) are presented for both methods "Improved Handle-Bar" and "One-Hand" and for both experiments (rotation without and with scaling). A better performance with the "Improved HandleBar" method is clearly visible from the average times and angular distances, as these values were always lower than the ones obtained with "OneHand". For all variables (total time, time to 5°, and angular distance) Wilcoxon tests rejected the equality hypothesis (with $p < 0.05$ for all cases: 0.00015 for total time, < 0.0000001 for time to 5° and 0.000312 for angular distance) meaning that the difference between the "Improved HandleBar" and the "OneHand" is significant in both experiments. It is clear from the box plot analysis that users spent more time aligning the 3D objects with "OneHand"; in particular, regarding the variable Time below 5°, users took almost twice as much time with the "OneHand" to reach an acceptable accuracy (5° error) than with the "Improved HandleBar" method.

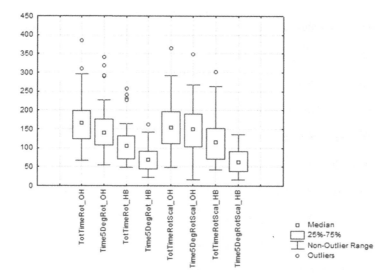

Fig. 8. Times (total time and time below 5°, in seconds) with "OneHand" (OH) and "Improved HandleBar" (HB) methods for the rotation only and rotation with scaling tests.

Table 1. Average performance values obtained with "OneHand" (OH) and "Improved HandleBar" (HB) methods for the rotation only and rotation with scaling tests.

	Rotation		Rotation and scaling	
	OneHand	HandleBar	OneHand	HandleBar
Angular distance (degrees)	5.24	2.79	4.52	3.07
Total time (min:sec)	02:31	01:57	02:44	02:12
Time below 5° (min:sec)	02:00	01:05	02:10	00:58
Scaling factor	–	–	0.995	0.997

Data collected during the experiment, especially during the rotation only test suggests the "Improved HandleBar" method attained a much better acceptance among participants. Accordingly, the results obtained from the questionnaires concerning the first test (Fig. 9) show that, in terms of overall satisfaction, participants evaluated the "Improved HandleBar" method more positively than the "OneHand". Specifically, variables evaluating the easiness in obtaining the desired position and the intuitiveness of the "Improved HandleBar" were much higher than the ones for "OneHand". Moreover, when asked directly which method was more satisfactory and which had less annoying features, participants preferred the "Improved HandleBar" method. These differences were validated by a Wilcoxon matched pairs test (p < 0.05) that shows significant differences between methods concerning "Easy to obtain position", "Intuitive manipulation", "Annoying characteristics", and "Overall satisfaction".

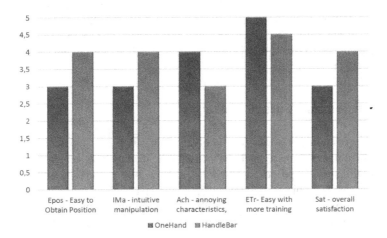

Fig. 9. Questionnaire results for the rotation only test obtained with "OneHand" (OH) and "Improved HandleBar" (HB) (median values in a 5 point Lickert-type scale: 1-completely disagree, 5-completely agree).

Similar results were obtained concerning the rotation with scaling test (Fig. 10). Despite a smaller difference between methods, we can still observe a slight user preference for the "Improved HandleBar" over the "OneHand" method, namely regarding "Easy to obtain position", "Easy with more training" and "Overall satisfaction".

The differences for these three questions were validated with a Wilcoxon matched pairs with $p < 0.05$.

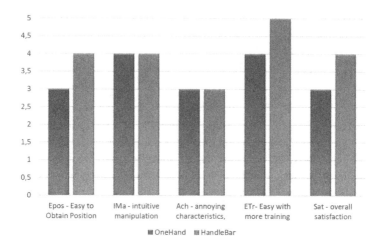

Fig. 10. Questionnaire results for the rotation with scaling test obtained with "OneHand" (OH) and "Improved HandleBar" (HB) (median values in a 5 point Lickert-type scale: 1-completely desagree, 5-completely agree).

From these results, it is clear that the "Improved HandleBar", method introducing the missing DOF, was significantly better in terms of usability when compared to "OneHand". Furthermore, by observing the participants during the experiment, we noticed that after using the "Improved HandleBar" method, participants did not like at all the "OneHand" alternative.

6   Conclusion and Future Work

In this work we studied methods for 3D object manipulation using freehand gestures. Our goal was to integrate these methods into a public display system in the entrance hall of our department. We proposed and implemented two gesture based methods for manipulation of 3D objects: "OneHand", a cursor-based interaction method, and "HandleBar" a bi-manual interaction method. A preliminary study showed that both methods suffered from the lack of one DOF, leading to several cumulative rotations that were confusing to the users. Upon this preliminary test, users suggested a possible way to improve this issue by introducing the gesture of both hands moving up or down simultaneously to enable the rotation about the missing DOF. This improvement led to the development of a novel 3D object manipulation method that allows users to perform rotation around the three axes. An experiment involving 40 participants was conducted. Results revealed significant differences in several usability dimensions (both from data logged during the experiment and from questionnaires answers), suggesting that the "Improved HandleBar" provides a more efficient method for rotation and scaling of 3D objects method, clearly outperforming the "OneHand".

As future work we plan to test these methods with the Kinect ONE sensor which enables the detection of the wrists' orientation, not only allowing the improvement of our methods, but also the implementation of new manipulation approaches. Expanding our manipulation methods to afford object translation is also an envisaged direction for future developments. This would provide the possibility to manipulate objects in virtual worlds in a natural way by grabbing, moving, rotating and scaling objects simply using the hands as manipulation device. Some additional work on user representation in the virtual world may also be relevant. We have done preliminary tests replacing the handle bar by two virtual hands moving in space according to the user hands; yet, this did not lead to better performance, potentially due to occlusions problems.

Acknowledgements. The authors are grateful to all volunteer participants. This work was partially funded by National Funds through FCT - Foundation for Science and Technology, in the context of the projects UID/CEC/00127/2013.

References

1. Tuukka, M.T., Rauhamaa, P., Takala, T.: Survey of 3DUI applications and development challenges. In: 3DUI, pp. 89–96 (2012)
2. Ni, T.: A Framework of Freehand Gesture Interaction: Techniques, Guidelines, and Applications. Ph.D. thesis, Virginia Tech (2011)
3. Billinghurst, M., Piumsomboon, T., Huidong, B.: Hands in space-gesture interaction with augmented reality interfaces. IEEE Comput. Graph. Appl. **34**(1), 77–80 (2014)
4. Garber, L.: Gestural technology: moving interfaces in a new direction. Computer **46**(10), 22–25 (2013)
5. Wachs, J., Kölsch, M., Stern, H., Edan, Y.: Vision-based hand gesture applications. Commun. ACM **54**(2), 60–71 (2011)
6. Norman, D.A., Nielsen, J.: Gestural interfaces: a step backward in usability. Interactions **17**, 46–49 (2010)
7. Bowman, D.A.: 3D user interfaces. In: Soegaard, M., Dam, R.F. (eds.) The Encyclopedia of Human-Computer Interaction, 2nd edn. The Interaction Design Foundation, Aarhus (2014). https://www.interaction-design.org/encyclopedia/3d_user_interfaces.html
8. Dias, P., Sousa, T., Parracho, J., Cardoso, J., Monteiro, A., Sousa, Santos B.: Student Projects Involving Novel Interaction with Large Displays. IEEE Comput. Graphics Appl. **34**(2), 80–86 (2014)
9. Jankowski, J., Hachet, M.: Advances in interaction with 3D environments. Comput. Graph. Forum **34**(1), 152–190 (2015)
10. Bowman, D.A., Hodges, L.: An evaluation of techniques for grabbing and manipulating remote objects in immersive virtual environments. In: Proceedings of the 1997 Symposium on Interactive 3D Graphics, pp. 35–38 (1997)
11. Fisher, S., McGreevy, M., Humphries, J., Robinett, W.: Virtual environment display system. In: I3D 1986, Proceedings of the 1986 Workshop on Interactive 3D Graphics, pp. 77–87 (1986)
12. Freeman, W.T., Weissman, C.: Television control by hand gestures. In: Proceedings of International Workshop on Automatic Face and Gesture Recognition, pp. 179–183 (1995)

13. Boussemart, Y., Rioux, F., Rudzicz, F., Wozniewski, M., Cooperstock, J.R.: A frame-work for 3D visualization and manipulation in an immersive space using an untethered bi-manual gestural interface. In: Proceedings of the ACM Symposium on Virtual Reality Software and Technology - VRST 2004, pp. 162–165 (2004)

14. Karam, M.: A framework for research and design of gesture-based human computer interactions. Ph.D. thesis, University of Southampton (2006)

15. Kim, T., Park, J.: 3D Object manipulation using virtual handles with a grabbing metaphor. IEEE Comput. Graph. Appl. **34**(3), 30–38 (2014)

16. Cabral, M.C., Morimoto, C.H., Zuffo, M.K.: On the usability of gesture inter-faces in virtual reality environments. In: Proceedings of the 2005 Latin American Conference on Human-Computer Interaction - CLIHC 2005, pp. 100–108 (2005)

17. Vogel, D., Balakrishnan, R.: Distant freehand pointing and clicking on very large, high resolution displays. In: Proceedings of the 18th Annual ACM Symposium on User Interface Software and Technology, pp. 33–42 (2005)

18. Song, P., Goh, W.B., Hutama, W., Fu, C.W., Liu, X.: A handle bar metaphor for virtual object manipulation with mid-air interaction. In: Proceedings 2012 ACM Annual Conference on Human Factors in Computing Systems - CHI 2012, pp. 1297–1306 (2012)

19. Hespanhol, L., Tomitsch, M., Grace, K., Collins, A., Kay, J.: Investigating intuitiveness and effectiveness of gestures for free spatial interaction with large displays. In: Proceedings of the International Symposium on Pervasive Displays (PerDis 2012), pp. 1–6. ACM, New York (2012)

20. Bowman, D.A., Coquillart, S., Froehlich, B., Hirose, M., Kitamura, Y., Kiyokawa, K., Stuerzlinger, W.: 3D user interfaces: new directions and perspectives. IEEE Comput. Graph. Appl. **28**(6), 20–36 (2008)

21. Bowman, D.A., Kruij, E., LaViola, J.J., Poupyrev, I.: 3D User Interfaces: Theory and Practice. Addison Wesley Longman Publishing Co. Inc., Redwood City (2004)

It Made More Sense: Comparison of User-Elicited On-skin Touch and Freehand Gesture Sets

Hayati Havlucu[1], Mehmet Yarkın Ergin[3], İdil Bostan[1], Oğuz Turan Buruk[1(✉)],
Tilbe Göksun[2], and Oğuzhan Özcan[1]

[1] Koç University – Arçelik Research Center for Creative Industries (KUAR), İstanbul, Turkey
{hhavlucu16,idbostan,oburuk,oozcan}@ku.edu.tr
[2] Koç University, İstanbul, Turkey
tgoksun@ku.edu.tr
[3] Boğaziçi University, İstanbul, Turkey
m.yarkin.ergin@gmail.com

Abstract. Research on gestural control interfaces is getting more widespread for the purpose of creating natural interfaces. Two of these popular gesture types are *freehand* and *on-skin touch* gestures, because they eliminate the use of an intermediary device. Previous studies investigated these modalities separately with *user-elicitation methods*; however, there is a gap in the field considering their comparison. In this study, we compare user-elicited on-skin touch and freehand gesture sets to explore users' preferences. Thus, we conducted an experiment in which we compare 13 gestures to control computer tasks for each set. Eighteen young adults participated in our study and filled our survey consisted of NASA Task Load Index and 4 additional items of *social acceptability, learnability, memorability, and the goodness*. The results show that on-skin touch gestures were less physically demanding and more socially acceptable compared to freehand gestures. On the other hand, freehand gestures were more intuitive than on-skin touch gestures. Overall, our results suggest that different gesture types could be useful in different scenarios. Our contribution to the field might inspire designers and developers to make better judgments for designing new gestural interfaces for a variety of devices.

Keywords: Gestures · Comparison · On-skin touch · Freehand · User-elicitation · Mid-air · Embodied interaction · Skin gestures · On-body gestures

1 Introduction

Today digital artifacts come in various shapes and dimensions. With decreasing and increasing sizes of instruments (e.g. smart watches, wall-sized displays etc.), traditional ways of interacting with existing interfaces such as the pointer (WIMP) paradigm become more and more ineffective and impractical. One of the alternative methods of interaction that has a promising future is gestures. Until now, various gesture recognition devices and gestural interfaces have been presented for interaction [1–7]. The interaction modalities for these devices predominantly fall into three categories: handheld devices, touch gestures, and freehand gestures.

© Springer International Publishing AG 2017
N. Streitz and P. Markopoulos (Eds.): DAPI 2017, LNCS 10291, pp. 159–171, 2017.
DOI: 10.1007/978-3-319-58697-7_11

Among these gesture types, *on-skin touch gestures* and *freehand gestures* come forward as they offer an interaction model where intermediary devices, such as remote controllers, are no longer needed. Previous studies have explored these models separately with various device implementations [2, 7, 8] and user-centered studies [9–12]. However, there is still a gap in the field regarding a comparison of user experience of these two gesture types. There is not enough design knowledge, which informs designers about strengths and shortcomings of these modalities that points to appropriate application fields comparatively. To produce this design knowledge in this unexplored area, we aim to investigate users' preferences about these gesture types and see the conditions in which one would be advantageous to the other.

In order to make a comparison of on-skin touch and freehand gestures, we procured and adapted two user-elicited gesture sets: a skin-to-skin touch gesture set obtained by our previous study [13], and a freehand gesture set, obtained by Vatavu [14]. In this work, our goal was to explore users' intuitions and preferences regarding these gestures. Twenty participants evaluated thirteen computer tasks and their corresponding gestures, which were taken from each set, summing up to twenty-six gestures in total. We used the NASA Task Load Index (TLX) [15] to evaluate users' subjective evaluations about the gestures. We added four 7-point Likert scale items about social acceptability, learnability, memorability, and the 'goodness' [16] of gestures to this Index.

Our findings reveal that on-skin touch gestures were less physically demanding and more socially acceptable compared to freehand gestures. It suggests that on-skin touch gestures are more suitable for daily use where time and space are limited resources. They are more appropriate for controlling smaller personal devices such as smartphones. In comparison, freehand gestures were more convenient for large displays. Since they were found to be more engaging, they can be more suitable for entertainment contexts such as TVs or gaming consoles. Predominantly, our results suggest that different gesture types have different advantages in different contexts. Our work contributes to HCI community in inspiring designers and developers to choose and design new gestural interfaces for various devices and their ambient displays.

2   Related Work

2.1   Gesture-Based Interfaces

With varying size of displays, the need for new interaction modalities emerged to create better-suited methods for controlling vast amount of technological devices in different sizes. Interfaces with accustomed modalities such as WIMP paradigm have shifted towards interfaces with novel modalities such as gestural interfaces to fill the gap. Studies investigated gestural interactions with various application devices such as different home appliances [17] and ambient displays [18] with the aim of evaluating types of gestures proposed. Others tried to understand and define gestures for these diverse contexts [19, 20]. However, participatory experiments regarding mainly large screen implementations [1] revealed the users' preferences and shifted the focus to 'intuitiveness' of the gestures [21–23]. With the aim of achieving this intuition, several studies focused on designing gestures through user-elicitation methods instead of pre-defined design methods [24–26].

Moving on to user-centered approach of gesture design, Nacenta et al. underlines the importance of user-elicitation methods as they create more memorable results [27]. They further argue that users explicitly prefer user-elicited gesture sets over pre-defined sets as they seem more usable. On the other hand, the reason behind this preference is still ambiguous. Heydekorn et al. evaluate a user-elicited gesture set by conducting a usability test to clarify the ambiguity [28]. The participants of the study were able to use an interactive display, spontaneously through touch gestures they did not know of, which indicates the benefit of intuition for controlling ambient displays.

2.2 Gesture Types

There are many interaction modalities presented to control ambient displays; however, handheld devices, touch gestures, and freehand gestures predominantly adopted user-elicitation method in creation. Among these gesture types, on-skin touch gestures and freehand gestures stand out, because they offer an interaction model that excludes the use of intermediary devices, such as remote controllers or touch sensitive displays. In this section, we address these two gesture types that we incorporated in our study.

On-skin Touch Gestures. In this gesture type, the input is taken with the various contact methods of two skin-related items. There are different subsets under this category with various elicitation and implementation methods. As an example, Cahn et al. has created a set called Single-hand Microgestures (SHGMs), in which the users touch different parts of their palms with different actions to carry out the referent, using only a single hand [29]. Despite the fact that SHGM clearly creates a more subtle, discrete and mobile interaction with devices, it also lacks to propose an implementation method other than external hand tracking sensors. On the other hand, several studies proposed implementations of on-skin touch gestures through using an armband [2], a wristband [3] or a smart watch [5] for partial recognition of body parts. Skinput can even detect multiple parts of the body through acoustic transmission with an implementation of an armband [7]. All of these studies propose a method to measure the input of a single user. On the contrary, Nakatsuma et al. use another armband to measure the electrical capacitance between two users by active bioacoustics measurement [4]. It creates new application fields for on-skin touch gestures by adding a second user to the equation; however, lack of user experience is still an issue regarding on-skin gestures.

Freehand Gestures. In this gesture type, the input is taken by moving one's hand in mid-air. Studies investigated freehand gestures by evaluating and defining the gestures [30], and by understanding users' preference and creating a taxonomy [31]. While creating sets for freehand gestures, studies mainly focused on devices that will be controlled. As an example, Henze and Hesselmann created a user-elicited gesture set for music playback [32], where as several other studies focused on creating a user-defined gesture set for controlling televisions [33, 34]. These studies create an advantage for users to control necessary referents for specific devices; however, they also lack to evaluate the general perception of freehand gestures from users' perspective. To enhance the solution, some studies focused on feedback of freehand gestures in which users can understand if they performed the gestures right. Hood and Karvinen proposed haptic feedback regarding the issue [35, 36]. Nonetheless, it still lacks to fulfill users' experience over ambient devices.

2.3   Comparison of Gestures

Until now studies evaluated these gestures within the boundaries of their own sets. Both user preference and elicitation studies only concern a single type of gesture set, although there are several studies that compare a type to another. BodyScape is a device implementation that can both recognize freehand and on-skin touch gestures [6]. The study both compares and combines these two types of gestures for large displays. However, it does not compare every gesture one-by-one and it lacks to report the results of this comparison. Instead, what the study reports is a combination of freehand and freehand-on body elicitation study. Moreover, the on-skin touch gesture set they use to compare is not a user-elicited set, where some of the gestures have extreme actions like touching the feet. In another study, Jakobsen et al. compare touch and freehand gestures for large displays [37]. They reported that although touch gestures were faster to perform and easier to select small targets, when the affordance of movement was calculated freehand gestures were preferred over touch gestures. Both of these studies clearly investigate advantages of one type of gesture over another; however, they are limited to a single scenario of controlling a large display.

Adverting to the concern, Vatavu compares handheld and freehand gestures for ambient home entertainment displays [14]. He reports that users prefer handheld devices to perform gestures because they prefer buttons and familiar actions such as WIMP paradigm. The work illustrates users' experience towards two different gestures types, yet it does not compare usage scenarios with new interaction modalities, where there is no use of accustomed intermediary devices. The results demonstrate users' bias for already known interactions. On the other hand, what we strive for is to understand user's preference for new interaction modalities for different contexts.

The literature review suggests that despite the shift toward users' experience concerning different gesture types, there is still a gap in the field regarding a comparison of user experience for new modalities. There is a lack of design knowledge to inform researches about which gestures will be advantageous for varying technological devices and contexts. We aim to explore users' preferences comparatively for these gesture types to produce design knowledge in this uncharted area. Thus, we designed a study to compare on-skin touch and freehand gestures, and observe the conditions in which one would be advantageous to the other.

3   Methodology

3.1   Participants

Twenty individuals (12 females and 8 males) participated to our study. Participants' ages ranged from 18 to 26 ($M = 21.15$, $SD = 2.01$), and they were all university students with various level of education from undergraduate level to PhD. All participants were right-handed and regular technology users with no professional relationship to design and/or HCI. Although we have conducted a previous user-elicitation study for creating on-skin gesture set, none of the participants were engaged in creating that set and they performed the gestures for the first time in their lives.

3.2   Setting

We conducted the experiment in an audio studio located in our university to minimize the external stimuli and control for possible extraneous variables such as lighting. There were 3 computers in the room (Fig. 1), where the first one (A) recorded videos via two external cameras, one in front of the participant (A1) and one above (A2). The second computer (B) displayed the survey to the participants via an external screen (B1). The third one (C) transferred the videos and the actions of the gestures to a LCD TV (C1) that was visible to the participants. Also, one of the two experimenters (D) used this computer to perform wizard-of-oz (WoZ) actions. The interface displayed to the participants was an edited Microsoft Power Point presentation, where the actions of the tasks were controlled by a simple click of WoZ.

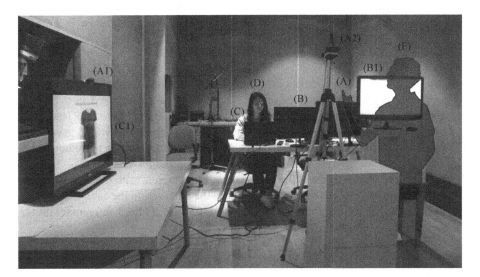

Fig. 1. The setting of the experiment: (A) Computer no. 1, (A1) Camera no. 1, (A2) Camera no. 2, (B) Computer no. 2, (B1) Survey screen, (C) Computer no. 3, (C1) LCD TV, (D) Wizard-of-oz, (F) Participant

3.3   Gesture Sets

Freehand.   We obtained the freehand gesture set from a previous work done by Vatavu [14]. In that study, he conducted a user-elicitation experiment with twenty participants (12 females and 8 males) with various technical backgrounds. The participants were all right-handed similar to our case. He collected the gestures using Xbox's Kinect sensor. Originally in his study, he obtained 22 freehand gestures for corresponding tasks with some task having more than one referent. However, for this study we chose 13 tasks, which correlated with our previous study [13], and chose the gestures with the highest agreement scores set by Vatavu (Fig. 2).

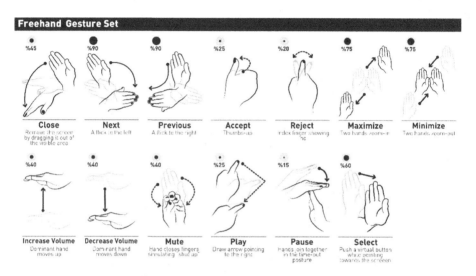

Fig. 2.   Freehand gesture set for 13 tasks

On-skin Touch.   We used the on-skin touch gesture set from our previous work [13]. Nineteen undergraduate students (9 females and 10 males) participated in that study creating two on-skin touch gesture sets, an intuitive and an exclusive set. These sets included 26 tasks each and again we selected 13 tasks that correlated with Vatavu's set [14]. We mainly chose the referents from the intuitive gesture set due to higher agreement scores; however, some of the referents were very similar for different tasks because of being intuitive. When this was the case, we gave the referent with the highest agreement score to the corresponding task and replaced the others from the exclusive gesture set. As a result, we obtained an on-skin touch gesture set with 13 referents with the highest agreement scores (Fig. 3).

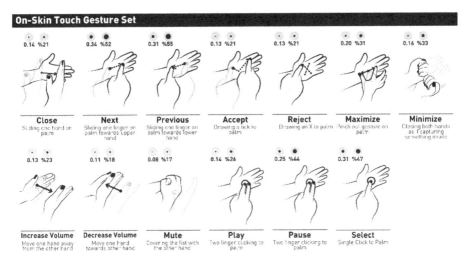

Fig. 3. On-skin touch gesture set for 13 tasks

3.4 Procedure

First, the participants were greeted to the setting and seated. Here, while the first experimenter informed the participant about the experiment and handed the informed consent forms, the second experimenter started the video recordings. Both the experimenters and the participants signed the two consent forms, one for the participant and one for the experimenters. Then, the participants were situated in front of the main screen where they were visible to the cameras. Here, participants were told that they would see two gesture sets on the screen, both containing the same 13 tasks but different 13 corresponding gestures. The order of these sets was counterbalanced for each participant such as first on-skin touch gesture set or first freehand gesture set. Also, the order of these tasks was randomized for each participant and each set.

As the process began, the participants were asked to watch the videos of the gestures with the task name on top twice and repeat the gesture when the command screen shows up. They were told if they repeat the gesture as they see, *'the machine'* would recognize the gesture and carry the necessary action for the corresponding task. We first presented a sample gesture (e.g. open menu) for each set to show them the process. After they successfully repeated the gesture and the WoZ initiated the action, they filled our 7-point Likert scale survey consisted of NASA Task Load Index (TLX) and our additional questions of social acceptability, learnability, memorability, and the goodness (Table 1). As the participants filled the surveys, we went over the questions together to make sure they were understandable. When the participants were done with the sample survey, we filled in their demographic information and chose their groups (e.g. on-skin gesture set first).

Table 1. 7-Point Likert Scale survey questions

No	Index code	Question
1	Mental demand	How mentally demanding was the gesture you performed?
2	Physical demand	How physically demanding was the gesture you performed?
3	Temporal demand	How hurried or rushed was the pace of the gesture you performed?
4	Learnability	How hard was it to learn the gesture you performed?
5	Memorability	How hard was it to remember the gesture you performed?
6	Performance	How successful were you in performing the gesture?
7	Effort	How hard did you have to work to accomplish you level of performance?
8	Frustration	How insecure, discouraged, irritated, stressed and annoyed were you?
9	Goodness	How fitting was the gesture you performed to the task?
10	Social acceptibility	How comfortable would you be in performing the gesture in public?

Next, we continued with our designated gestures. The participants again watched the videos twice, repeated until they were successful and filled the survey for each gesture. Mention that although we presented a single large display to control with gestures to shorten the process, we continuously reminded the participants to think for various and ambient devices they use. They were also encouraged to think out loud and comment on anything that comes to their mind. After they finished all 13 tasks for the first set, we again showed a sample gesture and repeated the procedure for the second set. Subsequently, we seated the participants again and had a semi structural interview about the process. Here we also informed them about the WoZ process. In total, the procedure lasted approximately 30 min.

4   Results and Discussion

4.1   Survey Results

Two of the participants were dropped from the analysis because they were outliers in multiple items, leaving 18 participants for the final analysis. Repeated measures ANOVA was conducted for the items in the 7-point Likert scale survey, controlling for order effects of seeing either gesture set first. Results showed that freehand gestures (M = 1.62, SD = 0.56) were found more physically demanding than on-skin touch gestures (M = 1.28, SD = 0.33), $F(1,16) = 10.55, p < 0.01$. Freehand gestures (M = 6.07, SD = 0.91) were also less socially acceptable than on-skin gestures (M = 6.62, SD = 0.42), $F(1,16) = 10.77, p < 0.01$. For all other items in the survey, mean differences between freehand and on-skin gestures were not significant, $p > 0.05$.

4.2   Mental Model Observation

In this section we will share the results of semi-structural interviews together with our insights regarding participants' behavior during the study. Predominantly, participants preferred freehand gestures (8 participants) over on-skin touch gestures (5 participants). However, another 5 participants expressed that both sets have advantages over the other considering various end devices, thus they want to use both of these sets. They indicated that the preference could easily shift from a device to another, so there should be a personalization option for the given sets, where the user can decide which modality to choose. In this section, we will discuss pros and cons of these gesture sets over the other in the given contexts.

Physical Demand. One of the significant items in our comparison analysis was physical demand. Four participants specified freehand gestures as *'large.'* Five further participants described them as *'tiring'* and *'difficult.'* On the other hand, 3 participants found on-skin touch gestures as *'easy.'* The significance of the result may be due to higher physical demand caused by the nature of freehand gestures. Freehand gestures are indeed take much space and effort in reality. Their use of larger space felt too much for some participants while the on-skin touch ones were easier because they require less effort.

Intuitive vs. Artificial. We observed that most of our participants perceived the palm as the multi-touch sensor. They transferred the metaphor of accustomed devices such as the smartphone or the tablet onto their hands and perceived on-skin touch gestures as similar. Therefore, we observed a legacy bias of standard smartphone touch gestures onto the on-skin touch gesture set, with 5 participants pointing that these gestures were *'habitual.'* One participant expressed this situation by referring to on-skin touch gestures as "transporting the touchpad to the palm." As a result, another participant indicated it to be *'artificial,'* pointing to its man-made qualities. They evaluated accustomed gestures (e.g., swipe left for "next") as *'boring.'* On the other hand, many of the freehand gestures were taken from daily life, which one naturally performs while manipulating actual objects. Two participants even reported that they are *'suitable for daily life.'* Another 2 participants found freehand gestures as *'intuitive.'* Additionally, the interviews revealed that the gestures which were derived from symbols (e.g., thumbs up for "accept") were more liked because they were claimed to be more memorable and that they "made more sense."

Social Acceptability. The other significant item in our comparison analysis was social acceptability. Twelve participants reported that they would prefer on-skin touch gestures in public context, while freehand gestures had less social acceptability on the survey questions. We believe this relates to many factors such as the size of the gestures, their relatively covert nature and their *'artificial'* quality. First, as many participants indicated, freehand gestures take up larger space and this constitutes a problem while performing gestures on the street or on crowded public transportation. The possibility of trespassing strangers' personal spaces was one of the main reasons why these gestures would not be socially acceptable in public. Second, on-skin touch gestures are usually performed within the palm area and can easily be concealed from public by correctly positioning the hand. Since they take small space, they can easily go unnoticed by public, providing the user with increased privacy in his use of the sensor. Finally, on-skin touch gestures are perceived to be more man-made while freehand gestures resemble gestures used in daily life communication. Therefore, some participants thought freehand gestures could be perceived as rude in the public context if strangers confused command gestures with communicative gestures. Since on-skin touch gestures are clearly directed towards an electronic device, these have a higher social acceptability.

Areas of Use. Participants suggested many application areas or contexts for both gesture types. A general overview reveals that on-skin touch gestures were mostly seen appropriate for controlling *'smaller personal devices'* or those require more *'precision.'* Two participants reported they would prefer these gestures for *'reading'* or 'writing'. On the other hand, freehand gestures were found more *'fun'* (2 participants) and *'immersive'* (1 participant), which resulted in them being suitable for *'large displays'* (7 participants). Five participants also indicated they can be used to control *'public displays'* such as an interface of an automat or a presentation for a meeting. Further, 2 participants indicated a use for 'gaming' correlating with immersion, another wanted to interact with *'holograms'* using freehand gestures. Participants believed they could have more fun with these gestures and increase immersion in multimedia by performing such large, intuitive gestures.

5 Conclusion

In this study, we compared user-elicited freehand and on-skin touch gestures through a user participatory experiment. In this experiment, twenty participants completed 13 tasks with the correlated gestures for each set and filled our survey. Our results revealed that on-skin touch gestures were less physically demanding and more socially acceptable. On the other hand, freehand gestures were found more intuitive. Further they were expressed as more fun and immersive.

From our results, future interaction designers should take account that smaller and artificial gestures like on-skin touch gestures are more appropriate modalities for publicly used devices such as mobile phones, mp3 players, smart watches or maybe even POS machines. They are preferred by the users because these gestures are divergent from one naturally performs. They have a lower possibility to confuse public because they are clearly to perform or control some action. Also, the subtler nature of these gestures helps to conceal the action if wanted. Moreover, this nature also enables smaller movements for the gesture, which made participants think that they are more appropriate for smaller devices and the devices with precision. In a sense, most of the devices we publicly use are small devices because they need to be easily carried and mobile. Thus, there is also a link between small devices preference and public use advantage of on-skin touch gestures.

On the other hand, designers should also account that intuitive and immersive gestures like freehand gestures are more appropriate modalities for fun contexts such as gaming, watching movies, listening music, sports or maybe even cooking and using other home appliances. Users preferred these gestures because compared to on-skin touch gestures, which were found boring, freehand gestures are more engaging. They need the use of larger parts of the body with wider motions ending up immersing the user in the action they perform. That is one of the reasons why they are also preferred to be used in private actions, because the true immersion of the self can hardly be achieved with spectators. Furthermore, immersion and wide motions of these gestures are the reason why they are preferred to control large displays. Controlling televisions to large billboards or even an automat was more convenient for our participants. Thus, we can speculate, it is even more convenient to make a presentation using these gestures to be more engaging, although it is a rather public environment.

Although, we presented advantages of these two gesture sets over another in different contexts to inform designers of the modalities, note that many of the participants preferred to customize these sets. They want to use both sets according to their needs, which can change over situations. For instance, they prefer to use on-skin gesture set to control their smartphones during a crowded bus trip, but they also prefer to use freehand gesture to control the same smartphone during a house party where they choose the music. Therefore, while both of the sets have clear advantages over another, interaction designers should also take account that these advantages are mainly context related and these contexts change over time. Thus, the most user-friendly way to approach the topic is to prepare a customizable interaction modality where users can adapt according to their needs.

References

1. Vogel, D., Balakrishnan, R.: Distant freehand pointing and clicking on very large, high resolution displays. In: Proceedings of the 18th Annual ACM Symposium on User Interface Software and Technology - UIST 2005, p. 33 (2005)
2. Harrison, C., Ramamurthy, S., Hudson, S.E.: On-body interaction: armed and dangerous. In: Proceedings of TEI 2012, pp. 69–76 (2012)
3. Matthies, D.J.C., Perrault, S.T., Urban, B., Zhao, S., Rostock, F.I.G.D.: Botential: localizing on-body gestures by measuring electrical signatures on t he human skin, pp. 207–216 (2015)
4. Nakatsuma, K., Takedomi, R., Eguchi, T., Oshima, Y., Torigoe, I.: Active bioacoustic measurement for human-to-human skin contact area detection, pp. 1–4 (2015)
5. Zhang, Y., Zhou, J., Laput, G., Harrison, C.: SkinTrack. In: Proceedings of the 2016 CHI Conference on Human Factors in Computing Systems - CHI 2016, pp. 1491–1503 (2016)
6. Wagner, J., Nancel, M., Gustafson, S.G., Huot, S., Mackay, W.E.: Body-centric design space for multi-surface interaction, pp. 1299–1308 (2013)
7. Harrison, C., Tan, D., Morris, D.: Skinput: appropriating the body as an input surface. In: Proceedings of the SIGCHI Conference on Human Factors in Computing Systems, pp. 453–462 (2010)
8. Gannon, M., Grossman, T., Fitzmaurice, G.: Tactum: a skin-centric approach to digital design and fabrication, pp. 1–10
9. Wobbrock, J.O., Aung, H.H., Rothrock, B., Myers, B.A.: Maximizing the guessability of symbolic input. In: CHI 2005 Extended Abstracts on Human Factors in Computing Systems, pp. 1869–1872 (2005)
10. Canat, M., Tezcan, M.O., Yurdakul, C., Tiza, E., Sefercik, B.C., Bostan, I., Buruk, O.T., Göksun, T., Özcan, O.: Sensation: measuring the effects of a human-to-human social touch based controller on the player experience. In: Proceedings of the 2016 CHI Conference on Human Factors in Computing Systems, pp. 3944–3955 (2016)

11. Mauney, D., Howarth, J., Wirtanen, A., Capra, M.: Cultural similarities and differences in user-defined gestures for touchscreen user interfaces. In: Extended Abstracts of the 28th International Conference on Human Factors in Computing Systems (CHI 2010), pp. 4015–4020 (2010)
12. Canat, M., Tezcan, M.O., Yurdakul, C., Buruk, O.T., Özcan, O.: Experiencing human-to-human touch in digital games. In: CHI 2016 (2016)
13. Bostan, İ., Buruk, O.T., Canat, M., Tezcan, M., Yurdakul, C., Göksun, T., Özcan, O.O.: Hands as a controller: user preferences for hand specific on-skin gestures. In: Proceedings of the Designing Interactive Systems Conference. ACM (2017)
14. Vatavu, R.D.: A comparative study of user-defined handheld vs. freehand gestures for home entertainment environments. J. Ambient Intell. Smart Environ. **5**, 187–211 (2013)
15. Hart, S.G., Staveland, L.E.: Development of NASA-TLX (Task Load Index): results of empirical and theoretical research. Adv. Psychol. **52**, 139–183 (1988)
16. Wobbrock, J.O., Morris, M.R., Wilson, A.D.: User-defined gestures for surface computing. In: Proceedings of the 27th International Conference on Human Factors in Computing Systems - CHI 2009, p. 1083 (2009)
17. Kühnel, C., Westermann, T., Hemmert, F., Kratz, S., Müller, A., Möller, S.: I'm home: defining and evaluating gesture set for smart-home control. Int. J. Hum Comput Stud. **69**, 693–704 (2011)
18. Vatavu, R.D.: Nomadic gestures: a technique for reusing gesture commands for frequent ambient interactions. J. Ambient Intell. Smart Environ. **4**, 79–93 (2012)
19. Camp, F., Schick, A., Stiefelhagen, R.: How to click in mid-air. In: Streitz, N., Stephanidis, C. (eds.) DAPI 2013. LNCS, vol. 8028, pp. 78–86. Springer, Heidelberg (2013). doi: 10.1007/978-3-642-39351-8_9
20. Shoemaker, G., Tsukitani, T., Kitamura, Y., Booth, K.S.: Body-centric interaction techniques for very large wall displays. In: Proceedings of the 6th Nordic Conference on Human-Computer Interaction Extending Boundaries - NordiCHI 2010, pp. 463–472 (2010)
21. Hespanhol, L., Tomitsch, M., Grace, K., Collins, A., Kay, J.: Investigating intuitiveness and effectiveness of gestures for free spatial interaction with large displays. In: Proceedings of the 2012 International Symposium on Pervasive Displays - PerDis 2012, pp. 1–6 (2012)
22. Jansen, B.E.: Teaching users how to interact with gesture-based interfaces (2012)
23. Nancel, M., Wagner, J., Pietriga, E., Chapuis, O., Mackay, W.: Mid-air pan-and-zoom on wall-sized displays (2011). To cite this version
24. Wu, H., Wang, J., Zhang, X.: (Luke): User-centered gesture development in TV viewing environment. Multimedia Tools Appl. **75**, 733–760 (2016)
25. Vatavu, R.-D., Zaiti, I.-A.: Leap gestures for TV: insights from an elicitation study. In: Proceedings of the 2014 ACM International Conference on Interactive Experiences for TV and Online Video, pp. 131–138 (2014)
26. Buruk, O.T., Özcan, O.: DubTouch: exploring human to human touch interaction for gaming in double sided displays. In: Proceedings of the 8th Nordic Conference on Human-Computer Interaction, pp. 333–342 (2014)
27. Nacenta, M.A., Kamber, Y., Qiang, Y., Kristensson, P.O.: Memorability of pre-designed and user-defined gesture sets. In: Proceedings of the SIGCHI Conference on Human Factors in Computing Systems - CHI 2013, p. 1099 (2013)
28. Heydekorn, J., Frisch, M., Dachselt, R.: Evaluating a user-elicited gesture set for interactive displays. In: Mensch & Computer, pp. 191–200 (2011)
29. Chan, E., Seyed, T., Stuerzlinger, W., Yang, X.-D., Maurer, F.: User elicitation on single-hand microgestures. In: Proceedings of the 2016 CHI Conference on Human Factors in Computing Systems, pp. 3403–3414 (2016)

30. Yoo, S., Parker, C., Kay, J., Tomitsch, M.: To dwell or not to dwell: an evaluation of mid-air gestures for large information displays. In: Proceedings of the Annual Meeting of the Australian Special Interest Group for Computer Human Interaction on - OzCHI 2015, pp. 187–191 (2015)

31. Aigner, R., Wigdor, D., Benko, H., Haller, M., Lindlbauer, D., Ion, A., Zhao, S., Koh, J.T.K.V.: Understanding mid-air hand gestures: a study of human preferences in usage of gesture types for HCI. Technical report MSR-TR-2012-11, 10 p. (2012)

32. Henze, N., Hesselmann, T., Pielot, M.: Free-hand gestures for music playback: deriving gestures with a user-centred process. Methodology, p. 16 (2010)

33. Zaiţi, I.-A., Pentiuc, Ş.-G., Vatavu, R.-D.: On free-hand TV control: experimental results on user-elicited gestures with leap motion. Pers. Ubiquit. Comput. **19**, 821–838 (2015)

34. Vatavu, R.-D.: User-defined gestures for free-hand TV control. In: Proceedings of the 10th European Conference on Interactive TV and Video - EuroiTV 2012, p. 45. ACM Press, New York (2012)

35. Hood, S.: The intuitiveness of bimanual, mid-air, gesture-based input methods which provide haptic feedback, pp. 5–7 (2012)

36. Karvinen, J.: Haptic feedback in freehand gesture interaction, 66 p. (2015)

37. Jakobsen, M.R., Jansen, Y., Boring, S., Hornbæk, K.: Should I stay or should I go? Selecting between touch and mid-air gestures for large-display interaction. In: Abascal, J., Barbosa, S., Fetter, M., Gross, T., Palanque, P., Winckler, M. (eds.) INTERACT 2015. LNCS, vol. 9298, pp. 455–473. Springer, Cham (2015). doi:10.1007/978-3-319-22698-9_31

MIDAS-M: A Software Framework for Supporting Multimodal Interaction on Heterogeneous Interaction Devices for Cloud Applications

Myunghee Lee[1], Gerard J. Kim[1(✉)], and Jeonghyun Baek[2]

[1] Digital Experience Laboratory, Korea University, Seoul, Korea
{lmh81,gjkim}@korea.ac.kr
[2] KMC Robotics, Seoul, Korea
jhbaik@kmcrobot.com

Abstract. In this paper, we present a software framework, called MIDAS-M (Mixing and matching heterogeneous Interaction Devices to Applications and Services) that enables an application to lend itself to many different types of interaction methods and accommodate users with different client devices in a flexible manner. In particular, we focus on the aspect of supporting "multimodal" interaction by defining and mapping events that are mixed and matched by different input/output components. The multimodal events defined this way can be realized on various client platforms according to their capabilities. We also describe a case study of applying MIDAS-M to developing a multimodal interface for a virtual apartment preview system, called the SMARTIS, and demonstrate its advantages.

Keywords: Cloud based interaction · Ubiquitous interaction · Multimodal interaction · Software framework

1 Introduction

Cloud computing allows and simplifies the instant access of rich information and high quality service anywhere by decoupling the core software functionality (on the server side) and the input/output (on the client side). That is, the client can be relatively computationally less capable supporting just the acquisition of user input, presentation of the output and communication these between the client and server. In many cases, the web environment is used to provide the interaction platform independence for the cloud client. The web environment basically supports only the standard keyboard and cursor/pointer/touch interaction. In the future, we can easily imagine a situation where users with variant client devices (and interaction capabilities) wanting to accomplish a given application task in a different way. For instance, in playing a first person shooting game, one might prefer to shoot using a hardware button, another by touch button, another by swipe gesture, and another by voice command. That is, sophisticated users will expect to choose the most usable form of interaction for themselves, depending on the given device (e.g. desktop, smart phone, pad, VR).

© Springer International Publishing AG 2017
N. Streitz and P. Markopoulos (Eds.): DAPI 2017, LNCS 10291, pp. 172–179, 2017.
DOI: 10.1007/978-3-319-58697-7_12

Traditionally, to accommodate the situation as described above, either separate client programs are developed for (or ported to) different devices and operating systems, enforcing a particular interface most suited for the given device, or a "large" client program is developed to cover all possible interaction possibilities. Practically, this has caused application services (cloud or local) to be compatible to only a small family or brand of devices and leaving no choices for the users in terms of the interaction possibilities.

In the line of such a need, we had developed present a software framework, called MIDAS (Mixing and matching heterogeneous Interaction Devices to Applications and Services), that enables an application to lend itself to many different types of interaction methods (namely, sensing and display) and accommodate users with different client devices in a flexible manner [1]. In this paper, we present an important extension to MIDAS, called MIDAS-M, for supporting "multimodal" interaction in the similar way. Using MIDAS-M, multimodal events can be defined in an abstract manner, and mapped to the application, e.g. to provide redundant and assured input/output delivery, alternative interaction methods, and/or interfaces matched in modalities by the task characteristics. The multimodal events defined this way can be realized on various client platforms according to their capabilities. We describe the MIDAS-M framework and present a case study of applying it to developing a multimodal interface for a virtual apartment preview system, called the SMARTIS.

2 Related Work

The objective of our work is similar to those of the migratory or plastic interfaces. Migratory interfaces are those that operate on changing operating platforms or interaction resources. Cameleon-RT [2] and BEACH [3] are examples of such software architecture/infrastructures in which multiple interaction devices could be managed and interact with the given application. Such middlewares enable a "generically" described interactive application to build their own "view" for a given physical interaction platform. Plasticity further requires the migrating interface to preserve the usability as much as possible by adaptation to the specific operating platform (e.g. the control panel lay out changed according to the size of the PDA) [4]. In these approaches, separate platform specific implementations and compilation processes are still needed, and they do not support the design of multimodal interaction in a flexible mix (different modalities) and match (to various devices) fashion.

TERESA [5] is an authoring tool for "One Model, Many Interfaces" [6] type of applications. With the help of TERESA, different user interface codes can be conveniently generated from abstract user interface descriptions. However, the output application still compiled for a specific platform with its interaction capabilities known ahead of time. The SEESCOA component system [7] uses abstract UI described in XML which is interpreted to compose user interfaces at run time. Mark up languages for the interactive web and cloud applications that describe UI objects, and interpreted and realized by different platform browsers, operate on similar principles [8, 9]. Gilroy et al. has developed a client middleware that adapts application's "presentation styles" (expressed in an XML format specification document) most suited for a given device at run time. This way, the menus, form-fills, dialogue GUIs are adjusted and presented according to the device capabilities and thus high usability can be expected [10]. Our work focuses on defining and managing multimodal interaction.

3   MIDAS-M Framework

Figure 1 shows the overall architecture of MIDAS-M. In the far left (and right), lie different input (and output) modules/platforms operating in different modalities or equipped with various sensors and displays. MIDAS-M takes the raw input signals from the input modules (which may be separate from where the application resides), and relays them to the application (possibly through the network) in the form of meaningful application "events." The "events" can be multimodal that combines the different input streams in different timings (but within a limited time window) and/or contributing factors. For example, a multimodal input might be defined as a successive input of a voice command and finger tracking data within 1 s, or a simultaneous input of voice and touch. Such definitions are specified by the developer using a separate authoring tool (Fig. 2) producing an XML based description of the multimodal events (Fig. 3), as an input to the MIDAS-M engine (middle part of Fig. 1). As illustrated in Fig. 3, the events

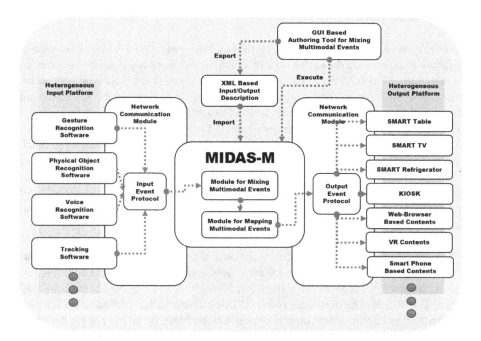

Fig. 1. MIDAS-M: A flexible architecture that decouples the application from interaction complexities and device heterogeneity. It also supports definitions of multimodal input and output events as mapped to the application in a neutral and generic way.

are assigned with unique identifiers and used in the given application to define their handlers.

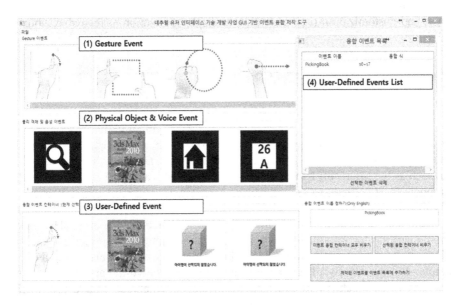

Fig. 2. The GUI based authoring tool to define multimodal events and mapping them to a given application. An example of an XML description of a multimodal event

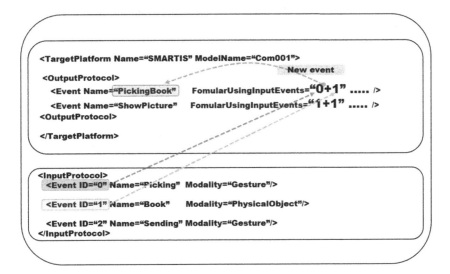

Fig. 3. An example of an XML description of a multimodal event. For instance, the output event, "PickingBook" is triggered by a combined (sequential) multimodal input event of "0" (hand gesture) and "1" (target object recognition).

Just like the multimodal input events, multimodal output events can be specified in the same way and used in the pertaining application. Important aspects of multimodal output event might include the timing, synchronization and heterogeneous device support and customization (e.g. according to display resolution, screen size, volume level, etc.).

4   A Case Application: SMARTIS

We demonstrate the flexibility of the MIDAS-M framework, in providing a variety of ways to interact and improving general usability, by applying it to the development of a virtual apartment previewing system, called the SMARTIS. It is composed of two main output displays, namely, a tabular and an upright monitors, and a number of sensors for input such as the Microsoft Kinect depth sensor, an RGB camera, touch screen, and a microphone.

With SMARTIS, the user can make commands in various ways for making selections (e.g. particular floor plan, apartment model/size, interaction/content modes, viewpoints), querying for information (e.g. price, location, options), zooming in/out, and navigating and exploring the scene. Many interactions are defined multimodally. For example, the "move forward" command (for navigating the virtual apartment) can be invoked by voice, touch or mid-air gestures separately or combined. Figure 4 shows the system in use and Table 1 summarizes the (multimodal) interfaces for various aforementioned tasks. The output is presented through the two monitors, e.g. the 2D floor plan on the flat monitor and 3D interior scenes on the upright, accompanied by sound/voice feedback where appropriate. Figure 4 shows the overall system set-up and its typical usage situation.

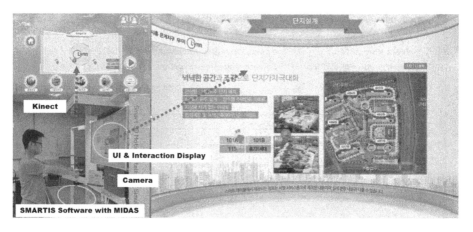

Fig. 4. A scene from interacting with SMARTIS (virtual apartment previewing system) using natural gestures, finger tracking, touch, multiple displays and voice commands.

Table 1. Multimodal interfaces for various tasks in SMARTIS.

	Task	Interface
Input	Navigation (Translation and Rotation)	Gesture
		Voice
		Touch
		Object recognition
	Select	Object recognition
		Gesture
	Zoom in/Zoom out	Gesture
	Capturing ROI	Gesture
	Mode change	Voice
		Gesture
		Touch
Output	Present 2D floor plan	Visual feedback (flat display)
		Sound feedback
	Present 3D apartment interior	Visual feedback (upright display)
		Sound feedback
	Present instructions	Visual feedback (flat/upright display)
		Sound feedback
	Command confirmation	Visual feedback (flat/upright display)
		Sound feedback

The input modules and the core applications in SMARTIS were developed separately on different operating platforms and run on separate computers communicating through the network. The whole system was internally integrated through the event language and protocol of the MIDAS-M, which defined the various input and output events (some of multimodal, see Table 1) and mapped to the core application logic. These event specifications were mostly carried out using the aforementioned authoring tool (Fig. 2).

Fig. 5. Another smart table based object manipulation application quickly developed using the same I/O modules and MIDAS-M framework.

The decoupled development, between the I/O and core application follows the well-known principle of separation of concerns [11] and the MVC (Model-View-Controller) development methodology [12, 13]. All the input/output modules are easily reusable in different multimodal combination for another application. Figure 5 shows a simple smart table based object manipulation application, quickly developed using same I/O modules and MIDAS-M middleware.

5   Discussion and Conclusion

In this paper, we presented MIDAS-M that supports multimodal interaction and interface-model decoupled application development. The multimodal events can be defined in a variety of forms to allow rich interaction and high usability of the target application. The framework was put to use to develop a commercially deployed product. It demonstrates that how MIDAS-M allows a flexible mixing and matching of and reusing of the I/O modules at compile or even run time to suit the various interactional needs. In addition to the logical decoupling between the I/O and core application, future MIDAS-M framework can be applied as a cloud middleware (e.g. for hardware/platform decoupling) in which clients only have to perform the necessary I/O functions with the sensors and input modules available to themselves.

Acknowledgement. The research was supported through the "Software Convergence Technology Development Program," funded by the Ministry of Science, ICT and Future Planning (S1002-13-1005), and also through the "Basic Science Research Program," funded by the Korean National Research Foundation (No. 2011-0030079).

References

1. Ahn, E., Lim, K., Kim, G.J.: MIDAS: a software framework for accommodating heterogeneous interaction devices for cloud applications. In: Streitz, N., Stephanidis, C. (eds.) DAPI 2013. LNCS, vol. 8028, pp. 339–348. Springer, Heidelberg (2013). doi: 10.1007/978-3-642-39351-8_37
2. Balme, L., Demeure, A., Barralon, N., Coutaz, J., Calvary, G.: CAMELEON-RT: a software architecture reference model for distributed, migratable, and plastic user interfaces. In: Markopoulos, P., Eggen, B., Aarts, E., Crowley, James L. (eds.) EUSAI 2004. LNCS, vol. 3295, pp. 291–302. Springer, Heidelberg (2004). doi:10.1007/978-3-540-30473-9_28
3. Tandler, P.: Software infrastructure for ubiquitous computing environments: supporting synchronous collaboration with heterogeneous devices. In: Abowd, G.D., Brumitt, B., Shafer, S. (eds.) UbiComp 2001. LNCS, vol. 2201, pp. 96–115. Springer, Heidelberg (2001). doi: 10.1007/3-540-45427-6_9
4. Calvary, G., Coutaz, J., Thevenin, D.: A unifying reference framework for the development of plastic user interfaces. In: Little, M.R., Nigay, L. (eds.) EHCI 2001. LNCS, vol. 2254, pp. 173–192. Springer, Heidelberg (2001). doi:10.1007/3-540-45348-2_17
5. Mori, G., Paterno, F., Santoro, C.: Design and development of multidevice user interfaces through multiple logical descriptions. IEEE Trans. Softw. Eng. **30**(8), 507–520 (2004). IEEE

6. Paterno, F., Santoro, C.: One model, many interfaces. In: Kolski, C., Vanderdonckt, J. (eds.) Computer-Aided Design of User interfaces III, vol. 3, pp. 143–154. Springer, Netherlands (2002)
7. Luyten, K., Vandervelpen, C., Coninx, K.: Migratable user interface descriptions in component-based development. In: Forbrig, P., Limbourg, Q., Vanderdonckt, J., Urban, B. (eds.) DSV-IS 2002. LNCS, vol. 2545, pp. 44–58. Springer, Heidelberg (2002). doi: 10.1007/3-540-36235-5_4
8. XHTML2 Working Group Home Page. http://www.w3.org/MarkUp
9. XAML Overview (WPF). http://msdn.microsoft.com/en-us/library/ms752059.aspx
10. Gilroy, S.W., Harrison, M.D.: Using interaction style to match the ubiquitous user interface to the device-to-hand. In: Bastide, R., Palanque, P., Roth, J. (eds.) DSV-IS 2004. LNCS, vol. 3425, pp. 325–345. Springer, Heidelberg (2005). doi:10.1007/11431879_22
11. Suh, N.P.: The Principles of Design, vol. 990. Oxford University Press, New York
12. Patterns, D., Pattern, C.: Model-View-Controller (2003)
13. Leff, A., Rayfield, J. T.: Web-application development using the model/view/controller design pattern. In: Enterprise Distributed Object Computing Conference, pp. 118–127. IEEE (2001)

Design and Evaluation of Cross-Objects User Interface for Whiteboard Interaction

Xiangdong A. Li[1(✉)], Preben Hansen[2], Xiaolong Lou[1],
Weidong Geng[1], and Ren Peng[1]

[1] Department of Digital Media, Zhejiang University, Hangzhou, People's Republic of China
{axli,dragondlx68,gengwd,pengren}@zju.edu.cn
[2] Department of Computer Science and Systems, Stockholm University, Kista, Sweden
preben@dsv.su.se

Abstract. Whiteboard has long been an important tool for education and communication, and nowadays it embraces display functions and other interactive features such as pen pointing and selecting of digital contents. Despite the enhanced interactivity, it is often time- and cost-consuming to implement specific apparatus for different whiteboard interactions. Therefore, we aimed at incorporating physical-world objects (e.g. Lego Rubik's cubes) as the cross-objects user interface for multiple whiteboard interaction tasks without incurring heavy development work. The user interface utilised electromagnetic technique to extract electromechanical signals and recognised normal objects, thus extended the generality. To further understand effectiveness of the user interface, we implemented a low-fidelity prototype and conducted within-subject evaluation. The results showed the cross-objects user interface was natural, responsive, and easy of learning as the conventional whiteboard. Moreover, the user interface outperformed over the conventional one in the perspectives of configuration efficiency and versatility of multiple interaction tasks. Given these findings, practical implications for future tangible user interface design for whiteboard interactions are discussed.

KeywordS: Cross-objects user interface · Whiteboard interaction · Physical icon · User study · User interface

1 Introduction

Whiteboard is an important tool to support user's learning and information exchanging in scenarios such as classrooms and conference rooms. As a presentation media that combined with annotating features, whiteboard allows multiple users to visualise and communicate their thoughts with marker pens that can be massively produced and applied in versatile interaction scenarios [1]. Due to the advances in display technologies, nowadays whiteboard has integrated graphic display functions (e.g. e-whiteboard [2]), and the interaction began to rely on assistant apparatus. In addition, natural interaction technologies are increasingly being embedded in whiteboard interaction (e.g. pressure-sensing drawing [3]). This introduces more peripheral equipment in

© Springer International Publishing AG 2017
N. Streitz and P. Markopoulos (Eds.): DAPI 2017, LNCS 10291, pp. 180–191, 2017.
DOI: 10.1007/978-3-319-58697-7_13

whiteboard interaction, with which numerous whiteboard applications are designed such as pick-and-drop pen for cross-computers file transfer [4] and cross-devices information sharing system [5]. So far, whiteboard has become not only an interactive tool but also a hub of apparatus that enables various interaction tasks such as idea sketching, sharing, and learning [6].

However, it is both time- and cost-consuming to implement specific apparatus for different whiteboard interaction tasks. For example, digital stylus replaced conventional marker pens, but which required extra system configurations to maintain consistent sensitivity across different whiteboard sizes and platforms [7]. Furthermore, adding or removing interaction modalities in whiteboard interaction faces other difficulties due to that the specifically developed apparatus are often deeply coupled with whiteboard tasks (or functionalities) [1]. Given these tightly-coupled apparatus, whiteboard interaction becomes uneasy of introducing new interaction metaphors derived from natural physical-world objects [8]. For example, whiteboard marker dispenser is designed useful in large size whiteboard, but it runs into practical difficulties when transferring to a small tablet due to the limited screen real-estate [9]. Similar problems are anticipated when users attempt to configure one marker dispenser for other purposes of use.

Increasing attentions are attracted to improving the generality of whiteboard's peripheral apparatus and meanwhile to lowering the development cost across interaction tasks [7]. To bridge the gap, we designed the cross-objects user interface that was capable of recognising everyday objects (Lego Rubik's cubes in this case) and configuring these as manipulation tool in whiteboard interaction. Furthermore, to understand effectiveness of the user interface, we constructed a low-fidelity prototype and conducted within-subject evaluation. The main contributions of the study are two-folder. Firstly, it pioneers the implementation of the cross-objects user interface that has generalising use in whiteboard interaction; secondly, it provides new understandings of how effective such user interface is used in whiteboard interaction.

The remainder of the paper is organised as follows. Section 2 give a literature review that mainly covers whiteboard interactions and cross-objects user interface. Section 3 describes methodological details of study as well as the data analysis. Section 4 gives a statement of study results, and Sect. 5 discusses the findings and related implications. Finally, Sect. 6 concludes the study results and implications.

2   Related Work

2.1   Whiteboard Interaction and Peripheral Apparatus

Whiteboard supports people sketching thoughts and sharing ideas. Various sizes and placements of whiteboard have enabled different forms of interactions such as industrial design sketching and multi-user collaborative tasks [10]. Particularly, whiteboard is a great colour tool for demonstrations, as it can highlight important features of objects with the stylus that incorporates different width and colour marks [11]. In addition, the interaction of whiteboard accommodates different types of learning styles [1]. Tactile users can benefit from touching and marking on the board, and such sense can be further developed by combining with other interaction modalities such as music and spoken discussions [12].

Whiteboard interfaces well with other peripherals [10]. With projectors, it displays images that collaborate with user's marking; and with sensor-integrated stylus, it enables spatial drawing in front of board [7]. As the recent Microsoft Surface Studio demonstrates, not only conventional stylus is embedded in an altered whiteboard system (which is a large size display screen), but also physical objects such as the cylinder dialler can be added as manipulation tool. Given these examples, we see an explicit trend of that the whiteboard interaction is increasingly integrating display and interactive technologies to facilitate different types of natural interactions. So far, apparatus is developed and integrated in whiteboard systems, so to expand the interaction range as well as methods.

However, the generality is often limited when the apparatus is specifically implemented for distinguishing interaction tasks. The limit not only refers to electronic apparatus that are developed for concrete functions, but also covers tangible user interfaces that involve everyday objects as manipulation tool [13]. For example, cross-screen file transferring requires specially developed stylus hardware and software [4]; spatial marking whiteboard needs corresponding pre-use calibrations and configurations that are troublesome to normal users [13]; and in the contexts of education, multiple users hold pens that require special wireless networks to synchronise connection and interaction status [14].

The generality problem is justified for two reasons. Firstly, there are various operation systems and configurable devices currently coexisting in whiteboard interaction environments. For example, whiteboard's image display functionalities can be realised through projectors and large scale flat screens; and the marking functionality can be implemented by digital stylus and fingers. The diversities of existing system and environment configurations raise the necessity of proposing interaction apparatus for specific scenarios and functionalities. Secondly, the tasks of whiteboard interaction are often distinguishing, that is, for example, selecting a distal item in whiteboard performs differently with spatial-stylus and finger-pointing methods [15]. This stimulates developers and researchers to explore novel whiteboard interactions at a specific task-oriented point of view. In the contrast, the reverse way – to make the interaction more generalising – is less concerned in current studies. The consequences are, firstly, it becomes uneasy of using natural object-based interaction metaphors due to the high implementation cost; and secondly, there are more difficulties in integrating new techniques and apparatus in existing whiteboard interaction platforms and scenarios.

2.2 Tangible User Interfaces and Cross-Objects User Interface

Tangible user interfaces, which were setup to *"make computing truly ubiquitous and invisible"*, have been considered as one of effective solutions to the generality problem in whiteboard interaction [16]. A body of research in computational systems emphasised on the importance of physical-world object modalities in interactions [17]. In addition, research systems began to rely on the physical artefacts as representations and controls for digital information [17], although the characteristics of the interactions with the artefacts have yet to setup systematic frameworks. To extend this limit, researchers take a significant step in the direction of "graspable user interfaces [16] ".

As [16] claimed, the digital-world information is being coupled into physical-world objects, so to transform physical objects into configurable interfaces. In the contexts of whiteboard interaction, researchers explored this concept and delivered implements. For example, making whiteboard a smart clustering of free-hand sketches [18], integrating ambient light system to add value in meeting and control rooms [19], and using large interactive surface to track user's deictic gestures [20]. The advantages provided by these systems include a tighter coupling of physical-world objects and cyberspace interfaces as well as the greater interactivity of whiteboard [21].

However, these systems were often tightly coupled with digital apparatus. For example, a spatial position recognition is uneasy of transforming to another whiteboard [17], not to mention the software toolkits that were tailored for special use [22]. To address this issue, a body of research constructed frameworks that were adaptive to different interactions. For example, implicit interaction was proposed to support interactions across different electronic whiteboards [2, 23] and framework of physical objects was imported to enable cross-device whiteboard interaction [5].

To enhance the generality of the apparatus, researchers used sensing technologies such as RFID to recognise and mark objects [24]. For example, digital stylus equipped with RFID tag has names and attributes to transfer digital files across devices and users [4]. This apparatus still required specific equipment and development work, but it provided inspirations of that everyday objects could be a part of unified user interface.

Object recognition often requires sensor embedment and that involves extra development setups. Electromechanical technique provides a new method of recognising everyday objects for whiteboard interaction, as it is capable of detect uninstrumented and electrical objects without extra equipment. In [25], researchers demonstrated that multiple mundane objects could be recognised through electromechanical signature, and a separate graphical user interface could be displayed on the host device. This technique could be further extended to recognise everyday objects that emit small amounts of unique electromagnetic signals, and configurations and interactions could be done through the host device. This provides the technical foundation of cross-objects user interface that extends whiteboard interaction while keeping high generality across the objects.

3   Method

Given the preceding understanding of whiteboard interaction and requirements for user interface that aims to enhance apparatus generality and meanwhile lower the development cost, we referred to the electromagnetic signal recognition technique and developed a cross-objects user interface for whiteboard interaction. In addition, we conducted a within-subject evaluation to investigate the effectiveness of this user interface. Below we describe methodological details.

3.1 Implement Cross-Objects User Interface

We prototyped a low-fidelity cross-objects user interface that consisted of three separate cubes disassemblied from a 3 * 3 Lego Rubik's cube by referring to the technique in [25] (Fig. 1). The cubes' electromagnetic signal patterns were manually extracted and trained beforehand. Thus, when the cubes were touched by user's hand, the mobile phone in the other hand received electromagnetic signals through user's body as conductive antenna, recognised the cubes on touch, and launched configuration interfaces in mobile phone. By changing the settings displayed in the mobile phone, the users configured functionalities of the cubes in whiteboard interactions.

Fig. 1. Disassembled cubes as the cross-objects user interface

The cubes attached magnetic pads to stick on and move around the whiteboard surface. The whiteboard was a conventional board at sizes of 900 * 1800 mm. A projector was setup in front of the whiteboard to display contents during the interaction. In addition, a webcam was attached on the top surface of the projector to recognise positions and numbers of cubes, so the contents were accurately displayed around the cubes. Both the projector and webcam were connected to a laptop. The mobile phone ran an application that stored the cubes' configurations and communicated with the laptop through Bluetooth. A full map of study apparatus setup is illustrated in Fig. 2.

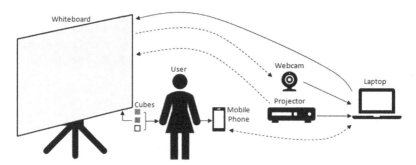

Fig. 2. Study apparatus setup

3.2 Evaluation of Cross-Objects User Interface

To understand effectiveness of the user interface in whiteboard interaction, we conducted within-subject comparable evaluation. We recruited 15 undergraduate students. None of them had any previous experiences of cross-objects user interface, and none self-reported any body movement impairments. The participants were required to trial the cross-objects user interface and complete three whiteboard-related tasks: namely, sketching, erasing, and file transferring between the cubes. These represented the mostly frequent whiteboard interaction tasks [12]. Procedural flows of the evaluation procedures were as follows.

1. The participants received a 5-min introduction of the user interface given by experimenter, and then were given a 2-min trial of the cubes on whiteboard with mobile phone.
2. On the end of pre-study practice session, the participants were required to make open sketches on the whiteboard by firstly configuring the cubes as a drawing marker. The configuration process was done through the mobile phone. The sketches were an open task to circumvent unnecessary pressures on participants.
3. The participants were then asked to reconfigure the cubes to erase the sketches drawn earlier.
4. The participants were asked to reconfigure the cubes, displayed the contents stored in the cubes, and transferred these contents from one cube to another. This was an open task which aimed to encourage participants' exploration of the use of user interface.
5. After accomplishing all required tasks, the participants fulfilled 5-Likert questionnaires which contained 9 effectiveness-related questions and 1 overall satisfaction-realted question (see questions in Appendix 1). The questions asked participants to compare with conventional whiteboard interaction (including normal markers and plain whiteboard) and then to give ratings.
6. Following the questionnaires, informal interviews were hosted by experimenters and the feedbacks were logged.

The evaluation of effectiveness of the cross-objects user interface adopted three criteria derived from [26]. The criteria were used in evaluation of various interactive products such as intelligent tutoring systems with proven reliability and validity, particularly the criteria were suitable to reflect effectiveness of conceptual products that were not massively applied [27]. The criteria consisted of:

1. timeliness which measures how quickly a system is able to provide the user with the outputs (e.g. sketching and erasing in this case) they require; this reflects how the new user interface can help participants accomplish the given tasks;
2. throughput which measures how much work is done by the system over a period of time; this reflects how much work the new user interface can afford to be a productive tool in critical whiteboard interaction tasks; and
3. utilisation which measures the proportion of time a system resource is busy; this reflects how much resources of the new user interface are available to support participants' interactions.

The evaluation collected 15 questionnaires and interview logs, respectively. Each question in the questionnaire required the participants to compare with conventional whiteboard interaction and to give two respective ratings, one for the conventional whiteboard interaction and the other for the cross-objects user interface. The conventional whiteboard interaction was chosen as the comparison benchmark of evaluation, because the results were more intuitive when comparing the cross-objects user interface with the natural physical-world objects. All questionnaire results were transcribed into databases for later analysis, and the interview logs were examined by experimenters to annotate the key phrases.

Statistical analysis was conducted to compare the differences in the aspects of effectiveness between the conventional whiteboard interaction and the cross-objects user interface whiteboard interaction. The results are shown in Fig. 3.

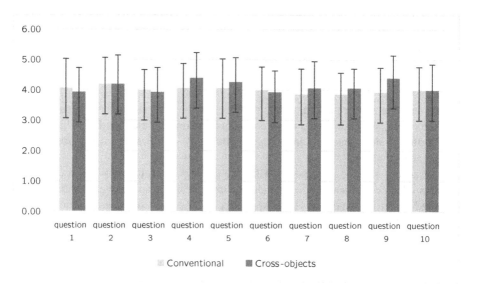

Fig. 3. Results of effectiveness of the cross-objects user interface

As Fig. 3 shows, the analysis reported significant differences in the results of question 5, 8, and 9 (Independent-Sample T-test, $p = 0.03$, 0.046, and 0.049, respectively). The rest questions did not report any significant differences between the interaction with conventional markers and whiteboard and the cross-objects user interface.

The overall reliability and validity of evaluation were great, as the results of question 10 showed, all participants successfully completed required tasks and rated equal overall satisfaction levels. The results of question 5 confirmed the participants' expectation of interactive functionalities embedded in whiteboard. The results of question 8 showed that the participants' willingness to deploy the cross-objects user interface was affirmative, and the results of question 9 showed that the participants were happy to extend the cross-objects user interface in broader applications. The results of other questions showed some advantages of conventional whiteboard interaction over the cross-objects user interface interaction. For example, question 1 (measuring the timeliness of learning) indicated that the conventional markers and whiteboard were still easier and quicker to learn, which was validated by the results of question 6 and interview feedbacks.

As the results of question 3 indicated, the participants might not be the same confident as in conventional whiteboard interaction when facilitating with the new user interface. The results of question 4 and 7 showed some advantages of the cross-objects user interface, although no significant differences were reported. Importantly, the results of question 2 (measuring the timeliness of naturalness) reported equal naturalness of the cross-objects user interface as conventional markers and erasers, which confirmed that the physical cubes and related metaphors of the cross-objects user interface were understandable to the participants. This was validated by interview results, as the participants commented *"it (the cubes) feels easy to understand, it's also quite intuitive"*.

4   Results

The preceding evaluation findings confirmed the overall effectiveness of the cross-objects user interface for whiteboard interaction, as the interface achieved equal results compared with conventional whiteboard interaction, particularly in several aspects of effectiveness the cross-objects user interface gained greater advantages. Taking all evidences together, we claimed that the cross-objects user interface was effective and it had great potentials to support various whiteboard applications with lightweight configurations.

5   Discussion

The intention of this research was not to deliver a one-for-all solution to the generality problem in whiteboard interaction, rather it was motivated to explore new avenues that could possibly incorporate physical-world objects to implement cross-objects user interface to support multiple whiteboard interaction tasks with less development work. Admittedly, many studies have proposed different systems that were aimed at maximising the use of apparatus across whiteboards. This study did not make significant differences in this regard.

However, the study stepped further towards the coupling of physical and virtual world and the coupling of everyday objects and digital information by adopting electromagnetic technique. Consequently, the study proposed the cross-objects user interface that was almost same natural as the conventional markers and whiteboard, and importantly the evaluation study showed that the new user interface was more configurable and adaptable across multiple whiteboard interaction tasks. Therefore, the main contributions of this study lay on two points, one is the implementation of the cross-objects user interface for whiteboard interaction, and the other is the understanding of the effectiveness of the cross-objects user interface. The latter understanding supplies generalising implications for future tangible user interface design and augmented reality user interface research.

The findings drawn from this evaluation are generally aligned with the conclusions of previous studies. For example, tangible objects as manipulation tools are naturally intuitive [28] and tangible bits take advantage of users' cognition habits that have been accumulated through biological evolvement [16]. Also, new understandings were added. For example, despite users learned the cross-objects user interface quickly, they appeared less confident in interaction.

Regardless of evaluation findings, the design of cross-objects user interface as well as its trials in the study give broader implications for user interface design in ubiquitous computing era. The form of using physical objects in whiteboard interaction is not new, as this has been done in previous projects such as [9, 13–16]. However, these objects were still bound to specific colours, shapes, and materials. Given the electromagnetic technique, researchers are now easy of introducing interaction metaphors from physical world, and they can configure the apparatus with minimum development efforts. Also, the cross-objects user interface realised foreground and background interaction environments, which focused on the interactive objects and the peripherals, respectively [29]. The peripherals are often neglected in conventional HCI research, but the cross-objects user interface helps users coordinate foreground and background interaction simultaneously.

In addition, the electromagnetic technique-based mundane object recognition can be further extended to a wider range of applications. In [25], the researchers have attempted to apply this technique in different everyday objects such as door handle, motor-bike, and toaster. Initially this technique was proposed to recognise electrical and electromechanical objects by identifying objects' electromagnetic signal patterns (also called 'signature'), and then enabled to infer object states. However, when this technique is able to accurately recognise objects' electromagnetic signatures, it could be extensively used as a connector between the objects and ubiquitous networks. As partially demonstrated in this study, the cubes could be assigned links that point to remote digital files assisted by the host device, which could be a wearable smart watch or any other digital artefacts. Therefore, not exaggeratingly, the cubes could be containing the whole internet contents when it is recognised with a unique identification and working links to contents. The cross-objects user interface also shed some lights in envisioning future user interface design, for example, an invisible user interface that supports user grabbing a box of milk in store and complete payment by touching the wallet.

Due to the early stage prototype development and preliminary exploratory study, the cross-objects user interface and the evaluation are noted with some limits. Firstly, low-fidelity prototype of cross-objects user interface was used in study. The interface was functional and fulfilled expected study requirements, however, to some extent it affected the participants' overall satisfaction. Secondly, the evaluation used a relatively small number of participants. We do not deny that a larger sample would be adding more credits to the study, but we also believe that the evaluation study that strictly followed methodological procedures provided a reliable and valid ground of understanding. Finally, the electromagnetic technique adopted in this study still has some limits due to its early stage development, these included the negative influences of object sizes and locations. The technical limits will be especially pushed forward in future work.

6   Conclusions

We have proposed a cross-objects user interface for whiteboard interaction, and evaluated effectiveness of the interface. Compared with conventional whiteboard interaction, we analysed how the cross-objects user interface performed in the perspectives of time-liness, throughput, and utilisation. Our study showed that the new interface was as natural, responsive, and easy to learn as conventional whiteboard interaction, and in some aspects (e.g. versatility) the cross-objects user interface outperformed over the conventional one. Given these findings, implications for future tangible user interface design for whiteboard interaction as well as for broader ubiquitous computing-related application design are discussed.

Acknowledgements. The authors would like to thank all participants. This research has been supported by the funding from Cloud-based natural interaction devices and tools (2016YFB1001300), Zhejiang Provincial Natural Science Funding (LQ15F020002), and China Knowledge Centre for Engineering Science and Technology (CKCEST-2014-3-2).

Appendix 1 (Evaluation Questionnaires, 1 - Strongly Disagree, 5 - Strongly Agree)

1. I can learn to use the cross-objects user interface quickly.
2. I feel like the use of cross-objects user interface is natural.
3. I think I can use the cross-objects user interface skilfully.
4. I feel like I can use the cross-objects user interface to draw something efficiently.
5. I feel like I am confident to use this new user interface to do some practical works, e.g. file sharing and transferring.
6. I think the configurations of the cross-objects user interface (the cubes) are easy and quick.
7. I think the cross-objects user interface has quick response in both configurations and interactions.
8. I feel confident that the cross-objects user interface has sufficient computing resources to support more complicated tasks.
9. I feel like this cross-objects user interface has great potentials for new applications in other contexts e.g. shopping.
10. I think the overall configurations and interactions with the cross-objects user inter-faces are smooth and satisfactory.

References

1. Madni, T.M., Nayan, Y., Sulaiman, S., Tahir, M., Abro, A., Khan, M.I.: Collaborative learning using tabletop and interactive whiteboard systems. Int. J. Bus. Inf. Syst. **20**, 382–395 (2015)
2. Ju, W., Lee, B.A., Klemmer, S.R.: Range: exploring implicit interaction through electronic whiteboard design. In: Proceedings of the 2008 ACM Conference on Computer Supported Cooperative Work, pp. 17–26. ACM (2008)
3. Haller, M.: Designing natural user interfaces: from large surfaces to flexible input sensors. In: 2015 8th International Conference on Human System Interactions (HSI), pp. 15–16. IEEE (2015)

4. Rekimoto, J.: Pick-and-drop: a direct manipulation technique for multiple computer environments. In: Proceedings of the 10th Annual ACM Symposium on User Interface Software and Technology, pp. 31–39. ACM (1997)

5. Hamilton, P., Wigdor, D.J.: Conductor: enabling and understanding cross-device interaction. In: Proceedings of the SIGCHI Conference on Human Factors in Computing Systems, pp. 2773–2782. ACM (2014)

6. Schmidt, D., Seifert, J., Rukzio, E., Gellersen, H.: A cross-device interaction style for mobiles and surfaces. In: Proceedings of the Designing Interactive Systems Conference, pp. 318–327. ACM (2012)

7. Kudale, A.E., Wanjale, K.: Human computer interaction model based virtual whiteboard: a review. Int. J. Comput. Appl. 0975–8887 (2015)

8. Yang, H., Han, S.H., Park, J.: User interface metaphors for a PDA operating system. Int. J. Ind. Ergon. **40**, 517–529 (2010). doi:10.1016/j.ergon.2010.04.002

9. Toennies, E., Kawamoto, N., Sharma, A.: Whiteboard Marker Dispenser. Mechanical Engineering Design Project Class. Paper 34 (2015)

10. Mangano, N., LaToza, T.D., Petre, M., van der Hoek, A.: Supporting informal design with interactive whiteboards. In: Proceedings of the SIGCHI Conference on Human Factors in Computing Systems, pp. 331–340. ACM (2014)

11. Camplani, M., Salgado Álvarez de Sotomayor, L., Camplani, R.: Low-cost efficient interactive whiteboard. In: 2012 International Conference on Consumer Electronics (ICCE). IEEE (2012)

12. Bell, M.A.: Why use an interactive whiteboard? A baker's dozen reasons. Teachers' Net Gazette 3 (2002). http://teachers.net/gazette/JAN02/mabell.html. Accessed 1st Dec 2016

13. Sra, M., Lee, A., Pao, S.-Y., Jiang, G., Ishii, H.: Point and share: from paper to whiteboard. In: Adjunct Proceedings of the 25th Annual ACM Symposium on User Interface Software and Technology, pp. 23–24. ACM, Cambridge (2012). doi:10.1145/2380296.2380309

14. Yucel, K., Orhan, N., Misirli, G., Bal, G., Sahin, Y.G.: An improved interactive whiteboard system: a new design and an ergonomic stylus. In: 2010 2nd International Conference on Education Technology and Computer (ICETC), pp. V3-148–V143-152. IEEE (2010)

15. Zhang, S., He, W., Yu, Q., Zheng, X.: Low-cost interactive whiteboard using the Kinect. In: 2012 International Conference on Image Analysis and Signal Processing (IASP), pp. 1–5. IEEE (2012)

16. Ishii, H., Ullmer, B.: Tangible bits: towards seamless interfaces between people, bits and atoms. In: Proceedings of the SIGCHI Conference on Human Factors in Computing Systems. ACM, Atlanta (1997). doi:http://doi.acm.org/10.1145/258549.258715

17. Ullmer, B., Ishii, H.: Emerging frameworks for tangible user interfaces. IBM Syst. **39**, 915–931 (2000)

18. Perteneder, F., Bresler, M., Grossauer, E.-M., Leong, J., Haller, M.: Cluster: smart clustering of free-hand sketches on large interactive surfaces. In: Proceedings of the 28th Annual ACM Symposium on User Interface Software & Technology, pp. 37–46. ACM (2015)

19. Perteneder, F., Grossauer, E.-M.B., Leong, J., Stuerzlinger, W., Haller, M.: Glowworms and fireflies: ambient light on large interactive surfaces. In: CHI, pp. 5849–5861 (2016)

20. Alavi, A., Kunz, A.: Tracking deictic gestures over large interactive surfaces. Comput. Support. Coop. Work (CSCW) **24**, 109–119 (2015)

21. Kim, M.J., Maher, M.L.: The impact of tangible user interfaces on designers' spatial cognition. Hum.-Comput. Interact. **23**, 101–137 (2008). doi:10.1080/07370020802016415

22. Cuendet, S., Dehler-Zufferey, J., Ortoleva, G., Dillenbourg, P.: An integrated way of using a tangible user interface in a classroom. Int. J. Comput.-Support. Collaborative Learn. **10**, 183–208 (2015)

23. Ju, W.: The design of implicit interactions. Synth. Lect. Hum.-Centered Inf. **8**, 1–93 (2015)

24. Marquardt, N., Taylor, A.S., Villar, N., Greenberg, S.: Rethinking RFID: awareness and control for interaction with RFID systems. In: Proceedings of the 28th International Conference on Human Factors in Computing Systems. ACM, Atlanta (2010). doi: 10.1145/1753326.1753674

25. Laput, G., Yang, C., Xiao, R., Sample, A., Harrison, C.: Em-sense: touch recognition of uninstrumented, electrical and electromechanical objects. In: Proceedings of the 28th Annual ACM Symposium on User Interface Software & Technology, pp. 157–166. ACM (2015)

26. Legree, P.J., Gillis, P.D.: Product effectiveness evaluation criteria for intelligent tutoring systems. J. Comput.-Based Instr. **18**, 57–62 (1991)

27. VanLehn, K.: The relative effectiveness of human tutoring, intelligent tutoring systems, and other tutoring systems. Educ. Psychol. **46**, 197–221 (2011)

28. Harvey, K.: Tangible Things: Making History Through Objects. Taylor & Francis, Boca Raton (2016)

29. Buxton, W.: Integrating the periphery and context: a new taxonomy of telematics. In: Proceedings of Graphics Interface, pp. 239–246. Citeseer (1995)

Experience Design of Social Interaction for Generation Y Based on Tangible Interaction

Yan Shi[1(✉)], Yuhui Guo[1], Zheng Gong[1], Bing Yang[2],
and Leijing Zhou[3]

[1] School of Media and Design, Hangzhou Dianzi University,
Xiasha Higher Education Zone, Hangzhou 310018, China
hzshiyan@gmail.com
[2] School of Computer Science, Hangzhou Dianzi University,
Xiasha Higher Education Zone, Hangzhou 310018, China
[3] Zhejiang University, Hangzhou 310058, China

Abstract. Generation Y of the mainland China has the features of "chameleon": adapting to social rules in society and showing distinct personality in their own small circles. This self-contradictory presentation differentiates it from other groups in a way that is integrated into the real world. We explore the experience design based on tangible computing in the hope of better communication and interaction of Generation Y in the physical environment. We have explored the design principle for Generation Y and the design prototype "chameleon cube" based on this concept: to design a space that allows the Generation Y to experience the public environment and enter into a self-review state, and in this installation, they can relax themselves and also to express individuality. Through experimental observation and data analysis, we verify that the products based on the "chameleon design principle" can explore the characteristics of the Generation Y group and help to enhance the communication skills of Generation Y.

Keywords: Generation Y · Tangible computing · Interactive experience

1 Introduction

The concept of "Generation Y" (Gen Yers) was first proposed by the American researchers, which defines that "Generation Y" was the generation born in 1982–1994 period and grew up with computers and the Internet. In China, opinions are divided on the definition of "Generation Y". This study defines "Generation Y" as a generation born in the period with the development and popularization of computers and the Internet in China, because the development of computer and Internet technology in China lags behind the United States, and the gradual popularization of computers and Internet technology is mature during 1983–1998, which is the important basis for this thesis to define the group born in this period as China's Generation Y.

Generation Y at China and abroad generally have the following several similar characteristics: (1) independent value orientation and self-centered (2) the Internet

© Springer International Publishing AG 2017
N. Streitz and P. Markopoulos (Eds.): DAPI 2017, LNCS 10291, pp. 192–202, 2017.
DOI: 10.1007/978-3-319-58697-7_14

environment and rapidly adapt to high-tech updates; (3) higher level of education, in the knowledge-based economic system and education requirements are relatively improved; (4) pay attention to the balance of life and work [1–3].

The social background of China's Generation Y is complex, and the political, economic, cultural and educational changes all influence the formation of the consciousness of Generation Y. China launched its reform and opening-up policy in 1979, and put forward the strategy of rejuvenating the country through science and education in 1995. At the same time, China has a long history of its traditional culture and family concept, which makes the family structure rather special and driven by the basic national policy of family planning, the unique 6 + 1 family structure was formed. Therefore, it is easy for Generation Y group to develop the self-centered character since childhood. However, this has also virtually put pressure on Generation Y as the focus of family has shifted to Generation Y, with the result that Generation Y tends to fail to meet the predefined expectations under high expectations, leading to a loss of confidence or transformation to a negative or rebellious attitude towards life.

Generation Y is deeply influenced by the traditional Chinese culture and the impact of Western culture. They are eager to express themselves but are bound by the traditional culture, which has caused the inner self-contradictions of China's Generation Y, that is, whether to express themselves bravely or to drift with the current and adapt to the society. Under the depressive contradiction, Generation Y group has developed its own unique characteristic: in the society, they can be very good at adapting to social rules, and in their own small circles, they can express distinct personalities. This phenomenon is just like the chameleon that changes its color of the skin as the environment changes, so we say that Generation Y of the mainland has chameleon features.

Generation Y is the group aged 18–32 in China, which is the current main crowd or in the near future. Most studies of Generation Y offer theoretical suggestions on employment outlook, work view, values, consumption view and learning methods etc. Few auxiliary installations or tools help Generation Y to better adapt to the real world.

This thesis will start from the virtual mode familiar to Generation Y in the way of Tangible Interaction to let the Generation Y better integrate into the real world and make Generation Y reflect and integrate into the real world naturally.

2   Related Work

Since 2000, many researchers began to study Generation Y. Interested in what was causing the change in the students; Stewart did a self-reported personality questions used to self-describe the behavior of individuals [4]. Arhin and Cormier demonstrated that Y group is more proficient at multitasking, visual learning, and using technology [5]. Other characteristics describing Generation Y include loyal, hard working, goal oriented, socially networked, team oriented, efficient multitaskers, interested in addressing social problems, and comfortable being assessed [6, 7]. This generation also possesses traditional values and has a strong family emphasis [8]. A weakness of Generation Y that is apparent in their narratives is their inability to write proficiently. This generation is well-versed in disruptive technology, including emailing, texting, instant messaging, blog-posting, and Facebooking [9, 10].

Many research focused on the family structure, parental work patterns and educational mode of Y generation [5, 7, 11–13]. Researches on generation Y consumer habits, purchasing power and so on [13]. Chung built the internet service marketing model according to the information environment change and information behavior characteristics of Generation Y users, and based on the model, discussed the service marketing strategies [14].

There are lots of studies on Generation Y group, most of which belong to theoretical or management classes. However, few designs have been made for the Generation Y, and installations are rarely designed to solve the problems of Generation Y group. Based on the previous researches, this thesis puts forward the design of products conforming to the style of Generation Y based on their characteristics, which helps guide the psychology and behaviors of Generation Y and promote better communication and integration into the society of Generation Y.

The goal of tangible interaction is to empower collaboration, learning, and design by using digital technology and at the same time takes advantage of human abilities to grasp and manipulate physical objects and materials [15]. From a broader perspective, human–computer interaction requires physical effort, by using body movement to control the character, scene, animation and so on. Therefore, applying the tangible interaction theory and the relevant computer technologies will be an important and effective approach for exploring how to let the Generation Y better integrates into the real world and making Generation Y reflect and integrate into the real world naturally.

3   Research Process

3.1   Pre-study

Generation Y is now in college student period and we carried out qualitative observation of students' characteristics in daily life in several places in a university for three weeks, three times a day in the early, middle and late periods, each lasting one hour. In the meantime, we conducted 60 semi-open and valid questionnaires. Specifically in the first week, we observed the learning state of the post-90s college students in the library and study rooms; in the second week, we observed the active state of the college students during recess time and on the way to class; in the third week, we observed and recorded the communication and frequency of playing mobile phone during the dinner.

After qualitative research, we have derived the basic characteristic of Generation Y, therefore we needed to design a product complying with this characteristic to meet the needs of Generation Y group. Then according to the initial installation designed, design the usage scenario and put into the practice. During this process, we modified the design according to three bases: a. according to the results of the test user feedback; b. according to analysis of the users' behavior recorded in the process of using; c. new design ideas and integration of new concept. Finally, we redesigned a product with new concept and put into practical applications. All the relevant feedback collected and new conceptions were integrated into the design of the new product and constant iterations were conducted to design products that suit Generation Y group.

The above observation and analysis led us to the conclusion that the post-90s college students of Generation Y group have a distinguished characteristic, which is, spending a lot of idle time on their cell phones, mainly the communication on the network. Whether it is in the class break or on the way to and after class or after dinner, they will habitually bow their heads to play the cell phone, which promoted the generation of a current popular vocabulary – "phubbing". And in our observation, in public occasions, people will have the demand of integrating into the groups, and show some restraint of their own personalities. This has resulted in a very contradictory psychology of the Generation Y group, being reintegrated into public life but reluctant be assimilated, wanting to express their own characteristics but fear of being regarded as outliers. This gave us the idea of designing a "chameleon prototype" motive power that can reflect the characteristics of the Generation Y group.

3.2   Prototype Building

We used the user-centered interactive design method to design and complete the initial installation. Guided by observational data and conclusions reached, to design a space that allows the Generation Y to experience the public environment and enter into a self-review state. In this installation they can relax themselves and express individuality. It took us two weeks to make a preliminary physical installation, test our installation again and again, and to invite users to use it and redesign it based on the advice given. Then, after a week of modification, our installation was gradually refined and placed at our Student Activity Center (where many students organize activities, so there were many experiencers who meet the criteria). After the deployment, we invited students to experience our installation, and then interviewed them with their experiences and got as much valuable advice and user surveys as possible. Every day we would carry out observations when more students are gathered here, interview them and obtain survey data.

4   The Design Principle of Chameleon Installation

Based on our literature review and design study, we determined the following design principles for installation of "Chameleon Cube".

4.1   Create Two Different Scenes

One of the two scenes is to cater to the public scene faced by Generation Y. In this scene, students will feel that they are being watched and their own behaviors will be restrained accordingly, the virtual group interacts with the person who is experiencing, and if it violates the principles of the public, the experiencer will be excluded and cannot continue to integrate into this scene. This will result in two kinds of results, one is that the experience fits in well and the other is that the experience is ostracized. The other scene is a private space where the experiencer can express his or her own emotions without worrying about the surroundings; meanwhile the experiencer can share his or her feelings or leave the true self.

4.2   Observe Without Disturbing the Experience

In the private space, we will record the real reflection of those who experience without disturbing them, and protect the privacy of the experiencers.

To evaluate how well our method can classify the art style between the Chinese and the foreign painting. Table 1 lists experiment results when using different methods.

Table 1. Key summary from the observed

Outside the "cube"		Inside the "cube"	Proportion agreeing to share the video
Status:	Status 1. Curious and excited to go inside to experience	Experience the contents of all sides inside excitedly	90%
		Experience calmly	69%
	Status 2. Invited and wait calmly	Experience excitedly and reluctant to get out of the experience area	65%
		Still relatively calm, see what themselves are like outside the "cube" and look pensive	23%

4.3   Close to the Real Environment

This installation is completely constructed in the real scene, which will not give the experiencer a sense of deliberateness or violation and can well guide the experiencers to integrate into the scenes set in our installation.

4.4   Focus on Sharing

According to Generation Y's characteristic of being willing to share, we especially provided the sharing function for the experiencers, so that they can pass the feelings they experienced here or the most true and lovely side to other experiencers, which will also encourage the following experiencers to use the installation.

4.5   Simple Interaction

For experiencers to integrate into the installation rapidly, we need to set the humanized interactive mode. Complex interaction demands a certain period of time of learning for the experiencers, which is not conducive to experience, so our interaction will be presented through the finger touch and other forms consistent with the interactive mode in mobile terminals. In the case of improper user interactions, the installation will automatically remind the experiencer, which can also promote a good experience process for experiencers.

5 Core of the Chameleon Prototype Installation

The installation of "Chameleon Cube" is a 60 × 60 × 60 cube installation, and the eight surfaces inside and outside the cube are made of mirror materials with very good mirror effect (Fig. 1). Inside the cube 4 iPads are embedded, being separately placed in the adjacent four internal mirror surfaces. These 4 iPads are set for different purposes. We will first mark the 4 iPads to divide them into A, B, C and D.

Fig. 1. Installation of "Chameleon Cube"

The function of A side is to shoot the emotions expressed by the experiencers in the cube. The cube can only hold one person, so the experiencer doesn't have to care what others think. The function of B side is to play the behavior images of the experience outside the cube. The C side will play the videos others agree to share and the personalities expressed by others in the cube. The function of D side is to play the video outside the cube of the corresponding experiencer being played in C side. The experiencer may watch but cannot do anything to the videos.

The four iPads are connected to the background server through WiFi and the video collection is to upload the recorded videos to the server after consent of sharing is obtained. The videos uploaded will be numbered and imported to the sharing library; meanwhile the experiencer can see the facial expressions showed by himself/herself.

Inside the cube installation are all four sides of the iPad, and the functions are different. We placed a tablet with touch screen inside the cube on which the experiencers can leave messages or write down suggestions for our installation. These messages or suggestions can be uploaded to our server and we will use them to improve our installation.

6   Technical Description of the Chameleon Installation

1. Set up the LAN. Equipment are switches, laptop, network cable and iPad. The architecture of LAN is as follows (Fig. 2):

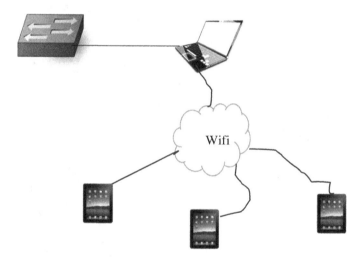

Fig. 2. The architecture of LAN

2. Wed server. Apache HTTP Server is an open source Web server project provided by Apache Software Foundation. It has several features of strong scalability, open source code and cross-platform. This system is to build a web server in the laptop, and the iPad can access to the video resources in the laptop through the wifi of the laptop.
3. Video and upload. The easiest way to take pictures and record videos in iOS is to use the UIImagePickerController. UIImagePickerController inherits from UINavigationController, which can be used to take pictures and record videos. Basic steps for recording a video: Steps to use UIImagePickerController to take pictures or record videos can usually be divided into the following:

(1) Create the UIImagePickerController object;
(2) Specify the pickup source. Normally we use the pickup source of the photo gallery or photo album when choosing pictures, this time we need to specify it as the camera type;
(3) Specify the camera, front camera or rear camera;
(4) Set the mediaType, which must be set if it is video. If it is photographing, this step can be omitted for mediaType default contains kUTTypeImage (note that the media type definition is in MobileCoreServices.framework);
(5) Specify the capture mode, taking pictures or recording videos. (For video recording, first set the media type and then set the capture mode);
(6) Display UIImagePickerController (usually opened as modal window);
(7) After taking pictures and recording videos, display/save photos or videos in proxy approach.

From the above, we can get the recorded videos, and then we will upload the recorded video to the server:

(1) Save the recorded video in the specified folder;
(2) First is the asynchronous export of block data. So after the completion of asynchronous operation, the results of asynchronous operation cannot be obtained immediately. Wait until the completion of block before continuing to obtain the results.
(3) VIDEO_EXPORTING_URL uses fileURL with no need of creating a file in advance. Session can directly create a file and write. If there is already a pointed file of fileURL, there can be problem of not being able to store.
(4) Loop playback

As a result of the use of web server, the realization of online broadcast function is achieved through the web. The specific method is to call the video price-control of html, and then use js to achieve the loop playback of video resources.

7 Discussion of Experience Results

The installation was hung below the ceiling center in one of exhibition rooms. Many visitors observed or experienced outside the installation, while one person is allowed to experience inside the installation. Our designed experience lasted for three days. At first, most students seemed not to notice this installation, and most were still "phubbing" or expressionless, walking without communication. About 2/3 of the students who noticed the cube would be curious and approach the "cube" to watch. Some of them didn't stay long and left immediately; some would stand outside one of the mirrors to observe themselves and the environment reflected (Fig. 3).

The students we invited to enter the "cube" were those who stood outside the cube for relatively a long time and who did not notice the cube or did not stay long after noticing it. In the second and third day, some interested students find us and expressed the wishes to experience the cube. Those who entered the "cube" are the respondents of the experiment and questionnaire. Due to limited objective circumstances, the

Fig. 3. The experience scene

experiencing time inside the cube is no more than 2 min. Iteration was used to improve the content of the questionaire. This process was shown as follow. Firstly, questionaire survey was conducted to get feedback. Secondly, the content of the questionaire was improved according to feedback. This cyclic process was ongoing till the test made every survey question clear in questionaire, which promoted the accuracy of the questionaire result. In actual, seven times cyclic iteration was implementated to reach the satisfying suevey questions. Later, 60 questionaires was selected randomly as the sample and divided into two groups on average as status 1 and status 2.

Table 2. The mean values of the valence and arousal levels

| | Status 1 | | Status 2 | | ANOVA F-values | |
	Outside the "cube"	Inside the "cube"	Outside the "cube"	Inside the "cube"	Status	Outside vs. Inside
Valence	5.6 ± 0.9	8.1 ± 1.1	4.6 ± 1.3	7.1 ± 1.3	6.5	11.8*
Arousal	5.0 ± 0.8	8.9 ± 0.8	4.9 ± 1.1	6.8 ± 1.5	9.9	7.9**

The values are the F values for all subjects
*p < 0.05; **p < 0.01; ***p < 0.001.

At the conclusion of data collection for each of the tasks the subject was asked to provide a subjective rating for his or her responses to the experimental "cube" using 10-point rating scales. The scales were used to designate the levels of valence (1 = very unpleasant, and 10 = very pleasant) and arousal (1 = lowest arousal, and 10 = highest arousal).

The mean values of the valence and arousal levels of all conditions for all subjects are reported in Table 2. ANOVA revealed a significant task effect for the mean value of valence and arousal level, indicating a higher emotion-induced arousal level during inside "cube" than that outside "cube". Table 2 showed the within-the-group sample comparison of the status 1 and the status 2 respectively, and then the sample comparison between the groups.

8 Conclusion

In this thesis, we show an exploratory design serving the Generation Y. Our results show that the design principle of our chameleon installation is appropriate. It promotes the Generation Y group to better express themselves and self-reflection, so as to better integrate into the real world and take the initiative to share with friends around their true side, which is of great help to us to study Generation Y. At the same time, this work provides a framework of ideas and methods for us to determine design principles for specific groups of people.

In future studies, we plan to add more interactions and functions to the chameleon installation for broader experience effects and explore the use of advanced sensor technology in our chameleon installations while conducting more detailed data recording and analysis. The experience summary and design process and methods described here can provide a valuable reference and innovative exploratory spirit for designing products that are more suitable for the Generation Y.

Acknowledgment. This research was supported by the Zhejiang Provincial Natural Science Foundation of China (Grant No. LQ14E050010, LQ14F020012), and the Social Science and Humanity on Young Fund of the Ministry of Education (Grant No. 16YJC760047)

Appendix

See Fig. 4

Questionnaire Feedback

This questionnaire is only for understanding of the level of post-experiential questionnaires. This questionnaire survey is absolutely anonymous, definitely it will not have any negative influence on your life and study. Thanks for your participation, thank you!

1. What do you think of the quantity of the survey questions in this questionnaire? (   )
A. Moderate   B. Overmuch   C. Too little

2. Do you understand every survey question in the questionnaire clearly? (   ) Which survey question you can't understand, list them please_____
A. Yes   B. No

3. Are you interested in the content of the survey question in this questionnaire?
A. Totally interested   B. Partially interested
C. Partially not interested   D. Totally not interested

4 You degree of satisfaction to this questionnaire is (10 marks in total):_____

5 What is your suggestion about this questionnaire?
_____

Fig. 4. Questionnaire feedback form

References

1. Williams, K.C., Page, R.A.: Marketing to the generations. J. Behav. Stud. Bus. **3**, 1–17 (2013)
2. Oblinger. D.: Boomers, etc., understanding the "new students". Educ. Rev. 44–45 (2003)
3. McCoy, S., Everard, A., Polak, P., Galletta, D.: The effects of online advertising. Commun. ACM **50**, 84–88 (2007)
4. Stewart, K.: Lessons from teaching millennials. Coll. Teach. **57**, 11–117 (2009)
5. Arhin, A.O., Cormier, E.: Using deconstruction to educate generation Y nursing students. J. Nurs. Educ. **46**, 562–567 (2007)
6. Howe, N., Strauss, W.: The next twenty years: how customer and workforce attitudes will evolve. Harv. Bus. Rev. **85**, 41–52 (2007)
7. Hill, K.S.: Defy the decades with multigenerational teams. Nurs. Manag. **35**, 32–35 (2004)
8. Murray, N.D.: Welcome to the future: the millennial generation. J. Career Plan. Employ. **57**, 36–42 (1997)
9. Sherman, R.O.: Teaching the net set. J. Nurs. Educ. **48**, 359–360 (2009)
10. Arhin, A.O., Johnson-Mallard, V.: Encouraging alternative forms of self expression in the generation Y student: a strategy for effective learning in the classroom. ABNF J. **14**, 121–122 (2003)
11. Elam, C., Stratton, T., Gibson, D.D.: Welcoming a new generation to college: the millennial students. J. Coll. Admiss. **195**, 20–25 (2007)
12. Mestre, L.: Accommodating diverse learning styles in an online environment. Ref. User Serv. Q. **46**, 27–32 (2006)
13. Dugas., C.: Generation "Y" faces some steep financial hurdles. USA Today (2010)
14. Chung, K.C., Fam, K.S., Holdsworth, D.K.: Impact of cultural values on young consumers choice of international tertiary education. Asia – Pac. J. Bus. Adm. **1**(1), 54–67 (2009)
15. Ishii, H.: Tangible bits: beyond pixels. In: Proceedings of the 2nd International Conference on Tangible and Embedded Interaction, pp. xv–xxv (2008)

Propositions for a Mid-Air Interactions System Using Leap-Motion for a Collaborative Omnidirectional Immersive Environment

Robin Vivian[(✉)]

PERSEUS Laboratory, UFR MIM, Université de Lorraine, Metz, France
`robin.vivian@univ-lorraine.fr`

Abstract. This paper describes a work in progress that exploring the potential of Leap-Motion acquisition system as a believable alternative to multi-touch device to interact with a large curve display: Hyve-3D immersive environment. This system could be used for collaborative ideation with local people working together in the same area and multiple Hyve-3Ds can be connected (via Internet) to share a single work space. Today, Hyve-3D uses a new paradigm of 3D interaction based on tactile device tracked in 6 Degree Of Freedom and it is possible to make immersive sketching with a tactile tablet. We believe that systems of Mid-Air gestures can be an important asset for carrying out, more simply, naturally some tasks. We believe that Leap Motion device must be, not an alternative but an additional solution. This paper proposes a classification of interactions and a distribution by devices. We will define a grammar of gestures and we will offer some technical solutions.

Keywords: Air gestures · Omnidirectional interaction · Immersive environment

1 Introduction

In 1991, Howard Rheingold [1] defines virtual reality (VR) as an experience in which a person is "surrounded by a three-dimensional computer-generated representation, and is able to move around in the virtual world and see it from different angles, to reach into it, grab it, and reshape it." Virtual experience has become a reality for ordinary consumer. A smartphone and a headset (Oculus, HTV vive or PlayStation VR) are terminals accessible for only a few euros. Tomorrow, our environment will become virtual. Today omnidirectional systems are developing in all areas (science, medicine, street views, datamining, etc.). The problem is no longer creating an environment but interacting with it. CAVE [2] was certainly the first omnidirectional interface but the CAVE has not produced any significant new control paradigms. At the beginning of the 2000's Hua, Brown and Gao [3] proposed a HMPD technology (Head-Mounted Projective Display) maned SCAPE. SCAPE was a technology that lies on the boundary of conventional HDMs and CAVE like projective display. SCAPE was a room display system allowing collaborative applications by improving the perception of the real world, by providing the capability to create an arbitrary number of individual viewpoints and by retaining

© Springer International Publishing AG 2017
N. Streitz and P. Markopoulos (Eds.): DAPI 2017, LNCS 10291, pp. 203–216, 2017.
DOI: 10.1007/978-3-319-58697-7_15

natural face-to face communication. One step further in immersive environment with the 240° curved screen i-Cone [4] (Fig. 1). They have developed an interaction paradigm allowing multiple users to share a virtual environment in a conventional single-view stereoscopic. They used spatially tracked PDAs as a common interaction device for every user of the system, combining ray casting selection and direct object motion in the virtual environment with system control for menus, tools, and modes on the "private" interface of each user's PDA.

Fig. 1. 240° i-Cone display

In 2010 Magnor et al. [5] proposed a paper presenting some results from computer graphics research, offering solutions to contemporary challenges in digital planetarium rendering and modeling. The user is immersed in a virtual world but the possibilities of interaction are narrow or nonexistent. Still in 2010, Benko and Wilson used also a dome display but introduced new interactions with an immersive omnidirectional environment. [6]. The grammar to exchange with information shows on screen of the dome is very limited. The interaction vocabulary consists of five different primitives: hand pinch, two hand circle, one hand clasp, speech recognition and interactions with an IR laser pointer.

2   Mid-Air Interaction, Related Work

To create a total immersion impression, the 5 senses must perceive the digital environment as real. Immersive technology can stimulate the senses through: 3D panoramic displays, surround sound, force-feedback, movement recognition devices, and artificial creation of tastes and odors. Today a little number of systems brings together all these vectors of interaction. Augmented reality systems strive to reproduce display, more or less realistically. The main difficulty is to design interactions from the operator to the system. The principal approach is to factor these 6 DOF into 2D spaces that are mapped to the x, y and sometime z axes of a mouse. This metaphor is inherently modal because one needs to switch between subspaces, and disconnects the input space from the modeling space. Wang [7] propose a bimanual hand tracking system that provides physically-motivated 6-DOF control for 3D assembly. This system is reserved to CAD/CAM that typically uses tasks such as manipulating the camera perspective and assembling pieces. It builds 3D interactions based on the recognition of the position of two hands in space and on the recognition of simple gestures based on a metaphor of the real world. Technically the principle is simple. The authors have two cameras which, in diving, film both hands of the operator (Fig. 2).

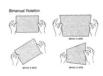

Fig. 2. Wang's 6 DOF interaction

The advantage of this solution is that it is able to detect the movements of the hands without additional artifact and without being intrusive. System haves a small set of gestures that are comfortable to use, precise, and easy to remember.

With a more "immersive" preoccupation, Hilligues et al. have developed the Holo-desk system [8]. The system combines a transparent screen and a Kinect to create the illusion that the user interacts directly with the virtual world (Fig. 3). The interaction space is located below the glass surface. The image is displayed by a screen above the display. The operator has the illusion that the objects are above his hands. A Kinect analyses the operator's hands movements and associates these movements to the scene.

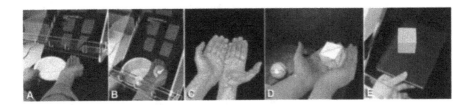

Fig. 3. Holodesk direct interaction with virtual objects

Mokup Builder [9] is a semi-immersive system consecrated to modeling and manipulating objects in 3 dimensions (Fig. 4). The authors argue that modeling in immersive environments provides three major benefits in the design process. The first one concerns the possibility of interacting with objects in real time. The second one is that operators work with various notions of scale of representation, in the construction and interaction spaces. Last one, immersive environments allow a stronger match between the subjective ideas of designers and the principles of intuitive conceptions.

The main freehand gestural interaction issue is the problem of gesture limits (begin/end). How can the application know when the movement is intended to be a gesture or action and not simply a human movement through space? More precisely, it is often difficult to precisely know the exact moment the gesture started or ended. When you use

Fig. 4. Mokup builder et son interaction environment

some tactile interactions, touch contacts provide straightforward delimiters: when the user touches the surface, they are engaged, and lift-off usually signals the end of the action. However, in the open air, we must consider the 3D environment in which we live.

In 2012 [10] Song et al. proposes a new handle bar metaphor as an effective visual control metaphor between the user's hand gestures and the corresponding virtual object manipulation operations. It mimics a familiar situation of handling objects that are skewered with a bimanual handle bar (Fig. 5).

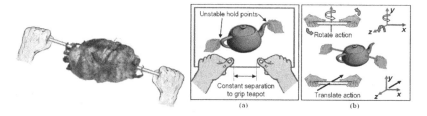

Fig. 5. (a) The metaphor of *two remote gripping-hands* projected into the 3D virtual space, (b) The metaphor of a *handle bar* extended from two clasp hands, which is used to pierce through the teapot for rotation and translation manipulations.

This method is concerned with enabling a single user to inter-actively manipulate single or multiple 3D objects in a virtual environment. The system is able to recognize three basic single-handed gestures: POINT, OPEN, and CLOSE. You execute different visual manipulation operations by moving, closing or opening one or two hands freely within the physical space. Homogenous bimanual gestures will perform basic rotation-translation-scaling (RTS). The handle bar metaphor provides 7 DOF manipulation (3D translation, 3D rotation, and 1D scaling) of virtual object and supports continuous transitions between operations. The results are rather interesting and the simplicity of the movements makes the learning times are almost zero (https://www.youtube.com/watch?v=p0EM9Ejv0r0). However, the system has some limitations. For some translations and rotations, the authors find it is difficult to interact with system continuously. The work carried out by Rodrigues et al. [11] compare the approach developed by Song to manipulation techniques, via 3D gestures, of virtual objects in semi-immersive or even immersive systems with a virtual reality helmet. The system developed by Rodrigues has five different modules (Fig. 6).

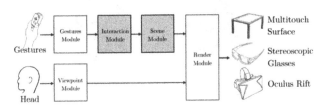

Fig. 6. Five manipulation modules

Authors observe that the mid-air interactions in immersive systems are most efficient and satisfying for all users. The main raison is the possibility to manipulate 6 DOF directly and the mining of natural gestures to interact with objects.

3 Hyve-3D

3.1 Presentation

With only plane display, the difficulty to represent and understand complex 3D shapes, proportion interpretation, the human scale, and the observer's fixed angle of vision have been described by Landsdown [12]. Creating sketches directly in 3D in VR opens up a new dimension in the application of sketching in architectural co-design. The main complexity with GUI arises in 3D interaction due to that 3D data need to be supplied via abstract 2D interfaces. This complexity make creative thinking more difficult. Structured interaction of the mouse with menus forces the user to make premature decisions, demanding more accuracy compared to pen-on-paper techniques. These difficulties distance an architect from creative task. The importance of sketching has been shown in several studies suggesting that different characteristic like ambiguity, abstraction or inaccuracy help architect in the conceptual design [13–15]. Sketches provide a medium of freedom with a flexible degree of abstraction, allowing multiple readings and interpretations.

Hyves-3D is an omnidirectional immersive concept for co-design in architecture [16–18]. Users are situated into 360° screen. They watch a display showing a 3D virtual environment. Hyve-3D is designed for local and remote collaboration. Users can be in the same room, or interconnected across the globe, in full-scale and real-time (Fig. 7).

Fig. 7. Hyves-3D screen and control remote

3.2 Hyves-3D Cursor and Navigation

Gyroscope and accelerometer are used to know physical position and orientation of the tablet. This information is used to manipulate the 3D cursor in virtual space. A 3D cursor is projected in the virtual world as a rectangular frame with the same ratio as the tablet display. A 3D Tracker (magnetic tracker system) is used to reproduce the device position from the real world to virtual world. Users can move and rotate the displayed 3D scene with multi-touch gestures (Fig. 8). When you sliding up on the screen when tablet is in horizontal position, you obtain a forward movement. The same gesture results in an upward movement when the tablet is held vertically or a climbing movement when the device is held diagonally. User can change the view by combining a navigation button and a single finger dragging.

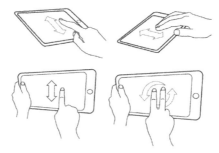

Fig. 8. Gesture and different 3D orientation for displacement in virtual world

When user don't press constraint or navigation buttons, the 3D cursor is fixed in space and it acts as a Drawing Area. Tactile display become a drawing tablet and Users can create freehand sketches by either finger or pressure-sensitive stylus (Fig. 9). The sketches create on the tablet are replicated on the Drawing space in virtual world. User can zoom the draw area using pinch gesture. For non-planar sketches (free 3D sketches), user can sketch while using one of the four constraint modes allowing the 3D cursor to move during sketching.

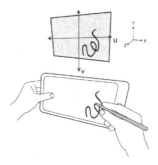

Fig. 9. Sketching in Hyves-3D

Objects can be selected using the 3D cursor via Butterfly-Net metaphor. The 3D objects intersected by the 3D cursor are alternatively selected/deselected. When an object is selected, affine transformations, such as moving, rotating, scaling, and duplicating, can be done.

4   Hyves-3D Interface Utilization

Different experimentations show that the actual interface is only used 28% during an activity [18]. For 72% of time, the system is on standby. By observing log-files from Hyve-3D application, Authors find out that all of the navigation, 3D cursor placement, and sketching were efficient (Fig. 10). In total, 38% of the active time was used for navigation which was followed by 34% for 3D cursor placement and 28% for sketching.

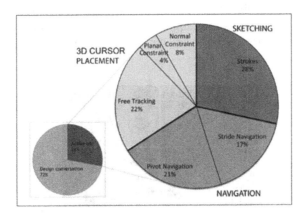

Fig. 10. Utilization of interface during observation

5 Leap-Motion

Leap Motion is an USB sensor device released in July 2013 by Leap Motion Inc. Leap motion controller is new interactive devices mainly aiming at hand gestures and finger position detection. It could detect palm and fingers movements on top of it (Fig. 11). He is designed to provide real-time tracking of hands and fingers in three-dimensional space with 0.01-millimeter accuracy. It allows a user to get information about objects located in device's field of view (about 150 degree with distance not exceeding 1 m). Details of how Leap Motion performs 3D scene capturing have not been revealed by Leap Motion, Inc. Hardware consists of three infrared LEDs which are used for scene illumination, while two cameras, spaced 4 cm apart, capture images with 50–200 fps framerates, dependent whether USB 2.0 or 3.0 is used.

Fig. 11. Leap motion device

Information sent by LeapMotion, are the position of a hand, but also physical properties such as the width and length of the hand and arm as well as the width and length of each digit and the four bones associated with each digit. In addition to these properties, the Leap recognizes certain movement patterns as "gestures" (Fig. 12). There are four currently recognized gestures: a circle, a swipe, a key tap, and a screen tap [19]. A circle gesture is simply a single finger drawing a circle; a swipe is a long linear movement of a finger; a key tap is a finger rotating slightly downwards and back up; and a screen tap is a finger moving forward and backward quickly. These four gestures, have their own properties, such as speed.

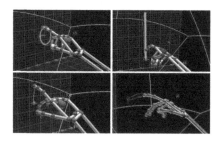

Fig. 12. Basic gestures recognized by leap motion

Hand gesture interfaces provide an intuitive and natural way for interacting with a wide range of applications. The LEAP motion controller has been specifically designed to interact with these applications. Leap motion is a perfect device to produce freehand drawing recognition algorithms to interpret the tracking data of the hand and finger movements. The device can detect four different hands and permits a collaborative work.

6 Grammar of Air Gestures in Omnidirectional Immersive Environment

Today, we find a lot of studies that present interest of mid-air gesture in unidirectional environment [7–10] or [11]. Studies in omnidirectional immersive environments are more confidential. The main reason is that it is not easy to possess these infrastructures. Omni-directional interfaces, such as CAVE displays [20], room displays [3], cone displays [4], or dome displays [5] offer an interesting solution. With these displays, research associated, are focused on problem of rendering. Interactions in immersive virtual environments have been an important research area with most solutions requiring the use of tracked/connected gloves or styli. One of more completed solution is the one proposed by Benko and Wilson [21] combine speech commands with freehand pinch and clasping gestures and infrared laser pointers. To interact with these omnidirectional environments with a gestural interface you need to build an intuitive grammar of gestures. Rovelo [22] has proved for an OVD system, that it is very difficult to find a consensual gesture to realize an interaction. It obtained different propositions to execute different actions like: play, stop, pause, forward. Evaluation shows too that gesture are different if you alone or if you work in a collaborative way (Fig. 13).

Fig. 13. Gesture for: play, pause, stop, skip scene, fast forward, go backward, pan and zoom and an example how participants mirrored gesture

   Our working hypothesis is that interactions in omnidirectional immersive systems, like Hyves-3D, cannot be efficiently performed with a single type of device. We believe that a mid-air gestures device can be a complementary mode of interaction to realize a set of specific tasks like sketching or moving in virtual world. All Hyves-3D interactions can be grouped into 4 categories:

- Moving interaction (Forward, backward, up, down, position in space, go back, turn etc.).
- Drawing interaction (sketching, erasing, coloring, etc.).
- Working interactions (working zone, working stats, collaborative exchanges, etc.).
- Manipulation interaction (single object selection, multi-objects selection, rotation, position, scale, assembly, etc.).

Today, moving inside a virtual Hyves-3D environment is a little constraining. For example, navigating in virtual world require: activate the moving mode (navigation button), to define an orientation of tactile tablet, dragging gesture moves in the desired 3D direction [18]. For a long displacement, the same dragging gesture has to be reproduce in large numbers. The movement is jerky and the time to realize an action could be long. A sketch is built on tablet. Users have on a reduce screen, the projection of only one part of all the virtual world. Architect quick sketches with a pen on the screen of tablet and observes the result on hemispheric display. We note two problems. First one is the user have only a restrictive representation of the world on tablet. If the sketching hang over his 3D cursor projection, to realize a large sketching becomes complicated. The second one is that user needs visually to go back and forth from tablet to large display and loses the complete perception of environment.

A Mid-Air gestures interface, and more specifically the leap motion device, could be used by at least two categories: drawing (sketching) in space and fluid displacements in the scene (showing the direction).

- Drawing is space is:
  - Natural
  - Efficient
  - Not limited to tablet screen
  - Accurate
- Moving in the virtual world showing a direction:
  - Intuitive gestures without learning forward, up, scale, turn, etc.
  - Continuity of movement as long as the gesture is performed.

Most of the mid-air gesture frameworks provide standard gestures that are easy to use for interactions linked to the system or the device functionalities. However, more complex gestures are often difficult to implement and to describe. Kammer et al. [23, 24], for tactile interactions, contributes to formalize gestures interactions, complex or not. They have described a formalization of gestures for multi-touch contacts based on semiotics, which describes all phenomena associated with the production and interpretation of signs and symbols. In this context, they have created a syntax based on atomic gestures and able to describe gestures or sequences of gestures (Fig. 14).

```
1F(HOLD(o))  +  1F(SEMICIRCLE(o))
```

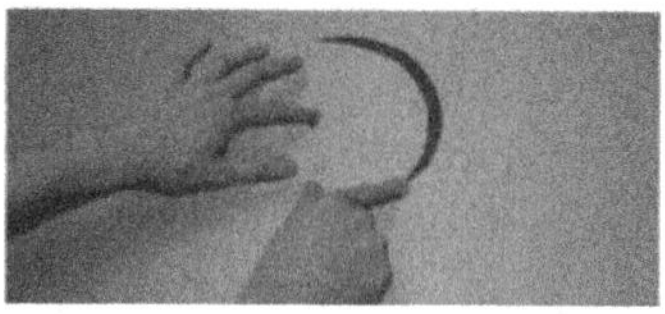

Fig. 14. Rotate gesture described by GeForm grammar and resulting gesture

Based on this approach, we propose a pseudo formalization of LeapMotion interactions. Derived from the extended Backus-Naur form (EBNF), we define blow the language of interaction. In the EBNF, the following characters represent operators (by order of increasing importance):

- + concatenation
- | choice
- = definition
- ; termination

Sketching and moving in virtual world we defined six atomic gestures; all are recognized by LeapMotion (Table 1):

Table 1. Different gestures used for our application.

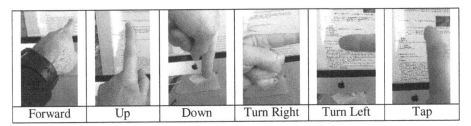

| Forward | Up | Down | Turn Right | Turn Left | Tap |

Moreover, LeapMotion device has the possibility to detect that user grasps a pencil (Fig. 15).

Fig. 15. Pencil detection and Line Drawing with LeapMotion[©]

LeapMotion Interactions can be described by the following pseudo expressions:

LeapInteraction ::= Mov*| Sketch*
Sketch ::= Tap + Draw* + Tap
Draw ::= Tool + Line *
Tool ::= True| False
Mov ::= Gesture*
Gesture ::= Forward | Up | Down | Turn Right | Turn Left;

Note that backward it's just a Forward with opposite direction (or after a rotation Right/Left of 360°).

7   LeapMotion and Hyve-3D

A technical difficulty is that LeapMotion device need must be integrated to Hyves-3D environment. The first possibility is to adapter this device on central consol. To realize a mid-air interaction, users have to returned compulsorily at the middle of working space. This solution is the easier to develop but the less adapted to free interactions in all space. The second one is to couple current interface (iPad) and Leap Motion (like additional trackers used today). For this we have designed a base on which we fit Leap Motion (Fig. 16).

Fig. 16. Ipad-leap assembly

However, it is by no means a perfect solution. To access of mid-air gestures, user can for example to turn Ipad. System can detect the iPad orientation and turn off current action to activate sketching and moving way. The disadvantage of this solution is the necessity to still have a wire connection (to server computer) and to separate interaction modes. The last solution is to couple LeapMotion with an Arduino system by USB and create another separate enter point. The system must will be self-powered and exchanges with server will be done by WIFI. The last both solutions are investigated today.

8   First Evaluation

We conducted a first comparative investigation on the satisfaction rate when users manipulate both interfaces to move in a virtual world. It was impossible for use to develop an application in hyves-3D (SDK under development). We had simulated a close progression with basic movements realized in Hyves-3D: Forward, Backward, Up, Down, Turn Right, Turn Left. The same dragging gesture was reproduced for long displacement with iPad. The focus group constituted with 15 members (8 men – 7 women) aged from 27 to 50 years old (avg 32.6). Everybody have used a tactile tablet but nobody the device LeapMotion (4 have used a Kinect to play to tennis game). Users had to move in a pseudo-labyrinth with two devices: IPad and LeapMotion. The time to realize progression was not controlled. Users were asked to indicate their printing on a Likert scale (5 level, 0: unhappy– 5 happy). We don't have indicated the gesture to perform for backward move. The only gestures presented were those in Table 1 (without Tap). The users had to rotate 360° to go back.

The results show that on the majority of movements the Mid-air gestures obtain better satisfaction score for this area of utilization (Table 2).

Table 2. Average scores

	Forward	Backward	Up	Down	Turn right	Turn left
Ipad satisfaction	3.1	3.1	2.7	2.7	3.1	3.1
Leap satisfaction	4.2	2.8	4.2	3.2	4.1	4.1

The only one gesture where the score is better when focus group used a tablet is for backward move. In first time users try to turn wrist with index finger pointing to themselves. It was not a comfortable position and they didn't obtain the intended result (not defined in our application). In addition, the wrist was sometimes occluded by the arm (One tried to turn around device).

We also found that to indicate right or left direction, users preferred to use opposite hand.

9   Conclusion and Future Works

This work in progress try to prove that Mid-air gesture is an intuitive solution to interact with an omnidirectional immersive system. According to our previous studies on tactile interaction, we propose a pseudo grammar and a set of gestures reserved for sketching and moving in virtual world. The first results show that Mid-air gestures are well adapted to carry out different actions like the displacement in 3D space. The satisfaction rate is promising and high and scoring above IPad. The next step is to integrate the Mid-air device to Hyve-3D environment. When all technical problems will be solved, we hope to prove that such interfaces are more efficient that tactile interactions used today. We hope quickly solve technical solutions and integrate Leap Motion device in an omnidirectional immersive environment and realize more evaluations in situ. We hope to prove too that drawing lines in 3D, by reproducing identically the natural gesture, should be more efficient and more easy and, in the medium term, generalize LeapMotion to a large set of interactions like manipulation of objects, modeling and the management of environment.

References

1. Rheingold, H.: Virtual Reality. Summit, New York (1991)
2. Cruz-Neira, C., Sandin, D.J., DeFanti, T.A., Kenyon, R., Hart, J.C.: The CAVE, audio visual experience automatic virtual environment. Commun. ACM **35**, 64–72 (1992)
3. Hua, H., Brown, L.D., Gao, C.: Scape: supporting stereoscopic collaboration in augmented and projective environments. IEEE Comput. Graph. Appl. **24**(1), 66–75 (2004)
4. Simon, A., Göbel, M.: The i-Cone – a panoramic display system for virtual environments. In: Proceedings of Pacific Conference on Computer Graphics and Applications, pp. 3–7 (2002)
5. Magnor, M., Sen, P., Kniss, J., Angel, E., Wenger, S.: Progress in rendering and modeling for digital planetariums. In: Proceedings of EUROGRAPHICS 2010 (2010)
6. Benko H. Wilson A.D.: Multi-point interactions with immersive omnidirectional visualizations in a dome. In: ITS 2010, pp. 19–28, Saarbrucken (2010)

7. Wang, R., Paris, S., Popovic, J.: 6d hands: markerless hand-tracking for computer aided design. In: Proceedings of the 24th Annual ACM Symposium on User Interface Software and Technology (2011)
8. Hilliges, O., Kim, D., Izadi, S., Weiss, M., Wilson, A.: Holodesk: direct 3d interactions with a situated see-through display. In: Proceedings of the SIGCHI Conference on Human Factors in Computing Systems (2012)
9. De Araujo, B.R., Casiez, G., Jorge, J.A.: Mockup builder: direct 3D modeling on and above the surface in a continuous interaction space. In: GI 2012 - 38th Graphics Interface conference, May 2012, Toronto, Canada, pp. 173–180. Canadian Information Processing Society (2012)
10. Song, P., Goh, W.B., Hutama, W., Fu, C.-W., Liu, X.: A handle bar metaphor for virtual object manipulation with mid-air interaction. In: CHI 2012, Texas, pp. 1297–1306 (2012)
11. Rodrigues, V., Mendes, D., Ferreira, A., Jorge, J.: Mid-air manipulation of 3D models in (Semi-)Immersive virtual environments. In: SciTecIN 2015, pp. 100–108 (2015)
12. Landsdown, J.: Visualizing design ideas. In: MacDonald, L., Vince, J. (eds.) Interacting with Virtual Environments, pp. 61–77. Wiley, Toronto (1994)
13. Gross, M.D., Do, E.Y.-L.: Ambiguous intentions: a paper-like interface for creative design. In: Proceedings of the ACM Symposium on User Interface Software and Technology, Seattle, WA, 6–8 November 1996, pp. 183–192. ACM, New York (1996)
14. Daru, R.: Sketch as sketch can: design sketching with imperfect aids and sketchpads of the future. In: Pittioni, G. (ed.) Proceedings of the eCAADe Conference: Experiences with CAAD in Education and Practice, Munich, Germany, 17–19 October 1991, pp. 162–172. eCAADe, Munich (1991)
15. Goel, V.: Sketches of Thought. MIT Press, Cambridge (1994)
16. Dorta, T., Lesage, A., Pérez, E.: Design tools and collaborative ideation. In: Proceeding CAAD Futures 2009, pp. 65–76 (2009)
17. http://www.hyve3d.com
18. Dorta, T., Kinayoglu, G., Hoffmann, M.: Hyves-3D and 3D-Cursor: architectural co-design with freedom in virtual reality. IJAC 4(2), 87–102 (2016)
19. Chan, A., Halevi, T., Memon, N.: Leap motion controller for authentication via hand geometry and gestures. In: Tryfonas, T., Askoxylakis, I. (eds.) HAS 2015. LNCS, vol. 9190, pp. 13–22. Springer, Cham (2015). doi:10.1007/978-3-319-20376-8_2
20. Cruz-Neira, C., Sandin, D.J., DeFanti, T.A.: Surround-screen projection-based virtual reality: the design and implementation of the CAVE. In: Proceedings of ACM SIGGRAPH 1993, pp. 135–142 (1993)
21. Benko, H., Wilson, A.: Multi-point interactions with immersive omnidirectional visualizations in a dome. In: ITS 2010, pp. 19–28 (2010)
22. Rovelo, G., Vanacken, D., Luyten, K., Abad, F., Camahort, A.: Multi-viewer gesture based interaction for omidirectional video. In: CHI 2014 (2014)
23. Kammer, D., Henkens, D., Henzen, C., Groh, R.: Gesture formalization for multitouch. Softw. Pract. Exper. 45(4), 527–548 (2015)
24. Kammer, D., Wojdziak, J., Keck, M., Groh, R., Taranko, S.: Towards a formalization of multi-touch gestures. In: ACM International Conference on Interactive Tabletops and Surfaces, ITS 2010, pp. 49–58. ACM, New York (2010)

Smart Cities

A Smart City Application for Sharing Up-to-date Road Surface Conditions Detected from Crowdsourced Data

Kenro Aihara[1,2(✉)], Piao Bin[1], Hajime Imura[3], Atsuhiro Takasu[1,2], and Yuzuru Tanaka[3]

[1] National Institute of Informatics,
2-1-2 Hitotsubashi, Chiyoda-ku, Tokyo 101-8430, Japan
{kenro.aihara,piaobin,takasu}@nii.ac.jp
[2] The Graduate University for Advanced Studies, Hayama, Japan
[3] Hokkaido University, N-13, W-8, Sapporo, Hokkaido 060-8628, Japan
{hajime,tanaka}@meme.hokudai.ac.jp

Abstract. This paper introduces a smart city application to share road conditions. The application is based on a mobile sensing framework to collect sensor data reflecting personal-scale, or microscopic, roadside phenomena using crowdsourcing. To collect data, a driving recorder smartphone application that records not only sensor data but also videos from the driver's view is used. To extract specific roadside phenomena, collected data are integrated and analyzed at the service platform. One example is estimating road surface conditions. The paper shows our method to estimate road surface type (RST) and road surface shape (RSS). Features are defined in Sequential Forward Floating Search (SFFS) algorithm from collected data. By using random forest as classifier, average recall was about 91% in the 50 km/h – 80 km/h range. The result may support to build a service that provides detected road conditions from up-to-date crowdsourced mobile sensing application.

Keywords: Smart city · Road condition detection · Mobile sensing · Crowdsourcing · Cyber-physical systems

1 Introduction

Road surface conditions have long been a concern in society because they have a significant impact on transport safety and driving comfort, especially in snowfall areas. It can be seen that about 50% of accidents have occurred on frozen road surfaces. Therefore, it is important to detect frozen road surfaces effectively.

In areas of snowfall, the road surface can have many different states, which will change with weather and volume of traffic. The changes are mainly influenced by two factors: (1) The substance that covers the road surface, such as asphalt, water, snow, and ice, which is called the road surface type (RST); and (2) The shape of the road surface, such as its roughness or frequency of potholes, which is called the road surface shape (RSS).

© Springer International Publishing AG 2017
N. Streitz and P. Markopoulos (Eds.): DAPI 2017, LNCS 10291, pp. 219–234, 2017.
DOI: 10.1007/978-3-319-58697-7_16

Automatically estimating road surface conditions is a critical activity in transport infrastructure management, and many approaches have been proposed. Most make use of expensive sensors to detect road anomalies, or evaluate the road roughness index, however a common problem of these approaches is the high cost of setup and execution. Modern smartphones contain various sensor types such as an accelerometer, gyroscope, and Global Positioning System (GPS), which allow the smartphone to track its position and motion states with a high degree of precision. Because the penetration rate of smartphones is increasing, crowdsourced mobile sensing, used for collecting low-cost smartphone sensor data, has become possible; this allows for the use of an in-vehicle smartphone to monitor and estimate road surface conditions. Estimating road conditions using such sensors, which are usually loosely placed in the car, nonetheless poses a significant challenge.

In this paper, we propose a smart city application "around-the-corner." which enables citizens to share road conditions including traffic and surface conditions. The keys to establish the application are collecting data on road and estimating road surface conditions, by using a motion sensor embedded in a smartphone. To solve the former issue, we proposed a methodology of crowdsourced mobile sensing framework [1], which can collect sensor data reflecting microscopic roadside phenomena using crowdsourcing. In our study, a published smartphone application called 'Drive around-the-corner.' is used. This provides an online driving recorder service to collect both sensor data and videos, recorded from the view of the driver; by using this application, users benefit from a free record of their driving, and we obtain large amounts of low-cost sensor data. Then, we estimate road surface conditions which contain both the RSS and RST factors by analysing such collected sensor data. We have been developing a web application "around-the-corner." to show detected conditions and road events, such as heavy traffic and road constructions.

2   Related Work

2.1   Estimation of Road Surface Conditions Using Acceleration Sensors

For paved roads, most existing work relates to the RSS; for example, the road roughness, or road anomalies such as potholes. The International Roughness Index (IRI) [14] is a standard global index of road roughness, and study [4] shows that the IRI and the Root Mean Square (RMS) of the vertical component of acceleration values, have a high correlation. Using this relationship, it is possible to calculate approximate values of the IRI, however a limitation of the study [4] is that the parameter must be manually adjusted for different vehicles. Another study [15] provides a spring and damper model, which can automatically estimate vehicle parameters including a damping ratio and resonant frequency, and can then use these parameters to calculate approximate values of the IRI. A further study [11] also evaluates the roughness index, but focuses mainly on detecting the changing road conditions. Other research has studied the detection of road surface anomalies, such as potholes; one study [2] provided an improved Gaussian Mixture Model (GMM) for detection of road potholes.

Table 1. Summary of related works

		Estimation target		Estimation accuracy	Robustness	Estimation cost and granularity
		RST	RSS			
Accelerometer	[4]	N	Y	Y	Y	N
	[2,11,15]	N	Y	Y	Y	Y
In-vehicle camera	[8,12,13]	Y	N	N	N	N
	[16]	Y	N	Y	Y	N
Fixed camera	[7]	Y	N	Y	Y	N

2.2 Estimation of Road Surface Condition Using Cameras

In contrast to normal paved roads, most work on snow covered roads concerns the RST, and uses image processing techniques. Studies [8,12,13] use standard in-vehicle camera devices, such as a driving recorder or smartphone. Among these studies, [8,12] can determine wet or snowy conditions with a high degree of accuracy; however, they cannot detect frozen roads that are the most dangerous in snowy areas. Study [13] can detect frozen roads, but with an accuracy of less than 60%. Study [16] also uses an in-vehicle camera to estimate the road surface condition with a high level of accuracy, but it is necessary to attach two polarizing films to the lens. Finally, study [7] used a fixed camera placed at representative points on major roads, and to improve accuracy the study also used weather data; the geographical area covered however, was limited.

2.3 Summary

Table 1 shows a summary of the related work discussed in this section. A common problem is that no single study supports both RSS and RST. Additionally, approaches using motion sensors such as an accelerometer are more robust than those using cameras. For these reasons, in our study we have estimated new road surface conditions using both the RSS and the RST. Furthermore, we have provided a method to estimate newly defined road surface conditions using motion sensors only.

3 Social Drive Recording Service: "Drive around-the-corner."

In February 2015, we developed a drive recorder application called "Drive around-the-corner. (Drive ATC)" This application was made available to the public in February 2016[1]. Drive ATC collects driving behavior logs, records events, and delivers information regarding the vehicle's current position (Fig. 1).

---

[1] https://itunes.apple.com/app/drive-around-the-corner./id1053216595.

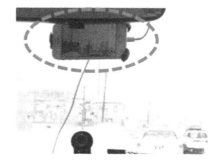

Fig. 1. Smartphone mounting positions.

Table 2. Data collected by Drive around-the-corner.

Type	Attributes
Location	Latitude, longitude, and altitude with accuracy
Heading	True_north with accuracy
Move	Speed, course
Acceleration	x, y, z
Rotation rate	x, y, z

The service can be accessed via the iOS application. Before commencing a journey, users mount their smartphone in a holder and connect a power-supply cable if necessary, and then open the application. The application records driving behavior logs and videos, and uploads them to the service platform.

3.1 Sensing Functions

Onboard Location and Motion Sensors. The Drive ATC application obtains location and motion data from onboard sensors. While users are driving and using the application, behavior logs and movies are recorded. The data that are collected are pooled in the local data store and then transmitted to the service platform. The data that are collected are shown in Table 2.

Movies. The Drive ATC application records two types of movies, one to be uploaded and the other to be saved locally. To reduce traffic to the service platform, uploaded movies are transferred intermittently, the frame rate being adjusted in accordance with the speed of the vehicle.

Because these movies are uploaded via a mobile network such as 3G or LTE, they should be compressed. The movies that are saved locally are of higher quality and can be used as evidence in the event of an accident.

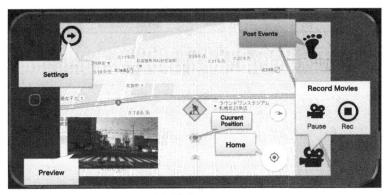

(a) Main screen

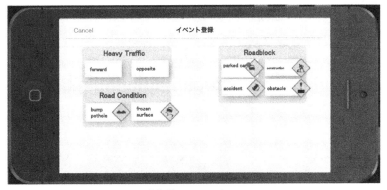

(b) Event options

Fig. 2. The "Drive around-the-corner." application. Traffic information, user-posted events, events extracted from sensor data, and footprints, are shown on the main screen map. (Color figure online)

3.2 User Functions

Map with Event Information. When the Drive ATC application is opened, it shows a map of the current location (Fig. 2a). Roadside events are retrieved from the service platform and shown on the map. For example, the yellow icon located at the center of Fig. 2a denotes road construction. This information has previously been posted by other Drive ATC users.

Posting Event. To enable users to report a roadside event to others while they are stationary, the application provides them with the ability to post event information. After tapping the footprint marker in the top right corner, users are requested to select an event that they recognize (Fig. 2b). There are eight possible events grouped into three categories: heavy traffic, road condition, and roadblock. The selected event is posted to the service platform with details of the current time and location.

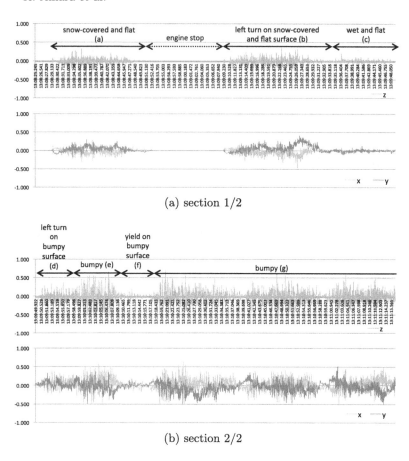

(a) section 1/2

(b) section 2/2

Fig. 3. An example of recorded acceleration data (Color figure online)

3.3 An Example of Collected Data

Figure 3 shows an example of acceleration data collected from a vehicle in Sapporo. The green line represents the z-axis (vertical) offset acceleration value for gravity. The blue and red lines represent the x-axis (the axle direction of the car) and y-axis (the heading direction), respectively. Figure 4 illustrates scenes from the journey shown in Fig. 3.

At first, the car travels on a wide road covered with snow (Fig. 4a). The surface of the road is frozen, but even. The acceleration, represented by the green line in Fig. 3a of this segment oscillates below $0.3 \, \text{m/s}^2$. Next, the car stops for a red light. The car's engine is automatically shut down by the start–stop system, and the oscillation falls to the minimum level. Then, the car moves to the next intersection and turns left onto a wet road. The increase in transverse acceleration represented by the red line in Fig. 3a indicates the left-hand turn. The acceleration increases significantly because this wet road is more stable than the previous frozen road (Fig. 4b).

(a) a broad flat road, covered with snow   (b) a wet road

(c) a narrow bumpy frozen road   (d) a narrow snow-covered road

Fig. 4. Example scenes (Color figure online)

The car then turns left onto a narrower road. The road is frozen, but is uneven because the ice is thawing. The car travels very slowly and pitches wildly (Fig. 4c). Its acceleration reaches more than $0.5\,\mathrm{m/s^2}$, and even rolling and yawing are recognized because the car slips and drifts on the road (Fig. 3b).

4 Detecting Road Surface Conditions

In previous studies, many road monitoring systems have used image processing techniques [3, 16] whereby the video cameras are usually placed at representative points on the main roads or mounted on the dashboards of vehicles. However, the effectiveness of the cameras may be impacted by factors such as low light levels at night time or snowfall. Further, this method cannot identify the surface conditions when a frozen road surface has been covered by a layer of snow.

To enable the detection of road surface conditions from the collected data, we studied a methodology for estimating the condition of snow-covered roads using the collected motion values. This method extracts features from both the time domain and the spectral domain of data collected from accelerometers and gyroscopes.

4.1 Road Surface Condition Definition

We define a set of both road surface types (RST) and road surface shapes (RSS). The set of RST includes four elements: paved, sherbet, compacted snow, and

(a) flat road surface with asphalt   (b) frozen road surface with bumpy

(c) frozen road surface with potholes   (d) mirror-like frozen road surface

(e) sherbet road surface with potholes   (f) flat road surface with snowfall

Fig. 5. Three kinds of road surfaces

frozen. A sherbet road surface means that the road surface, which is covered by snow, contains water or ice. The set of RSS also includes four elements: Smooth, bumpy, potholes, and potholes/bumpy. A smooth surface shape means that the road is flat, regardless of whether snow has fallen. Tables 3 and 4 show details of these; the new road surface conditions are defined by the cartesian product of these two sets.

Figure 5 shows some examples of the defined road surface conditions. Figure 5b, c, and d show frozen road surfaces with different RSS. In snowy areas, these are the most dangerous road types; even cars fitted with winter tires may slip. Figure 5e shows a sherbet road surface with some potholes; although this kind of road is less hazardous than frozen roads, it will affect vehicle speed. Figure 5f shows a road covered with compacted snow; although the road has a covering of snow, driving on this kind of road is usually normal.

Table 3. Road surface type definitions

Road surface	Definitions
Paved road	The surface is paved with asphalt or concrete, and with no snow or ice on the surface
Sherbet	The surface is covered by mixed water and snow ice
Compacted snow	The surface is covered with dry snow
Frozen	The surface is covered with ice

Table 4. Road surface shape definitions

Road surface	Definitions
Smooth	A flat road surface with no bumps or potholes
Bumpy	A flat road surface with many raised parts
Potholes	A road surface with some large holes
Bumpy & potholes	A mixed road surface with bumps and potholes

4.2 Estimating Road Surface Conditions

As mentioned in Sect. 2, most related work has focused only on vertical direction acceleration when estimating road surface conditions, when in fact road surface conditions generate other vehicle in-motion values. We, however, realized in our preliminary experiment that not only vertical but also horizontal acceleration values of frozen and rough road are greater than of compacted and smooth road. The reason for the horizontal motion may be due to the car slipping in a horizontal direction despite the driver preference to keep the driving direction forwards only. We, therefore, can assume from this example that the motion values may reflect both the type and shape of the road surface. If this assumption is true, we can use motion values to classify only road surface conditions that include both type and shape.

4.3 Feature Extraction

In the field of human activity recognition, many effective features have been published using motion sensor data; in our study, these were used as an initial feature set. In our method, signals from each axis of the accelerometer and gyroscope are segmented into windows of 2 s, with a 50% overlap between two consecutive windows. We use x_a, y_a, and z_a to denote the three axes of the accelerometer, and use x_g, y_g, and z_g to denote the three axes of the gyroscope. For both the accelerometer and gyroscope, the x-axis is the direction of the car axle, the y-axis is the direction in which the car is heading, and the z-axis is the vertical direction. Table 5 shows the details of the initial feature set. The extracted features have 67 dimensions in total.

Table 5. Initial set of features for estimating road surface condition

Type of feature	Features
Mean	$mean_t$ $(t \in \{x_a, y_a, z_a, x_g, y_g, z_g\})$
Standard deviation	std_t $(t \in \{x_a, y_a, z_a, x_g, y_g, z_g\})$
Correlation	$correlation_t$ $(t \in \{x_a\_y_a, y_a\_z_a, z_a\_x_a, x_g\_y_g, y_g\_z_g, z_g\_x_g\})$
Energy	$energy_{t_i}$ $(t \in \{x_a, y_a, z_a, x_g, y_g, z_g\}, i \in [0, 4])$
Entropy	$entropy_t$ $(t \in \{x_a, y_a, z_a, x_g, y_g, z_g\})$
Max	max_t $(t \in \{x_a, y_a, z_a, x_g, y_g, z_g\})$
Min	min_t $(t \in \{x_a, y_a, z_a, x_g, y_g, z_g\})$
Mean speed	msp_t $(t \in \{x_a, y_a, z_a, x_g, y_g, z_g\})$

4.4   Features Selection

A good feature set helps to improve the efficiency of the classification algorithms and enables accurate classification. Numerous feature selection algorithms have been published. Among them, the PCA, Relief-F, and SFFS are three popular algorithms for feature selection. To select the best features from the initial feature set, we compared these three algorithms to choose the best one. In this study, we determined the criteria of choice as the number of features that provide the best accuracy with the random forest classifiers. For evaluating the accuracy, we used the ten-fold cross-validation approach.

PCA is a mathematical algorithm that reduces the dimensionality of the data while retaining most of the variation in the data set [6]. It accomplishes this reduction by identifying directions, called principal components, along which the variation in the data is maximal. Using this algorithm to select features, we gradually increased the number of PCA components beginning with two PCA components and calculated the accuracy each time for all the 67 PCA components. Finally, the least number of features that provided maximum accuracy were selected.

Relief-F is a filter-based feature selection method used for the weight estimation of a feature [9,10]. The weight of a feature of a measurement vector is defined in terms of the feature relevance. The features were sorted according to their relevance in decreasing order. The most relevant feature was first added and the accuracy of the given dataset was found using random forest classifiers. Subsequently, the successive relevant features were added sequentially, and the accuracy was calculated each time until all the 67 features were added. Finally, the least number of features that provided maximum accuracy was selected.

SFFS is a wrapper-based feature selection method [5]. It uses a classification scheme as a wrapper around which the whole feature selection is carried out. It starts with an empty set for the desired selected features "X". The features are to be selected from a larger set of features "S". Let's be the most significant feature in S with respect to X, which provides the least accuracy when included in X. At each iteration, the most significant feature in S is included in X if its inclusion does not increase the accuracy. Similarly, the least significant feature in X is found and removed if its exclusion helps improve the accuracy.

4.5 Classification

In this study, we use the random forest classifiers to classify the road surface conditions based on the folders for cross validation. A random forest classifier is an ensemble learning method that constructs a multitude of decision trees at training time. It is one of the most successful ensemble learning techniques that has proved to be very popular and powerful in pattern recognition and machine learning for high-dimensional classification and imbalanced problems.

According to the study [2], different speeds of a vehicle will affect the values of the frequency and the amplitude of the motion, even for a vehicle driving on the same road under the same conditions. In this study, we divided the velocity domain into intervals of 10 km/h. The road-surface condition was classified across different speed ranges using the random forest classifier.

4.6 Experimental Results and Discussion

Datasets. The road condition labels were manually generated by three people living in an area of snowfall. The actual ground conditions were determined by voting results from these three people. In addition to the road surface conditions, the acceleration and gyro are also affected by the car, driver, smartphone, and the mount. To reduce these factors, we used the same car and driver, with the same smartphone and mount; differences in motions should thus be affected only by road conditions and driving behavior. We used the dataset from one user, and Fig. 6 shows the numbers of each road condition at different speed ranges. Because the drive recorder application was used during daily driving, imbalances inevitably occurred in the collected data.

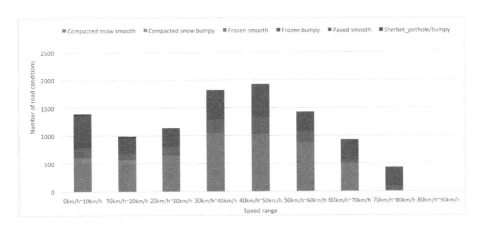

Fig. 6. Numbers of each road condition at different speed ranges

Feature Selection and Classification Accuracy. To select the best features from the initial feature set, we compared three kinds of feature selection algorithm: The PCA, the Relief-F, and the SFFS. Each algorithm is evaluated against the accuracy of the random forest, with ten folders for cross validation. Figure 7 shows the selected features from three feature selection algorithms, and Fig. 8 shows the performance index comparisons for random forest classifiers, combined with the feature selected algorithms; the SFFS algorithm is most effective, with fewer features and higher accuracy in each speed range.

Based on the results above, we decided to use SFFS as the feature selection algorithm. In this study, the classification was evaluated against the recall of the random forest, with ten folders for cross validation. The recall is defined as

$$Recall = \frac{TP}{TP + FN} \tag{1}$$

where TP is the number of true positives, and FN the number of false negatives. Figure 9 shows the results of the SFFS + Random forest classification across

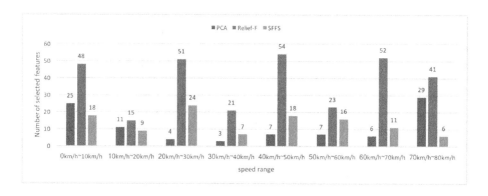

Fig. 7. Selected features from three feature selection algorithms

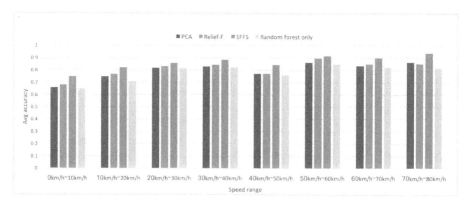

Fig. 8. Performance index comparisons for random forest classifiers, combined with the feature selected algorithms

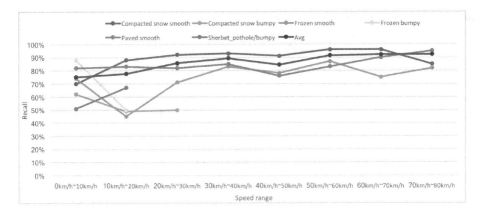

Fig. 9. Results of the SFFS + Random forest classification, across different speed ranges

	0km/h	10km/h	20km/h	30km/h	40km/h	50km/h	60km/h	70km/h	80km/h
corr_az_ax									
Std_gx									
energy_gz_4									
energy_gx_1									
energy_gy_4									
corr_gy_gz									
entropy_az									
max_az									
energy_ay_1									
mean_gx									
min_gz									
energy_az_0									
energy_gz_0									
energy_gx_2									
energy_gx_4									

Fig. 10. Details of the selected features by using the SFFS in different speed ranges

different speed ranges; the results show that the best average of recall, of about 91%, was obtained in the 50 km/h – 80 km/h range. We, therefore, could confirm that the road surface conditions can be effectively classified by using only the motion values when the speed is greater than 50 km/h. In particular, we could confirm that the most dangerous frozen road can be classified by using only the motion values.

Figure 10 shows the details of the major features selected by using the SFFS. The most common features in different speed ranges are the correlation between the directions of the vertical and the car axle, the standard deviation of the pitching of the vehicle, and the high frequency energy.

Discussion. From the experimental results, we can see that the more complex RSS such as bumpy and potholes are distributed in the low-speed range, and accuracy of the classification between them is very low. One of the reasons is that we have not quantitatively defined the RSS.

In this paper, we have described an estimation method for the road-surface condition by using only one vehicle. However, in the future, we need to estimate the road surface conditions by using multiple vehicles. Many factors influence vertical motion values. One of the factors is the type of vehicle. Length of the wheelbase and the strength of the suspension differ depending on the type of vehicle, and we believe these aspects have an influence on the motion values. The other factor is the individual's driving style. We infer that the motion values change differently, depending on the individual's driving technique and experience. We need to verify the relationship between these factors and the motion values in the future.

5   Web Application: "around-the-corner."

Users can access the service website to check on the current situation and review their journey and driving performance[2]. Figure 11 illustrates the website, which

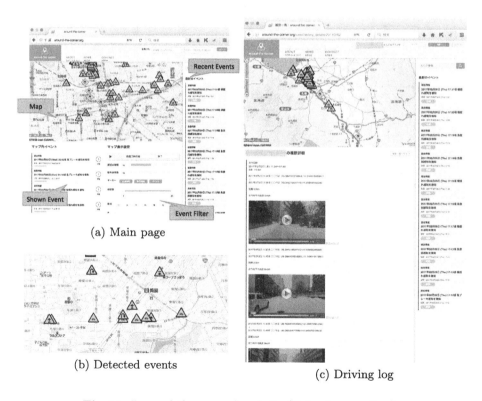

(a) Main page

(b) Detected events

(c) Driving log

Fig. 11. "around-the-corner." website (Color figure online)

---

[2] http://around-the-corner.org/.

mainly consists of a map and a list of detected events. All visitors to the website can view event information in either map or list form (Fig. 11a). On the right of the main page, up-to-date events are listed. When they select one event on the list, the icon of the selected event will be placed on the map. Each event is represented on the map by a corresponding icon. Under the map, shown events on the current map are listed. Displayed events can be filtered by users with the controller in the page. Users can set the target time period, time range, days of the week, month, and types of events.

Events include both detected based on collected and anonymized data and posted by users. Figure 11b illustrates some detected events, such as hard braking and lateral vibration, on map.

Registered users can also log in and access their own driving records. Figure 11c illustrates an example of driving records. The drive route is denoted by a red line. And also, they can view a timeline of the drive under the map including uploaded images. They can also play back uploaded movies.

6   Conclusion

This paper introduces a smart city application to share road conditions. The application is based on a mobile sensing framework to collect sensor data reflecting personal-scale, or microscopic, roadside phenomena using crowdsourcing. To motivate users to get involved in the service, it must deliver the useful information or service to them. It, therefore, is quite important to extract useful information from collected data.

In the experiment of detecting road surface conditions, we could obtain the result of about 91% average recall in the 50 km/h – 80 km/h range. We suppose that the result supports to build a web service that provides detected road conditions from up-to-date crowdsourced mobile sensing application.

We have been improving a method to estimate road conditions. We need to gather more data (and users) to evaluate our methodology and approach.

Acknowledgments. The authors would like to thank City of Sapporo, Hokkaido Government, Hokkaido Chuo Bus Co., Ltd. for their cooperation with this research.

This research was supported by "Research and Development on Fundamental and Utilization Technologies for Social Big Data" of the Commissioned Research of National Institute of Information and Communications Technology (NICT), Japan. And also it was partly supported by the CPS-IIP Project in the research promotion program "Research and Development for the Realization of Next-Generation IT Platforms" of the Ministry of Education, Culture, Sports, Science and Technology of Japan (MEXT).

References

1. Aihara, K., Bin, P., Imura, H., Takasu, A., Tanaka, Y.: On feasibility of crowd-sourced mobile sensing for smarter city life. In: Streitz, N., Markopoulos, P. (eds.) DAPI 2016. LNCS, vol. 9749, pp. 395–404. Springer, Cham (2016). doi:10.1007/978-3-319-39862-4_36
2. Chen, K., Lu, M., Tan, G., Wu, J.: Crsm: crowdsourcing based road surface monitoring. In: 2013 IEEE 10th International Conference on High Performance Computing and Communications & 2013 IEEE International Conference on Embedded and Ubiquitous Computing (HPCC_EUC), pp. 2151–2158. IEEE (2013)
3. Feng, F.: Winter Road Surface Condition Estimation and Forecasting. Ph.D. thesis, University of Waterloo, Ontario, Canada (2013)
4. Fujino, Y., Kitagawa, K., Furukawa, T., Ishii, H.: Development of Vehicle Intelligent Monitoring System (VIMS). In: Proceedings of the SPIE, Part 1 edn., vol. 5765, pp. 148–157 (2005)
5. Jain, A., Zongker, D.: Feature selection: evaluation, application, and small sample performance. IEEE Trans. Pattern Anal. Mach. Intell. 19(2), 153–158 (1997)
6. Jolliffe, I.: Principal Component Analysis. Springer, New York (1986)
7. Jonsson, P.: Classification of road conditions: from camera images and weather data. In: 2011 IEEE International Conference on Computational Intelligence for Measurement Systems and Applications (CIMSA), pp. 1–6. IEEE (2011)
8. Kawai, S., Takeuchi, K., Shibata, K., Horita, Y.: A method to distinguish road surface conditions for car-mounted camera images at night-time. In: 2012 12th International Conference on ITS Telecommunications (ITST), pp. 668–672. IEEE (2012)
9. Kira, K., Rendell, L.A.: A practical approach to feature selection. In: Proceedings of the Ninth International Workshop on Machine Learning, pp. 249–256 (1992)
10. Kononenko, I.: Estimating attributes: analysis and extensions of RELIEF. In: Bergadano, F., Raedt, L. (eds.) ECML 1994. LNCS, vol. 784, pp. 171–182. Springer, Heidelberg (1994). doi:10.1007/3-540-57868-4_57
11. Nomura, T., Shiraishi, Y.: A method for estimating road surface conditions with a smartphone. Int. J. Inf. Soc. 7(1), 29–36 (2015)
12. Omer, R., Fu, L.: An automatic image recognition system for winter road surface condition classification. In: 2010 13th International IEEE Conference on Intelligent Transportation Systems (ITSC), pp. 1375–1379. IEEE (2010)
13. Qian, Y., Almazan, E.J., Elder, J.H.: Evaluating features and classifiers for road weather condition analysis. In: 2016 IEEE International Conference on Image Processing (ICIP), pp. 4403–4407. IEEE (2016)
14. Sayers, M.: On the calculation of international roughness index from longitudinal road profile. Transp. Res. Rec. 1501, 1–12 (1995)
15. Yagi, K.: A measuring method of road surface longitudinal profile from sprung acceleration, and verification with road profiler. J. Jpn. Soc. Civ. Eng. Ser. E1 (Pavement Eng.) 69(3), I-1–I-7 (2013)
16. Yamada, M., Ueda, K., Horiba, I., Tsugawa, S., Yamamoto, S.: A study of the road surface condition detection technique based on the image information for deployment on a vehicle. IEEJ Trans. Electron. Inf. Syst. 124(3), 753–760 (2004)

Building a Platform Society Towards Sustainability Based on Internet-of-Things

Hina Akasaki, Fumiko Ishizawa, Mizuki Sakamoto, and Tatsuo Nakajima[✉]

Department of Computer Science and Engineering, Waseda University, Tokyo, Japan
{h.akasaki,f.ishizawa,mizuki,tatsuo}@dcl.cs.waseda.ac.jp

Abstract. In this paper, we present a case study for designing a social platform towards environmental sustainability based on Internet-of-Things. The case study we investigate encourages low carbon communities, in particular, to aim for a car-free city. A car-free city promises to make our society more sustainable; however, people must be guided to choose a desirable lifestyle. We will show how our design framework helps to build a better car-free city without affecting citizens' success. We also show an augmented bicycle prototype that is an Internet of Things (IoT)-enhanced bicycle for promoting bicycle-sharing within communities. Bicycle sharing can help to achieve a car-free city, and IoT-based daily artifacts can contribute to building an effective social platform.

Keywords: Social platforms · Human behavior · Persuasive affordance · Gamification · Low carbon communities · IoT-based technologies · Augmented bike

1 Introduction

Our society must urgently solve a variety of fundamental social issues. For example, in the modern urban lifestyle, people generally consume large amounts of natural resources, which will render future life unsustainable. Internet-of-Thing (IoT) technologies dramatically improve the efficiency of natural resource use; however, the improvement will be limited in the future if we only consider technological factors. We must change our attitudes and behaviors and improve our daily lifestyles to reduce the use of natural resources. Guiding human behavior is crucial to achieving a sustainable society [16]. There are several manners in which to guide human behavior. A typical approach is to use social norms or public policies [11]. A government may conduct public campaigns to promote a sustainable lifestyle to maintain its country's wealth. However, this approach will only be able to improve people's average behavior, and some people may not change their behavior. The situation may be problematic because people who do not change their behavior may receive benefits without contributing effort, and other people will think their situation unfair. Finally, most people may stop contributing to the campaign. Thus, the social situation does not change and may become worse.

We present a case study for designing a social platform towards environmental sustainability based on Internet-of-Things. The case study we investigate encourages low carbon communities [6, 7], in particular, to aim for a car-free city. A car-free city

© Springer International Publishing AG 2017
N. Streitz and P. Markopoulos (Eds.): DAPI 2017, LNCS 10291, pp. 235–251, 2017.
DOI: 10.1007/978-3-319-58697-7_17

promises to make our society more sustainable [3]; however, people must be guided to choose a desirable lifestyle. We will show how our design framework helps to build a better car-free city without affecting citizens' success. We also show an augmented bicycle prototype that is an Internet of Things (IoT)-enhanced bicycle for promoting bicycle-sharing within communities. Bicycle sharing can help to achieve a car-free city, and IoT-based daily artifacts can contribute to building an effective social platform.

The remainder of the paper is organized as follows: In Sect. 2, we present some issues that occur when designing persuasive affordances and an overview of alternative reality. The case study described in Sect. 3 seeks to develop a social platform to encourage low carbon communities to increase environmental sustainability. In Sect. 4, we discuss some lessons learned from the case study, and Sect. 5 concludes the paper.

2   Persuasive Affordances, Alternative Reality and Seligman's PERMA Model

Recently, digital marketing and social media practitioners have adopted an approach to develop information services based on game-based concepts, termed *gamification* [4]. The idea is to use game mechanics, such as the mechanics in online games, to render a task entertaining, encouraging people to conscientiously complete target goals. In traditional gamification, a set of game mechanics is widely adopted to motivate human behavior; however, incorporating game mechanics into the real world is not easy. Thus, simple mechanics such as badges, leaderboards and points are typically used. However, the gamification definition above suggests enhancing digital services with *"affordances for gameful experience,"* which suggests that exploiting the semiotic or rhetorical aspects of video games offers a novel approach to guiding collective human behavior and enhancing our daily lives. Gamification employs the use of affordances to motivate users to engage in the systems with gameful experiences. These affordances are often referred to as motivational affordances [13].

We refine motivational affordances to the persuasive affordances [14] because our focus also includes unconscious social influences [2]. The most common persuasive affordances used in gamification are points, badges, and leaderboards. Other affordances observed in academic studies and commercial applications include levels, challenges, rewards, feedback, clear goals, avatar/theme, and progress. In [15], the authors propose gameful digital rhetoric that is a framework to incorporate pervasive affordances in the real spaces with five types of abstractions named rhetoric.

Alternative Reality makes it possible to connect the real world with the virtual world from a single temporal perspective [12]. The worlds can also be seamlessly integrated because the virtual world consists of real landscapes, objects and persons. This means that it may be possible to enhance the real world by presenting fictional occurrences along with real events, and thus people experience an enhanced hybrid world in the real world rather than in a fictional world (as in a movie). Incorporating fictionality into real space strongly influences human attitudes and behavior. Thus, this approach can be used to guide people towards a more desirable lifestyle.

In *Alternative Reality*, a user watches a sequence of scenes on an HMD. The sequence consists of several scenes. Some scenes are captured from contemporary scenes in the real world. The scenes are recorded by a 360-degree camera and shown on the HMD in real-time. However, some scenes in the sequence are not real scenes; such scenes may actually be constructed through VR techniques and are fictional. Additionally, the virtual scenes may include several events that do not occur in the contemporary real world. Typically, these scenes are constructed using 3D models of real persons, objects and landscapes in advance, but some real persons who are not actually present may appear. One of the important requirements of *Alternative Reality* is that the user feels that these real and virtual scenes are continuous and, thus, is not aware of the boundary between the two scenes. Therefore, he/she feels that the virtual scenes are actually happening in the real world. The most important issue in achieving this immersion is blurring the boundary between fiction and reality.

Seligman defined a well-being theory [17] as a theme of positive psychology. In his book, he identified five factors necessary for humans to flourish in the PERMA model, including *positive emotion, engagement, relationships, meaning,* and *achievement*. The factor of human well-being steers people toward desirable behavior. For example, a husband and wife who have positive images of one another can create a fruitful married life. Additionally, positive emotions reduce the risk of catching a cold or an infectious disease. Seligman claims that people without positivity tend to think that there is no way to improve their everyday lives whereas people with high positivity can act to have more meaningful and productive lives [17]. Therefore, developing a social platform should consider how such a platform helps people achieve human well-being to guide their desirable human behavior. If the requirement is satisfied, diverse people are willing to use the platform.

3   Building Social Platforms Based on IoT-Based Technologies

3.1   Social Platforms for Low Carbon Communities

Low carbon communities works with communities to find sustainable energy solutions [6, 7]. Low carbon communities' activities involve working with households, businesses, schools and community groups to increase awareness of climate change. A car-free city is a population center that relies primarily on public transportation, walking, or cycling within the urban area [3]. Car-free cities greatly reduce petroleum dependency, air pollution, greenhouse gas emissions, automobile crashes, noise pollution, and traffic congestion. With increasing awareness of the urgent need to respond to global warming by reducing carbon emissions and recognizing the social benefits of car-free living, increasingly more city planners, advocates, and everyday urban dwellers are demanding ideas for new manners in which to build cities.

Recently, a variety of urban areas have offered a public bicycle-sharing system [18]. The public bicycle-sharing system is a service in which bicycles are made available for shared use to individuals on a short-term basis. The sharing schemes allow people to borrow a bike from one point and return it to another point. This social platform appears to be effective in encouraging car-free cities. The system is currently available in 50 countries on five continents, including 712 cities, utilizing approximately 806,200 bicycles at 37,500 stations. However, in most cities, the system does not work well primarily because riding bikes in cities is not enjoyable. Typically, the landscape in cities is boring although some small areas in the cities are quite attractive and people generally enjoy riding bikes in those areas.

In this study, we chose a fictional Yokohama city to discuss a manner in which to encourage a car-free city. This area is one of the most popular sightseeing destinations for youth in Japan. In the city, several interesting areas to visit are not accessible by public transportation. Therefore, the majority of young people use their own cars or rental cars to move around the city.

Yokohama has some interesting areas in which people enjoy riding bikes, as shown in Fig. 1. In the *Minato-Mirai* area, there are an amusement park and a museum; in the *Red Brick Warehouse* area, there are many fancy shops; the *Yamashita Park* area is a nice place to sit on a bench; in the *Yamanote* area, there are several historical houses; and in the *China Town* area, there are many excellent Chinese restaurants. However, the landscapes between these attractions are not interesting although each area has its own excellent characteristics that attract visitors.

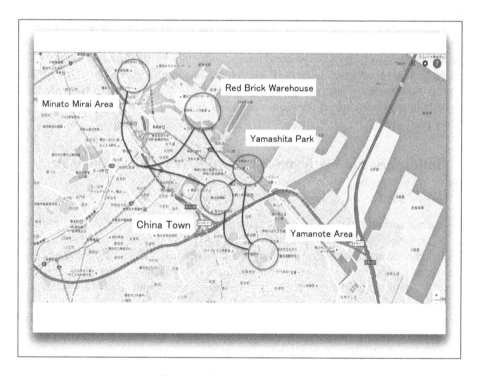

Fig. 1. A fictional yokohama city

3.2   Augmented Bike Concept

In this study, we enhance the city experience to encourage people who visit this Yokohama city to use the public bicycle-sharing system. To discuss our approach, we adopted a research method called design fiction [1] or speculative design [5]. Design fiction or speculative design is a method of critical design that uses fictional and narrative scenarios to envision, explain and raise questions regarding possible future designs for society. Critical questions regarding emerging technology in everyday situations have presented preferable futures as opposed to predicting the future. As shown in Fig. 1, we assume that each area in the Yokohama city is completely car-free. Thus, people can walk or bicycle without worrying about car traffic. In addition, we assume that there are bicycle paths depicted as green lines in these car-free areas and that people ride *Augmented Bikes,* described in the next section, on those paths.

When riding *Augmented Bikes,* people must wear head-mounted displays (HMDs). In the car-free areas, riders can directly see the landscape of the areas. The camera attached to their head-mounted display captures the real-world view of the landscape and shows the view on the HMD. However, when riders are on bicycle paths in car-free areas, the head-mounted display produces landscapes constructed by 3D models or videos capturing scenery pleasing to bike riders. In addition, the HMD makes bicyclists aware of other bikes on the paths to avoid collisions. If people enjoy riding the *Augmented Bikes* in the car-free areas, the public bicycle-sharing system will become more popular.

Incorporating fictionality into the real world is not an easy task. Traditional gamification mechanisms such as points and badges can easily be embedded in reality; however, these mechanisms do not satisfy the requirement of achieving all five factors in the PERMA model. Incorporating fictionality based on *Alternative Reality* into real space addresses the pitfalls because the real world's meaningfulness is increased by enhancing the meaning of the real space. Also, the enhancement makes people more positive.

Augmented Bike is a digitally enhanced daily artifact that augments rental bicycles using *Alternative Reality* with VR and AR technologies. When a new wearable device such as Google Glass or a contact-lens-type display becomes popular and most people wear the device in the near future, the devices can be used for facilitating a car-free city by augmenting rental bicycles with the new wearable devices and motivating people to use a rental bicycle. Using an *Augmented Bike*, people can easily rent a bike by touching their IC cards or using a fingerprint or an implanted IC chip that contains their personal information. Let us imagine a situation in which people always use an HMD and the display does not impede their sight, unlike a current HMD such as Oculus Lift[1]. The *Augmented Bike* enhances people's view and shows additional information on the HMDs that they wear. In addition, traveling distance and trail information are recorded on their smartphones, and people can check the information anytime. Figure 2 presents an overview of the *Augmented Bike* prototype.

---

[1] https://www.oculus.com/.

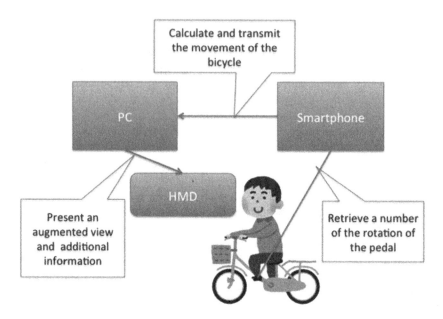

Fig. 2. An overview of augmented bike

When using the *Augmented Bike*, an application program displays the images that enhance a user's current real view on an HMD based on *Alternative Reality* and shows pop-up information regarding the images to provide the rider with additional information. We also developed an application program that records traveling distance and trail information, and we offer some persuasive affordances using graphical changes.

3.3   Scenarios and Their Analyses

In this subsection, we use the case study to explore strategies to design social platforms for sustainability. The research question is how to make diverse people feel good while riding bikes on public bicycle paths. We use a scenario-based analysis [8] to analyze our approach to low carbon communities. We show scenarios in which some persons do not like to use the public bicycle-sharing system of *Augmented Bikes*. The purpose of the analysis is to determine what types of features are missing while using the public bicycle-sharing system and to discuss some solutions to overcome the pitfalls. We analyze the user experience when a user rents a car to go sightseeing, uses a rental bike, and rides on an *Augmented Bike* based on the scenario analysis. A persona in the scenarios stays in Yokohama, one of the most famous cities in Japan, for a week. The developed persona is used in the scenarios as follows.

Rin likes to travel and to tour sightseeing spots; however, she is not happy that it takes so long to get from spot to spot. Because cars are fast and comfortable, she often rents a car and drives it to travel around. Unless the street is particularly beautiful, she drives without enjoying the scenery. Rin likes sightseeing, and she wants to protect the beautiful scenery of sightseeing spots although Rin believes that there is nothing she can do to protect the scenery.

In the following first scenario, Rin drives a rental car.

i. *Rin travels to Yokohama, a famous tourist spot in Japan, and decides to stay there for a week. Rin rents a car and tours and goes sightseeing by car. She decides to drive to the Yamanote area, Yamashita Park, the Yokohama Red Brick Warehouses, and the Minato-Mirai area.*

ii. *The road between her hotel and the Yamanote area is a plain residential street. Rin is bored while driving the car. Finally she arrives at the Yamanote area and looks for a parking space. Because of the consecutive holidays, all parking areas near the park are already full. Rin feels stressed from looking for a parking space but finally finds a space a short distance from the Yamanote area and parks the car. It takes a few minutes for Rin to walk from the parking lot to the Yamanote area. The walk from the parking area is boring; thus, Rin walks quickly without thinking. Rin finally arrives at the Yamanote area and enjoys the scenery.*

iii. *Next, Rin drives to Yamashita Park, which is famous for its beautiful seaside scenery. Again, Rin has trouble finding a parking space and then walks along the seaside road. Rin enjoys the scenery of the park and feels comfortable in a sea breeze.*

iv. *Then, Rin drives toward the Yokohama Red Brick Warehouses. The road to the Red Brick Warehouses is a main street, and the traffic is heavy. Rin becomes irritated when she is caught in a traffic jam. After enjoying the shopping at the Red Brick Warehouses, Rin decides to go to see the scenery around the Minato-Mirai area, but the traffic is quite heavy.*

v. *After going back to the hotel, Rin falls asleep immediately because she is tired from looking for parking and being caught in a traffic jam.*

Using a rental car makes it difficult to enjoy the scenery because the typical streets in a city have been developed based on their efficiency, not people's well-being. Looking for parking or being caught in a traffic jam can become stressful. However, if Rin uses a rental bike, the scenario changes.

i. *Rin travels to Yokohama, a famous tourist spot in Japan, and decides to stay there for a week. She learns that there is a widely utilized bicycle rental service in Yokohama. Because she is concerned about the environment, she decides to rent a bike to tour Yokohama. The Yamanote area is near her hotel; thus, Rin plans to start from the Yamanote area and then go to the Yokohama Red Brick Warehouses through Yamashita Park and to the Minato-Mirai area to enjoy the scenery.*

ii. *Rin rents a bike near her hotel and starts to pedal. The road between her hotel and the Yamanote area is a plain residential street, and the ride is boring. Finally, she arrives at the Yamanote area. The bike is slower than a car, which causes some tension; however, when she arrives at the Yamanote area, Rin feels a sense of achievement. In addition, all of the parking spaces she saw near the park were full, making Rin think it was a good idea to rent the bike. Rin enjoys the beautiful scenery of the Yamanote area.*

iii. *After that, Rin goes to Yamashita Park, which is famous for its beautiful seaside scenery. She pedals along a seaside road in Yamashita Park. She enjoys the scenery of the park and feels comfortable in the sea breeze.*

iv. *Then, she pedals toward the Yokohama Red Brick Warehouses. The road to the Red Brick Warehouses is a main street, and the traffic is heavy. Although Rin avoids being caught in a traffic jam, the scenery on that road is dull and the air is bad. She feels bored while she rides the bike. After enjoying shopping at the Red Brick Warehouses, she decides to go to see the scenery in the Minato-Mirai area; however, the traffic is heavy and the scenery is miserable. Pedaling along the road with the dull scenery makes Rin jealous of cars that can move faster and arrive at their destination earlier.*

v. *After going back to the hotel, Rin immediately falls asleep because all the pedaling made her tired. She thinks that it is hard to ride a bike and that it takes more time than driving a car. She wants to use a rental car next time.*

As shown in the above scenarios, using a rental bicycle solves the problem of stress caused by traffic and parking difficulties. However, riding a bicycle is more difficult than driving a car and more time-consuming. Unpleasant scenery while riding a bicycle is worse than in a car. However, a user's sense of achievement is greater after pedaling around the city.

We analyzed these two scenarios with the Seligman's PERMA model's five factors of well-being that we mentioned in the previous section. Positive emotions are not satisfied while driving a rental car. Riding a rental bicycle may create positive emotions because the rider can tour without looking for a parking space; however, riding along streets with unpleasant scenery destroys those positive emotions. Achievement is satisfied when the user arrives at the destination. At this point, bikes create a stronger sense of achievement than cars. Meaning is not satisfied at all when using a rental car. Even if the user understands that biking contributes to protecting the environment, it is difficult to believe that one single action truly contributes to environmental protection. Relationships is not satisfied by either a rental car or a rental bicycle. Engagement may become stronger using a rent-a-cycle than a rental car because people can feel the wind on their bodies.

Our basic approach is to adopt game elements that increase the factor in the PERMA model that is not well-satisfied in the above scenarios. According to the framework, *positive emotions (P)* can be increased by introducing characters, *achievement (A)* can be increased by introducing goal-setting, *meaning (M)* can be increased by introducing dynamic graphical changes, and *relationships (R)* can be increased by introducing a close sense of others. In this case, we introduced user reviews of sightseeing spots or the surrounding scenery. *Engagement (E)* can be increased by music and special graphic effects. To achieve this goal, we believed that incorporating fictionality into real space based on alternative reality was a promising direction. In particular, introducing a character and enhanced fictional sights is consistent with introducing fictionality.

From the above analysis, the scenario when a user uses the *Augmented Bike* becomes the following.

i. *Rin travels to Yokohama, a famous tourist spot in Japan, and decides to stay there for a week. She learns that there is a widely utilized bicycle rental service in Yokohama. Because she is worried about the environment, she decides to rent a bike to tour Yokohama. The Yamanote area is near her hotel; thus, she plans to start from the Yamanote area and then cycle to the Yokohama Red Brick Warehouses through Yamashita Park and finally to the Minato-Mirai area to enjoy the scenery.*

ii. *Rin rents a bike near her hotel. The rental bicycle is equipped with Augmented Bike functionalities. Rin installs the Augmented Bike application on her smartphone and confirms her my-page. Scenery is displayed on her my-page; however, the scenery is not beautiful. A cute character is also displayed on her my-page. Rin wears an HMD and starts pedaling.*

iii. *The road between her hotel and the Yamanote area is a plain residential street. Then the scenery displayed on her HMD changes into a beautiful seaside road. Rin enjoys the virtual scenery while she pedals to the Yamanote area. All of the parking spaces that she sees near the park are full, making Rin think it was a good decision to come by bike. Rin enjoys the beautiful scenery of the Yamanote area.*

iv. *After that, Rin goes to Yamashita Park, which is famous for its beautiful seaside scenery. Yamashita Park naturally has beautiful scenery. The scenery displayed on her HMD changes into the actual view of Yamashita Park, and cool music appropriate to the sea is played. She pedals along a seaside road in Yamashita Park. When Rin has traveled nearly halfway across Yamashita Park, a pop-up window appears in the corner of her HMD. The window displays a user review: "The flowerbeds in Yamashita Park are so beautiful." Rin decides to drop in there for a short visit. The flowers in the flowerbeds really are beautiful, and Rin enjoys scenery that could not have been seen from a car. Rin appreciates the user who wrote the review.*

v. *Next, Rin pedals toward the Yokohama Red Brick Warehouses. The road to the Red Brick Warehouses is a main street, and the traffic is heavy. The scenery is terrible; however, the scenery displayed on her HMD is a beautiful tree-lined road. Rin enjoys the virtual scenery while she pedals to the Red Brick Warehouses. After enjoying shopping at Red Brick Warehouses, she decides to go see the scenery near the Minato-Mirai area. Although the traffic on the road is heavy and the scenery is unpleasant, Rin enjoys the virtual scenery on her HMD.*

vi. *After going back to the hotel, Rin checks the my-page of her smartphone application. The graphic of the earth is a little cleaner than when Rin had looked in the morning. The character in the application joyfully says, "The earth becomes cleaner, thanks to you. Rin feels that she can contribute to protecting the environments and scenery, and this makes her happy. In addition, there is a map on the application, and the roads she has ridden on are colored. This gives her a sense of achievement. She wants to use a rent-a-cycle from now on, and to color more roads on the map in the near future.*

Thus, the *Augmented Bike* overcomes the drawback that biking is boring when a user is in an area with drab scenery. A normal bicycle cannot increase positive emotions, achievement, relationships and meaning; however, the gamification-based approach with the framework we introduce in this paper can overcome such pitfalls, and the user will feel positive about the experience although pedaling can be difficult.

3.4   A Current Augmented Bike Prototype System and Its User Study

The current *Augmented Bike* consists of the following two parts. The first part runs on a desktop computer and delivers sound and movies to an HMD. The second part runs on a smartphone, and is connected to the first part. The first part changes the current view that a user sees according to the location. As shown in Fig. 3, the boring view when a user

Fig. 3.   Changing a user's view in augmented bike

rides on a bicycle on a usual cycle road between sightseeing places is changed to a more attractive view. The current prototype adopted Oculus Lift as an HMD. Of course, the current HMDs are too big and heavy to carry and the angle of its vision is narrow for the practical uses, but the contact-lens-shaped displays are recently developed and the technologies will make *the Augmented Bike* concept more practical in the near future [10].

The second part running on a smartphone records the road that a user passes through on its map and reports the travel distance as a feedback to him/her (Fig. 4). As the screenshots showed in Fig. 5, it displays the picture of polished earth before using *Augmented Bike* and cleaned earth after the cycling.

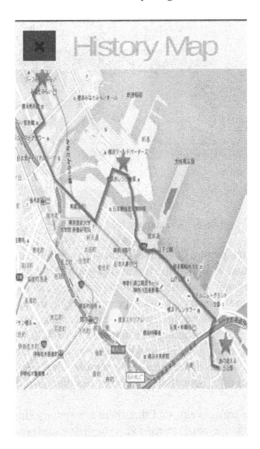

Fig. 4. Route map

As a user experiment, we recruited five participants. We asked the participants to use the *Augmented Bike* prototype system and discussed with them about the advantages and disadvantages of our current approach. They also investigated potential pitfalls for making our prototype system more practical. The five participants are male and early twenties.

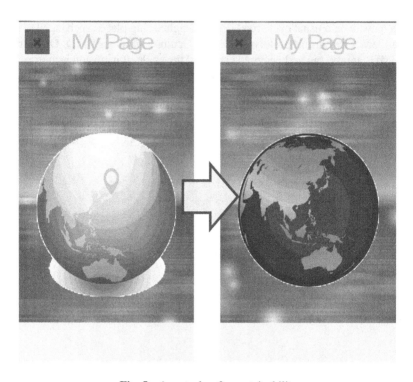

Fig. 5. A metaphor for sustainability

The approach that the picture of earth becomes clean after enough cycling seems to motivate participants and to notice them that using a bicycle is more environmental-friendly than to use an automobile because riding on a bicycle does not excrete carbon dioxide. However, from the interview after the experiment, the approach did not motivate the participants well because the approach does no make them to feel their actual contribution to make our environment sustainable. In addition, we found that the approach is not enough strong as an incentive to use a rental bicycle. The approach more directly related to individuals is requires, for example, showing the effects related to their health issues or to offer economic incentives like the discounts of local shops or restaurants.

Furthermore, some participants said that there are few cycling roads especially in Japan. When cyclers run on a usual car roadway, they have some risks of traffic accidents with automobiles, but on the pedestrian area they may hit and injure pedestrians. There are many dangerous places for cyclers in Japan and there are also few bicycle parking lots. Many cyclers currently do not understand the importance of traffic rules because they need no licenses to ride on bicycles. There are also some cyclers inherently with bad manners and dangerous driving. To promote rental bicycling more safely, it is necessary to prepare enough cycling roads and parking lots and to establish more appropriate traffic laws for bicyclers.

We assume that *Augmented Bike* is used in the outside environment, but our experiment was conducted in our laboratory setting because our prototype system currently requires a powerful desktop computer to process and deliver a movie to a participant's HMD. Thus, it is difficult to safely conduct the experiments in the actual outside environment. The current prototype system attached acceleration sensors to the indoor exercise pedals. The HMD that a participant wears presents movies that were taken with a 360-degree camera (bublcam[2]). The movies are switched according to the participant's situation as described before. The display rate of the movies is changed according to the value retrieved from the acceleration sensors. In our scenario, the road where participants passes in the experiment presents boring scenery and is familiar with them. Thus, the prototype system shows a movie of boring scenery while the system assumes that the participant takes a bicycle in a cycling road, between sightseeing places and the scenery is changed while the system assumes that the participant arrives at a sightseeing place. However, because of the indoor experiment, the boring road is an unknown place for the participants, thus the effect of the change of scenery could not be investigated well. In the next step, we like to conduct an outdoor experiment with a powerful portable computer for making the experiment close to the scenarios described in the previous section, then we will be able to conduct the effect of the scenery change in more details.

The Participants who like cycling claimed another opinion about the relationship between game mechanics used in the *Augmented Bike* and the Seligman's five factors. However, we could not analyze the detailed reasons well due to the current limited number of participants, but in the next step, we also like to investigate the issues and more appropriate approach to promote to use rental bicycles. One issue that we found is that the Seligman's five factors are related to the total user experience, but the game mechanics are related to a part of the experience [9]. Thus, although some games mechanics may enhance the five flourished factors, there are other many possibilities to decreased the five factors in the actual user experience while riding an *Augmented Bike*.

From the insights extracted in the above experiment, the most important finding is that the flourished five factors should not used for designing game mechanics in a platform society to enhance the human flourishness. We need to focus on how the total user experience should be designed not only game mechanics because game mechanics may have unexpected effects on user experience according to a user's current situation.

4   Lessons Learned from Designing Flourishness in a Platform Society

This section examines the two lessons learned from designing and evaluating the *Augmented Bike*. The first lesson involves design strategies to encourage diverse people. The basic idea of the proposed approach in the paper is to define multiple frameworks with which to design services. The frameworks offer different angles to investigate how each person responds to the services and how to enhance the services to motivate each participant. In this paper, we defined a persona, created scenarios regarding the persona, and examined whether the scenarios worked well. If we identified potential pitfalls, we

---

[2] https://www.bublcam.com/.

discussed which framework should be reconsidered. The approach allows us to overcome potential pitfalls by considering different personas incrementally.

The above approach potentially raises two issues. The first issue is how many personas must be examined before the design finally becomes saturated. The second issue is more serious. To extract multiple frames, we generally consider an average number of people. For example, in [17], Seligman proposed five factors to enhance our lives. However, the model only shows that the possibility becomes higher if people satisfy all of these factors. Some people may feel well-being in areas in which other people do not. However, when designing social platforms as social infrastructures, diverse people must be satisfied using the platforms, and we must investigate improved strategies for *designing for diversity*.

The second lesson is how we can use IoT-based technologies to design social platforms. The most important power of IoT-based technologies is to model our real world and change the strategies according to the current conditions in the model. This approach offers a powerful technique to guide human attitudes and behavior. However, constructing an accurate digital model of the real world is difficult; in particular, there is no manner in which to construct a completely generic model because of the frame problem identified by the artificial intelligence research community.

Changing the meaning of the real world is an effective manner in which to change human behavior; currently, however, there is no systematic manner in which to guide the meaning, and it is difficult to predict the effect on behavior changes. In addition, if there are inconsistencies between the enhanced world and the real world, people may not make correct decisions. For example, in the *Augmented Bikes*, if people are not aware of potential risks while riding, the possibility of accidents becomes higher. It may also be a good idea to replace humans' five senses. For example, a human's visual sense can be replaced by the auditory sense. However, it is not clear whether humans can correctly understand the meaning of the real world when their five senses are replaced. The necessity remains to investigate the best manner in which to enhance the meaning of the real world without biasing human decision-making and leading to accidental decisions.

To build a social platform, a concept named crowdsourcing is a promising approach to promoting a community's willingness to achieve their goals. This approach has been shown to be successful in several service areas [15], and it is desirable to integrate the concept in our case study to motivate the community's activities. In addition, to encourage people, a concept called procedural rhetoric is promising for designing persuasive affordances based on digital game concepts. The concept offers an interesting direction that complements the gamification concept to design better persuasive affordances. Procedural rhetoric [21] will become a powerful theoretical foundation utilizing digital games' full powers to persuade people to enhance their communities. However, currently, it is not clear how the design of procedural rhetoric is related to the Seligman's five factors. We need to investigate how the meaning is assigned to procedural rhetoric and how the meaning enhances the five factors. However, as presented in the previous section, we also need to investigate how the meaning is used to design the total user experience offered by a platform society.

Libertarian paternalism is a legitimate concept with which public institutions may influence human behavior without sacrificing freedom of choice. In [19], Thaler and

Sunstein defined libertarian paternalism as paternalism that "... *tries to influence choices in a way that will make choosers better off, as judged by themselves*"; the concept of paternalism implies a restriction of choice although it is libertarian that "*people should be free to opt out of specified arrangements if they choose to do so.*" Choice architecture allows designers to design how choices can be presented to people and how the presentation affects their decision-making [20]. Thus, the libertarian paternalists support the intentional design of choice architecture to nudge people toward personally and socially desirable behaviors such as saving for retirement, choosing healthier foods, or reducing their energy consumption.

In 2010 the British government commissioned research into influencing behavior by policy. What the research produced was a report called MINDSPACE that offers guidelines for implementing the libertarian paternalism concept as public policy [10]. Our approach to enhancing the meaning of real space in which people live by augmented reality and virtual reality technologies is implementing the libertarian paternalism concept using information technology. Currently, there is scant research on how to coordinate policies and technologies to achieve a better society. We expect our approach to become a first step in a promising direction.

5   Conclusion and Future Direction

In this paper, we discussed design strategies to build social platforms for diverse people. Our modern society is becoming increasingly complex, and we are becoming busier and more stressed. The well-being of our society is one of the most important social issues of the near future. In particular, our social platform must consider a thriving society in a manner that extends beyond our daily lives. We presented a case study to demonstrate the effectiveness of the proposed design framework. The case study promotes low carbon communities by using IoT-based technology. We developed *Augmented Bikes* to enhance people's enjoyable experiences in an urban setting without sacrificing our immediate environment.

Libertarian paternalism is a legitimate concept with which public institutions may influence human behavior without sacrificing freedom of choice. In [19], Thaler and Sunstein defined libertarian paternalism as paternalism that "... *tries to influence choices in a way that will make choosers better off, as judged by themselves*"; the concept of paternalism implies a restriction of choice although it is libertarian that "*people should be free to opt out of specified arrangements if they choose to do so.*" Choice architecture allows designers to design how choices can be presented to people and how the presentation affects their decision-making. Thus, the libertarian paternalists support the intentional design of choice architecture to nudge people toward personally and socially desirable behaviors such as saving for retirement, choosing healthier foods, or reducing their energy consumption.

Acknowledgement. The author would like to thank to Monami Takahashi for her helps to include the discussions about the Augmented Bike prototype system.

References

1. Blythe, B.: Research through design fiction: narrative in real and imaginary abstracts. In: Proceedings of the International Conference on Human Factors in Computing Systems (2014)
2. Cialdini, R.B.: Influence: The Psychology of Persuasion, Revised edn. Harper Business, New York (2006)
3. Crawford J.H.: *Carfree Cities*, Intl Books (2000)
4. Deterding, S., Dixon, D., Khaled, R., Nacke, N.: From game design elements to gamefulness: defining "ramification". In: Proceedings of the 15th International Academic MindTrek Conference: Envisioning Future Media Environments, pp. 9–15 (2011)
5. Dunne, A., Raby, F.: Speculative Everything: Design, Fiction, and Social Dreaming. MIT Press, Cambridge (2013)
6. Fraker, H.: The Hidden Potential of Sustainable Neighborhoods: Lessons from Low-Carbon Communities. Island Press, Washington, D.C. (2013)
7. Foletta, N., Henderson, J.: Low Car(bon) Communities: Inspiring Car-free and Car-lite Urban Futures. Routledge, New York (2016)
8. Fahey, L., Randall, R.M.: Learning From the Future: Competitive Foresight Scenarios. Wiley, New York (1997)
9. Hagen, U.: Designing for player experience how professional game developers communicate design visions. In: Proceeding of Nordic DiGRA 2010 (2010)
10. Ho, H., Saeedi, E., Kim, S.S., Shen, T.T., Parviz, B.A.: Contact Lens with Integrated Inorganic Semiconductor Services. IEEE, Micro. Electro. Mech. Syst. **21**(1), 403–406 (2008)
11. Institute of Government: MINDSPACE: Influencing Behavior through Public Policy, CabinetOffice (2010)
12. Ishizawa, F., Nakajima, T.: Alternative reality: an augmented daily urban world inserting virtual scenes temporally. In: Caballero-Gil, P., Burmester, M., Quesada-Arencibia, A. (eds.) Proceedings of the 10th International Conference on Ubiquitous Computing & Ambient Intelligence. LNCS, vol. 10069, pp. 353–364. Springer, Cham (2016)
13. Jia, Y., Xu, B., Karanam, Y., Voida, S.: Personality-targeted gamification: a survey study on personality traits and motivational affordances. In: Proceedings of the 2016 CHI Conference on Human Factors in Computing Systems (2016)
14. Sakamoto, M., Nakajima, T.: Search of the right abstraction for designing persuasive affordance towards a flourished society. In: Proceedings of the 9th International Conference on Design and Semantics of Form and Movement (2015)
15. Sakamoto, M., Nakajima, T., Akioka, S.: Gamifying collective human behavior with gameful digital rhetoric. Multimed. Tools Appl. (2016). doi:10.1007/s11042-016-3665-y
16. Sakamoto, M., Nakajima, T.: Making citizens' activities flourish through a crowdsourcing-based social infrastructure. In: Konomi. S., Rousso, G. (eds.) Enriching Urban Spaces with Ambient Computing, the Internet of Things, and Smart City Design, IGI Global (2016)
17. Seligman, M.E.P.: Flourish: A Visionary New Understanding of Happiness and Well-being. Atria Books, New York (2011)
18. Shaheen, S.A., et al.: Public Bikesharing in North America during a period of rapid expansion: understanding business models, industry trends, and user impacts, MTI Mineta Transportation Institute, Report 12-29 (2015)
19. Sunstein, C., Thaler, R.: Libertarian Paternalism is Not an Oxymoron. Univ. Chicago Law Rev. **70**(4), 1159–1202 (2003)

20. Thaler, R.H., Sunstein, C., R., Balz, J.P.: Choice architecture. In: The Behavioral Foundations of Public Policy (2014)
21. Treanor, M., Schweizer, B., Bogost, I., Mateas, M.: Proceduralist readings: how to find meaning in games with graphical logics. In: Proceedings of Foundations of Digital Games (2011)

Knowledge-Based Approach to Modeling Urban Dynamics

Sonja Gievska[✉] and Petre Lameski

Faculty of Computer Science and Engineering, University of Ss Cyril and Methodius in Skopje,
Skopje, Republic of Macedonia
sonjag@gwu.edu, lameski@finki.ukim.mk

Abstract. The model representing the complexity of the pedestrian mobility has to incorporate the nature of the modeled phenomenon by accounting the interdependence between human behavior and urban environment. Our efforts are directed towards correlating emergent behavior patterns of different types of pedestrians to contextual knowledge that will help us map realistic pedestrian behavior into agent's decision making capabilities. We propose that agent's beliefs, goals and decision-making strategies should be derived directly from the integrated urban knowledge. Causal probabilistic models that are based on Bayesian inference are proposed as a potential solution to some of the challenges in the pedestrian agent modeling.

Keywords: Pedestrian modeling · Bayesian inference · Multi-agent simulation

1 Introduction

Urban systems are complex systems, very difficult to delimitate, evolving through space and time. If the general structures of urban systems are complex, the behaviors that can be observed are far from being entirely stochastic [2]. Our knowledge of urban phenomena might have been deepened on many levels, though its modeling and computational representation is still an open problem [6]. The idea of a city as an urban space that is sustained by human connections requires suitable models that recognize the sound interplay between physical and phenomenological aspects of the urban system. Our approach to urban modeling resembles the anthropological view [14]; a network perspective of a city as an interconnection of people, urban elements and their dynamic relationships and processes. This alternative perspective places humans and their experience, rather than urban form, at the center stage of the metropolis view.

Agent-based models possess suitable capabilities required for modeling structural and behavioral properties of real-world urban systems, since the complex agencies are directly modeled and the behavioral properties of the agencies can be explicitly specified in terms of meaningful operations and applicable knowledge rules. Multi-agent models provide facilities for simulating the entities, processes and interactions involved in urban dynamics, making them applicable to a wide range of urban problems, and suitable for dealing with both the macro-level (societal) and the micro-level (individuals) aspects of urban systems.

© Springer International Publishing AG 2017
N. Streitz and P. Markopoulos (Eds.): DAPI 2017, LNCS 10291, pp. 252–261, 2017.
DOI: 10.1007/978-3-319-58697-7_18

There is a very natural way to simulate various moving entities in a city (e.g. pedestrians, transportation) within multi-agent models. Models of pedestrian mobility vary in the level of detail, abstraction and design approach [11–13]. Trajectory patterns can be considered as spatiotemporal evidence of movement behavior i.e., the footprints of the confrontation between the physical urban system and individuals' behavior that give rise to the structure of the city. In [11], data mining techniques play a fundamental role for extracting patterns from trajectory data gathered by means of location-based and sensing technologies. Pedestrian behavior at the microscopic level (e.g. pedestrian speed, inter-pedestrian positions) and its implications to agent modeling is presented in [12]. Suitability of an extensive set of algorithms for representation of real-world pedestrian trajectory data is discussed in [13].

Our long-term goal has been to layout a foundation for developing a multi-agent system that will accommodate our future exploration of different research scenarios related to pedestrian mobility. Our interest is in the manifestations generated by interconnecting elements at a higher level of aggregation and abstraction, rather than the behavior of individuals at a microscopic level. Our efforts are directed towards correlating emergent behavior patterns of different types of pedestrians to contextual knowledge that will help us map realistic pedestrian behavior into agent's decision making capabilities. The premise was that the more that is known about the factors affecting behavior, trends and processes before we start modeling, the better design choices for agent modeling could be expected.

2   Urban Knowledge

Creation of a knowledge base that pertains to urban modeling is of crucial importance for creating more effective urban environment models, both for holistic views of a city or specialized scenarios of a particular urban area. There is an urgent need for converging knowledge representation that requires unity of models, strategies and perspectives, contributed by the relevant disciplines and experts (Fig. 1). The knowledge base should provide a means for integrating and interconnecting traditional urban knowledge data such as urban maps, photographs, cadaster data, and various unstructured data (A), as

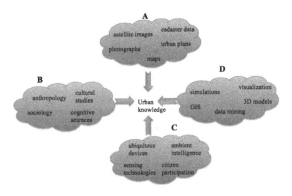

Fig. 1. Integrated urban knowledge base

well as empirical studies and social surveys (B). This effort needs access to heterogeneous data, solicited and gathered by experts in various fields (e.g. architects, city planners, social science experts) with various solicitation and analytical methods. Semantic heterogeneity, terminology differences, inconsistency, redundant data and interoperability are some of the problems that might be encountered.

The new directions in information technologies aimed at pervasiveness and intelligence have increased the amount of raw data collection with a potential to increase our knowledge of different aspects of social urban life. The employment of a number of tools and intelligent techniques could support the process of capturing and visualizing the observable manifestation of behavior trends and patterns i.e. the urban dynamics (C). Correlating observable and emergent patterns of behavior with other urban-related knowledge that can help us make sense of the underlying complex systems is an imperative (D). Extracting qualitative knowledge from large quantities of data is just the beginning of the search for meaning and plausible explanation of urban dynamics.

Validation is critical when modeling complex dynamic systems, hence integrated urban knowledge have been recognized to serve both purposes, interpretation and understanding of the studied behavior, and as a captured and measured historical and empirical manifestations against which model outcomes could be evaluated.

Our long-term goal has been to layout a foundation for developing a multi-agent system that will accommodate our future exploration of different research scenarios related to pedestrian mobility. The first phase in designing agents that will represent real-life pedestrians was to create an appropriate urban context representation as a basis for modeling pedestrian mobility.

We have examined the ways in which human movement decisions might be influenced by various demographic, situational and environmental factors that characterize the context in which pedestrians move.

Table 1. Urban knowledge categories related to pedestrian movement.

Type of knowledge	Knowledge category
Environmental factors	• Street type (characteristics) • Destination/attractors • Integration value • Visual fields • Level of services • Level of comfort • Popularity
Situational factors	• Traffic intensity • Season • Time of day • Seasonal/daily events
Individual/group factors	• Stereotypical type • Preferences • Demographics • Visit frequency

A variety of urban context data (situational and environmental) and additional pragmatic factors were identified and investigated to have a prominent role in establishing appropriate urban knowledge for our particular research (Table 1). Some of these categories represent invariant properties of the urban context that can be obtained from domain-specific urban knowledge, and the specifics of the particular scenario. Others should be drawn from the information gathered from a variety of sources (e.g., social studies, ambient and smart technologies). The set of selected categories could be broken down into three groups: (1) environmental factors, (2) situational factors reflecting the particularities of a given situation, and (3) characteristics to account for the individual and group perspectives. The justification for the selection of the characteristics is based on the theory and empirical evidence reported in relevant literature.

Pedestrian agents will be situated in a particular urban environment, which may have a profound effect on their decision-making strategies and behavior. A number of environmental factors that describe the local urban context should be explored in order to establish their impact on pedestrian movement. The environmental factors capture the physicality and the dynamics of the urban space where the human mobility takes place. Steady progress has been made toward identifying and understanding what factors may have an impact on pedestrian movement trough a certain urban space. Street morphology [2, 12], level of integration value [10], spatial configuration [2], visual fields [4], level of service and comfort [7], etc. have been pointed out to affect human movement in different urban context scenarios. Identifying the attractors and possible destinations is a way to reason about pedestrians' goals and plans.

The inclusion of situational factors attributes substantially greater sensitivity in agents' behavior, namely, the ability to adapt to temporal constraints, or the particularity of a given situation (2). Recognizing situations associated with daily events, random gatherings, excessive traffic and crowd-related behavior are crucial since they are more likely to affect pedestrian behavior. Temporal aspects of pedestrian dynamics should be accounted for, which may sometimes constrain the goal-oriented behavior of pedestrians, other times may generate new incentives, goals and plans.

Individual and group categories are included to support the representation and reasoning about a particular situation as a pedestrian views it (3). These categories lie somewhere on a specialization scale from generic to individual. Generic categories target stereotypical pedestrian groups (e.g., preferences, emergent behavior), as opposed to individual user characteristics specific to a single user. Demographic characteristics such as: age, gender, etc., should be accounted for if their effect is known to manifest in the domain under investigation. The behavior of pedestrians who are frequent visitors of an area may exhibit different patterns from pedestrians, who visit it rarely or for the first time.

3 Agent-Based Modelling of Pedestrian Dynamics

Agents can only perform as well as their representations of the task they are trying to perform and of the world they are trying to perform in [15]. We can gather evidence and capture the footprints of human behavior, though the explanation and interpretation used for modeling purposes must be interdisciplinary, theoretically and empirically plausible contributions. We propose that agent's beliefs, goals and decision-making strategies should be derived directly from the integrated urban knowledge. Movement decisions correlated to goals, surroundings, and situational circumstances have to be appropriately accounted for. Our modeling efforts are directed toward gathering evidence of the pedestrian behavior. An agent model that is derived from realistic pedestrian behavior is expected to represent pedestrian complex interactions with the physicality and particularity of the urban space.

Pedestrian behavior can be described at three major levels: strategic, tactical, and operational level [7]. Human actions and behavior are purposeful and meaningful; people do not move in urban spaces for inexplicable reasons, they move because of the activity they are engaged in. This goal-directed behavior of pedestrians is represented at the strategic level. The tactical level is an expression of short-term decisions regarding pedestrian movement within a particular urban area (e.g. sequence, route, temporal constraints). At the operational level, a pedestrian makes swift decisions as a response to immediate environmental and situational circumstances (e.g. daily events, traffic intensity). Models of pedestrian mobility may vary in the level of detail for the pedestrian strategic, tactical or operational behavior to suit the research purposes.

Individual pieces of urban knowledge or a collection of categories do not constitute a model. The efforts to find out how those pieces of information are related to each other and affect pedestrian mobility are far more challenging. How can all of this information be combined to support agent's reasoning capabilities that closely approximate realistic pedestrian patterns? We argue that causal probabilistic models that are based on Bayesian inference provide a potential solution to some of the challenges in the pedestrian agent reasoning. It provides a formal method for quantifying uncertainty by combining diverse types of evidence including both subjective beliefs (expert and participants) and objective data. Explanations of behavior derived from realistic causal model are more likely to match the reality, because the model accounts for deeper and richer relationships underneath data and simplistic statistical analysis.

Bayesian Belief Networks (BBNs) are suitable for representing the causal relationship between different pieces of information, as well as the rules for how to use, maintain, and reason with urban-related knowledge. The Bayesian network representing agent's reasoning and decisions regarding pedestrian movement is shown in Fig. 2. It should be noted the figure depicts variables and relations only on the highest level; in practice the network could be quite complex. As shown, the agent movement decisions are related to the states of three hypothetical (non-observable) variables: Strategic Movement Decisions, Tactical Movement Decisions, and Operational Movement Decisions. Each of the hypothetical variables is linked to the relevant urban knowledge categories (drawn as oval boxes), which correspond to the categories discussed in previous section (Table 1). Once the knowledge categories are identified, a suitable classification would be needed to categorize them.

The decisions at higher abstraction levels (strategic) seemed to only partially describe a particular movement behavior. Examination of lower-level decisions was needed especially for describing short-term decisions (tactical level) and random situations. Hence, the goal-oriented view (strategic level) would be contrasted with inherent

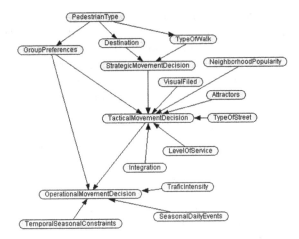

Fig. 2. High-level dependencies between urban knowledge categories for pedestrian agent reasoning

attitudes, preferences and randomness in human and crowd behavior. The strategic movement decisions are expected to generate the space of possible routes to a chosen destination, while tactical movement decisions would simulate a path selection at each intersection. Human randomness, group fuzziness and crowd behavior are necessary for more realistic modeling of pedestrian movement in an uncertain environment and will be derived as a final decision, i.e. operational movement decision.

To apply the proposed framework for modeling pedestrian mobility in a particular urban domain requires: (1) a selection of the knowledge categories relevant in that particular domain; (2) an identification of the sources of information and intelligent techniques needed for establishing the states of variables; and (3) a construction and training of the Bayesian network which includes the relationships amongst the urban categories and the specification of the conditional probabilities implied by the relationships.

4 Case Study

Skopje's Old Bazaar, a mediaeval city fragment with a unique appearance was the focus in our case study, a sample solution that may, by analogy, suggest ways to tackle problems that might be encountered in another context. The Old Bazaar historically has always been a center of commerce, which determined the structure of its urban space and the distribution of its buildings and visitors. Consequently, the area of the Old Bazaar has been and still is mainly constituted of places of trade, commerce and services, with few cultural and historical sites that serve as attractors for tourists.

Agents modeling have started by identifying different agent types to represent distinct entities and processes at play in the enclosed urban area. Several aggregated agent types were selected to represent different pedestrians at strategic level, namely, tourists, transit pedestrians, employees and visitors of various service providers (public, private). One should note that visitors to religious facilities and people in search for nightlife entertainment represent different stereotypical groups that entail different modeling strategies. Space-syntax models were deemed more suitable for modeling tourist agent behavior, while utility-based approach was employed for modeling other agent types.

A number of realistic trajectories were collected from the history of pedestrian activity [10], which were used to establish the space of possible routes associated with aggregated pedestrian types. The visualization of the recorded pedestrian data has revealed several patterns with specific spatial and time distribution. It provided insights into both movement patterns and overall system behavior. The selection and categorization of the taxonomic factors was followed by the phase of constructing the BBN-based model to serve as agent knowledge representation. The urban context factors were interrelated and built into agents reasoning mechanism. The Bayesian network was constructed and trained off-line with the pilot study data as a training set. The training set was used to adjust the corresponding causal probabilities of the BBN nodes. Agent design went through iterative refinements, empirically consistent with the existing knowledge (surveys, historical data, statistics, observations).

A number of environmental factors that described the local context in terms of urban structure were explored in order to establish their impact and sensitivity during pedestrian route-finding decisions (tactical behavior). The overall integration value of the street network in the Old Bazaar indicates that highly-integrated streets are the ones in the middle of the area, while the peripheral streets have lower integration values [10]. The exhibited pattern coincides well with the most frequented pedestrian routes. Data analysis has confirmed pedestrian preference for streets that are visually open and connected to the other parts of the route. The observed preference of wider non-deserted, though not overly crowded streets, has been considered [10].

The identification of attractors governing pedestrian dynamics within our context of interest was one of the objectives for gathering exhaustive context knowledge. Each urban entity or area, private and commercial, identified as a possible attractor or destination, were enriched by several context attributes such as type, functionality, ownership, working hours, demographics, number of employees, frequency of visitors, etc. The pedestrian routes and paths were described according to their accessibility, obstacles, sun exposure, street lights positions, dimensions, and throughput, in order to take into account how the characteristics of the real environment affect and constrain the pedestrian movement. Entities and areas outside the Old Bazaar perimeter were also included to account for the fact that their attraction, prominence and affordance may distinctively affect different agent type's behavior by extending the space of destinations.

We have examined how much the states of the variables linked to movement decisions influence the beliefs about that node. The results have confirmed that neighborhood attractions, the street type and the visual fields were most likely to produce the greatest change in the associated beliefs. Street features, nearby attractor buildings, and time of the day were found to have significant impact on the movement preferences across the pedestrian types.

Situational factors that characterize the particular scenario have been accounted for to simulate the exhibited behavior on an operational level. The immediate attraction to ongoing events, such as festivals, concerts, exhibitions and gatherings have been taken into account. We concluded that a number of influential factors affect the way humans negotiate the urban space, which points at their relevance for inclusion in the causal probability models for agent reasoning.

Heterogeneity in the real world, observed through anthropological surveys and empirical studies, provided valuable insights for distinguishing relevant aggregated agent types as well as for rules governing their goal-directed behavior. The results of all participants were aggregated to distinguish behavior and patterns based on a particular scenario and context, rather than of individual participants, so that aggregated agents can make independent decisions within previously established behavioral guidelines.

We have used knowledge discovery to help us in identifying and interpreting patterns relevant to our agent modeling. A number of data mining exploration studies to discover the associative and causal relationships between factors have been conducted and are still in progress. Discovering meaningful relationships between urban knowledge categories and the emerging collective behavior has been a crucial step in increasing the quality of the current agent design and future validations. Our aim was to improve our understanding of how stereotypical pedestrians behave, and how their movement was guided (affected) by the various situational and environmental factors expected to influence their interaction with this particular urban area.

Samples of movement behavior of three agents presented in Fig. 3 represent the following situation: (a) a tourist pedestrian agent on a way to a historical site visits a random lines of authentic filigree jewelry shops, (b) a transit pedestrian agent on its way to a selected destination randomly stops at a nearby shop, and (c) a transit pedestrian agent who takes the originally established shortest route to a selected destination point. The popularity of attractors is based on empirical studies results (e.g., traffic/visit frequency, surveys).

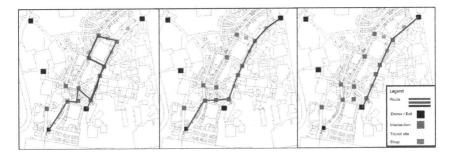

Fig. 3. Simulated agent behavior. (a) A tourist pedestrian agent visiting several places of interest. (b) A transit pedestrian agent visiting a random shop. (c) A transit pedestrian agent taking the shortest route to destination without any stops (https://www.youtube.com/watch?v= 2un0eyFHpq0). (Color figure online)

Each time a specified situation arises (e.g., intersection, event, nearby attraction), the agent deliberates and makes a decision, either by generating a new route or staying on the same course of movement. If a new goal is established, network beliefs will be recalculated and updated. If the goal remains unchanged, the originally established route will be followed, or the original route could slightly deviate to accommodate a random choice (e.g., lunch time, local happening). Color coding (different route colors) is used to represent the points of deliberation and new decisions.

During simulation, a number of agents of different types simultaneously move through the area. The distribution of agents for each agent type reflects the real-life statistics and frequencies, their behavior is autonomous and different, but within previously established behavioral guidelines. For example, we may have agents of a certain type, one who selects less crowded path, while the other chooses to mix with the crowds (out of curiosity). The presence of multiple pedestrian agents on the scene would result in strengthening or weakening of the level of attraction of a certain entity, and even generate new attractions on the run.

5   Conclusions

This paper has presented a knowledge-based approach to modeling pedestrian mobility in urban spaces. Bayesian belief networks were proposed to provide a suitable representation of the causal relationship between different pieces of urban information and to integrate rules for agent's reasoning and decision making. The knowledge space is expected to provide a starting point with enough possibilities to account for the complexity and the relationship among urban dynamics of different nature and with the same depth as it was explored in our case studies. Experimentation with multi-agent models are expected to lead the way to a better understanding of the general processes and conditions at play in the urban world.

Acknowledgements. The research has been performed within the framework of the MUSE-Modelling Users Societies Environments research project supported by the Faculty of Computer Science and Engineering, University of "Ss. Cyril and Methodius" in Skopje, Macedonia.

References

1. Batty, M.: A generic framework for computational spatial modeling. In: Heppenstall, A.J., Crooks, A.T., See, L.M., Batty, M. (eds.) Agent-Based Models of Geographical Systems. Springer Science + Business Media BV, Dordrecht (2011)
2. Bretagnolle, A., Daude, E., Pumain, D.: From theory to modeling: urban systems as complex systems. CyberGe: Eur. J. Geogr. **355**, 1–17 (2005)
3. Fruin, J.J.: Design for pedestrians: a level-of-service concept. Highw. Res. Rec. **355**, 1–15 (1971)
4. Hillier, B., Hanson, J.: The Social Logic of Space. Cambridge University Press, Cambridge (1984)
5. Hillier, B., Hanson, J.: Space is the Machine–A Configurational Theory of Architecture. Cambridge University Press, Cambridge (1996)
6. Hillier, B.: The knowledge that shapes the city: the human city beneath the social city. In: Proceedings of 4th International Space Syntax Symposium, London (2003)
7. Hoogendoorn, S.P., Bovy, P.H.L.: State-of-the-art of vehicular traffic flow modelling. Proc. Inst. Mech. Eng. - I **215**(4), 283–303 (2001)

8. Krafta, R.: Modelling intraurban configurational development. Environ. Plan. B: Plan. Des. **21**, 67–82 (1994)
9. March, L., Steadman, P.: The Geometry of Environment: An Introduction to Spatial Organization in Design. RIBA Publications, London (1971)
10. Marina, O., et al.: Modelling pedestrian mobility as a designer's tool in urban protected areas. In: Proceedings of 11th International Conference on Reliability and Statistics in Transportation and Communication 2011, Riga, Latvia (2011)
11. Nanni, M., Trasarti, R., Giannotti, F., Pedrechi, D.: Advanced knowledge discovery on movement data with the GeoPKDD system. In: Proceedings of EDBT 2010 International Conference on Extending Database Technologies, Lausanne, Switzerland (2010)
12. Torrens, P.M., et al.: An extensible simulation environment and movement metrics for testing walking behavior in agent-based models. Comput. Environ. Urban Syst. **36**, 1–17 (2012)
13. Willis, A., et al.: Human movement behavior in urban spaces. Environ. Plan. B: Plan. Des. **31**, 805–828 (2004)
14. Wolfe, A.W.: Anthropologist view of social network analysis and data mining. Soc. Netw. Anal. Min. J. **1**(1), 3–19 (2011)
15. Wooldridge, M.: Introduction to Multiagent Systems, 2nd edn. Wiley, Hoboken (2009)

A Service Infrastructure for Human-Centered IoT-Based Smart Built Environments

Denis Gračanin[1(✉)], Mohamed Handosa[1], and Hicham G. Elmongui[2]

[1] Virginia Tech, Blacksburg, VA 24060, USA
gracanin@vt.edu
[2] Alexandria University, Alexandria, Egypt

Abstract. Smart built environments enhanced with technology can improve the lives of individuals, groups, and the broader community. Internet of Things (IoT), a collection of networked and interacting embedded devices, could provide the necessary infrastructure and enabling technologies to design, develop and deploy smart built-environments. We describe an approach to modeling IoT-based smart built environments that uses a large-scale virtual environment where a building model is aligned with the physical space. This approach takes advantages of affordances and embodied cognition in a large physical space to model user interaction with built spaces. The built space contains 'smart objects' with embedded sensors/actuators/controllers (e.g., kitchen appliances). A 'smart object' has the corresponding virtual object in the virtual environment. We build on our work on the conceptual design of interaction middleware and context sensitive interaction interoperability frameworks to develop support for a living ecosystem of services, a service framework, to support interactions with a smart built-environment. We illustrate the proposed framework on a case study, a living lab for smart built-environments that includes a kitchen, a living room, a bathroom, an office, and a bedroom.

Keywords: 3D user interactions · Internet of Things · Built environments

1 Introduction

Internet of Things (IoT), a collection of networked and interacting embedded devices, in connection with pervasive computing, could provide the necessary infrastructure and enabling technologies to design, develop and deploy smart built-environments. Designing and deploying IoT into the built environments provides capacities that can change how systems behave and how users interact with them. Such smart built environments enhanced with technology can improve the lives of individuals, groups, and the broader community. IoT could support sustainable and comfortable living through design, simulation, planning, monitoring, optimization, and visualization tools. Similarly, ambient intelligence would allow us to learn about people activities, their responses and interests,

© Springer International Publishing AG 2017
N. Streitz and P. Markopoulos (Eds.): DAPI 2017, LNCS 10291, pp. 262–274, 2017.
DOI: 10.1007/978-3-319-58697-7_19

how to make intuitive and data-based decision about what people want, and which action to perform.

The physical and social structures within a built environment are subject to continuous change. Thus, adding information technology and related services into our homes has to be done considering the multitude of activities architectural space support. House is a social place where family and friends meet and interact. As a consequence, service support for multiple users must accommodate for resource and preference conflicts. The conflict-resolution approach, while based on priorities and access control, also depends on the context and ambient intelligence. At the intersection of interaction design and built environments is thinking about how to "architect interaction."

The design factors range from cultural, environmental, to more specific interaction goals such as effective navigation to the exit of a building. However, the common design goal for the services is to enhance the user experience and achieve the desired comfort level by providing easy and flexible ways to interact with the surrounding environment as well as to provide automatic actions based on decisions inferred from collected data and user preferences.

In the context of energy and living comfort, an energy-efficient house is effective only if the inhabitants are comfortable. Therefore, quantitative measures such as energy consumption or temperature must be augmented with more qualitative or subjective measure based on the individual and group preferences and desired comfort level. There are many efforts along those lines (e.g., Nest thermostat) but we are still lacking a comprehensive, holistic approach that should overcome the disconnect between quantitative and qualitative measures.

We build on our work on the conceptual design of interaction independence middleware and context sensitive interaction interoperability frameworks to develop support for a living ecosystem of services, a service framework, to support interactions with a smart built-environment. These services are created and destroyed over time based on the evolution of users' needs and habits [14].

User tasks in built environments usually involve interaction with physical objects that respond to user actions with some kind of feedback. Services should allow users to both issue commands and receive feedback. They exist on multiple scales ranging from the design of door knobs to the placement of buildings.

The services are organized into layers. The IoT layer services provide connectivity and communication to embedded devices, sensors and actuators. The data layer services provide data collection and data fusion. The resource layer services support resource management (e.g., energy, water). The comfort layer services allow users to manage comfort settings. Finally, the UI layer services support multi-modal interactions across a variety of interface and interaction devices in a smart built-environment. In addition, the service management subsystem manages the service life-cycle and deals with user collaboration and conflict resolution, context awareness, behavior detection and safety/security/privacy issues.

Technology does not only dominate our work lives but has become an integral part of our domestic lives as well. Instead of replacing existing media, new technology is adapted for the existing patterns of use [9]. The 'smart house', or 'home of the future', such as the Aware House built by Georgia Tech, augments the traditional home with a rich computational and communicational infrastructure, such as "smart" devices and sensors that can detect and interact with the inhabitants of the house in novel ways.

We illustrate the proposed framework on a case study, a living lab for smart built-environments [17]. We describe the implementation of the framework and provide several examples of service creation and supporting multi-modal interactions in a single-user and multiuser setup. These examples demonstrate service for kitchen activities and proactive light control in a living room. We also present a corresponding simulation testbed that uses an enclosed space $50 \times 40 \times 40$ feet with real-time tracking and spatial audio capabilities to provide a multiuser mixed-reality/virtual reality environment. Several users can simultaneously move in the physical space and interact to test the service ecosystem before its deployment in the living lab.

2   Related Work

The new sensor, mobile, and control technologies have a great promise in connecting users to their environment. Smart built environments (e.g., a smart house) enhanced with technology can support better living to improve the lives of individuals, groups, and the broader community, including increased awareness of information in the user's surroundings, integrated control over factors in one's surrounding and home environments, and increased ability to support a sustainable living for both individuals and groups. A smart house can be used in many contexts, such as residence, office, store, classroom, etc., or can be a part of a larger place that includes the surrounding area and other buildings. Each smart house or building and their inhabitants contribute to the overall data collection, including participatory sensing and crowd-sourced data, thus supporting a 'smart city' [20].

The notion of a smart home, aware home, or green home has been explored toward incorporating environmentally friendly initiatives and techniques into the built-home environment. Technology plays a key role in monitoring information generated by these homes and in controlling certain aspects of the home. Awareness can be raised through the use of mobile notification systems, which attempt to deliver current, important information to the user in an efficient and effective manner. Some key Human-Computer Interaction (HCI) related questions regarding the presentation of information via mobile and other devices: enabling individuals to understand how their decisions may impact the environment, and enabling groups to reach consensus on decisions.

In addition, supporting interactions with built environments raises some unique usability challenges. Given the multitude of devices that all the inhabitants of the space can each interact with, it becomes apparent that these interactions can become quite complex. For example, they can depend on a given augmented device, the identity of the user that wants to interact with it, the presence of other users in the same or other location, the time, and any other contextual information. As users can take on different roles in the household, there is a potential for conflicting rules within policies, in which case a conflict resolution mechanism needs to be put in place.

Harrison and Dourish emphasized the difference between space and place, defining a place as space with added socio-cultural understandings [11,18]. They argue that "place, not space, frames appropriate behavior." The physical and social structures within the home are subject to continuous change. Thus, adding information technology into our homes has to be done considering the multitude of activities architectural space support.

Aipperspach et al. discussed the dangers of introducing information technology into the home without considering potential detrimental effects on its inhabitants [2]. They suggest the idea of a semi-smart home, where areas are intentionally kept free of technology, except for so-called tourist devices (devices that may visit certain areas, yet have a specific 'home').

Nissenbaum introduced the concept of contextual integrity to address concerns about the effects of information technology on privacy from the perspective of the law [24]. Contextual integrity is based on norms of appropriateness and norms of information flow and can be used to determine whether privacy expectations have been violated.

Crabtree and Rodden studied domestic routines as related to communication and collaboration [9]. They introduce three major concepts: ecological habitats as places where communication media live, activity centers as places where media are produced and consumed, and coordinate displays as places where media are made available to coordinate activities.

The concept of Internet of Things (IoT) [6] describes the pervasive presence of things or objects which use a unique addressing scheme to interact with each other and cooperate with their neighbors to reach common goals. These physical objects have a social existence that could be supported through the IoT (an Internet of social things) [23].

The applications of IoT range from automation and manufacturing to assisted living and e-health. Designing and deploying IoT into the built environments provides capacities that can change how systems behave and how users interact with them. IoT could support sustainability through design, simulation, planning, monitoring, optimization, and visualization tools [15].

The IoT architecture and the corresponding implementation [10,22] differ from the traditional network architecture. A large number of devices have to be connected, most of them with limited computing and networking capabilities. The IoT devices will be deployed in various contexts [3], including wearable devices, house appliances/sensors, embedded devices/smartphones, manufacturing plants and environmental sensors. The can span large urban areas to support 'smart cities' [20].

The evaluation of IoT and distributed sensor systems includes real-world testing, miniature prototypes and software simulations [5]. Sensor device emulators could be used to fully replicate the behavior of the deployed sensors. While software simulations are more convenient compared to the real-world testing, most of them focus on the low-level networking aspects, with well-defined topologies and arrangements of objects. However, recent efforts are focusing on efficient simulation methodologies for large-scale IoT systems in urban environments from an application-layer perspective [8].

Distributed test system frameworks for open-source IoT software have been proposed [26] to support continuous integration techniques and a permanent distributed plugtest for network interoperability testing. Since one of the key function of IoT systems is data collection and processing, it is important to understand how data analytics solution will work for IoT systems. Benchmark toolkits, such as IoTAbench [4], support testing of IoT use cases.

Three-dimensional (3D) Virtual Environments (VEs) allow users to explore virtual worlds without actually 'being there.' VEs have been used in a variety of applications including education, training, architectural walkthroughs, scientific visualization, art, and entertainment [7]. Although VE applications can be used for many different purposes, there are some fundamental interaction tasks used in VE applications.

3D Distributed Virtual Environment (DVE) is a software system in which multiple users interact with each other in real-time, even though those users may be located around the world [27]. DVEs are challenging applications due to several reasons. First, DVEs are multimedia-rich environments that include 3D graphical objects as well as audio and video streams. Second, users interact in real-time, such as in multi-player online games. Third, the number of users could reach hundreds or thousands in a single application who can compete or collaborate individually or in groups. That, in turn, implies the high variations in users' requirements.

Experience with 3D user interfaces and interactions with the virtual worlds can be a starting point for interaction with the real world and architectural artifacts [16,19]. By providing a virtual world that models the architectural space and is connected to controls, sensors and actuators in the architectural space, we can use human-computer interaction based approaches and interaction techniques to support human-architecture interactions.

VE applications, such as Second Life [28], can be used to map or represent real-world sensors and embedded devices to virtual devices and objects. 3D user interface and visualization enable users to evaluate IoT computing applications using a VE to interactively test various IoT configurations [12,21,25].

3   Approach

We build on the preliminary work [13] that uses Virginia Tech's Cube facility (http://www.icat.vt.edu/facilities/living_labs) that provides an enclosed space (dimensions $50 \times 40 \times 40$ feet) with real-time tracking and spatial audio capabilities. Several users can simultaneously move in the physical space and view the simulation results from different points of view. The physical location and orientation of a user is used in real-time to determine the corresponding view in the VE. The user can also observe other users and collaborate to change the simulation (Fig. 1).

Fig. 1. The users navigating the virtual environment and the corresponding physical space (Cube).

The modeling framework (Fig. 2) provides a connection between the real world IoT-based collection of devices, sensors, and actuators and the corresponding virtual world representations [1]. Each sensor is modeled based on the set of the corresponding environmental and control parameters. The physical space and virtual space can synchronize their state by sharing the same IoT server. The IoT server records both sensory readings and user commands and keeps track of the most recent ones.

Besides mirroring a physical space state and providing a 3D virtual user interface to interact with it, the virtual space can serve two other purposes. First, it can simulate a non-existing physical space, where the virtual sensors will produce virtual streams of data and user commands will change the state of the virtual model. This allows for exploring different user interaction designs and techniques before implementation in the physical space. Second, it can playback a history of events stored at the IoT server, including both sensory readings and user commands. This can help exploring and studying different usage patterns by having the ability to reproduce them in VE settings.

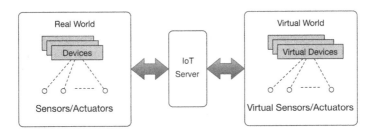

Fig. 2. Mapping between the real and virtual worlds.

Constructing a VE to clone a physical IoT-based built space involves a set of steps. First, identifying the characteristics of the built space structure to be modeled in the VE. Second, identifying the list of devices to be modeled together with their physical characteristics. Third, identifying the set of sensors to be modeled together with the corresponding equations for producing virtual data streams, as needed. Fourth, determining the set of virtual actuator representing the set of supported functionalities for each device (e.g. turn on/off). Fifth, finding how a user will trigger different actions upon virtual actuators. Finally, building the VE model and integrating it with the IoT server as well as providing the user interface for accepting user commands.

Creating the list of devices starts with the initial requirements gathering and preliminary design. The built environment under design is first analyzed from the energy perspective to identify components (appliances, consumer electronics, lights, etc.) that consume energy and should be monitored. Next, user interactions are studied to identify components (things) that a user interact with. In addition to the obvious choices (appliances, light switches) that already provide control capabilities, the designer can also select purely mechanical devices such as doors or drawers that then need to be equipped with embedded controllers, sensors and actuators.

Identifying, for each device, its physical characteristics for modeling purposes means that the control parameters (e.g., the warmer temperature or the extent of drawer opening) are used in equations modeling the real-world actions (e.g., energy consumption or the time needed for the warmer drawer to open). The individual sensors and actuators are registered with the IoT server so that the sensory readings and user commands are automatically recorded. Identifying the set of virtual sensors that will produce virtual data streams is based on the developed physical models for the individual devices to mimic the data generated by the real world sensors. Identifying the basic functionalities of the device and related actuators determines all possible user interactions. For example, a microwave can have a very elaborated user interface with many buttons/keys. Determining the virtual actions that the device can perform through the virtual actuator determines what are the visual manifestations of user actions (e.g., changes in position/orientation/size). Initially, only a basic subset of interactions is supported in the VE and then gradually expanded as the development progresses.

Representing the devices in the VE means that a sufficiently detailed model (geometry, parts, animation) has to be developed to accurately represent the user's actions and their consequences. Pressing a button in the VE to open a warmer drawer must result in the drawer moving with the appropriate speed that results from the user action in the VE.

Synchronizing the physical built-space and the VE using the same IoT server allows for creating a very flexible testbed. First, since the real world data is stored on the IoT server, the recorded data can be replayed and studied in the VE. Second, the developed physical models can be compared to the real world measurements and refined as needed. Third, once the VE is sufficiently accurate, the VE can be used to observe user interactions and behavior in a physical space (Cube) that matches the real world scale. Finally, the VE can be used, through the IoT server, to control the real world system.

In short, the system is developed in an iterative, bottom-up fashion where the IoT server is connected to both the real world devices and the virtual devices modeled in the VE. Modeling individual devices and composing them into a larger built environments produces reusable artifacts.

4 Case Study

Figure 5 shows the FutureHAUS prototype (http://www.futurehaus.tech/) consisting of several modules (a kitchen, a living room, a bathroom, an office, and a bedroom) that leverages the use of prefabricated architectural components for a home. The components can be accessed and controlled through a whole-house interface which manages and monitors appliance performance and energy use. The modules are instrumented with IoT-based electronic sensors and actuators that facilitates the use of the living space makes it more energy efficient. The goal is to integrate smart technologies into a prefabricated system while elevating the human experience of all household activities (e.g. cooking, and socializing).

The initial idea and the architectural conceptual (Fig. 3 top left) were used to create the corresponding VE (Fig. 3 center and Fig. 4). After exploring and refining the VE (Figs. 1 and 3 bottom left) the modules were constructed (Fig. 3 bottom right and Fig. 5).

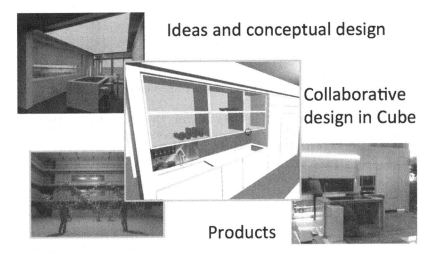

Fig. 3. Kitchen and living room modules.

The kitchen has a set of devices (appliances), where each device has an IoT-based embedded controller controlling a set of sensors and/or actuators. The living room has controllable color lights and a sofa with pressure sensors. A local network connects the controllers to the IoT server. The controllers communicate with the IoT server by sending sensory readings periodically and receiving user

Fig. 4. VE for the built environment.

Fig. 5. Kitchen and living room modules.

commands, if any, before triggering the actuators to execute them. Applications and users can interact with the system by querying the readings or posting commands. The list of devices includes an inductive cooktop, a faucet, a dishwasher, a coffee maker, an oven, a warmer, a refrigerator, a microwave, LED lights, and a sofa.

4.1   Device Modeling

Modeling each device should consider different sets of parameters representing the physical characteristics of the device, the environmental parameters that can affect those characteristics, and the control parameters. For example, the warmer model considers its power consumption, temperature, and the length of its drawer. The environmental parameters include room temperature and humidity. The control parameters include the desired warmer temperature and the open percentage of the warmer's drawer. Different warmer characteristics were represented using basic physical models. For example, the energy consumption was initially approximated using Eq. 1.

$$E = \frac{T_{select} - T_0}{T_{max} - T_0} P_{max} t \tag{1}$$

where T_{select} is the desired warmer temperature, T_{max} is the maximum warmer temperature, T_0 is the initial warmer temperature, P_{max} is the maximum power and t is the elapsed time. This physical model (equation) can be further modified based on the real-world measurements.

Different appliances were individually designed and tested in terms of modeling and user interactions. Figure 6 shows a VE setup for a virtual warmer and a virtual refrigerator.

Fig. 6. FutureHAUS warmer and refrigerator appliances.

4.2   Light Control

Exploring different types of interaction techniques with IoT devices in a built environment, we have developed a smartphone application as well as a 3D user interface to control the LED-lights in the living room module as shown in Fig. 7. The smartphone application maps the layout of the living room lights to a 2D GUI allowing the user to control the color and intensity of individual lights through the smartphone. However, there are some limitations associated with the use of a smartphone for controlling devices. First, mapping devices that exist in a 3D space to a 2D GUI can be tricky for both users and developers. Second, relying on a smartphone to control devices places an explicit barrier between users and devices. Third, switching between different applications/screens to control different devices can be frustrating to the user. The 3D version of the user interface tries to address those limitations associated with the use of 2D GUIs by allowing for hands-free control of lights using a gestures-based interaction technique. The user can control different parameters of individual lights by simply pointing at the light source of interest using one hand and changing its color/intensity using the other hand. This allows for a seamless interaction while avoiding explicit intermediary devices.

Fig. 7. Left: The living room with LED-lights. **Right:** Gesture-based lights control.

5   Conclusion

The current implementation demonstrates the feasibility of the proposed approach. The users can explore the VE while navigating and interacting in the physical space that matches the built environment under study. One of the main challenges is how to quickly develop sufficiently accurate physical models of individual appliances and other devices. Our experience with the case study points out that for a well-defined application domain such built environments, it's feasible to build a library of models that can be reused.

We are continuing our work to model all of the house modules. The ongoing work proceeds in several directions, including preparing user studies and exploring additional application domains, such as manufacturing systems, and training.

Acknowledgments. This work was supported, in part, by a grant from Virginia Tech Institute for Creativity, Arts and Technology (ICAT).

References

1. Ahmed, H., Gračanin, D.: Context sensitive interaction interoperability for serious virtual worlds. In: Debattista, K., Dickey, M., Proença, A., Santos, L.P. (eds.) Proceedings of the 2nd International Conference on Games and Virtual Worlds for Serious Applications (VS GAMES 2010), pp. 159–166, 25–26 March 2010
2. Aipperspach, R., Hooker, B., Woodruff, A.: FEATURE: The heterogeneous home. Interactions **16**(1), 35–38 (2009)
3. Anderson, J., Rainie, L., Duggan, M.: The internet of things will thrive by 2025. Technical report, Pew Research Center, Washington, D.C. 20036, May 2014
4. Arlitt, M., Marwah, M., Bellala, G., Shah, A., Healey, J., Vandiver, B.: ioTAbench: an internet of things analytics benchmark. In: Proceedings of the 6th ACM/SPEC International Conference on Performance Engineering, pp. 133–144. ACM, New York (2015)

5. Armac, I., Retkowitz, D.: Simulation of smart environments. In: The Proceedings of the IEEE International Conference on Pervasive Services, pp. 322–331, 15–20 July 2007
6. Atzori, L., Iera, A., Morabito, G.: The internet of things: a survey. Comput. Netw. **54**(15), 2787–2805 (2010)
7. Bowman, D.A., Kruijff, E., LaViola, J.J., Poupyrev, I.: 3D User Interfaces: Theory and Practice. Addison-Wesley, Boston (2005)
8. Brambilla, G., Picone, M., Cirani, S., Amoretti, M., Zanichelli, F.: A simulation platform for large-scale internet of things scenarios in urban environments. In: Proceedings of the First International Conference on IoT in Urban Space, pp. 50–55. ICST (Institute for Computer Sciences, Social-Informatics and Telecommunications Engineering), Brussels (2014)
9. Crabtree, A., Rodden, T.: Domestic routines and design for the home. Comput. Support. Coop. Work **13**(2), 191–220 (2004)
10. daCosta, F.: Rethinking the Internet of Things: A Scalable Approach to Connecting Everything. Apress L. P. (2013)
11. Dourish, P.: Re-space-ing place: "place" and "space" ten years on. In: Proceedings of the 2006 20th Anniversary Conference on Computer Supported Cooperative Work (CSCW 2006), pp. 299–308, 4–8 November 2006
12. Eastman, C., Teicholz, P., Sacks, R., Liston, K.: BIM Handbook: A Guide to Building Information Modeling for Owners, Managers, Architects, Engineers, Contractors, and Fabricators. Wiley, New Jersey (2008)
13. Gračanin, D., Eck II., T., Silverman, R., Heivilin, A., Meacham, S.: An approach to embodied interactive visual steering: bridging simulated and real worlds. In: Proceedings of the 2014 Winter Simulation Conference (WSC), pp. 4073–4074, December 2014
14. Gračanin, D., Matković, K., Wheeler, J.: An approach to modeling internet of things based smart built environments. In: Proceedings of the 2015 Winter Simulation Conference (WSC), pp. 3208–3209, 6–9 December 2015
15. Gračanin, D., McCrickard, D.S., Billingsley, A., Cooper, R., Gatling, T., Irvin-Williams, E.J., Osborne, F., Doswell, F.: Mobile interfaces for better living: supporting awareness in a smart home environment. In: Stephanidis, C. (ed.) UAHCI 2011. LNCS, vol. 6767, pp. 163–172. Springer, Heidelberg (2011). doi:10.1007/978-3-642-21666-4_19
16. Gračanin, D., Zhang, X.: CaffeNeve: A podcasting-capable framework for creating flexible and extensible 3D applications. ACM Computers in Entertainment **11**(1), 1–30 (2013)
17. Handosa, M., Gračanin, D., Elmongui, H.G., Ciambrone, A.: Painting with light: gesture based light control in architectural settings. In: Proceedings of the 2017 IEEE Symposium on 3D User Interfaces, 18–19 March 2017
18. Harrison, S., Dourish, P.: Re-place-ing space: the roles of place and space in collaborative systems. In: Proceedings of the 1996 ACM Conference on Computer Supported Cooperative Work (CSCW 1996), pp. 67–76. ACM, New York (1996)
19. Lazem, S., Gračanin, D.: Social traps in second life. In: Debattista, K., Dickey, M., Proenča, A., Santos, L.P. (eds.) Proceedings of the 2nd International Conference on Games and Virtual Worlds for Serious Applications (VS GAMES 2010), pp. 133–140, 25–26 March 2010
20. Lea, R., Blackstock, M.: Smart cities: an IoT-centric approach. In: Proceedings of the 2014 International Workshop on Web Intelligence and Smart Sensing, p. 12:1–12:2. ACM, New York (2014)

21. McGlinn, K., Hederman, L., Lewis, D.: SimCon: a context simulator for supporting evaluation of smart building applications when faced with uncertainty. Pervasive Mob. Comput. **12**, 139–159 (2014)

22. Mukhopadhyay, S.C. (ed.): Internet of Things: Challenges and Opportunities. Smart Sensors, Measurement and Instrumentation, vol. 9. Springer, Cham (2014)

23. Nansen, B., van Ryn, L., Vetere, F., Robertson, T., Brereton, M., Douish, P.: An internet of social things. In: Proceedings of the 26th Australian Computer-Human Interaction Conference on Designing Futures: The Future of Design, pp. 87–96. ACM, New York (2014)

24. Nissenbaum, H.F.: Privacy as contextual integrity. Wash. Law Rev. **79**(1), 119–158 (2004)

25. Prendinger, H., Brandherm, B., Ullrich, S.: A simulation framework for sensor-based systems in second life. Presence Teleoperators Virtual Environ. **18**(6), 468–477 (2009)

26. Rosenkranz, P., Wählisch, M., Baccelli, E., Ortmann, L.: A distributed test system architecture for open-source IoT software. In: Proceedings of the 2015 Workshop on IoT Challenges in Mobile and Industrial Systems, pp. 43–48. ACM, New York (2015)

27. Singhal, S., Zyda, M.: Networked Virtual Environments: Design and Implementation. SIGGRAPH Series. ACM Press, Addison Wesley, Reading (1999)

28. Varvello, M., Picconi, F., Diot, C., Biersack, E.: Is there life in second life? In: Proceedings of the 2008 ACM CoNEXT Conference (CoNEXT 2008), pp. 1–12. ACM, New York (2008)

Food Ordering Service System Design for Chinese Urban Commuters Based on Internet of Things

Xinhui Hong[✉]

Department of Industrial Design, Academy of Arts and Design, Fuzhou University,
No. 852 Ligong Road, Jimei District, Xiamen, Fujian, People's Republic of China
id_hxh@foxmail.com

Abstract. Based on users' needs as the starting point, this thesis investigated the related services of current situation of domestic and foreign through the huge data analysis of consumption trends in Chinese City family meals. It combined the method of service design with the technology of Internet of Things to re-plan the "service blueprint", and explore the innovation strategy of the food ordering service system design Chinese urban commuters. Also, it enhanced the satisfaction of user experience, and created a higher commercial value and social value.

Keywords: The Internet of Things · Urban commuters · Food ordering service · Service system design

1 Introduction

In recent years, with the rapid development of urbanization, the pace of life of urban residents in China was getting faster and faster, especially the commuters. For advocating "food for the people" of the Chinese people, a series of "eating problems" became the real trouble to more and more Chinese urban commuters. Where to eat? What to eat? And how to eat?" "The Research Report of Chinese Takeaway Food Delivery Internet Market" which was released in March 2016 by Analysys showed, in 2015, the scale of the Internet Chinese food takeaway market reached 45.78 billion Yuan, with an increase of 201.1%. The monthly number of active Internet caterers also increased from 152.211 million in January to 22.753 million in December, up by 49.5% in just one year. In the further research, we found that the key factor which caused the surge in food takeaway market was from the "buy food difficult" problem which was brought by the expansion of the city, as well as consumers' appeal which was "seeking fast", "seeking convenience" and "seeking delicious". In 2016, IKEA released "China's urban home life report" also showed that, although the cooking time was constantly "compressed", aside from health (60.3%), safety (47.2%) and saving money (31%), the Chinese were willing to go home and enjoy a good time with their families to cook. After all, compared to "eating out" or "take-away delivery", "home cooking" was full of more love for their loved ones and family responsibilities, but also the Chinese people to maintain family ties and friendship special ties.

© Springer International Publishing AG 2017
N. Streitz and P. Markopoulos (Eds.): DAPI 2017, LNCS 10291, pp. 275–285, 2017.
DOI: 10.1007/978-3-319-58697-7_20

So, can we integrate "Internet of Things" technology with "service design" methodology, so that urban office workers could enjoy the cooking time, and meanwhile, simplified pre-dinner preparation to make the Chinese people "eat" more healthy and happier? With this idea, I studied the status of domestic and foreign related services, which helped to analysis of Chinese urban family dining table consumer trends. I hoped to create a good user experience from the start, and combined with the application of Internet technology re-planning "service blueprint" to explore the possibilities of Chinese urban office workers set food service system designed to enhance the user "at home to eat"; the health, convenience, and happiness and a sense of accomplishment.

2   Status of Domestic and Foreign Related Services and User Demands

2.1   Existing Procurement Approach for Fresh Product in the Domestic and Aboard

The traditional market, the modern super and fresh electricity providers were the three major ways for consumers to buy fresh products. Traditional markets included farmers market, roadside paving and mobile vendors. The modern business covered large supermarkets, supermarkets and convenience stores. However, the fresh electricity refers to use the e-commerce direct sales of fresh products on the Internet. With the accelerated pace of work and life, data technology and distribution channels, the development of online shopping was recognized, accepted and loved by more and more consumers. BCG's "2016 China Fresh Consumption Trend Report" showed that the Chinese fresh category online sales growth would continue to maintain a rapid momentum. From 2012 to 2016, the fresh electricity supplier market size from 40 billion yuan soared to 950 billion yuan. There were 7% of urban fresh consumption occurred online, and the penetration was expected to reach 15–25% by 2020. For Chinese urban office workers, online shopping not only had a lower price, but also more rich categories, more timesaving and save trouble. They often used their fragmentation time of the work to online shopping, and received the package after work when getting home on the next day.

In addition, the market for fresh purchase launched different types of innovative products and services. Some businesses such as Farmigo to create an "online agricultural sales" platform, the geographical location of the consumers to "food community" as the unit. And the local small and medium farms connected to make it easier for consumers to buy fresh, local, affordable, healthy and sustainable food. Staying at home would be able to get fresh, cheap, rest assured the ingredients. Some businesses such as the United States Instacart were the use of "purchasing" in the form of buyers' online order. The nearby purchasing got the orders to help buyers to go to the store to buy food, and sent goods to buyers, so you can eliminate the need for consumers to personally remove over-shopping time, and the purchasing those who pay the time for remuneration. There were also many businesses offering semi-finished products, "ready to cook", for busy young consumers with cooking recipes to help them solve the pain points of having no time to buy and cleaning ingredients, but eager to eat at home. It was said that this "ready to cook" of the earliest origin of a Swedish mother, she noted that many families because there was no time to purchase so could not cook at home. Based on this demand, she founded Middagsfrid in 2007, the ingredients Dishes packaged in the form of distribution to the customers' door. Compared to traditional fresh products, they not only saved cooking time and reduced the difficulty of cooking, but also could reduce the waste of food. This model was popular after the introduction, and soon expanded to Germany, Switzerland, Belgium, Denmark, the United States and other countries and regions, such as Blue Apron, Hello Fresh. The domestic daily fresh and young had a large group of loyal users.

2.2   User Requirements

Per the literature data and the user interview method, we had collected and sorted out the existing problems of the online ordering service, and found that the problems were mainly concentrated in the following aspects:

- In terms of ordering

Most foreign products were ordered weekly, and fixed number of times per week to match a fixed number of distribution time needed to be determined in advance; most of the domestic used of the first set after the mining method, and the customer ordered online after the purchase by the business, cleaning, deployment, delivery. It was a great opportunity on temporary changes in the number or change the chances of a trip, but the flexibility to modify or cancel the order is not.

- In terms of distribution

Whether it was door-to-door, or in the subway, or the district's storage box from the mention, distribution and storage were mostly black box. The users could not monitor if the temperature and humidity meet the storage conditions of different types of fresh, and sometimes might be due to delivery or delivery of the time difference, or cold chain logistics equipment failure caused by fresh or even deterioration.

- In the selection of dishes

The selectivity of dishes was too small on some platforms. However, the users were easily to get tired. And some platforms had rich dishes, but classification is not clear enough. So, the users often felt unable to start, they needed to spend a lot of time to carry out the selection. It was too tangled for the choice of patients with difficulties.

- In terms of packaging

For the protection of fresh products that did not spill and absorb the smell, most businesses used disposable lunch boxes and plastic bags for packaging materials, also supplemented by ice bags, cardboard boxes, foam boxes and so on for distribution. Although the packaging material to make the product even more refined, a large amount of waste from overpacking could be hazardous to the environment.

- In the cooking process

If the processing of food was too difficult to order, it was easy to dampen the enthusiasm of the consumer cooking; if it was just heating the finished product, it was similar as take-away fast food experience. Also, it was difficult to find when the "chef" sense of accomplishment. It was possible to consider different pre-processing levels to choose from and to provide cooking opportunities while cooking was easy.

- In terms of safety and health

In addition, it was difficult to know the freshness of ingredients, and the safety of food ingredients. The hygiene of the processing process and the degree of standardization of the storage links were not known, it was difficult to establish a continuous sense of trust.

From the above user feedback, it was not difficult to see the current consumers of food service were the main concern: the safety of raw materials, food freshness, and the nutrition, distribution timeliness and experience the pleasure, but also required environmental protection. They not only pursued higher quality products, but also more professional, reliable products and services, as well as innovative life solutions.

2.3 Characteristics of Chinese Urban Commuters in Need of the Food Service

According to January 5, 2017, the first financial business data center, combined with the release of the Tmall's "2017 Chinese family table consumption trend report" showed that Chinese consumers were increasingly willing to quality control, nutritional balance, convenient processing and rich variety of ingredients pay. And 28-year-old 35-year-old young white-collar workers were the main line of consumer groups. This information was based on the analysis of purchasing data of Alcatel-Lucent's Livestock Platform. In the follow-up study, we also used this age group as the core user group for food service. And through interviews, behavior habits, consumption characteristics and product expectations, such as in-depth research to the user portrait in the form of the user classification (Table 1). The characteristics of a more typical user group were as follows for differentiated services to prepare the follow-up.

Table 1. User classification and demand summary

User Type	House-work beginners	Foodies	Nutritionists
Key features	Just set up a small family, the couples were not good at cooking. Mortgage pressure, work overtime was often happened	Senior foodie, and has no resistance to food. Whether it is the Chilean king crab or Xinjiang sheep scorpions is heart love; like watching the A Bite of China, and the other food TV shows	It's the hard period during career, so the healthy body was important for work. And they very concerned about the family's health and food security
User goals	Usually making a table full of love dinner for family. Inviting friends at the weekend to home and have dinner	Learning from the masters who cooked a variety of novelties in TV, and then got more attention from friends	Quickly cooking out nutritious and delicious dishes. First, they could solve the kids' picky eaters' problem. Second, adjusting the physical function of the elderly and kids through diet therapy
Key requirements	Cooking process was simple, with a reasonable diet of meat and vegetables. And it finished with the tasty dish	The best way to get all the ingredients was one-stop shop. The "fresh" was important to fresh ingredients; especially the look of the ingredients must be better	Nutrition was very important. It was not just a meal to achieve nutritional balance, but to ensure adequate intake of a variety of trace elements in a week or even longer
Product attitude	It's more convenient than supermarket, more economy than restaurant and warmer than carry-out food, as long as the price was reasonable and cooking convenience which was worthy of long-term ownership	The price was not matter, but the fresh mattered a lot. They could invite couple friends to taste the new dishes together	The price is not the most important issue. The key was whether there was adequate nutrition, reasonable recipe. Also, they need know some basic knowledge of food
Knowledge and experience	Online shopping experience; cooking experience was not rich; less concerned about nutrition	Online shopping experience and cooking experience is more abundant, so is food experience	Online shopping experience and cooking experience was more abundant, also focused on nutrition
Product demands	It's best to eat with a good number of dishes, rich variety of dishes can be prepared. Every day dinner, materials were fully entrusted. For the temporary overwork or friends visiting could easily cancel or modify the order	It's best to recommend some imported fresh products seasonally, and come up with couple cooking tutorials. According to the recommended recipes, all the necessary ingredients could be purchased at one-stop	Presenting more detailed nutritional information of ingredients to provide a wide range of recipes options; ordering process was more convenient and flexible, or even automatically made the order

3 New Technology and New Ideas for Food Service Innovation

3.1 Possibility of Internet of Things Technology Applications

Internet of Things was through the radio frequency identification (RFID), global positioning system (LBS), infrared sensors, laser scanners and other information sensing equipment, based on the agreement, connected the items with the Internet. Using information exchange and communication to achieve the intelligent identification of goods, positioning, tracking, monitoring and management of a network. In addition to food traceability, RFID can also be used in logistics links, with temperature sensors, humidity sensors and other instruments on the distribution of food throughout the monitoring, flexible adjustment of temperature and humidity protection of fresh food; using of LBS positioning technology can track the location of buyers and ingredients. Through the cloud could automatically dispatch scheduling, allowing the material come after users. By using infrared or Bluetooth equipment, a microcomputer processor smart appliances can automatically set the cooking time and duration based on food labels on the QR code or bar code; the use of weight sensors for eggs, milk, rice and other common consumption of raw materials observing, automatic order replenishment could reduce memory burden. It collected the information of the existing ingredients in the home through the image recognition technology and the radio frequency video recognition technology which can automatically generate the recipes according to the category and quantity for the users' reference; sharing the seasonal weather and body status information in the large data platform and intelligently orders the personalized menu. Also, according to the nutritional intake of the period proposed food with recommendations. The integration of the Internet of Things technology can fully realize the autonomy of buyers, and use the machine learning without manual intervention to complete the automated procurement, record and analysis, to reduce the new generation of consumers' physical and mental burden.

3.2 Importance of Service Design

Service was a series of activities that formed a process and have value to the end user[1]. The "Design Dictionary", published by the Board of International Research in Design, considers "service design" to set the function and form of a service from the customer's perspective. Its goal was to ensure that the service interface was the customer felt useful, available and desirable; and at the same time, the service providers felt it was efficient and recognizable[2]. From the definition of service design by experts and organizations, it was not difficult to find that the core of service design was "user-centric", but only considering users was not enough. It should do the system planning for the explicit or implicit contact between the user and the service in the overall service flow. Therefore, we need to import the service design concept to help us define the scope of the problem, and indicate the direction to solve the problem, describe the scene of each link, so as to

---

[1] Saffer (2007).
[2] Michael and Marshall (2008).

reconstruct the user service model and innovate the service design scheme. Among them, the service blueprint was an accurate description of the service system tools. It was by means of the flow chart, through the continuous description of the service delivery process, service tasks, staff and customer roles and tangible evidence of service to visually display the service. By combing the service blueprint, designers could more intuitively provide the service process steps and content, as well as the completion of the method of service-by-item design to identify customers with business and service personnel contact points, and from these touchpoints to enhance the service of the user experience.

3.3 Integration and Innovation for New Opportunities

Compared to 2015, China's fresh electricity market in 2016 with 80% growth. We can see more and more Chinese consumers have begun to try or used to buy fresh products online. However, it was said that 2016 was also a fresh electricity business failures, layoffs, contraction and the acquisition of the event occurred in this year, which indicating that the existing related products in the business model and user experience there was still room for further improvement. In this case, if it could flexible use the application of tools in the Internet of Things technology, and clever use of methods at the service level design thinking, hardware and software around the integration of innovation. On the one hand through the equipment, carrier innovation to improve service performance and quality, and on the other hand, improving the interactive mode and consumption patterns of innovation optimizing the service experience and value. Through the construction of high-quality network service system designed to design the overall solution would help users to enhance viscosity, branding, and contribute to industry sustainable development as well.

4 Design of Service System for Chinese Urban Commuters Family

Consumers of fresh electricity business were more widely. If we just blindly pursuit of large and comprehensive services, the short term could be formed brand awareness, but there was no precise positioning which was difficult to form consumer stickiness. We started with the largest family of three as the breakthrough point, and conducted in-depth analysis of user behavior and needs, to explore the service system design of food service innovation strategy.

4.1 System Elements of Food Service

1. Service demander

Using online food ordering service system. Users' profile (Fig. 1): Family of three, 6 years old kid called Baby Bean who was picky eaters, and his parents were career-oriented. Usually, the breakfast had bread, fried eggs and milk, which could finish quickly. They had lunch at school, offices or the fast-food restaurants. For the dinner, they ate at home which seemed it was time to improve the meal quality, and also enjoyed the happy time with family.

Profile:
Father | IT Engineer 40 years old Hatarakiman, Overseas Educated Doctor
Mother | Middle School Teacher 36 years old Strong Sense of Resposiblities, Concern about Nutrition
Baby Bean | Primary School Student 8 years old   Picky
Income: 20,000 RMB/month
Daily Activity: On weekdays, Little Bean was doing homework on the small desk after dinner. His parents were sitting on the same desk to write code and check the homework.
On weekends, parents would spend one day on taking Little Bean to library, science museum or park.
Sometimes they went to suppermart.
Daily Meal:
Breakfast | Toast, Milk, Eggs
Lunch | Fast Food
Dinner | Chinese Food(Four dishes one soup), may have a little change.
Mother was in charge of cooking, meanwhile, baby and father would help.

Family of Three: Father, Mother and Little Bean

Fig. 1. Target users profile

2. Service provider

Electronic business platform, logistics channels and suppliers were the three major providers. Service process: the user completed the selection of ingredients and determined the location of the delivery through the APP was provided by the business platform; the electronic business platform arranged the dispatcher to sort, process and storage the food ingredients based on the order, and then dispatched the delivery staff to send at the right time. The user followed tutorial to complete the cooking dishes, or by the smart kitchen electrical identification labels finishing automatically after the completion of programming dishes cooked. Users could take pictures and upload them to the cloud. They can also record the service experience. The database of the business platform would record the nutritional information of the uploaded dishes and the user feedback, so that it could generate a database of health and user preferences. After meal, the hostess used the gap between counseling children's homework to check APP, browse the notifications of "tomorrow specials" and "healthy recipes".

3. Service carrier

APPs on the phone offered the online food service; the cold chain logistics equipment for distributing materials; a smart box with RFID module and one with temperature humidity monitoring; an intelligent terminal equipped with an RFID module which could detect and record information which could be controlled by voice; and a smart kitchen appliance with Microcomputer processing functions; a weight sensor rice boxes or egg boxes and other kitchen intelligent hardware.

4. Service environment

For service needs, home, on the road, office, any place could use mobile phones. For the service providers, they need clean and standardized food preparation space (real-time video visualization), stable and reliable transport links (real-time data visualization).

5. Support Resources

Internet of Things system, large data platform, cloud computing platform, mobile payment platform, food supply platform, logistics and distribution platform, security system, etc.

4.2 Service Design Blueprint

Order service system should be a scientific food and logistics management, intelligent service delivery, visual information presentation and other elements of the ecological system. It used the technology of the Internet of Things to connect the service demander, the service provider and the corresponding physical entity. The user can easily and naturally start the human-computer interaction in different scenes, and then trigger the relevant subsystems to respond and finally complete the service with manual assistance task (Fig. 2).

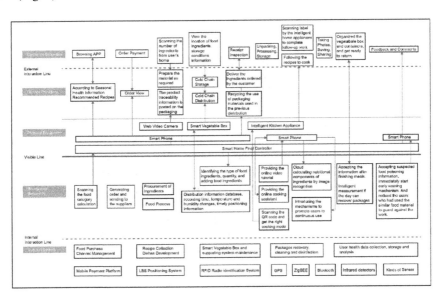

Fig. 2. Chinese urban family's food ordering service design blueprint

4.3 A Representative Service Scenario

After defining the service blueprint, we use the story-situational method to sort out the circulation of the food and the circulation of information, and verify the rationality of the food ordering service system design for Chinese urban commuters based on IOT (Fig. 3).

Father, Mother and Baby Bean. Parents arrived home at almost 18:30 from the late peak traffic every day. At the noon break, mother opened app and thought about the dinner. At this time, one notification reminded her, "rice box weighs less than 500 g,

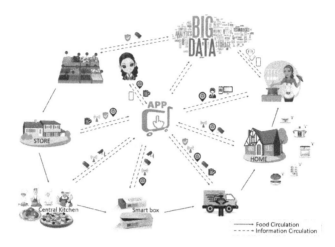

Fig. 3. Information architecture of IOT (Color figure online)

and need for replenishment." She remembered that when she cooked noodles yesterday, the rice was not much left, so she put the first shopping cart quickly. Also, it showed, "purchased on Oct. 5th, 350 g ham and 300 g cucumbers. She thought that was the weekend shopping to the supermarket. She worried about those materials were not fresh after putting a long time. Then she opened the recommended recipes, and checked "ham", "cucumber". And it produced a bunch of recipes, which was ham fried cucumber, cucumber brewed, fried cucumber, ham scrambled eggs, Orléans pizza … Suddenly, mom noticed baby hate eating cucumbers, but maybe he could accept when putting in the pizza. Then she clicked on the "triple package", and the system provided a set of flour, cheese, onions, Orleans seasoning powder and other pizza may be used to produce ingredients. Mom selected the "corn soup" and "fried article", or "pre-preparation" along the shopping cart page "with recommended". And then she cleared the total price, confirmed delivery address, and returned into the work of tension. Her mind also flashed his son devoured the scene. In the case of no traffic jams, her company was 20 min' drive from home. After work, she opened APP and click "go home". The system began to lock her LBS location tracking, and scheduled dispatcher to the central kitchen to pick up. She just stepped into the house and changed clothes, the "ready to go" package was delivered. In fact, before this, mother did not do pizza, but the cake has been reconciled, onion, green and red peppers had also been shredded. While preheating oven, Mom diced the ham and cucumber. And then followed recipes from APP, in the steps of scanning the label on the QR code. The oven automatically adjusted the oven time to start baking. At the same time, French fries and broth were also guided by the APP tutorial from the pan. Less than 20 min, the spicy Italian-style dinner was on the table. Baby was enjoying this meal, and showed the perfect praise on his mother's first attempt.

5   Conclusion

Using the technology of the Internet of Things, users can reduce the burden of physical and mental processes in the procurement and cooking tasks while increasing the perceptual and control of each service touch point. Nowadays, in China, the consumers in many cities had changed from price sensitivity to quality sensitivity. With the transfer of consumption hot spots from material to non-material, the design of product service system became more and more important. Under the combined actions of technology-driven vertical innovation and experience-driven horizontal innovation, it was believed that in the future, not only the young people but also the elderly people with the aged at home could easily enjoy the service quality optimization to the daily life. And even through data storage, mining and analysis, the large data played a greater role to comprehensively promote the user value, business value and social value.

References

Xin, L., Jikun, L.: Possible opportunity: the concept and practice of product service system design. Creat. Des. **16**(05), 15–17 (2011). China

Saffer, D.: Designing for Interaction: Creating Smart Applications and Clever Devices. New Riders, Berkely (2007)

Michael, E., Marshall, T.: Design Dictionary: Perspectives on Design Terminology, p. 355. Birkhauser, Boston (2008)

Liu, B., Ye, G., Xiong, C.: Research and design of intelligent kitchen catering system. Design **16**(13), 100–101 (2016). China

CBNData & TMall.com: Chinese family table consumption trend report (2017). China. http://www.yicai.com/data/cbndata/

Real-Time Visualization of the Degree of Indoor Congestion with Smartphone-Based Participatory Sensing

Tomoya Kitazato$^{(\boxtimes)}$, Kyoichi Ito, Keisuke Umezawa, Masaki Ito, and Kaoru Sezaki

Institute of Industrial Science, The University of Tokyo,
Komaba 4-6-1, Meguro, Tokyo, Japan
{t-kitazato,k-ito,k-umezawa}@mcl.iis.u-tokyo.ac.jp,
{mito,sezaki}@iis.u-tokyo.ac.jp

Abstract. Real-time visualization of the degree of indoor congestion is very useful to improve users' experience in public spaces such as an event space or a shopping mall by helping users to identify crowded places to avoid congestion. However, it is difficult to develop a low-cost congestion visualization system. We designed a low-cost system for real-time visualization of indoor congestion degree with smartphone-based participatory sensing. The system is cost-effective, using Wi-Fi access point fingerprint-based indoor localization and Bluetooth-based congestion sensing with smartphone-based participatory sensing. In this paper, we develop a prototype of the proposed system. Moreover, we evaluate the prototype system from two aspects: first, how low is the cost of the system for sensing; second, how close is the relationship between congestion and the number of Bluetooth devices. We experimented in two places and found that the proposed system is cost-effective and the number of Bluetooth devices does have a relationship with the degree of congestion.

Keywords: Mobile computing · Participatory sensing · Bluetooth · Indoor localization

1 Introduction

Real-time visualization of the degree of indoor congestion is very helpful to improve users' experience in public spaces such as an event space, and it is also helpful for managers trying to equalize the density of people. In a public space, people gather in some popular shops or exhibition booths and shape the crowd around them. This crowd can often be the cause of trouble. For example, because of the narrow space available for walking, pedestrians are prone to falling over, and there is a high possibility that others will be tripped. If the degree of indoor congestion is visualized, users can identify crowded places to avoid congestion, and they can also reduce their waiting times. Moreover, managers of public facilities can equalize the density of the people to prevent problems caused by

© Springer International Publishing AG 2017
N. Streitz and P. Markopoulos (Eds.): DAPI 2017, LNCS 10291, pp. 286–301, 2017.
DOI: 10.1007/978-3-319-58697-7_21

crowding. Therefore, visualization of the degree of indoor congestion helps in keeping public spaces safe and in improving users' experience and management of facilities.

However, visualization of indoor congestion is difficult because it costs too much. If we install fixed sensors in all areas of a public space, the costs would be too high. For example, when the event space covers an area of $20,000\,m^2$, if the manager wants to sense congestion in each $400\,m^2$, 50 sensors would be needed. It is also a difficult task to install sensors in all areas. Sensors would need to be placed in each individual part and there would also be the need to calibrate sensors in some cases. This process would cost much time and human resources. Moreover, the layout of an event space changes frequently because of the changes of the contents. Sensors would need to be reinstalled to manage these frequent changes.

As mentioned above, visualization of the degree of congestion is helpful, but it is difficult because of the large costs involved. Hence, we propose a low-cost method for the visualization of the degree of indoor congestion with smartphone-based participatory sensing in this paper. In our proposal, we use the smartphones of the visitors in an event space as sensors and scan Bluetooth devices and Wi-Fi access points around them. Then, the degree of congestion of each area can be visualized from the scanned data.

The contributions of this work are:

- the proposal of a low-cost system for the visualization of the degree of indoor congestion;
- the development of a prototype system; and
- the experimental evaluation of the proposed system.

The rest of the paper is organized as follows. Section 2 highlights the related work and Sect. 3 presents the requirements of the low-cost visualization system. Section 4 shows how we designed the system. Section 5 demonstrates the implementation of the prototype system and an evaluation is given in Sect. 6. Finally, Sect. 7 concludes our paper.

2   Related Works

Sensing pedestrian flow and pedestrian density has attracted a lot of attention, and it is an active area of study and development. Previous research has developed methods of sensing pedestrian flow and pedestrian density, but suitable methods for short-term low-cost sensing are limited.

The service-based visualization of the degree of congestion has already been published by some enterprises, because of the spread of smartphones [1,2]. Users' smartphones upload their positions obtained from a global positioning system (GPS) sensor when users use the map services, then the server of the enterprise processes the data and visualizes congestion. However, we cannot use GPS in an indoor environment because GPS signals are weakened by interference from the roofs or walls of buildings.

Light detection and ranging (LiDAR)-based pedestrian-flow sensing is an example method of pedestrian-flow sensing [3, 12]. In [3], the degree of congestion of the entire event space is clearly visualized. However, LiDAR is too expensive that to cover the whole space. Moreover, LiDAR is not good at responding to changes of the layout in spaces, because LiDAR detects pedestrians by detecting the difference between the obtained image and the background image of the space. Therefore, we need to prepare a background image when we change the layout of the space.

Audio-based and acceleration-based congestion classification is useful for estimating the smoothness of pedestrian flows [6]. They proposed a method to measure congestion by collecting sound and the acceleration of surroundings from smartphones. In their research, they analyzed the relationship between step intervals and congestion and the relationship between surrounding sounds and congestion by fast Fourier transformation (FFT). However, it is difficult to use this method in our case, because we need to measure the congestion in a public space such as an event space. Here, the sounds and the exhibition style are different in each case, for example, it is very loud in a music concert, but it is very quiet in a museum.

Bluetooth-scan-based sensing is the method we have chosen. In recent years, many Bluetooth devices have entered daily life such as smartphones, portable headsets, and wearable bands. A previous experiment in scanning Bluetooth devices in a museum has succeeded in analyzing the flow of visitors [11]. The authors installed fixed sensors at seven significant places in the museum and collected the MAC address emitted by Bluetooth devices. They reported that about 8.2% of visitors activated Bluetooth on their mobile device while in the museum. Moreover, previous research used the number of devices, the mean signal strength, and the variance of the signal strength of scanned Bluetooth devices for categorizing the degree of congestion [10]. They also classified the degree of congestion using a classifier tree with six features of the scanned Bluetooth devices [9]. This research succeeded in classifying crowd density with over 75% recognition accuracy on seven discrete classes.

As we have shown above, there are various methods for congestion sensing. Many of these methods achieved congestion sensing, but only the Bluetooth-based sensing is useful for our goal of a low-cost system of real-time visualization of indoor congestion. A detailed discussion of the method of selection for sensing is described in Sect. 4.3.

3 Requirements

The method for congestion sensing in public space needs to be low cost. In public spaces, we need frequent preparation for sensing because the layout of the public space can often change. For example, in a museum, the contents of a special exhibition change about every 3 months. In an exhibition hall, the layout changes more frequently. In extreme cases, changes can occur every day. Thus, we consider a method to reduce the costs of sensing.

We focused on three aspects of costs for sensing: time, money, and labor. Time means the time required for preparation and sensing. Installing sensors in all areas of the event space would require a large amount of time. Some types of sensors also need calibration for sensing. Money means the costs of purchasing and installing sensors. For example, LiDAR is a very elaborate sensor, but it often costs over US$5000. In addition, if we need to install many sensors in the space, these costs are multiplied. We also want to reduce the labor required for preparation and sensing. Installing sensors in a large space can require a lot of labor, and installing sensors in areas such as the ceiling can be a difficult task.

4 System Design

4.1 System Overview

In this section, we design the real-time visualization system of the degree of indoor congestion. In our system, there are three components: preparation for indoor localization, data collection, and visualization, as shown in Fig. 1. To localize sensing points, we need to prepare for indoor localization with methods such as an installation of sensors and calibration of sensors. After that, participants collect data to visualize congestion. Then, the system rotates the cycle of collection and visualization. We describe the design of each of these three components.

Fig. 1. Process of visualization

4.2 Preparation for Indoor Localization

We decided to adopt a Wi-Fi fingerprinting-based indoor localization method for the system because of its low-cost installation. In a fingerprint-based approach, we make a fingerprint by recording the received signal strength indicators (RSSIs) of Wi-Fi access points at each area in advance. We can localize the object by comparing the RSSIs of Wi-Fi access points with the fingerprint. Hence, we only need to scan Wi-Fi access points in each area in this method when we prepare for indoor localization.

There are two reasons why we selected the Wi-Fi access points fingerprint-based approach for localization. First, some methods need some installation for indoor localization, but in the Wi-Fi access points fingerprint-based approach, Wi-Fi access points are often already installed in public spaces. Second, in this method, we do not need to know the positions of Wi-Fi access points, unlike in other Wi-Fi-based methods.

Indoor localization is an area of active research. However, some methods need to install expensive sensors and some methods need to calibrate or replace sensors frequently. There are four approaches to Wi-Fi-based indoor localization: triangulation by the signal strength of multiple access points, fingerprinting of the signal strength of access points, triangulation by the angle of arrival of signals, and triangulation by the time of flight of signals. Recent research has realized decimeter-level indoor localization [5,7]. As mentioned previously, unlike in other Wi-Fi-based approaches, in a fingerprint-based approach we do not need to know the positions of Wi-Fi access points. Radiofrequency identifiers (RFIDs) are also used for indoor localization. In the RFID-based method, reference RFID tags are deployed, and a reader can measure the signal strength from RFID tags. Then we can locate the position of the target RFID tag by comparing the signal strength of the target RFID tag with those of reference RFIDs. RFID-based localization has also realized decimeter-level localization [8]. A RFID tags are cheap sensors, but we would need to fix many reference RFID tags before localization. LiDAR and cameras can also be used for localization. They can localize pedestrians without pedestrians holding any devices, but they need calibration for installation and they are expensive.

4.3 Data Collection

In the data-collection phase, we need to collect congestion data and location data to visualize the degree of indoor congestion. We can collect location data by just scanning Wi-Fi access points. Hence, we need to consider a method to obtain congestion data.

We adopted a Bluetooth-based method for congestion sensing because of its low cost and precision. Bluetooth is a wireless communication technology at 2.4 GHz and is implemented on many devices such as smartphones, portable audio players, and smart watches. A Bluetooth device can scan other devices on its protocol and we now introduce the scanning process. The core architecture of Bluetooth is composed of three elements: controller stack, host stack, and host–controller interface (HCI). The controller stack defines the lower-level layers as a physical protocol including the physical layer and radio transceiver, and the host stack defines the higher level layers as logical protocols including application programming interfaces (APIs) and profiles. HCI delivers data between the host stack and controller stack. Bluetooth Low Energy (LE) is the controller stack that is available from Bluetooth version 4, and this protocol has no compatibility with legacy Bluetooth (the Basic Rate/Enhanced Data Rate (BR/EDR)). In Bluetooth BR/EDR, to discover other devices, a Bluetooth device can broadcast inquiry messages, and a device that can be discovered responds to inquiry messages with its ID. In this way, a Bluetooth device can discover nearby devices in BR/EDR. In Bluetooth LE, a Bluetooth device can enter the advertising mode to show its existence, and other devices can scan the advertising device by entering the scanning mode. Then, Bluetooth devices can also discover nearby devices in LE [4]. Bluetooth devices are categorized into three classes by their power: devices that can communicate within 1 m are categorized as class 3, within 10 m as class 2, and within 100 m as class 1. Almost all smartphones and headsets are class 2, so they can communicate within 10 m.

Now, we compare methods for congestion sensing from the five points of view of time cost, money cost, labor cost, indoor support, and precision of sensing congestion in public spaces. We compare service-based (with GPS), LiDAR-based, audio- and acceleration-based, and Bluetooth-based. GPS is a low-cost sensor in participatory sensing because we do not need to install sensors or purchase any equipment owing to pedestrians' smartphones already including GPS modules. However, we cannot use GPS indoors, so the service-based method is difficult to adapt. The LiDAR-based method is not low cost because the sensors need to be installed and calibrated. Moreover, LiDAR sensors are far too expensive. The audio- and acceleration-based method is low cost and supports indoor sensing. However, as we mentioned in Sect. 2, this method is specialized to detecting the smoothness of pedestrian flow, so it is not suitable for our purpose. The Bluetooth-based method is good for low-cost sensing in participatory sensing because pedestrians' smartphones already have Bluetooth modules, so we do not need to prepare additional equipment. Moreover, the Bluetooth-based method is available indoors and the precision of congestion estimation is good. Thus, we consider that the Bluetooth-based method with participatory sensing is the best method of congestion sensing. In Table 1 we present a comparison of the sensing methods.

Table 1. Comparison of methods for our use

Method	Time cost	Money cost	Labor cost	Indoor support	Precision
Service (with GPS)	✓	✓	✓	✗	✗
LiDAR	✗	✗	✗	✓	✓
Audio & Acceleration	✓	✓	✓	✓	✗
Bluetooth	✓	✓	✓	✓	✓

4.4 Visualization

In the visualization phase, we considered two elements. First, we visualize the congestion map on the participants' smartphones. Second, the server interpolates the congestion data if there is no data from some areas. In participatory sensing, it is difficult to rally participants without rewards. So we decided to visualize the congestion map on participants smartphones. Participants can receive beneficial information as the reward for participation. It is possible that there is no congestion data from some areas, so we decided to interpolate missing data using a spatiotemporal data interpolation method. There are labor costs involved if someone needs to collect data in each period. Congestion data are spatiotemporal data, so we consider that we can interpolate data with some methods.

5   Implementation

5.1   Overview of Our Prototype System

In this section, we describe the details of our implementation. The system is composed of two elements: a smartphone application and a server application. The smartphone application is implemented as an Android application. This application manages the scanning of Wi-Fi access points and Bluetooth devices, and visualization of the congestion map. The main functions of the server application are the localization of smartphones, congestion estimation, data storage, and data interpolation. An overview of the prototype system is shown in Fig. 2.

In preparation for the indoor localization phase, managers send information about the positions and Wi-Fi access points data using the smartphone application. Then, the server application stores the data of Wi-Fi access points in the database of Wi-Fi access points. In the data-collection phase, the smartphone application automatically scans Wi-Fi access points and Bluetooth devices and sends data to the server. The server application stores the data in the congestion database. In the visualization phase, the server application interpolates the missing data by kriging. When the smartphone application requests the congestion data, the server application returns the interpolated data and the smartphone application visualizes the data on the map. We now demonstrate the details of each phase.

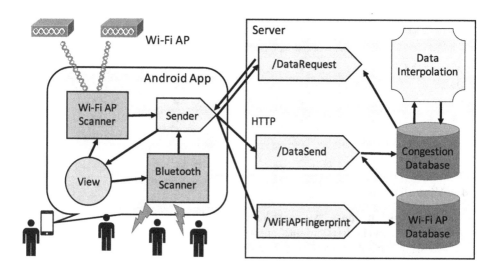

Fig. 2. System overview

5.2   Preparation for Indoor Localization

The manager of a public space can easily make a Wi-Fi fingerprint using the Wi-Fi scan mode of the smartphone application. In the Wi-Fi scan mode, the smartphone application sends the position and data of Wi-Fi access points to the server. Then the server application stores received data in the database. We can make a Wi-Fi access point fingerprint by simply doing this in each area.

The detailed usage of the Wi-Fi scan mode is described in the following. First, the manager fills in forms about the position (building name, level, room number (specification of the place), latitude, and longitude). Second, the manager pushes the send button, the smartphone application then scans the Wi-Fi access points and sends the information about the scanned access points and the input position to the server. A sample image of the Wi-Fi scan mode is given in Fig. 3a.

The Wi-Fi scan mode has a data delete function. If the manager sends data with delete checked, corresponding data will be deleted from the database on the server. Moreover, the smartphone application stores the history of sent data, so the manager can fill in the forms from history.

5.3   Data Collection

A participant can collect location data and congestion data by just holding their smartphone with the smartphone application installed. The smartphone application automatically scans Bluetooth devices and Wi-Fi access points every 30 s. After scanning, the application sends the data to the server as a JavaScript Object Notation (JSON) object over Hypertext Transfer Protocol (HTTP). The server receives the data from smartphone applications, then the server localizes the positions of the participant from scanned Wi-Fi access points data by comparing Wi-Fi fingerprints. After localization, the Bluetooth data are stored in the database with the localized position. When the server estimates the congestion, the server looks up the Bluetooth data and counts the number of Bluetooth devices. Hence, participants can achieve data collection for visualizing congestion by just walking around with the smartphone application.

5.4   Visualization

When a participant wants to see the real-time congestion map, they can load the congestion map by pushing the request button. When the request button is pushed, the smartphone application requests congestion data from the server. Then the server returns congestion data as a JSON object over HTTP. The smartphone application visualizes the degree of congestion by painting colors on the map. At present, we have decided to paint the high-density areas red and the low-density areas blue.

If the server does not have Bluetooth data from some areas, the server interpolates the congestion with kriging. In the prototype implementation, the interpolation program always runs in the background. The program interpolates the data and stores the interpolated congestion in the database.

(a) Wi-Fi Scan View

(b) Congestion View

Fig. 3. Screenshot of the smartphone application

6 Evaluation

We set up two experiments for evaluating our system. First, we evaluated the cost to prepare for indoor localization. We take the cost of setting up the system into account and then we need to evaluate this. Second, we evaluated the relationship between congestion and the number of Bluetooth devices. Previous research has already evaluated Bluetooth-based congestion sensing, but these approaches did not consider how wide an area is covered by the scanning Bluetooth devices. Thus, we need to evaluate the Bluetooth-based congestion-sensing method.

We performed our experiments at Makuhari Messe International Exhibition Hall 9–11 and at the Yaesu Shopping Mall. Makuhari Messe is the one of the largest exhibition halls in Japan. Tokyo Auto Salon 2017 was being held at the Makuhari Messe Hall during our experiment. Tokyo Auto Salon 2017 is an automotive industry showcase and demonstrate the latest technologies of automobile companies. The Yaesu Shopping Mall is the one of the largest shopping malls in Japan. The experimental environments are shown in Table 2. We partitioned the two venues into grid cells (20 m × 20 m) as shown in Fig. 8. Red stars denote sensing points, red lines denote main thoroughfares, and yellow rectangles denote booths or shops.

6.1 Cost to Prepare for Indoor Localization

We made Wi-Fi access points fingerprints by scanning Wi-Fi access points at each grid cell at Makuhari Messe International Exhibition Hall 9–11. Only three

Table 2. Information about the experimental space

Place	Area	Grid cells	Participants	Bluetooth scans	Map
Makuhari	18,000 m^2	40	3	56	Fig. 8a
Yaesu	15,000 m^2	37	3	37	Fig. 8b

people were involved. The instruction of usage of the application took 10 min. After that, we scanned Wi-Fi access points at 40 grid cells. It took 30 min to scan all the grid cells. Thus, it took only 40 min to prepare for indoor congestion visualization in the main hall.

6.2 Relationship Between Congestion and Number of Bluetooth Devices

To evaluate the relationship between congestion and the number of Bluetooth devices, we scanned the Bluetooth devices and counted the number of people in Makuhari Messe and the Yaesu Shopping Mall. We first describe how we collected the Bluetooth data and the pedestrian data. For scanning Bluetooth devices, we developed an Android application. By using this application, an Android smartphone scans Bluetooth BR/EDR devices for about 12 s and scans Bluetooth LE devices for 5 s. We scanned Bluetooth devices from three smartphones simultaneously, then we pick up all device data (Address, RSSI) scanned by three smartphones and if scanned devices are duplicated, selected the device whose RSSI is maximum. We counted the number of pedestrians in different ways between Makuhari Messe and the Yaesu Shopping Mall. In Makuhari Messe, we took photographs using a Ricoh Theta S and counted the number of people from the photographs. We counted the number of people within a distance of 10 m. In some photographs, we also counted the number of people within a distance of 15 m. In the Yaesu Shopping Mall, we counted the number of surrounding people within a distance of 15 m. The scenes of our measurements are shown in Fig. 4d.

The results of the experiments are shown in Fig. 5. For the sake of simplicity, we assigned IDs to the obtained pedestrian data as shown in Table 3. The lines on the graphs are regression lines. We consider the $y = ax$ model about the relationship between the number of pedestrians and the number of Bluetooth devices. In Fig. 5b, we can see a relationship between the number of Bluetooth devices and the number of pedestrians, but this is not visible in Fig. 5a.

Table 3. Assigned IDs to data

ID	Place	Pedestrian count range
A	Makuhari Messe	10 m
B	Makuhari Messe	15 m
C	The Yaesu Shopping Mall	15 m

(a) Environment of Makuhari Messe   (b) Environment of the Yaesu Shopping
                                     Mall

(c) Photograph of Makuhari   (d) Measurement in Makuhari Messe
Messe by a Ricoh Theta S

Fig. 4. Experiment

We calculated Pearson correlation coefficients between the number of pedestrians and the number of Bluetooth devices to examine the relationship between them. Before calculating the Pearson correlation coefficients, we applied the Shapiro–Wilk test to both the Bluetooth data and the pedestrian data for an α level of 0.05. The p-values of the tests are shown in Table 4. We cannot reject the null hypothesis that the data are from a normally distributed population except for Bluetooth LE data of C. Hence, we calculated the Pearson correlation coefficients, and the results are shown in Table 5. As shown in Table 5, the number of pedestrians and the number of Bluetooth devices has some correlation in data B and C, but it has hardly any correlation in data A. We considered that the reason why we could not find a correlation in data A was the short radius of counting pedestrians. In light of these results, our application detected Bluetooth devices out of range of 10 m.

We also calculated the Pearson correlation coefficients with various thresholds of RSSI of Bluetooth devices because we considered that the RSSI thresholds exclude some influence of distant devices. The results are shown in Fig. 6.

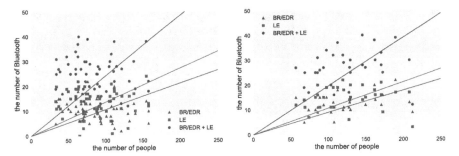

(a) Pedestrian data A and Bluetooth data   (b) Pedestrian data B and Bluetooth data

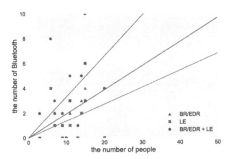

(c) Pedestrian data C and Bluetooth data

Fig. 5. Relationship between the number of pedestrians and the number of bluetooth devices

Table 4. The p-values of the Shapiro–Wilk test

	A	B	C
Pedestrian	0.147	0.284	0.867
Bluetooth BD/EDR	0.353	0.203	0.163
Bluetooth LE	0.184	0.493	**0.005**
Bluetooth BD/EDR + EL	0.601	0.391	0.196

Table 5. Pearson correlation coefficient between the number of pedestrians and the number of bluetooth devices

	A	B	C
Bluetooth BD/EDR	−0.211	**0.310**	**0.521**
Bluetooth LE	−0.007	**0.188**	**0.248**
Bluetooth BD/EDR + EL	−1.115	**0.303**	**0.401**

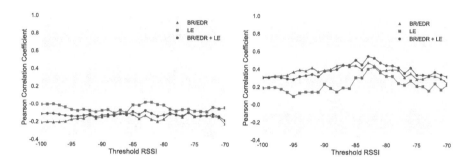

(a) Pedestrian data A and Bluetooth data   (b) Pedestrian data B and Bluetooth data

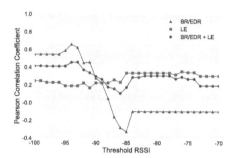

(c) Pedestrian data C and Bluetooth data

Fig. 6. Pearson correlation coefficient between the number of pedestrians and the number of bluetooth devices with various RSSI thresholds

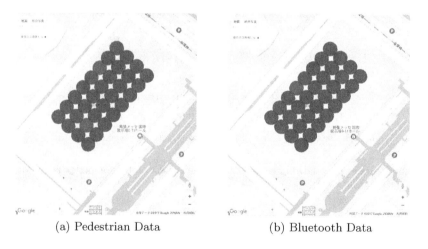

(a) Pedestrian Data   (b) Bluetooth Data

Fig. 7. Visualization of pedestrian data B and corresponding bluetooth data (Color figure online)

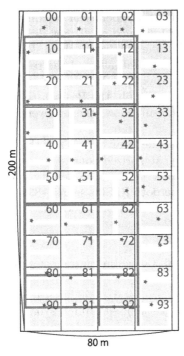

(a) Makuhari Messe Layout

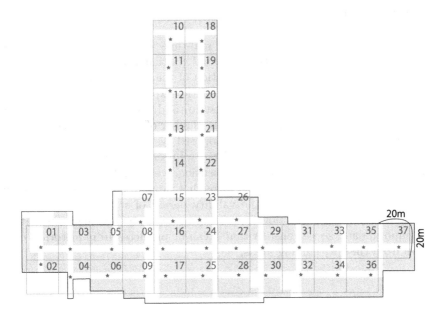

(b) The Yaesu Shopping Mall Layout

Fig. 8. Layouts of the experimental space (Color figure online)

In Fig. 6a, the Pearson correlation coefficient is constantly low. It is possible that we cannot exclude the influence of distant devices. In Fig. 6c the shape of the graph is particularly different from others. We consider that the environment of the Yaesu Shopping Mall affected the results. The Yaesu Shopping Mall has many walls unlike Makuhari Messe, and walls can interfere with the Bluetooth signal. However, in Fig. 6b, the Pearson correlation coefficients have a peak around −83 dB. This result shows the achievement of removing the noise of distant devices.

Finally, we visualized the pedestrian data B and the corresponding Bluetooth data as shown in Fig. 7. We categorized congestion degrees into four classes as shown in Table 6 and red color means high density and blue color means low density. The threshold of Bluetooth RSSI is set as −83 and the Bluetooth devices include both Bluetooth BR/EDR and Bluetooth LE. In this setting, the Pearson correlation coefficient is 0.482.

Table 6. Congestion degree categories

Category	1	2	3	4
Density (people/m^2)	–0.1	0.1–0.2	0.2–0.3	0.3–

7   Conclusion

In this paper, we proposed a system of real-time visualization of the degree of indoor congestion with smartphone-based participatory sensing. Then, we demonstrated the design and implementation of the prototype system. We also set up two experiments, and the results of the experiments show the ease of preparing and installing the proposed system, and also show the relationship between the number of pedestrians and the number of Bluetooth devices. These results support the applicability of our proposed system.

As future work, we have two tasks. First, we need to investigate the validity period of scanned data. In participatory sensing, we cannot control the sensing interval in one area, so it sometimes happens that we cannot obtain data for some period. Thus, we need to decide the validity period of scanned data. Second, we consider developing a function for predicting congestion. Congestion data is spatiotemporal data, so we consider that it can be predicted from historical data and data from the surrounding areas.

References

1. Konzatsudo Map [density map]. http://lab.its-mo.com/densitymap/
2. Yahoo! Chizu [yahoo! map]. http://map.yahoo.co.jp/maps?layer=crowd&v=3
3. Asahara, A., Sato, N., Nomiya, M., Tsuji, S.: LiDAR-based pedestrian-flow analysis for crowdedness equalization. In: Proceedings of the 23rd SIGSPATIAL International Conference on Advances in Geographic Information Systems (2015)
4. Bluetooth SIG Inc.: Bluetooth core specification version 5.0 (2016)
5. Kotaru, M., Joshi, K., Bharadia, D., Katti, S.: SpotFi: Decimeter level localization using WiFi. SIGCOMM Comput. Commun. Rev. **45**, 269–282 (2015)
6. Nishimura, T., Higuchi, T., Yamaguchi, H., Higashino, T.: Detecting smoothness of pedestrian flows by participatory sensing with mobile phones. In: Proceedings of the 2014 ACM International Symposium on Wearable Computers (2014)
7. Vasisht, D., Kumar, S., Katabi, D.: Decimeter-level localization with a single wifi access point. In: 13th USENIX Symposium on Networked Systems Design and Implementation (NSDI 2016) (2016)
8. Wang, J., Katabi, D.: Dude, where's my card? RFID positioning that works with multipath and non-line of sight. In: Proceedings of the ACM SIGCOMM 2013 Conference on SIGCOMM (2013)
9. Weppner, J., Lukowicz, P.: Bluetooth based collaborative crowd density estimation with mobile phones. In: 2013 IEEE International Conference on Pervasive Computing and Communications (PerCom) (2013)
10. Weppner, J., Lukowicz, P.: Collaborative crowd density estimation with mobile phones. In: Proceedings of ACM PhoneSense (2011)
11. Yoshimura, Y., Sobolevsky, S., Ratti, C., Girardin, F., Carrascal, J.P., Blat, J., Sinatra, R.: An analysis of visitors' behavior in the Louvre Museum: a study using bluetooth data. Plann. Des. Environ. Plann. B **41**, 1113–1131 (2014)
12. Zhao, H., Shibasaki, R.: A novel system for tracking pedestrians using multiple single-row laser-range scanners. IEEE Trans. Syst. Man Cybern. Part A Syst. Hum. **35**, 283–291 (2005)

Radioactive Soundscape Project

Hiroki Kobayashi[1,2(✉)] and Hiromi Kudo[1]

[1] Center of Spatial Information Science, The University of Tokyo,
Kashiwa, Chiba 277-8568, Japan
{Kobayashi,kudo3}@csis.u-tokyo.ac.jp
[2] PRESTO, Japan Science and Technology Agency, Kawaguchi, Japan

Abstract. Acoustic ecology data have been used for various types of soundscape investigations. Counting sounds in the soundscape is considered an effective method in ecology studies and offers comparative data for human-caused impacts on the environment. One particularly valuable dataset of broadcasted recordings from the "difficult-to-return zone (exclusion zone)" area, 10 km from the Fukushima Daiichi Nuclear Power Plant was collected by Hill H. Kobayashi and H. Kudo in the Oamaru District (Namie, Fukushima, Japan) in 2016. These audio samples, which have not yet been analyzed (a total of over 700 h in MP3 format), were continuously transmitted in a live stream of sound from an unmanned remote sensing station in the area. In 2016, the first part of that collection of audio sample covering the transmitted sound recording from the station was made available on the project website. The data package described here covers the bioacoustics in the area. We expect these recordings to prove useful for studies on topics, which include radioecology and the emerging dialects for future observations.

Keywords: Acoustic ecology · Radioecology

1 Introduction

According to the Chernobyl nuclear disaster report of the International Atomic Energy Agency [1], it is academically and socially important to conduct ecological studies concerning the levels and effects of radiation exposure on wild animal populations over several generations. Although many studies and investigation were conducted around the Chernobyl nuclear power plant, there were little audio samples. At last, twenty years after the Chernobyl disaster, Peter Cusack made recordings in the exclusion zone in Ukraine [2]. To understand the effects of the nuclear accident, long-term and wide-range monitoring of the effects of nuclear radiation on animals is required because there is little evidence of the direct effects of radioactivity on the wildlife in Fukushima [3]. Immediately following the Fukushima Daiichi Nuclear Power Plant disaster, whose remnants are shown in Fig. 1, Ishida (a research collaborator at the University of Tokyo) started conducting regular ecological studies of wild animals in the northern Abukuma Mountains near the Fukushima Daiichi Nuclear Power Plant, where high levels of radiation were detected. Ishida reported that it is essential to place automatic recording devices (e.g., portable digital recorders) at over 500 locations to collect and analyze the vocalizations of target wild animals [3]. For monitoring such species, counting the

© Springer International Publishing AG 2017
N. Streitz and P. Markopoulos (Eds.): DAPI 2017, LNCS 10291, pp. 302–311, 2017.
DOI: 10.1007/978-3-319-58697-7_22

recorded calls of animals is considered an effective method because acoustic communication is used by various animals, including mammals, birds, amphibians, fish, and insects [4, 5]. In addition to using visual counts, this method, in particular, is commonly used to investigate the habitat of birds and amphibians [6]. Furthermore, the ecological studies of the environment near urban areas are being conducted using cell phones [7]. However, it is difficult to use such information devices in the exclusion zone as these areas do not have infrastructure services. Therefore, it is necessary to develop a monitoring system capable of operating over multiple years to ensure long-term stability under unmanned operating conditions.

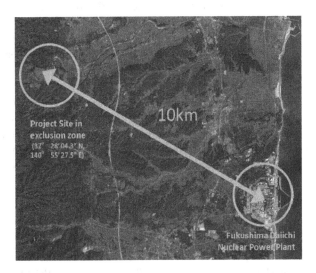

Fig. 1. Location of project site in exclusion zone (37° 28′ 04.3″ N, 140° 55′ 27.5″ E), which is 10 km from Fukushima Daiichi Nuclear Power Plant.

2   Background

As introduced above, in ecological studies, it is desirable to develop a technology that most effectively supports a study with minimal resources. More specifically, we aim to establish a long-term continuously operating ubiquitous system that delivers, in real time, environmental information, such as sound. Researchers worldwide are conducting ecological studies by recording and analyzing the spatial information of wild animal vocalizations [3]. To record vocalizations of wild animals whose behaviors are difficult to predict, it is necessary to continuously operate a monitoring system. As it is difficult to conduct system maintenance due to the severe environmental conditions of wild animal habitats (e.g., when out of infrastructure service areas and in radioactive environments), system redundancy becomes crucial.

We have previously researched and developed proprietary systems that deliver and record remote environmental sounds in real time for ecology studies [8]. Since 1996, this system has been almost continuously operational at the Iriomote Island (Okinawa).

To date, the basic research at the Iriomote Island has expanded to include 18 domestic and international sites, including Los Angeles and the San Francisco Bay area in the United States, Sanshiro Pond at the Hongo Campus of the University of Tokyo in Japan, Kyoto Shokokuji Mizuharu in Suikinkutsu, Mumbai in India, and the Syowa Station in Antarctica (under construction). We have worked with project collaborators and introduced our system to the University of Tokyo Chichibu Forest, Otsuchi in Iwate, Shinshu University, the University of Tokyo Fuji Forests, the University of Tokyo Hokkaido Forest (under construction), the University of Tokyo International Coastal Research Center, and at an uninhabited island in Iwate [10]. We have also demonstrated [10] that (a) the transmission of live sound from a remote woodland can be effectively used by researchers to monitor birds in a remote location, (b) the simultaneous involvement of several participants via Internet Relay Chat to listen to live sound transmissions can enhance the accuracy of census data collection, and (c) the interactions via Twitter allowed public volunteers (e.g., citizen scientists) to engage with and help the remote monitoring of birds and experience the inaccessible nature using novel technologies.

With these achievements, the Radioactive Soundscape project aims to collect, share, and analyze the soundscape data at over 500 locations in the exclusion zone by performing the following activities: (1) Distributing these sound data in the exclusion zone to the public via the Internet, in order to make the live sounds in the area publicly available for listening in real time and (2) distributing these sound data to the public via the Internet.

3   Methods

This project installed the first transmitter station [9] in the exclusion zone area (10 km from the Fukushima Daiichi Nuclear Power Plant). A map of the exclusion zone in Fukushima (Japan) is shown in Fig. 2. The transmitter station is located at the Oamaru district in the Namie town, Fukushima (37° 28′ 04.3″ N, 140° 55′ 27.5″ E). We chose this site in the exclusion zone because it is one of the most difficult areas for long-term

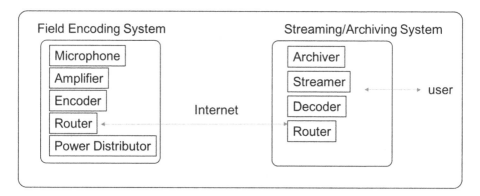

Fig. 2. System diagram of live sound system: field encoding system (left) and streaming/archiving system (right).

and continuous investigations. First, the difficult-to-return zone is the most radioactively polluted zone in Fukushima. Second, no remote sensing method at the surface level is available due to the lack of power and information infrastructure. Third, field surveys are required; however, the amount of workable hours is extremely limited due to radiation exposure concerns. Further, frequently used portable recorders require regular replacement owing to the memory and battery capacities, which is impractical for long-term and continuous investigations.

This project aims to collect, share, and analyze the soundscape data at over 500 locations in the exclusion zone. Therefore, for the first location, we developed a "Live Sound System" and a "Streaming/Archiving System" that enables us to perform the following activities: (1) Distribute the sound data in the exclusion zone to the public via the Internet in order to make the live sounds in the difficult-to-return zone publicly available for listening in real time and (2) distribute the sound data to the public via the Internet. The Live Sound System, as illustrated in Fig. 3, comprises separate subsystems: a "Field Encoding System" (to digitize the live sounds in the forests) and a "Streaming/ Archiving System" (to conduct live sound delivery via the Internet and archive the sound data in a recorded file). The technical operational testing notes of the Live Sound System can be found in our previous study [10].

Fig. 3. The first transmitter station at project site in exclusion zone.

The Field Encoding System (Fig. 2) established in the remote forest includes the antenna depicted in our previous study [10]. This system comprises two blocks: an audio block and a transmission block. The microphones (omnidirectional SONY F-115B microphones) are individually connected to the amplifier (XENYX 802, Behringer) of the audio block and their outputs serve as input to the audio encoder (instreamer100, Barix) to convert the microphone sounds into MP3, the format used for subsequent digital sound delivery. As there was no prior Internet connection at the exclusion zone site, we incorporated a satellite Internet service, which was provided by IPSTAR in April 2016. We subscribed to IPSTAR's "Dual" service plan, which provides the largest upload bandwidth of 2 mbps for approximately US $125 per month. There is also a daily limit (2 GB) on data usage per customer. These characteristics of the service plan are important because the research funds required to conduct a long-term ecological study are likely to fluctuate over time. The power supply to the Field Encoding System is provided by a local electric company via a special contract. Indeed, the company needed to reconstruct the infrastructure in the exclusion zone after the devastating damage caused by the earthquake. This reconstruction was important for the long-term continuity of the project. To continuously operate the system using solar panels or other independent power sources, frequent system maintenance at the site would be required.

The Streaming/Archiving System is located in the server room in our laboratory and has a normal bandwidth Internet connection, allowing simultaneous public access to transmissions (Fig. 2). Two servers are used, one for streaming and the other for archiving. The servers were established in the laboratory due to technical difficulties (e.g., the previously mentioned problems with power supply and data download limits) involved in the setup and operation of such a server at the relevant site. The processed audio signal is sent from the microphone, encoded into an MP3 live stream in the Field Encoding System, and transferred to the Streaming/Archiving System. The MP3 live stream can then be simultaneously played on MP3-based audio software worldwide. We use a standard single package of Linux Fedora 14 as the operating system and the Icecast 2 software as the sound delivery server. We have used Icecast 2 in our projects since the beginning and have experienced only minor problems, e.g., a slight delay (0.5 s) in the sound transmission. However, the signal strength of our system is affected by severe weather, such as heavy rain or snowstorms, and this could cause communication delays with the satellite network. To address this, we adjusted the amount of information that could be received by the network (via the Linux TCP Receive Window) to ensure that interruptions do not occur when transmitting sounds on the streaming server. Finally, to share the encoded live sound with listeners at high availability, the archiving server stores all the MP3 sound format files that are sent from the Field Encoding System through the Streaming Server. According to the Radioactive Soundscape project, it was important to make live transmissions publicly available for listening purposes and have access to the archive to experience changes over a day as well as across all the seasons.

This project started with a year of literature search (2011), fundraising with government approval (2012–2014), and the installation of a transmitter station with satellite Internet (2015). Finally, based on official preparations and approvals, a local electric company agreed to sign a service contract with us in 2016 after an intensive feasibility survey of the all transmission facilities at the location. The final construction was completed at the end of March in 2016 in Fig. 3. This project aims to operate the system for 24 h in a day and 365 days a year. Prior to this project, we had experience in operating a similar system for more than 10 years. Therefore, it is possible to operate this project until approximately 2030.

4   Data Records

The Radioactive Soundscape project aims to collect, share, and analyze soundscape data (mp3, 160 kbps, 2ch, mono) at over 500 locations in the exclusion zone. The data records with the organization must meet the following requirements:

1. Identify the project names from the filename
2. Identify more than 500 stations from the filename
3. Identify the event schedule (time) from the filename

For each level, we provide a registry of all the campaigns, stations, and events in universal resource locator (URL) queries. Filenames that indicate the project, station, and start of timestamp are built using a consistent syntax that has the following format:
projectname_station#_date(yyyymmddhhMM).mp3,
e.g., RS_1_201103111426.mp3.
Furthermore, every 24 files (1 day) is archived in a single TAR file.
e.g., RS_1_20160609.tar
The archived sound recordings are stored in the project web site.

5   Technical Validation

We provide a technical validation of the Radioactive Soundscape project data via the Checker file-validation software. Checker 0.96 (http://cgjennings.ca/checker/) performs a technical validation of the received MP3 format data. In addition, it measures the background noise by examining the quietest part of the data. A soundscape is defined as a set of various sounds that are spontaneously generated in a particular environment and that continually change, diurnally and day-to-day over a passage of time. It can be compared to a chorus defined by the geography or other physical aspects and the acoustic properties of an area. From the viewpoint of informatics, the amount and duration of bioacoustic information contained in sounds are small compared with the other continuously present environmental sounds, such as wind and running water. In contrast, the bird and animal calls are only a small fraction of the total soundscape.

Figure 4 shows the measured background noise of the samples (total duration = 742 h) from July 9, 2016 to June 8, 2016 that was validated by the software. The change in the background noise traits, such as the anthropogenic noise and the hum of the electricity power, determine the quality of the long-term structure of the data and the dynamics of the food webs and other ecological networks across the received recording. When the system is continuously operated by recording and broadcasting the sound for 24 h in a day over the entire year, it produces environmental factors (i.e., anthropogenic noise). The quality of the digital signal processed by the real-time audio-processing software decreases as the recording system operates over extended periods. In majority of the cases, the processed signal contains numerous heat-related "hum" sounds. Heat is generated by the recording system itself because it must operate in the extremely high moisture and temperature environment of the site. Therefore, to solve the heat problem, it was essential to set up a continuously operating cooling system. However, it is extremely difficult to configure a hardware mechanism to reliably operate under unmanned conditions.

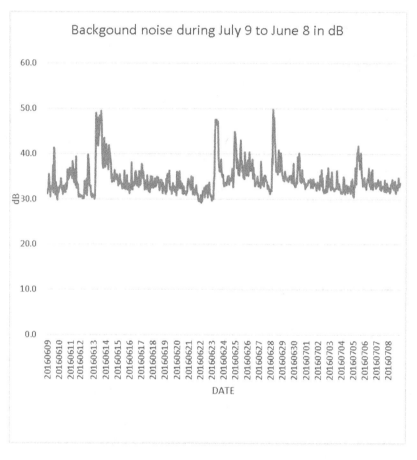

Fig. 4. The measured background noise in dB from July 9, 2016 to June 8, 2016.

6   Discussion

It has been 30 years since the Chernobyl nuclear disaster. In that time, wildlife has returned and appears to be thriving in the surrounding forests [1]. Although 20 million wild animals were killed in the immediate aftermath of the disaster, it is believed that a very small number of wild animals survived and adapted to the changing environment. These animals evolved and prospered in high-radiation areas. However, it took a long time to establish research organizations to conduct ecology studies, and the evolutionary process of the surviving animals remains unknown. Insight into the survival and evolution of radiation-exposed wild animals may result in insights into agriculture and forestry, animal husbandry, and medical care. However, long-term ecological studies of wild animals and their radiation exposure levels are required [3]. During the recovery from the Fukushima Nuclear Power Plant Disaster, the journal Nature (http://www.nature.com/news/2011/110527/full/news.2011.326.html) has pointed out the importance of ecological studies from the very beginning of a disaster. As described introduction, Ishida (research collaborator) of the University of Tokyo, who has conducted ecological studies since immediately after the disaster, has stated that it would be extremely difficult to continue conducting ecological studies on an ongoing basis [3]. However, the domain of human computer interactions can address these issues, and the authors claim with confidence that the proposed project will address these issues successfully through our project web page in Fig. 5.

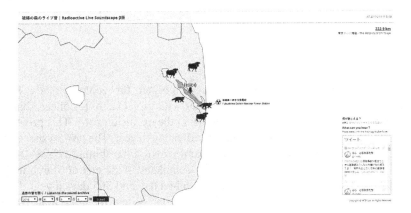

Fig. 5. Web interface for radioactive live soundscape http://radioactivelivesoundscape.net/

7 Future Direction

Investigations into natural environments consider living creatures and their natural environments, and are important to review the value of biological diversity from various perspectives. It is currently possible to obtain ecological information about wild animals in remote areas using various ubiquitous systems. However, an information and electrical power supply infrastructure is essential to the operation of these systems, and thus, they are limited to the areas serviced by such infrastructure studies around the Fukushima Daiichi Nuclear Power Plant. To abate this limitation, researchers have started using wearable sensors for wild animals (Fig. 6). To collect the data recorded by the wearable sensors, it is necessary to recapture the monitoring subjects; thus, wearable sensors are limited to collecting data from the recaptured subjects' habitats. To solve the problems with existing systems, the proposed project will develop "a system where wild animals carry a wearable sensor; record the spatial information in their territory through individual actions; share the information obtained through group actions, with reduced power requirements; and eventually upload the shared information on the Internet.

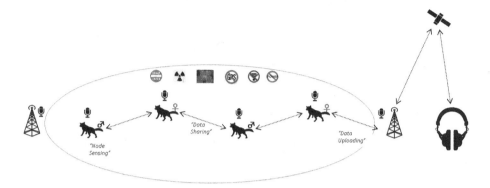

Fig. 6. Proposed sensing system-concept image

8 Conclusion

This paper presents Radioactive Soundscape project for ecology study for the Fukushima Daiichi Nuclear Power Plant disaster. This project aims to collect, share, and analyze sound-scape data at over 500 locations in the exclusion zone. This project also aims to operate the system for 24 h in a day and 365 days a year. The project successfully installed the first transmitter station in the Namie town, Fukushima (37° 28′ 04.3″ N, 140° 55′ 27.5″ E). The final construction was completed at the end of March in 2016. This project aims to operate the system for 24 h in a day and 365 days a year. Prior to this project, we had experience in operating a similar system for more than 10 years. Therefore, it is possible to operate this project until approximately 2030.

Acknowledgement. This study was supported by the JSPS KAKENHI Grant 26700015, 16K12666, MIC SCOPE Grant 142103015 162103107, JST PRESTO 11012, Telecommunications Advancement Foundation, Moritani Scholarship Foundation, Tateisi Science and Technology Foundation, and Mitsubishi Foundation.

References

1. Chernobyl Forum: Expert Group "Environment" & International Atomic Energy Agency. Environmental consequences of the Chernobyl accident and their remediation: twenty years of experience; report of the Chernobyl Forum Expert Group "Environment." International Atomic Energy Agency (2006)
2. Cusack, P.: Sounds from Dangerous Places. ReR Megacorp (2012)
3. Ishida, K.: Agricultural Implications of the Fukushima Nuclear Accident. In: Nakanishi, T.M., Tanoi, K. (eds.) 119–129. Springer, Japan (2013). Chap. 12
4. Krebs, J.R., Davies, N.B.: An introduction to behavioural ecology. Blackwell Scientific Publications, Hoboken (1993)

5. Searcy, W.A., Nowicki, S.: The Evolution of Animal Communication: Reliability and Deception in Signaling Systems. Princeton University Press, Princeton (2005)
6. Heyer, W.R.: Measuring and Monitoring Biological Diversity: Standard Methods for Amphibians. Smithsonian Institution Press, Silver Hill (1994)
7. Hans, S., Peet, M.: Ecology: Birds sing at a higher pitch in urban noise. Nature **424**, 267 (2003). doi:10.1038/424267a
8. Kobayashi, H.: Basic research in human-computer-biosphere interaction. Ph.D. thesis, The University of Tokyo (2010)
9. Kobayashi, H., Kudo, H.: Acoustic ecology data transmitter in exclusion zone, 10 km from Fukushima Daiichi Nuclear Power Plant. LEONARDO/J. Int. Soc. Arts Sci. Technol. MIT Press (accepted)
10. Saito, K., et al.: Utilizing the cyberforest live sound system with social media to remotely conduct woodland bird censuses in Central Japan. Ambio **44**, 572–583 (2015). doi:10.1007/s13280-015-0708-y

Civic Tech and Ambient Data in the Public Realm

Challenges and Opportunities for Learning Cities and Smart Cities

H. Patricia McKenna[✉]

AmbientEase and the UrbanitiesLab, Victoria, Canada
mckennaph@gmail.com

Abstract. This work highlights issues associated with the sharing and using of data for learning and solution making in smart cities and learning cities. Moving beyond dichotomous dystopian and utopian views of civic tech, smart cities, and urban data initiatives, this paper explores everyday understandings of data through diverse voices. Theoretically this work uses the contructs of awareness, learning, openness, and meaningful engagement to explore civic tech and ambient data in 21st century cities. Using an exploratory case study approach, data were collected through interview and survey from individuals in small to medium to large sized cities, mostly in Canada but also extending to Europe. In parallel with this study ancedotal evidence was gathered from people across the city through group and individual discussions enabling further analysis, comparison, and triangulation of data. This work contributes to theorizing of the ambient data concept in the context of smart cities; further develops the learning cities component of smart cities; formulates and operationalizes an ambient data framework for smart cities; and sheds light on the complex challenges of aware technologies as opportunities for increased human potential. Going forward, this opening of an ambient data space provides opportunities for further development, debate, and exploration for both practice and research.

Keywords: Ambient data · Ambient privacy · Awareness · Civic tech · Engagement · Learning · Learning cities · Openness · Smart cities

1 Introduction

In the context of the wicked issues facing education [1] and urban areas [2] in the 21st century, this work explores data challenges and opportunities for smart cities [3]. Schmitt [4] points to the importance of urban data emanating from "the city's inhabitants and its infrastructure" in real time, "producing a constant flow" that may be understood "as the new building material of the future dynamic city." Gordon and Mihailidis [5] claim that civic tech "typically refers to work within government" but that this space "has grown significantly" to include many businesses, groups and individuals. Where Townsend [6] noted that, "we experience the symbiosis of place and cyberspace everyday", Konomi and Roussos [7] claim that, "we are now going beyond the last decade's conception of smart cities" and moving "towards a deeper level of symbiosis among smart citizens, Internet of Things and ambient spaces." As such, this work focuses on the problems

© Springer International Publishing AG 2017
N. Streitz and P. Markopoulos (Eds.): DAPI 2017, LNCS 10291, pp. 312–331, 2017.
DOI: 10.1007/978-3-319-58697-7_23

associated with the sharing and using of data for learning and solution making in technology-pervasive urban environments. Moving beyond dichotomous dystopian and utopian views [6] of civic tech, smart cities, and urban data initiatives, this paper explores the potentials and opportunities identified by Hespanhol and Tomitsch [8] in relation to 'responsive ambient' interfaces and what Florida [9] refers to as the "legitimately exciting use of new data" in cities.

This work is significant in that it explores everyday understandings of data in smart cities from multiple perspectives through diverse voices; contributes to theorizing of the ambient data concept in the context of smart cities; and further develops the learning cities component of smart cities in relation to ambient data. The main objective of this paper is to explore existing and emergent understandings of data in contemporary urban environments, characterized by pervasive and aware technologies, in shedding light on complex challenges as opportunities for increased awareness, learning, openness, and meaningful engagement. A review of the research literature on smart cities and learning cities in relation to data, and more particularly real-time data, is provided in developing the theoretical perspective for this work and formulation of an ambient data framework. Using an exploratory case study approach, data collection techniques included a combination of interview and survey. In parallel with this study, qualitative data were also collected through group and individual discussions with a range of people across the city. Content analysis was used in the deductive and inductive analysis of data from the literature review and interviews/discussions, respectively. Additional details on methodology are provided in Sect. 3 of this paper.

What follows is the theoretical perspective for this paper including the research questions and propositions under exploration, the methodology, and a presentation and discussion of findings. The contributions of this work are identified along with the limitations and mitigations, followed by the conclusion.

2 Theoretical Perspective

This section provides a review of the literature for smart cities and learning cities in relation to data, data challenges, and data opportunities. With this background, formulation of an ambient data framework for learning cities and smart cities is advanced in support of an inquiry into the research questions and propositions for this paper.

2.1 Smart Cities and Learning Cities

Townsend [6] defines smart cities as "places where information technology is combined with infrastructure, architecture, everyday objects and even our bodies, to address social, economic, and environmental problems." Referring to the smart city as a work in progress, and claiming that "there isn't any single place we can go to see a smart city in its entirety" because building such a thing is "a long, messy, incremental process", Townsend [6] poses what he considers to be the "more important and interesting question" of "what do you want a smart city to be?" Albino et al. [10] conducted a review of the literature and found that the smart city label "is a fuzzy concept" that "is used in ways that are not always consistent." Incorporating the people component of smart cities enables an understanding of social infrastructure in cities and key drivers such as creativity, education, learning, and knowledge [10].

Nam and Pardo [11] identify a learning city in relation to the three main dimensions of a smart city (technology, people, and institutions) where "the critical factor in any successful city is its people and how they interact." While "a smart city is also a learning city" according to Nam and Pardo [11], "learning cities are actively involved in building a skilled information economy workforce" and fostering "social learning for strengthening human infrastructure." UNESCO describes a learning city as one that "effectively mobilizes its resources in every sector to promote inclusive learning from basic to higher education" [12] extending to workplaces, new technologies, and a culture of lifelong learning. In response to "why learning cities?" UNESCO maintains that "learning throughout life is becoming increasingly relevant in today's fast-changing world where social, economic and political norms are constantly being redefined." Indeed, UNESCO provides guidelines for building learning cities [13], arguing that, "a learning society must be built province by province, city by city, and community by community" [12]. Adams Becker et al. [1] note the "move away from traditional lecture-based programming" towards "more hands-on scenarios" where "university classrooms will start to resemble real-world work and social environments that facilitate organic interactions and cross-disciplinary problem solving." Kearns [14] identifies three generations of learning cities, claiming that "Gen 1 Learning Cities were European in their orientation" and "Gen 2 reflected their East Asian environment" and speculates that "emerging Gen 3 Learning Cities well be fully international in drawing on ideas and experience from anywhere" in order to address "the big global issues confronting cities."

The civic technology landscape is described by the USDN [15] as "an interface for local government and community members to virtually interact" where the interaction is intended to solve something. For example, the use of "open data to improve communications or to spot trends in public transit use." As distinct from the term smart cities, civic tech is said to be "the softer, community-facing side of technology" forming "a new normal for interaction between citizens and their governing bodies" while providing "a door to big data access and use through local crowdsourcing."

Differences. Citing a possible reason for the lack of a generally agreed upon definition for smart cities, Albino et al. [10] point to application of the term in "hard domains" including physical infrastructures for energy, transport and the like "where ICT play a decisive role" and in "soft domains" where "ICT are not usually decisive", as in, "education, culture, policy innovations" to name a few.

Picking up on "so called soft factors", Laitinen and Stenvall [3] refer to the progression of smart cities to smart learning environments, arguing that, "the learning dimension is becoming more central" requiring "more investments in training and in continuing education" in fostering the "learning and innovation capacity" of smart cities. With the purpose of creating "something new and unique" Laitinen and Stenvall [3] note that smart cities programs can be understood as a learning process involving universities "with many different partners/stakeholders."

Visible perhaps in the smart cities and learning cities landscape is the deep learning concept which Goodfellow, Bengio, and Courville [16] explain "was known as cybernetics in the 1940–60s" undergoing a name change to "connectionism in the 1980s–1990s" with "a current resurgence under the name deep learning beginning in 2006." Pointing to "the diminished role of neuroscience in deep learning today" Goodfellow et al. [16] note that "modern deep learning draws inspiration from many fields." Goodfellow et al. [16] are careful to distinguish computational neuroscience as "the effort to understand how the brain works on an algorithmic level", from deep learning, as the building "of computer systems that are able to successfully solve tasks requiring intelligence." Deeper learning approaches in a higher education context are described by Adams Becker et al. [1], based on the work of the William and Flora Hewitt Foundation, as "content that engages students in critical thinking, problem-solving, collaboration, and self-directed learning."

Similarities. Albino et al. [10] highlight the types of emerging metrics for assessing smart city initiatives, citing the work of Zygiaris [17] who developed a measurement system based on six layers of a smart city. The six layers include: *city layer* (context); *the green city layer* (environmental sustainability); the *interconnection layer* (diffusion of green economies); the *instrumentation layer* (real-time smart meters and infrastructure sensors); the *open integration layer* (apps to communicate and share data, content, services, and information); the *application layer* (real-time responsive operation); and the *innovation layer* (foster new business opportunities). It is worth noting that school, as in education and learning, is located in the interconnection layer and data is situated in the instrumentation layer as well as the open integration layer.

Learning is occurring in a technology context where again, a layer approach is used in deep learning [16], described by Goodfellow et al. as "a type of machine learning" utilizing "a technique that enables computer systems to improve with experience and data." Deep learning is advanced for use "in complicated real-world environments" through "representing the world as a nested hierarchy of concepts, with each concept defined in relation to simpler concepts" [16]. Adams Becker et al. [1] identify a range of wicked, as in highly complex, challenges for higher education including next generation learning management systems (LMS) as "more flexible spaces that support personalization" and natural user interfaces (NUIs). NUIs are "allowing humans to interact with machines similarly to how they interact with each other" incorporating "taps, swipes, touching, motions, body movement, and increasingly, natural language."

2.2 Data in Smart Cities and Learning Cities.

In 2014 the World Council on City Data (WCCD) was launched along with ISO 37120 [18], an international standard for *Sustainable development of communities: Indicators for city services and quality of life*. The standard is based on the framework of the Global City Indicators Facility [19], consists of 100 indicators (46 of which are core) categorized into 17 themes, and is designed to measure the social, economic, and environmental performance of a city. Lea points to the complexity of the smart city standardization landscape [20], providing an overview and noting the work of The British Standards Institution

(BSI) in development of data standards for interoperability and data sharing – *PAS 182, Smart city concept model: Guide to establishing a model for data* [21].

Van Zoonen [22] provides a preliminary overview of the city data landscape, shedding light on the diversity of data in smart cities in terms of size, regularity, purpose, complexity, ownership, and visibility, to name a few. Florida [9] points to the complexity of relations between data and cities, highlighting the importance of "nuanced human reasoning about cities" in the midst of "new data sources and analytic techniques." Gil-Garcia, Zhang, and Puron-Cid [23] identify from the research literature "three approaches to the use of data in government" in smart cities as: (a) data that is "captured from both physical and virtual sensors" and is "related to the concept of Internet of Things" (IoT); (b) data emerging from an "enterprise computing and communication platform for interconnecting and integrating" content "from various public services"; and (c) leveraging of the first two types of data "for complex analytics, models, and simulation to make better operational decisions." Laserson [24] describes deep learning in relation to smart sensors and the Internet of Things (IoT) enabling the transforming of building automation. Herrmann, Hildebrandt, Tielemans, and Diaz [25] demonstrate the purpose and value of interdisciplinary collaborations in the investigation of complex challenges associated with location-based data when explored from engineering, legal, and ethical perspectives.

UNESCO provides a framework of the key features of learning cities along with a more detailed listing of key features and measurement indicators [26]. Data sources are identified as a combination of official city data, expert reviews, and statistical data in survey/review results.

As noted by Schmitt [4], while data generation and collection have always occurred in cities, "new today is the ability of any person using computational devices to generate large amounts of data" that is "real time data." As such, "the entire city becomes an information organism" the visualization of which "creates new knowledge about the city and is able to make the invisible visible." It is the "constant flow of data" produced by "the inhabitants of the city" that gives way to the notion of ambient data. From a legal perspective [27], EDRM defined ambient data as "data stored in non-traditional computer storage areas and formats, such as Windows swap files, unallocated space and file slack." For the purposes of this paper, the ambient data concept is expanded for use in the context of smart cities and learning cities. For example, Schmitt [4] calls for the need to "derive a connection between data, activities, and locations in a meaningful sense by establishing relations between data" in forging "the new building material" of the dynamic city.

2.3   Data Challenges for Smart Cities and Learning Cities

Lea [28] argues that smart city issues "are not strictly" about "technologies," suggesting that, "the problems are more around exposing data, sharing data and using the data" in the two areas of "infrastructure data" and "citizen data." Cohen et al. [29] explore emerging tensions among innovators and entrepreneurs engaging with local governments and citizens including those related to open and generative data. Fruehe [30] points to the importance of whether data is "accurate, secure, and actionable." In addition to concerns with trust around the sharing of data, Gurevich, Hudis, and Wing [31] describe the inverse privacy problem as – "the inaccessibility to you of your personal information" in a "safe scenario" such as "your favorite supermarket." Cinnamon and Schuurman [32] highlight the data divide in the context of spatial turns focusing on volunteered geographic information (VGI) enabled through the "techno-social revolution in geospatial technology and data."

Kurose and Marzullo [33] note that "the rapid increase in the quantity of personal information being collected and retained" together "with the increased ability to analyze and combine it with other information" gives rise to "concerns about privacy." Kurose and Marzullo [33] highlight the importance of "investment in research and development in privacy-enhancing technologies" (PETs) and "encouraging cross-cutting research" of a multi-disciplinary nature involving "not only computer science and mathematics, but also social science, communications, and legal disciplines." The goal of the strategy according to Kurose and Marzullo [33] is to "produce knowledge and technology that will enable individuals, commercial entities, and the Federal Government to benefit from technological advancement and data use while proactively identifying and mitigating privacy risks" and aiming to "inspire parallel efforts in the private sector."

From a legal perspective, Solove [34] claimed the privacy concept to be in disarray, such that "nobody can articulate what it means." Van Zoonen [22] refers to the privacy paradox involving "people's clearly expressed concerns about their privacy" juxtaposed with "a simultaneous lack of appropriate secure behavior." Acknowledging this "disorder in the field", Van Zoonen [22] identifies three consistent and persistent "factors influencing people's concerns about privacy" as "the type of data, the purpose of data collection and usage, and the organization or persons collecting and using the data." Van Zoonen develops a smart city privacy challenges framework as a sensitizing instrument in a 2 × 2 frame of data as personal or impersonal in relation to the purposes of service or surveillance.

Concerned with "autonomic smart environments" that "take an unprecedented number of decisions both for the private and the public good", Hildebrandt and Koops [35] point to the novel concept of ambient law to address the challenges of "errors, loss of autonomy and privacy, unfair discrimination and stigmatisation, and an absence of due process." More recently, Hildebrandt [36] argues that "technological infrastructures matter" and "require our attention" at a time now when "data-driven agency builds on an entirely different grammar." According to Hildebrandt [36], the era of data-driven agency is resulting in a shift away from "the linearity and sequential processing demands of written text" using instead "the building blocks" of "information and behavior."

Williamson [37] refers to the neuro-turn for smart cities where, "transformed by actors such as IBM into brain/code/spaces", education is being driven by learning algorithms such that "nonconscious computing brains are embedded in the functioning of the environment and intended to weave into the cognitive experience of citizens."

2.4 Data Opportunities for Learning Cities and Smart Cities

Goldsmith and Crawford [38] articulate the notion of the responsive city, highlighting community engagement and "data-smart governance" with a shift "from a compliance model to a problem-solving one." Russon Gilman [39] looks "beyond open data" in promoting partnerships and providing "access to the tools and computing power" in order to "engage people who are typically disconnected from 'data' to create their own framework to analyze and understand data" in support of finding "creative uses for the data." Townsend [40] challenges engineers to design for urban inclusion and the work of Janet Echelman [41] who "explores the cutting edge of sculpture, public art, and urban transformation" provides vibrant examples of what is possible through her collaborations with "aeronautical and mechanical engineers, architects, lighting designers, landscape architects, and fabricators." Echelman "creates experiential sculpture at the scale of buildings that transform with wind and light" advancing the idea of working with data to "use it to do serious things in a playful manner" [42]. For example, Echelman describes a request from the Biennial of the Americas in Denver to "represent the 35 nations of the western hemisphere and their interconnectedness in a sculpture." Echelman noticed the "earthquake in Chile" and how the ensuing "tsunami that rippled across the entire Pacific Ocean shifted the earth's tectonic plates, sped up the planet's rotation and shortened the length of the day." Based on Tsunami data shared by NOAA (National Oceanic and Atmospheric Administration), Echelman translated the data into an artistic rendering titled 1.26 that "refers to the number of microseconds that the earth's day was shortened." This visualization of data provides an artistic rendering of the interconnectedness of 35 nations that now forms "part of the fabric of the city" of Denver.

Recognizing the need to modernize law in the face of pervasive, aware, and smart technologies, Hildebrandt [36] identifies the opportunity to rethink and redesign the "architecture of the Rule of Law" through the "framing of law *as* information." As such, Hildebrandt [36] calls for "collaboration between lawyers and computer scientists" that is "in-depth as well as hands-on" in order to "redesign the upcoming data-driven architectures to accommodate human action, to safeguard the fundamental uncertainty and indeterminacy it assumes" while protecting "the pinch of freedom and autonomy that defines us."

Data figures strongly in four of the 14 dimensions of smartness in government identified by Gil-Garcia, Zhang, and Puron-Cid (e.g., integration, evidence-based decision making, equality, openness) [23]. Collaboration figures in six of the dimensions (e.g., integration, evidence-based decision making, effectiveness, citizen engagement, openness, resiliency, technology savviness) while education figures strongly in six (e.g., integration, creativity, equality, entrepreneurialism, citizen engagement, openness). It is worth noting that information figures strongly in nine dimensions (e.g. integration, evidence-based decision making, citizen centricity, effectiveness, equality, citizen engagement, openness, resiliency, technology savviness) while knowledge figures in five (e.g., integration, creativity, entrepreneurialism, citizen engagement, technology savviness). And finally, relationships figure strongly in two of the dimensions (e.g., citizen engagement and technology savviness). Gil-Garcia et al. [23] cite the work of Gil-Garcia, Pardo, and Burke [43] where "government inter-organizational information integration" is advanced as including "components in a continuum from social to technical aspects" as – "trusted social networks, shared information, integrated data, and interoperable technical infrastructure." Lämmerhirt, Jameson, and Prasetyo [44] advance a framework for collaboration in "making citizen generated data work."

Lee et al. [45] identify the value of smart city data hubs for interoperability in that "federation of smart city functionality can focus on hub integration, rather than the integration of individual city sub-systems" enabling developers to "more easily create reusable applications that work in multiple cities." Lea et al. [45] point to the importance of this type of open innovation platform for "the variety and quality of data streams generated by city infrastructure and citizens." Fan, Chen, Ziong, and Chen [46] articulate the Internet of Data (IoD) concept, noting that "data standing alone has little or no meaning" and that "when they interoperate" it is "the information of the relations between data" that "become more significant and useful." In the context of the architecture of collaboration for a smart city, Snow, Håkonsson and Obel [47] define infrastructures as "systems that connect actors" allowing them "to connect with one another" and "access the same information, knowledge, and other resources." Russon Gilman [39] argues that "interactive and fun" initiatives "help build civic involvement with government, encourage experimentation, and collaboration within governments." Further, Russon Gilman [39] notes that, "educating more people about the innovative work of government can build stronger, more resilient systems while also fostering more trust in governance institutions." In an interview, O'Malley describes the work of the MetroLab, highlighting the importance of "using data in city government" for application to human services problems based on "new ways of governing and getting things done" that are "very much aided by technology" [48].

Gurevich et al. [31] argue that "shared data decays into inversely private." The "sharing back" of such data from, say Fitbit, can have benefit for people in terms of learning about their exercise patterns for example. As such, Gurevich et al. [31] argue that inversely private data will be enormously influential in evolving social norms around data sharing and use.

Data innovation is advanced in a development context as "the use of new or non-traditional data sources and methods to gain a more nuanced understanding of challenges" [49]. Further, the combining of data sources is used "to reframe issues and shed new light on seemingly intractable problems" possibly drawing on an array of digital spaces such as "social media, web content, transaction data, GPS devices" in seeking "more complete, timely, and/or granular information" [49].

2.5   Research Questions, Propositions and Ambient Data Framework

The literature review and theoretical perspective provided in this paper enables formulation of an ambient data conceptual framework for learning cities and smart cities (Fig. 1). The framework is operationalized for use in this paper in responding to the research questions under exploration in this study. As depicted in Fig. 1, this work is concerned with urban data generated through city infrastructures and human infrastructures. Challenges are explored in relation to the constructs of awareness, learning, openness, and engagement. And it is these challenges that simultaneously provide opportunities for: exposing, sharing, and using data; data privacy, trust, and control; and data purpose, value, innovation, and other emergent elements.

Urban Data

Fig. 1. Ambient data framework for learning cities and smart cities

The research questions for this paper focus on the key constructs of awareness, learning, openness, and engagement, as follows.

In contemporary urban environments:

Q1: How is awareness aided by data?
Q2: How does learning benefit from data?
Q3: What are the challenges of openness for data in relation to civic tech in the public realm?
Q4: What is the opportunity for engagement with data as a building material?

The research questions are formulated as propositions for exploration as follows:
In contemporary urban environments:

P1: Ambient data forms part of the critical infrastructure by contributing to greater awareness for action, creativity, and interactions
P2: Enabled by ambient data, learning becomes more adaptive, contextual, situational, and emergent
P3: Openness is supported by ambient data, driving new conceptualizations of sharing, privacy, and other complex challenges
P4: Opportunities for more meaningful engagement arise shedding light on the purpose, value, and innovative aspects of ambient data as a connective and connecting element of the urban social fabric.

3   Methodology

The research design for this study employed an emergent and exploratory case study approach, said to be particularly appropriate for the exploration of contemporary phenomena in a real-world context [50].

A website was used to describe the study and enable people to participate. Demographic data were gathered at sign up including age range, city, and self-identification in one or more category types (e.g., city official, student, instructor, local business, community member, or visitor). Participants were invited to complete an online survey with the option to discuss smart cities and their experience of the city. More specifically, questions invited discussion of learning cities and smart cities and provided the opportunity to think about the city as an emergent environment for leveraging data while exploring challenges, opportunities, practices, and approaches.

Interview data served as the main source of qualitative evidence for this study along with responses to open-ended survey questions. In parallel with this study, group and individual discussions were also conducted with a wide range of people in small to medium to large cities in Canada (e.g., from Langford to Victoria to Vancouver to Toronto).

Content analysis was used as an analytic technique for qualitative data involving inductive analysis to identify emerging terms on the one hand, and deductive analysis of terms from the literature review on the other. Qualitative data gathered from discussions in parallel with this study supported further analysis, comparison, and triangulation of evidence.

Diverse voices emerged from this work across multiple cities and countries from individuals involved in business (e.g., architectural design, ecology, energy, sustainability, technology, tourism); government (e.g., city councilors, policymakers, IT staff); educators (secondary and postsecondary, researchers/lab directors); community members (IT professionals, urban placemakers and designers, engagement leaders, policy influencers); students (postsecondary – engineering/design/computing/education/media).

Overall, data were analyzed for an n = 51 spanning the age ranges of people in their 20 s to their 70 s with 35% females and 65% males. Response to the study was received mostly from Canadian cities (e.g. Langford to Victoria to Ottawa to St. John's) and also extending to cities in Europe (e.g. Jyvaskyla to Valetta). This study spans a 1.5-year timeframe from mid 2015 through 2016.

4   Findings

Findings are presented in response to each of the four propositions for this study in relation to the key constructs of awareness, learning, openness, and engagement.

Awareness. A community member in Greater Victoria identified the desire to share information with city officials about bike path areas requiring improvement for increased safety stating that "I would love to have an app that" enables me to "tell the city that" a particular street or road "needs a bike lane." City IT staff noted that "historically we published datasets that have very little value" adding that now there is a focus on "normalizing the dataset" and "making sure the data has some value and structure." Citing concerns such as privacy regulations, City IT noted the tendency toward "being very conservative when it comes to data collection" in relation to "the purpose, and how we track, how we manage" the data. A student in Valetta suggested that "as we work out how to sort out the data that is constantly being made" and "built, essentially in social media" spaces, "we will know more" about "what to do with it." Regarding technology in smart cities, an educator in St. John's observed that, "we're not smart on how we use it" calling for "improved communication about the transportation system" and "anywhere Internet" as "particularly useful." A student in Valetta commented that "an absolute goal of smart cites" should be "total, free wifi" in urban areas. An urban environmental designer in Victoria commented that "I guess its kind of a tradeoff of awareness of what's around, what I can perceive without the technology to what is perceived through the technology." A community engagement leader speculated on whether there are "roles for technology" in the transition of downtown parking, as in, "an app that could help me find parking or the closest open stall" and "maybe even reserve it by paying." An innovation designer for education and cities in Vancouver observed that "young people are not really interested in the archive, the data management" and "they're not interested in holding on to things in some ways" thus, contributing possibly to the notion of ambient data. An IT leader in higher education in Greater Victoria added that for youth "their legacy is change, their life's work is not materials, its social, social capital" aided by technology. Yet, referring to the physical coming together of people in the city, the innovation designer suggested that, "the meeting becomes the technology that changes everything."

Learning. An urban environmental designer commented that, "one thing I'm learning is" the importance of "using data from technologies to improve aspects of the city" on the one hand, and "the human component" on the other "in order to enable all those connections to happen." An IT professional in a higher education institution (HEI) in Vancouver pointed to the importance of data sharing to verify the anonymized presence of people in buildings on campus for security, safety, and emergency purposes. Another IT professional in an HEI described smart cities and learning cities activities in terms of collaboration between the university and the local city indicating that, "we've been working on whole systems on the campus looking at everything from environmentally friendly all the way out to how we integrate new building into the infrastructure" and "working with" the city "on tying things in" since "the city has been working on a fiber project across all the city." Regarding emergent opportunities for learning from urban data flows, city IT staff commented that, "we are a little immature with respect to that level of data mining." Indeed, it was noted that opportunities to share data exist "even inside the processes of City Hall" whereby "we're slowly getting those connections so that engineering and planning" can work together. Regarding data analytics, learning challenges and opportunities were identified by City IT staff in that, "we're starting to look at the tools to help us mine the data that we already have an interest in." City IT staff added that, "going outside of our little silos" and "getting that semi-structured, that unstructured data and trying to then look at it through a different lens is alien to us because we're not data scientists" acknowledging that "we're very much immature in that overall data sense." As such, City IT staff commented that, "the idea of data between two different datasets, we're just starting to look at the tools that would give us the visualizations of that." An educator in St. John's commented that, "I'm always looking for the more visual stuff" as in, how cities present "the visual sense of the city." An educator in Jyvaskyla pointed to the potential of a mobile application for civic purposes "that people could use to capture ideas, to capture evidence of problems on the move, capture evidence of potential solutions and evidence of impact." Noticing the use of infrared camera technology by downtown businesses to gather data on pedestrian volume and movement in certain areas, a community engagement leader in Victoria stated "I'd love to do some of that kind of stuff with some of our public spaces, like plazas" in order "to have some of that anonymous kind of count" data.

Discussing apps for civic engagement such as PlaceSpeak, a community engagement leader highlighted such platforms as a way to "encourage people to do some observations of space and people and post stuff" in a space "that's interactive" as a kind of activity to "look at any given space and analyze what's working here and what isn't and what could improve it."

Openness. On a community level in Victoria the issue was identified of "not being able to find out really what's going on in the city." City IT staff commented that, "fundamentally there is a desire to be very, very open with public data" while adhering to "privacy regulations" and being cognizant of "the public's preferences." An educator in St. John's suggested the need to "provide user friendly and not too dense information on what's happening at a particular point" in the city "so that you can access information and know what's going on in real time almost." An educator in Jyvaskyla suggested that civic apps "could be used from ideation to real life experimentations" establishing "proof of concept" and the "next stages of open innovation" and "capturing the evidence of the impact." Referring to a mobile app for urban spaces, the educator pointed to the capability of being "able to open this kind of feedback" potential to anyone in the city as a way "to transform contributions both in terms of unique ideas and patterns into the design of some urban space or buildings" as in "city smart infrastructure" emphasizing "energy and resources" enabling city officials "to listen and understand what people want in the form of evidence." A community member in Toronto noted that, "the number one requested dataset from the city by the public is zoning and development data," adding that this "is not currently available as open data to cities around Canada at least." An IT professional at a higher education institution in Vancouver raised the issue of learning to work across systems and infrastructures of data involving buildings and room bookings, for example, and "how we exchange that data in a way that is safe" to generate "real occupancy information" in conjunction with "devices of people to verify that someone is actually in the room." A student in Valetta speculated on ways to address the wicked challenges of personal data privacy in order to "devise ways whereby you can create some kind of security to anonymize data and thereby make the data itself open and shared in some way that would still provide some kind of smart delivery too, so you could actually make use of the data" which could be "learning data, information data about people, things, events, places."

Engagement. A community member in Victoria referred to "a lot of advantages to having" smartphone data "to enhance the urban experience and to be able to get from point a to be faster." City IT staff cited the example of an eTownHall, enabled through the use of technology, observing that, "bringing questions in and sharing answers through Twitter, Facebook" provided "a dataset of documented engagement." As such, City IT staff noted that "using different tools to interrogate and present data becomes that much more important and it contributes to how we successfully engage with the citizenry." Commenting on city dashboards, a student in Valetta stated that "you can take this kind of data and rather than just present numbers you can make beautiful artistic visualizations" adding that "this is how to get people on board." An educator in St. John's commented that "much more collaboration is necessary" in how technology is used.

An educator in Jyvaskyla pointed to a mobile app in terms of data that is "evidence-based so the decision-makers can show at any meeting" that "people said this and that is why we decided to do it." Hinting at unspoken elements in support of engagement, the educator commented that "if we forget about the technology for a moment its almost" as if "we assume there is this wireless connectivity between us happening." A community member in Toronto pointed to the importance of "marketing and communications" when releasing a dataset, identifying what could potentially be built with the data, adding the need to point out that "the government just doesn't have the means to make it happen and we're hoping the people will." Regarding zoning and development data, the community member stated, "imagine if there was an app that told you all the notifications on this corner" and because "people would be affected, they would pay attention and they would suddenly be engaged" since "their environment is being changed" and "right now, nobody knows what's happening." Regarding urban parking, a community engagement leader wondered whether technology could help with getting more clarity on whether there is an oversupply or undersupply of parking in terms of "people's perception" versus actual data.

In summary, Table 1 provides an overview of findings for this exploration of ambient data in relation to the four constructs of awareness, learning, openness, and engagement. Associated challenges and opportunities are identified in the context of learning cities and smart cities.

Table 1. Overview of findings.

Constructs	Ambient data	Challenges	Opportunities
Awareness	Bike path feedback	Safety	Real-time sharing
	City datasets	Privacy	Value
	Social media	Analysis	Purposes/uses
	Parking apps	People + tech	Purposes/uses
Learning	Urban space feedback	People + tech	Real-time sharing
	University + city (smartness)	Collaboration	Purposes/uses
	Unstructured info/ tools	Analysis	Real-time sharing
	Public space uses/ patterns	People + tech	Analysis
Openness	What's happening in the city	Privacy	Real-time sharing
	Civic apps	People + tech	Real-time sharing
		Analysis	Listen + act
Engagement	Urban experiences	People + tech	Real-time sharing
	Documented engagement	People + tech	Real-time sharing
	City information	Visualization	Real-time sharing

A range of ambient data types for learning cities and smart cities are highlighted from city datasets to civic apps. Challenges presented by ambient data are identified in relation to analysis, collaboration, people and technology interactions, privacy, safety, and visualization. Opportunities presented by ambient data are also identified, including but not limited to: analysis, real-time sharing, purposes/users, value, and the potential for listening and action by decision-makers.

While this overview (Table 1) is not intended to be exhaustive, it does provide an early glimpse of the emerging ambient data landscape for small to medium to large-sized learning cities and smart cities in Canada and extending to Europe. Further, Table 1 provides an indication of how all four propositions under exploration were supported in this study.

Regarding proposition 1, ambient data is seen to form part of the critical infrastructure by contributing to greater awareness for action, creativity, and interactions in relation to bike paths, city datasets, social media, and parking apps.

For proposition 2, enabled by ambient data, learning becomes more adaptive, contextual, situational, and emergent in relation to urban spaces, university/city collaborations, and urban data analysis including emerging data sources and tools.

For proposition 3, openness is supported by ambient data, driving new conceptualizations of sharing, privacy, and other complex challenges in relation to real-time sharing and analysis and the development and use of civic apps.

For proposition 4, opportunities for more meaningful engagement arise shedding light on the purpose, value, and innovative aspects of ambient data as a connective and connecting element of the urban social fabric in relation to everyday urban experiences, documented engagement using social media and other aware technologies during eTownHalls, and the visualization of city information.

5   Discussion

The exploration of ambient data in relation to the four constructs of awareness, learning, openness, and engagement is depicted in terms of opportunities for learning cities and smart cities in Fig. 2. This glimpse of the emerging fabric of ambient data in smart cities and learning cities provides a rendering of the four constructs as overlapping and interweaving, yielding a continuously unfolding interplay of elements characterized as adaptive, contextual, connective, and interactive that enable action, sharing, creativity, purpose, value, and other emergent potentials. This dynamic urban fabric of data is giving way to opportunities for a rethinking of the information landscape, in support of innovative initiatives such as inverse privacy while contributing to a discourse, practice, and research space for ambient privacy.

Individuals in both Canadian and European cities identified the need to do more with the data being generated in urban contexts. Further, concern with data delivery was highlighted in terms of "mechanisms for delivery" in Canada and as "smart delivery" in Europe. Encapsulated in the words of a student in Europe – "the more that technical infrastructure can be made to constantly reciprocate the data flows that are happening between people, formal and informal, the better" – is support for real-time data opportunities and possibly emergent understandings of the ambient data concept.

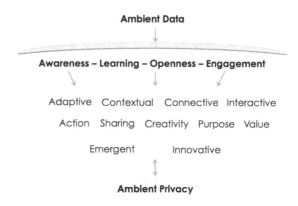

Fig. 2. Ambient data opportunities for learning cities and smart cities

In a higher education context, IT professionals identified multi-purpose opportunities for leveraging and exposing "some of the information in a way that is safe" to "make it available for other things." The need for data sharing opportunities was identified on the community level in the words "nobody ever really knows what's happening" in the city and reinforced by individuals in other cities. Of particular note is the opportunity identified by city IT staff in gaining new literacies associated with data sharing, analysis, and use – improving skills within and across organizations to advance beyond current levels of maturity.

Questions about dataset veracity were identified on the one hand by city IT staff in terms of completeness of datasets and on the other by a student with respect to social media data where people are said to often mix fictional elements into their profiles whether for fun, privacy, or other reasons. Urban collaborations and civic tech platforms such as PlaceSpeak provide an example of the potential for building trusted spaces for learning cities and smarter cities based on emerging understandings of ambient data and other evolving collaborative opportunities.

City IT staff highlighted the importance of evolving approaches to sharing whether infrastructure, data centers, datasets, and the like as opportunities, emphasizing that "trying to get" existing mindsets "to change is the biggest challenge." Engagement of people meaningfully in the city and with technology-based initiatives is seen to be key in coming to contemporary understandings, interpretations, and directions for deeper learning as it relates to education on the one hand and people and technology interactions on the other. The visualization of data for more meaningful engagement was identified with the suggestion that data be combined and rendered in more artistic ways.

Speculating on the innovative potential of data collection, sharing, and analytics, a city IT professional was particularly fascinated to observe the accidental, serendipitous, and unintended uses that occur when new mechanisms for sharing data are made available. In this context of emergent purposes and value for data collection, sharing, and use, the challenges posed open opportunities for increased data literacies in relation to privacy, security, analysis, and visualization. In response to privacy requirements to fully know in advance what the purpose, use, and value of data collection will be, it is precisely the accidental, serendipitous, and unintended opportunities that reflect the "human action" identified by Hildebrandt [36] and "the fundamental uncertainty and indeterminacy it assumes."

It is worth noting that the civic tech engagement platform, PlaceSpeak, is architected to incorporate Privacy by Design (PbD) principles [51]. However, the embedding of privacy into applications and systems may prove to be too brittle, in some cases, a criticism leveled by Townsend [6] about systems that are not highly adaptive, responsive, or resilient. Going forward, and in parallel with PbD, perhaps opportunities exist for more adaptive and flexible privacy architectures conceptualized as ambient privacy [52]. The privacy requirement that data purpose be knowable and provided up front prior to the granting of use may be a sound principle in traditional information environments but less tenable in the emergent, uncertain environments of 21st century cities. As such, more flexible, adaptive, and dynamic privacy principles are required, perhaps in the form of new conceptualizations of privacy as ambient privacy [52], inverse privacy [31], and the like. As such, this work points to the potential for an extending of Sassen's [53] urbanizing concept and the need for smart city technologies to be able to "work within a particular urban context", to McKenna's articulation of urbanizing the ambient [54], to the urbanizing of ambient data for smart cities and learning cities.

In summary, multiple learning opportunities emerged in this work from the perspective of those in higher education, city governments, and urban communities contributing to evolving understandings of learning cities and smart cities.

6   Contributions

This work is significant in several ways in that it: (a) explores the ambient data concept in the context of smart cities; (b) theorizes and operationalizes a conceptual framework for ambient data as dynamic, real time, and adaptive enabled by aware, pervasive, and other emerging technologies and human factors; (c) extends the discourse space for ambient data to civic technologies, the public realm, and other emergent socio-urban intersections; and (d) relates deep learning conceptualizations to learning cities and smart cities involving the interactive people and technologies dynamic.

7   Challenges and Mitigations

A key limitation of this study was sample size, mitigated by the diverse voices and rich content shared from multiple, small to medium to large sized cities in several countries. Challenges related to geographic location, size, and urban characteristics are mitigated by the potential to extend this work to other cities, including megacities and regions exceeding 10 million people. The challenge of studying emergent, invisible, and ambient data is mitigated by opportunities to creatively discover and collaboratively explore the opportunities and potentials for the making of spaces, infrastructures, and environments to advance understandings through real-world research and practice.

8   Conclusion

This work explores and theorizes ambient data in urban environments in the context of 21st century smart cities. Through the interactive dynamic of people – technologies – cities, the constructs of awareness, learning, openness, and engagement are explored in relation to ambient data and associated challenges.

Key contributions of this paper include: (a) conceptualization of ambient data in contemporary urban environments; (b) further development of the research and practice literature for smart cities, learning cities, and ambient data; (c) theorizing and operationalization of the ambient data framework for learning cities and smart cities; and (d) the opening of a discourse space for evolving understandings of data as dynamic, emergent, and continuous in the context of smart cities and learning cities. Of particular value in this work is the emergence of the diverse voices of people across the city from business to city officials to postsecondary educators and students to community members and information technology staff (e.g., city and higher education institutions). Also of note is the literature review that introduces a range of challenges and opportunities for data, and more particularly ambient data, in contemporary society. What can be learned in the process of smart city discussion and development is highlighted along with emerging understandings of the deep learning concept in relation to people on the one hand and to technologies on the other, in the context of learning cities and smart cities.

A key take away from this work is the importance of the ambient data concept, opening the way for new discourse spaces and explorations in both research and practice for learning cities and smart cities. It is hoped that the notion of ambient data will contribute to opportunities for innovating data related challenges from sharing to privacy to collaboration going forward.

This work will be of interest to urban innovators, educators, learners, city officials, community members, and anyone concerned with evolving approaches to civic tech and ambient data for learning cities and smarter cities.

References

1. Adams Becker, S., Cummins, S., Davis, A., Freeman, A., Hall, C., Ananthanarayanan, V.: NMC Horizon Report: 2017 Higher Education Edition
2. Charoubi, H., Nam, T., Walker, S., Gil-Garcia, J.R., Mellouli, S., Nahon, K., Pardo, T.A., Scholl, H.J.: Understanding smart cities: an integrative framework. In: Proceedings of the 45th Hawaii International Conference on System Sciences, pp. 2289–2297. IEEE Computer Society Press, Washington (2012)
3. Laitinen, I., Stenvall, J.: From smart cities to smart learning environments: a comparative study. Seminar Series 2015–2016. University of Glasgow, Pascal International Exchanges, Glasgow (2016)
4. Schmitt, G.: Smart cities. Massive Open Online Course (MOOC), edX. ETH Zurich, Zurich, Switzerland (2016)
5. Gordon, E., Mihailidis, P.: Civic Media: Technology, Design, Practice. MIT Press, Cambridge (2016)
6. Townsend, A.M.: Smart Cities: Big Data, Civic Hackers and the Quest for a New Utopia. WW Norton, New York (2013)

7. Konomi, S., Roussos, G.: Enriching Urban Spaces with Ambient Computing, the Internet of Things, and Smart City Design. IGI Global, Hershey (2017)
8. Hespanhol, L., Tomitsch, M.: Strategies for intuitive interaction in public urban spaces. Interact. Comput. (2015). doi:10.1093/iwc/iwu051
9. Florida, R.: The complex relationship between data and cities. The Atlantic CityLab (2016). http://bit.ly/1OJwgnq. Accessed 29 July 2016
10. Albino, V., Berardi, U., Dangelico, R.M.: Smart cities: definitions, dimensions, performance, and initiatives. J. Urban Technol. (2015). doi:10.1080/10630732.2014.942092
11. Nam, T., Pardo, T.A.: Conceptualizing smart city with dimensions of technology, people, and institutions. In: Proceedings of the 12th Annual International Conference on Digital Government Research, pp. 282–291 (2011)
12. UNESCO: Global network of learning cities. UNESCO Institute for Lifelong Learning (2015). http://uil.unesco.org/lifelong-learning/learning-cities. Accessed 9 Jan 2017
13. UIL: Guidelines for building learning cities. UNESCO Institute for Lifelong Learning (2015)
14. Kearns, P.: Learning cities on the move. Aust. J. Adult Learn. **55**(1), 153–168 (2015)
15. USDN: The Civic Technology Landscape: A Field Analysis and Urban Sustainability Directors Network Recommendation. Urban Sustainability Directors Network, Chicago (2015)
16. Goodfellow, I., Bengio, Y., Courville, A.: Deep Learning. MIT Press, Cambridge (2016)
17. Zygiaris, S.: Smart city reference model: assisting planners to conceptualize the building of smart city innovation ecosystems. J. Knowl. Econ. **4**(2), 217–231 (2013)
18. WCCD: WCCD ISO 37120 Created by cities, for cities. Data for Cities, World Council on City Data, Toronto (2017). http://www.dataforcities.org/wccd/. Accessed 10 Jan 2017
19. GCI: Global City Indicators Facility. Global Cities Institute, University of Toronto, Toronto (2013). http://www.globalcitiesinstitute.org. Accessed 11 Jan 2017
20. Lea, R.: Making sense of the smart city standardization landscape. IEEE: Standards University (2016). http://www.standardsuniversity.org/e-magazine/november-2016-volume-6-issue-4-smart-city-standards/making-sense-smart-city-standardization-landscape/. Accessed 10 Jan 2017
21. BSI: PAS 182 Smart city concept model: guide to establishing a model for data interoperability. British Standards Institute (2014). https://www.bsigroup.com/en-GB/smart-cities/Smart-Cities-Standards-and-Publication/PAS-182-smart-cities-data-concept-model/. Accessed 11 Jan 2017
22. Van Zoonen, L.: Privacy concerns in smart cities. Gov. Inf. Q. **33**(3), 472–480 (2016)
23. Gil-Garcia, J.R., Zhang, J., Puron-Cid, G.: Conceptualizing smartness in government: an integrative and multi-dimensional view. Gov. Inf. Q. **33**(3), 524–534 (2016)
24. Laserson, J.: Smarter sensors: how deep learning is transforming building automation. Smart Buildings Magazine (2016). http://www.smartbuildingsmagazine.com/features/smarter-sensors-how-deep-learning-is-transforming-building-automati. Accessed 15 Jan 2017
25. Herrmann, M., Hildebrandt, M., Tielemans, L., Diaz, C.: Privacy in location-based service: an interdisciplinary approach. ScriptEd **13**(2) (2016). https://script-ed.org/article/privacy-in-location-based-services-an-interdisciplinary-approach/. Accessed 4 Jan 2017
26. UIL: UNESCO global network of learning cities: guiding documents. UNESCO Institute for Lifelong Learning, Hamburg (2015). http://uil.unesco.org/fileadmin/keydocuments/LifelongLearning/learning-cities/en-unesco-global-network-of-learning-cities-guiding-documents.pdf. Accessed 11 Jan 2017
27. EDRM: EDRM glossary. Duke Law Center for Judicial Studies (2017). http://www.edrm.net/resources/glossaries/glossary/glossary-a/ambient-data. Accessed 4 Jan 2017

28. Lea, R.: Smart cities: technology challenges for the IoT. SenseTecnic Blog (2015). http://sensetecnic.com/technology-challenges-for-the-iot/. Accessed 8 Sept 2016

29. Cohen, B., Almirall, E., Chesbrough, H.: The city as a lab: open innovation meets the collaborative economy. Special issue on city innovation. Calif. Manag. Rev. **59**(1), 5–13 (2016)

30. Fruehe, J.: The internet of things is about data, not things. Forbes (2015). http://onforb.es/1IsjPCK. Accessed 4 Aug 2016

31. Gurevich, Y., Hudis, E., Wing, J.M.: Inverse privacy: seeking a market-based solution to the problem of a person's unjustified inaccessibility to their private information. Commun. ACM **59**(7), 38–42 (2016)

32. Cinnamon, J., Schuurman, N.: Confronting the data-divide in a time of spatial turns and volunteered geographic information. GeoJournal **78**(4), 657–674 (2013)

33. Kurose, J., Marzullo, K.: Priorities for the national privacy research strategy. The WhiteHouse Blog (2016). https://www.whitehouse.gov/blog/2016/07/01/priorities-national-privacy-research-strategy. Accessed 4 Jan 2017

34. Solove, D.J.: A taxonomy of privacy. Univ. PA Law Rev. **154**(3), 477–560 (2006)

35. Hildebrandt, M., Koops, B.-J.: The challenges of ambient law and legal protection in the profiling era. Mod. Law Rev. **73**(3), 428–460 (2010)

36. Hildebrandt, M.: Law as information in the era of data-driven agency. Mod. Law Rev. **79**(1), 1–30 (2016)

37. Williamson, B.: Computing brains: learning algorithms and neurocomputation in the smart city. Inf. Commun. Soc. **20**(1), 81–99 (2017)

38. Goldsmith, S., Crawford, S.: The Responsive City: Engaging Communities Through Data-Smart Governance. Jossey-Bass, San Francisco (2014)

39. Russon Gilman, H.: The future of civic technology. Brookings Institute Techtank (2015). https://www.brookings.edu/blog/techtank/2015/04/20/the-future-of-civic-technology/. Accessed 15 Oct 2016

40. Townsend, A.: Can engineers build inclusive smart cities? Speech delivered to Delft University of Technology, Delft (2015). https://medium.com/@anthonymobile/can-engineers-build-inclusive-smart-cities-d6754d82e81#.93kep5khh. Accessed 25 Nov 2016

41. Echelman, J.: About (2013). http://www.echelman.com/about/. Accessed 15 Jan 2017

42. Echelman, J.: Janet Echelon: taking imagination seriously. TED Talk (2011). https://www.ted.com/playlists/11/the_creative_spark. Accessed 16 Jan 2017

43. Gil-Garcia, J.R., Pardo, T.A., Burke, G.B.: Conceptualizing inter organizational information integration in government. In: Scholl, H.J. (ed.) E-government: Information, Technology, and Transformation. M.E. Sharpe, Armonk (2010)

44. Lämmerhirt, D., Jameson, S., Prasetyo, E.: Making citizen generated data work: towards a framework strengthening collaborations between citizens, civil society organizations, and others. Datashift, Civicus; Open Knowledge (2016). http://civicus.org/thedatashift/wp-content/uploads/2015/07/Making-citizen-generated-data-work.pdf. Accessed 15 Jan 2017

45. Lea, R., Blackstock, M., Giang, N., Vogt, D.: Smart cities: engaging users and developers to foster innovation ecosystems. In: Smart City Workshop, Proceedings of the 2015 ACM International Joint Conference on Pervasive and Ubiquitous Computing and Proceedings of the 2015 ACM International Symposium on Wearable Computers, pp. 1535–1542. ACM, New York (2015)

46. Fan, W., Chen, Z., Ziong, Z., Chen, H.: The internet of data: a new idea to extend the IoT in the digital world. Front. Comput. Sci. **6**(6), 660–667 (2012). Springer

47. Snow, C.C., Håkonsson, D.D., Obel, B.: A smart city is a collaborative community: lessons from smart Aarhus. Calif. Manag. Rev. **59**(1), 92–108 (2016)

48. Williams, J.: O'Malley lays out MetroLab goals, charges leaders to encourage tech officials. StateScoop (2016). http://statescoop.com/omalley-lays-out-metrolab-goals-charges-leaders-to-encourage-tech-officials. Accessed 15 Jan 2017
49. UNDP & UN Global Pulse: A guide to data innovation for development: from idea to proof of concept. United Nations, United Nations Development Program and UN Global Pulse, New York (2016)
50. Yin, R.K.: Case Study Research: Design and Methods. Sage, Los Angeles (2013)
51. Cavoukian, A.: Privacy by Design: The 7 Foundational Principles. Privacy and Big Data Institute, Ryerson University, Toronto (2017)
52. McKenna, H.P., Arnone, M.P., Kaarst-Brown, M.L., McKnight, L.W., Chauncey, S.A.: Ambient privacy with wireless grids: forging new concepts of relationship in 21st century information society. Int. J. Inf. Secur. Res. 3(1–2), 408–417 (2013)
53. Sassen, S.: Urbanizing technology. LSE Cities (2012). https://lsecities.net/media/objects/articles/urbanising-technology/en-gb/. Accessed 26 May 2015
54. McKenna, H.P.: Urbanizing the ambient: why people matter so much in smart cities. In: Konomi, S., Roussos, G. (eds.) Enriching Urban Spaces with Ambient Computing, the Internet of Things, and Smart City Design, pp. 209–231. IGI Global, Hershey (2017)

Art and Cultural Heritage in Smart Environments

Intelligent Painting Based on Social Internet of Things

Zhiyong Fu[✉], Jia Lin, Zhi Li, Wenjia Du, Jieye Zhang, and Shuxiong Ye

Tsinghua University, Beijing 100084, China
fuzhiyong@tsinghua.edu.cn, ninjalinjia@yahoo.com,
bettercallme@foxmail.com, duwenjia@126.com, jeococo@qq.com,
ysx15@mails.tsinghua.edu.cn

Abstract. Because of social computing, people are more interconnected to things and vice versa. Social computing transforms the Internet of Things to a new form called "Social Internet of Things". The social Internet of Things needs a social approach to the Internet of Things. It is equally true that design in the context of social computing also requires a social approach to the Internet of Things. A human-object mixed social interaction model or a social approach is demonstrated in this paper and based on which a children-centered social thing, specifically an intelligent painting device is shown in this paper, whose objective is to create a superpower interaction for children and mix the human-human social network with object-object machine network to form a social network consisting of humans and objects and emotions, which focuses more on machine emotion, children behavior and children emotion.

Keywords: Social computing · Internet of Things · Social approach · Social interaction · Emotion

1 Introduction

Social computing is a cross-disciplinary research and application field with theoretical underpinnings including both computational and social sciences [1]. In the context of Internet of Things where things are connected to each other due to ICT development and with the arrival of social computing, whose unique feature is that it pays more attention to social intelligence rather than social information processing and it holds that technology development shall serve for society and appropriate social knowledge and theories shall be incorporated into technology development, a new form of Internet of Things comes into being and is named "Social Internet of Things". Social Internet of Things focuses more on machines and objects' social behaviors on the basis of objects being interconnected. Social computing and social Internet of Things provide designers a research area called social things, which owns certain social approach to the Internet of Things, addresses technological and social aspects of the Internet of Things [2]. The design research area "social things" brings new challenges in designing social smart products that are not only smart and networked but also social, playing a role in human social network to create a two-way social interaction between objects' network and human's social network.

N. Streitz and P. Markopoulos (Eds.): DAPI 2017, LNCS 10291, pp. 335–346, 2017.
DOI: 10.1007/978-3-319-58697-7_24

The purpose of this paper is to design and implement an intelligent painting product intended for children in the design research area of social things. The social things and social Internet of Things are necessarily a guide for this children-centered product design and additionally how significant the role that color plays in children growing process basically explains why the painting products gain popularity among children. The study finds that people have color perception from the infancy and by the impact of color environment, color can not only stimulate children's visual nerve, but also are related to the development of children's intelligence, emotional stability, personality formation. Color magically affects people's mental state. The color of children's living environment has a great relationship with children's intellectual development, and personality development.

2   Related Work

The related literature proposes basic concepts and do some research in regard to Internet of Things, social computing, social Internet of Things, social things. The Internet embodies a great many objects that provide services and information to people. Billions of objects are expected to take a major active role in the future network, bringing physical world data into the world of digital content and services, which results a networking paradigm, called the Internet of Things [3]. Social computing whose definition is that Computational facilitation of social studies and human social dynamics as well as the design and use of ICT technologies that consider social context helps to form the social Internet of Things (SIoT). SIoT has a development process. A first idea of socialization between objects has been introduced by Holmquist et al. whose focus was on solutions that enable smart wireless devices, mostly wireless sensors, to establish temporary relationships [4]. The concept of Embodied Microblogging (EM) also challenges the current vision of IoTs. It proposes that the augmented everyday objects will play the role in mediating the human-to-human communication and supporting additional ways for making noticeable and noticing activities in everyday life [5]. Objects are able to participate in conversations that were previously reserved to humans only [6]. Later there is a view that if things are involved into human's network, the social networks can be built based on the Internet of Things [7]. An individual can share the services offered by smart objects with friends or their things and human's social network is utilized by things as an infrastructure for service discovery and access [8]. The integration between the IoT and the social networks is investigated and a few interesting exemplary applications are described [9]. The exploitation of social networks in the context of the IoT has been investigated to propose to exploit human social network relationships to share the resources offered by a given smart thing [8]. Recently the name Social Internet of Things began to appear in the published papers. This happens in form of interesting attempts to explore the social potentialities of the Internet of Things building blocks [10]. The Social Internet of Things (SIoT) is characterized as an IoT where things are fit for building social associations with different items [11].

Then the design research area on social computing which addresses both techno-logical and social aspect namely "social things" is analyzed [2]. In this paper, the author describes some areas and applications that social things is applied. For example, social things are capable of facilitating the learning to make learning a more effective and more enjoyable social experience. Combined with the application area of social computing [1], entertainment software, which focuses on building intelligent entities (programs, agents, or robots) that can interact with human users. The idea of intelligent painting device based on models of social things that are expatiated in the next part is shaped into and taking account of children psychology which is analyzed [12] and color meaning for children which is analyzed [13], the proposed painting device is children-centered to facilitate education and communication.

3   Model of Social Thing

3.1   Social Thing Model I

When humans play with objects or machines, usually machines act in two ways, one is machine-like and the other is human-like. The machine-like way shows that the objects or machines really behave like themselves, in other words, they are just machines or objects. In the case of machine-like behavior, people find it hard to interact with the objects responding to humans by just obeying the orders and doing what humans know what they are going to do, which is not surprising at all. Nevertheless, the human-like way gives objects or machines human characteristics including human behavior, human emotion and human personality. Thanks to these features, objects behave like humans and that makes it natural and easy for humans to interact with objects. Objects with emotion tend to attract human's attention and encourages humans to have a further conversation with objects out of curiosity, which promotes an emotional social interac-tion between humans and objects. Playing with objects seems not that dull, but more like talking to objects and it creates an entrance for objects to enter human's social network, for in human's social network, humans talk to each other, exchange feelings with each other. Now that objects are capable of communicating with humans in a mental state. Thus, it is possible for objects to show some kind of emotion of personality to human, for example being naughty, lazy, rebel, passionate, shy, cold, aggressive, and friendly. Therefore, it is easier that objects become a certain member of human social network in which people regard object as a pal, a friend, a child or even a teacher, not the objects or machines lacking emotion. What mentioned above about objects with emotion and what influence they have on human social network offer a kind of social approach to the Internet of Things. This model is shown in Fig. 1.

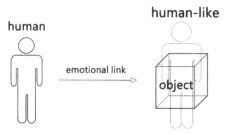

Fig. 1. Social thing model I

3.2 Social Thing Model II

The Internet of Things creates an environment where objects are able to exchange information with each other with the help of sensors and actuators. One object sends an order or message and the other receives the order or message, and gives a feedback. The messages and orders the objects send and receive, together with the feedbacks the objects give are merely mechanical ones including sensor data, wireless data, network data and so on. It is a rigorous technical environment where objects are communicating, talking, sharing only by rigorous code and data. Appropriate and even precise reply shall be given as long as data sending and data transmission is correctly executed. Though objects seem to be talking to each other but still it is a non-emotion way of communicating.

For human's world, the social network comes into being when people have a partner or a circle of friends to communicate with. The way people communicate is emotion-driven. It is always said that people express emotions. That is to say, by means of saying, feeling in heart can be conveyed to other people. Accordingly, people's talking to people is different from objects' talking to objects and it is a emotional way.

With the advance of Internet and Internet of Things, Web 2.0 services and tools emerge to support effective online communication for social communities. The Internet of Things technology is combined with social networks, which leads to the formation of one aspect of social Internet of Things using objects as a communicating medium and has the purpose of social entertainment and social interaction. That offers an inspiration that if there is a link line drawn between certain object and certain human based on the model 1 which suggests that objects with emotion is more likely to interact with humans. The non-emotion machine communication network will be incorporated into human's social emotional communication network. In this situation, feelings of human are not only transmitted in human social network, but also exchanged between two mechanical objects and data are even flown back to human. Consequently, machine's and human's networks have a mixture. Information, specifically, emotional information is on the move in this mixed network. The data transmission becomes emotional thanks to that emotional link connecting humans to machines. These mentioned above is shown in Fig. 2.

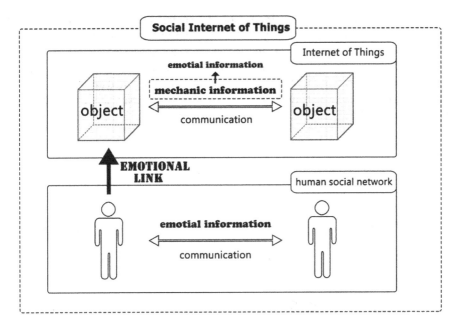

Fig. 2. Social thing model II

3.3 Social Thing Model III

In the network of objects and machines, there is an asymmetric relation among objects. For example, Bluetooth, ZigBee, 6LoWPAN networks of sensors/actuators and RFID identification systems are typically asymmetric because there is always a master machine and several slave machines. The master machines send messages to their own slave machines and all slave machines can receive the master orders and it is called broadcasting. Even if this situation looks like human behavior and human relationship existing between a human employer and human employees, it is still an analogy. Basically, it is still a mechanical communicating way that excludes emotion. However, provided that there is a connection established between a person and a master machine and the connection is an emotional bond, there emerges a possibility that master-slave machine communicating pattern is added emotion elements. Considering that in human social network, a group of people often work or play together. During this so called "co-" process, people's feeling, thoughts are shared and expressed among a group where there is also human's master-slave communicating pattern which, however, have emotional features and is different from object ones mentioned above. Thanks to the bond connecting people and a certain master object, the feelings can be conveyed from human's world to objects' world, just like social thing model mentioned above based on object-human connection discussed in social thing model I. Further, if there are more links between a person and a master object, the coordination between human social network and master-slave object network will reach a better state in which people find it more convenient and interesting to co-play, co-work and take advantage of social objects to more directly express their emotions for social objects which at that time act emotional mediums that are very easy to be noticed when lying in front of people. As a result, feeling runs to master object, and object sends a emotional message to all slave objects which receives the emotional message and shows them. Spontaneously the emotional links between master objects and slave objects are created and even there will be emotional lines appearing between two objects which didn't have any communication before. The social thing model III is shown in Fig. 3.

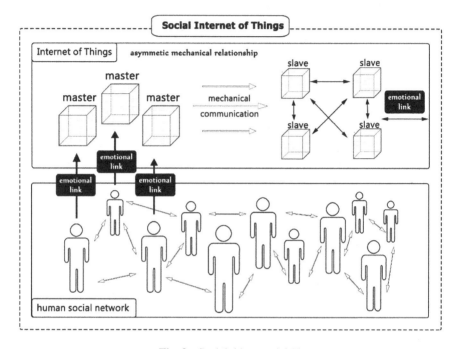

Fig. 3. Social thing model III

4 Case Study

To prove the practical function of three social thing models mentioned in Model part and to develop a children-centered, superpower-way and intelligent painting device, this paper elaborates the making process of an intelligent painting device.

The first step is survey, what is discussed above about the significance color has for children growth lays a foundation for the popularity of color products including education-oriented color books and color toy and color painting products. By investigating current color painting products, we notice that there are some defects which are listed as below.

1. consumption of materials is too great,
2. For children, limited cognitive level, not sensitive to color
3. the painting work cannot be preserved permanently

4. parents are not able to participate in the painting creating process in the distance

Apart from the four defects, we also conclude that current painting products lack so called "personality". In children's eyes, they are just toys they can play not some human-like things they can communicate with.

What's more, we notice that the painting process of current painting device can be divided into four sections. Comparing, choosing, imitating and creating. For each section, we will discuss where the super-way interaction inspiration comes from and apply the above social thing models into practice by additionally taking personality lacking into account. Here the latter three sections are chosen to analyze.

For "choosing" section, in consideration of the problem that children have limited cognitive level and are not sensitive to color, we develop a "superpower" way to pick color by making use of color sensor to pick color from real world. For example, you can pick "red" from a red apple and "green" from a green leaf. For children, picking color from real world seems that they have superpower that enables them to be the owner of the real color world. It is a part of "superpower" interaction.

For "imitating" section, We first analyze the children's behavior and psychology: imitating figures action in fairy tale, and animation; hoping to apply their favorite color in their works and wanting items to have their own exclusive features, based on which we abandon the traditional third-party painting physical media, such as paint, brushes, and fine sand to establish natural user interface of finger grasping movements. The natural finger grasping movements let children feel that they have a superpower that they really catch color in their hands. It is also a part of "superpower" interaction.

For "creating" section, this is the section that we apply the above social thing model into practice. We design two versions of our painting product and each version of product has its own superpower interaction and own mode to connect with object network with human network. For the first version, when children catch color in their hands, they can touch then release to let color "runs" to the target object or target planar. The pattern that color runs to the object has "superpower" interaction features. For the second version, children pick color then open one hand to shoot a color light to light a object with picked color, which is like ironman's manipulator and that also seems to give children a superpower ability of lighting an object.

The second version designs and develops some functions including saving painting object (painting scheme actually), sharing painting object with friends and parents to make objects more interconnected to human. For two versions of our product, picking color and lighting objects with picked color, which technically, is a one-to-many, object-to-object communication between color sensor and LED lights. The object-to-object communication doesn't come to end because Internet enables colored objects to share themselves then painting scheme can be saved in the cloud. The saved painting objects/schemes can be shown in children's different terminals in order to let children see some dimensional color painting effects on terminals and form a human-to-object communication mode.

Besides, the function saving in the second version is saving some copies of painting objects in the cloud like in real life you have pasted some color material stored and take out when deciding to continue the painting process. This saving function transforms former single Internet of Things to object-human communication mode. Children communicate with their own products. Moreover, the function sharing in the second version provides children with two modes. One is a parent-child communication mode and the other is friend sharing mode. In parent-child communication mode, the color painted through object-to-object mode can be simultaneously displayed for parents on mobile and PC terminals and in addition parents are capable of changing color online and thanks to Internet of Things, some parts of the painting product in front of children can turn to corresponding color. It is a process of remote parent-child communication interactive education and a social Internet of Things called "human-object-human" remote parent-child communication using intelligent painting toy and Internet as media, which is a typical instance of social thing model II especially in one scenario when children collect different colors outside and back home to show colors to their parents, or the other scenario when children pick color and light different colors to express their inner feeling in a color way with their parents.

As for the other sharing mode, friend sharing mode, it is referred to previously that painting objects are able to saved in the cloud and are accessible by other children. Shared painting objects can be downloaded for children to appreciate the idea or experience thoughts and emotions that are hidden in the shared painting objects.

Two scenarios in parent-child communication mode, friend sharing mode and remote parent-child communication as well, typically creates a line between a emotional child with a non-emotional painting object thus to have a mixture of object network and human network where emotions are on the move in this mixed circle, which perfectly stands for the meaning of social thing Model II.

Both versions of our painting products allow many children to paint one big painting object together. From a technical aspect, it is a master-slave mechanical mode addressed in Model III. Here by wireless communication technology called NRF, multiple color-picking sensors conduct a object-object Internet of Things communicating mode with one painting device. The color sensors send picked color to that painting object at the same time. From a experience aspect, because there is a obvious link between the master object and a child, so this is a typical instance of Model III. Several kids are painting together, which gives rise to co-playing behavior pattern, extends the object-object Internet of Things to human-human communication and forms a human-object-human social Internet of Things of co-communicating by taking the intelligent painting product as a tool.

To overcome the defects of lacking personality, more specifically, to make the color display of this intelligent painting device more interesting and more resemble human behavior and personality, we refer to social thing model I to design some human-like color display ways that have human personality trait. The examples are shown as follows.

Well-behaved way

- It is the most normal situation and the painted one shows the corresponding color in a stable state.

Naughty way

- When children paint one object, the neighbor one is lit while the lighted one is not lit.

- The painted one is flashing in a unstable state and with a fast speed
- The painted one doesn't show the right color at the beginning. Maybe several seconds later comes the right shown color

Rebel way

- The painted one shows the complementary color

Lazy way

- The painted one is too lazy to show color, it is flashing in a slow and unstable state, like yawning
- The painted one is only showing color for a while

Passionate way

- When a painted one is lit, its neighbor ones are lit together creating a "spreading" feeling.

Indifferent way

- The painted one is indifferent, sometimes shows color sometimes refuses to show.

Impulse way

- The painted one is breathing to a brighter state

Shy way

- The painted one is breathing to a dimmer state

Moody way

- The painted one changes shown color at irregular intervals

The color display ways described above endows the intelligent painting product human personality and thanks to which it is easier that painting objects become a certain member of children social network in which children regard painting objects as a pal, a friend, a child or even a teacher, not the objects lacking emotion. It perfectly instantiates social thing model I.

5   Evaluation and Discussion

The evaluation part contains two stages. The first stage is that ten children are invited to take part in our intelligent painting product prototype testing. Two testing sections are arranged and one is to let each child experience the emotional color displaying way to see whether the human-like color showing way arrest children's attention or not, which is shown in Fig. 4. Through testing and observing, the conclusion is drawn that some emotion expressing ways really catch children's eyes such as naughty way, lazy way, passionate way, which verify social thing model I. While other human-like ways, for instance, well-behaved way and rebel way confuses the child in a way for during the process of testing, they are more likely to have questions. However, if we give children extra explanations, we find that children are able to understand but it loses the meaning of human-like way. So here we notice the limitation of some emotional color displaying ways, lacking the knowledge of common human behavior leads to confusion and also for children, imitating human personality only in a visual way is not enough. The other section is that several children play painting product together and as a result, we find that children show great interest for co-painting and our intelligent painting product can increase children engagement. What's more, via observing and coding, we see that when playing the painting product together, it is more natural and common for children to communicate with each other, what they communicate is painting scheme as well as thoughts and feelings, that to some extend verifies the social thing model III.

Fig. 4. Emotional color displaying evaluation (Color figure online)

The second stage is that five parent-child groups receive remote parent-child proto-type testing, which is shown in Fig. 5. The testing result reveals that children find it more interesting to communicate with their parents and even shy children in daily life is more willing to play this painting with parents. Interview to children is conducted and shows that for children, this painting product is considered as emotional media through which

Fig. 5. Parent-child prototype testing

children show their color thinking and inner feeling to their parents, just like a bond. The bond has what social Internet of Things means and can be thought as a verification of Model II.

6 Future Work

Considering that there are some limitations to human-like emotional color display. Further research on human behaviors and relationship between human social things and object social things need to be done.

Also, social Internet of Things is yet in its infancy and what now it focuses more on objects' own social network built by themselves without human's intervention. Current intelligent painting device, though, imitates human behavior in some ways but still can only called smart objects rather than social objects. So how to make this intelligent painting product more intelligent so as to become social agents still has a long way to go. Specifically, it is possible for the painting product to be exerted a function of detecting human's emotion and forming their own social networks to form a color emotion world by communicating and cooperation to comfort sad people, to inspire and encourage people at a loss and to really join in human's social network without people's leading.

References

1. Karjalainen, J., Nyberg, T.R., Mohajeri, B., Gang, X., Zhu, F., Hu, B.: On implementing location-based services in Guangzhou, China. In: Proceedings of 2014 IEEE International Conference on Service Operations and Logistics, and Informatics, Qingdao, pp. 458–463 (2014). doi:10.1109/SOLI.2014.6960768
2. Hu, J.: Social things: design research on social computing. In: Rau, P.-L.P. (ed.) CCD 2016. LNCS, vol. 9741, pp. 79–88. Springer, Cham (2016). doi:10.1007/978-3-319-40093-8_9
3. Atzori, L., Iera, A., Morabito, G.: From "smart objects" to "social objects": the next evolutionary step of the internet of things. IEEE Commun. Mag. **52**(1), 97–105 (2014). doi: 10.1109/MCOM.2014.6710070
4. Holmquist, L.E., Mattern, F., Schiele, B., Alahutha, P., Beigl, M., Gallersen, H.: Smart-its friends: a technique for users to easily establish connections between smart artefacts. In: Proceedings of ACM UbiComp 2001, September–October 2001
5. Nazz, E., Sokoler, T.: Walky for embodied microblogging: sharing mundane activities through augmented everyday objects. In: Proceedings of the 13th International Conference on Human–Computer Interaction with Mobile Devices and Services, MobileHCI, September 2011
6. Mendes, P.: Social-driven internet of connected objects. In: Proceedings of the Interconnecting Smart Objects with the Internet Workshop, March 2011
7. Ding, L., Shi, P., Liu, B.: The clustering of internet internet of things and social network. In: Proceedings of the 3rd International Symposium on Knowledge Acquisition and Modeling, October 2010
8. Guinard, D., Fischer, M., Trifa, V.: Sharing using social networks in a composable web of things. In: Proceedings of IEEE Percom 2010, March–April 2010

9. Kranz, M., Roalter, L., Michahelles, F.: Things that twitter: social networks and the internet of things. In: Proceedings of the Pervasive 2010, the Citizen Internet of Things 2010 Workshop CIoT 2010: What Can the Internet of Things Do for the Citizen? May 2010

10. Boucouvalas, A.C., Kosmatos, E.A., Tselikas, N.D.: Integrating RFIDS and smart objects into a unified internet of things architecture. Adv. Internet Things **1**, 5–12 (2011)

11. Tripathy, B.K., Dutta, D., Tazivazvino, C.: On the research and development of social internet of things. In: Mavromoustakis, C.X., Mastorakis, G., Batalla, J.M. (eds.) Internet of Things (IoT) in 5G Mobile Technologies, pp. 153–173. Springer International Publishing, Cham (2016)

12. Radu, I., MacIntyre, B.: Using children's developmental psychology to guide augmented-reality design and usability. In: 2012 IEEE International Symposium on Mixed and Augmented Reality (ISMAR), pp. 227–236. Atlanta, GA (2012). doi:10.1109/ISMAR.2012.6402561

13. Cycowicz, Y.M., Friedman, D., Duff, M.: Pictures and their colors: what do children remember? J. Cogn. Neurosci. **15**(5), 759–768 (2003). doi:10.1162/jocn.2003.15.5.759

Guidance Method to Allow a User Free Exploration with a Photorealistic View in 3D Reconstructed Virtual Environments

Sho Iwasaki[✉], Takuji Narumi, Tomohiro Tanikawa, and Michitaka Hirose

Graduate School of Information Science and Technology, The University of Tokyo,
7-3-1 Hongo, Bunkyo-ku, Tokyo 113-8656, Japan
{iwasaki,narumi,tani,hirose}@cyber.t.u-tokyo.ac.jp

Abstract. Architectural reconstruction based on photographs is important for digitally archiving historic buildings. In addition, freely exploring a reconstructed Virtual Environment (VE) enhances users' understanding of and interest in the background cultural information. However, reconstructed models often have errors as well as terribly distorted views when viewed from a point distant from where the pictures were taken. Because of this problem, it is difficult to allow users to freely explore in a VE while keeping photorealistic views.

In this study, we propose a new method that enables both free exploration and high rendering quality by implicitly guiding users to the well-rendered viewpoints. First, we evaluate the rendering quality of the reconstructed model with view-dependent texture mapping. Second, by combining the evaluation results, we create a type of potential field that defines which direction to guide the users. Experimental results suggest that our proposed method can decrease the distortion in the views during VE exploration, and can possibly allow free exploration in VEs.

Keywords: User guidance · Image-based rendering · 3D reconstruction · Virtual environment · Digital museum

1 Introduction

Image-based rendering and modeling makes it possible to digitally archive and explore historic places and architectures. Exploring virtual environments (VEs) with free interaction is expected to not only enable users to intuitively understand the size and atmosphere, but also to promote their interest in the historical and cultural background information [1, 2]. Actually, interactive museum exhibits that use image-based rendering and modeling can effectively convey information [2].

A three-dimensional (3D) reconstruction method makes it possible to explore a virtual environment freely without being constrained by the camera positions [3]. Three-dimensional reconstruction estimates the 3D structure of a target object selected from images and generates a 3D model of it. Structure from Motion (SfM) is an essential 3D reconstruction technique. In the SfM workflow, the feature points in the images are detected, and then the positions in 3D space of these points and the cameras are estimated

© Springer International Publishing AG 2017
N. Streitz and P. Markopoulos (Eds.): DAPI 2017, LNCS 10291, pp. 347–357, 2017.
DOI: 10.1007/978-3-319-58697-7_25

geometrically. Generally, further reconstruction, e.g., dense-point reconstruction and surface reconstruction, will be made based on the results of SfM.

Many studies have investigated methods for reconstructing 3D models from images and applying 3D reconstruction to Virtual Reality (VR) [3, 4]. However, 3D reconstruction often makes errors, depending on the conditions in which the pictures were taken and the materials or shapes of the target objects. For example, a glass or wall with a plain texture is very difficult to reconstruct from only images because their feature points cannot be detected. Then, these errors cause a view distortion when exploring the VE and decrease the sense of immersion. Moreover, the decrease in the sense of immersion decreases the users' interest and their understanding of the target.

Incidentally, many studies have been conducted on user guidance in VE, and several studies have proposed methods with which users are guided unconsciously [5]. These techniques enable users to keep the feeling of free exploration while leading them to pre-defined viewpoints in the VE. We think that, with these guidance methods, we can help users avoid locations with distorted views and guide them to photorealistic views as they explore.

Therefore, in this paper, we propose a new guidance method that leads users implicitly and keeps their views photorealistic while allowing free exploration. In this method, we evaluate the rendering quality at each viewpoint in the VE, and generate a type of potential field, which we refer to as a guidance field, whose value is the result of the evaluation. Then, users are guided according to the guidance field. In addition, we conducted preliminary experiments to examine the effectiveness of the guidance field in decreasing the view distortion.

2 Related Work

In this section, we first describe studies on 3D viewers for VR using 3D reconstruction technology. Second, we describe related studies on user-guidance methods in VE.

2.1 3D Viewers for VEs Reconstructed from Multiple Images

"Photosynth" [6] by Microsoft and "Photo tourism" [3] by Snavely et al. are famous 3D viewer applications that enable the interactive exploration of VEs reconstructed using images.

Photosynth is a web service that enables users to easily construct panoramic views from several photos on a web browser. It has two viewer modes. In one mode, users can look around panoramically from a single point; in the other mode, users can move around a single target object and look at it from 360°. However, users can only move to the left or right, and the exploratory degrees of freedom (DOF) are very small.

Snavely et al. proposed a 3D viewer named "Photo tourism," which enables the interactive exploration of VEs reconstructed using numerous images on the web. They employed several interfaces to view the VEs. Basically, users smoothly transition between photos and only view them from the positions from which they were taken. Although the authors also implemented the viewer mode using the standard 6-DOF, the views could not be kept photorealistic and the quality of the views could be low if the users' viewpoints were away from the photos [7].

These days, other 3D reconstruction methods using prior knowledge, or methods using images and a 3D sensor in combination, have been proposed. However, the views are still distorted, depending on the users' viewpoint and view direction, even when using the latest 3D reconstruction methods or 3D sensors [8, 9].

2.2   Guidance Methods for Exploration in VEs

Galyean proposed a guidance method called "the river analogy," which contains the users' exploration around an "anchor" moving along a predefined path in the VE [10]. In this method, the users are tied to the anchor by a virtual spring; if the user goes too far from the anchor, he is pulled back near it. This method makes it possible to keep users near the predefined path and prevent them from leaving the desired positions. However, with Galyean's original method, since the anchor moves from moment to moment, there is a high possibility that the users will be forced to move and their free exploration may be hindered.

Tanaka et al. proposed another guidance method that slightly alters the user inputs and implicitly leads them to the predefined positions [5]. A type of potential field is generated depending on the distance and direction from the target position, and it defines the alterations against the users' input. If the alteration is very small, the users may not feel a sense of incompatibility or sometimes do not even notice the guidance; thus, this guidance method can keep the feeling of free exploration. We extended this method and propose a new method that generates a potential field and slightly changes the users' viewpoints to less distorted view positions.

3   Design of Proposed Method

3.1   Overview

In this section, we explain the algorithm for our proposed guidance method, based on evaluating the rendering quality, and the manner of generating the guidance field, which defines where to guide the users. Figure 1 shows our method's workflow. Generating the guidance field mainly consists of three processes:

1. 3D reconstruction of VE,
2. Evaluation of rendering quality, and
3. Generation of a guidance field, based on the evaluation results.

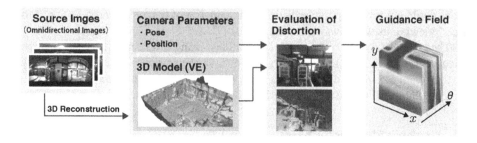

Fig. 1. Our method's workflow.

3.2   3D Reconstruction of VE

Our 3D reconstruction workflow and processes are similar to previous studies [4]. The workflow is as follows:

(1) Feature points are detected in the images and the feature correspondences are acquired.
(2) The cameras' poses and positions are estimated from the feature-correspondence results. Simultaneously, the feature points' positions in 3D space are estimated; these are called sparse space points.
(3) Based on the camera parameters, dense space points are reconstructed using a multi-view stereo method.
(4) Finally, the surface of the target objects is reconstructed and a 3D model is generated.

We used the Agisoft [11] for processes (1) to (3) and a Poisson Surface Reconstruction [12] implemented on MeshLab [13] for process (4).

3.3   Evaluation of Rendering Quality

To realize photorealistic views, we evaluate the rendering quality. In this paper, we use rendering quality and view distortion to mean opposite things. Before we define our evaluation of the rendering quality, we explain the texture-mapping method used in our 3D viewer. We employ view-dependent texture-mapping [14].

View-dependent texture-mapping is a texture-mapping method which selects a texture image projected onto the model, depending on the current viewpoint and view angle. Specifically, an image that is taken from an angle or position close to the current view angle or position is selected as the texture. Therefore, the texture mapped onto the VE changes dynamically as users walk or look around in the VE. The camera positions used to calculate the distance from the current viewpoint were already recovered in the 3D reconstruction process.

We employ view-dependent texture-mapping because the method is compatible with the models generated by 3D reconstruction. It is almost impossible to reconstruct object structures in detail; therefore, reconstructed 3D models sometimes have rough meshes and errors. View-dependent texture-mapping can visually remove the roughness and the errors. In other words, by switching textures based on the view positions and angles, the views look natural even if the 3D model contains errors. Specifically, if the texture is projected onto the mesh from almost the same angle as the current view angle, the generated view will be very natural, regardless of the roughness of the 3D model. Thus, view-dependent texture-mapping is very effective for reconstructed models.

Let us now return to the evaluation of rendering quality. The rendering quality of the mesh whose texture was selected by the view-dependent texture-mapping depends on the following three elements: the current viewpoint, the target mesh position, and the point where the texture image was taken. Thus, the evaluation of rendering quality, which is defined for each mesh, can be defined using the geometric information. Buehler et al. [15] proposed using the angular error, expressed as follows (Fig. 2(a)):

$$\varphi_k^{ULG} = \cos^{-1}\left(\hat{v}_c \cdot \hat{v}_v\right), \tag{1}$$

where $\hat{v}_v$ denotes the direction vectors between the current view points and the k-th mesh centers, and $\hat{v}_c$ denotes the direction vectors between the camera centers and the k-th mesh centers. When the texture is projected obliquely against the mesh face, the texture image will be stretched and the value calculated by Eq. 1 will sometimes not correspond to the visually observed rendering quality. Thus, we propose a new evaluation, which is a simple change from Eq. 1. We consider the normal vector of the mesh, i.e. (Fig. 2(b)):

$$\varphi_k^{proposed} = \cos^{-1}\left(\hat{v}_c \cdot \hat{v}_v\right)\cos^{-1}\left(-n \cdot \hat{v}_c\right), \tag{2}$$

where n denotes the normal unit vector of the k-th mesh. If the texture is obliquely projected onto the mesh, the angle between $-n$ and $\hat{v}_c$ increases, as does the value of $\varphi_k^{proposed}$. Moreover, the value of $\varphi_k^{proposed}$ decreases if the rendering quality is high.

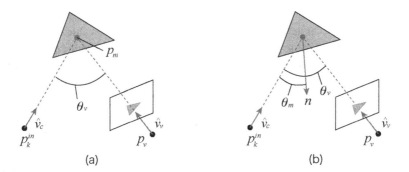

(a)   (b)

Fig. 2. Evaluation of rendering quality. p_v, p_k^{in} and p_c are respectively the positions of the user and the camera with which the texture image was taken, and p_k is the position of the k-th mesh. (a) The evaluation used in a previous study [15] employs θ_v, the angle between the vectors $\hat{v}_c$ and $\hat{v}_v$, which are direction vectors from p_v and p_c to p_k, respectively. (b) Our proposed method considers the normal unit vector n of the mesh and uses the angle θ_m between $\hat{v}_c$ and n.

In this paper, because we generate the texture from a single omnidirectional image, only the meshes visible from the camera position are rendered with the texture.

Thus, the rendering quality can't be defined for the meshes invisible from the cameras, and we defined their rendering quality as the constant value $C_{invisible}$. Figure 3 shows the result of our proposed evaluation.

(a) View Image   (b) Buehler et al.' s method   (c) Proposed method

Fig. 3. Result of evaluating the rendering quality. (a) View image. The area circled in red is natural and the area circled in blue is distorted. (b) The result of applying Buehler et al.'s method [15] to the view. The rendering quality of the two circled areas is almost the same. (c) Result of our proposed method. The values correlate well with the visual distortion. (Color figure online)

3.4 Guidance Field Based on the Rendering-Quality Evaluation

We next describe how to generate a guidance field based on the rendering-quality evaluation and how to lead users according to the guidance field. We defined the view distortion at each viewpoint as the average evaluated rendering quality in the view there. Then, we used it as the value of the viewpoint guidance field. Consequently, the guidance field is defined as follows:

$$\Phi = \frac{1}{m} \sum_{p \in D} \varphi_k^p, \tag{3}$$

where p denotes a pixel in the view screen, and D and m denote a set of pixels in the view screen and the total number of pixels, respectively. φ_k^p is the value of the rendering quality of the k-th mesh, which is projected onto pixel p. That is, the value of the guidance field is the sum of the rendering quality on the screen at that viewpoint. Finally, the user's locomotion and rotation are altered by the following equations, respectively:

$$v_{guide} = -\nabla\Phi, \tag{4}$$

$$v_{output} = v_{input} + g(\Phi)Gv_{guide}, \tag{5}$$

where v_{guide} denotes the vector indicating which direction to guide the user, v_{input} denotes the user's input vector, and v_{output} denotes the vector indicating the total changes of the user's position and rotation. The function $g(\Phi)$ defines the strength of the guidance and the matrix G defines the strength balance between locomotion and rotation. With guidance according to Eq. 4, the user will be guided to less distorted view points.

4   Experiment

To evaluate our proposed guidance-field method, we conducted preliminary experiments by applying our method to real data. First, we describe the VE used in the experiment. Second, we describe the experimental procedures and results.

4.1   VE Used in the Experiment

3D Reconstruction and Model. We reconstructed "Kikusuiyu," one of the most famous Japanese public bathhouses. The bathhouse was closed in September 2015. We photographed the bathhouse with an omnidirectional camera, the Ladybug3, with a resolution of 4096 × 2048 pixels (Fig. 4(a)). We took pictures along the five straight paths (Fig. 4(b)). For 3D reconstruction, we used 44 omnidirectional images, which are each about 30 cm away from the next picture.

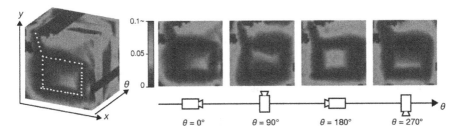

Fig. 4. Guidance field. (*left*) Overview of the guidance field $\Phi(x, y, \theta)$. The white dots indicate the positions where the texture images were taken. (*right*) Cross sections of the field at four typical directions.

We applied 3D reconstruction, mentioned in Sect. 3.1, to these images, and simplified the 3D model by applying a Quadric Edge Collapse Decimation, implemented in MeshLab. The resulting 3D model contains 30,022 vertices and 59,987 faces (Fig. 4(c)).

Guidance Field. We generated the guidance field for the VE according to Eq. 3. In this experiment, the user can only move horizontally, and only rotate around the vertical axis. Therefore, the guidance field is expressed as $\Phi(x, y, \theta)$.

To generate the guidance field, we calculated the rendering quality for 1600 points (40 × 40 grid with an interval of almost 15 cm), and 36 directions with a 10-degree interval at each point. $C_{invisible}$ was 0.25. The aspect ratio and field of view are 4 × 3, and 70°, respectively, which is the same as that used in our 3D viewer. We excluded 64 points where the user can see beyond the 3D model and outside of the VE. Since the rendering quality differs even at the same position and angle, depending on the texture image projected onto the meshes, we generated guidance fields for each of the 44 texture images. Then, we integrated these guidance fields by employing the smallest distortion value at each position and angle. The final generated guidance field is shown in Fig. 5.

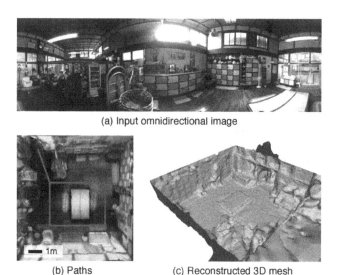

(a) Input omnidirectional image

(b) Paths

(c) Reconstructed 3D mesh

Fig. 5. Input data and result of the 3D reconstruction. (Color figure online)

In Fig. 5, the view distortion is small in the blue areas; conversely, the rendering quality is low in the red areas. The white points denote the positions where the texture images were taken. It can be seen in the figure that, near these points, the guidance field value is small; i.e., the rendering quality is high.

Texture Mapping. We employed view-dependent texture-mapping, but used a different method to select the texture image for the with- and without-guidance conditions. For the with-guidance condition, the texture with the smallest rendering quality at the viewpoint was selected. For the without-guidance condition, the texture nearest the current viewpoint was selected.

4.2 Detailed Procedure

We prepared two typical scenes that assume exploration in the VE, which we call Scene 1 and Scene 2, and compared the views in each scene with and without our proposed guidance method.

In Scene 1, the virtual user moves straight without rotating. This assumes simple locomotion. The start position is $(x, y) = (3.7, 4.2)$ and the start direction is $225°$ from the x-axis. The moving speed is constant at 0.83 m/s. In Scene 2, the virtual user rotates without locomotion. This assumes that the user is simply looking around. The start position is $(x, y) = (2.9, 0.5)$ and the start direction is the positive y-axis direction, which is $90°$ from the x-axis. The virtual user rotates clockwise at a constant speed of $40°/s$.

Through the experiments, the aspect ratio is 4×3 and the field of view is $70°$. The function $g(\Phi)$ and the matrix G in Eq. 5 are defined as follows: $g(\Phi) = \alpha|\Phi|$, where $a = 4.8 \times 10^3$, and $G = diag(1, 1, 25)$, respectively. The units are meters and degrees, also respectively.

4.3   Results and Discussion

Figures 6 and 7 show the viewpoint transitions and the transitions of the evaluated distortion values for the views in Scene 1 and Scene 2, respectively.

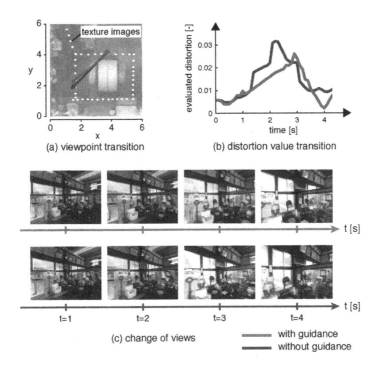

Fig. 6. Views with and without guidance in Scene 1. The white dots in (a) depict the positions where the texture images were taken.

Figure 6 shows that, in Scene 1, our proposed guidance method slightly altered the virtual user's moving path, and decreased the distortion in the views; the average evaluated distortion value four seconds from the start was 0.015 without guidance and 0.012 with guidance. Figure 6(a) shows that the viewpoints are led near the positions where the texture images were taken. Consequently, the evaluated distortion was kept lower with the guidance than without it, from $t = 1.5$ to $t = 2.5$. However, the value was reversed at $t = 3$. We think it is mainly because the proposed method only leads users to current lower potential viewpoints according to Eq. 4, and does not consider time-series information or path planning. Figure 6(c) shows that the guidance altered not only the moving path but also the view directions.

Figure 7 shows that, in Scene 2 as well, the guidance method slightly altered the virtual user's viewpoints and kept the evaluated distortion in the views. In Scene 2, although the virtual user's input was only rotation without locomotion, the virtual user was led by the guidance near the positions where the textures were taken (Fig. 7(a)). The average evaluated distortion value for four seconds from the start was 0.021 without

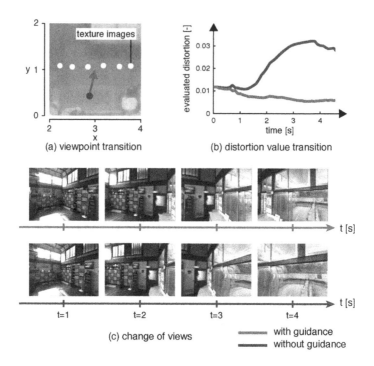

Fig. 7. Views with and without guidance in Scene 2. The white dots in (a) depict the positions where the texture images were taken.

guidance and 0.0078 with guidance. In Fig. 7(c), the view at t = 3 without guidance is terribly distorted, but the view with guidance is not.

These results suggest that our proposed guidance method efficiently decreases the distortion and keeps the rendering quality in the views. We also think that the alterations of the users' positions and directions each time are small enough to not hinder free exploration.

5   Conclusion

Both free exploration and high visual quality are important for exploration in VEs. In this paper, we proposed a new method that maintains high rendering quality while allowing free exploration by slightly altering the users' viewpoints and view direction according to the guidance field generated by evaluating the rendering quality.

Experimental results showed that our proposed guidance method could maintain the view quality and suggested that it could provide both free exploration and high view quality.

In future work, we plan to examine whether the guidance-based alteration disturbs the users' exploration in real scenes. It is also important to investigate what types of alteration the users notice easily. We think that the users will more easily notice the direction change while moving straight, as in Scene 1, than the viewpoint change while rotating, as in Scene 2, because the former alteration sometimes results in moving the users away from their destination in VE. For real use, we must consider these things when designing the guidance method.

Acknowledgements. This research and development work was supported by the MIC/SCOPE#162303009.

References

1. Cairncross, S., Mannion, M.: Interactive multimedia and learning: realizing the benefits. Innovations Educ. Teach. Int. **38**(2), 156–164 (2001)
2. Narumi, T., Hayashi, O., Kasada, K., Yamazaki, M., Tanikawa, T., Hirose, M.: Digital diorama: AR exhibition system to convey background information for museums. In: Shumaker, R. (ed.) VMR 2011. LNCS, vol. 6773, pp. 76–86. Springer, Heidelberg (2011). doi:10.1007/978-3-642-22021-0_10
3. Snavely, N., Seitz, S.M., Szeliski, R.: Photo tourism: exploring photo collections in 3D. In: ACM Transactions on Graphics (TOG), vol. 25, pp. 835–846. ACM (2006)
4. Musialski, P., Wonka, P., Aliaga, D.G., Wimmer, M., Gool, L.V., Purgathofer, W.: A survey of urban reconstruction. In: Computer Graphics Forum, vol. 32, no. 6, pp. 146–177. Wiley Online Library (2013)
5. Tanaka, R., Narumi, T., Tanikawa, T., Hirose, M.: Guidance field: potential field to guide users to target locations in virtual environments. In: 2016 IEEE Symposium on 3D User Interfaces (3DUI), pp. 39–48. IEEE (2016)
6. Microsoft Corporation. Photosynth. https://photosynth.net/
7. Snavely, N., Garg, R., Seitz, S.M., Szeliski, R.: Finding paths through the world's photos. In: ACM Transactions on Graphics (TOG), vol. 27, no. 3, p. 15 (2008)
8. Furukawa, Y., Curless, B., Seitz, S.M., Szeliski, R.: Reconstructing building interiors from images. In: 2009 IEEE 12th International Conference on Computer Vision, pp. 80–87. IEEE (2009)
9. Xiao, J., Furukawa, Y.: Reconstructing the world's museums. Int. J. Comput. Vis. **110**(3), 243–258 (2014)
10. Galyean, T.A.: Guided navigation of virtual environments. In: Proceedings of the 1995 Symposium on Interactive 3D Graphics, p. 103-ff. ACM (1995)
11. Agisoft PhotoScan User Manual, Professional Edition, Version 1.2. http://www.agisoft.com/pdf/photoscan-pro_1_2_en.pdf
12. Kazhdan, M., Bolitho, M., Hoppe, H.: Poisson surface reconstruction. In: Proceedings of the Fourth Eurographics Symposium on Geometry Processing, vol. 7, pp. 61–70 (2006)
13. Cignoni, P., Callieri, M., Corsini, M., Dellepiane, M., Ganovelli, F., Ranzuglia, G.: MeshLab: an open-source mesh processing tool. In: Scarano, V., De Chiara, R., Erra, U. (eds.) Eurographics Italian Chapter Conference. The Eurographics Association (2008)
14. Debevec, P.E., Taylor, C.J., Malik, J.: Modeling and rendering architecture from photographs: a hybrid geometry- and image-based approach. In: Proceedings of the 23rd Annual Conference on Computer Graphics and Interactive Techniques, pp. 11–20, ACM. (1996)
15. Buehler, C., Bosse, M., McMillan, L., Gortler, S., Cohen, M.: Unstructured lumigraph rendering. In: Proceedings of the 28th Annual Conference on Computer Graphics and Interactive Techniques, pp. 425–432. ACM (2001)

Wearable AR Platform for K-Culture Time Machine

Eunseok Kim[1], Jungi Kim[1], Kihong Kim[1], Seungmo Hong[2], Jongwon Lee[3],
Noh-young Park[4], Hyerim Park[4], Hayun Kim[4], Jungwha Kim[4],
and Woontack Woo[4(✉)]

[1] Augmeted Reality Research Institute KAIST, Deajeon, Korea
{scbgm,k.junki34,kihongkim}@kaist.ac.kr
[2] Postmedia Corporation, Seoul, Korea
hsm@postmedia.co.kr
[3] Department of Computer Engineering, Chungnam National University,
Daejeon, South Korea
uranos1@cnu.ac.kr
[4] UVR Lab KAIST, Deajeon, Korea
{nypark,ilihot,hayunkim,jungwhakim,wwoo}@kaist.ac.kr

Abstract. AR technology has been rapidly accepted in the cultural heritage
domain, which requires wide context information for complete understanding as
providing an enhanced experience to the user with related information of the
physical world. However, currently, there are several limitations for seamless AR
such as applications in outdoor environments and wearable platforms. To address
this issue, we introduce our AR platform in this paper that supports the outdoor
AR and wearable platform. Through the standardized metadata schema-based
data retrieval, time-space correlated AR content containing the assorted context
information can be provided to users. In addition, vision- and sensor-based spatial
data composition technology supports stable 3D outdoor tracking. Finally, an
immersive visualization provisioning module, which integrates the aforementioned component, provides a 360-degree panorama virtual reality for wearable
platforms and the outdoor AR in mobile platforms. Using this platform, we expect
a seamless context-aware AR service in the cultural heritage domain.

Keywords: Augmented reality · Wearable AR · 3D outdoor tracking · 360-
degree panorama VR · Cultural heritage domain

1 Introduction

Following the development of mobile augmented reality (AR) in the 2010s, AR technology has been confirmed to have applications in various fields. Because AR technology effectively transmits various additional information related to reality, it is used
as an immersive delivery method in the commercial field, and it is utilized as a new
medium for enhancing the learning effect of users in the field of education and training.

Following these trends, AR technologies are actively applied in the field of cultural
heritage. In general, an in-depth understanding of cultural heritage requires a historical,
economic, and cultural context of the cultural heritage, apart from a description of itself.

© Springer International Publishing AG 2017
N. Streitz and P. Markopoulos (Eds.): DAPI 2017, LNCS 10291, pp. 358–370, 2017.
DOI: 10.1007/978-3-319-58697-7_26

For this purpose, information that can improve understanding is provided to visitors in various forms, such as text-based description and various audiovisual materials. Consequently, AR technology, which increases human recognition abilities, is attracting attention as the next generation technology in the field of cultural heritage, as a means for effectively providing a large amount of additional information to visitors [1].

Major research projects that use AR technology in the cultural heritage domain are classified into applications in museum-oriented indoor environments and applications in site-oriented outdoor environments. For example, the ARCO System [2], ARTSense Project [3], and Project CHESS [4] are representative examples that use AR technology in indoor environments. The ARCO System was developed in the early stages of the applications of VR and AR in museums. Although it was an early attempt, the ARCO System established a data structure that considers users, technologies, interoperability, and operational practices to provide reusability and interoperability. The ARCO system is considered a novel precedent for the later AR projects that were executed in Europe. In the cases of the ARTSense Project and Project CHESS, these projects attempted to apply AR in indoor environments such as European museums. The ARTSense Project is characterized by the provision of user adaptive services based on user context information acquisition. On the other hand, the CHESS project provided a storytelling user experience and supported a content authoring tool, which was used by the general public to create and share the content.

On the other hand, there have been several projects that attempted to deploy AR in outdoor environments. Archeologuide [5] was the first attempt to apply outdoor AR in the cultural heritage domain; it visualized the 3D model of an ancient Greek temple as an augmented reality from an outdoor site based on a PC-based hardware platform. Archeologuide is considered a pioneering example of proving the hardware feasibility of augmented reality in an outdoor environment. Since then, Mobi-AR [6] has been providing urban tourism support applications using augmented reality technology in a mobile environment. Mobi-AR detects the location of users using embedded sensors and vision algorithms and provides related information through the mobile device. Particularly, to address the issue of computing power and battery depletion, which are considered inherent limits of mobile platforms, a remote server is dedicated to the calculation of user localization. Project ORCHESTRA is the first example of AR implementation based on wearable platforms of optical see-thorough HMD devices in the cultural heritage domain. Although it focused on user interaction that is suitable for wearable environments based on vision technology [7] and user evaluation through demonstration [8], this project proved that it is still difficult to utilize wearable devices for augmented reality due to the technical limitations of hardware. In view of this technological trend, present augmented reality technologies are in a transition period from mobile platforms to wearable platforms.

Moreover, we have tried to apply AR technology in the cultural heritage domain through K-Culture Time Machine Project [9, 10]. The K-Culture Time Machine Project aims to integrate heterogeneous cultural heritage databases in Korea and create time-space correlations between cultural heritages and provide time-space correlated content through AR technology. For this purpose, we have studied the integration of heterogeneous cultural heritage databases according to time and space, and we have standardized this aggregation method, while providing users with an immersive experience through AR technology. In this paper, we introduce the wearable AR platform, which is the latest development in the K-Culture Time Machine Project.

2   Wearable AR Platform for K-Culture Time Machine

The wearable platform of K-Culture Time Machine Project consists of two part. The first part retrieves time-space correlated content and multimedia data and incorporates the information into a standardized metadata schema. To provide these contents and multimedia data, heterogeneous databases have been aggregated with mitigating ontology. The second part provides the AR experience to user in outdoor environment. To support AR visualization in outdoor environments, spatial data composition component constructs spatial information of a heritage site based on vision and sensor information. In addition, an experience provisioning module is developed to provide immersive experiences to users. The following sections will provide a detailed description of each part of the project.

2.1   Standardized Metadata Schema-Based Data Retrieval

Standardized metadata schema-based data retrieval module performs the dynamic content retrieval for the wearable AR visualization and its overall process is described in Fig. 1. The content retrieval process consists of two main flows. First, an ontology, constructed according to the time-space correlation defined by existing Korean Cultural Heritage Data Model (KCHDM) [11], is parsed by an SPARQL query. Second, a multimedia content DB, which contains the multimedia content related to the cultural heritage, is established and parsed with a MySQL query. Such information is integrated into the

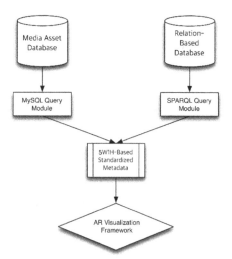

Fig. 1. Overall workflow of the data retrieval process

revised standardized metadata for AR content [12], and visualization of the AR content is performed based on this data structure.

For the time-space correlated content integration, the Korean Cultural Heritage Data Model (KCHDM) [13], which is the ontology standard for aggregating heterogeneous data from Korean cultural heritage institutions, was developed and adapted into the retrieval process. KCHDM consists of 31 classes and 41 properties to link cultural heritage entities semantically. Through the time-space correlation generation technique proposed in the previous study [10], a conceptual relationship model among cultural heritage entities based on KCHDM can be developed semi-automatically.

However, the conceptual relationship model from the previous process needs to be modified in order to develop the cultural heritage knowledge base for the wearable AR. Although KCHDM has 31 classes, we used only 5 super classes, including actor, event, thing, time-span, and place, due to the simple and intuitive user interface of the wearable platform. Figure 2 is an example of a knowledge graph for the wearable AR platform of K-Culture Time Machine.

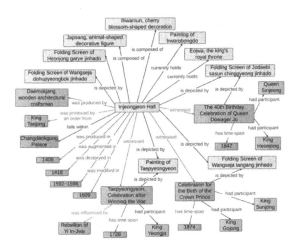

Fig. 2. An example of a knowledge graph for injeongjeon hall of the Changdeokgung palace [13]

In addition to modifying classes, the process of mapping web resources to the relationship model is needed. The conceptual relationship model does not include information from web resources that present a certain cultural heritage entity, but includes information on only the relationship between cultural heritage entities. Therefore, we used the properties "has description" for text descriptions and "has representation" for multimedia content in order to map web resources onto the relationship model. In addition, the data-type property "has url" was used for presenting the locations of web resources in order to load content in the wearable AR platform. After these modification processes, the final relationship model is stored in the web database as Web Ontology Language (OWL) format.

To parse the information from the OWL format, the SPARQL Query method is utilized in the data retrieval process. Using the dotNefRdf library [14], which is an open source.NET Library for Resource Description Framework (RDF), ontology of OWL format can be parsed into C# data structures, and it can be utilized in visualization platforms by parsing the ontology into standardized 5W1H metadata schema implemented with C# data structures. Using ontology data parsing, detailed descriptions and media content for each cultural heritage, which are in raw database of the concerned authorities, and the spatio-temporal correlation between cultural heritages are parsed into the standardized metadata schema.

Multimedia database includes video content related to cultural heritages such as historic TV dramas and movies. To support the interoperability and reuse of AR content, existing metadata schema and its design principles [15, 16] are referred for building our multimedia database. The features of the referred existing metadata sets are as follows. First, the metadata set of W3C [17], the de facto standard of metadata schema, aims at enhancing the interoperability of different descriptions of media resources. It has 28 critical multimedia metadata properties proposed by W3C by analyzing 18 multimedia metadata formats and 6 multimedia container formats. Second, existing metadata schema for the AR content is used for considering the characteristics of AR and supporting the AR visualization [18]. It supports expandability and context-aware features for AR visualization, based on the 5W1H-based metadata schema. Third, the metadata set for broadcast content distribution [19] is used for designing a data structure for the metadata schema. For covering the video resources thoroughly, we adopted a multi-layered hierarchical structure for the video [20]. In the hierarchy, video and sequence have the same meaning of program and episode as shown in [19]. Therefore, it was used for designing the video and sequence classes to implement the multimedia database. Figure 3 shows the process of establishing a multimedia database.

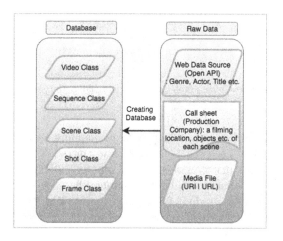

Fig. 3. Implementing a multimedia database

To parse video content from the database, a multimedia–parsing module is developed using SQL query with POST. When the name of the cultural heritage entity is given, the module retrieves scenes and shot data with the same entity value. These parsed data are restructured into the standardized 5W1H metadata schema with C# data structure. Through this process, the content can be retrieved and visualized in the AR system.

As an integrating container, standardized metadata schema is adapted for background data structure of the wearable AR platform. We had worked on the standardizations of an aggregation method for heterogeneous cultural heritage database [11] and integrating metadata for AR content [12]. Currently, we are revising the AR content metadata standard to integrate the two previous standards. The main improvement is adding the MAR ontology structure to include the KCHDM and other elements of ontology. To support the service, user information is added and a lot of common information is arranged. The result of the revision is shown in Figs. 4 and 5.

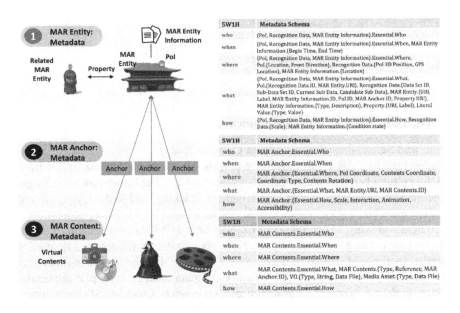

Fig. 4. Revised 5W1H metadata schema for AR content

According to the schema, background content data structure of the visualization module is developed and information is parsed as discussed above. From the KCHDM ontology, information on cultural heritages and their relevance and related content are parsed. On the basis of that, contemporary video content of multimedia database complements the data of the information content. After this process, the visualization module can provide the AR/VR scene and related contents from the contents data.

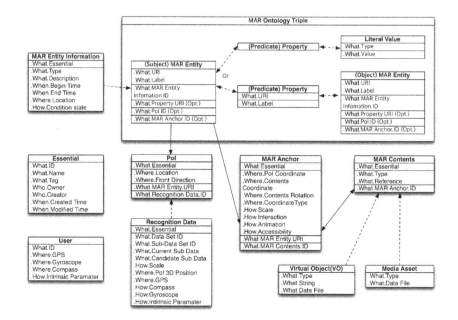

Fig. 5. Revised 5W1H metadata structure for AR content

2.2   Wearable AR Platform Development

Vision- and Sensor-based Spatial Data Composition

To support outdoor AR environment, we proposed a vision-based outdoor AR framework for cultural heritage sites in previous research [21]. The framework was designed to incorporate computer vision-based camera tracking and ontology-based data-authoring technology. Our framework design includes: (1) visual data generation, (2) AR content authoring, (3) mobile optimization, and (4) AR content visualization.

In the visual data generation module, 3D keypoints and keyframes are automatically generated by the SfM (structure-from-motion) pipeline. For the feature extraction and matching process, we use ORB [22] to reduce computational costs for real-time camera tracking. In the AR content authoring process, we connect associated 3D coordinates of a PoI (Point of Interest) with virtual content. Figure 6 shows the content authoring process. In order to stabilize the camera position estimation and tracking, our framework was designed using the multi-threading architecture. Finally, the content visualization module integrates 3D visual data and content authoring results to visualize the AR content with the current 6DoF (Degree-of-freedom) camera position of the mobile device. Figure 7 shows real-time AR content visualization results.

Fig. 6. AR content authoring process

Fig. 7. AR content visualization

Immersive Visualization Provision

The immersive visualization module provides an enhanced experience to the user by generating an AR/VR scene for cultural heritages. The AR module provides mobile-based AR experience to the visitor with related information and multimedia content of cultural heritages. On the other hand, the VR module provides mobile - and wearable-based remote experience to a user exploring sites of cultural heritage from remote environment based on 360-degree panoramic images.

The AR visualization module aims to provide enhanced experience to the visitors of the cultural heritage site. Based on the vision - and sensor-based spatial data composition, user localization of object-level accuracy in large-scale outdoor environment is present due to the hybrid tracking method. Moreover, a user can search for related information and multimedia content with dynamic access to raw databases through the user interface.

The VR visualization module was developed to address the space constraints of the AR where users must be on the site and for immersive VR experience. The VR visualization module provides users with a VR experience through mobile and wearable platforms based on 360-degree panoramic images. The user's time-space constraints required by the AR module are solved via the VR module through a remote experience of the cultural heritage site.

On the mobile platform, users can explore cultural heritage sites like the street view feature of the existing maps service such as Google maps. In addition, the same information and multimedia content provided by the AR module are also supported by the VR module. Through this feature, a user can explore a cultural heritage site in a remote environment. On the other hand, on the wearable platform, immersive experience on the cultural heritage site and 3D reconstruction of the cultural heritage, which is currently perished, are provided.

3   Prototype and Future Expansion

A prototype was developed to verify the proposed platform. This prototype targets an area from Sejong-ro to Changdeokgung Palace in Seoul (Fig. 8). The prototype supports mobile AR visualization, and mobile and wearable VR experience based on 360-degree panoramic image. The prototype provides AR visualization based on detailed object-level robust tracking in the outdoor environment and provides a virtual experience from the Sejong-ro to the Changdeok Palace based on 360-degree panoramic images. The smartphone VR HMD was utilized to solve issues such as limited viewing angle of the current optical see-through HMD, battery depletion and insufficient computation power of devices, and barriers to user entry that requires purchasing expensive HMD. To provide the 360-degree panoramic view, Google VR SDK was implemented.

Fig. 8. 360-degree panoramic image-based VR experience using the prototype

However, there are some issues that need to be addressed in order to visualize assorted content on mobile and wearable platforms. First, for a digital cultural heritage, all content has authenticity issues. If the digital contents of cultural heritage are not validated by historical records, there could be a risk of conveying false information to users. In this prototype, we solved the issue of authenticity by directly utilizing the contents of the existing cultural heritage database built on the basis of historical data, or developing content by referring to them. On the other hand, 3D model data and large volume of contents may consume a lot of resources to be visualized on mobile and wearable devices. For this case, we optimized the content with the appropriate level of data for mobile and wearable devices and made it available to users.

For future expansion, we plan to develop several features such as: (1) advanced video content retrieval and (2) view-point guidance. First, using the integrated metadata schema and content parsing module, advanced video content retrieval can be enabled. Until now, when searching for video content, users were able to use limited information of a video such as title, actor, and genre. Moreover, it has been impossible to search for video clips based on the content of a scene or shot unit. However, based on the integrated metadata schema, users can search related multimedia based on not only the user's location and position but also the temporal and spatial data of the content. As shown in Fig. 9, a user can watch various video clips related to certain PoIs, watch video clips filmed in one location sequentially, and watch video clips based on the same time background in PoI. This would provide new media experience in cultural heritage sites by providing various TV drama or movie clips, which are temporally and spatially related to the historical site.

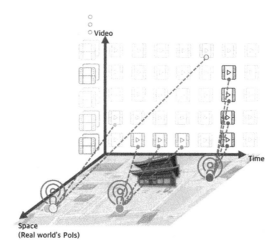

Fig. 9. Advanced video contents retrieval based on multimedia database

In addition, using the integrated metadata schema could provide immersive experience with view-point guidance (Fig. 10). Each frame of a video contains various information such as date, GPS, compass, and altitude, a service can guide users to the exact point of the video clip to be watched. At this point, users can watch the real world as the background of the video clip on the device screen. Furthermore, when a tourist visits the filming location, oftentimes, it looks different from the scene because of several reasons such as different seasons, different time (day or night), and computer graphics. If the database has data related to the filming date or object, it would be possible to provide more immersive experience by augmenting the scene to the real world based on the context-awareness of an environment, content, and a user.

Fig. 10. View-point guidance based on metadata of contents

4 Conclusion

In this paper, we presented a wearable AR platform for the cultural heritage of the K-Culture Time Machine project. In the back-end, heterogeneous cultural heritage databases were aggregated with standardized metadata schema, and extensive spatial data composition was performed to support vision-based rigorous tracking in an outdoor environment. In the front-end, the platform provided AR/VR visualization to provide the additional information, historic knowledge, and assorted multimedia content for cultural heritages.

To verify the platform, we developed a prototype targeting the cultural heritage of Seoul. With several additional functionality expansions discussed above, a usability test would be part of a future study.

Acknowledgments. This research is supported by Ministry of Culture, Sports and Tourism(MCST) and Korea Creative contents Agency(KOCCA) in the Culture Technology(CT) Research & Development Program 2014.

References

1. Damala, A., Marchal, I., Houlier, P.: Merging augmented reality based features in mobile multimedia museum guides. In: Anticipating the Future of the Cultural Past, CIPA Conference 2007, 1–6 October 2007 (2007)
2. Patel, M., White, M., Mourkoussis, N., Walczak, K., Wojciechowski, R., Chmielewski, J.: Metadata requirements for digital museum environments. Int. J. Digit. Libr. **5**(3), 179–192 (2005)
3. Damala, A., Stojanovic, N., Schuchert, T., Moragues, J., Cabrera, A., Gilleade, K.: Adaptive augmented reality for cultural heritage: ARtSENSE project. In: Ioannides, M., Fritsch, D., Leissner, J., Davies, R., Remondino, F., Caffo, R. (eds.) EuroMed 2012. LNCS, vol. 7616, pp. 746–755. Springer, Heidelberg (2012). doi:10.1007/978-3-642-34234-9_79
4. Pujol, L., et al. Personalizing interactive digital storytelling in archaeological museums: the CHESS project. In: 40th Annual Conference of Computer Applications and Quantitative Methods in Archaeology. Amsterdam University Press (2012)
5. Vlahakis, V., et al.: Archeoguide: first results of an augmented reality, mobile computing system in cultural heritage sites. Virtual Reality, Archeology, and Cultural Heritage (2001)
6. Marimon, D., et al.: MobiAR: tourist experiences through mobile augmented reality. Telefonica Research and Development, Barcelona, Spain (2010)
7. Caggianese, G., Neroni, P., Gallo, L.: Natural interaction and wearable augmented reality for the enjoyment of the cultural heritage in outdoor conditions. In: De Paolis, L.T., Mongelli, A. (eds.) AVR 2014. LNCS, vol. 8853, pp. 267–282. Springer, Cham (2014). doi: 10.1007/978-3-319-13969-2_20
8. Barile, F., et al.: ICT solutions for the OR. C. HE. STRA project: from personalized selection to enhanced fruition of cultural heritage data. In: 2014 Tenth International Conference on Signal-Image Technology and Internet-Based Systems (SITIS). IEEE (2014)
9. Ha, T., Kim, Y., Kim, E., Kim, K., Lim, S., Hong, S., Kim, J., Kim, S., Kim, J., Woo, W.: K-culture time machine: development of creation and provision technology for time-space-connected cultural contents. In: Yamamoto, S. (ed.) HCI 2015. LNCS, vol. 9173, pp. 428–435. Springer, Cham (2015). doi:10.1007/978-3-319-20618-9_43

10. Kim, E., Jo, J., Kim, K., Kim, S., Hong, S., Kim, J.-I., Park, N.-y., Park, H., Matuszka, T., Kim, J., Woo, W.: AR reference model for K-Culture time machine. In: Yamamoto, S. (ed.) HIMI 2016. LNCS, vol. 9735, pp. 278–289. Springer, Cham (2016). doi:10.1007/978-3-319-40397-7_27

11. Telecommunications Technology Association (TTA), Context-based Metadata Model for Cultural Heritage Data Aggregation, Korea, TTAK.KO-10.0850

12. Telecommunications Technology Association (TTA), Metadata Schema for Visualization and Sharing of the Augmented Reality Contents, Korea, TTAK.KO-10.0851

13. Kim, H., Matuszka T., Kim, J.I., Kim, J., Woo, W.: An ontology-based augmented reality application exploring contextual data of cultural heritage sites. In: 2016 12th International Conference on Signal-Image Technology & Internet-Based Systems, pp. 468–475. IEEE (2016)

14. dotNetRDF, An Open Source.NET Library for RDF. http://www.dotnetrdf.org/

15. Heery, R., Patel, M.: Application profiles: mixing and matching metadata schemas. Ariadne **25** (2000)

16. Duval, E., Hodgins, W., Sutton, S., Weibel, S.L.: Metadata principles and practicalities. D-lib Mag. **8**(4), 16 (2002)

17. Lee, W., et al.: Ontology for media resources 1.0. W3C recommendation 9 (2012)

18. Kim, E., Kim, J., Woo, W.: Metadata schema for context-aware augmented reality application in cultural heritage domain. In: Digital Heritage 2015 proceedings (2015)

19. Hyun, B.J.D.: Metadata element and format for broadcast content distribution (2014) http://mpeg.chiariglione.org/standards/mpeg-a/augmented-reality-application-format

20. Hunter, J., Armstrong, L.: A comparison of schemas for video metadata representation. Comput. Netw. **31**(11), 1431–1451 (1999)

21. Noh-young, P., et al.: All-in-one mobile outdoor augmented reality framework for cultural heritage sites. In: 2016 International Workshop on Visions on Internet of Cultural Things and Applications. IEEE (2016)

22. Rublee, E., et al.: ORB: an efficient alternative to SIFT or SURF. In: 2011 International Conference on Computer Vision. IEEE (2011)

Flyer Mapping in Art Museums: Acquiring Implicit Feedback Using Physical Objects

Tomoyo Sasao[✉] and Shin'ichi Konomi

Center for Spatial Information Science,
The University of Tokyo, Kashiwa, Chiba 277-8568, Japan
{sasaotomoyo,konomi}@csis.u-tokyo.ac.jp

Abstract. In this paper, we present our study that analyzes collections of flyers in different museums using statistical modeling techniques and show that sensing and analyzing interactions with physical flyers can uncover invisible differences among museums, thereby demonstrating the feasibility of our approach that focuses on visitors' interactions with physical objects to characterize physical spaces. Moreover, our study suggests the potential of multi-tiered analyses according to the structures of social practices around physical objects.

Keywords: Urban sensing and analysis · Physical objects · Civic computing

1 Introduction

Civic computing integrates computational capabilities in urban public spaces by exploiting pervasive smart devices and objects. Urban spaces are increasingly acquiring the capability to sense, store and process the data that mirror people's usage of various spaces in cities. Existing approaches to capturing usage patterns of urban spaces heavily rely on location-sensing technologies such as GPS. However, location data are only useful so far as people are interested in location-related features. It is often difficult to infer one's preferences related to physical objects or non-physical dimensions of urban spaces by simply applying statistical algorithms to mobility datasets.

Retail stores have been using automatic identification technologies such as barcodes and RFIDs, thereby collecting data that enable analysis of people's preferences about commercial physical objects. However, many physical objects in urban spaces are not sales items, and therefore we know little about people's interactions and preferences around non-commercial physical objects or spaces that are not intended for economic activities. Direct observation could be used but it is generally too labor-intensive to collect sufficiently comprehensive data for meaningful quantitative analysis.

In this paper, we propose an approach to modeling and visualizing people's interests and preferences related to non-commercial physical objects, and present the results of our study to test the feasibility of our approach. In particular, our study analyzes sets of physical flyers placed at key locations in museums using statistical modeling techniques to show that visitors' interactions with a collection of flyers reveal collective interests of the visitors to a museum. Investigating several museums in Japan based on this approach reveals similarities and differences of the museums according to the collective interests

© Springer International Publishing AG 2017
N. Streitz and P. Markopoulos (Eds.): DAPI 2017, LNCS 10291, pp. 371–379, 2017.
DOI: 10.1007/978-3-319-58697-7_27

of their visitors. Moreover, our study suggests the potential of multi-tiered analyses according to the structures of social practices around physical objects.

2 Related Works

There are different sources of data that can be used to model and/or visualize characteristics of physical spaces based on people's perceptions and interests. We can classify such data sources into explicit data sources, i.e., the ones requiring explicit user inputs as in the cases of voting, experience sampling, and crowdsourcing, and implicit data sources, i.e., the ones without requiring explicit inputs as in the cases of opportunistic crowdsensing, social media streams, activity sensing using physical objects, and so on.

Among the technologies for supporting explicit user inputs, situated voting devices [5, 6, 8, 11] can be used for capturing perceptions and interests of diverse urban inhabitants who may or may not own mobile devices. VoxBox [5] is a tangible system for gathering opinions on a range of topics in situ at an event through playful and engaging interaction. Game of Words [6] is a crowdsourcing game for public displays, which allows the creation of a keyword dictionary to describe locations.

An apparent limitation to explicit data sources is the need for users to input data manually for the sake of data collection. Implicit data sources can minimize such a burden on users without significantly degrading the quality of collected data or increasing privacy concerns. Indeed, researchers have examined if opportunistically-captured location information can be used to infer interests by investigating the relationship between explicit place ratings and implicit aspects of travel behavior such as visit frequency and travel time [4]. Although, such approach could potentially be useful in making a rough estimation of users' interests, crowd sensing and social media streams can be more useful when one must derive detailed categories and clusters that reflect people's perceptions and interests. CSP [2] exploits opportunistically captured images and audio clips from smartphones to analyze words spoken by people, text written on signs or objects and thereby classifying places into various categories. Livehoods [3] derive clusters of urban areas based on the data from a location-based online social network.

Implicit data can be captured by sensing people's interactions with physical objects, thereby potentially making it easy for anyone, including people who do not own smartphones, to have their perceptions and interests be heard without the burden of explicit inputs. Although conventional approaches rely on mobile phones to sense people's interactions with physical objects, vision-based techniques or stationary sensors can be employed as well, depending on the settings and constraints. Physical mobile interaction [1] allows users to interact with tagged physical objects such as physical posters using mobile devices. FlierMeet [7] is a system that allows users to capture interesting flyers from bulletin boards and upload it to a server that groups and tags flyers based on various context-based and content-based features. A key limitation to these existing systems is the relative inattention to modeling and visualization of urban spaces. Our study complements the existing works by looking into the usefulness of this type of implicit data in potentially modeling and visualizing physical spaces based on the implicit physically-based 'feedback' from all.

3 Flyers: Physical Objects that Draw the Interest of Visitors

Our study focuses on collections of physical flyers that are placed on shelves, tables, etc. in museums (see Fig. 1). In this section, we discuss why people's interactions with flyers can be useful for inferring their detailed perceptions and interests, and also describe contexts and uses of flyers.

Fig. 1. Sets of flyers made available for visitors at different museums in Japan.

Flyers often include summarized information about events, products, restaurants, stores, etc. and typically used for advertisement. Compared to plain business documents, flyers are often visually appealing to draw interest of the people that they target. They also fit in bags and wallets easily.

Different collections of flyers are available at different places including hotels, cafes, restaurants, bookstores, shops, beauty salons, cleaning shops, hospitals, etc. It is generally free of charge to put flyers at these places. However, one may have to pay to put flyers at supermarkets, convenience stores, train stations, and post offices. Also, even when it is free of charge, one might have to obtain a permission. The selection of flyers available at these locations is influenced by these social and economic contexts.

We have visited twenty museums and galleries in Japan to observe the locations and layouts of flyers in the museums, ten of which we conducted focused observation to measure people's interactions with flyers. Figure 1 shows flyers made available for visitors at some of the museums. We collected all the flyers at the museums to analyze their contents, and counted the number of people who took each flyer during a 60 min period except for mori museum and ide museum, at which we concluded the observation in 52 and 45 min, respectively (see Tables 1 and 2).

Table 1. Rate of flyer takers gender-segmented in each museum

		Mori	Ide	Bun	Hachi
Male	Visitors	84	22	11	81
	Flyer takers	12	10	4	5
	%	14.3	45.5	36.4	6.17
Female	Visitors	200	27	50	122
	Flyer takers	50	18	21	17
	%	25.0	66.7	42.0	13.9

Additionally, we informally interviewed a curator of at one of the venues. She mainly talked about her gallery in Tokyo, but believes that large museums select and distribute flyers in the same way as her gallery. The gallery receives quite a large number of flyers and they have to select the ones they provide in the gallery. This is in line with what we observed in the museums, and we understood that some museums are more selective in choosing the flyers than others.

In selecting flyers, the ones that match the style of the ongoing exhibition are often prioritized. That is, they select a different set of flyers when a new exhibition starts at the gallery. The number of flyers they provide in the gallery also changes exhibition by exhibition. In general, there are less flyers in the gallery during the exhibitions organized by the gallery than during the ones organized by people who rent the gallery for a short period of time.

The gallery also distributes their flyers to advertise the exhibitions they host. There seem to be five factors that influence this process as they send their flyers to:

1. the venues that the artist of the exhibition used in the past for his/her personal exhibition,
2. the venues the gallery has connections with,
3. the venues that match the artist's style,
4. the venues that many people visit, and
5. the venues that the artist has connections with.

In relation to the fourth factor, she may consider using a popular art magazine since the flyers included as supplemental material of their publication will be distributed to many venues. The rest of the factors are targeted towards a small number of selected recipients based on social networks and artistic styles. Thus, flyers are preselected to some degree before being selected by the venues in which they are displayed.

Usage of flyers is sometimes monitored by counting remaining flyers on a monthly basis. In other cases, the effects of flyers are assessed by looking at the increase/decrease of the visitors at the venues that the flyers advertise. In case flyers include discount coupons etc., the number of used coupons may be considered as a relevant quantitative indicator.

Table 2. Rate of flyer takers age-segmented in each museum

		Mori	Ide	Bun	Hachi
10's	Visitors	6	0	0	34
	Flyer takers	1	0	0	0
	%	**16.7**	**0.0**	**0.0**	**0.0**
20–30's	Visitors	219	10	44	79
	Flyer takers	36	4	16	10
	%	**16.4**	**40.0**	**36.4**	**12.7**
40–50's	Visitors	59	28	17	50
	Flyer takers	25	17	9	7
	%	**42.4**	**60.7**	**52.9**	**14.0**
60's	Visitors	0	11	0	40
	Flyer takers	0	7	0	5
	%	**0.0**	**63.6**	**0.0**	**12.5**

4 Flyer Analysis and Mapping

We have analyzed the textual contents of all the flyers we collected at four museums ("Mori", "Ide", "Bun", "Hachi") in Japan by modeling each flyer document based on a machine learning technique. The four museums are a subset of the ten museums at which we conducted focused observation and their data are complete for statistical analysis. We present the results focusing on the museum-by-museum differences of their collections of flyers.

4.1 Method

We have scanned the 147 flyers we collected and extracted textual contents by using Google Drive's OCR functionality. As it is more difficult to extract accurate textual data from freely-formatted colorful flyers than others, we also used an online database of flyers including their images and textual descriptions. For the 50 (34%) flyers that have corresponding online digital versions, we use their online descriptions, and we use the OCR-generated text for the remaining 97 flyers (66%).

As Japanese text does not have spaces between words, we next decompose text into sequences of words by using morphological analysis software [10]. Subsequently, we modeled the textual contents of each flyer by applying the Doc2Vec algorithm [9] and generating vector representations for variable-length pieces of texts. We used the gensim package of Python to compute them with the following parameters: dm = 0, size = 300, window = 15, alpha = .025, min_alpha = .025, min_count = 1, and sample = 1e-6, and epoch = 20. Using the resulting models of flyers, we have analyzed their relative positions in a 2-dimensional space based on principal component analysis. Finally, we have followed the same procedure to analyze pairwise similarities between museums in two different ways, (1) by treating the entire set of flyers at each museum as a document, and (2) by treating the set of the flyers that visitors took at each museum as a document.

4.2   Results

According to the visualization of flyers based on principal component analysis (see Fig. 2), in which each dot represent a flyer, flyers from each museum seem distributed without apparent concentration around specific spots. The lightest gray dots show the distribution of all digital flyers in the online database as a reference.

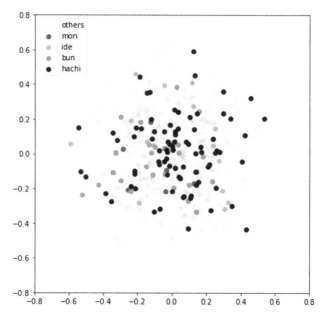

Fig. 2. Visualization of flyers based on principal component analysis.

We next show the results of our analysis of pairwise similarities between museums by treating the entire set of flyers at each museum as a document. As shown in Fig. 3, the three museums ("mori", "ide" and "bun") are rather similar, i.e., the textual contents of the flyers that provide indicate their similarity according to our statistical analysis.

Finally, we show the results of our analysis of pairwise similarities between museums by treating the set of the flyers that visitors took at each museum as a document. As shown in Fig. 4, the similarities between the museums are much smaller in most cases. Differences among the museums have been highlighted by considering not only the presence of flyers but also visitors' interactions with them.

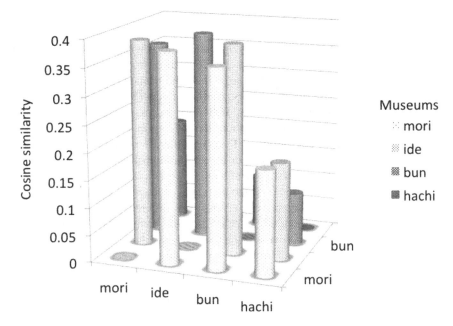

Fig. 3. Pairwise similarities between the four museums by treating the entire set of flyers at each museum as a document.

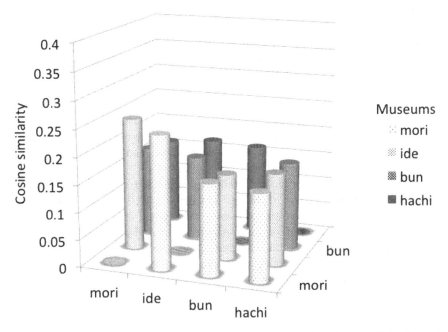

Fig. 4. Pairwise similarities between the four museums by treating the set of the flyers that visitors took at each museum as a document.

5   Discussion

Our results show that sensing and analyzing interactions with physical objects can uncover invisible differences among places. We focused on the two-step selection process of flyers, firstly the selection by the people who manage places (e.g., curators) (S1), and then the selection by the visitors who take flyers (S2). Although both steps may reflect some inherent characteristics of individual places, our results show that the second step is generally more revealing about the differences of places.

Figure 2 suggests that collections of flyers at different museums are rather uniformly distributed. We examine this further by computing pairwise similarities, which is visualized in Fig. 3, and the results reinforce our observation about Fig. 2 to some degree, in that most of the museums exhibits mutual similarity except for the 'hachi' museum. This suggests that step S1 can reveal some differences of places but other differences could not be uncovered. It could be that many museums are not too selective about the flyers they provide or they employ similar selection criteria.

Figure 4 suggests that we could uncover invisible differences among places by sensing visitors' interactions with physical objects. Such differences are arguably based on the interests of visitors rather than the intentions of the people who manage places. By modeling what we call the two-step or two-tiered selection process, we could begin to understand not only similarities and differences of places but also multi-tiered meanings of places based on what people do with physical objects.

6   Conclusion

We have analyzed collections of flyers in different museums using statistical modeling techniques and shown that sensing and analyzing interactions with physical flyers can uncover invisible differences among museums, thereby demonstrating the feasibility of our approach that focuses on visitors' interactions with physical objects to characterize physical spaces.

Our results have suggested the potential of two-tiered analysis according to the social practices around fliers in museum settings. We believe that our approach can be applicable to other environments in which people visit and interact with physical objects including but are not limited to flyers.

Our future work includes studies involving automatic sensing of flyers using cameras and embedded sensors in shelves or tables, as well as improved statistical analyses possibly including non-textual features of physical objects.

As our approach can be used for non-commercial physical objects, we hope that our approach can help pave the way to characterize, evaluate, and potentially improve all kinds of urban spaces, with or without commercial activities, by building on inclusive computing environments for the civics.

Acknowledgment. This work is partially supported by JSPS KAKENHI Grant No. 15J08542.

References

1. Broil, G., Paolucci, M., Wagner, M., Rukzio, E., Schmidt, A., Hußmann, H.: Perci: pervasive service interaction with the internet of things. IEEE Internet Comput. **13**(6), 74–81 (2009)
2. Chon, Y., Lane, N.D., Li, F., Cha, H., Zhao, F.: Automatically characterizing places with opportunistic crowdsensing using smartphones. In: Proceedings of the International Conference on Ubiquitous Computing, pp. 481–490. ACM Press (2012)
3. Cranshaw, J., Hong, J.I., Sadeh, N.: The Livehoods project: utilizing social media to understand the dynamics of a city. In: Proceedings of the 6th International AAAI Conference on Weblogs and Social Media, pp. 58–65 (2012)
4. Froehlich, J., Chen, M.Y., Smith, I.E., Potter, F.: Voting with your feet: an investigative study of the relationship between place visit behavior and preference. In: Dourish, P., Friday, A. (eds.) UbiComp 2006. LNCS, vol. 4206, pp. 333–350. Springer, Heidelberg (2006). doi:10.1007/11853565_20
5. Golsteijn, C., Gallacher, S., Koeman, L., et al.: VoxBox: a tangible machine that gathers opinions from the public at events. In: Proceedings of the 9th International Conference on Tangible, Embedded, and Embodied Interaction - TEI 2015, pp. 201–208 (2015)
6. Goncalves, J., Hosio, S., Ferreira, D., Kostakos, V.: Game of words: tagging places through crowdsourcing on public displays. In: Proceedings of the 2014 Conference on Designing Interactive Systems (DIS 2014), pp. 705–714 (2014)
7. Guo, B., Chen, H., Yu, Z., Xie, X., Huangfu, S., Zhang, D.: FlierMeet: a mobile crowdsensing system for cross-space public information reposting, tagging, and sharing. IEEE Trans. Mob. Comput. **14**(10), 2020–2033 (2015)
8. Koeman, L., Kalnikaite, V., Rogers, Y.: "Everyone is Talking about It!": a distributed approach to urban voting technology and visualisations. In: Proceedings of the ACM CHI 2015 Conference on Human Factors in Computing Systems, pp. 3127–3136 (2015)
9. Le, Q., Mikolov, T.: Distributed representations of sentences and documents. In: International Conference on Machine Learning - ICML 2014, vol. 32, pp. 1188–1196 (2014)
10. Morita, H., Kawahara, D., Kurohashi, S.: Morphological analysis for unsegmented languages using recurrent neural network language model. In: Proceedings of the 2015 Conference on Empirical Methods in Natural Language Processing, vol. 2, pp. 2292–2297, September 2015
11. Taylor, N., Marshall, J., Blum-Ross, A., et al. Viewpoint: empowering communities with situated voting devices. In: Proceedings of the ACM CHI 2012 Conference on Human Factors in Computing Systems, pp. 1361–1370 (2012)

The Construction of Art in Virtual Reality and Its Education

Jin Sheng[✉]

School of Media Arts and Communication, Nanjing University of the Arts,
Nanjing, China
nysmsj@163.com

Abstract. The rapid development of virtual reality has brought opportunities to colleges and universities, challenging them to produce skilled graduates in the field. From the perspective of arts colleges and universities, the question of how to build an educational system of digital arts content in virtual reality has become a forward-looking subject in today's digital art education. The Virtual Reality Art discipline of Nanjing University of the Arts has been refining its art curriculum through the creation and development of this academic major, in line with market demand and the university's existing educational characteristics. This has greatly promoted the overall development of the discipline, providing some guidance and reference for the development of related majors in other Chinese institutes.

Keywords: Virtual reality art · Digital content · Arts curriculum
Education guidance

1 Introduction

2016 marks the first year of completed virtual reality education (for graduates of Nanjing University of the Arts?). This does not signify the emergence of virtual reality but the beginnings of its social and cultural value. Virtual reality, which is centered on realistic experience, features multi-source information fusion in an environment simulated by a computer system, and offers interactive behavior with three-dimensional dynamic viewing, allowing users to experience the illusion of immersion.

As various sectors of society begin to apply virtual reality technologies, soon these technologies will be increasingly integrated into all aspects of daily life. The advancement of this technology does not, however, represent progress in artistic content. Without art, no technology can offer aesthetic and visual enjoyment, no matter how good the technology is. Consequently, cultivating virtual reality specialists with artistic skill is a top priority. The design and structuring of academic majors in colleges and universities, as well as in the cultivation of skilled graduates, should be closely related to the needs of society, as the curriculum system and education orientation influence the success of the discipline. In this way, markets, academic majors, and education systems are closely connected, and as such changes in the market will bring about changes in academic majors and education. Nanjing University of the Arts is the first art college in China to offer Virtual Reality Art as an academic discipline, found in

© Springer International Publishing AG 2017
N. Streitz and P. Markopoulos (Eds.): DAPI 2017, LNCS 10291, pp. 380–392, 2017.
DOI: 10.1007/978-3-319-58697-7_28

the Department of Digital Media Art, in the School of Media. There are three majors offered within the discipline: Interactive Media Art, Game Art, and Virtual Reality Art. In Virtual Reality Art, fifty-one undergraduates have already completed the course and graduated with good employment prospects. Most of them are going on to work in digital technology, broadcasting and television, e-commerce platforms, as well as cultural and art institutions. The high employment rate of these graduates shows that skilled workers in virtual reality art are in high demand in today's society.

2   Arts and Architecture Systems in Virtual Reality

Virtual reality art describes any digital visual content presented through virtual reality technology. It is a new and independent art form, of which the main characteristics are hypertext, interaction, and immersion. This interactive art experience is based on virtual reality technology, allowing the artist to more fully express concepts and enable viewers to enjoy the experience when applied to life. In the present era of the Internet, people need not only a technical experience but also an aesthetic experience of their inner world. Therefore, only when the arts environment is created in virtual reality and such features of art (figurativeness, originality, emotionality, aesthetics) are emphasized can a full range of art experiences be offered to satisfy better the spiritual and cultural needs of the viewer.

2.1   Figurativeness of Art in Virtual Reality

Wang Bi, one of the main propagators of metaphysics in the Wei and Jin Dynasties, proposed in *Zhou Yi Lue Li-Ming Xiang*: "夫象者，出意者也。言者，明象者也。尽意莫若象，尽象莫若言。言生于象，故可寻言以观象；象生于意，故可寻象以观意。" In other words, profound truth is understood through metaphor. If the deeper truth is understood, it is not necessary to find out whether the image (象) exists; if the deeper form (象) is understood, language is not required to describe this image. This is what is meant by, "Hold onto the truth and forget the image, grasp the image and cast away the language." The same is true in the figurativeness of art in virtual reality. The interactive actions in virtual reality are in themselves graphic, expressing artistic ideas and thoughts through participatory actions. The image (象) is the cloak of the profound truth (意), and the truth (意) is the kernel of the image (象).

Concept of Artistic Figurativeness. Artistic images are the means used to reflect the truth "意" of the real world. They come from the perfect fusion of subjectivity and objectivity, and their creation is founded in subjectivity. The expression of artistic images can be divided into visual images, aural images, language images, and a variety of integrated images. In terms of its reflection on the real world, the core of an artwork is its artistic image. Artistic images include three aspects: the unity of subjectivity and objectivity, the unity of content and form, and the unity of individuality and universality [1].

In virtual reality, art figurativeness found in artistic images is not only added to the virtual action, but also to the mental process of artistic creation. It is the dynamic performance of psychology and behavior. Therefore, art figurativeness is a multidimensional and special form that reflects the mental and thinking process of artists using virtual artistic behaviors. It is an attribute that not only reflects on life, but also vividly evokes the perceptual experience, thoughts, and feelings.

Features of Artistic Figurativeness. The first feature of art figurativeness is its multidimensional nature. Artistic images can be multidimensional. Some may be two-dimensional, such as QR codes and emoticons. These are simple, clear, and highly expressive. Some are three-dimensional such as three-dimensional contouring in games or cubic buttons, which have a strong spatial form. Some are four-dimensional dynamic graphics, such as dynamic three-dimensional images and interactive games, which leave strong visual impressions and a clear sense of space. Others are multidimensional combinational forms such as integrated forms consisting of various graphics and shapes found in interactive media. They have strong maneuverability and convertibility, able to interconvert and interactively change. All of the above shows that, in virtual reality art forms, figurativeness is multidimensional in nature.

The second feature of art figurativeness is its dynamic nature. In virtual reality, art is not just a human-machine interaction, but also the interaction between mind and body. Changes in the mind lead to psychological (dynamic) changes, and then bodily (dynamic) changes. Only when the mind and the body are both involved can one experience the joy and excitement of interactive art.

Time is another characteristic of art figurativeness. Since art is dynamic in virtual reality, it carries the concept of time. From freeze-frame to frame-by-frame motion, virtual images are all centered on the progression of time. Random image changes may make the viewer feel anxious, which is the only way to increase the enjoyability of art using time (Fig. 1).

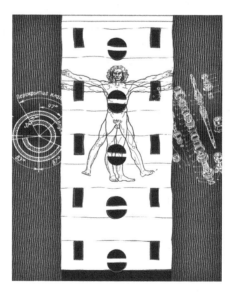

Fig. 1. 2016 graduation project: *Windows 2016*

2.2   Originality of Art in Virtual Reality

Originality implies that a work of art comes from independent creation and can be deemed as non-imitative and differential. Originality can be divided into original work and recreated work. Original work is the product of the author's independent ideas, with strong exclusivity. Recreated works differ from existing ones in their presentation. They are not simply reproductions of existing works, but newly recreated works may also be regarded as original in form. Original works refers to not only one artist's individual creation, but also those works completed by two or more artists. They can come from a single spark of independent inspiration, or the collision of thoughts.

Hegel once mentioned in Aesthetics Lectures on Fine Art [2] that "Real artistic originality is the integration and unity of the subjectivity of the artist and the objectivity of the object's features." That is to say, the originality of art is reflected by meaning or profound truth conveyed -"意." The image (象) is thus the independent creativity derived from the artist's deeper thinking and reflection. From these works the soul (灵魂) can come into being.

Concept of Artistic Originality. The originality of art in virtual reality is not merely adding a visual and mysterious veil to the "concept of artistic originality." From the creators' and the viewers' perspective, it is not just simply digital content, but virtual dynamic concepts blended into an artistic creation. The viewer is incorporated in the work, becoming an integral part of the artwork. The ideas stemming from interaction and resonation between subjective works and an objective audience are what artists seek in their final result. This is because the response of an objective audience enhances the originality of art.

Features of Artistic Originality. The originality of art is first and foremost in its uniqueness. Independently created works of art are the goal of every artist, and this is the same for artistic originality in virtual reality. During the creative process, artists must compare their subjective concepts with other works. The use of digital technology is the same, in that unique form and content are the core of the work.

The second feature of artistic originality is ingenuity. Artworks should be non-imitative and unique. The subjective arbitrariness of artists is not the original purpose in art. The pursuit of the bizarre, the grotesque, and the ugly will only distort the original concept. Originality is the denial of imitation and plagiarism. It requires that works of aesthetic value be created independently by an individual or a team from concept to content.

The third feature of artistic originality is its re-creative nature. Virtual reality art relies on computerized three-dimensional space for interaction and communication. Therefore, re-creative nature implies giving traditional art forms new concepts and forms (Fig. 2).

Fig. 2. 2016 graduation project: *Shadow in Tree Holes*

2.3   Emotionality of Art in Virtual Reality

According to the Dictionary of Psychology [3], "Emotion is the attitude and experience that people have when determining whether an objective satisfies their needs." At the same time, psychology courses often teachthat, "Moods and emotions are the attitude and experience that people have regarding an objective. Moods tend to refer to the attitude and experience of meeting basic individual desires, while emotions tend to refer to the attitude and experience of meeting social desires and needs." Therefore, embedded in the variety of emotional expressions of an artist, as well as in the passionate creation of artistic works, are forceful and individual psychological characteristics.

Concept of Artistic Emotionality. The source of artistic theories is no doubt emotional. After all, art design serves human beings, triggers human emotions, and thereby creates resonation and sublimation. Emotional expressions in works of art no doubt reflect the artists' values and thoughts. Artists' ideological orientation throughout the creative process also determines the form of emotional expressions found in the art produced.

In the artistic creation of virtual reality, interaction is the only way that allows participants to perceive the art and thus to experience emotion. This means that to take the human element in virtual reality design into full account and create a user-centered design, the design must incorporate an emotional performance, just as the user and his emotions are a complete system. Emotions are two-way, offering a relationship of equality. Its meaning is open and uncertain. The emotions evoked by artworks are their interaction with the viewer. Their value lies in achieving the aim of emotional communication. Clarifying the concept of artistic emotionality in virtual reality can trigger the emotions of the viewer and more comprehensively and more purposefully, thereby enabling works of art to meet the emotional needs of the viewer.

Features of Artistic Emotionality. The first feature of artistic emotionality is intuition. In the process of artistic experience, the viewer feels and perceives artistic images, makes value judgments, and develops initial aesthetic emotions. Intuition is the result of this focus on emotions.

The second feature of artistic emotionality is complexity. Each individual's situation, thinking, and mentality will directly affect the expression of emotion. Different viewers will have varied aesthetic experiences and evaluations of the same work of art. Today, art aesthetics is anti-traditional, and a work of art will evoke different feelings or even contrary feelings for diverse groups of people. The resulting emotions may be entirely opposite to one other.

The third feature of artistic emotionality is generality. The viewer makes his or her own examination and evaluation of the artistic content. He or she would use rational thought to make reasoned judgment of art pieces, and then develop a response emotionally and subconsciously, thereby further enriching the perception of these artworks. This is one characteristic of focusing on rational results (Fig. 3).

Fig. 3. 2016 graduation project: *Colorful College*

2.4   Art Aesthetics in Virtual Reality

Aesthetics is a form of perception instilled through personal feelings that individuals have towards human society and natural phenomena. It is also the expressive form of human emotion, changing with the development of social civilization. Varied social environments and individual characteristics may produce different aesthetic results.

Concepts of Art Aesthetics. In traditional art appreciation activities, art and viewer are independent entities, and the appreciation experience is unidirectional. Although virtual reality art still has some of the aesthetic features of traditional art, compared with traditional art forms, virtual reality art aesthetics also engages some new features. In the interactive experience process between the viewer and artworks, immersion brings new forms of expression to art, changing the way the viewer appreciates the works of art and giving the viewer a unique aesthetic experience. In virtual reality, artistic aesthetics is more diverse. The aesthetic subject and the aesthetic object form a relationship of interaction, communication, and development, by which aesthetic beauty is expressed. Both the creative process of the artist and the aesthetic process of the viewer then resonate in a variety of aesthetic experiences.

Features of Art Aesthetics. In virtual reality, art aesthetics offers a dual experience of interactivity and immersion, which features bilateral communication. This gives both the aesthetic subject and the viewer an artistic role. They are the creators and recipients of art, able to experience creation and re-creation.

In virtual reality, art aesthetics offers multidimensional experiences which are created through multi-sensory interactive methods and interactive rendering of different dimensions. It also offers virtual experiences: 1. Simulation of the real world, which connects the real world to virtual reality so as to strengthen perceptions of the real world; 2. Simulation of mixed situations, which mix virtual reality with physical reality. The exploration of mixed environments where simulation and reality coexist has contributed to the rapid development of virtual reality (Fig. 4).

Fig. 4. 2016 graduation project: *Phantom*

3　Educational Guidance on Art in Virtual Reality

In 2012, a "China Virtual Reality Art Research Center" was jointly set up by more than thirty universities. The Center is the first authoritative exchange and dialogue platform in China that is dedicated to the development of Virtual Reality art. Its purpose is to integrate knowledge from all aspects of China and create a reference system and standard of value that combines technology and art. In the past four years, its development has revealed an increasingly wide range of applications and social demand for virtual reality.

The Department of Digital Media Art in the School of Media is different from similar departments in other colleges and universities across China. It offers three major directions: Interactive Media Art, Game Art, and Virtual Reality Art. Complementary and distinctive, these courses intersect one another. This kind of structure is professional and well-reasoned. The direction of the Virtual Reality Art course is to take advantage of media art, virtual interaction, and laboratory education and to focus on making the teaching professional, advanced and practical. Following the rapid development of digital technologies, and taking advantage of comprehensive art disciplines in the university, versatile and advanced graduates are produced that can adapt to the needs of today's information and network industry, as well as conduct research and development into digital architectural representation, virtual scene interactions, and special effects in the digital space (Fig. 5).

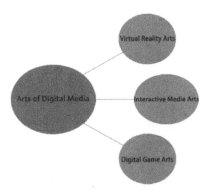

Fig. 5. The Majors of Department of Arts of Digital Media, School of Media Arts and Communication, Nanjing University of Arts

3.1   Education Guidance on the Curriculum

Virtual reality can be divided into "virtual reality technology" and "virtual reality art." Among colleges that began studies in virtual reality relatively early, Beijing University of Aeronautics and Astronautics as well as Nanjing University of the Arts are doing well. As an engineering college, the Beijing University of Aeronautics and Astronautics pays attention to the scientificity of applying virtual reality technologies to aerospace science and technology. As a comprehensive art college, Nanjing University of the Arts focuses more on visual effects and graphics offered in virtual reality.

The curriculum structure of Virtual Reality Art is divided into basic specialized courses, key specialized courses, and elective courses. Among these, basic specialized courses are the intersection between the three majors of the Department of Digital Media Art, covering the fundamental knowledge that all students of the Department must master. These courses include Theoretical Foundations, Artistic Foundations, and Technical Foundations, providing a theoretical, artistic, and technical basis for the discipline. In Theoretical Foundations, the education of artistic theories and artistic thought are highlighted to conceptually improve student aesthetics. In Artistic Foundations, the training of modeling abilities is emphasized, improving students' creative and imaginative thinking through modeling experiments and digital media innovation. In Technical Foundations, students need to master relevant professional software, as well as complete a relevant work, rendering together the theoretical and artistic foundations by means of technology.

The key specialized courses include Spatial Foundations, Professional Enhancement, and Professional Creation. Spatial Foundations focuses on the cultivation of spatial understanding and space cognitive ability; Professional Enhancement is the learning and application of core knowledge of virtual reality; Professional Creation cultivates student comprehensive ability of professional creation from two aspects - experimental and commercial.

The elective courses provide students with other relevant expertise. The whole curriculum system first lays a solid foundation from theory to technology, and then embarks on step-by-step professional development from a professional perspective, followed by artistic development using other specialized knowledge. This kind of curriculum system effectively guarantees the cultivation of versatile and advanced skilled graduates (Figs. 6, 7, 8, 9 and 10).

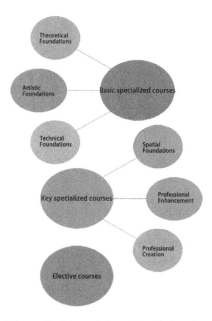

Fig. 6. The curriculums of the major of virtual reality art

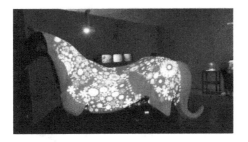

Fig. 7. 2015 graduation project: *Walk*

Fig. 8. 2015 graduation project: *GOLEM Universe Creatures*

Fig. 9. 2015 graduation project: *Across Limitation*

Fig. 10. 2015 graduation project: *Dreamland*

3.2   Education Guidance of the Methods

Traditional education methods are simple. Teachers repeat what the book says and add speculative commentary. These methods are rigid and isolated from reality. To improve on these education methods, Nanjing University of the Arts conducted an experimental reform. Throughout the course, in addition to classroom teaching and course creation, laboratory sessions and project work are emphasized. Laboratory sessions are mainly research-oriented while project work focuses on practical creative projects. The coordination of a variety of learning styles ultimately enhances the overall teaching results.

With regards to laboratory education, the national-level Media and Arts Experimental Education Demonstration Center and the Virtual Reality Educational Laboratory Center of Jiangsu Province (a provincial-level key laboratory) have changed some courses to laboratory projects so as to allow for multi-disciplinary experiments. Of these, the "1+X" joint task training of the third year is representative. "1" refers to oneself, and "X" refers to the partner. Students from different majors form a working group, led by teachers of different specialized courses, to create a work combining different concepts with a cross-discipline approach. Each of these teams must complete the project in 45 days, followed by an exhibition. This training method is conducive to fostering students' ability to demonstrate empathy and understanding and perform cross-discipline cooperation. This will lay a foundation for their graduation project in the fourth year (Figs. 11 and 12).

This education method offers a combination of practical projects and courses. Virtual reality art is sometimes a creative expression of three-dimensional modeling and at other times the recreation of something in the real world. For example, an ongoing project led by the Cultural Department of Jiangsu Provincial Government, "Nanjing - the changes of a city," represents and recreates the urban changes seen by Nanjing across 2000 years. Incorporating this project into the curriculum may improve student artistic and technical skills and enable them to understand the overall operation of real-world projects. Such a combination will help students to further understand the relationship between art and society.

In the six years since founding the academic major of Virtual Reality Art, the department teaching methods and curriculum are being constantly adjusted to be more

Fig. 11. Project: *Circle*

Fig. 12. Project: *1+1*

effective. The department aims to provide students with broadened horizons and inspire greater creativity. Three objectives of the curriculum structure are thus embodied: the cultivation of artistic expression, creativity in the field of real-world application, and breakthrough in creative design ability.

3.3   Education Guidance on Creative Thinking Experiments

In recent years, the academic discipline of Virtual Reality Art in Nanjing University of the Arts has been closely combining the development of China's contemporary art with the development of the academic discipline. For example, "Contemporary Art Ethos" and "Digital Media Innovation" are two courses that lead students to participate in concrete activities of media creation. They offer students insight into various exhibitions of contemporary art, allow them to experience an art atmosphere, and establish an awareness of creative thinking.

By visiting exhibitions of contemporary art, students can enter into "dialogue" with great artists. During this course, after visiting each exhibition, students are allowed to select an artist and their works, analyze these works, express their views, and then demonstrate understanding of the artist by creating a work of art from the artists' perspective, and then comparing the artworks. The most critical point of contemporary art is expressing a certain kind of conceptual thinking. Some artists create pieces revolving around a certain concept, and their way of thinking serves to inspire students. For students, this is the subtle training of their creative thinking.

Apart from courses, professors and scholars at home and abroad are invited to conduct "master's workshop" experimental lectures. For example, in May last year, Mr. Dominic, a celebrated documentary director from Switzerland, was invited to lecture in a two-week "master's workshop" for the School of Media. Students from different majors formed various working groups to plan, discuss, and revise together on topics assigned by the director. Eventually, the students themselves produced artistic documentary pieces.

4 Conclusion

At present, much research on virtual reality remains at the technical or commercial level. Compared to this technological aspect, research on digital content with artistic value is experiencing a slow development. Construction of the artistic systems stands vacant. However, with consistent progressive involvement of virtual reality in real life, artistic pursuit and perfection in this area are inevitable results. Therefore, virtual reality should employ artistic expression on a technical and commercial basis so as to meet the spiritual and cultural needs of the people. Virtual reality should not just build a technological framework. It should instill it with the energy of culture and art.

Nanjing University of the Arts is mature in virtual reality art education. The disciplinary classification is sound and interdisciplinary support is strong. Through exchanges with other universities, the rationality of its teaching methods in the academic major of Virtual Reality Art has been proven. The teaching philosophies mentioned above are not universal but are founded in the education foundations of the college. Each school has its own disciplinary system, and it can be hoped that Nanjing University of the Arts may inspire other institutions as they establish departments related to digital media art.

References

1. Li, Z.: The painter portrays to the reflected object shape and holds himself aloof from the world, exploring the figurative expression painting in the art practice. A Thesis Submitted for the Degree of Master, p. 13 (2014). (in Chinese)
2. Zhao, B.: Hegel's theory of art imagination and creativity. J. Soc. Theory Guide **10**, 35 (1997). (in Chinese)
3. Lin, C., Yang, Z., Huang, X.: The Comprehensive Dictionary of Psychology, pp. 940–942. Shanghai Educational Publishing House, Shanghai (2003). (in Chinese)

Painting Image Classification Using Online Learning Algorithm

Bing Yang[1]([✉]), Jinliang Yao[1], Xin Yang[2], and Yan Shi[3]

[1] School of Computer Science and Technology, Hangzhou Dianzi University,
Xiasha Higher Education Zone, Hangzhou 310018, China
363621700@qq.com
[2] Computer Science and Technology College, Dalian University of Technology,
Linggong Road, Ganjingzi District, Dalian 116024, China
[3] School of Media and Design, Hangzhou Dianzi University,
Xiasha Higher Education Zone, Hangzhou 310018, China

Abstract. Recent years have witnessed a growing interesting in studying of painting images. It is obvious that there exists a deep gap between painting images and natural images, due to special characteristics of painting images. Therefore, general image classification methods are not suitable to be applied directly to the painting images. This paper demonstrates a simple, yet powerful on-line learning algorithm to classify the category of painting images. Specifically, we use the multi-features combining of local and global features as the image descriptor, and then K-means is applied to initialize the dictionary. We resort to the online learning method to optimize the dictionary which then served as a codebook for spare coding of multi-features. Finally, we facilitate the linear support vector machine to classify images. The experimental results on two painting image datasets show that, compared with the traditional image classi-fication method, our method has improved the accuracy of image classification. What's more, from the practical viewpoint, our online learning mechanism can be also useful for many other pattern recognition tasks. Based on the research results of this paper, it can be applied in various fields such as art field and art analysis, the research of this paper provides a new way for art researchers to explore the potential of computer-aided analysis of painting works and promote the development of art research. Painting image classification could be used in social internet of things such as in museum, to make people understand the painting more in-depth.

Keywords: Painting image classification · Multi-features · Online learning

1 Introduction

Image classification [1, 2] is one of critical issues in the field of computer vision and pattern recognition. Learning based methods [3] have achieved a lot of success in recent years. However, in these researches, the objects to be classified mainly focus on natural images while ignoring the digital painting images. On the other hand, with the development and wide application of digital technology, more and more painting images gradually digitized, making large-scale paintings art analysis possible. It is

© Springer International Publishing AG 2017
N. Streitz and P. Markopoulos (Eds.): DAPI 2017, LNCS 10291, pp. 393–403, 2017.
DOI: 10.1007/978-3-319-58697-7_29

obvious that there exists a deep gap between painting images and natural images [4, 5], due to special characteristics of painting images. For instance, to paint one object, some painters may use several brushworks while others paint it heavily and complicatedly. Therefore, classification of painting images [6] is treated as a more challenging task, and general image classification methods are not suitable to be applied directly to the painting images. To overcome this problem, in this paper, we propose an effective online learning algorithm to classify the painting images by using multi-features.

Specially, in this paper, we extract local and global features as the image descriptor and use K-means to initialize the dictionary. After that, we establish the codebook by using online learning and optimization. According to the created codebook, sparse coding scheme is then applied on the extracted multi-features. Finally, we utilize the simple linear svm to achieve a high accuracy rate on painting image classification. The experimental results on two painting image datasets show that, compared to the traditional classification methods, the proposed algorithm highlights the classification accuracy, and what's more, the online learning mechanism makes this method a promising future in real applications.

Based on the research results of this paper, it can be applied in various fields such as art field and art analysis, and fully display the value of combining art and computer intelligence analysis, promote the historical and cultural value of Chinese ancient painting, and satisfy people's need of spiritual and cultural life. In the field of engineering practice, the research of this paper provides a new way for art researchers to explore the potential of computer-aided analysis of painting works and promote the development of art research, which has important academic significance and application value. Painting image classification could be used in social internet of things such as in museum, people can use the phone to shoot images, to identify the author of the painting, the classification of painting, or even the aesthetic style of the painting and so on. All of the information is pushed through the background information using the network to the user's telephone, aiming to let users understand more of paintings. Even through the comparison of painting classification, people could simulate the same painting scenes with different aesthetic styles.

2   Related Work

Painting images are being extensively digitized in order to preserve them and make them to be more widely available and easily accessible. Thus, researchers now could conveniently get painting samples to commence their work. Research on painting images by using computer, is recognized as one task combining technical with art which attracting more and more interests.

Recent years, there exist many research topics on painting images in field of computer vision and machine learning. These topics include classification based on aesthetic style, aesthetic visual quality assessment of paintings, annotation on different dynasties paintings, etc.

The study on image classification has developed rapidly and attracted interests of many researchers. Unfortunately, some methods don't work on painting images even though they catch the amazing performance on natural images. To overcome this problem, Li et al. [7] compared van Gogh's paintings with his contemporaries by statistically analyzing a massive set of automatically extracted brushstrokes and developed an extraction method by exploiting an integration of edge detection and clustering-based segmentation. Yelizaveta et al. [8] employed the serial multi-expert framework with semi-supervised clustering methods to perform the annotation of brushwork patterns. Keren [9] proposed an algorithm under the estimation that for one artist, his paintings are of the same aesthetic visual style. Xu et al. [10] presented an image aesthetic style leaning method based on texture synthesis by using Markov random field as the prototype. Then, they applied the algorithm to the Dunhuang fresco image and got a satisfying result.

Although aforementioned progresses have been made, how to effectively use the computer to classify these massive painting images to facilitate further study of the researchers is still far from solved. Therefore, in this paper, we propose a painting image classification method based on online learning mechanism and multi-features. Evaluation results on established painting image datasets verify that our method can produce a better classification accuracy compared to state-of-the-art classification methods.

3 Our Method

The flowchart of our method is as shown in Fig. 1 which includes three major steps: feature extraction, online learning and image classification.

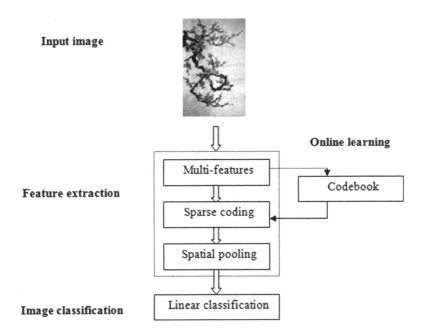

Fig. 1. The flowchart of our proposed method

3.1   Image Feature Extraction

Feature extraction plays an important role in image processing. Different features represent different characteristics of images, and they have diverse capacity to discriminate images. Local features could describe the detail of images, while global features show the panorama of the object to be classified. In order to take full advantage of the information in the image, we choose a combination of local features and global features to construct the descriptor of painting images. The extracted features are described as follows:

(a) Local Feature:

- Point feature [11]

  In this paper, we use SIFT (Scale Invariant Feature Transform) to extract the characteristics of image points. Built on the image scale space, SIFT algorithm is looking for extreme points in the scale space. Finally, the dimensions of the SIFT feature vector is chosen as 128.

- Shape features

  As a dense feature, we select HOG (Histogram of Oriented Gradient) operator to describe the contour of the image, which can be utilized to depict the similarity between same labeled images and the difference between images of different categories visually.

(b) Global Feature:

- Spatial variations of color

  This feature tries to identify the differences in color palette used by different painters. To measure the spatial variation of color, we apply the following method which is similar to Florin's method [12]: For an input painting image, its R, G and B channels are normalized by division by the intensity of painting image. At each pixel, we could determine the orientation of the plane that best fits a 5*5 neighborhood centered on the pixel of interest in the R, G and B domains respectively. Thus, at each pixel, we obtains three normals: n_R, n_G and n_B. The average of the areas constructing facets of the pyramid determined by these normals is taken as a measurement of the spatial variation of color around the pixel.

$$f_a = SV(I) \tag{1}$$

It is intuition that for painting images created by different painters, the color palate is distinguishable. Therefore, the spatial variation of color is different from each other.

- Arithmetic average brightness

  It is intuitively rational that brightness affects people's impression on a painting. Artists use a series of techniques to represent bright condition of a scene. We choose arithmetic average brightness to demonstrate the brightness attribute of paintings. The arithmetic average brightness is calculated as following:

$$f_b = \frac{1}{W * H} = \sum_{x=1}^{W} \sum_{y=1}^{H} B(x, y) \tag{2}$$

where $B(w, h) = (I_R(w, h) + I_G(w, h) + I_B(w, h))/3$, and the I_R, I_G, I_B are the R, G, B channel of the painting image, W and H mean the weight and height of image.

3.2   Online Learning

3.2.1   Sparse Coding Scheme

Assuming the descriptor of one painting image denoted by symbol M, which is a D-dimensional feature vector: $M = [m1, m2, \ldots, mN] \in R^{D \times N}$, totally having N eigenvectors. The initial codebook trained using K-means is represented by $B = [b1, b2, \ldots, bS] \in R^{D \times S}$. Lazebnik et al. [13] used VQ (vector quantization) to encode image features to generate the codebook. The VQ encoding is formulated as following:

$$\arg \min_{C} \sum_{i=1}^{N} \|f_1 - Bc_1\|^2 \quad s.t. \|c_i\|_p = 1, \|c_i\|_{l^1} = 1, c_i \geq 0, \forall i \tag{3}$$

Where $C = [c_1, c_2, \ldots, c_N]$ is the codebook trained by vector quantization. $\|c_i\|_p = 1$ means that for c_i, which corresponds to feature vector m_i in the codebook, there is only one non-zero element in it. Calculating one codebook using VQ method is fast, however, many research exposed that the accuracy rate is not too high. Therefore, we consider the sparse coding scheme for better performances.

Generally speaking, "sparse" means there are only a small amount of elements that have non-zero values. Some researches [14, 15] pointed out that data sparse expression has following obvious advantages: its calculation is very fast but with low computational complexity, its interpretability is better and its prediction to new data is much more quick.

The target of sparse coding is to approximately represent input vectors by a linear weighted combination of a series of basic vectors. We could then obtain high-level representation [16] by using basic vectors via sparse coding. Specially, assuming the input vector is $\vec{\xi}$, $\vec{\xi} \in R^D$ and its basic vectors denoted according to $\vec{b_1}, \cdots, \vec{b_n} \in R^K$, while the corresponding weights are $\vec{s} \in R^n$ then we have $\vec{\xi} \approx \sum_j \vec{b_j} \cdot s$. Note that, the dimension (K) of basic vector may be greater than D.

To compensate the loss energy in VQ encoding, a regular term such as L1-norm is added in sparse coding. Thus, the sparse coding of each vector can be calculated as following:

$$\arg \min_{C} \sum_{i=1}^{N} \|x_i - Bc_i\|^2 + \lambda \|c_i\|_{l^1} \tag{4}$$

To seek the optimal solution of Eq. 4, we could obtain the optimal solution of B or C respectively but not simultaneously. The authors in [17] proposed an interactive method to solve this problem: For fixed B, the optimization of C is then converted into a linear regression problem. For fixed C, the Eq. 4 will treated as a least-squares optimization problem.

3.2.2   Online Optimization

In this paper, we use the concept of online optimization. The training procedure of codebook is often based on batch learning rather than online optimization in traditional image classification methods. This means that once trained, it will never change across the whole classification process. However, the initial codebook may be not perfect. Hence updating it online will be more suitable for image classification when the number of train samples is increasing. The online optimization algorithm is described as following: for an image feature set, we first acquire the initial codebook B_{init} using K-means, then B_{init} is updated by looping all feature vectors M. In each iteration, according to B_{init}, feature vector m_i could be coded as sparse code c_i by using Eq. 3. Then, based on c_i, the updated B_{init} will be resolved reversely. The pseudo-code is given in Algorithm 1.

```
Algorithm 1: Online optimization of codebook
input: Binit ∈ R^(D×S), M ∈ R^(D×N)
output: B
for i = 1 to N do
{coding with the initial codebook Binit }
```

$$c_i \leftarrow \arg\min_c \left\| m_i - B_{init}c \right\|^2 + \lambda \left\| c_i \right\|_{l^1}$$

```
{online optimize codebook}
       ΔB ← -2c₁(m₁ - Bc₁),  ω = √(1/i)
         B ← Binit -ωB/|c₁|₂
end for
```

From Algorithm 1, we can find that: starting from the initial codebook created by K-means, the online optimization update the codebook using feature sets of training samples to generate a codebook with higher accuracy for next step. Compared with the method using off-line optimization, the training time is enlarged while the classification accuracy has been improved and the flexibility increased. The detailed analysis is given in the Sect. 4.

3.3   Linear Support Vector Machine

Support vectors machine (SVM) [18, 19] is currently considered as a primary method to efficiently build linear classifiers from data, yielding state-of-the-art performance. Generally speaking, SVM is essential a machine learning method based on statistical learning theory. It seeks the optimal hyperplane to divide data into two classes by solving quadratic programming problems. Given a feature set $\{x_i, y_i\}$, $i = 1, \cdots, l$ where $y_i \in \{-1, 1\}$ denotes sample labels of two classes, the linear classification equation is formulated as: $wx_i + b = 0$, where w, b are parameters to be solved. Under linearly separable situation, solving the SVM is equivalent to find a hyperplane that has maximum classification distance as:

$$y_i = f(x) = wx_i + b \tag{5}$$

subject to $y_i (wx_i + b)$.

Supposing an image I_i and its feature vector m_i is coded as c_i. Then, for binary image classification, SVM needs to solve decision equation:

$$f(c) = \sum_{i=1}^{N} \alpha_i \kappa(c, c_i) + b \tag{6}$$

Where $\{(c_i, y_i)\}_{i=1}^{N}$ denotes the training set, $y_i \in \{1, -1\}$ represents the image label.

In SPM method [13], it was found that using non-linear kernel function, the classification results could gain high accuracy, and some other researchers [20] also reported similar conclusions. However, Yang et al. [16] discovered that, by using linear kernel, SVM would achieve higher accuracy than that using non-linear kernel, when applied on sparse coding. Therefore, in this work we decide to take the linear kernel of the absolute value of the pool (absolute value pooling) as the kernel function of support vector machine.

4 Experiment Results

In this section, we utilized established Chinese-foreign art style image database as well as image database that taken from the Dunhuang frescoes in [21, 22] to validate our method. To measure the performance of our method, we will compare our method with the non-linear SPM algorithm (KSPM) [13], and linear SPM algorithm (LSPM) [16].

4.1 Chinese-Foreign Art Style Image Database

We have constructed a Chinese-foreign art style image database consisting of 1000 images, and the number of each art style images is 500. To objectively and correctly measure our algorithm, the database is subtly designed as follows: for the Chinese wash paintings, the composition time spans from the Tang Dynasty to the modern, and the content includes person, scene, flower, animal, mountain, bamboo and so on; for the foreign art paintings, images differ according to region style: Baroque and Rococo, classicism, romanticism, realism, impressionism, Fauvism and so on, and the content includes religious paintings, landscapes, portrait and so on. Figure 2 shows several images with each art style from the dataset. From the sample images, we could see the characteristics of the two -different art style.

(a) The Chinese wash paintings

(b) The foreign art paintings

Fig. 2. Chinese-foreign art style image database

To evaluate how well our method can classify the art style between the Chinese and the foreign painting. Table 1 lists experiment results when using different methods.

Table 1. Classification accuracy rate (%) on Chinese-foreign art style image database

Algorithm	30 training images	45 training images	60 training images
KSPM	80.67	83.86	85.63
LSPM	92.14	94.18	95.50
Our method	95.71	96.00	96.25

From the Table 1, we can conclude that, compared with the KSPM, we can achieve 13% higher classification rate averagely, and 2% higher for LSPM. We believed this is due to the fact that multi-features and online learning are suitable for the art style representation.

4.2 Dunhuang Murals

In addition to Chinese-foreign art style image database, we verified the feasibility of our method on Dunhuang Mural images. The images are all captured from Dunhuang Mogao Grottoes. Totally, there are 1005 images and 10 categories. As shown in Fig. 3, different from traditional images, Dunhuang Murals have their own characteristics: for example, due to its long history, the figure of the Buddha is surrounded by background disrupters while the line is vague and the object is hard to distinguish (Table 2).

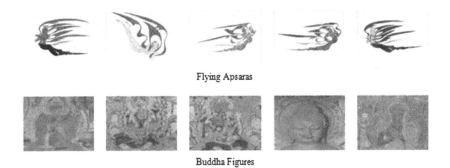

Flying Apsaras

Buddha Figures

Fig. 3. Dunhuang Murals

Table 2. Classification accuracy rate (%) on Dunhuang Murals

Algorithm	15 training images	30 training images	50 training images
KSPM	12.67	15.23	20.53
LSPM	21.65	27.34	31.00
Our method	25.35	31.64	35.91

Due to the obvious weakness before mentioned, the classification accuracy of Dunhuang Murals is lower than the results of Chinese-foreign art style image database. However, when compared with KSPM and LSPM methods, our method also achieves better performance, and this verifies the practicality of the proposed method.

4.3   Discussion

As can be seen from the above experimental results, compared with the previous algorithms, our method improves the classification accuracy by using online learning and multi-features. On the other hand, we find that the linear kernel function used in this paper is better than the nonlinear kernel.

In addition, there are some factors which influence the performance of our method. The discussions are organized as following:

- **The size of the codebook**

Intuitively, if the codebook is too small, it will lose the ability to distinguish different objects. Otherwise if too large, it may be unable to match samples. In this experiment, we test three different sizes of the codebook, e.g., 512, 1024, and 2048 respectively. The classification accuracy is shown in Table 3:

Table 3. The classification accuracy using different codebook size

Size	30 training images	45 training images	60 training images
512	92.14	92.35	93.09
1024	95.71	96.00	96.25
2048	96.07	96.28	96.60

The experimental results demonstrate that when the size of codebook increases, the classification accuracy also increases at the cost of time consumption. Taking into account both of accuracy and speed, the codebook size is selected as 1024 in this paper.

• **The training of the codebook**

In Table 4, we compare the performance by using the codebook generated by the K-means with that trained by online optimization algorithm.

Table 4. The classification accuracy using different codebook generation strategies

	30 training images	45 training images	60 training images
K-means	88.26	88.50	89.38
Online optimization	95.71	96.00	96.25

As shown in Table 4, after online optimization the codebook, the classification accuracy has improved by about 7%. Our method relies on the initial codebook generated by K-means, and further updates the codebook through online optimization by using the image feature. Therefore, in the training stage, the time consumption of our method is increased. However, there are no differences in the testing stage. In other word, the online optimization attempts to improve classification accuracy at the cost of increasing training time consumption.

5   Conclusion

In this paper, we propose an effective online learning algorithm to classify the painting images by using multi-features. We first combine the local features and global features to construct the image descriptor. Then, according to the initial codebook generated by K-means, we apply sparse coding scheme to code the image descriptor and establish online codebook. Finally, linear support vector machine is used to classify the images. The experimental results demonstrate the efficiency and feasibility of our method, and online codebook generation scheme makes our method more applicability for practical applications. In addition, we also find that our method is superior to state-of-the-art methods.

Acknowledgment. This research was supported by the Zhejiang Provincial Natural Science Foundation of China (Grant No. LQ14F020012, LQ14E050010), and the National Natural Science Foundation of China (Grant No. 61402143, and 61202280).

References

1. Li, F.F., Fergus, R., Perona, P.: Learning generative visual models from few training examples: an incremental Bayesian approach tested on 101 object categories. In: Proceedings of the 2004 IEEE Computer Society Conference on Computer Vision and Pattern Recognition, pp. 832–841 (2004)
2. Griffin, G., Holub, A., Perona, P.: Caltech-256 object category dataset. Technical report 7694, Califonia Institute of Technology (2007)

3. Prince, M.: Does active learning work? A review of the research. J. Eng. Educ. **93**(3), 223–231 (2004)
4. Bar, Y., Levy, N., Wolf, L.: Classification of artistic styles using binarized features derived from a deep neural network. In: Agapito, L., Bronstein, M.M., Rother, C. (eds.) ECCV 2014. LNCS, vol. 8925, pp. 71–84. Springer, Cham (2015). doi:10.1007/978-3-319-16178-5_5
5. Saleh, B., Abe, K., Arora, R.S., Elgammal, A.: Toward automated discovery of artistic influence. Multimed. Tools Appl. **75**(7), 3565–3591 (2016)
6. Stork, D.G.: Computer analysis of lighting style in fine art: steps towards inter-artist studies. In: Proceedings of the SPIE 7869, Computer Vision and Image Analysis of Art II, p. 786903 (2011). doi:10.1117/12.873190
7. Li, J., Yao, L., Henddriks, E., Wang, J.Z.: Rhythmic brushstrokes distinguish van Gogh from his contemporaries: findings via automated brushstroke extraction. IEEE Trans. Pattern Anal. Mach. Intell. **34**(6), 1159–1176 (2012)
8. Yelizaveta, M., Tat-Seng, C., Ramesh, J.: Semi-supervised annotation of brushwork in paintings domain using serial combinations of multiple experts. In: Proceedings of the ACM International Conference on Multimedia, pp. 529–538 (2006)
9. Keren, D.: Recognizing image "style" and activities in video using local features and naïve Bayes. Pattern Recogn. Lett. **24**(16), 2913–2922 (2003)
10. Xu, W., Wei, B., Pan, Y.: Learning of image rendering style based on texture synthesis. Eng. J. Wuhan Univ. **36**(3), 115–119 (2003)
11. Csurka, G., Bray, C., Dance, C., Fan, L.: Visual categorization with bags of keypoints. In: ECCV Workshop on Statistical Learning in Computer Vision, pp. 1–22 (2004)
12. Moorthy, Anush K., Obrador, P., Oliver, N.: Towards computational models of the visual aesthetic appeal of consumer videos. In: Daniilidis, K., Maragos, P., Paragios, N. (eds.) ECCV 2010. LNCS, vol. 6315, pp. 1–14. Springer, Heidelberg (2010). doi:10.1007/978-3-642-15555-0_1
13. Lazebnik, S., Schmid, C., Ponce, J.: Beyond bags of features: spatial pyramid matching for recognizing natural scene categories. In: Proceedings of the IEEE International Conference on Computer Vision and Pattern Recognition, pp. 2169–2178 (2006)
14. Olsshausen, B.A.: Sparse coding of time-varying natural images. J. Vis. **2**(7), 603–608 (2002)
15. Olsshausen, B.A., Field, D.J.: Sparse coding with an overcomplete basis set: a strategy employed by V1? Vis. Res. **37**(23), 3311–3325 (1997)
16. Wang, J., Yang, J., Yu, K., Lv, F., Huang, T.S.: Locality-constrained linear coding for image classification. In: Proceedings of the IEEE Conference on Computer Vision and Pattern Recognition, pp. 3360–3367 (2010)
17. Yang, J., Yu, K., Gong, Y., Huang, T.S.: Linear spatial pyramid matching using sparse coding for image classification. In: Proceedings of the IEEE Conference on Computer Vision and Pattern Recognition, pp. 1794–1801 (2009)
18. Cortes, C., Vapnik, V.: Support-vector networks. Mach. Learn. **20**(3), 273–297 (1995)
19. Chang, C.C., Lin, C.J.: LIBSVM: a library for support vector machines. ACM Trans. Intell. Syst. Technol. **2**(3), 1–27 (2011)
20. Zhou, X., Cui, N., Li, Z., Feng, L.: Hierarchical gaussianization for image classification. In: Proceedings of the 12th IEEE International Conference on Computer Vision, pp. 1971–1977 (2009)
21. Li, Q.: Dunhuang art in the period of Tibetan domination. Dunhuang Res. **02**, 1–20 (1998)
22. Zhang, Y., Zhang, Z.: On the Amitayur-Buddhan belief amid the Belief of The Saddharma-pundarika during The Northern Dynasties at Dunhuang: on the scene of Amitayur-Buddha in Preach in cave 285 of Mogao Grottoes as example. Dunhuang Res. **01**, 1–9 (2007)

The Study and Application of Smart Art Community Service with "ESPSAS" Internet of Things Platform

Jheng-Chun Yang and Su-Chu Hsu[✉]

Department of New Media Art, Taipei National University of the Arts, Taipei, Taiwan
jerrysvy@gmail.com, suchu.hsu@gmail.com

Abstract. In this research, we developed "ESPSAS" platform of IoT. It is based on ESP-12F, and the platform consists of three systems, thing system, website system and communication system. The platform solves the issues in art creation: the need for light, cheap chips in volume. In addition, another feature of the ESPSAS platform is its connection design. We propose a double-registered synchronization that confirms the complex communication within the thing system. We have already installed "ESPSAS" IoT Platform at Taipei Nan-men Elementary School in Taiwan and has run "Windflower ESPSAS" project, allowing students in elementary school to be makers and to create their own windflower things and to decorate the campus with social network art creation as their community cultural development on campus. Owing to the structure design of the windflower IoT thing and ESPSAS platform we developed, the windflower is a spinning pinwheel by day, a colorful lantern by night. People can appreciate the spinning of their own windflower on campus remotely via cellphone, and alter its light color remotely with cellphone. This study utilizes IoT technology to equip things and interfaces with transparency in a space, so that individual's emotional memory may become transparent and extend from the campus into the cloud. We look forward to the applications of this outcome to more artistic design and creative fields in the days to come.

Keywords: Community cultural development · Internet of Things · ESP-12F · Maker · Social network art · MQTT

1 Introduction

On the World Semiconductor Council (WSC) in May 2014, it was said the next trend shall be the Internet of Things (IoT), which proclaims, "The next big thing is the Internet of Things" [1]. The IoT has been commonly associated with smart life in recent years, but less with art creation, though, especially with community service. Our "Windflower ESPSAS" project is a research but also a social network art that uses IoT on community cultural development. It is also a rare case in the world that combines traditional artisanship, IoT and art social service to achieve the community cultural development on campus. We encourage elementary school students to be makers and create windflowers with traditional Taiwanese bamboo-pinwheels and digital chips. Hence, we decorated the campus with everyone's windflower through social network art. Due to the design

© Springer International Publishing AG 2017
N. Streitz and P. Markopoulos (Eds.): DAPI 2017, LNCS 10291, pp. 404–415, 2017.
DOI: 10.1007/978-3-319-58697-7_30

of bamboo structure and the embedded IoT chip, the windflower is a spinning pinwheel by day, a colorful lantern by night. One thing worthy of mentioning is that "Windflower ESPSAS" project was executed through the "ESPSAS" IoT platform we developed. Therefore, people can appreciate the spinning of their own windflowers on campus remotely via cellphone, and alter its light color remotely with cellphone. Thus, individual's emotional memory may become transparent and extend from the campus into the cloud.

The IoT nodes used in the social network art creation and design oftentimes requires chips that are light, cheap and in volume, and the platform also need to fit the freedom and flexibility in art creation. We had inquired and experimented many chips in vain. As such, we developed the "ESPSAS" IoT platform (abbreviated as ESPSAS) of our own. The name is derived from the IoT board "ESP-12F" plus "Smart Art-Design Service". That is, this IoT platform is developed for art-design service. Our ESPSAS is built with ESP-12F as its core thing hardware, featuring cheap in price, small in size, light in weight, and easy to assemble with Wi-Fi connectivity. We use it as a board to connect other electronic components and keep it in a minimum size, so that it can be inserted into the small things used in art creation. On ESPSAS, we developed various communication modes: "peer-to-peer", as well as "one-to-many" and "many-to-many". As long as a thing is connected to our platform, people can link, operate and interact with the thing via the webpage on the cellphone. The research and application of "Windflower ESPSAS" can be extended to diverse art designs and creative application in the future.

2   Related Work

2.1   The Board and System of IoT

The "Internet of Things" was proposed in 1999 by Kevin Ashton from the U.K. [2]. It is an internet working among things, which allows the things to transmit and receive data and automatically response to the data. Human can also give orders to the things or retrieve data collected by them. Back then, Ashton built the IoT with RFID, a near-field-communication IoT system. The IoT nowadays covers a wider range and scope, such as smart family life and smart monitoring system, and things can connect to one another from afar. The wireless communication technology commonly adopted are Wi-Fi, Bluetooth, IEEE 802.15.4 and RFID, in which Wi-Fi is most popular and able to connect to the Internet directly without a gateway to convert signals. Our ESPSAS uses Wi-Fi for the communication among things as well.

Introduction of ESP-12F.   The ESP modules commonly seen on the market are ESP-01 to ESP-14. These modules have many merits, a board suitable for DIY next to Arduino and Raspberry Pi. Particularly for ESP-12F, it is a module equpped with the IoT chip ESP8266, featuring Wi-Fi connectivity and microcontroller [3]. ESP8266 is cheap, light and stable with low energy consumption. After its launch in August 2014, it has become a trend throughout the world with strong community support [4] and various open-source development and projects.

There are numerous electronic boards available for the IoT, some of which require additional communication modules while others do not. Our ESPSAS uses ESP-12F as the electronic board because its module is small enough (16 mm × 24 mm) with more pins (22 in total), larger memory (4 MB) and an on-board antenna [5].

ESP module can serve as a board, but transistors and resistance have to be installed due to its physical limitation, nevertheless. There are many boards on the market equipped with ESP module since it is easier for pin insertion and a port for power input. Yet, the size of it will be two to three times of its original size, unable to fit into our smaller art things. On our ESPSAS platform, ESP-12F, electronic resistance and power supply module are assembled directly to serve as a board. Then, we stack vertically to expand the module chips while keeping the size of the area close to that of the electronic board. Thanks to this vertical stacking technique, we are able to keep the area of the board small enough to fit into small things.

Communication Protocol of IoT. The common protocols used for data transmission of IoT are HTTP REST, CoAP and MQTT [6]. Most of the IoT platforms today are based on these three protocols to provide cloud service and data analysis. Developers use the API provided to allow things to transmit data over the cloud. Some services like Arduino Cloud[1] even integrate with hardware. Nonetheless, such service has its limitation, like the limit on fee collection or the limit on connection. ESPSAS platform we developed uses MQTT protocol [7]. In addition to the merits of low energy consumption, stable connection and strong expansion capability, it carries many-to-many connectivity, too. It can also mount a cloud server to maximize the development flexibility for the service on the platform.

2.2 Application on Community Cultural Development

Community cultural development refers to the improvement of the neighborhood with local cultural at its core conducted by the residents and art workers to increase the well-being of the community as a whole. There are new creative communities emerging worldwide that combine with digital media to help foster community consensus and improve the neighborhood, in order to usher in new energy and innovative idea for the community [8]. PRIXARS ARS Electronica Festival opened the "Digital Community" in 2004 [9] to encourage the world to construct virtual or authentic communities with digital approach, so as to influence the society and better the life of the people. Many of the awarded works are online collective art creation. That shows that is has become an important trend and power to develop communities with digital approaches across the world.

There are already renowned cases of Digital Community across borders. The project "canal*ACCESSIBLE", launched by a Spanish artist Antoni Abad in 2006, invited some 40 physically-challenged individuals. They photographed, tagged, and put on description on a digital map through their cellphones as they roamed in the city of Barcelona and found any unfriendly facility or environment, so that the general public as well as

---

[1] Details in https://cloud.arduino.cc.

the government could see the problems and improve as such [9]. A similar case is "FixMyStreet" website, created by a British NPO "mySociety" in 2007. They focused on the streets and public infrastructure instead, however. The users found problems and published those onto it, which were relayed to the government to urge the government to act on it or encourage people to solve them voluntarily [9]. "El Campo de Cebada" in Madrid, Spain in 2010 is a movement that the local citizens developed the idle lands owned by the government. After negotiations, the development was led by the citizens with support from the government. People and the government cooperated instead of fought against each other, and all the information and resources were open to the public [9]. The work "Hello Lamp Post"[2] by Pan Studio in the U.K., in 2013 was based on SMS service platform, inviting people to interact and converse with the facilities on the street like lamp posts and mailboxes via text messages as if these objects had been intelligent and human. Our "Windflower ESPSAS" project is more close to "Hello Lamp Post", which is embedded with the concept of IoT. We combine traditional bamboo handicraft to design windflower things in maker's way, to realize the community cultural development on campus at Taipei Nan-men Elementary School in Taiwan.

3   Structure of ESPSAS IoT Platform

Our ESPSAS Platform consists of three systems: thing system, website system and communication system (see Fig. 1). The thing system is the process to insert chips into thing to equip it with Wi-Fi connectivity. The website system serves as the platform for the communication between users and things with webpage as the user interface. The communication system is the bridge to connect the thing system and the website system.

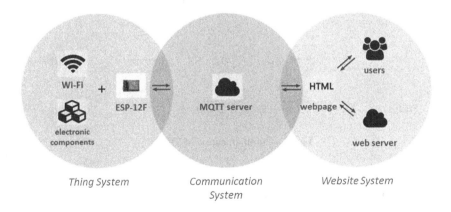

Fig. 1. The integration and operation of ESPSAS platform

- **Thing system:** A thing has to be equipped with wireless connectivity, sensors or functions to execute orders to be called as an IoT thing. This system is intended to

---

[2] Details in http://www.hellolamppost.co.uk/.

transform an ordinary thing without IoT connectivity to an IoT thing after being embedded with some IoT electronic devices. Our windflower thing system includes the assembling of ESP-12F board, the design of electronic architecture, the writing of firmware, power supply and Wi-Fi setup. Since ESP-12F uses Wi-Fi to communicate, it is vital to set up a space with Wi-Fi access. ESP-12F needs to be activated within a space accessible to Wi-Fi to be able to access the Internet. For example, for a windflower to be able to detect rotation speed and lighting, the electronic installation process is as followed: (a) electronic architecture design (ESP-12F board, full color LED light, small motor and power supply); (b) electronic welding; (c) firmware writing; (d) connection testing. During the connection testing, ESP-12F will automatically connect to a Wi-Fi AP. Should the connection fail, it will require manual set-up to connect. It then will automatically connect to the designated AP next time when it is on.

- **Website system:** It includes web server, database, website structure, interaction interface, monitoring and management, so that the data of the thing system's operation can be retrieved in real time, which can be visualized and transcribed in text. A user can connect to things via webpages. Each URI of webpage corresponds to a single thing, and each URI is therefore deemed as the single access portal to the interactive interface of that specific thing.
- **Communication system:** Message Queue Telemetry Transport (MQTT) protocol is used to handle the connection between the thing system and the website system like a bridge for communication. MQTT plays the role of connection relay. It is a publish-subscribe-based "lightweight" machine-to-machine (M2M) communication protocol for use on top of the TCP/IP protocol [7]. The data published by the publisher will be relay to the subscriber via a MQTT server; then the publisher and the subscriber on the same topic can be seen as connected (see Fig. 2).

Fig. 2. Communication of MQTT

4   Method of "Windflower ESPSAS"

"Windflower ESPSAS" Project is the first collective online action art using IoT technology in community cultural development in Taiwan. The IoT thing windflower is composed of traditional Taiwanese bamboo-pinwheel[3], which is inserted with ESP-12F module as the key thing for the project execution. The windflower is a spinning pinwheel by day, a colorful lantern by night. Through a website, people can see how the windflower spins remotely anytime anywhere. Also, they can set the colors of windflower's led light remotely from the webpage. Our community cultural development on campus at Nan-men Elementary School has two installations of windflower - "Windflowers on Pillars" and "Windflowers on Tree Rings" (see Fig. 3).

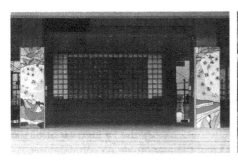

Fig. 3. Two windflower installations - "Windflowers on Pillars" and "Windflowers on Tree Rings"

4.1 Making of Windflower

Our "Windflower Maker Workshop" at the school allowed children to be makers and create their own windflowers (see Fig. 4), including bamboo handcraft, windflower painting and installation. Hence, each windflower is one of kinds as they carry the memories of the children's design. We designed 38 windflowers in total, 30 of which is installed on "Windflowers on Pillars" while 8 of which are installed on "Windflowers on Tree Rings". It is more than a maker movement, but a community cultural development on campus; furthermore, it is a digital interactive public art.

The materials used on windflower are bamboo strips, thin bamboo sticks, fix balls, cardboard, electric wires, small motors, full-color LED and ESP-12F board. The main features of windflower are light and spinning. Therefore, on the structural design, we use full-color LED for the lighting and small motor for spinning. Figure 5 is the illustration for the assembling of the electronic components with the bamboo pinwheel. Before the assembling, the electronic components are attached to a thin bamboo stick. The electronic components are extended by wires with plug and socket connected together. You can see the light of LED. After assembling, the fix ball holds the bamboo pinwheel and the small motor together. There are four reasons why a small motor is used: (a) small enough to be placed in the bamboo pinwheel; (b) cheap with a price range

---

[3] Bamboo-pinwheel is a traditional Taiwanese handcraft. It is composed of four thin bamboo strips woven into a ball. The bamboo ball has eight bamboo protrusions, which can be attached with eight flower pedals. Such structural design allows the bamboo-pinwheel to spin when the wind blows. For more details, check: https://www.youtube.com/watch?v=cCZkczvLG4A.

Fig. 4. Windflower maker workshop

US$0.3–1; (c) to avoid wire twist; (d) accurate rotation speed. One thing worthy of mentioning about (c) is that we take the advantage of voltage change when the small motor revolves and turns it into the rotating speed of the pinwheel, cleverly solving the issue of wire twist of the sensor due to the rotation. As for (d), the voltage variation the board detects is analogue signal range 0–1023 and the magnitude of voltage range 0–1 V [3]. Due to the rotation of the bamboo pinwheel, the value is somewhere from 0 to 60, so there is no overloaded issue. Besides, since it is a direct numerical conversion without mathematical translation, it is an effective and accurate value that can be used directly.

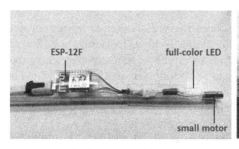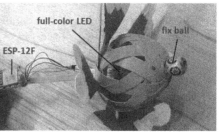

before assembling   after assembling

Fig. 5. Assembling of electronic components with a bamboo pinwheel

4.2 Scenario for Interaction

The installed windflower thing will automatically connect to a Wi-Fi AP, and communicate constantly with MQTT on the cloud 24/7. A user needs only to scan the QR code or type the link to access the online website[4] of our project. Each windflower on either "Windflowers in Pillars" or "Windflowers in Tree Rings" has a unique ID. On the webpage, one may access to a specific windflower by accessing the webpage of certain ID. As soon as the link is established successfully, one may see the visualization of the

---

[4] Details in http://fbilab.org/windflower.

windflower, check its real action, and even give it orders. Should there is an issue with the link, the system would prompt the user as well. Children or adults alike can see how the windflower spins via the webpage through the online platform during the day (see Fig. 6). If the users browse the webpage on a cellphone, they can even see the animation of windflower's spinning. By night, they can see how the windflower glow and set as well as alter the colors of the light on the windflower. If we stand in front of the public art "Windflowers on Pillars" or "Windflowers on Tree Rings", we can see the animated windflowers on webpage and check the synchronization of the real windflowers on campus. If we are away, we can still tap into the memories of the windflowers and enter the campus through the cloud via the platform.

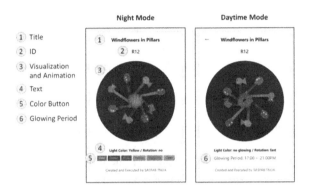

Fig. 6. The webpage of windflower

4.3 The Link Between Thing and Webpage

The link between the thing and the webpage is based on the system of ESPSAS platform. There are four presumptions in our design of our platform.

- Each windflower has one ID of its own.
- Each windflower has one corresponding webpage (URI: http://.../id).
- Each windflower and webpage use ID as their reference for MQTT topic; for instance, it may be "myWindflower/id" to subscribe and publish onto the MQTT server.
- Each windflower and webpage will subscribe to the MQTT server first at the initial setting, which is required only once.

Since the MQTT server needs to receive the subscription of windflower only at the beginning and the link stays connection without further subscription. As for publishing, it is an action has to be taken repeatedly. Therefore, when the thing and the webpage are at the initial setting, they will subscribe and only need to subscribe once.

The windflower has the detection abilities of rotation speed and lighting. Based on the four presumptions, we shall further elaborate on the communication processes of rotation speed mode and lighting mode respectively.

Rotation Speed Mode. The main purpose of rotation speed mode is to allow people to check the spinning of the windflower on campus online simply by clicking on the windflower webpage on the cellphone. That is, the webpage will send a request via the link to retrieve the rotation status of the windflower. In the mode of rotation speed, the "thing-webpage" communication is unidirectional. The communication process from the webpage to the windflower is presented as Fig. 7.

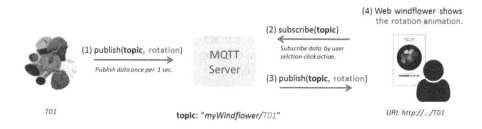

Fig. 7. Rotation speed mode – the communication flow from the windflower to the webpage

(1) The thing, when connected, will publish the data of rotation speed constantly per second to the MQTT server.
(2) When the user clicks on the windflower on the webpage, the webpage will send the subscription request of certain windflower topic to the MQTT server.
(3) As the MQTT server is constantly receiving the rotation speed data, it would also match according to the topic request sent by the webpage and publish the corresponding rotation data of the windflower to the matched webpage.
(4) As the webpage at the user end receives the rotation data, it would convert the data and present the rotation data with the animation of a windflower spinning. The larger the value is, the faster the animated windflower spinning will be, along with a text to indicate the speed of the rotation.

As long as the thing-webpage link sustains, such flow would execute repeatedly and feed the data of the thing to the webpage as they are synchronized.

Lighting Mode. There are two main functions in lighting mode: to allow the user to check the lighting of the windflower on campus when they click on the windflower over the webpage on the cellphone; to allow the user to alter the light color of the windflower on campus over the webpage. In lighting mode, the "thing-webpage" communication is bidirectional. We shall discuss it in two directions respectively: from webpage to windflower and from windflower to webpage.

From Webpage to Windflower. The link from webpage to windflower means people can view the lighting of the windflower on campus at the time as they click on the windflower on the cellphone's webpage. That is, the webpage will send a request to retrieve the lighting of the windflower in real-time. The flow from webpage to windflower is presented in Fig. 8. In the flow chart, (1)–(3) are the same as that of Rotation Speed Mode; the only difference is the data transmitted, which is light color here. On (4), the webpage will treat the light color as a parameter to execute the light visualization and text prompt of the windflower.

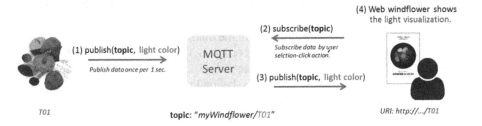

Fig. 8. Lighting mode – the communication flow from webpage to windflower

From Windflower to Webpage. The communication from windflower to webpage means people can alter the light color of the windflower on campus on the webpage, and the windflower sends out requests to learn about the alternation and react accordingly. The communication flow from the windflower to webpage is presented in Fig. 9.

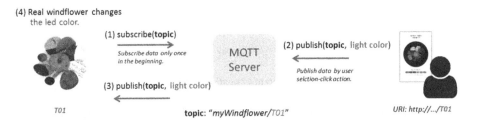

Fig. 9. Lighting mode – the communication flow from windflower to webpage

(1) The windflower subscribes once to the MQTT server initially for the light color.

(2) The user clicks on the light color of the windflower over the webpage, and the webpage will publish the data of the selected color of the windflower to the MQTT server.

(3) The MQTT server receives the data of the selected color, matches the topic, and publishes the updated light color to the matched windflower accordingly.

(4) The windflower in reality changes the light color according to the data received.

This direction of the communication flow differs with the other direction of the flow in the data publishing of the webpage. When the webpage publishes, it requires a user to operate and publish, while the thing publishes automatically. In the Figs. 8 and 9 above, the flows may appear logical if we view them in two different directions. However, if we observe from the angle of "topic", we will see when the two topics are identical, it will not be able to tell which direction the data came from, and therefore results in the confusion of program logic. To avoid such situation, we tag a codename of the subscribed target after the original topic like "myWindflower/id". For example, the topic for the subscription for windflower is "myWindflower/id/thing"; the topic for the subscription for webpage is "myWindflower/id/webpage". The same applies to the publishing.

As such, if we combined the scenarios discussed above, the overall flow of the communication can be illustrated as Fig. 10. As we separate topic into two different ones, we can thus distinguish the direction of the transmission accordingly. In the flows, (1)–(7) is the flow of user giving light color order. (1.1) is that the windflower publishes its light color to the MQTT server per second. (1.2) is that it only needs to do the subscription to the MQTT server once at the beginning. (4) is that when the webpage is connected, it will receive the light color of the windflower and present the light visualization and text prompt accordingly. (7) is that when the windflower in reality receives the color alternation selected by the user, it will change the light color accordingly.

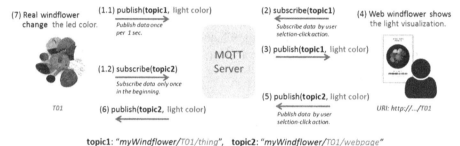

topic1: *"myWindflower/T01/thing"*,   topic2: *"myWindflower/T01/webpage"*

Fig. 10. The overall communication flow of lighting mode

In addition, our Platform has another feature: to ensure the thing receives data and to ensure the synchronization of both ends, we adopt "double-registered synchronization" in the communication. Hence, only after the other end confirms the transmission can this end be notified as order transmitted.

5   Conclusions and Future Work

"Windflower ESPSAS" Project is the first social network art using IoT technology in community cultural development in Taiwan. It is not only a public art installation, but a long-term project.[5] The elementary school partner will throw activities related to windflower from time to time, inviting children, parents and residents in the neighborhood to partake (see Fig. 11). This work is not merely a result of Maker Workshop and an art installation, but something transforms the campus into a more friendly space with aesthetic. It helps to promote the education of the Internet of Things as well as community interaction. On top of that, it creates a memory shared by the community on the cloud as well. This study, with the technology of IoT, aims to achieve the goal digital art workers try to accomplish for a long time – media transparency, i.e. connecting things via IoT on the cloud so as to make it transparent, as emotional memories are connected at the same time.

---

[5] Details in http://sasfab.org/?p=4502.

Fig. 11. "Windflower ESPSAS" project at Nan-men Elementary School

The ESPSAS platform we developed builds a framework with three systems: thing, website and communication. Such framework is easy to extend and use as it saves a huge amount of time for base development. In addition, the ESPSAS platform is the solution to the issue in art creation: the need for light, cheap chips in volume. Besides the basic webpage and thing communication function, we also developed the administrator page, auto-control page for us to monitor, operate and execute at certain time, as well as synchronize and auto-control among the things. We shall continue optimizing ESPSAS platform in the future, and apply the result to more artistic design and creative fields.

References

1. SciTech Report.: Celebrities talking about new trends in internet of things. SciTech Report, vol. 390, p. 25 (2014)
2. Ashton, K.: That 'internet of things' thing. RFiD J. **22**(7), 97–114 (2009)
3. Espressif IOT Team.: ESP8266EX Datasheet Version 5.3 (2016). http://espressif.com/sites/default/files/documentation/0a-esp8266ex_datasheet_en.pdf
4. ESP8266 Community Forum. http://www.esp8266.com
5. AI-THINKER: ESP-12F WiFi Module Version 1.0 (2015). https://www.elecrow.com/download/ESP-12F.pdf
6. Al-Fuqaha, A., Guizani, M., Mohammadi, M., Aledhari, M., Ayyash, M.: Internet of things: a survey on enabling technologies protocols and applications. IEEE Commun. Surv. Tutor. **17**(4), 2347–2376 (2015). doi:10.1109/COMST.2015.2444095. IEEE Press, New York
7. Banks, A., Gupta, R.: MQTT Version 3.1.1. OASIS Standard (2014). http://docs.oasis-open.org/mqtt/mqtt/v3.1.1/os/mqtt-v3.1.1-os.html
8. Goldbard, A.: New Creative Community - The Art of Cultural Development. New Village Press, Oakland (2006)
9. Banerjee, I., Fischer-Schreiber, I.: Digital Communities 2004–2014 - Selected Projects from Prix Ars Electronica. Ars Electronica, Vienna (2015)

Geometry-Aware Interactive AR Authoring Using a Smartphone in a Wearable AR Environment

Jeongmin Yu, Jinwoo Jeon, Jinwoo Park, Gabyong Park,
Hyung-il Kim, and Woontack Woo[✉]

KAIST UVR Lab., Daejeon, South Korea
{jmyu119,zkrkwlek,jinwooaa,gypark,hyungil,wwoo}@kaist.ac.kr

Abstract. This paper presents an augmented reality (AR) authoring system that enables an ordinary user to easily build an AR environment by manipulating and placing 3D virtual objects. The system tracks users' hand motions via an RGB-D camera which built-in an optical see-through (OST) head mounted display (HMD), and interactive features applied to virtual objects by the pre-defined hand gestures. In addition, the virtual objects and dynamic paths are placed by using a smartphone in a real-world space. To implement this system, three cored technologies are needed: (i) segmentation of regions of spaces and real-world objects (ii) hand tracking and gesture recognition for manipulating virtual objects, (iii) dynamic path placing of virtual objects using a smartphone wearing an OST HMD. We implement a prototype of the proposed system for testing its feasibility. To the end, we expect that our system enables simplify AR technology usage to ordinary users who are unfamiliar with professional AR authoring tools.

Keywords: AR contents authoring · Hand-augmented virtual object interaction · Wearable AR environment

1 Introduction

Augmented reality (AR) technology enables users to approach supplementary information by mixing with virtual objects in the real world in real-time with many kinds of devices such as mobile smartphones, tablet, head mounted display (HMD), and high performance PCs [1]. Using this technology, the users can be worked with digital virtual contents in various real-world spaces such as industry sites, cultural performance venues, classrooms and so forth. Owing to these attributes, AR technology is applied to various fields such as tele-educations, military, games, repair/maintenance, and gallery/ exhibition [2].

For the past few decades, many researchers have been developed on AR authoring systems/tools to easily manipulate AR contents for an ordinary user. The AR authoring methods are classified two categories: AR-based libraries and GUI-based authoring tool. The popularly used AR libraries for authoring are MRT [6], DWARF [5], osgART [4], AR Toolkit [3], so forth. Among them, ARToolKit library is popularly used because it can be transferred into other computing/program languages such as FLARToolKit

© Springer International Publishing AG 2017
N. Streitz and P. Markopoulos (Eds.): DAPI 2017, LNCS 10291, pp. 416–424, 2017.
DOI: 10.1007/978-3-319-58697-7_31

(Flash ActionScript) and NyARToolKit (Java). However, these can be only accessible and practically useful for professional programmers.

GUI-based AR authoring tools give more intuitive interaction to users. Utilizing these tools, users are able to perform AR authoring process as a manner of the point-and-click. The widely used AR authoring tools are AMIRE [7], DART [8], ATOMIC Authoring Tool [10], ComposAR [9], and these are used without having to write any program code. Even though these GUI-based authoring tools are easier to use than AR libraries, users should still acquire the specialized knowledge of the tool and just work in PC environment. Meanwhile, recently intuitive AR authoring systems using smart devices or natural user interface (e.g., hand gestures) are developed which enables a user to easily build an AR world in an in-situ environment and manipulate 3D virtual content to it. [11] shows manipulation the AR contents using multi-touch interface of smart mobile device and [12] proposes an AR authoring method for unknown outdoor scene using mobile devices. Project Tango [13] is a mobile authoring system which forms a 3D map of unknown indoor scene using a depth sensor. However, these systems have a cumbersome point that a user should see the augmented spot through a narrow mobile device display.

In this paper, to overcome above mentioned shortcomings, we present a geometry-aware interactive AR authoring system which enables an ordinary user to easily build an AR world in an in-situ environment through manipulating and placing virtual objects. The proposed system tracks users' hand motions via an RGB-D camera which built-in an OST HMD, and interactive features applied to virtual objects by hand gestures. Then the user can easily add and delete dynamic paths of virtual objects to real-world environment. To develop this system, three core technologies are needed: geometry awareness by segmentation of space and object regions, manipulating virtual objects by hand tracking and gesture recognition, and placing virtual objects and dynamic paths with a smartphone wearing an OST HMD. Through a preliminary prototype system implementation, we confirm its feasibility as a future AR authoring tool. We expect that the proposed system can be applicable to many AR applications such as education/training, urban planning, games and etc.

The remainder of this paper is organized as follows. The proposed overall system is presented in Sect. 2. In Sect. 3 introduces preliminary implementation and its result. Lastly, the conclusions and future works are presented in Sect. 4.

2 Proposed Authoring System

Figure 1 shows the proposed overall system diagram of AR authoring. In this system we use a smartphone wearing OST HMD (e.g., Microsoft Hololens) for placing of AR virtual objects, and use an egocentric RGB-D camera which is built in an OST HMD and a wearable sensor (e.g., smartwatch) for accurate hand tracking and gesture recognition. Utilizing hand tracking and gesture recognition, interactive features can be applied to a virtual object (i.e., enlargement, shrinkage, rotation). Then, the authored virtual objects are placed in real-world environment using rotation and touch direction information from the sensors (e.g., IMU and touch screen) built into a smartphone.

The detail methodological description of geometry-aware interactive AR authoring is presented as follows.

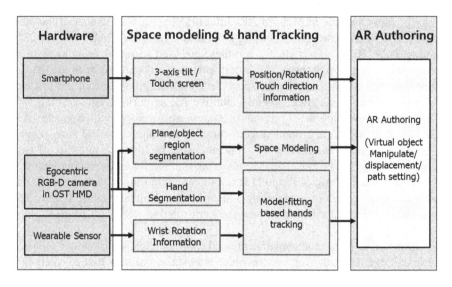

Fig. 1. The proposed AR authoring framework.

2.1 Segmentation of Space and Real-World Object Regions

The indoor space consists of objects and structures such as walls, floors, and ceilings. The object regions can be easily estimated by removing structures of planes. Figure 2 shows the procedure of the proposed irregular space/object segmentation. First, we calculate local surface normal vectors on a RGB-D image. Then, we cluster the normal vectors and calculate the plane corresponding to the structure. Finally, using the connected component labeling (CCL) algorithm, we segment the object regions of the plane regions from a RGB-D image.

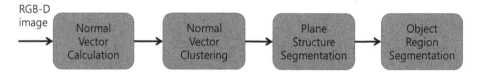

Fig. 2. Procedure of segmentation of space and object regions

2.1.1 Segmentation of Plane Regions

We first calculate the local surface normal vectors from a depth camera to estimate a planar area. After the azimuth and elevation of normal vectors are calculated, these are quantized and accumulated into a histogram. The normal vectors in the same bin are likely to exist in the same plane or parallel planes. In other words, the normal vectors included in the local maxima and neighbors are belonging to objects that are planes of indoor structures. Otherwise, these are parallel with indoor structures. After classifying the planar regions, we segment their boundaries from the image. The boundaries are mostly generated by two cases. The first occurs at the intersection of the two planes. In this case, the normal vector of the adjacent region is different from the normal vector of the two planes. However, in most cases, when the wall and the other wall are met, they can be occluded by objects. In this case, the intersection line of two plane parameters is the boundary. The second is when the two planes are parallel. In this case, the normal vectors of the boundary have similar normal vectors to the planar regions, but the distance values are different. By using this property, it is possible to obtain the outline information of the planar regions. The planar parameters that are the furthest or lowest in the each group are used as the plane of indoor spatial structure.

2.1.2   Segmentation of Real-World Object Regions

The objects can be separated using the previously calculated plane geometry information. By calculating dot product between the 3D point and the parameter matrix main plane, the distance between the point and the plane can be calculated. If this value is less than a user-defined threshold, the point belongs to the plane. Otherwise, it belongs to the object. This process can be performed on all points to obtain the binary image of the planes and objects. Then, CCL algorithm performs to segment the objects from indoor space.

2.2   Manipulating of Virtual Object Hand Tracking/Gesture Recognition

2.2.1   Method for Hand Tracking

The proposed hand tracking algorithm employs a model-based method as Fig. 3. The method first defines a 3D geometric hand model whose joints are controlled by 26 parameters. Then, it solves an optimization problem to find the 26 parameters. To do so, we define an objective function to quantify the error between the rendered hand model and observation. The objective function E is defined as the following equation.

$$E = \sum_{i=0}^{width-1} \sum_{j=0}^{height-1} D(o(i,j), r(i,j)) \tag{1}$$

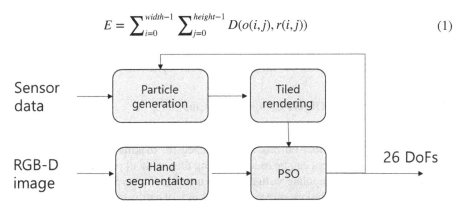

Fig. 3. Flowchart of the proposed hand tracking method.

Where o(i, j) is depth value of pixel (i, j) in a depth image from a depth camera, and r(i, j) is depth value of pixel (i, j) in depth image from rendered model. The function D(,) is Euclidean distance between two inputs. The objective function is optimized based on particle swarm optimization (PSO) algorithm [14], and the particle update rule is set as [15]. However, this method has a weakness of error accumulation after occurring tracking failure. To alleviate this, the data from wrist sensor is passed to the particle generation module. The particles are generated within the boundary decided by the data from the wrist sensor and the solution in the previous frame. This method is useful to reduce search range that the particles move.

2.2.2   3D Contents Manipulation

The optimized hand parameters are used to manipulate virtual objects as scaling, rotation, translation which shown in Fig. 4. To do this, the meshes are created by vertices transformed by the hand model parameters. The method for scaling and rotation becomes intuitive if the interaction system can detect the touch points between the mesh of the hand model and a virtual object. After detection of more than two collisions by finger models, the virtual object is translated or rotated by the wrist parameters of the hand model. With respect to the scaling, it requires a gesture to conduct it. We defines it as one click. After one collision detection of one finger, the scaling parameter of the virtual object is controlled by the area of the five fingers. To go back from the scaling mode, the user would touch the virtual object with one finger.

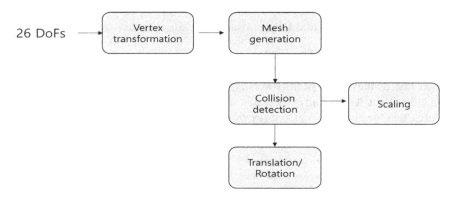

Fig. 4. Flowchart of the proposed virtual object manipulation.

2.3   Placing of Virtual Object Using a Smartphone

There are various methods using a bare hand [17, 18] and a smart device as input interface for manipulating virtual objects are developed for making an AR environment. Among them, smart devices can be used for a long time without physical fatigue, so we propose a method to manipulate virtual objects using it. Figure 5 shows the flowchart of the authoring system. The system requires two kinds of hardware such as a smartphone and an OST HMD. Utilizing these, users can manipulate virtual objects and insert dynamic paths into real space.

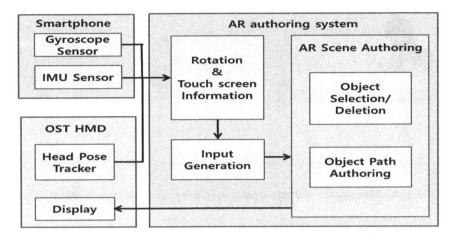

Fig. 5. Flowchart of the proposed virtual object manipulation system.

2.3.1   Rendering and Inserting of Dynamic Paths

Utilizing a casual smartphone as a tool for manipulating virtual dynamic paths and virtual objects, our system allows a user to create his/her own content in augmented reality environment. We have two advantages in terms of dealing with dynamic paths for virtual movable objects and increasing user's immersion.

First, a user can arbitrarily make and manipulate virtual paths with a simple inter-action on a touch screen and a built-in IMU of a smartphone. Basically, without any special and expensive tools like an HTC VIVE controller, it is very familiar for the users to use a smartphone to interact with virtual objects. Exploiting a smart phone as a mouse, a user moves a cursor and selects a virtual object or a specific menu in a form of graphic user interface on an HMD. For example, when creating and modifying a dynamic path, it can be easily done by selecting and transferring one of key positions which compose a dynamic path as shown in Fig. 6. In this case, selection and transfer is performed by finger tap and drag and drop respectively. Because paths are managed in a list container, it is possible to insert and delete key positions stably and dynamically. After completing path manipulation, a user can assign a path to movable objects by dragging and dropping them onto the specific path's key position. Then, with a proper animation assigned by a user beforehand, the objects start to move along the path they have.

Second, in terms of rendering 3D virtual objects, we exploit static LDR image, extracted in a form of spherical environment map via a Ricoh Theta 360 digital camera, as a distant light to enhance the realism of augmented objects. Different from [16], a high dynamic range image (HDRI) is not used in our system for the simple process. However, an LDR image also gives acceptable results without extremely glossy materials. Furthermore, because users typically perform authoring in a limited indoor and scarcely dynamic space, static distant light of an LDR image can enhance user's immersion by producing realistic visual results.

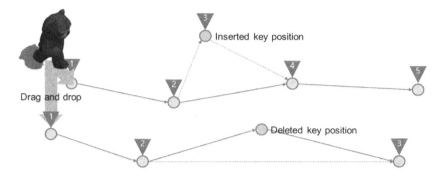

Fig. 6. Manipulation of dynamic paths and placing to movable virtual objects.

3   Implementation

3.1   Hardware and Software Configuration

We configured our prototype system using commercially available devices. Our system consists of a computing unit for computation, an OST HMD for visualization, HMD tracker for 6DOF HMD pose tracking, a near-range depth sensor for hand tracking, and a smartphone for AR authoring. Smartphone and computing unit are connected with Wi-Fi communication. We used a Microsoft Hololens, which is a computing device and an OST HMD with inside-out tracker. In addition, we tested various Android OS smartphones.

System modules are implemented and integrated with Unity Engine and Windows Universal Platform. Also, smartphone application is implemented with Android SDK. Figure 7 illustrates configuration of proposed system.

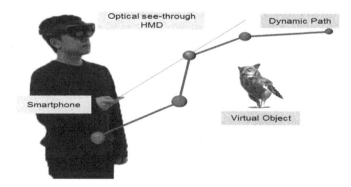

Fig. 7. Configuration of proposed system

3.2   Initial Implementation Result

Figure 8 shows initial result of our AR Authoring system prototype, which uses smartphone to author augmented space. User wearing optical see-through HMD can use one's own smartphone to select, place, and manipulate virtual objects in user's physical space. Also, user can generate dynamic path of virtual object by just manipulating key-points, and dragging virtual object into generated path. Our system enables a user to generate and organize a user-friendly augmented space without any professional programming or software skills.

Fig. 8.   User's view of our prototype system. User uses smartphone to select UI or virtual objects (left), and generate dynamic path of augmented objects (right).

4   Conclusions and Future Works

In this paper we have presented a geometry-aware interactive AR authoring system using a smartphone wearing an OST HMD, which enables an ordinary user to intuitively organize an AR space without any professional programming and tools. The proposed systems contain three core technologies: geometry awareness by segmentation of space and object regions, manipulating virtual objects by hand tracking and gesture recognition, and placing virtual objects and dynamic paths with a smartphone wearing an OST HMD. Preliminary implementation result shows its strong possibility as a future AR tool. We expect that the proposed AR system can be applicable to many AR applications such as education, training, urban planning, games, and so forth.

As the future works, we plan to develop hand tracking and recognition for manipulating virtual objects and light estimation for rendering virtual objects.

Acknowledgements.   This work was supported by National Research Foundation of Korea (NRF) grant funded by the Korea government (MSIP) (NRF-2014R1A2A2 A01003005) and by ICT R&D program of MSIP/IITP. [R7124-16-0004, Development of Intelligent Interaction Technology Based on Context Awareness and Human Intention Understanding].

References

1. Azuma, R.: A survey of augmented reality. Presence **6**(4), 355–385 (1997)
2. Azuma, R., Baillot, Y., Behringer, R., Feiner, S., Julier, S., MacIntyre, B.: Recent advances in augmented reality. IEEE Comput. Graph. Appl. **21**(6), 34–47 (2001)
3. Kato, H., Billinghurst, M.: Marker tracking and HMD calibration for a video-based augmented reality conferencing system. In: Proceedings of the 2nd IEEE and ACM International Workshop on Augmented Reality (1999)
4. Looser, J., Grasset, R., Seichter, H., Billinghurst, M.: OSGART – a pragmatic approach to MR. In: Industrial Workshop at ISMAR (2006)
5. Bauer, M., Bruegge, B., Klinker, G., MacWilliams, A., Reicher, T., Riss, S., Sandor, C., Wagner, M.: Design of a component-based augmented reality framework. In: ISMAR (2001)
6. Freeman, R.: Mixed reality toolkit. MSc VIVE Final Year Project Report (2004)
7. Grimm, P., Haller, M., Paelke, V., Reinhold, S., Reimann, C., Zauner, J.: AMIRE - authoring mixed reality. In: IEEE International Augmented Reality Toolkit Workshop (2002)
8. MacIntyre, B., Gandy, M., Dow, S., Bolter, J.D.: DART: a toolkit for rapid design exploration of augmented reality experiences. In: UIST (2004)
9. ATOMIC Authoring Tool. http://www.sologicolibre.org/projects/atomic/en/
10. Seichter, H., Looser, J., Billinghurst, M.: ComposAR: an intuitive tool for authoring AR applications. In: ISMAR (2008)
11. Jung, J., Hong, J., Park, S., Yang, H.: Smartphone as an augmented reality authoring tool via multi-touch based 3D interaction method. In: Proceedings of the 11th ACM SIGGRAPH International Conference on Virtual-Reality Continuum and Its Applications in Industry, pp. 17–20 (2012)
12. Langlotz, T., Mooslechner, S., Zollmann, S., Degendorfer, C., Reitmayr, G., Schmalstieg, D.: Sketching up the world: in situ authoring for mobile augmented reality. Pers. Ubiquit. Comput. **16**(6), 623–630 (2012)
13. https://www.google.com/atap/project-tango/
14. Kennedy, J., Eberhart, R.C.: Particle swarm optimization. In: International Conference on Neural Networks, pp. 1942–1948 (1995)
15. Park, G., Argyros, A., Woo, W.: Efficient 3D hand tracking in articulation subspaces for the manipulation of virtual objects. In: CGI (2016)
16. Paul. D.: Rendering synthetic objects into real scenes: bridging traditional and image-based graphics with global illumination and high dynamic range photography. In: ACM SIGGRAPH 2008 Classes (2008)
17. Ha, T., Feiner, S., Woo, W.: WeARHand: Head-worn, RGB-D camera-based, bare-hand user interface with visually enhanced depth perception. In: IEEE ISMAR, pp. 219–228 (2014)
18. Jang, Y., Noh, S., Chang, H., Kim, T., Woo, W.: 3D finger CAPE: clicking action and position estimation under self-occlusions in egocentric viewpoint. IEEE Trans. Visual Comput. Graphics **21**(4), 501–510 (2015)

Smart Environments for Quality of Life

A Preliminary Study of Smart Seat Cushion Design

Shijian Luo[1,2(✉)], Yun Wang[1], Yan Gong[2], Ge Shu[2], and Na Xiong[1]

[1] Creative Design Manufacturing Collaborative Innovation Center,
China Academy of Art, Hangzhou 310024, China
wy_james@126.com
[2] Department of Industrial Design, Zhejiang University, Hangzhou 310027, China
sjluo@126.com, 27006683@qq.com, 413076256@qq.com

Abstract. With the development of economy and the increase of social pressure, the proportion of working time for people is increasing year by year, which directly leads to the continuous expansion of the number of sedentary population. A large number of studies have shown that a sedentary lifestyle has become a global public health problem, which has a negative impact on human life. Unhealthy sitting posture can lead to many diseases. When people sitting for a long time, the unbalanced force may lead to some diseases such as sitting sores and lumbar disc herniation, lumbar spine injury etc. Therefore, it is necessary to study the pressure distribution in the sitting position. Smart seat and mobile application designed for sedentary people is an effective tool for the prevention of these diseases, the pressure center of the body posture can be detected and analyzed, in order to guide people to the correct posture, help prevent disease due to unbalanced posture.

The smart cushion is composed of three parts: pressure data acquisition module (internet of things), data receiving and processing module, data storage and analysis module. This study expounds the theory of sitting posture, explains the mechanism causing pathological effect and psychological effects of sedentary, and then makes a literature review, describes the research status of the pressure distribution of sitting posture, thermal comfort and cushion design, as a standard reference for subsequent design. This study gives definition and classification of sedentary population, puts forward the scheme of smart cushion and mobile application for the sedentary people, and focuses on the function, design and implementation of each module. Finally, it shows the hard and soft system, and tests normal subjects and patients with lumbar spine disease using the smart cushion. The analysis and experimental results show that the design of the smart cushion scheme is reasonable and feasible, and can realize the dynamic and real-time measurement of the pressure center in the sitting posture, and cumulative effect calculation.

Keywords: Sedentary crowd · Sitting balance · Force center · Multi-channel acquisition · Smart equipment

© Springer International Publishing AG 2017
N. Streitz and P. Markopoulos (Eds.): DAPI 2017, LNCS 10291, pp. 427–443, 2017.
DOI: 10.1007/978-3-319-58697-7_32

1 Introduction

In the era of knowledge economy, the refinement of social division of labor and the progress of science and technology liberated human physical burden gradually. The number of mental workers increased, and more and more work needs to be done with long time sitting at the desk. Professor Blackburn of University of Minnesota said that sitting was the change of civilization in the history of the most profound impact on human. This is the cause of metabolic disorders, and sedentary will not only cause disease, but also fatal.

Research from the World Health Organization (WHO) shows that each year about two million people died due to sedentary lifestyle, and it has become the first independent factor of the chronic non-infectious disease, a world-recognized public health and social problem. Therefore, while enjoying the rich material life brought by the social development, the sedentary crowd's health problems should be taken seriously.

From scientific researches, there are three main theories about the sedentary hazards.

1.1 The Sitting Theory

Sang et al. (2015) proposed the necessary conditions in good posture: there are the most appropriate pressure distribution on intervertebral discs between each vertebrae, and the most appropriate, the most uniform static load distribution on the attached muscle tissue. If people sit on a chair in a way that is not in the natural shape of the spine, the intervertebral disc is subject to an abnormal pressure distribution, which can cause waist discomfort over a long time. When the angle between the trunk and thighs maintains about 115°, the spine is close to the natural shape, while the lumbar part must be supported. People who use a back about 90° will feel uncomfortable, because the trunk upright sitting posture will produce a lot of spine twisting force, at this time the weight of the upper body will also have a negative effect on the lumbar spine. The posture with trunk forward will straighten the originally lordotic lumbar, and makes it bend backward. This affects the normal curvature of thoracic and lumbar vertebra, leading to kyphosis (Namkoong et al. 2015). At the same time the increasing isometric trunk muscle strength for head supporting will cause fatigue in neck and back.

Sitting in a chair, people are in a dynamic state of stability. By constantly adjusting the position slightly, people eliminate abnormal pressure on the spine, which is called sitting posture. In addition to the spine, legs and pelvis are equally important, we can regard them as a simple mechanical lever support system: the hip (pelvis) is an unstable inverted triangle when sitting, and the surface between human body and seat is two piece of circular ischial tuberosity bones with little muscle attachment. The 25 cm^2 sciatic tuberosity and the muscles under it bear the load of the weight of human body, which is sufficient to cause pressure fatigue. From a physiological point of view, this fatigue will restrict the blood circulating to the capillary, thereby affecting the nerve endings, leading to pain and numbness, etc. The two points on a seat cushion carry on most of the weight of human body, which has great mechanical instability. Under upright sitting position, the center of body gravity will deviate from the vertical of ischial tuberosities (about 2.5 cm in front of navel), which further aggravated the instability. Only by increasing the leverage effect provided by the legs and feet can people offset this instability. For example, sitting with leg crossed, arms relying on the desktop or supporting on the handrail, etc. are common ways to solve this instability. Good posture is often in a nearly natural state to balance the pressure of the body and reduce body discomfort. And its specific performance is waist straight naturally, two shoulders flush, and body slightly bent forward (backward). At the same time, sedentariness should be avoided in order to make the body relax in a half-dynamic state.

1.2 The Sedentary Pathological Hazards

The soft tissue of the human hip is a multi-layer structure, which is composed of the skin, fat, gluteus maximus and the capillary and nerve endings inside. Under the sitting position, the force between the hip and the seat surface is mainly made up of the pressure and shear stress from different directions, and they act on gluteus maximus together. If the gluteal soft tissue is excessively oppressed for a long time, then it will cause hip muscle contraction, and capillary blood flow slowdown or closed (Sugimura and Wada 2004), resulting in sitting discomfort or tissue damage, mainly manifested as fatigue, numbness and pain (Nakamura and Csikszentmihalyi 2014).

The force between the hip and the seat is mainly divided into pressure and shear stress, in which the shear stress is divided into horizontal shear stress and compressive shear stress with the same units. Usually, the maximum pressure is concentrated on the soft tissue of the 25 cm^2 region below the sciatic bone. The pressure is derived from the vertical direction of the erect body and the supporting force of the seat surface; the horizontal shear stress comes from the frictional force parallel to the contact surface from the opposite direction. The compressive shear stress is formed by the pressure from the same direction but of different values. It usually appears in the area under uneven stress.

Improper posture will result in uneven distribution of body pressure, which may be one of the causes of lumbar spine disease, such as lumbar spine injury (Hu et al. 2015). The long-term poor posture will cause unbalanced pressure distribution of hip and back. While it is the spine and pelvis that mainly support the sitting human body, if the body is in a forward position for a long time, the protruding lumbar will be straightened and bend backward, which will finally lead to kyphosis. It is the same while under a left-leaning or right-leaning posture. The deformation could result in spinal injury. The treatment of kyphosis and spinal cord injury is quite a large expenditure annually, and the price our families and society pay for it is imponderable. It is of great significance to measure the pressure distribution of sitting posture and to study the relationship between the pressure distribution and the occurrence of lumbar disease.

1.3 The Sedentary Psychological Hazards

Not only the physical impact, but also sedentary people's psychological impact cannot be ignored. However, psychological change is a complicated and step-by-step process, and at present there is no research to determine there is a strong correlation between sedentariness and psychological aspects such as emotion and fatigue. But there are experimental results from relevant medical institutions show that in the process of sedentariness, the continuous accumulation of metabolic substance will make the glycogen level decrease, and when it reduces to a certain level, people's working efficiency will be decreased. Mental activity also consumes a lot of energy, so sedentary people, although not involve in physical activity of high intensity consumption, are still easy to feel physically and mentally exhausted. This fatigue is also related to people's sense of work and the characteristics of brain processing. In modern society, the social division of labor becomes more and more detailed, and people often doubt about the meaning of work because of the lack of connection to their external factors. In addition, when work is disturbed or interrupted, people will also generate the negative feeling of fatigue. Psychologist Mihaly madean explanation of this phenomenon of mental activity. "Flow" refers to people's sense of fullness and excitement when they give full attention to something. "Entropy" refers to the mentality of confusion when people are unable to concentrate on their work. In the state of "entropy", the efficiency, creativity and autonomy of human will be reduced. People will doubt their own value, and thus become depressed and anxiety, and sedentariness will increase these psychological factors, which undoubtedly will aggravate the negative feelings of sedentary people. Sedentary people are more likely to be affected by the surrounding environment. Coupled with the pressure of work and life, these will make people lose their passion and sharpen the entropy state. In addition, people's daily communication in contemporary society is becoming more and more dependent on the social network, the reduction of face-to-face communication between people is more likely to lead to communication barriers. If the psychological pressure cannot be timely troubleshooting, it is more easily to lead to mental illness.

In the past twenty years, PC and mobile phones have greatly promoted the development of the Internet. The Internet of things and smart device have become a hot field and trend that cannot be ignored. Smart device is a concept of science and technology arisen after the smart phone. Through the combination of hardware and software, such as upgrading traditional equipment or developing new equipment, products are given smart features with Internet of things. Smart enables the equipment to connect with the device, achieve the loading of Internet services, and form the typical architecture of "cloud + terminal" with the additional value of big data. Smart device has been extended from wearable devices to smart TVs, smart home, smart cars, health care, smart toys, robotics and other fields, which typically includes Google Glass, Samsung Gear, Jawbone, Tesla, LETV TV etc. In this paper, the design of the smart cushion for sitting posture correction of the sedentary crowd is to detect the sitting time and the pressure distribution of these people, and then give advice such as stand to rest or adjust the sitting position at the right time.

2 The Device Design

2.1 The Design Aim of Smart Cushion

The outcome can be used in home-care and office-care, for example, the health examination and health care of desk workers and the elderly. In addition, it is effective to help people get rid of bad habits and improve the quality of life.

Sitting balance is an important indicator to measure whether people's sitting posture is healthy or not. The daily monitoring and analysis of sitting balance of sedentary people, can not only help them to get a more comprehensive understanding of their sitting posture, but also dig deeper on the relationship between the center of sitting pressure and human health. And sufficient amount of data can reflect the general habit of sitting posture. The existing sitting pressure distribution measurement system has the disadvantages of high cost, importability and complexity.

Based on the measurement of sitting pressure data of the sedentary crowd, the smart cushion can display, store and carry out preliminary analysis.

The smart cushion needs to meet the following requirements:

(1) The cushion design should conform to ergonomics, which helps disperse the pressure generated by the weight of the ischial tuberosity and the hip. Its materials should ensure the thermal comfort of human body.
(2) It can record the data and store the data to the cloud server with Internet of things. It cannot only display the measured data in real time, but also compare it with the measured data in history and make relevant evaluation based on measurement data.
(3) The device system is stable, easy to use, suitable price, and easy to promote. It can be used by the social.

2.2 The Cushion Design

Kazushige et al. studied the static and dynamic pressure distribution on cushion made of polyurethane foam. The results show pressure distribution in the various parts of the body both in short time and long time, and foam with low stiffness has better effect of than that of high stiffness. Stepen Spdglr et al. (Yost and Oates 1968) made impact testing on wheelchair cushions of different materials, and the results indicate that contour foam cushion could reduce impact loading, showing remarkable resilience.

In this study, the design of smart cushion is based on contour foam cushion with low stiffness.

2.3 The Size of Cushion

This study chooses the physical parameters of 50% digits, namely sitting depth 457 (male), 433 (female), hip width 344 (male), and 306 (female) as the dimensions of the cushion design reference. Based on the size of general office chair and the characteristics of cushion materials, the overall dimensions of the cushion is 44 cm × 34 cm × 7.5 cm, as shown in Fig. 1.

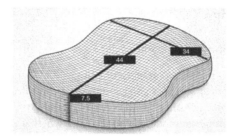

Fig. 1. The shape of cushion

The ischial tuberosity is not a anatomical landmark, but rather a curved bone area. The distance of the high pressure areas depend on the forward/backward rotation of the pelvis, since the ischial bones converge towards the pubis. According to general human physiological characteristics, referring to the distance between ischiums under upright sitting position, the placement of pressure transducer is shown as in Fig. 2, the measured pressure is F_{ul}, F_{ur}, F_{dl}, F_{dr}.

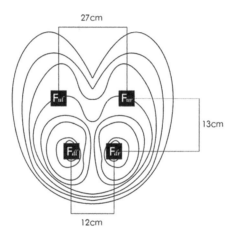

Fig. 2. The position of the sensors

2.4   The Material of the Cushion

Memory foam was created in 1962 in a study by NASA. During the design of escape system of Apollo command capsule, this material was developed and used to absorb the tremendous impact generated when the rocket takes off and the spacecraft returns to the atmosphere, or in some unexpected circumstances (such as crash), as well as improve the protectiveness and comfort of the seat[33]. Memory foam is a polyurethane polymer with open cell structure, with special viscoelastic property and strong ability of impact absorption. The molecule is very sensitive to temperature, so it is also called the temperature sensitive memory foam.

As material for cushion, it is under the pressure that is near static pressure. The molecular structure of memory foam material will flow to fit the deformation, and spread force to the entire surface, shown as in Fig. 3.

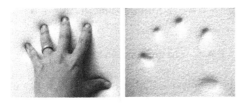

Fig. 3. The material of memory foam

The choice of memory foam as a the cushion is based on its two characteristics:

(1) Thermal properties: it could react to the human body temperature and gradually become soft. While absorbing the human body pressure, it can also help people adjust to the most comfortable posture. As for the lower part not exposed to the human body, it still maintains full supporting ability;

(2) Viscoelastic characteristics: though under compression and subsidence, it will not rebound strongly, and will gradually return to its original shape when the pressure is removed;

The pressure of human skin blood circulation is 36 mmHg, and the memory foam could distribute the pressure evenly and reduce it to less than 36 mmHg thus enhance blood circulation.

3   Function Module Design

The framework of the multi-channel pressure acquisition system is shown in Fig. 4.

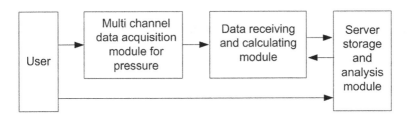

Fig. 4. The multi-channel pressure acquisition system

The pressure acquisition module realizes the basic data acquisition. It comprises a pressure sensor, a signal amplification circuit and a digital to analog conversion module. The pressure sensor and digital circuit are used to collect data. The Arduino board realizes the conversion between analog signal and digital signal. Pressure acquisition module itself does not analyze or store data, but by the other two modules (mobile phones and server) for processing. Its basic structure is shown in Fig. 5.

Fig. 5. The pressure acquisition module

In order to ensure the simpleness and feasible of data viewing, it uses the mobile phone as the actual data receiving and analyzing terminal. The pressure acquisition module transmits the real-time data to the mobile phone through the Bluetooth. The mobile phone receives the data and calculates and displays the relative value of the force, the pressure center and the impulse. When the measurement is completed, the data is uploaded to the server. At the same time, users can obtain their historical measurement data and some other relevant data through the network (such as their sitting habits, family sitting habits, etc.). The overall function of the mobile phone is shown in Fig. 6.

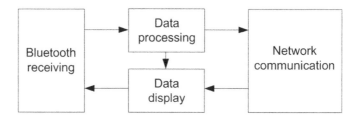

Fig. 6. The overall function of the mobile phone

The function of each module is as follows:

Bluetooth receiving module: By calling the system API and Bluetooth pairing and connecting, it could achieve the real-time monitoring of data collected by the acquisition module.

Data processing module: Achieve the real-time processing of the received data, data transmitted to the mobile phone through Bluetooth is pressure values with range of 0~50 kg, so calculation is necessary to get the relevant useful parameters (pressure center, impulse).

Data display module: It is the visual part of the program responsible for displaying useful information to users such as the real-time measurement interface, historical data and the proposed interface on App.

Network communication module: Based on the HTTP protocol, this module uses Web Service to communicate with the server, upload data and query the overall data and historical data.

Storage and analysis module: It stores the data of measurement each time in the cloud to ensure the consistency of the data at different mobile terminals, and collect data for analysis. The server is also responsible for data storage and analysis and the maintenance of user tables and measurement data tables. The user table records the user's basic information, such as height, weight, etc., for reference in the server analysis. The measurement table records the measurement results of each user each time, which is divided into 5 parts: the pressure of four measuring points and their force center. When the measurement is completed, the mobile terminal sends the request to the server, and the server stores the data and returns the corresponding test result.

4 Device Implementation

Device implementation of the overall system requires the acquisition of 4 channels pressure signal, after A/D conversion and the initial processing by the serial port to the host computer. The pressure sensor using a common half bridge strain sensor. A/D and DSP processing part using Arduino Uno programmable board. Power supply uses 3 AAA batteries.

4.1 Component Selection

The system requires the pressure signal to be a low frequency biological signal, usually not more than 2 Hz. Because of the long duration of the data acquisition, high sampling rate will lead to excessive data. According to the sampling law, the acquisition frequency of this system is determined as 5 Hz. Pressure sensor's parameters are shown in Table 1. The full load output of the sensor at 5 V voltage is 5 mv, and the input range of the Arduino Uno A/D is 0–5 V, so the amplification of the amplifier circuit is about 1000. The accuracy of the coordinates accuracy is 0.2%, requiring the accuracy of A/D more than 9 bits, and Arduino Uno with 10 bit A/D converter can meet the requirements.

Table 1. The component selection

No.	Content	Numerical value	No.	Content	Numerical value
1	Range	50 kg	9	Output temperature coefficient	0.1% F.S/10
2	Accuracy	0.10% F.S	10	Input impedance	$1000 \pm 10\ \Omega$
3	Sensitivity	$1.0 \pm 15\%$ mv/V	11	Output impedance	$1000 \pm 10\ \Omega$
4	Creep	0.1% F.S	12	Insulation resistance	$\geq 2000\ M\Omega$
5	Nonlinear	0.05% F.S	13	Supply voltage	10
6	Hysteresis error	0.05% F.S	14	Operating temperature range	$-10\ °C$
7	Repeatability error	0.05% F.S	15	Allowable overload load	150% F.S
8	Zero temperature coefficient	0.3% F.S/10			

4.2 Operational Amplifier

Because the output pressure signal is too small to carry on the A/D conversion directly. Amplifier is necessary to realize the preamplifier, which is to amplify and buffer the input signal to improve the resolution, so that the voltage range of the signal could match that of the A/D conversion circuit. According to the previous magnification of 1000, the INA128 operational amplifier of TI can meet this requirement, which is a universal instrument amplifier with low power and high precision. The operational amplifier design and small size enable it to obtain a wide range of applications. The feedback current input circuit can provide wide bandwidth even at high gain. Any increased profit between 1~10000 can be determined by a single external resistor.

INA128 magnification G is

$$G = 1 + \frac{50\,k\Omega}{R_g}$$

After calculation, The R_g is 50 Ω.

The main Features of INA128 are as Table 2.

Table 2. Theparameter of INA128

No.	Content	Numerical value	No.	Content	Numerical value
1	Low offset skin	Maximum 50 μV	5	Input protection	To ± 40 V
2	Low temperature drift	Maximum 0.5 μV/°C	6	Wide supply voltage range	From ± 2.25 to ± 18 V
3	Ibias	Maximum 5 nA	7	Low quiescent current	700 μA
4	High resistance against CMR	Minimum 120 dB			

4.3 Digital Circuit Part

The function of the digital circuit includes the A/D conversion of analog signal, the initial processing and the serial communication to the host computer. The parameters of the selected Arduino Uno programmable board are shown in Table 3.

Table 3. The parameter of Aduino Uno

No.	Content	Numerical value	No.	Content	Numerical value
1	Processor	ATmega328	8	3.3 V pin DC current	50 mA
2	Working voltage	5 V	9	Flash Memory	32 KB
3	Input voltage (recommended)	7–12 V	10	SRAM	2 KB
4	Input voltage (range)	6–20 V	11	EEPROM	1 KB
5	Digital IO pin	14	12	Working clock	16 MHz
6	Analog input pin	6	13	A/D accuracy	10
7	IO pin DC current	40 mA			

Table 4. The mean value of the pressure center in the 10 sitting postures

No.	Abbreviation	Sitting type	Pressure center
1	N	Natural sitting	$0.1 \pm 0.7, -0.6 \pm 0.4$
2	LF	Left leaning	$-8.1 \pm 2.5, 2.8 \pm 3.1$
3	F	Forward	$-1.4 \pm 1.9, 4.6 \pm 0.8$
4	RF	Right leaning	$8.9 \pm 3.0, 3.7 \pm 2.4$
5	L	Left-leaning	$-6.9 \pm 1.1, 1.2 \pm 0.7$
6	UR	Erect	$0.7 \pm 0.3, 0.6 \pm 0.2$
7	R	Right -leaning	$5.3 \pm 1.8, -0.4 \pm 1.6$
8	LB	Left back tilt	$-5.3 \pm 1.7, -4.1 \pm 2.2$
9	B	Backward	$1.2 \pm 0.3, -3.1 \pm 1.7$
10	RB	Backward	$4.1 \pm 1.7, -3.6 \pm 0.8$

4.4 Circuit Design

The amplifier circuit is shown in Fig. 7, where Rg is 50 Ω, R1a and R1b are adjustable resistors that are used to adjust the static bias of the circuit.

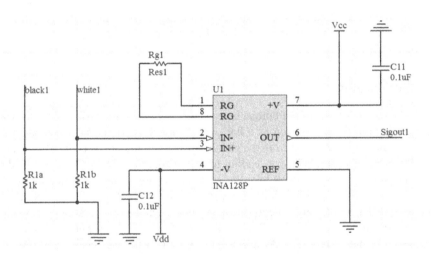

Fig. 7. The signal amplifier circuit design

4.5 Design of Data Receiving Module

The data acquisition module does not store the data, so data receiving is realized by APP. Through the data processing and storage can it real-time display sitting posture to users, and record and summary long-term sitting habits.

APP mainly includes three modules, the detection module, query module, setting module. The detection module is mainly responsible for the collection and calculation of data in real time, to show users their sitting posture, and record sitting habit; query module is responsible for providing historical data; setting module mainly carries on the entry of basic information such as weight and height.

5 Data Calculation

Calculation is mainly related to the data center of pressure and the impulse of each sensor. With 9600 baud rate, the real-time calculation is used to avoid excessive memory occupation and independent storage space. Among the characterization indexes of body pressure distribution, the asymmetry is related to sitting balance, which is shown as follow.

$$C_V = \frac{\sum_{i=1}^{N/2} |P_{iL} - P_{iR}| \cdot \Delta s}{\sum_{i=1}^{N/2} |P_{iL} + P_{iR}| \cdot \Delta s} \tag{1}$$

ΔS is the action area of a single sensor P_{iL}, P_{iR} are the pressure of the first i left and right measuring point

The larger the C_V is, the less balanced the body pressure distribution is.

The smart cushion collects and analyzes the signal of four pressure sensors, and calculates the pressure center and compares it with that of the natural sitting posture. It also calculates the impulse within a period of time of each sensor, in order to provide guidance of sitting behavior.

5.1 Mathematical Model

The mathematical model of the human body itself is highly symmetrical. Overlooking the cavity profile, it can be seen as a flat oval. When a person is fixed on seat, poor posture would show deviation from the standard value of the state, specifically refers to the adjustment of sitting behavior leading to the change of coordinates of centroid of the upper part of the body. If we take the geometric center of the four sensors for the origin, and the pressure center under standard posture as the first reference point, we could establish a two-dimension coordinate system. Then the real coordinate deviation caused by sitting behavior could reflect the change of centroid. So we need to transform the centroid deviation into quantity available to sensors, and give specific and scientifically reliable formula, as shown in Fig. 8.

For analysis purpose, the formula is built on the base of the following assumptions:

(1) Ignore the individual differences in the body part, and under the standard sitting posture trunk is both front-back and left-right symmetrical;
(2) The centroid related inertia parameters can be measured or simulated by functions or empirical formula;
(3) The effect of non observed variables such as the environment, physiological state of mutation and other uncontrollable factors on the observed quantities is small.

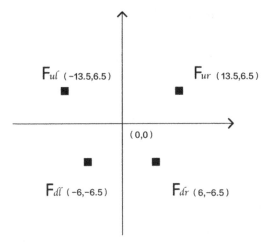

Fig. 8. Pressure center calculation reference coordinate system

5.2   Calculation of Pressure Center

The original stress distribution is simulated by the shape function, and the pressure is taken as the shape function F (x, y). Because the pressure values of four points F_{ul}, F_{ur}, F_{dl}, F_{dr} are known, there are 4 parameters a_1, a_2, a_3, a_4,

$$F(x, y) = a_1 xy + a_2 x + a_3 y + a_4$$

Four points can be substituted and get a_1, a_2, a_3 and a_4
Set the Force as

$$F_k = \int_\Omega F(x, y) dx dy \tag{2}$$

Then the coordinate of Force is

$$x_c = \frac{\int_\Omega F(x, y) \cdot y \cdot dx dy}{\int_\Omega F(x, y) dx dy} \tag{3}$$

$$y_c = \frac{\int_\Omega F(x, y) \cdot x \cdot dx dy}{\int_\Omega F(x, y) dx dy} \tag{4}$$

5.3   Impulse Calculation

Impulse is the effect of a Force varying with time on the an object. It is the integral of force to time:

$$I = \int F dt \tag{5}$$

The impulse of the four points of Ful, Fur, Fdl, Fdr can be calculated.

6   The Whole Device Realization and Experiment

6.1   Device Acquisition Section

The whole device was completed according to the above analysis and design, as shown in Fig. 9.

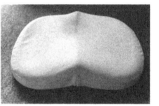

Fig. 9.   The whole device

6.2   Implementation of Mobile Terminal

The main factors that affect the App interface design of medical mobile products are user, business, scene and product. Users' difference in physical and psychological aspect and difference in scenarios will determine the App interface design, while the user's behavior habits determine their operating logic.

The design of mobile App for sedentary family, follow the development flow of App interface design. Through the user interviews and survey data of qualitative research

Fig. 10.   Impulse display interface of each measuring point of pressure center detection

and quantitative research to determine the demand for products → information architecture design → interaction design → visual interface design. In this section, the pressure center setting interface and the detection interface, as shown in Fig. 10.

6.3   Test and Analysis

Subjects

15 healthy people without lumbar spine disease were tested. Informed consent of all subjects. The age is 26.5 ± 1.4 years, the weight is 71.5 ± 8.4 kg, the height is 174.4 ± 3.4 cm and the BMI is 23.4 ± 2.09.

Experimental preparation

Test cushion is of 44 cm long, 34 cm wide, 7 cm high, placed on a height adjustable office chair with a back and no handrails. The seat surface length 47 cm, width 43 cm, nylon mesh fabric material, steel structure.

Because of the difference of individual body, it is difficult to define a pressure center suitable for everyone. The specific method used in this paper is: The subjects are seated, and adjust the seat to the comfortable height according to their daily habit of sitting posture. Then take natural sitting posture, namely the trunk and thighs about 150°, when the spine is close to the natural form. The observer record the center of pressure at this time as a reference point of the subjects.

Due to the limited storage space, in actual use, the phone does not store all the original data. Data testing and analysis are carried on by PC. The pressure center collection interface is shown in Fig. 8, and the pressure center coordinate data in real time is shown in Fig. 11.

Experiment design

A total of two tests carried out in this paper, the center of pressure acquisition test for validating the feasibility and rationality of this design, which perform as realizing the dynamic real-time measurement of people's pressure center, and calculating the cumulative effect; sedentary pressure center acquisition test aims to give preliminary exploration of the sedentary pressure distribution.

Multi seat pressure center acquisition test

When start, the observer records time, and ask every subject to change posture following a certain order LF - F - RF...... nine postures in total, each position for 5 s, to record the coordinate of the pressure center in this period of time, explore the pressure center under different sitting postures. The table is the mean value of the pressure center measured under 10 kinds of sitting posture for 15 persons (Table 4).

Sedentary stress center collection test

The subjects sit uninterruptedly in the testing chair for in 30 min, during which they can adjust themselves to maintain a comfortable position, and track the pressure center in this period. Because the sampling rate is high, so take the arithmetic mean value of the pressure center in 1 min as the pressure center within this period of time. The pressure center track drawing 10 min, 20 min, 30 min, as shown in Fig. 12.

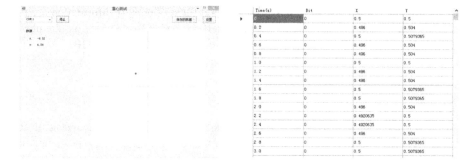

Fig. 11. The pressure center interface and the pressure center coordinate data

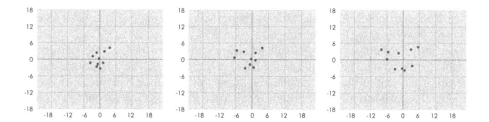

Fig. 12. The pressure center tracks of the 15 subjects in each 10 mins

6.4 Test Result Analysis

Test 1 shows that the smart cushion can basically reflect the balance of human sitting posture. According to the coordinates of the pressure center, the balance of sitting posture can be determined. The test results show that the design is feasible.

Results of test 2 show that in the 30-minute test time, pressure center changes from denseness to divergence. It indicates that over time, the amplitude of the change of pressure center increases, and it can be inferred that in the earlier period the subjects' sitting behavior is more singular and stable, latter they adjust posture to relieve the fatigue caused by sedentary.

7   Discussion

This paper describes the research at home and abroad of pressure distribution, sitting thermal comfort and cushion design, and analyze and summarize the pathological and psychological mechanisms of the influence of sedentariness. According to the anthropometric data of Chinese, this paper builds an smart cushion prototype, and realizes the hardware prototype of each module and illustrates the key technology of the software module used. It also puts forward an algorithm for simulating sitting balance. At the end this paper presents the mobile terminal prototype, sums up the results and makes analysis and prospect.

Design and fabricate a 4-point sensor array. The distribution of the sensor array is in accord with the characteristics of the human body pressure distribution, and the sensor has the advantages of stable conductivity and appropriate price, which makes the whole sensor array cost-effective and has great potential in commercial applications.

By calculating the pressure center to reflect the balance of human sitting posture, and display it to the users through a simple and intuitive form in the mobile terminal so users are available to the real-time results of adjusting sitting position. By calculating the cumulative effect of the force, reflecting the long-term sitting habits of the user, in order to further explore the balance of sitting posture and its pathological basis. When the smart cushion is finished, which could detect social problem of sittingsedentariness.

Considering the cost and practicality, the number of sensor points is less. In the future, we can increase the number of sensor points and improve the resolution of the system.

The relationship between the sitting balance and path physiology has not yet been studied quantitatively and qualitatively. The analysis needs a large sample of normal and diseased people to get the correlation between body pressure distribution data and disease, thus can provide guidance for sitting behavior.

In this paper, the stability of the sensor and the circuit has a lot of room for improvement, and joint research is necessary for investment.

Acknowledgement. This research was supported by the National Science and Technology Program (No. 2015BAH21F01) and Zhejiang Philosophy and Social Science Key Project (No. 11YD09Z).

References

Hu, L., Lin, Z., Zhang, J.: Study on the force of hip soft tissue in sitting position. Furniture **3**, 50–53 (2015)

Lu, J., Zhang, F., Shen, L.: Sitting posture theory and chair design principle and its application. J. Jiangnan Univ. (Nat. Sci. Ed.) **4**(6), 620–625 (2005)

Nakamura, J., Csikszentmihalyi, M.: The Concept of Flow: Flow and the Foundations of Positive Psychology, pp. 239–263. Springer, Netherlands (2014)

Namkoong, S., Shim, J.M., Kim, S.J., et al.: Effects of different sitting positions on skin temperature of the lowerextremity. J. Phys. Ther. Sci. **27**(8), 2637–2640 (2015)

Sang, W.L., Kim, S.Y.: Effects of hip exercises for chronic low-back pain patients with lumbarinstability. J. Phys. Ther. Sci. **27**(2), 345–348 (2015)

Sprigle, S., Chung, B., Meyer, T.: Assessment of the ISO impact damping test for wheelchair cushions. Assistive Technol. **22**(4), 236–244 (2010)

Sugimura, Y., Wada, C.: An analysis of the force and angle necessary to develop a standing-up assistive device. In: SICE 2004 Conference, vol. 3, pp. 2416–2420. IEEE Xplore, (2004)

Winkel, J., Jørgensen, K.: Evaluation of foot swelling and lower-limb temperatures in relation to leg activity during long-term seated office work. Ergonomics **29**(2), 313–328 (1986)

Yost, C.A., Oates, R.W.: Human survival in aircraft emergencies. NASA CR-1262, 1–55 (1968)

Human-Sensing: Low Resolution Thermal Array Sensor Data Classification of Location-Based Postures

Bruno Pontes[✉], Marcio Cunha, Rafael Pinho, and Hugo Fuks

Informatics Department, Pontifical Catholic University of Rio de Janeiro, Rio de Janeiro, Brazil
{bpontes,mcunha,randre,hugo}@inf.puc-rio.br

Abstract. Ambient Assisted Living (AAL) applications aim to allow elderly, sick and disabled people to stay safely at home while collaboratively assisted by their family, friends and medical staff. AAL, recently empowered by the Internet of Things, introduces a new healthcare connectivity paradigm that interconnects mobile apps and sensors allowing constant monitoring of the patient. Preserving privacy in the course of recognition of postures and classification of activities is one of the challenges for human-sensing and a critical factor of user acceptance, so there is a demand for solutions that do not require real live imaging in AAL.

This paper addresses this challenge through the usage of a low resolution thermal sensor and machine learning techniques, discussing the feasibility of low cost and privacy protecting solutions. We evaluated decision tree models in two tasks of human-sensing, presence and posture recognition, using data of different days and volunteers. We also contribute by providing public domain datasets, collected in a bedroom and a bathroom, which are described in this paper.

Keywords: Household monitoring · Human-sensing · Machine learning · Privacy · Thermal sensors · Low resolution

1 Introduction

Driven by an aging population, rising health care costs, lack of professional staff and remote support in most developed countries, there is a growing demand to provide a better delivery of health and social care services for elderly, sick, convalescent and disabled people [1]. Ambient Assisted Living (AAL) is a field of research focusing on IT support for healthcare, comfort and control applications for home environments. AAL facilities often require sensors, actuators and wearable devices, and generally require easy installation and low energy consumption. Current developments in wireless and mobile communications integrated with advances in pervasive and wearable technologies have a radical impact on healthcare delivery systems. Currently, the patients' continuous monitoring is considered the most relevant aspect in healthcare and privacy is always a concern and critical aspect for user acceptance [2, 3]. There is a demand for solutions that avoid real images, videos and cameras, especially in rooms such as the bathroom and the bedroom. There are solutions for Human Activity Recognition (HAR) [4] based on wearable sensors, but they are more often employed in outdoor studies where the environment imposes additional limitations and concerns to non-wearable

© Springer International Publishing AG 2017
N. Streitz and P. Markopoulos (Eds.): DAPI 2017, LNCS 10291, pp. 444–457, 2017.
DOI: 10.1007/978-3-319-58697-7_33

sensors, since it requires the user to wear the equipment for extended periods and the researchers to track battery, positioning and calibration of the sensors.

This paper studies the usage of Low Resolution Thermal Array Sensor (LRTAS) technology in household monitoring of daily activities in the bathroom and the bedroom. Our goal is to generate a thermal mapping dataset and explore it with machine learning models to investigate the feasibility to recognize the human-sensing properties of presence and posture [5]. LRTAS technology was chosen by the authors to preserve users' privacy given that it is not possible to generate body images from the sensor data output.

This paper is organized as follows. The next section discusses related works of household monitoring of daily activities. Section 3 presents the prototype devised for the experiment and the environment setup. Section 4 details the thermal mapping dataset and the classifier developed for presence and posture recognition. Section 5 concludes the paper and describes the next steps of this research.

2 Related Works

2.1 Activities of Daily Living

Several articles [6–8] show that healthcare professionals understand that the best way for detecting emerging medical conditions before they become critical is to look for changes in activities of daily living (ADLs). These routine activities comprise eating, getting in and out of the house, getting in and out of bed, using the toilet, bathing, dressing, using the phone, shopping, preparing meals, housekeeping, washing clothes and administering proper medications. For tracking the ADLs, a distributed mobile infrastructure composed of sensors, actuators, microcontrollers, communication networks must be installed in the patients' homes.

Several approaches to recognize ADLs in AAL have been considered in several papers [9–11]. One is the setup of a large and invisible infrastructure of sensors such as cameras and hidden microphones, presence sensors embedded into walls and ceilings, water pipes sensors and strain sensors under floorboards. Although this approach provides access to a wide variety of information, the cost of installing and maintaining it is usually very high.

Another approach is to use multiple low-cost sensors that cheapen the implementation and facilitate the setup throughout the home [8, 12, 13]. The disadvantage of this approach is that these sensors are obtrusive and ask for regular maintenance, like battery changes or corrections in their positions (e.g., sensors fixed on the doors of medicine cabinets, kitchen, refrigerator, walls, doors, etc.). According to Fogarty et al. [14], the elderly reject such sensors because they interfere with the look of their homes or create feelings of embarrassment or loss of privacy related to a need for assistance. A third approach is to use wearable devices [15], considering that the elderly, sick or convalescent may opt to avoid using such devices, by forgetting to use them every day or being unable to use them due to their health condition or disability.

2.2   Activity Recognition

The goal of activity recognition is to recognize common human activities in real-life settings. Accurate activity recognition is challenging because human activity is complex and highly diverse. Everyday activities at home roughly break down into two categories [16]. To the first category belong the activities that require repetitive motion of the human body and are constrained by its structure, such as walking and exercising. Studies indicate that these activities are easier to recognize by using on-body sensors [15]. The second category, however, contains activities is easier to recognize by looking for patterns in how people use things, and not by how they move around [16]. For these categories, objects used while performing activities such as grooming, cooking and socializing may provide more useful information than the body's movement or posture.

Homes and their furnishings have highly variable layouts, and individuals perform activities in different ways. The same activity (e.g. brushing teeth) may result in a significantly different sensor activation profile based upon the habits of the home dweller and the particular layout of his or her home. Successful research, however, has so far focused on recognizing simple human activities. Recognizing complex activities remains a challenging and active area of research. Specifically, the nature of human activities poses the following challenges [17]:

- *Recognizing concurrent activities.* People can perform several activities at the same time, such as watching television while talking to friends.
- *Recognizing interleaved activities.* Certain real-life activities can be interleaved. For instance, if a friend calls while you are cooking, you could talk to your friend while you continue to cook.
- *Ambiguity of interpretation.* Similar situations may be interpreted differently. For example, an open refrigerator may be related to several activities, such as cooking or cleaning.
- *Multiple residents.* More than one resident may be present in many environments. An AAL system needs to recognize the activities residents perform in parallel, even when a group performs them.

Researchers have been using several probability-based algorithms to build activity models for many years. The Hidden Markov Model (HMM) and the Conditional Random Field (CRF) are among the most popular modeling techniques. However, many activities may have non-deterministic natures in practice, where some steps of the activities may be performed in any order or in different time frames due to disability or limitation of each patient. In practice, because many activities are concurrent or interleaved with other activities, HMM and CRF have difficulty in representing multiple interacting activities and are incapable of capturing long-range or transitive dependencies of the observations [18].

To overcome these issues and to embrace the complexity and ambiguity in ADLs, other algorithms like Multi-Layer Neural Network (MLNNK) and Fuzzy Logic (FL) are being used to take advantages of the Autonomic Computing symptoms and activity model databases to be more flexible and efficient. The MLNNK-based algorithm shows better accuracy than both HMM and CRF-based algorithms. The accuracy of MLNNK is over 23% higher than CRF and about 14.6% higher than HMM [18].

Fuzzy Logic has shown better recognition accuracy compared to MLNNK. Fuzzy-logic-based algorithm shows an 11% improvement in the recognition accuracy of time slice activities. When algorithms utilize activity and symptoms knowledge base, both MLNNK and fuzzy logic show at least 27% improvement in activity recognition accuracy [18], showing the importance to have a collaborative analysis and decision database to share as much as possible how, when and where an activity can be started, paused or finished.

Although those accuracy improvements indicate active research in this field, (i) the comparison of results is severely hindered by the lack of published datasets and (ii) the verification of results is not possible. As acknowledged in [19], "the recognition algorithms rely heavily on the dataset". Publication of datasets is an imperative step towards the maturity of a research area, and as a form of contribution the authors published the dataset, along with detailed information about the sensor type, position and orientation, to enable verification and comparison of the achieved results.

3   Thermal Sensing Prototype

The prototype built for human-sensing uses the OMRON D6T-44L low-resolution array thermal sensor and the Arduino UNO microcontroller. This sensor provides a 4 × 4 matrix with temperature values, and it communicates with the microcontroller through Inter-Integrated Circuit (I2C) protocol.

Figure 1 illustrates the prototype that was installed on the bedroom and bathroom ceiling, to capture sensor data. In this figure, there are the Arduino microcontroller and the D6T-44L sensor connected to a protoboard, and also a five-meter cable that was used

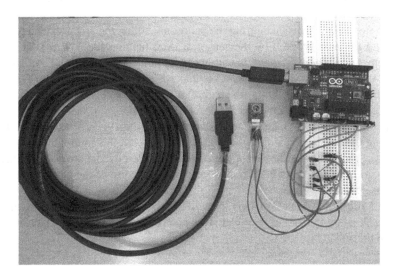

Fig. 1. Prototype used in this work.

to transmit data to a laptop. Processing (https://processing.org/) was the program used on the laptop side to receive and persist data, sent by Arduino through serial port. The USB port, which was used connected to the laptop, is next to the sensor in Fig. 1 to get a sense of sensor dimensions.

Figures 2 and 3 illustrate the bedroom where the study took place and, Figs. 4 and 5 illustrate the bathroom. The green shaded part of these figures represents the approximate field of view covered by the thermal sensor.

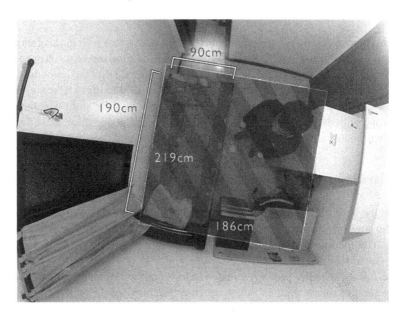

Fig. 2. Sensor field of view in the bedroom. (Color figure online)

The photo of Fig. 2 was taken from the bedroom ceiling, the green shaded rectangle representing the area covered by the sensor at floor height (40,734 cm^2). The bed is 190 cm long and 90 cm wide, and is within sensor field of view (SFoV). An area next to the bed is also within SFoV, where a volunteer is standing. The photo of Fig. 3 was taken from the wall, and illustrates the bedroom (267 cm) and bed height (46 cm), the bed to ceiling distance (221 cm) and SFoV angle (44.2°).

The photo of Fig. 4 was taken from the bathroom ceiling, the green shaded rectangle representing the SFoV area at floor height (30,690 cm^2). In this figure, the volunteer is sitting on the toilet and the shower stall is on the left. The covered area by the sensor in the bathroom is smaller than bedroom covered area, because of the bathroom's height (236 cm) is smaller.

Figure 5 illustrates, approximately, how SFoV covers the volunteer's 173 cm high, when he is standing in front of the toilet. This photo was taken from the bathroom wall just above the sink.

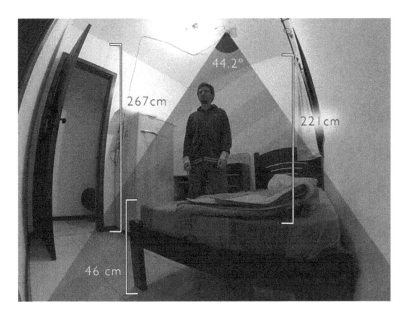

Fig. 3. Standing volunteer, sensor field of view angle and, bedroom and bed heights. (Color figure online)

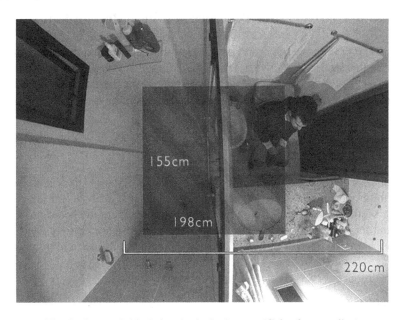

Fig. 4. Sensor field of view in the bathroom. (Color figure online)

Fig. 5. Standing volunteer, sensor field of view angle and bathroom height. (Color figure online)

4   Building Classifiers for Presence and Pose Recognition

The process of developing the proposed solution for presence and pose recognition is presented in this section. First, we describe the dataset that was generated in this work. Next, a brief analyzes and an explanation of how feature extraction was done are presented. Finally, we describe the proposed machine learning models for two tasks of human-sensing properties.

4.1   Data Collection

Five volunteers participated in the data collection, Table 1 presents their characteristics and the number of instances in the dataset. The results and analyzes presented in the following sections were done using only the data generated in the bedroom. The full dataset and the programs' source code, that were used to make analyzes and feature extraction, both described in this work, are available for public use in http://www.softwareofplaces.com/research.

The bedroom data was labeled with the following classes:

1. Lying on the bed.
2. Lying on the bed using blanket.
3. Sitting on the bed.
4. Sitting on the floor.
5. Lying on the floor.
6. Standing.

7. Standing wearing winter clothes.
8. None.

All volunteers performed all poses mentioned above. The bedroom data collection occurred in five different days, in room temperatures ranging from 21 °C to 29 °C. The None class refers to a persisted data when there was no one inside the SFoV. The None class data was used to calculate the threshold temperature value, used in the proposed background subtraction method, and to train and evaluate the generated machine learning models to recognize human presence.

Table 1. Characteristics of the volunteers and the dataset.

Subject	Genre	Age (y.o.)	Height (m)	Weight (kg)	Bathroom instances	Bedroom instances	Total instances
A	Male	28	1.83	74	0	1,593	1,593
B	Male	27	1.80	75	1,198	2,611	3,809
C	Male	30	1.79	79	954	3,053	4,007
D	Male	29	1.73	66	1,119	5,668	6,787
E	Female	27	1.60	64	1,188	21,406	22,594
None	–	–	–	–	201	9,339	9,540
Total	–	–	–	–	4,660	43,670	**48,330**

4.2   Exploring the Dataset

Some data from the dataset was used to evaluate the prototype performance, and to make a brief analysis of clothing, distance and room temperature, on the sensor data reading. The data persistence frequency had an average of 2.7 instances per second, *i.e.,* one instance persisted every 0.37 s. Despite this average frequency, in 3.69% of the data

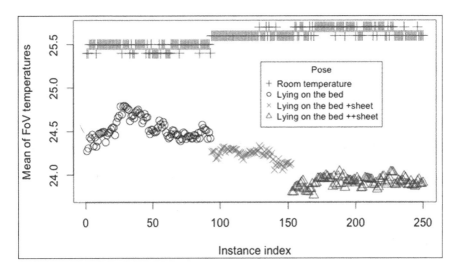

Fig. 6. The lying on the bed pose being performed with different sheets.

analyzed, two consecutive instances had a greater than one second interval between them.

Figure 6 illustrates three different lying on the bed data sets. The difference is the use of two kinds of sheet, a thinner and a thicker one, represented by *+sheet* and *++sheet* respectively. Each instance temperature, with degree Celsius value on the chart y-axis, is the SFoV temperatures' mean. The chart also contains the room temperature values for each instance. The temperature averages were lower when the volunteer used a sheet, and even lower when the volunteer used a thicker sheet, compared to when the volunteer performed the pose without using any sheet.

The temperatures shown in the Fig. 7 chart are from two different lying pose data sets, with the room temperatures of each instance, and it was calculated in the same way as the Fig. 6 chart temperatures. The temperature averages measured by the sensor had higher values for the pose performed on the bed. In addition to the distance, the fact that the lying on the floor pose was performed right beside the bed, which creates a kind of shadow and hides part of the volunteer's body from the SFoV, causes temperatures to be lower. The correct lying on the floor pose recognition is important, because this pose can be interpreted as a possible risk situation, such as a faint, followed or not by a fall.

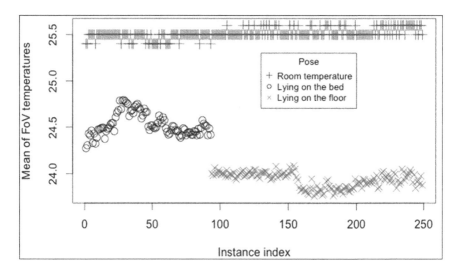

Fig. 7. The same pose being performed at different distances from the sensor.

Figure 8 illustrates data from four poses being performed on three different days, each one at different room temperatures. To calculate y-axis values, we selected the highest SFoV temperature for each pose data set instance and calculate its mean, resulting in only one value for each pose and day. These temperatures increase in a way not proportional to the increase in room temperature. The standing +clothes pose means that the volunteer wore winter clothes, and is the pose with the lowest temperature values. The data from Figs. 6, 7 and 8 are from volunteer D.

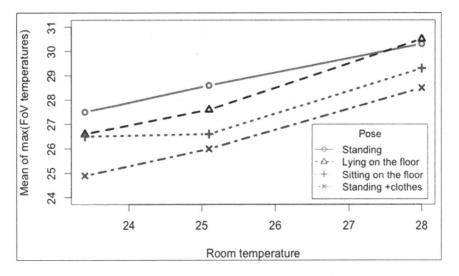

Fig. 8. Poses performed at different room temperatures.

4.3 Feature Extraction

We used eight classes of information to extract the features used by the machine learning models. These features were extracted from the sensor's output temperature values and a predefined value, which was used in the background subtraction method, which aims to reduce the task complexity by removing the pixels from the SFoV which are not associated with the heat source being analyzed, which in our case, is a person.

The first step in extracting features is to apply background subtraction using a predefined value to calculate a threshold temperature. To find this value, we analyzed the room temperature and the highest SFoV temperature value of the None class data, so we get a ratio between these two temperatures. The threshold value for each instance was calculated by multiplying the ratio value found with the current room temperature, so the pixels with a temperature value less than the threshold value were removed.

The first feature is the difference of the threshold temperature and the highest temperature of the SFoV. The second is the number of pixels with temperatures higher than the calculated threshold. Standard deviation, summation, and temperatures' average of the pixels not removed, are the third, fourth and fifth features. The sixth, seventh, and eighth feature values are binary. The sixth feature had its value set to 1 if the two highest temperature values are neighbors in the SFoV matrix, and 0 otherwise. The last two features are relative to the location with the highest and second highest temperature value. For the extraction of these two features, each SFoV pixel was associated with a location. In the bedroom case, two binary values were generated for each of these two features, referring to the bed and floor locations.

Figure 9 illustrates a print from the SFoV temperatures viewer. At the print moment, there was a volunteer performing the standing pose, at 23.4 °C. The following features were extracted from this instance: 4.5, 6, 1.5, 148.1, 24.7, 0, 0, 1, 0 and 1. The threshold temperature was 22.4 °C, it was calculated as 90% of room temperature. The last four values refer to the seventh and eighth features, and it means that the pixel with the highest and second highest temperature value are in the floor area.

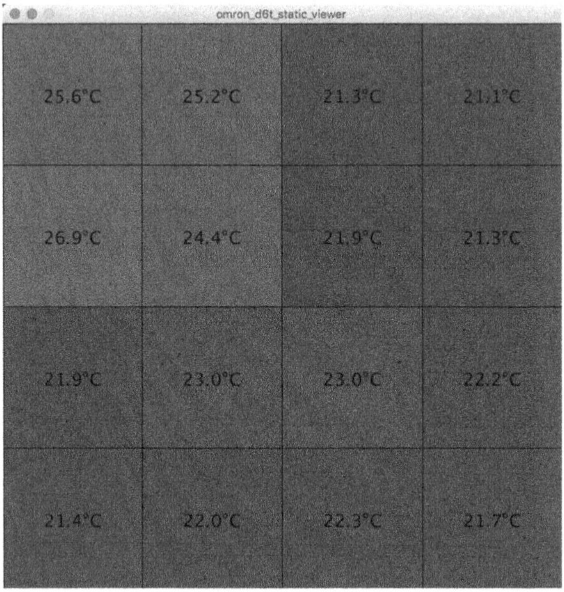

Fig. 9. Print from the SFoV temperatures viewer. This instance is from a volunteer performing the standing pose in the bedroom, at 23.4 °C.

4.4 Machine Learning Models

The J48 algorithm was used to build the machine learning models, its use was given through the Weka GUI (http://www.cs.waikato.ac.nz/ml/weka/), which is a machine learning framework. J48 is a supervised learning algorithm that builds decision tree predictive models.

In pose recognition task, we used five classes: lying on the bed and on the floor, sitting on the bed and on the floor, and standing. The lying on the bed using blanket labeled class data are part of the lying on the bed class. The joint purpose was to create more generic models to recognize poses. The standing wearing winter clothes labeled class data are part of the standing class, also with the intention of creating more generic models. None class data were not used to recognize poses. To recognize a person presence, data from all classes that had a volunteer in SFoV were labeled as Presence. Thus, this task had two classes: Presence and None.

4.5 Evaluation

The generated data in the bedroom were divided into three datasets, in order to evaluate models' recognition at different temperatures. Dataset 1 was collected on three days, and it was used to generate the recognition models. The collection of datasets 2 and 3 were done on different days, one day for each, and were used only to evaluate the models. Accuracies relating to dataset 1 are based on 10-fold cross-validation (Table 2).

Table 2. Pose and presence recognition accuracies.

Human-sensing task	Dataset	Accuracy (%)
Pose	1	90.67
	2	75.95
	3	60.06
Presence	1	99.57
	2	99.94
	3	91.65

The highest room temperature measured in datasets 1, 2 and 3, were 25.1 °C, 25.9 °C and 29.1 °C, respectively. Room temperatures measured in datasets 2 and 3 practically do not vary, but dataset 1 contains data with room temperatures varying approximately 4 °C.

The pose and presence recognition had accuracy above 90% in the test that used dataset1. The lowest accuracies occurred in the tests that used dataset 3. Figs. 10 and 11 illustrate the confusion matrices of these tests. The main diagonal of each matrix represents the instances correctly classified by the models. Figure 10 shows that the pose recognition model was quite wrong in the classification of the poses performed next to the bed. Figure 11 shows that the model failed to classify all none class instances.

a	b	c	d	e	<-----	classified as
526	33	0	0	0	a =	Lying on the bed
85	183	0	0	0	b =	Sitting on the bed
0	0	259	238	50	c =	Standing
0	0	89	79	0	d =	Sitting on the floor
0	0	135	67	1	e =	Lying on the floor

Fig. 10. Confusion matrix of pose recognition in dataset 3.

a	b	<-----	classified as
1,745	0	a =	Presence
159	0	b =	None

Fig. 11. Confusion matrix of presence recognition in dataset 3.

5 Conclusion and Future Works

This work presents an approach to the pose and presence recognition tasks using data from a low resolution thermal array sensor. These tasks are part of the human-sensing taxonomy proposed by [5] and assist in the recognition of ADLs.

The proposed solution obtained 90.67% accuracy in pose recognition and 99.57% in presence recognition in a bedroom, using a low cost and privacy protecting prototype. These results were obtained using a dataset containing room temperatures similar to the room temperatures of the data used to generate the recognition models. The next step of our research is to further investigate the effects of different room temperatures on the accuracy of the recognition models.

The results presented in this work indicated a strong dependency between the two tasks of recognition and data diversity. Our models performed poorly when they were evaluated on datasets generated at higher room temperatures. Thus, we suggest that more data, at different ambient temperatures, number of participants and room layouts, be made available in the literature. In this way, it will be possible to generate more generic predictive models, capable of recognizing human pose and presence in varied situations.

References

1. Pereira, C.V., Esteves, M.G.P., da Justa Medeiros, S.P. de Souza, J.M., Antelio, M.: How the crowd can change collaborative work in patient care. In: IEEE CSCWD, pp. 527–532 (2013)
2. Doyle, J., et al.: Requirements gathering for the delivery of healthcare data in aware homes. In: 2011 Proceedings of the 5th International Conference on Pervasive Computing Technologies for Healthcare (PervasiveHealth) and Workshops. IEEE (2011)
3. McCreary, F., Zafiroglu, A., Patterson, H.: The contextual complexity of privacy in smart homes and smart buildings. In: Nah, F.F.-H., Tan, C.-H. (eds.) HCIBGO 2016. LNCS, vol. 9752, pp. 67–78. Springer, Cham (2016). doi:10.1007/978-3-319-39399-5_7
4. Aehnelt, M., Urban, B.: Follow-Me: smartwatch assistance on the shop floor. In: Nah, F.F.-H. (ed.) HCIB 2014. LNCS, vol. 8527, pp. 279–287. Springer, Cham (2014). doi: 10.1007/978-3-319-07293-7_27
5. Teixeira, T., Dublon, G., Savvides, A.: A survey of human-sensing: methods for detecting presence, count, location, track, and identity. Technical report, ENALAB, Yale University (2010)
6. Lawton, M.P., Brody, E.M.: Assessment of older people: self-maintaining and instrumental activities of daily living. Gerontologist 9, 179–186 (1989)
7. Rogers, W.A., Meyer, B., Walker, N., Fisk, A.D.: Functional limitations to daily living tasks in the aged: a focus groups analysis. Hum. Factors 40, 111–125 (1998)
8. Tapia, E.M., Intille, S.S., Larson, K.: Activity Recognition in the home using simple and ubiquitous sensors. In: Ferscha, A., Mattern, F. (eds.) Pervasive 2004. LNCS, vol. 3001, pp. 158–175. Springer, Heidelberg (2004). doi:10.1007/978-3-540-24646-6_10
9. Abowd, G., Mynatt, E.D.: Charting past, present, and future research in ubiquitous computing. ACM Trans. Comput. Hum. Interact. (TOCHI) 7, 29–58 (2000)
10. Chen, J., Kam, A.H., Zhang, J., Liu, N., Shue, L.: Bathroom activity monitoring based on sound. In: Proceedings of the International Conference on Pervasive Computing (Pervasive 2005), pp. 47–61 (2005)
11. Rowan, J., Mynatt, E.D.: Digital family portrait field trial: support for aging in place. In: Proceedings of the ACM Conference on Human Factors in Computing Systems (CHI 2005), pp. 521–530 (2005)

12. Beckmann, C., Consolvo, S., LaMarca, A.: Some assembly required: supporting end-user sensor installation in domestic ubiquitous computing environments. In: Davies, Nigel, Mynatt, E.D., Siio, I. (eds.) UbiComp 2004. LNCS, vol. 3205, pp. 107–124. Springer, Heidelberg (2004). doi:10.1007/978-3-540-30119-6_7

13. Wilson, D.H., Atkeson, C.: Simultaneous tracking and activity recognition (STAR) using many anonymous, binary sensors. In: Gellersen, H.-W., Want, R., Schmidt, A. (eds.) Pervasive 2005. LNCS, vol. 3468, pp. 62–79. Springer, Heidelberg (2005). doi: 10.1007/11428572_5

14. Fogarty, J., Au, C., Hudson, S.E.: Sensing from the basement: a feasibility study of unobstrusive and low-cost home activity recognition. In: Proceedings of UIST, pp. 91–100 (2006)

15. Ugulino, W., Cardador, D., Vega, K., Velloso, E., Milidiú, R., Fuks, H.: Wearable computing: accelerometers' data classification of body postures and movements. In: Barros, L.N., Finger, M., Pozo, A.T., Gimenénez-Lugo, G.A., Castilho, M. (eds.) SBIA 2012. LNCS, pp. 52–61. Springer, Heidelberg (2012). doi:10.1007/978-3-642-34459-6_6

16. Kasteren, T., Noulas, A.K., Englebienne, G., Kröse, B.J.A.: Accurate activity recognition in a home setting. In: UbiComp, pp. 1–9 (2008)

17. Kim, E., Helal, D.C.: Human activity recognition and pattern discovery. IEEE Pervasive Comput. 9(1), 48–52 (2010)

18. Medjahed, H., Istrate, D., Boudy, J., Dorizzi, B.: Human activities of daily living recognition using fuzzy logic for elderly home monitoring. In: Proceedings of IEEE on Fuzzy System, pp. 2001–2006 (2009)

19. Yang, X., Lianwen, J.: A naturalistic 3D acceleration-based activity dataset & benchmark evaluations. In: IEEE International Conference on Systems Man and Cybernetics (SMC), pp. 4081–4085 (2010). ISSN: 1062-922X

Ambient Information Design to Amplify Connections Between New Empty Nest Parents and Their Children

Zhenyu Cheryl Qian[1(✉)], Yue Ma[1], Yingjie Chen[1], Yafeng Niu[2], and Chengqi Xue[2]

[1] Purdue University, West Lafayette, IN, USA
{qianz,ma173,victorchen}@purdue.edu
[2] Southeast University, Nanjing, China
{nyf,xcq}@seu.edu.cn

Abstract. Empty nest is a global social phenomenon that is constantly increasing during the recent decades. The loneliness and depression faced by parents and children lead to a decrease in life quality and other health problems especially for the families with international students. Remote family communication is crucial to reduce the symptoms and improve mental and physical health. Traditional verbal communication methods require synchronous interaction with a convenient time and a suitable environment. We aim to work on this issue from a perspective of immersive and transparent interaction through the ambient display. Based on a series of user research and iterations of concept development, our design outcome FAMILINK employs existing technologies and methods to offer a novel non-intrusive information communication experience. It constructs a cohesive system that generalizes collected data into ambient hologram display and projection and informs the user other family members' real-time statuses in an ambient approach.

Keywords: Ambient information design · User-centered design · Empty nest syndrome

1 Introduction

This paper introduces the motivation, design process, and evaluation outcomes of an interactive system FAMILINK that supports non-intrusive communications between new empty nest parents and their children. Coming from the analogy of young birds flying away from their parents' nest, *empty nest* refers to a kind of family in which the children have grown up and left home. This global social phenomenon is constantly increasing during the recent decades. The number of older adults who are living alone in rural areas has been sharply increasing as a result of the migration of younger adults to urban areas for employment [1]. Between 1900 and 2000, the percentage of Americans aged 45 to 64 who lived as a solo couple increased from about 10% to about 33% [2]. This phenomenon leads to a particular syndrome, empty nest syndrome, which refers to the grief that many parents feel when their children move out of home [3]. Such syndrome becomes very typical and more severe and in the families with international students. Remote family communication is crucial to reduce the symptoms and improve

© Springer International Publishing AG 2017
N. Streitz and P. Markopoulos (Eds.): DAPI 2017, LNCS 10291, pp. 458–471, 2017.
DOI: 10.1007/978-3-319-58697-7_34

family members' mental and physical health. With the rise of globalization and digital media technologies such as social media and mobile phones, new forms of maintaining connections to home are emerging among this present generation of transnational migrants (including international students) [4]. However, traditional methods of verbal communication, such as phone calls, text messages, and video chats require synchronous interaction with convenient time and a suitable environment (private and quiet). Such setting requirements make it inconvenient to communicate, especially given potential time zone differences and individuals' busy schedules.

Bearing these problems in mind, we aim to develop a system solution that can facilitate the connections between new empty nest parents and their children from a perspective of immersive and transparent interaction through the ambient display. Our design process included semi-structured interviewing, observation, iterations of concept development, prototyping, and usability testing in a gallery setting.

2 Background

2.1 Two Perspectives in the Empty Nest Phenomena

The children have grown up and left home to begin their adult lives in other cities or other countries is a typical stage in a family's cycle. It can be challenging emotionally for both the parents and the child. The parents of empty nest families commonly have a lower quality of life after their child's departure [5]. Common experienced loneliness and depression often cause stress and anxiety, which further exacerbates loneliness and depression [6]. These emotions have a synergistic effect in diminishing the well-being of elderly parents [7]. Tollmar & Persson [8] found that the elderly tend to keep meaningful items, which link to specific individuals; they may place a postcard or photo on a refrigerator, table, mirror, or furniture because these objects remind them of absent family members. Meanwhile, empty nest syndrome makes parents more prone to many problems such as drinking, smoking, weight gain, financial difficulties, various disorders, including cardiovascular disease, cancer, and asthma [7]. However, empty nest parents – especially the elderly – seldom communicate with other people in face-to-face interactions. Thus, for empty nest parents, one of the most practical ways is to build a connection to their remote child through communication, a lack of which is largely the initial cause of their feelings of loss and loneliness.

For many college students, especially in their first year, homesickness is a common problem. According to Thurber & Walton [9] and Johnson & Sandhu [10], many university freshmen have their first experience away from home during the first year, and all of the students must face challenges independently, such as making new friends, adjusting to new life routines, and making progress in school and life. For these young adults, the adjustments to these challenges are not easy and can easily cause depression. A change in the type and frequency of contact with primary caregivers makes the adjustment even more challenging [2]. Stress or anxiety disorders caused by separation from home is defined as homesickness, according to the DSM-IV [11]. Thurber also states that self-reports of homesickness typically have included negative emotions, cognitions focused on home, and physical symptoms [11]. Moreover, the frequency of contact to parents cannot be guaranteed because of the separation, which in turn creates more homesickness. Aside from homesickness, the challenges of adjustment can develop to be more complicated by the cultural differences between home and school [9, 12, 13]. Cultural adaptation problems are significantly common among international students; their lack of social support, overwhelming academic pressure, and even discrimination could be risk factors for depression among international students [14, 15]. In 2007, nearly 44% of international students reported that they had experienced depression problems that affected their well-being or academic performance [16].

To minimize the depression, loneliness, and homesickness experienced by international students, building effective and efficient means of connection with their parents – for the mutual benefit of both sides – is crucial.

2.2 Existing Technologies to Support Distanced Family Communication

Phone calls, texts, and video chats are commonly used communication methods in empty nest families. These methods require verbal talk or messages that are synchronous – real-time communication between users. Accordingly, the mismatch of parents' and child's daily schedules creates a major obstacle for such communication. For families with children who are international students, time zone difference makes the direct communication tougher. Apart from that, the emotional bond and sense of loneliness cannot be solved by verbal communication [17]. Sometimes, the feelings cannot be directly expressed by the language and some Social media, such as Facebook, Twitter, and WeChat, provides a different type of platform for empty nest parents and children to maintain a connection through sharing information online. By following posts and blogs, they can keep each other informed of their statuses and whereabouts. However, to maintain such a connection useful requires both sides to post either continuously or regularly. It took lots of efforts and sometimes against some people's personalities to post out their personally information and feelings. Moreover, emotional bonds and closeness have not improved through the social media.

A few recent efforts dedicated to dealing with this remote communication based on computer mediated technologies. *ShareTable* [18] is designed to facilitate meaningful, two-way interaction that goes beyond video chat. It is a method mimicking a real communication environment. Through *ShareTable,* a parent and child can play a board game together, color in a coloring book, or work on that evening's homework assignment as if they are still physically in the same room [18]. *Good Night Lamp* [19] consists of several internet-connected lamps distributed in different locations. When the big central lamp turns on or off, the other little lamps react accordingly. The little lamp owners, partner, children or friends, anywhere around the world can be informed about the big lamp owner's statuses: awake at night, sleeping at night or daytime. It is an ambient approach that communicates information or status without interruption to others' lives.

Inspired by these two projects, we want to propose and design a communication method that can facilitate the connections in the newly empty nest family based on immersive and transparent interaction through the ambient display. It should support the emotional bonding through a kind of "physically accompanied" and inform status in a non-intrusive manner.

3 Employ the User Studies to Identify Design Objectives

This project started from a series of semi-structured paired interviews with five international students and their newly empty nest parents to gather their experience of current communication methods and the essential information they exchange during the verbal communication. During the interviews, we encouraged the participants to brainstorm and describe their "ideal" experience to share their feelings and information with the distanced family members. The interviews were audio recorded and transcribed before analysis (Fig. 1). To filter out more explicit opinions from the shared information, we used a follow-up survey as a supplement method to identify subjects' preferences.

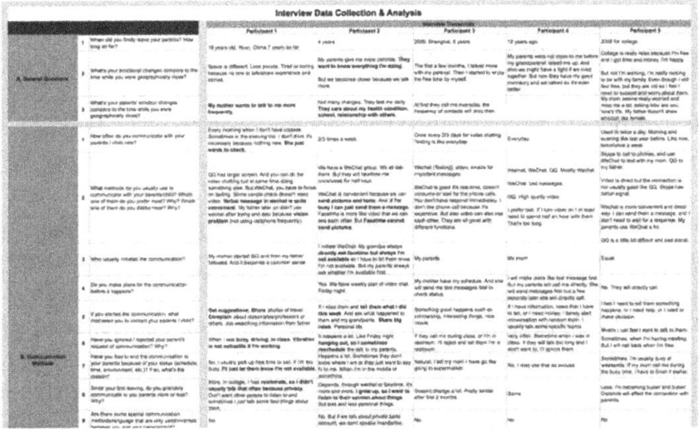

Fig. 1. Data analysis of semi-structured interviews with empty nest families

After integrating our findings from the literature review, existing technologies analyses, and user interview studies, we conclude our design objectives as follows:

- The system should *amplify the communication and connection* between empty nest parents and their children. Existing technologies have provided enough synchronous communication. Instead of reproducing the experience from the current tools, we want to focus on rebuilding the connection, implying the presence, increasing the emotional bond, and maintaining their overall connection.
- The interaction with the system should be *effortless*. The system can collect the data and learn the user's behavior patterns without inputting information manually. For example, through the smartphone's GPS, calendar, audio sensors, and motion sensors, the system would identify the user's location and roughly what the user is doing. Users' relative status and availability would be estimated and displayed.
- *Privacy* is one indispensable consideration in this design. The young adult wants the parents to know his/her availability but not everything in his/her life. The system can track lots of detailed data and activities, such as location, routine, personal events, etc. However, it does not display them directly to the other side. Instead, the data will be generalized into a relatively abstract visual display.

- The system should *share the information in an ambient approach*. Ambient information displays provide an alternate method of displaying information that does not require the constant attention of the user [20]. These displays may be of many forms such as lights, sounds, and physical objects. We choose to employ the ambient display as the primary communication method since the non-intrusive information it provides is suitable for settings of family connection.
- The system should display the information in a *straightforward and efficient* way. The user can read the information at a glance. Ambient information display indicates the information in general, simplified visual patterns rather than overwhelming texts. Because it is in real-time, users efficiently understand the information through just one glance. However, whether or not users pay attention to the information is voluntary.

4   Iterative Concept Development

The agile software development method has become a new trend to deliver faster, better, and cheaper solutions in the software engineering circles for decades [21]. Williams and Cockburn [22] argue that agile development is "about feedback and change," that agile methodologies are developed to "embrace, rather than reject, higher rates of change." We started to employ the method in the process of designing a repository to support authoring learning objects since 2008 [23]. The agile development method was introduced to this project for engaging potential users in the design process and adjusting the design on the way to maintain the match between user requirements and system design. During all the design stages, we show the new system structure and design ideas to the five families of participants and gather their feedbacks on the way. Based on the design objectives, we started sketching initial design ideas. In this section, we want to report three major iterations during the concept development process.

4.1   Round One

Figure 2 shows the illustration of system structure in the first round. There are two sides A & B to note the users on the two sides: the young adult and his/her parents. The system can collect the data such as calendar and GPS location from A's smartphone, analyze and calculate A's availability and physical location, and transfer into an ambient display to Side B. We sketched different possibilities of the ambient display. For example, right image in Fig. 2 shows A's availability through a circular stream graph. The center text shows the current location and the width of stream hint how busy A is. The display can be on the smartphone or a digital display on of the appliances in the kitchen or furniture in the living room. However, such an abstract screen display is neither exciting nor innovative. Some interview participants also expressed that the stream graph visualization is difficult to read and understand.

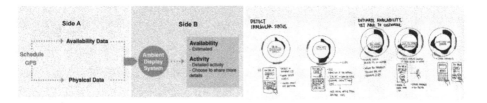

Fig. 2. Round one: system structure and one of the design ideas

4.2 Round Two

In the second round of concept development, we tried to introduce new elements to both the Side A (child data collection) and Side B (information display for the parents). On the one hand, we considered to incorporate a biosensor to collect emotional data and enrich the information about Side A. On the other hand; we proposed to present two layers of information in the ambient display system. At the first layer, only the general condition of A (positive/negative emotion) and essential status (busy, sleeping, entertaining, driving) would be displayed as a pattern. The vagueness of the information to maintain the privacy. If the display pattern looks regular from side B, parents know the child has a safe and ordinary day, the display will be merged into the surroundings. When any unusual patterns shows up from the display, parents can get alert and request more detailed data from Side A. Based on such a system structure (Fig. 3), we explored several ideas using different physical metaphors and patterns to indicate various emotional and availability status. The potential physical metaphors range from a lamp, a vase, a water bottle to a pen (Fig. 4).

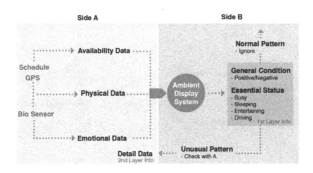

Fig. 3. Round two: system structure

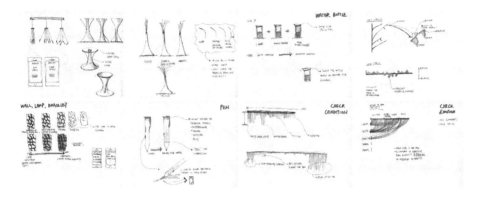

Fig. 4. Round two: design concepts of physical metaphors and display patterns

4.3   Round Three

The agile development methods [22] helped us to collect feedbacks and input from potential users and design experts quickly and led to a more refined system structure in round 3. Emotional data of Side A was eliminated based on potential users' choice. The system will only Side A's availability data and physical data from the calendar and GPS detection. Correspondingly, the availability status and an essential status of Side A would be showed to Side B through the ambient display system. The system would analyze an estimated availability (free to talk) through Side A's current schedule or location. Furthermore, side A can share a clear availability to Side B. Apart from the availability, only four essential statuses of A would be displayed in consideration of privacy (Fig. 5).

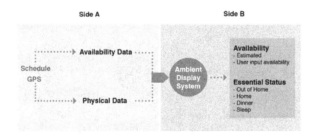

Fig. 5. Round three: system structure

Based on the 3rd round system structure, we proposed a new group of ideas to explore the possible experiences of carrying the ambient communication device. For example, the portable board concept (left image in Fig. 6) uses a mobile device to collect data and display the status through patterns on the physical screens. To imitate the analog of the family circle, the tangent rings model (right images in Fig. 6) is a representation concept using the location interactions between a larger ring (e.g. parents) and several small rings (e.g. children) to indicate the availability status in one family. These concepts have suggested more ambient representations than the previous two rounds. However, we are not confident if these concepts are intuitive enough that can enhance the bond between empty nest parents and children.

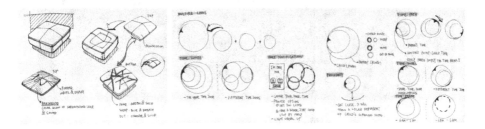

Fig. 6. Round three: design concepts

5   Prototype Development and Usability Testing

5.1   Integration of Family Dining Experience

The design solutions from previous three rounds of iteration focused on ambient information design to build up the information exchange. According to design experts' feedbacks, it is a very creative solution to build the communication through ambient information design. However, it only fulfills one of the design objectives we set up. The overall goal is to amplify the emotional bond between empty nest parents and children who are living in long distance. Thus, we started another round of interview to investigate what the actual bonding among family members is. Several of our participants mentioned their memories of dining together, and some described some details, which drew our attention to the family dining experience. Everywhere around the world, it is nearly the most common and an essential activity for all the family members to sit together and enjoy the dinner after a busy day. During the dinner time, family members chatted about what they met and heard, how they felt, and what they think during the daytime. That is the moment they can feel the bond noticeably. However, dining activity is a lost experience for empty nest parents and their children. We decided to virtually indicate the family members' presence and rebuild the dining experience.

5.2   The High Fidelity Prototype System FAMILINK

FAMILINK consists of a hologram projector and a phone app as the system setting that provides the cohesive communication experience. The hologram projector is suggested to place on the edge of a dining table to project dining pattern. Figure 7 indicates the system configuration and setting presented by a conceptual framework.

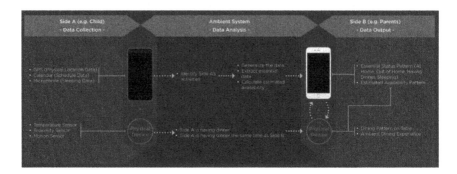

Fig. 7. Conceptual framework

Both of side A (child) and side B (parents) have the correlating hologram projector easily paired to the phone App. On A's side, they are used for data collection. In A's phone, the embedded GPS collects the physical location data, and the calendar provides schedule data and microphone gather the sleeping data. The hologram projector detects the dining activity through a temperature sensor, proximity sensor, and motion sensor. Even though the system can collect all of the detailed information from A, it will not transfer it directly to B. Instead, FAMILINK will extract critical status (out of the home, being home, having dinner and sleeping) from the data, estimate availability and dining activity as fuzzy ambient patterns. Thus, on Side B, the phone and hologram projector will display the abstracted visual patterns.

The core system of the app is "smart" enough to identify the user's behavior. For an instance, if the GPS detects A is at a school department building, or the calendar shows A is having a class, the app presents that A is busy and unavailable to talk. If the GPS detects A is in a park, and the calendar shows a blank slot, the app knows A is possibly in a high availability to chat. Thus, the availability status is estimated and calculated in the smart system through multiple resources. Regarding the essential statuses, it also relies on the GPS, sensors and pre-input home address to identify if A is at home, out of the home, sleeping or having dinner. Other than the availability and four essential statuses, none of other information would be sent to B for privacy consideration.

5.3   Physical Hologram Projector

In the physical design of the hologram projector (Fig. 8), there are three key components. The top and bottom shells are the primary displays of the holograms to indicate the status. The middle part incorporates functional portions such as LED indicator, power button, and heat dissipation grids. Proximity, motion and temperature sensors are embedded inside to detect the dining activities. A mini projector on the outside would project dining patterns on the dining table. Two hologram projectors are facing up and down inside to project hologram patterns.

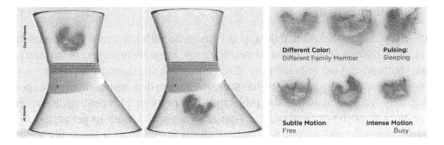

Fig. 8. Hologram projector design and essential status display patterns

The right image of Fig. 8 shows the ambient hologram patterns. Each pattern with identifying color code represents individual family members. Fluid motions are used to indicate the status information. The dynamicity of the pattern correlates to the family member's estimated availability. The pattern will pulse with breathing rhythm to show that A is sleeping. The sleeping status is detected by analyzing the breathing data through the microphone of A's phone. Estimated availability would be analyzed and calculated through multiple factors altogether intelligently, such as schedule, location, motion, etc. Then the availability will also be indicated through the dynamicity of the pattern. For example, if A is relatively free, B will see a slow and subtle motion on the pattern. If A is relatively busy, B will see a fast changing motion. The overall pattern appearance is fluid and continuous. As a matter of fact, the dynamicity of the pattern doesn't indicate the very accurate information. However, the consideration of the pattern dynamicity is to demonstrate a lively entity to remind B of the A's presence.

Having dinner status is displayed through the projection on the dining table to rebuild the shared dining experience. If A is having a dinner, A's projector detects his/her dining activity. And the data is analyzed and transfer to B. On B's dining table; the projector projects a dining pattern on the edge of the table in the corresponding color, which is from tracking A's dining activity. If by any chance, B is having dinner at the same time of A. The white dining pattern projected by B's projector starts to track B's dining activity. Then dining patterns from the two sides begin to merge gradually (Fig. 9). The overall dining experience not only strongly implies the presence of A, but also arouses the emotional bond and intimacy. Mentally the connection of A and B will be rebuilt and get amplified under the long-distance situation.

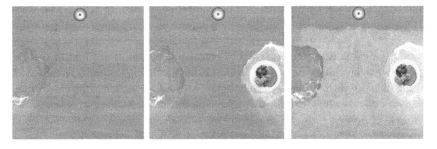

Fig. 9. Dining status and experience through projection

5.4 App Interface Design

The interface design of FAMLINK app is consistent with hologram projector setting and hologram pattern design. In the connection page, there are two areas in the interface: at home (bottom) and out of home (top). Such a location arrangement is consistent with the hologram project design. The app has the same pattern demonstration of out of home, at home and sleeping status as the projector. The purpose of repeating the ambient display on both of the project and the App is to allow the users to get access to the information anytime and anywhere. The projector is mainly used at home where dining activity would happen, while the phone App is in a portable environment. Secondly, having dinner status on the App displays as a fluid dining pattern behind the status pattern. When the user taps the pattern on the App, it will jump to a page with contact shortcuts including phone call, video call and messaging, which are synced to the corresponding apps (Fig. 10).

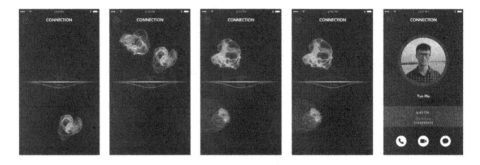

Fig. 10. Interfaces of connection menu

5.5 User Assessments in a Gallery Settings

FAMILINK design was exhibited at the Patti and Rusty Ruff Gallery for one week (Fig. 11). The topic of the exhibition is "Stay Connected in an Ambient Way." Instructional posters are for demonstrating the development of system structure and design concepts. Aside from the posters, three prototypes indicate the work scenario and user experience of the system. A video to introduce the prototype of the mobile App and pattern design was projected to the wall. The hologram prototype through an iPad and pyramid reflection rack were set up on a pedestal (bottom images in Fig. 11). We also moke up a dining environment with the dining pattern through a projection on the dining table.

During the exhibition week, audience were invited to sit at one end of the dining table, looking at the video demonstration, observing the flowing patterns on the tabletop, and filling up a survey to provide their thoughts. Most of the audience are undergraduate or graduate students who are living away from their parents. By the end of the show, we were able to collect 67 pages of survey answers. Here are some insights we concluded from these notes. People who appreciated the design mentioned that:

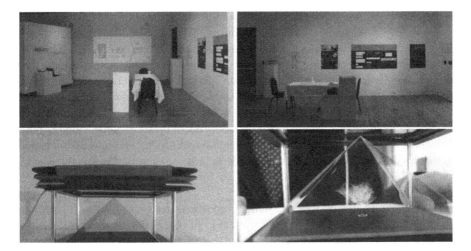

Fig. 11. Photos of final exhibition settings

- Ambient patterns are useful to strengthen the emotional bond with the loved ones. Their merging motion during the dining experience makes the connection closer.
- The ambient pattern would arouse some diverse emotions such as fulfillment, spiritual, contemplative, happy, sad, and relieved. This feeling relates to different family members.
- Ambient information design is a unique experience used in communication between family members in long distance situation. It is more about the feeling and emotion rather than direct verbal communication.
- This design could be used in any relationships that are in long distance situation, such as a couple or a pair of good friends.

  However, there are also some negative feedback and suggestions:

- More information on another side could be displayed according to users' needs. Otherwise, the patterns may also arouse sadness, anxiety and afraid.
- Users could customize the pattern appearance as a preference instead of "accepting the appearance objectively."
- Lots of college students do not always "sit down" to have a formal dinner. The design could be tailored to accommodate such a condition.

6   Conclusion

Ambient information design is a method that contributes to a subtle and non-intrusive digital experience. Although new technology and methods have been developed for enriching communication, visual representations through ambient patterns have never been explored in the context of long-distance communication. This communication could be non-verbal, asynchronous, and ambient. Knowing each other's status through an at-a-glance display redefines a new way to communicate. Our study aims to push the boundaries of how ambient communication amplify the connection and emotional bond between empty nest parents and their children. We employed an iterative design approach and agile software development method to ensure the quality, developing the system structures, and polishing the design outcomes based on potential users' feedbacks. A mobile application and a hologram projector construct a cohesive system FAMILINK, in which sensor collected data were abstracted into an ambient hologram display and projection. The first level interaction focuses on at-a-glance display of the fuzzy and essential status of another side including out of home, at home, having dinner, and sleeping statuses. The second level interaction focuses on creating a dining experience that implies the presence of another side to increase the emotional bond. The use of ambient information as the design solution for empty nest phenomena is a bold, innovative experiment.

We will continue the current research in three directions: (1) consider the feedback from exhibition audience and tailor the system to fit other kinds of users. (2) develop and testify a proper evaluation framework to assess ambient information system design, and (3) introduce and integrate more ambient design approaches in other projects to explore the potential domain.

References

1. You, K.S., Lee, H.: The physical, mental, and emotional health of older people who are living alone or with relatives. Arch. Psychiatr. Nurs. **20**(4), 193–201 (2006)
2. Fischer, C.S., Hout, M.: Century of Difference: How America Changed in the Last One Hundred Years. Russell Sage Foundation, New York (2006)
3. Raup, J.L., Myers, J.E.: The empty nest syndrome: myth or reality. J. Couns. Dev. **68**(2), 180–183 (1989)
4. Wong, J.W.E.: 'So that she feels a part of my life': how international students connect to home through digital media technologies. In: Tran, L.T., Gomes, C. (eds.) International Student Connectedness and Identity. CSTE, vol. 6, pp. 115–135. Springer, Singapore (2017). doi:10.1007/978-981-10-2601-0_7
5. Rodríguez, M.D., Gonzalez, V.M., Favela, J., Santana, P.C.: Home-based communication system for older adults and their remote family. Comput. Hum. Behav. **25**(3), 609–618 (2009)
6. Wang, J., Zhao, X.: Empty nest syndrome in China. Int. J. Soc. Psychiatry **58**(1), 110 (2011)
7. Liu, L.-J., Guo, Q.: Life satisfaction in a sample of empty-nest elderly: a survey in the rural area of a mountainous county in China. Qual. Life Res. **17**(6), 823 (2008)
8. Tollmar, K., Persson, J.: Understanding remote presence. In: Proceedings of the Second Nordic Conference on Human-Computer Interaction, pp. 41–50 (2002)
9. Thurber, C.A., Walton, E.A.: Homesickness and adjustment in university students. J. Am. Coll. Health **60**(5), 415–419 (2012)
10. Johnson, L.R., Sandhu, D.S.: Isolation, adjustment, and acculturation issues of international students: intervention strategies for counselors. In: Handb. Couns. Int. Stud. U. S., pp. 13–35 (2007)
11. Thurber, C.A.: The experience and expression of homesickness in preadolescent and adolescent boys. Child Dev. **66**(4), 1162–1178 (1995)
12. Tochkov, K., Levine, L., Sanaka, A.: Variation in the prediction of cross-cultural adjustment by Asian-Indian students in the United States. Coll. Stud. J. **44**(3), 677–689 (2010)

13. Tavakoli, S., Lumley, M.A., Hijazi, A.M., Slavin-Spenny, O.M., Parris, G.P.: Effects of assertiveness training and expressive writing on acculturative stress in international students: a randomized trial. J. Couns. Psychol. **56**(4), 590 (2009)

14. Constantine, M.G., Okazaki, S., Utsey, S.O.: Self-concealment, social self-efficacy, acculturative stress, and depression in African, Asian, and Latin American international college students. Am. J. Orthopsychiatry **74**(3), 230 (2004)

15. Wang, C.-C.D., Mallinckrodt, B.: Acculturation, attachment, and psychosocial adjustment of Chinese/Taiwanese international students. J. Couns. Psychol. **53**(4), 422 (2006)

16. Hyun, J., Quinn, B., Madon, T., Lustig, S.: Mental health need, awareness, and use of counseling services among international graduate students. J. Am. Coll. Health **56**(2), 109–118 (2007)

17. Wu, Z.-Q., Sun, L., Sun, Y.-H., Zhang, X.-J., Tao, F., Cui, G.-H.: Correlation between loneliness and social relationship among empty nest elderly in Anhui rural area, China. Aging Ment. Health **14**(1), 108–112 (2010)

18. Yarosh, S., Tang, A., Mokashi, S., Abowd, G.D.: Almost touching: parent-child remote communication using the sharetable system. In: Proceedings of the 2013 Conference on Computer Supported Cooperative Work, pp. 181–192 (2013)

19. Williamson, C.: Good night lamp: a family of house-shaped lamps. Design Milk, 05 February 2013. http://design-milk.com/good-night-lamp-a-family-of-house-shaped-lamps/. Accessed 03 Feb 2017

20. Jones, P.R.: Ambient information display. Citeseer (2007)

21. Dybå, T., Dingsøyr, T.: Empirical studies of agile software development: a systematic review. Inf. Softw. Technol. **50**(9–10), 833–859 (2008)

22. Williams, L., Cockburn, A.: Guest editors' introduction: agile software development: it's about feedback and change. Computer **36**(6), 39–43 (2003)

23. Qian, Z.C., Chen, Y.V., Woodbury, R.F.: Developing a simple repository to support authoring learning objects. Int. J. Adv. Media Commun. **2**(2), 154–173 (2008)

Breath Is to Be Perceived - Breathing Signal Sharing Involved in Remote Emotional Communication

Xiaotian Sun[✉] and Kiyoshi Tomimatsu

Kyushu University, Fukuoka, Japan
ginasun@foxmail.com

Abstract. In the city life with increasingly advanced technology, sociality tends to be more subtle. Although people, who have remote interpersonal intimacy, can watch or hear from each other, they cannot feel the real emotions from the other party. Especially, breath means existence in intimacy, and it is conductive to soothing emotion. This paper proposed a pair of interactive breathing sofa systems to communicate with each partner's breath tempo in real time. Also, the shared semi-virtual space and telepresence are established to enhance the emotional exchange and resonance in long-distance relationship. Each sofa can measure the user's breathing tempo and send it to the partner's sofa. In addition to strengthening emotional communication of long-distance relationship, the installation aims to design and realize the enhancement of remote emotional interaction, bio-signals communication, telepresence, and telepathy of ExtraSensory Perception.

Keywords: HCI · Bio-sensing and emotional communication · Breath control · Telematic breathing · Interactive media art · Sensors

1 Introduction

Sociality is increasingly subtle in people's daily life. People receive information and even acquire the sense of presence and accompany through communication. Although people, who have remote interpersonal intimacy, can watch or hear from each other, they cannot feel the real emotions from the other party. Especially, breath means existence in intimacy, and it is conductive to soothing emotion. Hence, we intended to study the feel of simple contentment, warmth and togetherness from the other party in a long distance, and to build an emotional comfort connection for the long-distance communication. Afterwards, a pair of sofas were designed to communicate with each other's breath tempo in real time. The goal of my work is to build virtual hyper-sensory experiences through biological breaths to enhance long-range intimate emotional communication.

2 Related Work

The distance communication by biological signal to promote the empathy experience of affinity was begun to study and explore in the 1960s. Sermon Paul created media art

© Springer International Publishing AG 2017
N. Streitz and P. Markopoulos (Eds.): DAPI 2017, LNCS 10291, pp. 472–481, 2017.
DOI: 10.1007/978-3-319-58697-7_35

"Telematic Dreaming" in 1992, it utilized the remote signal of the projector to carry out non-verbal personal communication through visual sense. The installation uses bed as a quiet and familiar place to establish a remote shared virtual space through communication so as to explore the subtle role of auditory sense, visual sense, and tactile sense in emotional communication [3]. With the continuous development of technology and the diversity of sensors, the multi-sensory digital experience is continuously explored. In the research field, masses of research deals with multiple interaction patterns at the same time under multi-modal interaction. The most typical interaction modality is gesture, voice and vision, but people generally ignore the hyper-sensory experience under the multi-sensory cooperation. "Lumitouch" is a pair of photo frames with remote interaction. When users touch one frame, the other one will light up. It takes visual stimulation as an emotional language of communication between loved ones [6]. "Mobile Feelings" is a mobile art project where users can send and receive body data over a wireless communication network. Through two wireless transmission devices that can be held in the palms, it can convey real-time heartbeat and respiratory data to users in long-distance touch [4]. The BreathingFrame is an interactive device based on the multisensory experience integrating visual sense, auditory sense, and tactile sense. Similarly, it also realizes the remote transmission of respiratory signals and communication through the physical inflatable airbag on the surface of the digital photo frame [1]. Media art 'The bed' is a bed as the carrier to provide intimate relations in the non-verbal communication installation. Bed as a familiar and safe place in the interaction through the visual vision and tactile sense to form a shared virtual space, connecting long-distance intimate relationship [5].

Except for olfaction and taste that have not yet been fully digitized for research, the sense utilized for digital interaction is still limited in the era of ubiquitous computing. At present, in addition to the full penetration of vision and hearing, touch technology interaction is the most common research point. It usually utilizes vibration, pressure, touch, stretch and other different mechanoreceptors to stimulate skin and enhance feelings. At the same time, the combination of telepresence and virtual space to enhance the hyper-sensory experience has become increasingly discussed.

3   Design of Breathing Sofa

Personally speaking, in psychology, people could exactly trust things or acquire the sense of presence only by strongly feeling the cognitive needs (seeing, hearing, smelling, tasting and touching) in terms of the sense of presence of both themselves and the others. Berkeley once pointed out that to be is to be perceived. The objective psychology believes that the signal we send out is proved to be real by receiving the others' response to our behaviors in the process of communication with other socialized people. Our sense of presence is based on the presence of our signal, thus helping us recognize the sense of presence and meet the needs of self identification [2]. Most kids tend to deliberately leave their footprints on the ground covered by snow. The kids identifying their movements acquire the sense of presence and prove their existence when they see their footprints on the ground. This is because the movement 'stepping' is our signal and the 'trace', in return, is the response from the outside world. It's not the movement we send signal but the others' active response that makes us feel the sense of presence. We acquire the sense of presence when recognizing our real signal actively commented by the others. From this perspective, people are looking forward to recognizing the sense of presence in emotional exchange. The sense of presence won't be felt without the interactive relationship.

For people who want to communicate, people want telepathy, which transcends language, text, body movements, and distance, without the need to deliver media, which is an extrasensory ability to communicate. If we regard the extrasensory perception as the senses of the senses that require the combined effects of the five senses, we may also quote the association of the senses (multi-sensory collaboration) proposed in Hara Design in Design [7]. People through the sense of experience, build awareness, Therefore, we decided to transfer association of the senses in distance.

Breath, as the physiological process promoting the gas exchange between organism and the outside world, not only features the information exchange, but also represents the presence of life. It occurs spontaneously all the time, and integrates the comprehensive function of the five senses to exchange information inside and outside the body. Therefore, we employ the perception of breath to enhance the sense of presence, satisfaction perceived and emotional resonance by people in remote communication. In this way, the communication and interactive relationship based on machines can be promoted.

Many previous experiments have proved that bio-signal sharing is conductive to the remote interpersonal intimacy. At present, research on the bio-signals as a means of communication mainly focuses on breath sharing. Similarly, for users without distance barrier, breath signals can be utilized to observe the other party's emotional state and mode, and to feel the other party's responses. This fully shows the value of the communication and exchange of breath signals.

Compared with other bio-signals, the advantage of breath signals is that they can make the two parties unconsciously and willingly interact with each other. Thus the breath signals have been applied to the devices to game interface control, emotion soothing, and media art. Moreover, breath is not only a symbol of the life, but also closely related to emotional changes. However, breath signals as the remote communication media haven't been adequately studied.

3.1 Prototype

This paper proposed a pair of interactive breathing sofa system. Each sofa can measure the user's breathing tempo and then send it to the partner's sofa. Intuitive feeling of relaxed, comfortable and semi-wrapped state of the sofa serves as a "personal space" and a unique interface between people because it is a space that is shared physically with the whole bodies touch and is a common medium used by the general population and the sensory- impaired. When two sofa connected through the network remotely, they formed a semi-virtual shared space. In addition to strengthening emotional communication of remote intimacy, the goal of our study is to design and realize sense enhancement remote emotional interaction, bio-signals communication, telepresence and telepathy in extrasensory perception (Fig. 1).

Fig. 1. Users seating on breathing sofa, and interactive with each other.

3.2 Hardware

In the design process, the belt-type pressure breathing sensor was utilized to detect breath signals of the users' abdomens and connect with Arduino. The cylinder was controlled by the driver and speed controller. This cylinder repeatedly compressed a gasbag partially filled with air by the detected breathing signal rate. The sofa was composed of the other gasbag, and the two gasbags were connected by air change tube exchanged air in the process of repeated compression of stepper motor. Consequently, the expansion and contraction of the gasbags in the sofa with the breathing rate were realized. Thus users can feel the breathing rate and the gasbag in the sofa in a partially wrapped state to strength the feeling (Figs. 2 and 3).

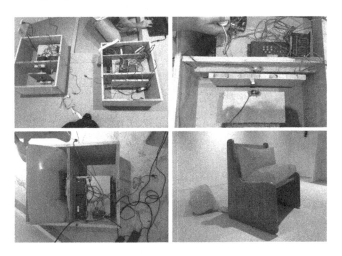

Fig. 2. Hardware

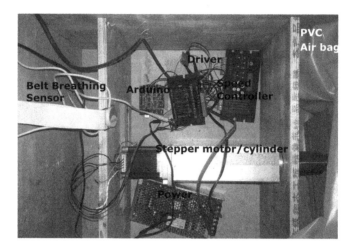

Fig. 3. Hardware

3.3 Communication

The WIFI Serial Server modules were equipped on the two sofas, respectively. The breathing sensor detected the breathing data and then realized the exchange in the cloud database by WIFI Serial Server module through the Internet. Thus one user can really feel the breath tempo of the other (Fig. 4).

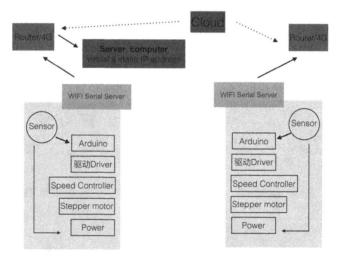

Fig. 4. Bidirectional communication diagram

4   Research Methods

4.1   User Study

We carried out an exploratory study to investigate the feasibility of Breathing Sofa for long-distance emotional experience. Our research direction is, in remote conditions, whether the emotional interaction, experience and communication can be enhanced through breath?

We selected 12 respondents in pairs, and divided them into six groups. We have chosen different genders, ages and relationships, including mother and child, couples, friends, grandchildren, and even strangers, so as to explore long-distance emotional experiences and interactions in a variety of relationships. The experiment was divided into four parts, namely, experimental information (personal information and relationship composition), emotion, experience and interaction. After recording the experimental information in the questionnaire, two people in the same group were in a separate room, sitting on the sofas with two breathing sensors(one for the installation, and the other concerted with a screen for testing breathing data) to watch a video (comedy, sensational or no emotion) in five minutes. Their emotions and breathing data were recorded. Then we began to experience the breathing dynamics of the other party, experience and guess the corresponding emotions and records. Five minutes after experiencing the other party's emotion, the result that whether one was affected by the mood of the other party was experienced and recorded. Also, whether the respiratory frequencies of both sides were gradually similar, and tended to calm? After 15 min, we had a five-minute interview. At last we compared the two results in one group to check the feasibility of Breathing Sofa, and classified the six research reports.

4.2   Findings

Based on the research result, there is no doubt that most participators could feel the existence of the other party and their emotional interaction through the breathing sofa system. Their views on the breathing sofa experience dramatically changed from doubt to expectation. Finally, they were willing to voluntarily sit on the sofa to share their breath, emotion and the quiet accompany with the others.

In the experiment, the breathing sensors tied on the user's abdomen and one connected with partner, the other one connected with computer. The test program detects a stream of the signal value of the intensity of respiratory pressure at each time node (per second) generated from pressure intensity between expiration and inspiration. When the user recorded a set of respiratory signals in the experiment, we mark the coordinate value signal and connected into line, made them into curve chart by taking the time and pressure signal as the axis, visualized the respiratory wave. It was compared the respiratory waves of users in the same group so as to get the conclusion evidently (Fig. 5).

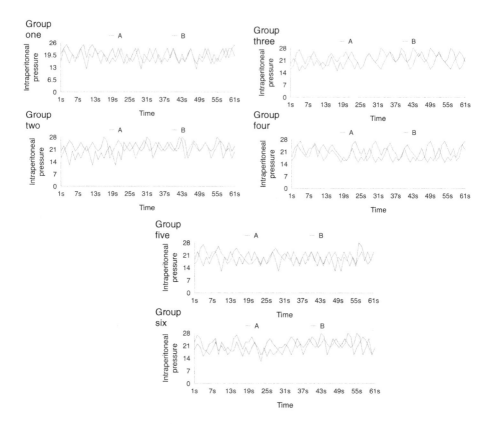

Fig. 5. Compare respiratory wave

Through experiments and interviews we divided the results into two parts. First, Emotions & Experience part: Whether the user can judge and feel the presence of the other party by breathing? Whether the user can guess through the installation and experience another user's emotions? Second, Interaction&Introspection: Whether the user can convey and communicate emotion through breathing? Whether the user can comfort the other party through this installation?

Emotions&Experience

Based on our observation of the interaction between the user and the Breathing sofa, we found that the first expectation was the immediate affective feedback. After wearing the respiratory sensor, visitors would feel the emotion and state of the other party, guess and immediately record. In the table, we compared the Emotions (user's own emotions) and the Experience (through the experience to guess the other's emotions), we found that at least eight people of experiments in the 12 people can accurately perceived the other party's emotion and state (Table 1).

Table 1. Experimental results

	Emotions (user's own emotions)	Experience (through the experience to guess the other's emotions)	Interaction (the feelings after interaction)
1A	Peaceful	Peaceful	Affected by the mood of the other party
1B	Happy	Peaceful	Affected by the mood of the other party
2A	Peaceful	Peaceful	Affected by the mood of the other party/Tend to calm
2B	Peaceful	Peaceful	Affected by the mood of the other party/Tend to calm
3A	Happy	Angry	Tend to calm
3B	Sad	Sad	Nothing to feel
4A	Peaceful	Depressed	Affected by the mood of the other party/Tend to calm
4B	Depressed	Peaceful	Affected by the mood of the other party/Tend to calm
5A	Depressed	Afraid	Nothing to feel
5B	Afraid	Peaceful	Nothing to feel
6A	Sad	Peaceful	Tend to calm
6B	Peaceful	Sad	Tend to calm

Interaction&Introspection

Also, as can be seen from the statistical data, four groups (group one, group two, group four, group six) of users could feel the convergence of their respiratory rate with the other users after interactive experience for a period of time, and both parties tended to calm. Also, as can be seen from the statistical data, four groups (group one, group two, group four, group six) of users could feel the convergence of their respiratory rate with the other users after interactive experience for a period of time, three groups (group two, group four, group six) parties tended to calm.

In the latter part of the curves of group one, group two, and group four can be clearly observed from the respiratory wave comparison chart, they are approaching the same. Indicating that their breathing frequency after a period of interaction time, respiratory frequency convergence. However, as a result of the unfamiliarity with the operation of the sensor, individuals' insensitivity to emotional breathing, and the sensor delay (such as data loss), users' accurate perception of the other party's emotion will be damaged sometimes. We believe that this dilemma can be solved by upgrading the sensor, optimizing the data processing algorithms, and the user's more practice feedback.

We obtained the positive answers, this proved that the Breathing sofa can carry out non-verbal communication and non-visual communication through unconscious breathing. First of all, the sofa as a carrier has provided the user with a relaxed semi-enclosed space. When the users experienced in relax, the can feel the actual presence and state of the other party. After a period of interaction, they can also feel the same embrace and comfort as in an intimate relationship. The respondent also said that he enjoyed the feeling and process of slow emotional comfort. Therefore, our assumption is reasonable. The user is not only the sensor, but also the receiver. In the distance, by enhancing the experience, the users are influenced psychologically and physically, and thus they change into a new way of communication. This is our purpose. In the using process, the device is not equipped with sophisticated sensors and operating interface, and users have no opportunity to change or manipulate this process. Therefore, we come to the conclusions as follows:

- The transmission and simulation of breathing signals can promote human emotional communication
- Breathing signal can be a way to communicate human emotions
- Breathing signal may become a new way of perception and interaction
- Extrasensory interaction can provide a more convenient way for people with sensory impairments to communicate
- There is a tendency that interaction and machines will become increasingly disappear and ubiquitous (Fig. 6).

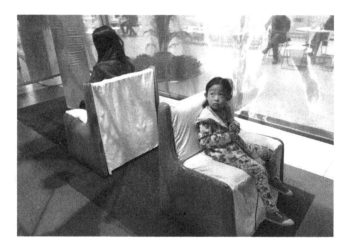

Fig. 6. Users seating on breathing sofa, and interactive with each other.

However, we also found many problems existing in the design and produce of the prototype. Firstly, the comfortableness needs to be improved or participators' comfortable experience will be affected. Secondly, in terms of the selection of materials, at the first stage we employed the wood and cloth commonly used in our daily life so as to avoid producing unfamiliar feelings to users compared to common home furnitures, thus cultivating the sense of presence and satisfaction by producing familiarity feeling and intimacy. Yet what we lack is the mystique and attraction. Therefore, we will make some changes in the selection of materials and promotion of fitness between body and sofa. Thirdly, hardware will also be improved because the cylinder presently used and the brake mode lead to its huge volume. Fourthly, the hysteresis and delay of signal won't be temporarily avoided in the process of remote transmission.

5   Conclusion

This research aims to create an installation and to study how the control of consciousness affects internal physiological process, and connects people with their own physiology through the datamation and informationization of breath. Breath information is stored and shared in remote transmission so as to explore the research and application of breath in enhanced experience of human-machine interaction. The future development will not be limited in daily communication. It can also realize remote communication between people with disabilities and realize emotional comfort and communication that are beyond life and death, time and space. Based on simple information transfer, users' emotions and feelings can be further improved so as to achieve better communication and interaction. On the one hand, users interact with the machine and the environment emotionally. On the other hand, they convey the machine to the role that coordinate and promote the emotional communication between users. In this way, the real existence and accurate transmission of biological signals will be further applied to the interactive design of affective computing.

References

1. Kim, J., Park, Y.W., Nam, T.J.: BreathingFrame: an inflatable frame for remote breath signal sharing. In: Tangible Embedded and Embodied Interactions, pp. 109–112 (2015)
2. Berkeley, G.A.: Treatise Concerning the Principles of Human Knowledge. Liberal Arts Press, New York (1957)
3. Sermon, P.: Telematic dreaming (1993)
4. Sommerer, C., Mignonneau, L.: Mobile Feelings– wireless communication of heartbeat and breath for mobile art. In: The Mobile Audience: Media Art & Mobile Tech, vol. 5, p. 269 (2003)
5. The Bed: A Medium for Intimate Communication, Chris Dodge, MIT Media Lab, Office E 15-351, 20 Ames Street, Cambridge, MA 02139 cdodge@media.mit.edu
6. Chang, A., Resner, B., Koerner, B., Wang, X.C., Ishii, H.: LumiTouch: an emotional communication device. In: Ext. Abstracts CHI 2001, pp. 313–314. ACM Press (2001)
7. Hara, K.: Designing Design. Lars Muller, Baden (2007)

Development and Evaluation of a Non-obtrusive Patient Monitoring System with Smart Patient Beds

Ruben van Dijk[1], Weifeng Liang[2], Biyong Zhang[3(✉)], and Jun Hu[1,4]

[1] Department of Industrial Design, Eindhoven University of Technology,
Eindhoven, The Netherlands
r.j.j.v.dijk@student.tue.nl
[2] Shengzhou Branch, The First Affiliated Hospital, Zhejiang University, Hangzhou, China
[3] BOBO Technology, Hangzhou, China
biyong.zhang@91ganlu.com
[4] School of Digital Media, Jiangnan University, Wuxi, China

Abstract. In Chinese hospitals, each patient is checked regularly during their night time. This happens to confirm that there are no emergency situations in which a patient is in need of immediate help. Because the regular checking can be very annoying for patients who are sleeping due to noise, we are looking for a solution to solve this problem using technology. The focus lies on non-obtrusive sensing technologies and on the social relation between patient and doctor. Two prototypes were developed, tested and evaluated on their usability to monitor patients from the central nurse station without disturbing them. The first prototype consists of a piezoelectric sensor with filtering circuit which measures the heartbeats. The second consists of a capacitive sensor capable of sensing the presence of a patient in the bed. Both sensors are placed under the mattress of the patient with as a result that they are not bothered while being monitored.

Keywords: Ballistocardiography · Capacitive proximity sensors · Monitoring · Patient-doctor relationship · Chinese hospitals

1 Introduction

In Chinese hospitals, there is a tension between patient and doctors [1, 2]. Patients experience long waiting lists, increasing out-of-pocket healthcare expenditure and the making of an appointment with a qualified doctor is difficult. That is the reason why patients want to make sure they receive good treatment once they are finally being treated. Due to this situation the patients raised awareness about their protective rights. However, the patients are lacking knowledge about the medical specialism of the doctors. On the other side the doctors are not satisfied with their jobs due to low income, long working hours and the feeling that they are not appreciated by the patients and society. But the management in Chinese hospitals is not always professional. Rules and regulations cannot be executed strictly. The levels of professionality of the Chinese doctors vary. This results in the making of mistakes by lower skilled or experienced doctors causing the loss of trust of the patients in the Chinese doctors [3]. The tension

© Springer International Publishing AG 2017
N. Streitz and P. Markopoulos (Eds.): DAPI 2017, LNCS 10291, pp. 482–490, 2017.
DOI: 10.1007/978-3-319-58697-7_36

between patient and doctor sometimes even results in violent conflicts [4]. Also it occurs that patients sue the hospital because they think they are not treated well. The Chinese hospitals want to avoid this. Therefore, there is a regulation in Chinese hospitals in which every patient has to be checked by a nurse regularly during the night, and normally the regular check happens every one hour or two hours. In this routine, the medical staff makes sure there are no emergency situations to avoid the blame in case a patient doesn't receive first aid in time. However, these actions can be annoying for the patients who are trying to sleep.

Except for the traditional regular checking solution, some other ways by using technology have been proposed as well. Zephyr BT is a kind of wearable sensor which can be used to extract the heart rate information of a patient [5]. Such kind of wearable sensors do satisfy the requirements of patient monitoring. However wearable devices reduce the comfort of sleeping based on the current applicable technology. Video Surveillance is another kind of popular solution, but the security and privacy concerns hinder the deployment [6]. Using Kinect Signature somehow improves the video surveillance solution technically [7]. The security and privacy concerns are not really overcome. Furthermore, the cost of the Kinect Signature is another weak point.

We turned this problem into a design opportunity to explore a low cost, non-disturbing and emotional secure solution. We wondered if non-obtrusive monitoring technology could be used to keep track of the patients heart rate and respiration, to make sure everything is OK without waking them in their night-time. In this way the hospital can provide better care for their patients and reduce the workload. This is what the Chinese hospitals are aiming for [8]. One important design challenge is the social part in this project: how to communicate to the patient that they are being monitored? The patient needs to have the feeling that he or she is taken care of and should trust the system. The method used in this design project is iterative design.

Related work includes the investigating of low-cost wireless occupancy sensors for beds [9]. In this research two solutions to sense presence of people in beds are compared: capacitive proximity sensors and accelerometers. Also the sleep trackers of the company Emfit are related to this project [10]. The company uses ballistocardiography as a method to sense heart beats [11] and calculate the BPM to tell the user something about their sleep quality. The sensor is placed under the mattress so there is no contact with the patient.

2   System Design

The designed system is a distributed system with interfaces [16, 17] on several heterogeneous platforms. The system consists of smart patient beds which are wirelessly connected to the computers at the nurse stations. The smart patient beds contain:

1. a piezoelectric sensor to measure the heart rate of the patient
2. a capacitive sensor to measure the presence of a patient in the bed
3. a feedback mechanism to communicate to the patient that he or she is being monitored (still to be designed)

The data from these sensors is sent wirelessly to the central nurse station. This information will be shown in the software which nurses are currently using. The nurses will receive a warning message on their desktop and mobile device when an abnormal situation is detected by the software e.g. the situation in which presence in the bed but no heartbeat is detected. In this way the nurses know when they should visit the patient and take action if needed (Fig. 1).

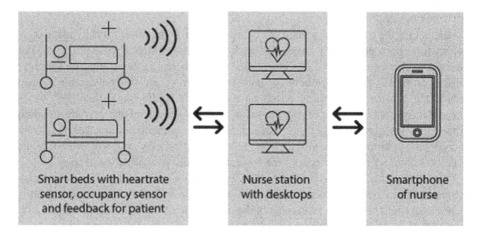

Fig. 1. Connection of smart devices in the system

2.1 Heart Rate Sensor

To measure the heartbeat of the patient lying in the bed the method ballistocardiography is used. In this method the ballistic forces of the heart are measured with a sensitive sensor which is able to capture the smallest vibrations. In this project the piezoelectric film of Emfit is used as the sensor. The sensor is placed under the mattress of the hospital bed. When the patient lies on the bed, the vibrations generated by his or her beating heart travel through the mattress to the piezoelectric sensor. At every heart beat the sensor is pressed very gently which generates a small voltage. This voltage can be measured with an Arduino Uno microcontroller by reading the input on the connected analog port.

Because the patient also makes other movements like breathing (small movements) and turning around (big movements) the signal needs to be filtered. This can be achieved with an electronic filtering circuit [12] and by filtering digitally. A prototype was designed to amplify the signal and filter frequencies below 1 Hz and higher than 5 Hz. Also a 16-bit Analog to Digital converter was added to the circuit in order to read the signal in a higher resolution. The components were soldered on perfboard in such a way that the board could be mounted on the Arduino Uno like a "shield" (Fig. 2).

Fig. 2. Prototype shield for Arduino Uno containing filtering circuit and 16 Bit Analog to Digital Converter (ADC) for higher signal resolution.

2.2 Occupancy Sensor

In order to know if a patient is in the bed or outside the bed another sensor is needed. A possible situation is that the patient is in the bed but the heart has stopped beating. In this case the nurses can be warned. Like discussed we focus on non-obtrusive sensor technologies. Capacitive proximity sensing is a suitable technology in this situation. Like the piezoelectric sensor, it can be placed under the mattress. Because the human

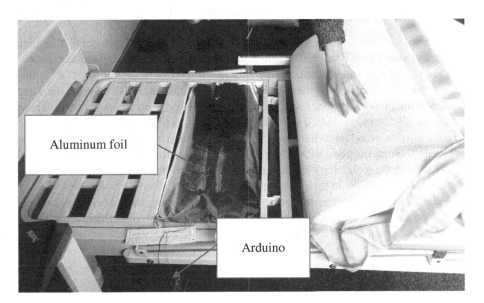

Fig. 3. Capacitive sensor experiment setup with aluminum foil over the full width of the hospital bed functioning as sensor.

body can hold an electrical charge, the presence of the human body in or near the bed can be sensed. There is no need for direct contact between the sensor and the human body. In this project aluminum foil is used as the capacitive sensor. A large surface was used for a bigger sensing range. The sensor was connected to a circuit with a resistor and to the analog port of the Arduino [13]. By playing with the resistor value the sensitivity of the sensor could be adapted (Fig. 3).

3   Evaluation

Both the heart rate sensor and capacitive sensor were tested and evaluated in the International SmartHealth Lab in Hangzhou. Also the heart rate sensor was demonstrated with real time output in The First Affiliated Hospital, Zhejiang University, Shengzhou Branch.

3.1   Heart Rate Sensor

The heart beat signal generated by the piezoelectric sensor was read with the Arduino. These values were visualized using a Processing code [14] which was developed for finger or ear pulse sensors. This code is also capable of calculating the BPM and IBI when using these sensors. Using the piezoelectric sensor without adapting the code will generate false values because the code is not calibrated for this sensor. But the plotted graph could show the typical heart peaks of a ballistocardiogram. Compared to a finger or ear sensor, the signal coming from a piezoelectric sensor contains more noise which has to be filtered. An algorithm designed to generate the BPM out of a signal coming from a piezoelectric sensor should be used instead. These algorithms already exist (Fig. 4).

The heart rate sensor was also demonstrated in The First Affiliated Hospital, Zhejiang University, Shengzhou Branch. The sensor was placed under the mattress of the hospital bed. The output was visualized using the built in Arduino serial plotter function. In this way the doctors could see the measured heat beats in real time. Also commercial sleep trackers with piezoelectric sensors with real time BPM were demonstrated. These trackers needed an interval of 10 s to calculate the BPM. A professional heart beat sensor from the hospital which uses the blood volume that flows through the fingertip as input was used to compare the two BPMs. The difference ranged from 0 to 5 beats. The hospital is interested in the technology but said the BPM needs to be more accurate before they would use such systems in their hospitals.

Because the piezoelectric sensor is so thin, a person lying on the bed does not feel the difference with the normal situation. Because there is no direct contact with the patient this solution is also hygienic (Fig. 5).

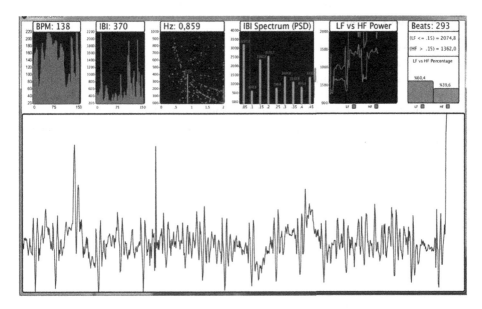

Fig. 4. Ballistocardiogram (BCG) of data processed by Arduino and visualized in Processing.

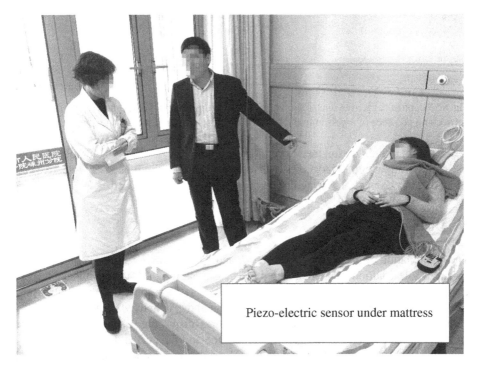

Piezo-electric sensor under mattress

Fig. 5. The prototype is tested and demonstrated to the doctors in The First Affiliated Hospital, Zhejiang University, Shengzhou Branch.

3.2 Occupancy Sensor

The capacitive sensor was only tested in the laboratory and not demonstrated in the hospital yet. Like shown in Fig. 6, the presence of a human body could be sensed clearly. Because the experimental Arduino setup was connected with a USB-cable to the laptop, the laptop itself functioned as a sensor as well. What also has to be taken into account is the hospital bed itself, because it built from metal parts. This influences the capacitance. It is important to calibrate the sensor first when it is placed in the bed before putting a patient in the bed.

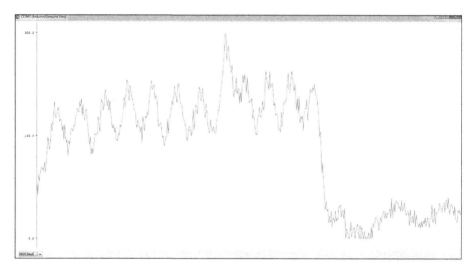

Fig. 6. Graph of capacitive sensor output made with Arduino serial plotter showing the difference between no presence of a person in the bed (left) and presence of a patient in the bed (right).

Instead of aluminum foil the next prototype could be made of a more durable material like copper foil, integrated together with the piezoelectric film. It needs a protective and strengthening layer of plastic and/or foam because it is easily folded.

4 Discussion

The combination of the piezoelectric sensor and the capacitive sensor is considered as an applicable solution for patient monitoring. Comparing with the inefficient regular checking, our solution provides a user-friendly way to reconstruct the relationship between nurses and patients. The nurses only visit and give help when the patients need help during the night time, without any redundant disturbing. In the meanwhile, the condition of the patients is monitored in real time and the nurses don't need to worry about the missing of any emergencies. Therefore, the responsibility of nurses is turned into the functionality of the monitoring system, it contributes to the improvement of the relationship between patients and nurses.

What still is missing is the feedback loop for the patient being monitored. The patients need to have the feeling that they are being monitored from a distance and trust that the nurses will visit them when they are in need of help. This could be a light or display next to the patients bed visualizing the sensed data e.g. in or out the bed, but this is just a simple example. The final solution for this situation still has to be designed and evaluated. The design will be evaluated with qualitative research by doing user test in which test subjects will lie in a hospital bed experiencing the feedback mechanism. After their experience they will be asked questions. Once a suitable design is found the design can be tested and evaluated in a pilot study in the hospital setting in China.

Like discussed in the chapter evaluation, the hospital is interested in the system. However, the demonstrated BPM calculating algorithm needs to be more accurate before they would use such systems in their hospitals. Qualified algorithms of BPM calculation already exist and are in practice. Future work includes the analysis and improvement of Heart Rate Variability (HRV)derived from BCG. Many diseases can be observed by analyzing HRV. In this case, the system could assist the nurses, especially to prevent critical situations. The same system or technology could also be used in retirement homes or used by elderly people living alone.

5   Conclusion

We presented and evaluated a non-obtrusive patient monitor system which could be used in Chinese hospitals. The system consists of a piezoelectric sensor to measure heart rate, a capacitive proximity sensor to measure presence of the patient in the bed and a feedback mechanism for the patient to communicate that they are being monitored. We conclude that ballistocardiography and capacitive proximity sensing are usable technologies to use in this context. The feedback mechanism still needs to be designed and evaluated in future work. Especially the effect on the patient-doctor relationship needs to be taken into account. "In the era of social networking and computing, things and people are more and more interconnected, giving rise to not only new opportunities but also new challenges in designing new products that are networked, and services that are adaptive to their human users and context aware in their physical and social environments" [15]. The effects on the social trust of this system is yet to be investigated.

References

1. Zhang, X., Sleeboom-Faulkner, M.: Tensions between medical professionals and patients in mainland China. Camb. Q. Healthc. Ethics **20**, 458–465 (2011)
2. He, A.J.: The doctor-patient relationship, defensive medicine and overprescription in Chinese public hospitals: evidence from a cross-sectional survey in Shenzhen city. Soc. Sci. Med. **123**, 64–71 (2014)
3. Tian, F., Han, C., Fu, M.: Several Impairing Factors and Countermeasures on the Harmonious Doctor- patient Relationship (2006)
4. Wu, D., Wang, Y., Lam, K.F., Hesketh, T.: Health system reforms, violence against doctors and job satisfaction in the medical profession: a cross-sectional survey in Zhejiang Province, Eastern China. BMJ Open **4**, e006431 (2014)

5. Kakria, P., Tripathi, N.K., Kitipawang, P.: A real-time health monitoring system for remote cardiac patients using smartphone and wearable sensors. Int. J. Telemed. Appl. **2015**, 1–11 (2015)

6. Braeken, A., Porambage, P., Gurtov, A., Ylianttila, M.: Secure and efficient reactive video surveillance for patient monitoring. Sensors **16**(1), 32 (2016)

7. Blumrosen, G., Miron, Y., Intrator, N., Plotnik, M.: A real-time kinect signature-based patient home monitoring system. Sensors **16**(11), 1965 (2016)

8. Jing, W., Otten, H., Sullivan, L., Lovell-Simons, L., Granek-Catarivas, M., Fritzsche, K.: Improving the doctor-patient relationship in China: the role of balint groups. Int. J. Psychiatry Med. **46**, 417–427 (2013)

9. Braun, A., Majewski, M., Wichert, R., Kuijper, A.: Investigating low-cost wireless occupancy sensors for beds. In: Streitz, N., Markopoulos, P. (eds.) DAPI 2016. LNCS, vol. 9749, pp. 26–34. Springer, Cham (2016). doi:10.1007/978-3-319-39862-4_3

10. Lekkala, J., Paajanen, M.: EMFi - new electret material for sensors and actuators. In: Proceedings of the International Symposium On Electrets, 1, pp. 743–746 (1999)

11. Parak, J.: Heart Rate Detection from Ballistocardiogram, pp. 1–5 (2012). Amber.Feld.Cvut.Cz

12. Karki, J.: Signal conditioning piezoelectric sensors. Sensors **48**, 1–6 (2000). Peterbrgh, NH

13. Badger, P.: Capacitive Sensing Library. http://playground.arduino.cc/Main/Capacitive SensorSignal

14. Dmainmon: Pulse Sensor Cardio Graph. https://github.com/dmainmon/Arduino-Pulse-Sensor-Amped-Cardio-Graph/tree/master/PulseSensorCardioGraph/Processing/CardioGraph

15. Hu, J.: Social things: design research on social computing. In: Rau, P.-L.P. (ed.) CCD 2016. LNCS, vol. 9741, pp. 79–88. Springer, Cham (2016). doi:10.1007/978-3-319-40093-8_9

16. Hu, J., Feijs, L.M.G.: An agent-based architecture for distributed interfaces and timed media in a storytelling application In: Presented at the 2nd International Joint Conference on Autonomous Agents and Multiagent Systems (AAMAS-03), Melbourne, Australia (2003)

17. Hu, J., Feijs, L.: An adaptive architecture for presenting interactive media onto distributed interfaces. In: Presented at the 21st IASTED International Conference on Applied Informatics (AI 2003), Innsbruck, Austria (2003)

Design of Internet Rehabilitation Service System with Individual Assessment Data for Autistic Children

Lie Zhang[1(✉)], Guobin Wang[2], Jiarui Wu[1], and Wei Wang[1]

[1] Department of Information Art and Design, Tsinghua University, Beijing 100084, China
zhlie@tsinghua.edu.cn, {wujiarui,ww}@ing4s.com
[2] Department of Environmental Art and Design, Beijing University of Technology,
Beijing 100124, China
06690@bjut.edu.cn

Abstract. As a subtype of pervasive development disorder, autism has unknown cause of disease and no completely rehabilitated cases to date. However, in the golden intervention period from 2 to 6 years old, scientific rehabilitation training may significantly improve the condition of the children patients. Therefore, in professional and timely initial assessment, diagnosis and continuous treatment, data continuity is of great importance to the rehabilitation service of autistic children. But, a lot of reasons such as shortage of professionals, irregular industry and limited coverage of rehabilitation institutions make professional and timely assessment and rehabilitation services not available to autistic children. In combination with the approach of designing an interactive service system, the application practice of the rehabilitation service system with individual assessment data of autistic children being the core in the internet environment was introduced in this article.

Keywords: Autism · Verbal behavior assessment · Rehabilitation training · Interactive design · Service design

1 Introduction

1.1 Background

Autistic disorder, also known as autism, is a subtype of pervasive development disorder. It is difficult for autistic patients inherently to establish normal emotional association with people in the surrounding environment, mainly featured by different levels of linguistic development disorder, interpersonal communication disorder, narrow interest and stark behavior mode. According to the Centers for Disease Control and Prevention, the incidence is 1/68. Based on our estimation, in China, there are more than autistic patients, including about 3 million children aged between 0–14 years old [1]. In view of great socioeconomic burden caused by autism has become a significant public health issue of common concern. Autism has unknown cause of disease and no completely rehabilitated cases to date. However, in the golden intervention period from 2 to 6 years old, scientific rehabilitation training may significantly improve the condition of the

N. Streitz and P. Markopoulos (Eds.): DAPI 2017, LNCS 10291, pp. 491–501, 2017.
DOI: 10.1007/978-3-319-58697-7_37

children patients. Therefore, in professional and timely initial assessment, diagnosis and continuous treatment, data continuity is of great importance to the rehabilitation service of autistic children. But, a lot of reasons such as great base of children patients, shortage of professionals, irregular industry and limited coverage of rehabilitation institutions make professional and timely assessment and rehabilitation services not available to autistic children.

New generation of internet has provided new development motives to social services, bringing about innovation in service mode. Unlike previous typical public benefit activity or charity donation, social innovation in the new era emphasizes the solution of social issues by utilizing new technological methods, innovative business mode, rigorous organizational behavior and people-centered service philosophy while realizing sustainable development of both the industry and all institutions.

1.2   Objectives

IngCare Project is just a social innovative project targeting initial assessment screening and rehabilitation data service under the guide of new technologies and concepts. By utilizing the internet platform, IngCare Project tries to establish a standardized, easy-to-use, far-reaching expert assessment and individual training data system which offers professional and efficient screening and treatment recommendations to all autistic children patients, including suspected people, in a timely manner, establish related Internet education and information service platforms on such basis, face with the pain points of the industry and reshape the industrial ecology through multi-discipline integrated innovation, thus rapidly improving the overall level of Chinese rehabilitation industry of autistic children and bringing health and happiness to autistic children and their families.

2   Status Quo and Related Studies

2.1   Related Domestic and International Studies About Autism

In 1943, Dr. Leo Kanner from US pioneered in offering the first autism case study in the world through clinical observation of 11 children [2]. After decades' in-depth research, a relatively mature rehabilitation theory system and approach in international community, such as TEACCH (Treatment and Education for Autistic and related Communication Handicapped Children), which was structured education carried out by Eric Schople from North Carolina, US in 1972, mainly for linguistic communication disorder among autistic children; ABA (Applied Behavior Analysis) is a branch system of psychology proposed and proofed through scientific experiment by Professor, B. F. Skinner, from psychology department, Harvard University at the earliest. It mainly discusses the function of environment in behaviors, with an aim to facilitate behaviors beneficial to society by changing surrounding environment. It has been extensively applied to areas such as special education (treatment of autism included) as a practical science; Floor-time, which was a game therapy created by Stanley Greenspan, an American psychiatrist and encouraged parents to sit on the floor and strengthen communication and exchange through games with children being the center and adults being the guide and assistant; and PECS (Picture Exchange Communication System), which was a linguistic communication system specifically designed for patients with language retardation (including autism patients). The biggest feature of the system was to allow language retardation children to express their inner minds through pictures and strengthen their communication with other persons.

2.2 New Research Trend with Support of Information Technology

The development of new generation of information technology is also supporting the innovation in the rehabilitation approach of autistic patients. Aids such as smart robot, interactive media game, APP, VR technology have been tried in China and internationally, resulting in certain rehabilitation effect. For instance, Acumen remote video autism therapy [3] (see Fig. 1) aims to assess and manage neurological disorder, introduce video observation, diagnosis and treatment concept through remote guidance such as video and website, and establish an information digital platform among children patients, families and doctors.

Fig. 1. Acumen remote video autism therapy.

However, in the meanwhile, the development of related products is still encountered with a lot of difficulties due to its own complexity of autism and unknown cause of disease. Like the foregoing mobile terminal APP as a new healthcare rehabilitation education means, there are up to 500 types available in app store. Few proved to be effective for rehabilitation scientifically, Acumen is one of a very few effective cases. In addition, existing digital products that support the rehabilitation of autistic children mostly are standalone ones and specific to local problems. To date, there is no systematic authoritative rehabilitation service product system available.

2.3   Status Quo of Domestic Use in China

Currently, more than 1000 special education institutions have been open that offers autism rehabilitation training throughout China. However, these institutions of different scales distributed in different regions are of varying quality. Many of them lack in systematic service mode and scientific regular assessment and rehabilitation service system, frequently causing inaccurate and incomplete assessment of autistic children, delayed optimal rehabilitation training period and consequently limited rehabilitation effect. Whereas rehabilitation teachers play a very important role in the entire rehabilitation education process, industrial faculty is greatly short relative to large demand, and high-level professional rehabilitation teachers who receive systematic education and have abundant experience are of critical shortage. It can be seen that in addition to rehabilitation technology and medical difficulty, the industrial ecology not effectively organized and regulated is also an important factor that restricts industrial development and the improvement of overall rehabilitation level.

3   Design of Internet Rehabilitation Service System Based on Special Assessment Products

3.1   Difficulties and Breakpoints for Autism Rehabilitation

Though we have had relatively deep understanding of the autism, the rehabilitation of autistic children internationally remains a difficulty, which is dependent upon the complexity of autism and individual difference of autistic children.

Firstly, many studies tried to find out the cause and mechanism of the autism, the cause of disease remains unclear and it's hard to launch a rehabilitation product that is specific to autism and has single effect. Secondly, a series of assessment and rehabilitation therapies specifically developed for autism in the international community have achieved certain effect, single product cannot adapt to most children patients due to wide individual deviation among children patients, and the rehabilitation treatment requires face-to-face specific training with experienced rehabilitation teachers, resulting in limited efficiency and popularity. Thirdly, verbal behavior capability of children has a lot of complex dimensions. In the book The Verbal Behavior Milestones Assessment and Placement Program, Dr. Mark Sundberg identified 170 milestones and 900 skills. Therefore, it is a great challenge for every rehabilitation teacher on how to familiarize and master the assessment of children's capability and take appropriate rehabilitation training methods specifically.

Rehabilitation courses or products that show significant effect for every autistic patient are not available in the market, and we have difficulty in developing and popularizing them with our current understanding and technology level. Rehabilitation treatment of the autism seriously depends upon experienced rehabilitation teachers and its core essentially is a kind of service. During our in-depth understanding and research, we have gradually found that in such an industrial ecology, data regarding professional children assessment and diagnosis and children's capability description remains the foundation and core of subsequent rehabilitation service. The acquisition of such data was seriously relied upon few highly-competent experts in the past, and such data could not be circulated and conveyed among experts, rehabilitation teachers, parents, schools, institutions and communities, resulting in reduced value. Therefore, an expert assessment data platform based on internet connectivity may definitely offer important support to the entire industry. In view of such background, we proposed the design of internet rehabilitation service system with assessment data of autistic individuals being the core and we would like to drive the integrated innovation in the autism rehabilitation industry through the service system idea and approach.

3.2 Structure of Internet Rehabilitation Service System for Autistic Children

Through analysis of each link of autism rehabilitation service and in combination with features and pain points of the autism industry as well as current technological system features, we built an internet rehabilitation service system with assessment data of autistic individuals being the foundation and core (See Fig. 2).

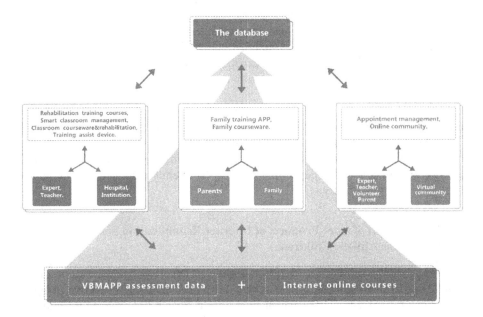

Fig. 2. Internet rehabilitation service system with assessment data of autistic individuals being the foundation and core.

The foundation and core of the system is the assessment product of autistic individuals "VB-MAPP Assessment Helper". It is an internet-based online assessment aid developed by us through our cooperation with and authorization from Mr. MARK L. SUNDBERG, the author of VB-MAPP, an internationally authoritative verbal behavior assessment system, and our introduction of the assessment system into China. Through learning, rehabilitation teachers may use online service to complete the assessment of autistic children and the system will automatically generate IEP (individual education program) to guide subsequent rehabilitation training.

In the meanwhile, we also launched an online cloud classroom about VB-MAPP system usage and autism rehabilitation training and engaged domestic famous authoritative autism experts to shoot online video courses for the purpose of popularizing autism rehabilitation education and training course system. Together with the cloud classroom, "VB-MAPP Assessment Helper" formed the data and education training support platform for the internet rehabilitation service system, which would provide data, education training and assistant product support service to healthcare institutions, families and virtual community, thereby forming the ecological system of rehabilitation service primarily.

For hospitals and other professional rehabilitation institutions, the system may provide training and professional qualification certification to professional rehabilitation teachers, and online "VB-MAPP Assessment Helper" service to various types of rehabilitation institutions, and based on above, offer smart classroom management, regulate training course systems, develop or improve courseware props and rehabilitation training assistant devices; for families, the system may provide training and assessment services to the parents of children patients and develop courseware and APPs suitable for family training; for virtual communities, the system may launch online forums, gather intelligence and enthusiasm from experts, teachers, parents and volunteers, make social publicity, facilitate integrated education, and offer rehabilitation training reservation management, and etc.

Meanwhile, data acquired by every product will be uploaded to a public cloud database, thus gradually forming the "Rehabilitation education database for autistic children". Once the database has accumulated sufficient samples, we will be able to further conduct big data based analysis and research and summarize the rules, which in turn facilitate the research of the medicine itself and the overall integrated innovation and development of the industry.

3.3   Development of Core Products of Internet Rehabilitation Service System for Autistic Children

The core of the system is "VB-MAPP Assessment Helper" online assessment. It is a Chinese digital version of assessment system developed based on The Verbal Behavior Milestones Assessment and Placement Program. Its launch has changed the situation where only few professional assessment staff is available in the industry, thereby rapidly popularizing professional assessment.

Designed with high complexity, the product system involves 170 milestones and nearly 800 skill milestone assessment standards in 14 areas, as well as 24 types of disorder assessment and 18 transition assessment links. The design also used 1596 assessment pictures totally and assistant methods such as various types of real props and counting and timing, through which a comprehensive assessment was conducted on children's verbal and behavior capability (see Fig. 3). Through careful analysis on function and usage flow, we mainly adopted linear interaction with diversified assistant tools to simplify the operation flow. Through iteration of multiple test versions, the product preliminarily converts a very professional and complex assessment system into a simplified, personalized, semi-automated operation flow. Through labeling and graphic means and a series of digital assistant tools such as quick recording and timers, we have significantly improved the efficiency of individual assessment with specialty and scientific nature guaranteed (see Figs. 4, 5 and 6). As a result, the professional assessment that cost two or three days in the past only takes three or four hours now, thus greatly reducing the burden on teachers and children patients.

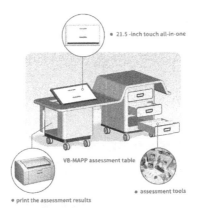

Fig. 3. VB-MAPPassessment system integrated with assessment table and assessment tools.

Fig. 4. Main screen of assessment menu: horizontal menu bar to realize autonomous switching among all links including milestone assessment, disorder assessment and transition assessment; longitudinal tab bar to realize quick recording function of assessment feedback; multi-tab display under Assessment closely associated with assessment tools. Click each table to realize the recording of assessment contents.

Fig. 5. Automatic scoring may be completed by the assessment staff through sliding correct assessment results from the left to the right assessment column.

Fig. 6. Use of assistant tools such smart timer.

Through online registration and cloud management, the product offers such services as online data storage, management and reservation, facilitating the connection among parents, assessment staff, experts and rehabilitation teachers (see Fig. 7). Upon completion of the assessment, the system will automatically generate VB-MAPP assessment result score form, assessment report and individual education program (IEP), facilitating the filing by users (see Figs. 8 and 9). Multiple assessment results may facilitate the comparison for the purpose of understanding the progress of the children.

Fig. 7. Online customer management system.

Fig. 8. Upon completion of the assessment, the system will automatically generate scoring scales such as milestone assessment, disorder assessment and transition assessment.

Fig. 9. The system will automatically generate IEP "Individual education program" target push.

The product also reduces the learning difficulty and entry threshold for assessment staff, which allows more professional rehabilitation teachers to quickly master the use of the product and improve the assessment skills and efficiency, thus reducing social education cost of professional assessment and rehabilitation training teachers and quickly increasing the quantity and quality of teachers.

Through improved scientific nature, professionalism and efficiency, the product significantly improves the social coverage of autistic children assessment and rehabilitation service generally and offer important support to the improved overall rehabilitation service capability.

3.4   Research Results of Internet Rehabilitation Service System for Autistic Children

By the end of 2016, the system has offered training services to more than 6000 front-line rehabilitation teachers, accounting for about 30% among all Chinese front-line rehabilitation teachers. "Cloud classroom" has been viewed for 2.9 million times totally, thus reducing a lot of education and training cost and improving training efficiency for the society; once the WeChat public account was launched one year ago, specialized knowledge about autism published in the system has been viewed for 3.41 million times totally; online public benefit Q&A has solved 1712 problems for 1004 parents; "Virtual community" has released 71064 posts and 35,000 topics, has 13,100 registered members consisting of teachers, parents and institutions, and 10.21 million page views, making it one of the most important virtual knowledge communities about autism in China [4].

4 Conclusion

The internet rehabilitation service system with individual assessment data of autistic children being the core seems build a "value chain" system. What exist in the value chain is not independent individuals, but a system consisting of a series of activities which are connected with various bonds and mutually dependent, thereby maximizing the overall efficacy.

In the internet rehabilitation service system, every online, in-line or offline link shows mutually penetrated and associated trend. Finally, it gathers all indispensable links and penetrates and integrates base critical data service, thus forming a complete B2B2C internet service system incorporating such functions as customer management, teacher management, institution management, course management and database management. The system has changed the management and service mode of conventional autism rehabilitation and education, and built the ecology of brand-new rehabilitation service industry. It realizes simple and efficient information exchange among children patients, parents, teachers, families, schools and the society, allows more people to understand autism, develops more qualified rehabilitation teachers, makes the demands of more families with autistic patients be satisfied, allows big data resources to play a bigger role through data storage, mining and analysis, and facilitates the development of scientific research of rehabilitation medicine, thereby generally improving the system service level of the entire industry, and offering practical help to autistic children patients, families with autistic patients, and even the society.

Acknowledgments. This article was supported by the National Social Science Fund Project in Arts - Development Status and Construction of Interaction Design Discipline (Ministry of Culture 13CB113).

References

1. Mei, L.: Chinese education autism rehabilitation industry development status report. In: Peishi, W. (ed.), pp. 5–165. Beijing Normal University Publishing Group, Beijing (2015)
2. Stehr Green, P., Stellfeld, M.: Autism and thimerosal-containing vaccines: lack of consistent evidence for an association. Am. J. Prey. Med. **25**(2), 101 (2003)
3. Xiaosou, L.: Acumen remote video new way to treat autism (online). vcbeat net (2014). http://www.vcbeat.net/786.html
4. Huani, Z.: IngCare internet educational project for children autism annual report (online). New media platform (2016). https://mp.weixin.qq.com/s?__biz=MzA5ODQyNTcyNQ==&mid=2650628644&idx=1&sn=4d3c6789973eca5e5b3569555cd4b49f&chksm=88980c36bfef8520ee37874815fd57790f23c1c722f9db021a628746a8ab42b3f49515892367&pass_ticket=KgOTRn%2FRzA0ZQLaxhPzQBb8jv30y%2B8jo03jzaAlme5M%3D#rd

Smart Environments for Learning and Creativity

Using Eye Tracking to Map Behaviors in an Online Course Prototype About Epilepsy

Ana Teresa Contier[1(✉)] and Laila Brito Torres[2]

[1] Unifesp, São Paulo, Brazil
anatcontier@gmail.com
[2] Instituto Israelita de ensino e pesquisa Albert Einstein, São Paulo, Brazil
laila.brito@einstein.br

Abstract. Human-computer interaction (HCI) design has its main focus on the needs of users, an approach known as user-centered design. Designing online courses is a field of human-computer research that integrates ubiquitous technology, cognition and design. The development of an online course is prototype-driven. Unfortunately, there is a lack of documented methods for assessing the design of a prototype course before it is presented to students. This paper should contribute to this need by proposing a method for evaluating online course designs based on eye tracking data, which can significantly help designers in analysing the public's behavior. Some of these measures include content fixation points, gaze position, duration and blink rate. Designers can also gather data about how stressed out or relaxed the test users are, how attentive they are and how they solve problems. Affectivity can also be measured and this can be used to create a more customized environment for content acquisition and learning. In this paper we set out to: (1) describe the general methodology of using eye tracking to design and evaluate an online course prototype (2) discuss interaction design challenges related to this methodology and its limitations. In order to guide our discussion we will refer to an actual ongoing online course project about epilepsy that will be used to train schoolteachers.

Keywords: Online course prototype · Eye-tracking · Learning

1 Introduction

Despite substantial innovations in antiepileptic drug therapy over the past 15 years, the proportion of patients with uncontrolled epilepsy has not changed, highlighting the need for new treatment strategies that should be associated with the dissemination of knowledge to improve the quality of life of the patient. Such strategies are associated with the preparation of professionals not only in health, but essentially linked to education, for a more efficient and early screening. Epilepsy affects over 50 million people worldwide, and, for a quarter of those affected, no combination of standard therapy—primarily medications and surgery—can control their seizures. The search for better drugs and surgical approaches, as well as preparation of professionals from multidisciplinary areas (especially teachers) for the overall gains of the person with epilepsy and more effective

© Springer International Publishing AG 2017
N. Streitz and P. Markopoulos (Eds.): DAPI 2017, LNCS 10291, pp. 505–513, 2017.
DOI: 10.1007/978-3-319-58697-7_38

public policies, should be reconciled. Thus, it is essential to use large-scale dissemination technologies, considering the geographical demands of Brazil, in the training/qualification of education professionals.

Epilepsy is a cerebral disorder characterized by the long-term predisposition to epileptic seizures and by the neurobiological, social, cognitive and psychological consequences of this condition; being a quite serious neurological disease, it is more prevalent than other diseases of its class [1]. The Ministry of Health, through Datasus, has recorded 157,070 new cases of epilepsy per year [2]. In Brazil it is estimated that between 1 and 2% of the population (2,050,000 to 4,100,000 people) have epilepsy [3]. Despite being underreported and the fragility of these data- as they do not reflect epidemiological reality- local studies have given a prevalence rate of epilepsy of 1.19% in the population of São Paulo and ranging from 1.65% to 2.03% in Porto Alegre [3, 4]. In addition, it is estimated that between 20% and 30% of people with epilepsy will not be able to control epileptic seizures with drug therapy [2]. The diagnosis occurs predominantly among children, especially in their first year of life, adolescents and patients of 65 years or older [2]. During childhood and adolescence, these individuals demonstrate a physiological process of neurological maturation and development of psychosocial structuring, which normally presupposes a phase that involves some personal conflicts. In pre-adolescents with epilepsy, this phase may be increased by the personal confrontation of the disease associated with the prejudice and stigma that are generated in all social environments, school, friends, and even in the family nucleus.

Teachers, when they have the proper knowledge, play a key role in introducing clarification, promoting acceptance of diversity among people and creating tools to eliminate discrimination. This comprehension of the teacher about epilepsy can have an effective and transformative impact on the social achievements of the students and the school and, consequently, on the professional life and social.

Despite this important role of the educator, little research is done in this field around the world, especially with intervention programs. Studies in different countries, including Denmark, the United States, Spain, and Greece, report insufficient teacher training on epilepsy, often associated with inappropriate and potentially harmful concepts of conditions involving the person with epilepsy [3, 5–8].

In 2008, the Brazilian Association of Epilepsy (ABE) began an intervention program in elementary schools in the state of São Paulo called "Epilepsy in Schools: Teaching Teachers", which was awarded by the International Bureau of Epilepsy (IBE). The content was delivered via face-to-face lessons and video conferencing in the "Knowledge Network" and evaluated through a questionnaire applied before (Phase 1) and after (Phase 2) the lecture "Epilepsy: Causes, Symptoms and Conduct" [9]. The evaluation consisted of 35 objective questions covering the following topics: Concepts and definitions of epilepsy (10); Treatment and adverse reactions of antiepileptic medications (10); Physical and occupational activities of the person with epilepsy (5); Stigmatizing popular knowledge (5); and Basic care during and after the crisis (5). A total of 1,153 educators, divided into two groups, participated in a face-to-face class (288 educators) taught in four Brazilian cities, as well as via videoconference (866 educators) transmitted to 74 cities in the state of São Paulo, including the capital. The results showed a use of up to 41% in the topic "Basic care during and after the crisis" and the greater ignorance

(74.6%) and worse utilization (0.1%) registered in the topic "Popular stigmatizing knowledge about epilepsy". The study concluded that joint efforts are needed to disseminate general knowledge about epilepsy and specific strategic planning on its stigmatizing conditions.

Making a course about Epilepsy available on the internet will probably engage a wider audience than if the material were taught exclusively in classrooms. In particular, this strategy may also allow schoolteachers from remote locations to become acquainted with current topics in Neuroscience that can help solve longstanding problems in children's education.

Translating the contents taught in a conventional classroom to an online environment requires attention to some fundamental differences between these two modalities. This includes handling instructional contents in interactive sessions promoting student engagement and increase their motivation along with the use of online features such as forums and chats that enable the dialogue between agents. Thus, the main challenge is to replicate actual social exchanges that are common in face-to- face implementations, since the observation of others and how they respond to one's own actions form the greater part of learning (enactive learning). The first step to decrease this distance is to develop a prototype and test it with the target public- in this case, teachers.

Furthermore, basic knowledge of neuroscience can stimulate a change of attitude towards special education students, fostering a positive approach when considering the behavior of such students as part of the normal spectrum of human differences, the so called neurodiversity [10].

In this context, the first step towards increasing teacher engagement and awareness would be made possible if there were a online course "Let's talk about Epilepsy" containing information about epilepsy and a guideline on how to proceed when dealing with specific situations. As Brazil is a continental country, access to the application should be facilitated by allowing teachers to download it on their cell and use it wherever and whenever they want.

However, this online approach has three major challenges. The first one is to ensure the adherence of these teachers along the course, bearing in mind that it is mostly composed of so-called digital immigrants, that is, people who are not so used to dealing with the language and the virtual tools used on the Internet [11]. The second one is the implementation of the course itself. The third challenge is the course structure and the definition of appropriate online activities to reduce transactional distance of the agentes [12] and allow their integrated action.

Considering these challenges, the purpose of this work is to present a methodology to evaluate an online course prototype. This methodology will evolve based on the use of eye tracking data collection during experimental trials. We will discuss the challenges and limitations of this methodology in a possible application on a e-learning about epilepsy aimed at schoolteachers.

2 Instructional Design

Currently, computing technologies and new transmaterials are incorporating more recip-rocal architectures and human-based (digitally enhanced) environment interaction [12, 13]. Online education is the integration between technologies, including hypertext and interactive communication networks, for the development of educational content and learning support. Nowadays, students can access this interactive material every-where, when they want. It is important to create materials that can teach students with the most efficiency. Research has proven that the results of learning a subject are increased when there is integration of text, images and diagrams [14, 15]. How can we design such efficient and integrated tools?

Some of the better-known (research based) approaches are user-centered/participa-tory, contextual designs and activity theory [13]. Most of these approaches are built on the assumption that a suitable design proposal is to be established through simulating a real interaction situation. The end result is to understand how the user responds to and interacts with the educational interface program.

The instructional designer is responsible for planning, preparing, producing every text, image and graphic, which are part of the course in a digital platform. The traditional instructional design model is called ADDIE. This acronym means: Analysis- identifying learning needs, setting instructional objectives, and surveying the constraints involved; Design and Development: planning instruction and the elaboration of instructional materials and products; Implementation: development of educational tools; and Evalu-ation: obtaining and reviewing feedback from the experience of users and technicians. Another approach is SAM (Successive Approximation Model), which was proposed by Michael Allen [16]. The main difference between these instructional design models is that the first is divided in five separate phases and the second is an iterative design incorporating a rapid prototyping, which means a continual basis feedback during implementation [16]. The various design versions of SAM, which are made of inter-mediary prototypes evaluated at the level of the user's experience, could be enhanced using eye tracker. It can provide insight into where students consume content based on the location on which they focus their eyes. To do this a camera is placed at the bottom of the computer screen to monitor eye movement. The information that is gathered through these eye-tracking devices shows us how interested the person is in the content and where they are placing their attention.

3 Eye Tracking

Eye tracker is a device to map and record eyes movement. It is performed by high resolution cameras that directly film the gaze and direction of eyes. This procedure is completely painless and does not include direct eye contact. There is no need for using glasses or any substance or medication during this recording procedure. Before starting to collect data, the system calibrates the viewers´eyes to ensure that the position of them is correctly mapped [17, 18] There are a various different types of eye tracking devices like head-mounted (used mainly in reading studies) and those that are integrated to monitors or standalone units, used preferentially in market and usability researches. Independent of type, the measures collected by these devices include content fixation points, gaze position, duration and blink rate. This data could be correlated to users' behavior: their stress, fatigue and attention during the tests. Sometimes users don't read a text, they scan for a useful information. Eye tracking data shows the large numbers of fixations on many screen parts and wandering gaze. This information is important for marketing, for example, following consumers eyes during their navigation on e-commerce platform shows what they see, how long they spend paying attention in some specific product, what they did before they decided to order [19]. Thus eye tracking helps to identify usability problems.

Eye-tracking data has been used to identify how subjects figure out causal and reasoning problems in online courses [20]. According to these authors the eye movement variables is correlated with the cognitive processes involved in learning. [21] emphasize that visual attention is correlated with the activities proposed in a context of learning. Other researchers developed interface guidelines to e-learning that were based on eye tracking data collection [22].

On the other hand, some authors [23–25] discuss some limitations of eye tracking. They argue this device can´t track peripheral vision and sometimes the interaction between facilitator and participant interferes in the result. Thus the data could not reflect the cognition. Another difficulty is the device itself; most of them are expensive and require specialized professionals to administer it. Also the devices need to be calibrated to each participant and much time is spent on this. Finally, Nielsen and Pernice [17] and Gueise [19] point out that there is not a pattern in research using eye tracking because each study has its own protocol to evaluate a specific site. This implicates difficulties in comparing studies because it is not possible to generalize findings neither user behavior.

Considering these challenges, we will start the discussion about instructional design by concentrating more on usability than learning to improve instructional design method.

4   Prototype

Our approach to the prototype's design is a multidisciplinary one. A team composed of neuroscientists, graphic designers, instructional designers and programmers, along with school teachers will be involved in all the design process. This collective construction is divided in two parts: prototype development and prototype evaluation.

4.1   Prototype Development

Neurocientists have a series of meetings with designers to decide: the content, the format, the public and protocol. The prototype "Let's alk about Epilepsy" addresses how to deal with a student that is having a seizure. First, one interactive infographic about this topic will be created and presented to the schoolteachers who will then answer a small quiz about it. The infographic format is best suited for this content, because it can portray many iconic elements making it easier to show the steps that the teacher needs to follow when a student has a seizure. The quiz is a multiple choice activity that will allow for scoring the schoolteachers responses.

According to Nielsen and Pernice [17] an adequate number of participants for eye tracking studies is 39. Following that guideline, this trial will include 40 teachers from 10 public schools in São Paulo (Brazil) that will be selected for participation.

We chose to use a lower priced eye tracking device that was created by Eye Tribe, a Danish start up. In December of 2016 the company was sold to Facebook. This portable device is installed on a computer. Like other eye trackers, it mainly measures:

- Gaze duration: the duration of gazes (fixations) on a certain area of interest.
- Number of fixations: the number of fixations on a certain area.
- Interval to first fixation: the amount of time until an area is first noticed.
- Density of fixations: the concentration of gazes in a particular area increases the density of fixations on that area

The analysis of these parameters will vary with context and care should be taken when trying to assess user intentions from eye movement patterns. For instance, high average gaze duration could be linked to very different causes, such as high level of engagement, high stress and even mind-wandering.

The programmers will work with the graphic designers to gather the Eye Tribe data and associate that with the images being displayed by the e-learning software.

The evaluation test will consist of the following steps inspired by recent studies [17, 19, 21, 22, 25]: pretest, data collection, data analysis.

4.2 Pretest

In this step, we will investigate the student's skills and experience in the following aspects: intimacy with equipment, experiences in training and calibration of eye tracker.

First of all, we explain to the participant what will happen in the trial. It is important to assure them that it is a safe, painless test. We could say, for example: "we will ask you to do two online activities that consist of one infographic and one quiz. During your navigation, this device (point to Eye Tribe) will record your eye movement. It is like a camera that films your eye. It is painless. You will help us to design better online courses". The designer needs to clarify them that there is no right and wrong in their actions and that a person will observe them during the test in order to note the sequence of activities that the participant will perform on each screen and that the participant should not worry about that.

The user signs an ethical agreement that assures him of the confidentiality of the study and of his rights. This agreement is also signed by the team who conducts the trial.

Before that, the user will answer a questionnaire on a computer. Our objective is to see his body position when he sits down to use the Web. In addition, we can inform him that he needs to focus only on the screen and he can't move his head a lot. This practice prepares him for the test. This is also an opportunity to ask him about his familiarity with the internet. These are the questions:

- Do you use your computer at work? Y/N
- Do you use the internet? Y/N
- Have you already done any e-Learning training? Y/N
- How was your experience? (*If you did an online course, please tell us about it*)

Finally, the Eye Tribe will be calibrated. This step is important to allow the data to be collected properly. The individuals who has ocular deficiencies can't participate in this study.

4.3 Data Collection

In the data collection step, eye tracking parameters will be collected. Another important data that can be collected in this step is "think-aloud" data. This consists of asking the participant to describe their interaction with what they see on the screen and could be used to better understand the relation between user intentions and eye tracking parameters.

4.4 Data Analysis

The objective of this step is to evaluate the efficiency of navigability and usability of the course. This should provide answers to questions such as:

- How intuitive is the navigation?
- More specifically, do participants know where to click?
- Are the instructions on how to explore the course satisfactory?

Gaze duration and time to first fixation could be used in determining if difficulty with some words or drawings in the infographic were the cause for problems in answering the quiz afterwards.

Additionally, there are software tools that help with statistical analysis of the eye tracking parameters and with the creation of visual representations of eye movements on top of the course images. Those can make it easier to identify improvements to the course material, i.e. low fixation densities could mean that information is more spread apart that what it should.

The results of the data analysis should then be used as seed for the next iteration within the context of the successive approximation model (SAM).

5 Conclusion

The increased use of technology applied to education requires more research about instructional design. Prototype-driven design and user-centric design are the basis of our methodology to the development of more effective courses in terms of usability.

Eye tracking is a tool that could help designers to evaluate the online course because mapping eye movements could give some clues about what needs to be changed in the course before it is launched. However there are some challenges to overcome, for example, lack of qualified professionals to do this type of test as well as a few standard protocols to follow.

In the prototype suggested "Let's talk about epilepsy", we propose an initial protocol to designing and evaluating e-learning material that takes into account the familiarity of the public with digital interaction. Finally, this proposal helps to start the discussion on different approaches to instructional design.

Acknowledgments. Associação Brasileira de Epilepsia (ABE), http://www.epilepsiabrasil. org.br

References

1. Fisher, R.S., Acevedo, C., Arzimanoglou, A., Bogacz, A., Cross, J.H., Elger, C.E., Engel, J., Forsgren, L., French, J.A., Glynn, M., Hesdorffer, D.C., Lee, B.I., Mathern, G.W., Moshé, S.L., Perucca, E., Scheffer, I.E., Tomson, T., Watanabe, M., Wiebe, S.: A practical clinical definition of epilepsy. Epilepsia **55**, 1–8 (2014)
2. Gomes, M.M.: Epidemiologia: distribuição, fatores de risco e considerações prognósticas. In: Guerreiro, C.A.M., Guerreiro, M.M., Cendes, F., Cendes, I.L (eds.) Epilepsia, pp. 11–21. Editora Lemos, São Paulo (2000)
3. Fernandes, J., Schmidt, M., Tozzi, S., Sander, J.: Prevalence of epilepsy: the Porto Alegre study. Epilepsia **33**, 132 (1992)
4. Marino Jr., R., Cukiert, A., Pinho, E.: Aspectos epidemiológicos da epilepsia em São Paulo. Arq. Neuropsiquiatr. **44**, 243–254 (1986)
5. Bishop, M., Boag, E.M.: Teachers – knowledge about epilepsy and attitudes toward students with epilepsy: results of a national survey. Epilepsy Behav. **8**, 397–405 (2006)
6. Holdsworth, L., Whitmore, K.: A study of children with epilepsy attending ordinary schools. II: information and attitudes held by their teachers. Dev. Med. Child Neurol. **16**, 759–765 (1974)
7. Kaleyias, J., Tzoufi, M., Kotsalis, C., Papavasiliou, A., Diamantopoulos, N.: Knowledge and attitude of the Greek educational community toward epilepsy and the epileptic student. Epilepsy Behav. **6**, 179–186 (2005)
8. Madsen, P.: Danish primary school teachers' knowledge about epilepsy in children. Ugeskr. Laeger **158**(14), 1977–1980 (1996)
9. Guilhoto, L., et al.: IBE Promising Strategies Program 2008 epilepsy at school: teaching the teachers - educational plan of the Associação Brasileira de Epilepsia with teachers of elementary school. Epilepsy Neurophysiol. **16**, 80–86 (2010)
10. Steven, K., et al.: Deficit, difference, or both? Autism and neurodiversity. Dev. Psychol. **49**(1), 59–71 (2013)
11. Prensky, M.: Digital natives, digital immigrants. On the Horiz. **9**(5), 1–6 (2001). MCB University Press
12. Moore, M.: Teoria da Distância Transacional. Revista de Aprendizagem Aberta e a Distância, São Paulo (2002)
13. Kaptelinin, V., Nardi, B.A.: Acting with Technology: Activity Theory and Interaction Design. MIT press, Cambridge (2006)
14. Hegarty, M., Mayer, R.E., Green, C.E.: Comprehension of arithmetic word problems: evidence from students' eye fixations. J. Educ. Psychol. **84**, 16 (1992)

15. Scheiter, K., Van Gog, T.: Using eye tracking in applied research to study and stimulate the processing of information from multi-representational sources. Appl. Cogn. Psychol. **1**, 1209–1214 (2009)
16. Allen, M., Sites, R.: Leaving ADDIE for SAM: An Agile Model for Developing the Best Learning Experiences. American Society for Training and Development, New York (2012)
17. Pernice, K., Nielsen, J.: How to Conduct Eyetracking Studies. Nielsen Norman Group, Fremont (2009)
18. Duchowski, A.: Eye Tracking Methodology: Theory and Practice. Springer Science & Business Media, London (2007)
19. Geise, S.: Eyetracking in media studies. theory, method and its exemplary application in analyzing shock-inducing advertisements. In: Research Methods in Media Studies, pp. 100–137 (2014)
20. Graesser, A.C., Lu, S., Olde, B.A., Cooper-Pye, E., Whitten, S.: Question asking and eye tracking during cognitive disequilibrium: comprehending illustrated texts on devices when the devices break down. Mem. Cogn. **33**, 1235–1247 (2005)
21. Nakayama, M., Shimizu, Y.: Evaluation of a multimedia learning exercise using oculo-motors. In: Proceedings of the 2006 Symposium on Eye Tracking Research & Applications, p. 46 (2006)
22. Zambarbieri, D.: E-TRACKING: eye tracking analysis in the evaluation of e-learning systems. In: Human-Centred Computing. Cognitive, Social and Ergonomic Aspects, pp. 617–21. Lawrence Erlbaum Associates Publication (2003)
23. Ross, J.: Eyetracking: Is it worth it. Diunduh dari (2009). http://www.uxmatters.com/mt/archives/2009/10/eyetracking-is-it-worth-it.php
24. Ehmke, C., Wilson, S.: Identifying web usability problems from eye-tracking data. In: Proceedings of the 21st British HCI Group Annual Conference on People and Computers: HCI... but not as we know it-Volume 1, September 3, pp. 119–128. British Computer Society (2007)
25. Nielsen, J., Pernice, K.: Eyetracking Web Usability. New Riders, Berkeley (2010)

Building Tools for Creative Data Exploration: A Comparative Overview of Data-Driven Design and User-Centered Design

Sara Diamond, Steve Szigeti, and Ana Jofre[✉]

OCAD University, 100 McCaul St, Toronto, ON M5T 1W1, Canada
{sdiamond,sszigeti,ajofre}@ocadu.ca

Abstract. Visualization scientists seek means to inspire insights from data, which require creative thinking on the part of analysts as well as cognitive reasoning. In information visualization a focus on the user has proven highly effective in the design of usable and engaging interfaces, although it has been argued that such a focus limits innovation in insights about the data and in the creation of metaphors for visualization. If a user-centered design recapitulates existing knowledge, then a design approach which derives exclusively from the data may provide more innovative results. Our approach considers both the designers and the users, whereby our goal is to elicit creativity in both the design of visualization tools and in their application. We compare user-centered design and data-driven design through tool sets that emerged from each of these methods. User-centered design methodologies were used in the creation of a custom interface for editors at a major national newspaper that visualizes measures of each story's popularity. Data-driven design methodologies were used to create a tangible user interface for data visualization. With UCD we built a tool that supported the use of data in editorial decisions and deployed familiar metaphors to encourage significant change in workplace practice. With DDD we unleashed creativity on the part of analysts which resulted in a more innovative approach on the part of designers and a gateway to new user communities. We compare strengths and weaknesses of each methodology through a reflection of our design outcomes.

Keywords: Data visualization · Design · Innovation

1 Introduction

"If we'd ask customers what they wanted, they'd ask for faster horses", is a popular quote attributed to Henry Ford to illustrate potential problems when involving users in the design process. User centered design often results in successful tool development and refinement. However, such results are incremental changes, not radical innovation [1]. This challenge of innovation in design lies at the center of how we visualize data.

Data visualization requires the adoption of appropriate visual metaphors, where the choice of metaphor is coupled with both qualities of the data and an understanding of potential data use. We use the term metaphor in the context of interface design, where

© Springer International Publishing AG 2017
N. Streitz and P. Markopoulos (Eds.): DAPI 2017, LNCS 10291, pp. 514–527, 2017.
DOI: 10.1007/978-3-319-58697-7_39

qualities of a familiar object and its behaviors in the real world are carried into the digital space to facilitate navigation [2], such as the icons for files and folders on a digital desktop. Metaphors in our usage includes familiar ways of representing numerical quantities such as graphs. In a data-driven approach, designers develop metaphors and interactions based on the data and its structure [3], while a user-centered approach first considers user hypotheses and requirements [4]. Innovation and creativity are tightly coupled, and the ability of data visualization tools to provide insight is a potential measure of creativity.

User-centered design (UCD) has been employed in the design of interfaces for decades and is increasingly prevalent within data visualization as it allows for the dynamic management of visual metaphors and underlying data structures within the context or culture of the user [2, 4, 5]. Many UCD approaches seek to understand their users through ethnography studies [6, 7] where users and their practices are studied by designers, and in more mature practice, through participatory engagement, where the intended user plays an active role in the design process [8, 9]. These practices were motivated by the need to capture tacit knowledge about work process within the design of technology through the recognition that systems designed without this knowledge were often flawed and less readily adopted. The best of UCD engages users through charrettes, self-documentation and prototyping.

It is important to recognize two subtle challenges related to a user-centered approach; (i) UCD caters its aesthetics to a particular user, thus reinforcing a normative approach to the data, and (ii) UCD begins with assumptions regarding users' queries of the data. Arguably a data-driven approach, lacking an initial focus on a specific user, may result in tools that are viable for a broader set of potential users and may reveal patterns from the data that do not conform to users' queries or assumptions.

Data-driven design (DDD) begins by considering the data in the absence of knowledge regarding its specific uses in order to foreground relationships within the data that may not have been previously considered. A DDD approach first considers the data and its structure, and then, in subsequent steps, looks at potential applications and user culture [3]. Raw data, in the absence of a known user, suggests the potential of analyses based on visualizations with new aesthetics and interpretations that may not have otherwise been proposed. As Benjamin Fry points out, aesthetics structure experiences in formal perceptual ways and provide interpretive tools with which to construct meanings [10].

While a user-centered approach has resulted in successful visualizations, the results will not necessarily be innovative [1]. Innovative ideas are fragile at their inception, and strong creative visualizations risk rejection [5], or are never invented due to a focus on perceived user needs. An approach induced through data-driven analysis could help guard against one of the dangers of UCD; namely, that questions and metaphors (such as familiar graphs) only recapitulate existing knowledge [5]. This is particularly relevant when the goal of the analytics tools is to prompt insight and creativity rather than to augment rapid decision making.

With both UCD or DDD, data visualization eventually requires the adoption of appropriate visual metaphors, where the choice of metaphor is coupled with both the qualities of the data and an understanding of potential data use. In DDD, designers involve users at later stages of the design process than in UCD. Namely, in UCD, the user is involved from the beginning, while in DDD, the user becomes involved after a prototype has been produced.

In this work, we compare both approaches to designing visualizations. In part 1, we examine the outcomes of a pilot study in which one team of designers explicitly engages in DDD, while the other team practices UCD to create visualizations. In part 2, we examine two case studies from our research. Our UCD case study is the design of a custom interface for editors at a major national newspaper that visualizes measures of each story's popularity, and our DDD case study is on the design of a tangible user interface for data visualization. The case studies illustrate (1) the creativity of designers working through the two approaches, and (2) how the tools might best support the creativity of the users: data analysts.

While research has considered the shortcomings of UCD as a means to innovate [11], there has been no comparative examination of the different outcomes of UCD and DDD in the domain of data visualization. Our research hopes to contribute an early step in this direction.

2   Part 1: Pilot Study

We begin our work by discussing a pilot study comparing different design approaches while using the same data to reduce a number of potentially confounding variables. The goal was (i) to evaluate the kinds of insights the DDD and UCD approaches provide from the data on the part of analysts, (ii) to compare the metaphors that emerge from these methods, and (iii) to develop a deeper understanding of both methods with a goal of potentially articulating new design methods, including those that support creativity on the part of designers.

In order to compare the outcomes of the UCD and DDD approaches, we assigned a team of graphic designers to each method. Both teams were provided with identical data sets. The UCD team worked closely with NLogic staff in order to understand user needs, whereas the DDD team had no access to existing users of the data.

2.1   Data Sets

Compiled by our industry partner, the data consists of detailed demographic information on radio listeners in Canada, and media consumption habits of the market research participants. Additionally, both teams had access to information regarding participant recruiting and data collection protocols.

2.2   Team Composition

Each of the two teams comprised three graphic designers and each is led by a researcher. The designers varied in their experience with developing metaphors and user interfaces, but all had existing design experience and training. In addition, a third researcher provided guidance to the teams and developed the experimental hypothesis.

2.3 Design Process

Both the UCD and the DDD teams worked through their particular design process in parallel. Figure 1 shows the procedure for both teams. The design process began with data analysis, then a design phase, followed by prototyping and then evaluation. The teams repeated the cycle in order to further refine the designs, aiming towards high fidelity prototypes. In each cycle, the main difference between the two teams occurred during data analysis and evaluation.

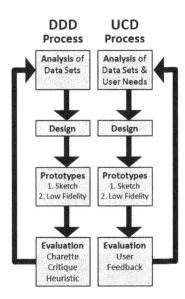

Fig. 1. The UCD and DDD design processes.

In these two phases, the UCD team's focus was on information provided by users, while the DDD team remained isolated from users. During the data analysis phase, the UCD team gathered data on the users, including developing personas, writing and administering questionnaires and conducting task-analysis [5]. The DDD team was provided with the raw data files, and guided on how to identify relationships in the data that would be interesting to visualize by users. Evaluation for the UCD team involves users, while the DDD team relied on the use of charrette's, critiques and heuristic evaluation [2].

Throughout the design process, the UCD and DDD teams did not communicate nor share experiences regarding their work. We believe this allowed us to better understand differences in the two approaches.

2.4 Observations

The themes emerging from the data were divided into three categories: (i) a focus on listener behavior and consumption patterns, (ii) a focus on geographical aspects of the data, and (iii) a focus on temporal qualities of the data. While these themes are consistent in both UCD and DDD, each team developed distinctly different insights and metaphors.

2.5   UCD Results

As expected, by working closely with users of existing NLogic information visualization tools, the early designs of the UCD team represented incremental improvements to the existing tools which were intended to correct shortcomings with existing data visualization metaphors and interfaces. Even when encouraged to try more unorthodox designs, the sketches remained tightly coupled with the results of user task analysis.

For example, Fig. 2 shows the use of a tree metaphor which is not only familiar in the field of information visualization, but the suggested interaction between user and prototype was identical to actions described in the needs assessment. This prototype changed one means of analyzing the data for another by altering the aesthetics of the interface and making improvements in usability, but failed to evoke new perspectives on the data. This is an important point, since the incorporation of a different metaphor ideally reveals something in the data that the previous metaphor did not.

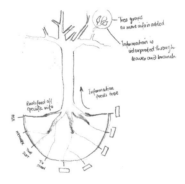

Fig. 2. UCD sketch: analogy of tree, where dynamic queries are performed through the roots, which in turn make the tree grow based on what it's been fed with.

2.6   DDD Results

In contrast to the UCD team prototypes, the prototypes that emerged from the DDD team made use of more granular data and considered the nature of how the data itself was collected. The designs introduced metaphors intended to present data about radio stations' listener demographics to a general audience in a novel way (for example via physical radio sets blaring in the hallways of the NLogic offices, as showed in Fig. 3). Some of the prototypes propose visualizations that allow technical staff at NLogic to monitor panelists' activity and identify potential anomalies and outliers in the data.

Fig. 3. DDD sketch: a wall of sound composed of physical radios, each representing a specific station, and of which the different components are mapped to data variables (Fig. 4).

The insights found in the work of the DDD team emerged from their focus on relationships within the data that existing tools did not foreground, rather than on existing user problems or needs. The technology used to present this data also moved beyond the traditional desktop interface (e.g., Figs. 3–5), which was not explored in the UCD approach.

We identified four key challenges to the methodology observed to date: designer bias, working with an industry partner, maintaining separation of design teams, and enforcing a DDD environment.

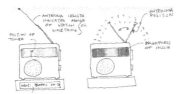

Fig. 4. DDD sketch: mapping radio components (antenna, displays, sounds etc.) to the data.

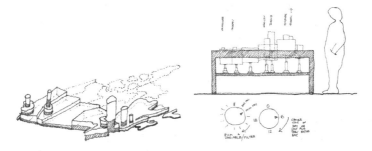

Fig. 5. DDD sketch: a physical model conveying the number of auditors per geographical regions through the elevation of these. Controls allow for the selection of different radio stations and various data filtering.

2.7   Existing Design Bias

During the first phase of sketching most of the designers came up with "typical" UI visualizations, including traditional widgets such as buttons and checkboxes to navigate the data. We believe this speaks to the existing preconceptions and training of many designers. Designers are trained to consider and imagine the user and hence bring assumptions about users to their work even in the absence of a clear definition of user needs. This bias can limit initial attempts at innovation and experimental design in both a UCD and DDD approach. Creative methods from the design world, such as probes and brainstorming techniques, have been created to subvert existing bias and focus on the user's immediate needs and expectations rather than the potential of a design [12].

2.8   Conducting Research with an Industry Partner

Conducting research in the context of an industrial partner presents several challenges. Sedlmair et al. [13] discuss issues that also arose in our work such as access to data, selecting an evaluation context, finding domain expert participants, confidentiality of information and engaging with complex work processes. Additional issues pertain to conducting concurrent design approaches involving the same lead researchers and representatives of the industrial partner who had contact with both design teams. While working on the same data visualization project, our comparative study imposed two separate approaches, which can cause potential confusion from our partners' point of view when exchanging information with one or the other team. It is essential to ensure that the representative of the industrial partner both have the time to devote to concurrent projects, and perfectly understand the design protocols of each.

2.9   Keep the Design Teams Separated, yet Synchronized

To guarantee a valid design protocol within the two design teams, they must not share information between each other. This can become an issue, when sharing the same work space, and organizational measures should be put into place so as to minimize the odds of the designers mistakenly exchanging information across teams. At the same time, we argue that it is preferable that the teams remain more or less synchronized in the overall design process and also for final evaluation with users.

2.10   Filtering Out Information from Users

While working with a large, complex database comprising many data tables and relations, it was necessary to maintain contact with our industrial partners, asking for clarifications and additional material (for example, the data collection protocol employed). In their answers to our questions, our partners sometimes provide user-contextual information that, if communicated to the DDD team, potentially introduces additional bias.

The design problems the two teams chose to address differed. On the one hand, the problems expressed by current users of the visualization tools employed to analyze the data shaped the design work of the UCD team, whereas the DDD team found problems to address via the data tables themselves. The raw data, in the absence of a known user, suggest visualizations, new aesthetics, uses and interpretations that may not have otherwise been proposed. We consider this a measure of creativity. While we did not expect to find examples of radical innovation (and we have not), we have found differences in outcomes from the UCD and DDD teams that are worth exploring further.

Importantly, the DDD team tended towards designs that communicated the statistical limitations of the NLogic dataset, which the designs of the UCD did not. This was a finding of particular interest to our industrial partner, who expressed struggles with reminding their clients of the limits of the data itself. Gathered from a large population sample, the increasing subdivision of the data results in sample sizes that are statistically insignificant (for example, from Canadian women (n = 1200) to women in Toronto (n = 200) to women between the ages of 18 and 24 (n = 42) to women who listened to over 3 h of radio per day (n = 8)). Clients had been considering the data at such a granular level, that the perceived correlations between data points was no longer valid.

In subsequent projects, described below, we continue to consider the differences between a UCD and a DDD approach to addressing design challenges. Work with The Globe and Mail (the Sophi Heads-Up Display) represents a UCD approach, whereas the Tangible User Interface research project emerged directly from our work with NLogic, continuing a DDD approach.

3   Part 2: Case Studies

3.1   User-Centred Design Case Study: The Sophi Heads-up Display

The Sophi Heads-up Display (HUD) is an analytics tool developed with a user-centered design approach for editors at Canada's The Globe and Mail newspaper. It overlays relevant data about articles' performances onto The Globe and Mail website, allowing news editors to easily make data-driven decisions throughout their workday. This technology represents a significant change within the editorial practices of newspapers. The Sophi HUD is a sign of the significant disintermediation occurring within media industries where data analysis increasingly supports traditional editorial decision-making. Such systems are intended to facilitate editorial decisions which are no longer purely intuitive but engaged with data regarding readership. The Sophi HUD shows article performance over time in relation to reader engagement with content and related advertisements. It introduced alerts on rapidly trending data, alerts editors to articles that may be underperforming in relation to editorial expectations, provided access to more granular data regarding an article (such as the number of readers and length of time of engagement over time) in order to help identify underlying reasons for the article's performance, and introduces a chart the editor can use to view and compare the popularity of all articles appearing on The Globe and Mail website that were published in the previous 24 h.

Design of the Sophi HUD was informed by intensive collaboration with The Globe and Mail employees. Data on editorial practice and requirements emerged from 20 semi-structured interviews with a broad representation of editorial team members. This data was supplemented by participant observation through job shadowing, cataloguing the data analysis tools that they were currently using, and undertaking design work in situ with users. These practices recognize that work environments influence cognitive processes and must be considered when designing a software system [14]. Our close interaction with editors and other stakeholders (including the data analytics team at the Globe and Mail) provided us with the context from which the requirements emerged, allowing us to modify our initial designs with a better understanding of the challenges faced by users of our proposed system.

The Sophi HUD has undergone a number of iterations, each informed by user feedback generated from interviews, training sessions, participatory design charrettes, and informal requests. The Globe and Mail has integrated the Sophi HUD into a number of editors' daily routines, and it continues to evolve as users learn from the data presented to them. The editorial team adopted the new tool at a time of significant transition in the use of data in making editorial decisions. The goal of this technology is to facilitate new kinds of insights, using data as well as "gut instincts". The Sophi HUD supports the creative problem solving requirements that are fundamental to editorial tasks, but does not provide a new way of thinking or metaphor regarding through the nature of how a digital newspaper is experienced by its readers.

The UCD approach was appropriate in this project because the users had very clear requirements and needs based on the data the organization collected. Innovation was not the goal; instead, we focused on developing improvements over tools that the editorial team had utilized, but which had not adequately addressed editorial needs. Both Chartbeat [15] and Parse.ly [16] are web analytics software products that are familiar to the editorial team users. Composed of a dashboard and a heads-up display system, these two products provided the users with examples of data visualization and analysis tools that could positively support editorial responsibilities. Knowledge of these software products, in particular their strengths and weaknesses, informed the design of the Sophi HUD. Further research would warrant a DDD approach to see if different kinds of realizations emerge from the data, once the editors become more familiar with the Sophi HUD.

3.2   Data-Driven Design Case Study: A Tangible User Interface for Radio Listenership Data

Emerging directly from our initial study with NLogic, the DDD group developed a series of metaphors making use of physical interfaces with the data. Sketches were developed which included proposals for a wall of transistor radios (where the position of the antenna and the volume represented different data points, see Fig. 4), a national map with 3D data representations (where the volume and height of the objects represented data points connected to specific geographic locations, see Fig. 5) and a table with mechanical functions that would raise or lower various columns, each representing an aspect of listenership data, inspired by the inForm interface from MIT [17]. While none of these sketches led to prototypes, when shared with potential users (our industrial partners) the notion of improving collaboration emerged as a design challenge. While the industrial

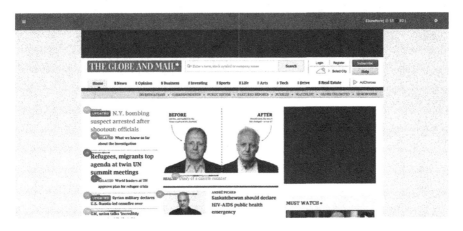

Fig. 6. The Sophi Heads-Up display.

partners explained that many collaborations take place remotely by means of telecommunications, they identified a need for a tool encouraging people to not only work on the same problem, but to work on it together at the same time in the same room (Fig. 6).

To address this design challenge, we created a prototype for a Tangible User Interface (TUI) for interactive data visualization. In this instance DDD processes focused on giving the designers the largest creative range possible, outside of immediate user needs. Research indicates that graspable tangible interfaces measurably increase collaborative behavior when compared to screen-based interfaces [18–22]. Our hybrid system combines a tabletop graspable user interface with a two-dimensional screen display; the users interrogate the data by manipulating tokens on the tabletop and the screen displays the results of the user's query. The tokens are tracked by means of a camera placed discretely beneath the transparent tabletop. The bottom of each object is marked with a fiducial marker, and the camera placed below the table captures the image of the fiducial markers in real time. The fiducial markers are read using open-source reacTIVision software [23]. The reacTIVision software outputs the position of the markers, if they are in the field of view of the camera, and this information is input into our software, which constructs the visualizations from a (user-provided) database (Fig. 7).

While the first prototype used NLOGIC's radio station listener demographic data to create a market research package for advertisers targeting radio air time [24, 25], this system can be (and has been) generalized to query various data sets. The software is designed to allow users to provide their own formatted data, and there are no specialized hardware requirements. The system consists of our software, a webcam, and fidicual markers with which to tag the tokens. The fiducial markers can be printed and attached to any object the user wishes to use to explore their data set.

We believe that the TUI combines embodied cognitive processes, with multiple perspectives on the data from collaborating users, thus opening up the possibilities of new discoveries about the data. As an outcome of a DDD approach, TUI represents an innovation that did not emerge from any existing analytics tools available to the user. Only by removing an understanding of the requirements and needs of users,

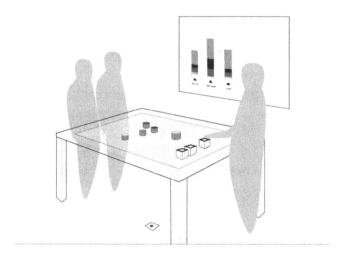

Fig. 7. Schematic of interactions with the tangible interface

was the design team able to propose conceptual tools that open a window on different interactions between - and with - data.

4   Discussion and Conclusion

Different design challenges require different approaches. In order to marshal the creativity of designers and the creativity of users, it is important to understand the broader requirements of a project: is innovation a necessary component or is there instead a need for incremental improvement over existing processes?

When the design challenge is focused on the improvement of an existing set of tools, then a UCD approach is most effective. Incremental improvement requires an acknowledgement that existing insights emerging from data sets should not be replaced, but rather that they need to be observed more efficiently or in a more nuanced manner. In other words, existing approaches provide cognitive aids that can be improved through the design process.

Where new or different insights are required, a UCD approach may prove less successful because of the fundamental focus on perceived user needs, and the constraints then returned to the analysts in the tool provided. Articulating user needs risks the elimination of innovative designs, particularly if there are existing data visualization tools used to analyze the data set.

However, while research has considered the shortcomings of UCD as a means to innovate [26], we have found it to be an effective means for creating tools that can support changes within workplace practices and allow prospective users to feel ownership and engagement with the technology. The Sophi HUD was found to be immediately useful for the editorial team at the Globe and Mail. Various users at the newspaper have adopted this visualization platform, and we continue to work closely with them to develop improvements and to meet their emerging needs. Sophi HUD emerged from close consultation with users in order to address the shortcomings of existing tools. As a result, workplace practices have changed dramatically as editors increasingly understand the relationship of readership data to their particular practice. The Sophi HUD has successfully supported the cognitive requirements of its users, proven by its adoption and continued use.

While the Sophi HUD was successfully designed to optimise the needs of a specific set of users, a key outcome of the DDD approach appears to be versatility of use. The TUI system fits a variety of users and situations. Since the initial design did not respond to a set of requirements and needs, there are fewer limits on how the tool may be applied. For example, the TUI system has been adopted by school teachers for classroom use. By not focusing a narrow set of user needs, we were able to create a software system that allows users to explore different data sets in different environments and situations. Whereas the UCD approach resulted in a tool with limited use cases, the DDD approach provides cognitive support for a wide variety of users and data sets. The application of the TUI is bound only by the creative capacities of potential users, which are broad.

The strength and weakness of each system (Sophi HUD versus TUI) is not necessarily found in the ultimate usefulness of the system – but rather in the appropriateness of the design processes to specific design challenges. Sophi HUD addresses a clear set of requirements. Editors have previously worked with similar software and were able to articulate the pros and cons of Chartbeat and Parse.ly. Thus, the design of the Sophi HUD incorporates the strengths of existing software, removes unnecessary functionality, and produces a bespoke tool that is tightly coupled with user needs and served effectively in a significant work force transition. The various methodologies incorporated in the UCD approach provided the designers with objectives and a clear direction in terms of constrained but effective creativity.

The DDD approach resulted in systems that users found to be a significant innovation over existing tools. It is doubtful that the TUI system would have emerged from a UCD approach, which insists on a tight connection between designer and user and a clarity of user requirements. The TUI represents innovation and a leap forward in terms of tools that the industry partner (NLogic) would incorporate into their work practice. However, the shift to using a tool that encourages curiosity and collaboration requires a fundamental shift in terms of work practice. The Sophi HUD was deemed trustworthy because it incorporated existing user relationships with a data visualization tool; the TUI asks the user to abandon their current work practice in exchange for both data insights that may be radically different from existing software applications, and for facilitated collaboration.

DDD is not an approach that eliminates the need for involving a user in the design process. We undertook user testing and feedback into various iterations of the TUI. In this process the design team identified a series of new uses for the TUI well beyond its original context. DDD re-orders the steps of designing for a user group – instead of gathering requirements and needs and then looking for means to address those needs, the designer first considers the data and the potential relationship of data points to propose tools of analysis which are then refined based on requirements and needs. The user should never be removed from the design process, but where they are positioned in the initial design stage may be the difference between iterative and innovative design outcomes.

The TUI has proven valuable to a broad range users and analysts, specifically in the field of education where the goal is to encourage free-ranging exploration of a wide range of data sets in a collaborative environment. On the other hand, the Sophi-HUD rapidly became an indispensable tool in the editorial room at The Globe and Mail. We will continue to explore and compare both the UCD and DDD design methods to better understand the context and applications in which each of these approaches best supports creativity and insight.

Acknowledgement. The authors with to thank Bianca Channer, Lan-xi Dong, Alex Gebhardt, Stephen Keller, Lauren Livingston, Anton Mwewa, Anne Stevens, Borzu Talaie and Phuong Ha Vu. We thank our industrial partners Jonathan Lee and David Phillips from NLogic and Gordon Edall from the Globe and Mail for their time and valuable input. We also note with thanks the important contributions of Fanny Chevalier (to the pilot study) and Jessica Peter (to the Sophi HUD case study). This research is supported by the BRAIN Alliance via the Ontario Research Fund - Research Excellence (ORF-RE) program. Additional funding provided by the NSERC Strategic Parternship program, MITACS, and the OCE-VIP program.

References

1. Norman, D.A., Verganti, R.: Incremental and radical innovation: design research vs. technology and meaning change. Des. Issues **30**(1), 78–96 (2013)
2. Rogers, Y., Sharp, H., Preece, J.: Interaction Design: Beyond Human - Computer Interaction, 3rd edn. Wiley, Chichester (2011)
3. Tufte, E.R.: The Visual Display of Quantitative Information, 2nd edn. Graphics Press, Cheshire (2001)
4. Espinosa, O.J., Hendrickson, C., Garrett, J.H.: Domain analysis: a technique to design a user-centered visualization framework. In: 1999 Proceedings of IEEE Symposium on Information Visualization, (Info Vis 1999), vol. 144, pp. 44–52 (1999)
5. Gould, J.D.: Human-computer interaction. In: Baecker, R.M., Grudin, J., Buxton, W.A.S., Greenberg, S. (eds.) The Art of Human Computer Interface Design, pp. 93–121. Morgan Kaufmann Publishers Inc., San Francisco (1995)
6. Button, G.: The Ethnographic Tradition and Design. Des. Stud. **21**(4), 319–332 (2000)
7. Salvador, T., Mateas, M.: Introduction to design ethnography. In: CHI 1997 Extended Abstracts on Human Factors in Computing Systems, CHI EA 1997, pp. 166–167. ACM, New York (1997)
8. Bjögvinsson, E., Ehn, P., Hillgren, P.-A.: Design things and design thinking: contemporary participatory design challenges. Des. Issues **28**(3), 101–116 (2012)
9. Schuler, D., Namioka, A.: Participatory Design: Principles and Practices. CRC Press, Boca Raton (1993)
10. Reas, C., Fry, B.: Processing: A Programming Handbook for Visual Designers and Artists. MIT Press, Cambridge (2007)
11. Greenberg, S., Buxton, B.: Usability evaluation considered harmful (some of the time). In: Proceedings of the SIGCHI Conference on Human Factors in Computing Systems, CHI 2008, pp. 111–120. ACM, New York (2008)

12. Gaver, W.W., Boucher, A., Pennington, S., Walker, B.: Cultural probes and the value of uncertainty. Interactions **11**(5), 53–56 (2004)
13. Sedlmair, M., Isenberg, P., Baur, D., Butz, A.: Information visualization evaluation in large companies: challenges, experiences and recommendations. Inf. Visual. **10**(3), 248–266 (2011)
14. Suchman, L.: Human-Machine Reconfigurations: Plans and Situated Actions. Cambridge University Press, Cambridge (2007)
15. Chartbeat | Building the Attention Economy (2017). https://chartbeat.com/. Accessed 7 February
16. Parse.ly | Audience Data & Content Analytics for Digital Media (2017). https://www.parsely.com/. Accessed 7 February
17. Follmer, S., Leithinger, D., Olwal, A., Hogge, A., Ishii, H.: inFORM: dynamic physical affordances and constraints through shape and object actuation. In: Proceedings of the 26th Annual ACM Symposium on User Interface Software and Technology, UIST 2013, pp. 417–426. ACM, New York (2013)
18. Antle, A.N., Wise, A.F.: Getting down to details: using theories of cognition and learning to inform tangible user interface design. Interact. Comput. **25**(1), 1–20 (2013)
19. Kim, M.J., Maher, M.L.: The impact of tangible user interfaces on spatial cognition during collaborative design. Des. Stud. **29**(3), 222–253 (2008)
20. Schneider, B., Jermann, P., Zufferey, G., Dillenbourg, P.: Benefits of a tangible interface for collaborative learning and interaction. IEEE Trans. Learn. Technol. **4**(3), 222–232 (2011)
21. Schneider, B., Sharma, K., Cuendet, S., Zufferey, G., Dillenbourg, P., Pea, A.D.: 3D tangibles facilitate joint visual attention in dyads. In: International Conference on Computer Supported Collaborative Learning (CSCL), pp. 158–165 (2015)
22. Ma, J., Sindorf, L., Liao, I., Frazier, J.: Using a tangible versus a multi-touch graphical user interface to support data exploration at a museum exhibit. In: Proceedings of the Ninth International Conference on Tangible, Embedded, and Embodied Interaction, TEI 2015, pp. 33–40. ACM, New York (2015)
23. Kaltenbrunner, M., Bencina, R.: . reacTIVision: a computer-vision framework for table-based tangible interaction. In: Proceedings of the 1st International Conference on Tangible and Embedded Interaction, TEI 2007, pp. 69–74. ACM, New York (2007). doi:10.1145/1226969.1226983
24. Jofre, A., Szigeti, S., Keller, S.T., Dong, L.-X., Czarnowski, D., Tomé, F., Diamond, S.: A tangible user interface for interactive data visualization. In: Proceedings of the 25th Annual International Conference on Computer Science and Software Engineering, CASCON 2015, pp. 244–247. IBM Corp., Riverton (2015)
25. Jofre, A., Szigeti, S., Tiefenbach-Keller, S., Dong, L.-X., Diamond, S.: Manipulating tabletop objects to interactively query a database. In: Proceedings of the 2016 CHI Conference Extended Abstracts on Human Factors in Computing Systems, CHI EA 2016, pp. 3695–3698. ACM, New York (2016). doi:10.1145/2851581.2890260
26. Crabtree, A., Rodden, T., Tolmie, P., Button, G.: Ethnography considered harmful. In: Proceedings of the SIGCHI Conference on Human Factors in Computing Systems, CHI 2009, pp. 879–888. ACM, New York (2009). doi:10.1145/1518701.1518835

The Foundation of the SEE BEYOND Method: Fashion Design and Neuroeducation Applied to the Teaching of the Project Methodology to Students with Congenital and Acquired Blindness

Geraldo Coelho Lima Júnior[✉] and Rachel Zuanon

Sense Design Lab, Graduate Program in Design, Anhembi Morumbi University, São Paulo, Brazil
glimadesign58@gmail.com, rzuanon@anhembi.br,
rachel.z@zuannon.com.br

Abstract. The SEE BEYOND teaching method is designed to include people with visual impairment in higher education fashion-design courses. This method employs a wide range of teaching material that is commonly used in Brazilian higher education institutions. Neuroscience is regarded as a field of knowledge that is essential for creating instruments and carrying out activities aimed at the sensory-motor stimulation of students, whether blind or with normal sight, and encourage them to be involved in the teaching methodology of the Fashion Design project. This article addresses the first of the three modules that structure the SEE BEYOND method: Foundation. The undertaking is combined with the following neuroscientific concepts: Identification, Abstraction, Appropriation and Consolidation. It examines the various ways the module can assist students with congenital and acquired blindness, particularly with regard to the following: (a) the recognition of contours and surfaces; (b) spatial perception based on the relation between two-dimensional and three-dimensional planes; (c) the creative process; (d) the links between the mould and garment; (e) the consolidation of skills; (f) and the exercise of self-criticism.

Keywords: Visual impairment · Fashion design · Neuroscience · Education · Project methodology

1 Introduction

The lack of research studies into the needs of students with visual impairments, or in more specific terms, in higher education Fashion Design courses, has led to the conception and development of the SEE BEYOND method which incorporates this sector in its training sessions. The title of this method consists of an acronym that forms the phoneme SEE, which is made up of the words Stimulate, Educate and Enlarge, which is then attached to the preposition BEYOND. Broadening the range of stimuli experienced by students with or without visual impairments, empowers the teaching/learning process and heightens our awareness of the features needed for compiling collections in fashion design.

© Springer International Publishing AG 2017
N. Streitz and P. Markopoulos (Eds.): DAPI 2017, LNCS 10291, pp. 528–546, 2017.
DOI: 10.1007/978-3-319-58697-7_40

Students with a lack of vision are supported by other sensory directions which can assist them in assimilating and making use of the content provided to achieve the pedagogical aims set out in a higher education training course. In this way, by following the stages of the SEE BEYOND method, touch, smell, hearing, taste and balance, can play a special role that very often goes unnoticed by people with normal sight.

On the basis of these assumptions, the SEE BEYOND method employs a wide range of teaching materials that are commonly adopted in Brazilian higher education institutions. In other words, it recognizes the value of creating and applying instruments and activities that are aimed at the sensory motor stimulation of students, both blind and with normal sight, and for teaching a methodology that can be employed for fashion design. This involves being structured into three modules: (A) Foundation; (B) Enhancement; (C) Materialization. In the sphere of (A) Foundation, the aim is to show the basis of knowledge about design and fashion so that it can serve as a theoretical framework for undertaking projects. With regard to (B) – Enhancement - it is devoted to teaching all the stages related to carrying out projects in fashion design. On the question of (C) – Materialization - all the knowledge acquired in the two previous phases is drawn on and applied to a project that involves forming a fashion collection.

The SEE BEYOND method regards Neuroscience as an essential field of knowledge for pedagogical and andragogical planning - "The brain is the organ of learning" (1). This is taken as a point of departure for this research study where an attempt is made to confront and overcome the obstacles raised by people with visual impairment and find ways of producing new kinds of knowledge. Discoveries in recent years about the development of the human brain, (largely brought about by examinations made through images), have allowed an understanding of a range of cerebral processes, including those linked to questions of learning, memory training and the consolidation of knowledge.

There has been an expansion of studies in the field of Neuroscience [2–12] and Neuroeducation [1, 13–15] which has allowed significant advances to be made in the area of education. This link between Neuroscience and Education is still being forged and has led to in-depth studies, particularly in this century. However, it is rooted in the studies of Luria [16] and Vygotsky [17], early in the 20th century who investigated the reactions and behavior of people with regard to learning as a means of creating knowledge and also belonging to their environment. This article is particularly concerned with the stages in which the module for Foundation (in the SEE BEYOND method) is structured and how it is expressed in neuroscientific concepts: Identification, Abstraction, Appropriation and Consolidation [18–24]. It seeks to ensure that the lesson content taught in fashion design to students with visual impairment or normal sight, can be understood, and assimilated, and thus exist as a memory that can be evoked in the two subsequent modules. This is achieved by employing teaching material that is especially prepared so that it can be made available to people with visual impairment while at the same time serving as teaching/learning resources for students with normal sight.

The Foundation module has a teaching schedule of 24 h and is structured in twelve face-to-face weekly sessions. It is supplemented by a chance to establish communication through other means, such as discussion groups in social network, and e-mails, as well as being able to carry out practical activities outside school that can lead to other kinds of knowledge being produced.

The feelings of touch and hearing are constantly being sought for this, either at the same time or alternately, when planning the features involved in the work [shape, silhouette, color, tissues, frameworks, modelling, trimming, finishing and improvements] [19, 25]; and as well as this, deciding how they should be linked in a chronological order. Fashion, defined as a system [26], is cyclical. Chronological order governs the principles of dressing which reflect society [27], as well as economic and technological change [28–31], and hence have an impact on Fashion Design.

It is hoped that both blind students and those with normal sight can retain this information through the mediation of sensory-motor stimuli and after this, process the mental images. "The mapped patterns constitute what we, conscious creatures, know as visions, sounds, tactile sensations, smells, tastes, pain, pleasure and things of this kind – in short, images. The images in our minds are the momentaneous maps that the brain creates from everything inside or outside of our body, whether concrete or abstract images, in progress or previously engraved in our memory" [4]. In other words, they enhance what has been learnt on the basis of mental maps that are present in individuals and upgraded in real time with regard to the surrounding environment [23] and have associations with their memories. In the sections that follow, the connections are made clear between the different phases of the module that forms the Foundation of the SEE BEYOND method and its neuroscientific concepts of Identification, Abstraction, Appropriation and Consolidation.

2   Identification

Each meaning has its sensory portal and the capacity of the individual to identify an object or environment originates "from the group of regions of the body around which the perception emerges" [5].

This interactive process between the environment and the body, which is directly linked to the brain, is detected by the sense organs or "sensory portals" [5]. In other words, (…) in the case of vision, the sensory portal includes not only the ocular musculature through which we move our eyes, but also the whole apparatus used to focus on an object. This includes the mechanism used to focus on an object by adjusting the size of the lens, the mechanism for adjusting the luminous intensity which dilates or enlarges the pupils (the shutters of the cameras of our eyes) and finally, the muscles around the eyes, by means of which we frown, blink or register delight. (…) Seeing does not just consist of obtaining an appropriate luminous pattern in the retina [5].

Understanding the sensory portals gives a broader idea of how to prepare the resources that are needed to establish the SEE BEYOND method. The study of the sensory portals of touch and sight are essential to achieve this end, as well as taste, smell, and spatial balance, which are all connected to the somatosensitive cortices [5].

All the information that originates from these portals has an intermediary station in the thalamus which leads on to the cerebral cortex where relations are established with the following: sensitivity, driveability, emotional behavior, memory and the activation of the cortex [5, 17].

When creating and planning the program content of the Foundation module, it was believed to be a limitation in the case of blind students and it was thus necessary to provide the resources that could make it possible for them to identify the objects they were given and make a connection between the objects and program content employed for each session of the module. For example, when there was a need to identify the silhouette and the contours of the human body, an articulated doll made of wood that was often used in design classes, was given to the blind students as a reference-point for the human figure. Following this, a board was used that reproduces the same articulation points that are found in a wooden doll. This was fitted with a cotton string on a two-dimensional surface, in a way that could allow a tactile reading of a three-dimensional object. This strategy achieves the purpose of offering a person with visual impairment two ways of representing the human figure, that is two-dimensional (the board) and three-dimensional (the doll). Thus relations can be established between two objects and the figure can be identified (Fig. 1).

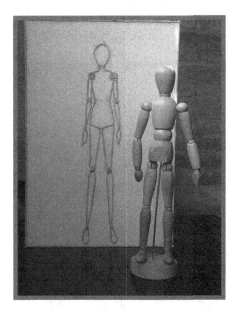

Fig. 1. Tactile board and doll, articulated in wood.

On this basis, the prospect of being able to represent the body in tactile boards is broadened to include representations of the dressed body so that items of clothing on the body and their distinct movements can be highlighted, as well as what they add to the history of fashion (Fig. 2).

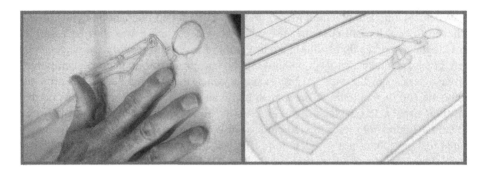

Fig. 2. Tactile boards.

Metal mini sculptures were also created on the basis of the articulated wooden doll and these – in parallel with the embossed designs – made it easier to identify the represented object and perhaps understand the spatial relationship provided by the area bordering each of them. That is, it was possible to locate the inside and outside of the mini sculptures and their relation with the body of the wooden doll (Fig. 3).

Fig. 3. Tactile board and mini sculpture.

In all the teaching material used in the SEE BEYOND method, it is understood that the recognition of the properties of the objects can occur by means of other sensory channels (touch, hearing, and taste which can be directly connected to odour through the identification of smells), as was the case found with people with visual impairment. However, in this stage of the Foundation module, touch is valued and becomes the sensory meaning that can most recognize these materials and their relations with the environment. In the opinion of Damásio [4], the preparation of the surrounding space is based on the ability of the individual to interact with it and with all the objects present there, through the mapping carried out by the brain. In the use of the word 'object', as described by this author, it is possible that a chair, the sea or wind can be designated as objects which in some way undergo an interaction with the brain; or the object can even be made unique for the individual in the way it is arranged and spread to different parts of the brain. Although there are distinct cortical regions that have special features that respond to particular stimuli, there is a process involving the interconnecting areas that form the cerebral. This is because (…) all the perceptive and cognitive tasks (such as the recognition of objects, decoding and recovery of memory, reading, memory of work, attention processing, motor planning and awareness), are the result of the distribution of large-scale cerebral network [2].

3   Abstraction and Appropriation

With regard to learning, different procedures are carried out by the human brain throughout the period of its life. The concept of Identification, outlined in the previous section, can be included as one of them. Abstraction and Appropriation are others that are also related since they are experienced by the individual when in contact with objects in his surroundings. Although they are different, they are interwoven and for this reason, are included here together.

It is by means of the brain that the individual assimilates, thinks, understands and acts. The brain intervenes in the meanings and (depending on how it perceives the outside world), controls its activities and human behavior. Every kind of acquired knowledge constitutes cerebral activities [5], and before it can form memories, the brain must enter into contact with the environment and with the objects that form it, whether a landscape seen from a distance or something much nearer that it is possible to touch.

In one way or another, the brain processes this information in accordance with the constancy and abstraction that establish close relations with vision and the other sensory meanings. Constancy is designed "to seek knowledge of the constant and essential properties" of objects and surfaces, when the information obtained, changes from moment to moment" [15].

A correlation between constancy and abstraction is necessary for the development and subsequent application of accessible resources in the realm of the SEE BEYOND method. As illustrated in the image below, by employing the plain mould, (which is shaped by the students) and with the aid of the articulated dolls, it is possible to create huge numbers of skirts that correspond to different historical periods. The handling of material and draping these on articulated dolls, invokes the concepts of abstraction, assimilation and appropriation. The dimensions of each of the moulds can be recognized by the differences between them when they are superimposed and at the same time, this stimulates the students and provides them with a capacity for abstraction and appropriation. The handling allows the students with visual impairment to make adjustments to the bodies of the articulated dolls and produce different volumes; as a result, this can provide a greater scope for abstraction among the possible shapes of this object.

Thus the process of abstraction begins to be a natural practice in this process which is pervaded by activities involving the identification and abstraction of the objects [19] (Fig. 4).

Fig. 4. Abstraction and Appropriation: a study involving two-dimensional and three-dimensional forms.

In addition, in the choice of prime materials employed for building teaching material, the same features are kept for each type of resource needed; this is a strategy adopted to preserve the concept of constancy.

With regard to abstraction, Zeki [21] states that this is "a critical step in the efficient acquisition of knowledge; without it, the brain would be enslaved to the particular. The capacity to abstract is also probably imposed on the brain by the limitations of its memory system, because it does away with the need to recall every detail."

The concept of abstraction can also be defined in other ways. Nee et al. [22] believe that there are different levels of abstraction which in turn are processed or detected in different areas of the prefrontal cortex. According to these authors, "abstraction refers to the degree to which processing/representation is tied to or divorced from particular instances" [22]. With regard to the kind of operation involved in abstraction, they put forward two theories – temporal and relational – each with its own operations and distinct responses to the stimuli received by the brain. In these cases, the kind of processing is tied to determined kinds of thoughts and intentions.

According to Nee et al. [22], temporal abstraction adopts the notion that the more abstract the objectives are (for example, "buying a car"), the longer will be the periods of responses related to the control of more concrete sub-objectives (for example, "going to the dealership", "having a test drive", etc.).

When employing the SEE BEYOND method, the concept of temporal abstraction can be applied when the objective is (i) how to make a *look* (Foundation) or a fashion collection (Materialization), both characterized as a more abstract objective, followed by; (ii) their respective sub-objectives (designing a model for an item of clothing; defining the textile materials; and completing the manufactured product).

The temporal differs from relational abstraction in so far as with regard to the latter, "the stimuli formed a pattern with one or more dimensions (e.g. shape, orientation, size) changing in an orderly manner across rows and down columns of the matrix" [22] (Fig. 5).

Fig. 5. Abstraction: (a) Design of the model; (b) definition of the textile materials; (c) preparation of the moulds; (d) manufacture.

In the sphere of the Foundation module, the concept of relational abstraction remains clear throughout the stages that follow the construction of the mould for the item of clothing and by working on the planned features (points, lines, shape and volume).

Points and lines are related to the measurements of the body. The relationship of shape x volume is established in a way that cam allow the students to have a clear idea of the correspondence between the volumes found in the items of clothing and the planned shape of the mould. At this time, memories are recovered of two-dimensional and three-dimensional factors (Fig. 6).

Fig. 6. Abstraction: (a) Identification of items of clothing; (b) Identification of details of the moulds.

The skirt was the element that allowed the teaching material to be prepared for an explanation of this subject. As a basis, the skirt was defined in the style that was worn in the 18th Century to establish the relation between shape and volume during a timeline. In this way, the volume given to a crinoline was re-established so that it was possible to highlight the pleated modelling and its variants with regard to its proportions (both width and length).

The framework of the crinoline which was worn as a support for skirts in the 18th and 19th Centuries, resembled the geometric shape of a cone. This was the point of departure in proposing the relation of the volume of the skirt and its structural folds over a period of time.

The importance of this image is that the plane can be traced from the volume.

In other words, what was first shown in a three-dimensional format can be revealed in a two-dimensional manner (Fig. 7).

Fig. 7. Abstraction: (a) tactile exploration of the embossed design; (b) recognition of the circular plane shape in paper; (c) identification of the volume in paper; (d) identification of volume in the crinoline- mini sculpture; (e) determining the space of the crinoline dress.

As mentioned earlier, there are two types of abstraction here and when making contact with objects, they must be investigated in different ways [15, 16]; however, this does not mean that they are processed differently in the brain. According to Gilead et al. [23], "[...] while the road from an abstract thought to concrete action appears paved and organized across fronto-parietal cortex, the opposite direction (turning a particular object into an abstraction) goes through multiple, sporadic, Less-charted paths".

Perlovsky and Ilin [24] adopt the position that the positioning of the abstraction of objects is grounded on recognizable factors (for example cultural) and hence forges a link with memory, together with the sensory perception that people have of objects or environments.

On the question of abstraction, at least three key factors are worth pointing out: (a) it occurs in the presence of a stimulus triggered by an object, e.g. an image, sound, smell, taste or texture; (b) there is a relation between the perception of the object, the memories linked to it and the appropriation of the image of this object by the brain; (c) cultural benchmark are important in so far as they act as a means of leading the abstraction to the appropriation.

These factors are significant within the teaching/learning process at several levels, particularly when those who are learning have visual impairment. However, it should not be overlooked that the same observations are applicable to students with normal sight because cerebral processes such as abstraction and appropriation are necessary for the learning of every human being. Appropriation entails a natural sequence in the process of abstraction which has a direct effect on the concept of appropriation. In other words, identification and continuous abstraction of objects means that the brain is able to make use of this information in a way that can lead to its appropriation and hence its consolidation in memory – the concept described in the next section.

4   Consolidation

Consolidation is closely linked to memory, a key factor when examining the learning process. It is a requirement of this activity that in the case of all human beings, the information obtained is in due course either saved or rejected, depending on its importance with regard to learning.

Memories are defined by their duration, i.e. whether they will last in the short, medium or long term. Each has its own particular importance in the life of an individual. Short-term memories are responsible for storing recent events and at the other extreme, there are those that involve keeping permanent records. Another way of categorizing them is to contrast the explicit memory which involves routine incidents that are dealt with on an everyday basis, with implicit memory which is linked to activities like riding a bike or brushing one's teeth. These become habits and conduct which can be recovered when requested [1].

The limbic system – a diverse set of cortical and sub-cortical regions that are essential for human behavior – is also bound up with the processing and consolidation of memory, in particular hippocampal training (explicit memory), and also the cognitive aspects of memory. As well as the Hippocampus, there is also the Amygdala brain region which makes connections with memory processes, in so far as it takes part in the acquisition, consolidation and recording of emotional memories. This region is responsible for the processing of the circuits involved in the emotions and emotional behavior [1, 9, 19].

Estrela and Ribeiro [19] explain that it is impossible to imagine any human activity, whether it be mental, motor or affective, in which memory does not play an active role. Without memory, it would be necessary to learn everyday how to carry out the same tasks such as walking, speaking, reading, recognizing people and objects etc.

In reality, it is owing to the fact that we have a motor memory that, for example, we do not have to think about all the stages and movements necessary to blink or raise our hands. And this means that we can always be in a condition to learn something new by making use of previously acquired knowledge, which is called long-term memory.

Thus when learning something new, the memory is able to establish relations that can complement what has already been taught and thus assist in broadening knowledge of a given subject.

In the context of the Foundation module, after the blind students have followed the steps of identification, abstraction and appropriation, when they handle the items of clothing, whether garments from a past historical era or those worn today, they will begin to evoke the memories that have been consolidated until then (Fig. 8).

Fig. 8. Consolidation: (a) tactile observation of items of clothing on display; (b) identification of the texture of an item of clothing.

As shown above, with regard to manufactured items, these students are encouraged to grope and identify the models which are arranged and displayed on the racks. This enables them to recover their memories with regard to shapes, textures, fabrics, volumes, silhouettes, colors, prints and differences between similar models. However, these lead to results that reflect the various ways of dressing in each historical period, as well as the different materials, information about the style, modelling and textile technology, the details of sewing, finishings, materials, timmings and processing used.

In so far as the items of clothing are touched by the students and the teacher provides additional verbal explanations with regard to the frameworks and their importance for fashion design, they form the strategy of the SEE BEYOND method by evoking other memories and consolidating those that are new.

However, it is essential to bear in mind that the memory of data, events and objects can create unreliable images for the same data, events and objects. Several systems interact with different processes of acquisition, assimilation and knowledge and later, the information is consolidated that can be recorded as memory of a long duration. A short memory can recover the whole context in which it is involved since both sensitive and motor factors are required for the memory of an item of information or object [4].

Consolidation is important not only with regard to the Foundation module but also for other modules in the SEE BEYOND method, and thus in every kind of teaching/learning process.

5   Results and Discussion

The scope of this article is restricted to outlining the results and respective discussions involved in the SEE BEYOND method, with students suffering from congenital or acquired blindness. In view of the need for an in-depth study to make a comprehensive inquiry feasible, those that apply to students with normal sight will be the object of a future article.

(a) Identification: outlines and surfaces

The different degrees of visual impairment resulting from congenital or acquired blindness entail different levels of reading and interpretation of the materials given to each of the students with this kind of handicap.

With regard to the Foundation module, some strategies are adopted when giving the silhouettes and shapes of items of clothing to the students. These include: [A] a tactile board with the outlines of a figure made of embossed cotton yarn; [B] a tactile board with a figure formed of embossed dots; [C] a tactile board with the outlines of an embossed figure in cotton yarn with the areas of the fabric filled with ethylene-vinyl acetate (EVA) porous plastic material.

From their birth, the reading and interpretation of tactile boards with outlines of cotton yarn or outlines of dots [A; B] has proved ineffective for students owing to the absence of memories attached to the mental images of the two-dimensional designs and this is owing to the nature of the condition of congenital blindness itself.

In contrast, in the case of students with acquired blindness, the strategy adopted in the tactile board [A], is found to be effective as far as its objective is concerned, which is to communicate information which can be retained about the silhouettes of the items of clothing. The same thing does not apply to the strategy employed in the tactile board [B]. As was found with those suffering from congenital blindness, the reading and interpretation of the silhouette of garments by means of embossed dots, also proved to be inefficient for students with acquired blindness (Fig. 9).

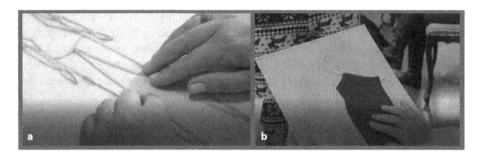

Fig. 9. (a) Identification: tactile reading of a two-dimensional embossed cord design; (b) tactile reading of a two-dimensional E.V.A mould for a design.

An effective strategy is obtained for both groups in the tactile board [C]. With the aid of this, both the students with congenital and acquired blindness are able to identify and learn the information related to the silhouette and to the shape of the garments. This shows the significant contribution made by using the space-filling two-dimensional designs. It also includes the chance to incorporate details in the items such as the pleated effects, cuttings and so on. The welcome given to this model of the tactile board by the students, is due to the fact that when they touch it, they are able to have a clearer understanding of the relation between the volume of the garment and the representation of the body which has been designed with the string.

(b) Relational Abstraction: spatial perception from the relation between the two-dimensional and three-dimensional planes
The purpose of increasing the chance of understanding the silhouettes and the shapes of the models of the dress by combining three-dimensional representations with two-dimensional designs, has proved to be a satisfactory strategy for stimulating spatial perception among both the congenital and acquired blindness groups. For this reason, the formal elements of the two-dimensional design are transposed to three-dimensional space as mini sculptures, in a way that can introduce another category of sensory-motor stimuli for the students. This resource enables the individual to form direct and simultaneous relations with the two-dimensional and three-dimensional representations, which provides them with the means to identify and understand the information regarding the designed items of clothing.

This strategy has an even more satisfactory effect on these groups when the three-dimensional representation, like the mini scuplture, is amplified to a human scale. This allows the student to appropriate the object and decide whether to drape it with a dress and feel it close to his body, and with regard to these two factors – the body and the accessory – to be aware of the surrounding space. It was found that this activity strengthens the understanding of the two-dimensional representation provided by the tactile boards. In addition, it expands the perceptual capacity with regard to the space of the classroom and the space that is formed between the body and the garment (Fig. 10).

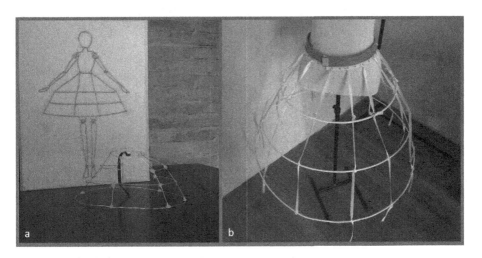

Fig. 10. Relational Abstraction: (a) the tactile board and mini sculpture; (b) crinoline in a human scale.

(c) Relational Abstraction: obstacles to linking the mould with clothes

During the stages of understanding the Foundation module, the process of transposing the parts of a two-dimensional plane mould for the volumetric structure of the three-dimensional body of the user, (in a way that can allow a garment to be made), represents another challenge to the capacity for abstraction of students with congenital or acquired blindness (relational) (Fig. 11).

Fig. 11. Temporal Abstraction: (a) definition of the fabric for the skirt; (b) definition of the fabric for the blouse.

In the case of these individuals, there is a complete lack of any understanding about how the two-dimensional mould formed on paper or cardboard modelling, can be related or adapted to the curves of the body shape. In other words, the capacity for relational abstraction which is required by this process is shown to be no longer applicable because of the methodological convention adopted in lessons on modelling, which recommends teaching this from a mould made of paper (Fig. 12).

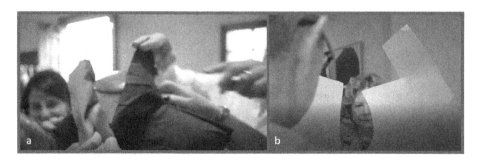

Fig. 12. Relational Abstraction: (a) recognition of the coat on a bust for modelling; (b) recognition of the mould of a coat.

The reversal of the stages in the process referred to can be configured as a responsible strategy for evoking consolidated memories about the structure of the manufactured dress to stimulate the relational abstractions needed for an understanding of how the dress and the mould should match. In other words, the initial stimulus begins to be the item of clothing mounted on the modelling bust and not the mould made of paper. From this, it can be determined to what extent it has a significant capacity to empower the relational abstraction of the students in question [32].

(d) Temporal Abstraction: challenges to the creative process
Within the Foundation module, the stage of conceiving and designing a "look", which is carried out on the basis of the information identified and learnt in the previous stages, reveals a significant difficulty arising from temporal abstraction for students with congenital and acquired blindness.

A challenging time is revealed that is full of anxiety and feelings of insecurity and this stems from the long periods of response to sub-objectives, even though all the sub-objectives have been assimilated. It involves: (i) obtaining an idea of their body measurements; (ii) understanding the design of the mouldings which represent their shapes and volumes; (iii) recognizing the different types of textile substrates; (iv) knowing the right time when these factors can be transposed into the planning of a "look" [a more abstract objective].

Even if the students feel they are able to apprehend the sub-objectives, they raise doubts about their own capacity for abstraction or in other words, new kinds of planning [the creative process] based on the memories consolidated until that time, whether they arise from knowledge acquired in the classroom or from their own private collection.

This conflict can only be overcome through a series of activities carried out by the teacher together with the students which is devoted to strengthening the sensory-motor stimuli and evoking memories.

(e) Appropriation: consolidated experience as a skill
The concept of appropriation is inherent in the progress made in each stage of the Foundation module. However, when undertaking the creation of a "look", this concept is much in evidence (Fig. 13).

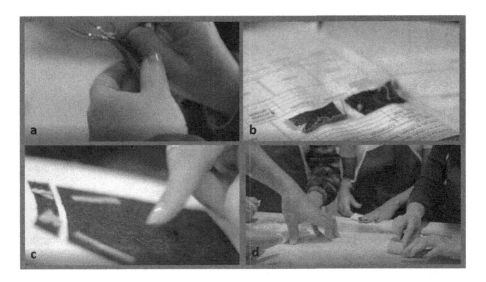

Fig. 13. Appropriation: (a) choice of trimming proportions; (b) definition of fabric; (c) tactile board with a model of the collection; (d) test of hand-made items.

This emphasis derives from associations between the memories that are formed and consolidated while this learning is obtained in this stage of the SEE BEYOND method. Moreover, it involves the individual ideas of each student for planning a project about clothes, which includes the definition of the projected design [shape, silhouette, color, fabrics, frameworks, modelling, trimming, finishing and processing]. In other words, the complexity of this planned process requires the capacity for appropriation of the student to be grouped on a particular skill. In this case, it is of crucial importance for the stimulus to be identified with the pro-activity, curiosity and creativity of the students with congenital or acquired blindness, as a strategy which can strengthen this skill.

(f) Consolidation: recognition and self-criticism

The detection of problems or defects in the prototype of the dress that will be manufactured, is aimed at making corrections and adjustments, and carried out (in a significant contribution to the acquisition of knowledge) during the sessions that are devoted to forming the Foundation module. This derives from the fact that the prototype will be tested on the bodies of students themselves with congenital or acquired blindness and not on the body of a mannequim, as is usually the case in fashion design. This means that in the body itself, it is possible to recognize if there is perhaps a lack of correspondence between the model created, the modelling carried out and the manufactured product obtained. Hence the planned choices of the students are not only provided but also felt in their bodies and this enables them to be self-critical about them (Fig. 14).

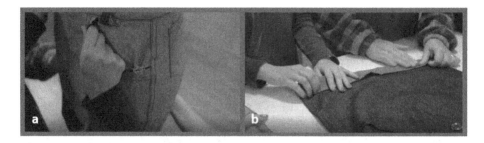

Fig. 14. Consolidation: (a) a clothes test; (b) finding the defects in an item of clothing.

6   Conclusion

The way information is received by students with normal sight differs from what has been found in the domain of those with visual impairment, where oral explanations are easily assimilated. However, a lack of vision has a direct effect on the recognition time of tactile information, which requires more time for a complete apprehension by the blind student.

In this area, the SEE BEYOND method is designed for planning and providing access to pedagogical and andragogical resources which can overcome the obstacles to the inclusion of people with visual impairment in higher education Fashion Design courses. This particularly involves helping them to become accustomed to creating fashion collections and carrying out the necessary steps for preparing them.

This article focused on the Foundation module, the first of the three modules that underpin the SEE BEYOND method, and explored the way it is interwoven with the neuroscientific concepts of Identification, Abstraction, Appropriation and Consolidation. The purpose of this was to pursue lines of thought about the perceptive process of people with congenital and acquired blindness, and the extent of collaboration in the conception and application of material suitable for the visually handicapped and aimed at planned learning.

The main positive outcomes that emerged from the observed results were as follows: (a) the adoption of "areas for filling activities" that were associated with two-dimensional design, proved to be a satisfactory strategy to enable students to perceive contours and surfaces, as well as the details involved; (b) the use of three-dimensional shapes was shown to be of crucial importance for spatial perception and forging a link between two-dimensional and three-dimensional representations. This was the case when the method was applied between the moulds and the items of clothing; (c) the information assimilated in the classroom did not guarantee the capacity for abstraction that is needed for the creative process. Hence, the participation of a teacher devoted to strengthening the sensory-motor stimuli and evoking memories, was found to be an overriding factor in the consolidation of knowledge and the strengthening of the skills of the students; (d) the reversal of the stages of the already established methodology might represent a necessary strategy for the apprehension of the teaching content learnt by the students. This is exemplified here by the exchange involved in the initial stimulus – a garment mounted on the dummy model, instead of a mould made of paper, as a point of departure to make it possible to understand the correspondence between the garment and the mould; (e) stimulating the pro-activity, curiosity and creativity of the student, as well as establishing a link between their personal experiences and what is learnt in the classroom. This proved to be essential to consolidate the kind of skills needed to carry out the projects; (f) the exercise of self-criticism was seen to be essential for the consolidation of learning. Within the method, there was thus evidence of ideas about planned choices when there was a correlation between the created model, the modelling carried out and the final manufactured object.

Further studies will focus on the results and achievements derived from the application of the Foundation module to students with normal sight with a view to broadening the perceptive capacities of this group and the benefits flowing from creative and practical planning. As well as this, future studies will address the two other modules that underpin the SEE BEYOND teaching method: Empowerment and Materialization.

References

1. Cosenza, R.M., Guerra, L.B.: Neurociência e educação: como o cérebro aprende (Neuroscience and education: how the brain learns). Artmed, Porto Alegre (2011)
2. Carter, R.: O livro do cérebro (The Book of the Brain). Agir, Rio de Janeiro (2012)
3. Damásio, A.: Em busca de Espinosa: prazer e dor na ciência dos sentidos (In search of Spinoza: pleasure and pain in the science of the senses). Companhia das Letras, São Paulo (2004)
4. Damásio, A.R.: E o cérebro criou o homem (And the brain created man). Companhia das Letras, São Paulo (2011)
5. Damásio, A.R.: O erro de Descartes: emoção, razão e o cérebro humano (The mistake of Descartes: emotion, reason and the human brain). Companhia das Letras, São Paulo (2012)
6. Drew, L., Bailey, S., Shreeve, A.: Fashion variations: student approaches to learning in fashion design. https://goo.gl/sBgBDS. Accessed Sept 2014
7. Izquierdo, I.: Memória (Memory). Artmed, Porto Alegre (2011)
8. Martin, J.H.: Neuroanatomia: texto e atlas (Neuroanatomy: text and atlas). AMGH, Porto Alegre (2013)
9. Maturana, H.R., Varela, F.J.: The Tree of Knowledge: The Biological Bases of Human Understanding. Palas Athena, São Paulo (2001)
10. Nicolelis, M.: Muito além de nosso eu: a nova neurociência que une cérebros e máquinas (Far beyond our being: the new neuroscience that combines brains and machines). Companhia das Letras, São Paulo (2011)
11. Feuerstein, R., Feuerstein, R.S., Falik, L.H.: Além da inteligência: aprendizagem mediada e a capacidade de mudança do cérebro (Beyond intelligence: mediated learning and the capacity for change in the brain). Vozes, Petrópolis, RJ (2014)
12. Ballestero-Alvarez, J.A.: Multisensorialidade no ensino de desenho a cegos (Multisensoriality in teaching design to the blind), Master's dissertation. USP, São Paulo (2003). https://goo.gl/s4QJJr. Accessed July 2014
13. Tabacow, L.S.: Contribuições da neurociência cognitiva para a formação de professores e pedagogos (Contributions of cognitive neuroscience to the training of teachers and educationalists). http://www.bibliotecadigital.puc-campinas.edu.br/tde_arquivos/3/TDE-2006-06-30T115909Z-1178/Publico/Luiz%20Tabacow.pdf. Accessed Sept 2015

14. Tokuhama-Espinosa, T.N.: The scientifically substantiated art of teaching: a study in the development of standards in the new academic field of neuroeducation (mind, brain and education science). Doctoral Research. Capella University (2008). http://pqdtopen.proquest.com/doc/250881375.html?FMT=ABS. Accessed Jan 2015

15. Luria, A.R.: A construção da mente (The making of mind). Ícone, São Paulo (1992)

16. Vygotsky, L.S.: Linguagem, desenvolvimento e aprendizagem (Language development and learning). Ícone, São Paulo (2010)

17. Ackerman, S.: Discovering the Brain. National Academies Press, Washington, D.C. (1992)

18. Machado, A.B.M., Haertel, L.M.: Neuroanatomia funcional (Functional neuroanatomy). Editora Atheneu, São Paulo (2014)

19. Sporns, O.: Network Analysis, Complexity, and Brain Function. https://goo.gl/ysBqrz. Accessed July 2014

20. Zeki, S.: Abstraction and idealism: From Plato to Einstein: how do we acquire knowledge? (2000). http://www.vislab.ucl.ac.uk/pdf/platotoeinstein.pdf. Accessed Jan 2016

21. Nee, D.E., Jahn, A., Brown, J.W.: Prefrontal Cortex Organization: Dissociating Effects of Temporal Abstraction, Relational Abstraction, and Integration with fMRI (2014). https://goo.gl/LxOdt3. Accessed Jan 2016

22. Gilead, M., Liberman, N., Maril, A.: From mind to matter: neural correlates of abstract and concrete mindsets (2014). https://goo.gl/VHBy9R. Accessed Jan 2016

23. Perlovsky, L., Ilin, R.: Brain. Conscious and Unconscious Mechanisms of Cognition, Emotions, and Language (2012). http://www.ncbi.nlm.nih.gov/pmc/articles/PMC4061812. Accessed Jan 2016

24. Sacks, O.: O olhar da mente (Mind eyes). Companhia das Letras, São Paulo (2010)

25. Estrela, J.B.C., Ribeiro, J.S.F.: Analysis of Relationship between memory and learning construction of knowledge (2012). https://goo.gl/SqPSFP. Accessed July 2014

26. Sorger, R., Udale, J.: Fundamental Principles of Fashion Design. Bookman, Porto Alegre (2009)

27. Jones, S.J.: Fashion Design: Manual of the Stylist. Cosac & Naify, São Paulo (2005)

28. Barthes, R.: Sistema da moda (The Fashion System). WMF Martins Fontes, São Paulo (2009)

29. Castilho, K.: Moda e linguagem (Fashion and Language). Editora Anhembi Morumbi, São Paulo (2009)

30. Chataignier, G.: Fio a fio: tecidos, moda e linguagem (Thread by thread: fabrics, fashion and language). Estação das Letras e Cores Editora, São Paulo (2006)

31. Hallet, C., Johnston, A.: Fabric for Fashion, a Complete Guide: Natural and Man-made Fibers. Laurence Kimg Publishing Ltd., London (2014)

32. Lima Júnior, G.C.: Cognitive processes in fashion design: designing and modelling projects for the visually handicapped. In: Zuanon, Rachel (org.) Projective Processes and Neurosciences in Art and Design. IGI Global, Hershey (2016)

Interaction/Cognition in Design:
The Red Bull Station's Classroom Case Study

Priscila Trovo[1(✉)], Adriana Valli[1], Nivia Ferreira[1],
and Agda Carvalho[1,2]

[1] Ph.D. and Master's Design Program,
Anhembi Morumbi University, São Paulo, Brazil
priscila.a.trovo@gmail.com, drivalli@gmail.com,
niviaboz@gmail.com, agdarcarvalho@gmail.com
[2] Graduate Program in Arts, UNESP, São Paulo, Brazil

Abstract. The present article aims at observing the possible interactions/ cognitions of users, based on the activities and events that take place in the built spaces of a public building wherein educational, ludic, creative and experimental experiences occur. In this investigation, we will focus on the building that houses the Red Bull Station in São Paulo, Brazil, in particular the spatial arrangements of the Classroom, as they have been adapted to provide great flexibility for the artistic practices that are developed following the curatorial and projectual proposal. In the proposed study, the object of analysis are three situations that occur in the venue's auditorium, which elicit and foster interactions and cognitions resulting from and rooted in a variety of content knowledge. The analysis of the aforementioned space is performed based on an understanding of the Classroom as a complex and fluid system, whereby the relations between the user and the built environment are alterable and articulated with the spatial configuration in which they occur. This condition foregrounds the great relevance of both the vision and the actual architectural design of the Classroom, as proposed by the Red Bull Station for the occupation/participation/experimentation of the user, whereby a crossover of educational, creative and cultural activities takes place. For this reason, the diversity of spatial arrangements provides a noteworthy experience, which stimulates and fosters open interactive engagements and encounters. The Red Bull Station's proposal is articulated with a significant level of complexity, which allows for a constantly changing space, affording projectual flexibility to the project. Ultimately, this expands the possibilities for interaction and fosters a dynamic creative and cognitive process. As a result of the study, it can be observed that the Classroom's projectual design provides much potential for interaction between the space and the user, and a high level of adaptability which enables a broad range of activities to be carried out.

Keywords: Interaction · Cognition · Classroom · Design · Spatial arrangements · Systemic complexity

1 Introduction

This paper is an investigation into the discussion of the possible user interactions/ cognitions that stem from the spatial arrangements of a built environment set up within a public building, where a range of educational, ludic, creative and experimental

© Springer International Publishing AG 2017
N. Streitz and P. Markopoulos (Eds.): DAPI 2017, LNCS 10291, pp. 547–560, 2017.
DOI: 10.1007/978-3-319-58697-7_41

activities is carried out. The study centres on a cultural venue called the Red Bull Station[1], which runs in a building located in the heart of São Paulo's city centre, in Brazil. The Red Bull Station's activities take place in the building's auditorium[2], and the programme follows a projectual approach that defies the notion of a centralized, rigid structure, operating with a high degree of flexibility and adaptability. The artistic practices developed in this space broadens users' experience by promoting experimentation, occupation and participation by the public. In addition, the programme fosters a process-based dynamics of interaction and cognition with a profusion of highly diversified content.

The Red Bull Station is housed within a historical building that was originally an old power station, shut down in the early 2000s[3]. With support from the Austrian company Red Bull GMbH, the space underwent extensive rehabilitation/restoration work, carried out by the architecture firm Triptyque, and was re-inaugurated in 2013. From then onwards, the Red Bull Station's programme has been run by curator and artistic director Fernando Velázquez, and the overall proposal follows many of the notions we propose to discuss here concerning a free-flowing approach to the configuration of spatial arrangements and their potential variations, promoting a range of situations for user interaction/cognition with the site itself.

In developing this reflection it is important to turn back to the first lines of investigation into the projectual conception of classrooms, auditoriums and other communal areas in schools or public venues as presented by architect Neufert et al. [1] in his reference book Architect's Data. He objectively and systematically drew up an instructional handbook for designing architectural projects, with protocols that determine the spatial requirements in building design and site planning. Neufert's guidelines are regarded as fundamental principles, and include scalability rules, rules for furniture arrangement and for the maximum capacity of users to occupy the projected spaces.

Following the same line of parameterisation of architectural projects, in Human Dimension and Interior Space [2], Panero and Zelnik describe the spatial relations of the human body in internal environments, drawing up projectual guidelines according

---

[1] The Red Bull Station is part of an international project known as the Red Bull Studios, set up in 10 cities across the world. As part of this discussion, we will focus on the Red Bull Studios São Paulo. http://www.redbullstation.com.br/ and http://www.redbullstudios.com/saopaulo [Accessed: 1 March 2017].

[2] Although the space is known as Auditório (Auditorium), for better understanding we will call it "Classroom", as this term encompasses the spaces wherein a variety of activities are held and afford a high level of dynamism to its spatial arrangements, which are modified according to the needs of the activities proposed.

[3] For the renovation of the building that houses the Red Bull Station, it was necessary to respect the regional norms for the preservation and conservation of cultural heritage, which, in this case, determined that the original façade of the building was maintained. This included the restoration of all parts of the façade that had been deteriorated with the passage of time, due to lack of maintenance and years of neglect. In regards to the configuration of the interior parts of the building, the regional norms did not specify preservation works as a requirement for occupancy and use of the building. Nevertheless, the architecture firm decided to maintain the identity of the building, including various finishes and surface materials, apparent structural elements, original internal doors, besides maintaining part of the collection of industrial parts and objects from the old power station.

to the activities or function developed in a wide range of spaces, including educational spaces such as classrooms and conference rooms. The authors present typical layouts and fixed spatial arrangements, employing predetermined frameworks and dimensions wherein ergonomics and anthropometry are used as the main reference.

Yet, it is possible to affirm that an extremely functional project, as those put forward by Neufert, Panero and Zelnik, ultimately renders the space rigid and inflexible, imposing limits on the user's use and occupation, and overlooks the activities proposed for the space as an important factor in its organization.

Following a different line of thought, in Lessons for Students in Architecture [3] Dutch architect Hertzberger puts forward reflections on classrooms that go beyond the physical demarcation of space. The author argues that built environments should stimulate appropriation by the user according to his desires, whereby "the point therefore is to arrive at an architecture that, when the users decide to put it to some different uses than those originally envisaged by the architect, does not get upset and confused and consequently loses its identity" [3].

In this way, it is possible to find holes in these investigations, as the spatial arrangements proposed by the authors do not take into account or anticipate changes in the activities being carried out in the space, thus limiting, to an extent, the possibilities for interaction and cognition, seeing that, once users are already acquainted with the spatial organization that has previously been set out for them, or come across traditional arrangements, the interaction is bound to be influenced by the norms of behaviour established by the projectual design.

However, when the user is faced with a more fluid spatial arrangement, one that is constantly changing due to the demands of certain activities, the projected place can potentially enhance interaction and cognition, seeing it enables greater movement and displacement of the body in space.

In this sense, the Classroom, located in Red Bull Station, dilates and broadens the meaning of occupation to include participation and experimentation in activities, expanding users' experience and interaction with a diversity of spatial arrangements, in turn promoting the interaction between users and content. Based on this observation, it is important to note that the configurations of spatial arrangements open other cognitive paths and enable an interactive experience that dialogues with the same space, but in different projectual situations, on account of the objects, furnishings and equipment being used and of the stimulus provided by the content itself. In this perspective, the Classroom is understood as a complex system where the spatial organization is promoted through the interaction of its agents, represented by all the elements that compose this space.

The relevance of this study lies in its ability to make us see the potential that resides in the space of the Classroom for educational activities and for experimentation, in other words, as a place where creative actions can unfold. Even though the cognitive process is unique for every individual, as an agent that takes part in a system, he comes under the direct influence of the interactions generated by the experience that the space produces, not only by means of its physical limits, but also from the interferences caused by the uses it is put to.

In this text, the analysis of space is understood as a complex system [4], particularly due to its adaptability and its free-flowing projectual proposal [5], which allows interaction between its agents, namely, in this case, the Classroom and the elements that compose this space, such as the furniture, equipment, content and the actual users. In this condition, it can be identified that when interaction takes place unpredictable behaviours manifest themselves, seeing that interaction and cognition are conditioned to the situation in which the agents find themselves [6]. Users' interaction will be analysed based on their distances and on the synaesthetic experiences that arise from this condition [7, 8], with the stimulation or inhibition of the senses.

Therefore, it can be accepted that the flexibility found in the Classroom at the Red Bull Station enables the study of interaction/cognition which this article sets out to investigate, as this space can be used to host events that range from small meetings, with an attendance of ten to fifteen people, to lectures for a public of up to 110 people. In addition, the type of furniture being used can also vary depending on the need of each particular project that is carried out in this built environment. The space can be furnished with tables for workshops, and rows of chairs for the audience can be arranged in front of a small stage that has been set up as part of the architectural plan, chairs can be arranged in a circle for debates, sofas and cushions can be laid out for film screenings, and ultimately the space can be used without any furnishings at all.

At the end of the study, the investigation performs an analysis of three situations of interaction and cognition, from events and activities - lectures, workshops and film screenings - held in the Classroom at the Red Bull Station, all of which entail changing the layout of the space, both in regard to the typology of the furniture as well as the way it is arranged. In this way, as part of the proposal for the Classroom there is a free-flow approach to occupation/participation/experimentation, seeing that its spatial arrangements constantly change their configuration and function according to a diversity of activities, whereby adaptability becomes a key, necessary element.

This study on the reorganization of a multi-use space and on the ways that the interaction that take place within it are promoted can potentially contribute to the broaden our understanding of existing spaces in other buildings and sites which share the same characteristics, and also to future projects developed by creators who seek to promote in-built spatial fluidity, allowing for a high level of dynamism in the process of interaction/cognition.

2   The Classroom's Interaction/Cognition and Its Systemic Complexity

This approach is based on a vision of the world, understood in this text as a systemic complexity, in which the events do not present a linearity nor a Cartesian order, for they are far from a functionalist and rationalized approach that reduces people to resources or means of reaching certain objectives [5].

The discussion with regards to the actions and the activities of the Classroom at the Red Bull Station is understood as a complex system, because the configuration of its different spatial arrangements allows for the adaptability of the space. These arrangements, in turn, unfold into a proposal of projectual design with fluid and flexible characteristics. The user of this space is open to the propositions that stimulate the articulations between the agents and expand the interactive and cognitive possibilities with the spatial experiences. It is emphasized that, in the events that occur in the Classroom, in a complex system, user's behaviours are not always predictable [4].

In this sense, the aim of this investigation is analysed as a space adaptable to the specifications of the three chosen activities, as, for each event there is a variation in the format of spatial arrangement.

These distinct formats explain the condition of adaptability because they are actions with particular characteristics. Activities in the form of lectures, workshops and film screenings were chosen to highlight, in this article, the possible projectual design variations in a system, and how this space, which is apparently static, is rendered dynamic by the action between agents. For each activity, the architectural project presents a reorganization of furniture and equipment, which attends to the content, occupation, participation and experimentation of the user.

As a result, the relations between the system's agents produce significations interaction patterns and temporary configurations that can always be redefined or readjusted [6], as can be observed in the three selected proposals, which will be developed further along.

Varela [6] also adds that the system possesses agents and agencies, in which, theses definitions depend on the scale in which the space is observed. An agency can be observed as a group of agents interacting with each other, in which, as the focus is modified, a new group can also be understood as an agency.

Another issue concerning the Classroom environment is that it promotes the formation, from lived experience, of creative and experimental processes, which is highly relevant, as according to Driscoll [9] it is necessary to consider that the cognitive process is not limited only to the formats and places of traditional learning. Learning is a persistent change in the performance or in the potential to perform, arising as a result of the learner's experience and interaction with the world.

Cognition becomes flexible and continuous, in establishing and enhancing connections, as well as making decisions, which are fundamental processes for the constant and desirable updating of knowledge. In this way, the cognitive process occurs in the collaborative networks promoted by the space. For this, the challenge of keeping the user engaged is identified, promoting spontaneous interactions with other agents which are involved in the process of interaction-cognition, such as the speakers, other users and interactions with the content itself.

According to Rogers et al. [10], one of the ways to analyse the spatial arrangement relates the interactions that occur from the user experiences, which are understood as: user – user, user – instructor and user – content.

The Red Bull Station Classroom has technological devices that interfere in the built environment when used. In the case of film screenings, the screen is positioned ion a particular spot, where there are no distracting elements or interferences between user and content. When it comes to a lecture, we become aware of the mediation of the content by the lecturer, and the screen is positioned in the foreground, functioning as a supporting tool.

According to Hall [7], the space's characteristics only become visible when the user's behaviour is observed, in other words, when particular activities are promoted where people behave in different manners. Still according to the author, human's sense of distance is not static and has very little to do with the linear perspective of a unique point of view. It is observed that perception is dynamic and is related to the action, that is, it interacts with the activities that are carried out in the Red Bull Station Classroom.

Cognition becomes flexible and continuous as it establishes and enhances connections. This condition enables the individual to make decisions and take new directions, which in turn are essential processes for the constant updating of knowledge. In this way, the interaction between the agents of the system, despite presenting a non-linearity, a high level of dynamism, an ambivalence and an ambiguity which insinuate a disorderly functioning [5], show an organization which manifests itself in a flexible manner, where the users constantly and continuously influence and are influenced by their surroundings and their relations with the environment.

3   Interactions According to Distances

The projectual proposal that concentrates on the spatial arrangements for the carrying out of particular activities determines the distances between elements that compose the space. These activities, in turn, are determinant in the interaction and in the sensorial experiences of the user. According to Hall [7], synaesthesia related to proximity results from the user's articulations with their surroundings. In the opinion of the author, users interact with the space as a consequence of their synaesthetic senses, such as vision, touch, smell and the thermal sense, can be inhibited or stimulated by the environment.

Therefore, it is possible to affirm that experiences will occur from interaction and from the synaesthetic relation of users with the environment and with the content as well. As stated by Dewey [11], experience is a transaction that that occurs between an individual and his surroundings, whereby the interaction between them generates longitudinal and transverse aspects.

Within this perspective, the user's experience is one of the most important factors when an activity is being carried out. In relating interaction and experience, it is possible to observe that the distances that arise between the users and the content enable particular senses to be enhanced. Thus, the more synaesthetic relations the user has, the greater his experience.

Hall [7] defines four distances related to the interaction of agents within a system, which are termed the intimate, personal, social and public distance.

3.1   Intimate Distance

The intimate distance indicates a relation in which sensory information is potentialized, wherein interaction occurs with all the senses, promoting a complete synaesthetic experience. Sensations of discomfort may occur when the distance between the agents is imposed by the spatial format, for example, in the case of an interaction in an elevator [7].

3.2   Personal Distance

The personal distance indicates a relation of proximity, but the sensory information between the agents regulates itself. This distance allows synaesthetic experiences to arise without sensations of discomfort, as in the intimate distance.

3.3   Social Distance

The social distance indicates impersonal relations between the agents, and the amount of sensory information is reduced. At this distance the synaesthetic experiences decrease and physical contact does not occur.

3.4   Public Distance

The public distance indicates a formal relation between the agents in which there is no sensory information from physical contact, and the sense of vision and hearing are compromised.

Scott-Webber [8] interprets Hall's theory [7] by analysing sensory information and behaviours oriented towards interaction, based on the distances between the agents in the proxemics zones, as can be seen in Fig. 1.

ATTRIBUTE	PROXEMIC ZONES			
	Intimate	Personal	Social	Public
Distance	0–18 inches	18–48 inches	48 inches–12 feet	12 feet–25 feet plus
Sensory Information	Vision is blurred	Normal vision	Reduction of sense of smell, ability to touch, visual details	Facial expressions and gestures are exaggerated
	Smell and sense of touch are fully engaged	Smell is strong and touching is engaged	Voices get louder	Considered a formal distance
	Body heat is experienced	Body heat is experienced	No body heat sensed	
	All senses are heightened			
Accepted Behavior	Physical contact	Grasping to just touching	No physical contact	No physical contact
	Kissing, hugging, nursing, or procreation	Holding hands, walking arm-in-arm	Impersonal business occurs	Formal behavior
			Interaction among casual acquaintances	
			Space used to screen others out	

Fig. 1. Proxemic zones [8]

4 Methodology

- The Classroom at the Red Bull Station was identified as a space in which the spatial arrangement articulates itself with a diversity of activities in the contemporaneous context, enabling a multiplicity of uses.
- The Classroom at the Red Bull Station was analysed as a complex system, taking into account characteristics of adaptability, complexity, flexibility and non-linearity in its spatial arrangement.
- To investigate the potentials for interaction offered by different spatial arrangements from this build environment, three configurations were selected, namely, lecture, workshops and film screening activities.
- Concepts of distances between agents, their interactions and perception of proxemics zones were articulated.

5 Results and Discussions

Interactions between agents in the system were investigated based on the selection of three spatial arrangements, which accommodate lecture, workshop and film screening activities, arriving at the following results:

5.1 Activity: Lecture

Spatial arrangement project: chairs placed in rows, sofas set against both sidewalls and a sofa set on the stage (Fig. 2).
Interactions analysed:

(a) Instructor – instructor: the lecturers are positioned at an intimate distance from each other.
(b) Instructor – user: the lectures and most of the agents are positioned at a public distance.
(c) User – content: users are positioned at public distance from the content exhibited on the projection screen.

The spatial format for the lecture activity predominantly promotes interaction at public distance, except for the lecturers themselves who are positioned at intimate distance from each other. In regards to the experiences of proxemics zones, a variation occurs between multiple sensory information from the agents at intimate distance, and also significant reduction of synaesthetic relations at social distance (Fig. 3).

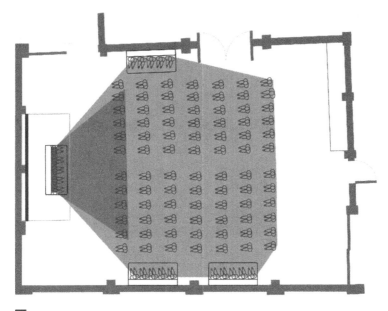

Intimate Distance (0-18 inches)
Personal Distance (18-48 inches)
Social Distance (48 inches-12 feet)
Public Distance (12 feet-25 feet plus)

Fig. 2. Spatial arrangement for the lecture activity

Fig. 3. Spatial arrangement for the lecture activity. Credit: Red Bull Station. Used with permition

5.2   Activity: Workshop

Spatial arrangements project: tables are arranged in the Classroom forming small groups (Fig. 4).

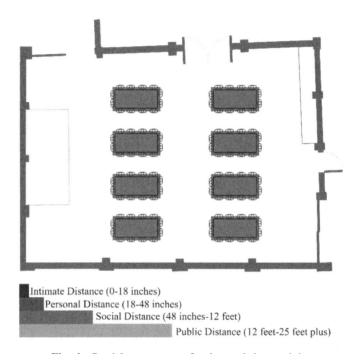

Intimate Distance (0-18 inches)
Personal Distance (18-48 inches)
Social Distance (48 inches-12 feet)
Public Distance (12 feet-25 feet plus)

Fig. 4. Spatial arrangement for the workshop activity

Interactions analysed:

(a) User – user: users interact at a predominantly personal distance.
(b) Instructor – user: the instructor manages to interact with all the agents at personal distance, according to his movement around the Classroom.
(c) User – content: users are able to interact with the content on the main screen at public distance, and with the content lying on top of the table, including computers, at intimate distance.

The spatial format for the workshop activity predominantly promotes interactions at social distance and this configuration allows the instructor's circulation around and between the tables. With regard to the user – content interaction, interactions vary between intimate and public distances. Regarding the experiences of proxemics zones, a relative stability and a balance in variation of sensory information may be considered, in relation to other arrangements (Fig. 5).

Fig. 5. Spatial arrangement for the workshop activity. Credit: Red Bull Station. Used with permition

5.3   Activity: Film Screenings

Spatial arrangement project: sofas and chairs are arranged facing the projection screen (Fig. 6).

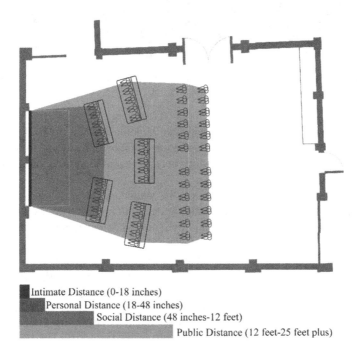

Intimate Distance (0-18 inches)
Personal Distance (18-48 inches)
Social Distance (48 inches-12 feet)
Public Distance (12 feet-25 feet plus)

Fig. 6. Spatial arrangement for the film screening activity

Interactions analysed:

(a) User – content: users interact with the content on the main screen predominantly at public distance.

The spatial format for the Lecture activity primarily promotes an interaction carried out at public distance. In regards to the experiences of proxemics zones, it is hoped that a reduction of sensorial information can be achieved. However, even though the users are positioned at a social and public distance from the screen, it is relevant to take into account the power of immersion of the exhibited content (Fig. 7).

Fig. 7. Spatial arrangement for the film screening activity. Credit: Red Bull Station. Used with permition

In this paper, we have investigated the hypothesis that the different spatial arrangements of the Red Bull Station Classroom, configured according to the activities being offered, promote different interactions between agents and broaden cognitive and synaesthetic experiences.

Here we consider the ways in which the projectual proposal interferes in the interaction of the user and how it potentializes cognition during the experiences with the various activities. It is important to highlight how systemic complexity is in effect in daily life, as this article recognizes that the lived experience of a situation of spatial adaptability and flexibility promotes a change in behaviour and dilates users' possible responses to occupation/participation/experience. Moreover, knowledge creation takes place as part of a dynamic creative process in which users are open to stimuli from their surroundings. In this way, this analysis identifies three spatial arrangements that encounter potential deviations, evolutions and directions according to each particular experience.

Another point of interest in this approach, which is important to note, is the relation between the elements in the space, as the connection established between the agents is realized in such a way that the interaction/cognition becomes unpredictable and flexible, and this condition, in turn, promotes a variety of openings and connections for each element in the space. Within this context technology is one of the crucial elements, because it is instrumental in improving and extending the content's reach and in stimulating user experience. Thus, the experience of the user in the built environment occurs through their interaction with the agents, arousing their synaesthetic senses.

6   Conclusions and Future Work

In this article, we have proposed to discuss the ways in which proposals for different spatial arrangements lead to synaesthetic experiences based on the interaction between agents of the complex system of the Classroom.

In relation to future developments, this investigation opens many windows of opportunities for analysing spaces like the Classroom, based on distances or types of interaction. It also opens up the possibility of performing this analysis in other spaces with similar characteristics, in order to find new projectual practices oriented towards spaces or venues like the Classroom.

In this sense, it is considered that the research study took on an exploratory character vis-à-vis the possibility of promoting interactions at different spatial distances. The study has opened new avenues both for a qualitative and quantitative investigation of interactions in a complex system like the Classroom, taking into account other projectual variables. By way of analysis of the interactions based on the distances between agents, designers can plan spaces that are aware of the action that different spatial arrangements can generate in users.

Additionally, spaces like the Classroom studied in this paper enable the participation of remote agents via technological interfaces and human-computer interaction (HCI), expanding the reach of the distances addressed in this article.

References

1. Neufert, E., Jones, V., Thackara, J., Miles, R.: Architects' data. St Albans, Herts, Granada (1980)
2. Panero, J., Zelnik, M.: Human Dimension and Interior Space: A Source Book of Design Reference Standards. Watson-Guptill, New York (2014)
3. Hertzberger, H.: Lessons for Students in Architecture. 010 Publishers, Rotterdam (2005)
4. Bertalanffy, L.V.: General System Theory: Foundations, Development, Aplications. George Braziller Inc., New York (1969)
5. Tescarolo, R.: A escola como sistema complexo: a ação, o poder e o sagrado. Escrituras Editora e Distribuidora de Livros, São Paulo (2014)
6. Varela, F.: O reencantamento do concreto. Cadernos de subjetividade 1(1), 72–86 (2003)
7. Hall, E.T.: The Hidden Dimension. Doubleday, New York (1966)

8. Scott-Webber, L.: In sync: environmental behavior research and the design of learning spaces. Society for College and University Planning (2004)
9. Driscoll, M.: Psychology of Learning for Instruction. Allyn & Bacon, Needham Heights (2000)
10. Rogers, Y., Sharp, H., Preece, J.: Design de interação: além da interação humano-computador. Bookman, Porto Alegre (2013)
11. Dewey, J.: Experience and Education. Simon and Schuster, New York (2007)

A Programming Cutting System to Enhance Productivity with Individualities

Cheng Yao[1(✉)], Ye Tao[1], Ting Zhang[2], Guanyun Wang[1], and Fangtian Ying[1]

[1] College of Computer Science and Technology, Zhejiang University,
38 Zheda Road, Hangzhou, China
{yaoch,taoye,guanyun,yingft}@zju.edu.cn
[2] International Design Institute, Zhejiang University, 38 Zheda Road, Hangzhou, China
zhangting5@zju.edu.cn

Abstract. As an alternative to traditional laser cutting, we present LaserLeast, a fabrication-oriented design system that produce 3D objects using a laser cutter to bridge the gaps in prototyping from software to hardware and further evoke energy- and resource-saving consciousness in rapid manufacturing context. The key idea behind our system is that it employs a line-based strategy to improve the original workflow at the 2D output arrangement stage by using two shapes sharing one cutting line, and create a line-based workflow without a 3D modeling stage using three customizable components (line shape, 2.5D technique, and assemble plug). We compare LaserLeast with the traditional strategy with two use cases to address the advantages and limitations and show that LaserLeast has the potential to stimulate the creativity of product designers and the human computer interaction community to enhance productivity in both design and laser cutting through the Internet.

Keywords: Laser cutting · Programming · 3D prototype · Individual design

1 Introduction

"The soul never thinks without an image." As Aristotle noted, image-oriented thinking has been used in science, philosophy, folk art, craft, visual communication, digital art, and other creative fields. Line is the most important element used to divide a plane into two mutually spaces, referred to as figure/ground principle in design discipline. Maggie Macnab [1] argued that the most effective use of this principle is when the figure and ground are represented as equal elements of meaning when both negative and positive space can be used toward a productive end. Inspired by figure/ground art works (e.g. Escher' tessellation work [2]), we explored how to apply the design principle to digital design and manufacturing of entity objects, and achieve its new value in fostering media literacy through good design which may be beneficial to the field of human computer interaction (HCI) research.

Cutting as a digital fabrication technique facilitates the generation of prototype in a range of HCI projects (e.g. chairs (SketchChair [3]), dresses (Dress-up [4]), custom capacitive touch sensors [5], and computational textiles [6]). From a fabrication

© Springer International Publishing AG 2017
N. Streitz and P. Markopoulos (Eds.): DAPI 2017, LNCS 10291, pp. 561–571, 2017.
DOI: 10.1007/978-3-319-58697-7_42

standpoint, digital cutting tools, such as milling machines and laser cutters, achieve much higher speeds by assembling the object from 2D plates rather than by additive fabrication methods such as 3D printing. However, this requires other manual labor in designing and cutting the joints for the assembly of 3D objects, and the actual fabrication costs decrease utilization and increase waste of material compared to additive fabrication. LaserOrigami [7] was designed to produce 3D objects using a laser cutter by folding and stretching the workpiece, rather than by placing joints, thereby eliminating the need for manual assembly. Similarly, LaserStacker [8] was proposed to use the laser cutter not only cut but also to weld to enable the building of non-planar objects by eliminating the assembly step. Because the assembly aspects have been well reviewed in the literature, here we focus on the potential and challenges of cutting prototypes from the standpoint of green design.

Here, we propose LaserLeast, a cutting fabrication-oriented design method built on the figure/ground design principle, aimed to evoke energy- and resource- saving consciousness in a rapid prototype context. The key idea behind our system is that it employs a line-based strategy to improve the original workflow at the 2D output arrangement stage. It does this by gathering two shapes sharing one cutting line and creates a line-based workflow without a 3D modeling stage using three customizable components to create at least two functional results. We conclude that the improvements of LaserLeast method to the development of a rapid prototype are as follows:

- Lowest waste and the meticulous arrangement of cut lines to minimize loss;
- Double productivity, cutting a single line to produce two useful pieces;
- Multiple results, cutting one piece for different purposes, as components for assembling one object or for assembly of several independent objects.

Based on the work, our main contributions include:

- Introducing a customizable high-design fabrication method named LaserLeast aimed to make 3D objects by laser cutting for the HCI community without gaps in prototyping from software to hardware.
- Integrating programming techniques, social Internet of things with a digital design system to cutting 3D shapes compared with previous methods, which has potential to create a global community for product innovation and exchange.
- Eliminating much of the waste produced during production by rearranging cutting patterns.
- Testing the usability of LaserLeast method through different cases and providing application examples to further explore the feasibility and expansibility of our method.

2   Theoretical Background

In design, gestalt, derived from a German word meaning "shape, form, figure, configuration, or appearance", refers to the physical parts and their arrangements that compose meaning through their relationship with other parts. More of an existential reality than a principle, the figure/ground relationship is the most elemental of gestalt principles [1].

A typical example in the last century is M. C. Escher's tessellation work [2] that shows multiple rotating images that fit seamlessly over a plane. In form creation by craft, Greg Payce [9] is recognized internationally for his unique ceramic works combining vase forms with precisely articulated profiles. When properly aligned, illusionary images, most often of human figures, appear in the negative spaces between the vases. In a starkly different approach to Western culture, Eastern philosophy approaches life as a both/and paradox, embodied by the rotational yin yang symbol. Opposites are seen as intrinsic parts of the whole or as essential and equal experiences. Above all, the basic tenet can be understood as a whole of interacting parts that harmonize, influence, and expand upon one other, meaning that "the whole is greater than the sum of its parts".

Based on this theoretical basis, we address the issue of sustainability from design to cutting fabrication. As Peek and Coleman [10] suggested, hardware and software are disjoint in their representations, their production methods, and their validation. There historically has been a gap between the capabilities of design in software and fabrication by hardware, because machine tools are not yet well-integrated systems, a requirement for automation or fabrication. An increasing number of researchers are looking into speeding up design-prototype iteration to allow creation of novel input and output methods (e.g. tabletop-based tangible editor [11] or low-fidelity fabrication [12–15]). To extend the use of digital cut machines in the field of HCI, we introduce a customizable high-design cutting platform applicable to a variety of low-cost materials in plane state able to build 3D objects.

3   System Description

LaserLeast system contains a fabrication-aware software platform aimed to bridge the gaps from software to hardware that exist in current strategies for the generation of prototypes using a laser cutter. The software platform is built on top of an open source algorithmic modeling platform, Grasshopper [16], which enables both graphic programming and a visual user interface. Currently, we have the basic toolsets to handle 2D structures and 3D simulation; more customized variations can be easily developed on top of the current platform.

3.1   Workflow

LaserLeast is designed with two goals in workflow (see Fig. 1): (1) improve original workflow at the 2D output arrangement stage; (2) create a programming 2D line workflow to replace the original 3D design and output arrangement stage.

Improving original workflow
Since different shapes require cutting space on a plane which can cause chaotic and failure surface position, we suggest a generation process to gather two shapes that share a single cutting line to achieve optimization of space and cut efficiency.

Creating line-based workflow

Based on the figure/ground principle, LaserLeast provides a designed line shape library with double 3D functions to increase controllability over the additional customizable components (e.g. line shape, 2.5D technique, and assemble plug).

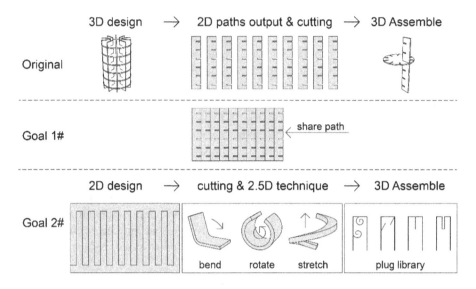

Fig. 1.   Workflow and design goals of LaserLeast.

3.2   Software

Pattern sharing

To achieve optimization of fabrication efficiency, we propose a software function by automatically arranging the cutting paths to make them sharing the same cutting path. This will help to solve the problem of low material utilization when prototyping or making using cutting method.

Customizable components

The system offer tools to customize the parameters of line shape, 2.5D technique, and assemble plug.

Specifically, in line shape design, we adopt array design to customize a basic shape, usually a long strip which can be linked in one line by consecutive double-square or central rotatable method, thus ensure each pattern separated by one line can get similar function. The system also provide the assemble element library which can be pinned in the designed line shape to provide different connection method and match different thickness materials.

To ensure all 2D features are properly executed in actual 3D work, we implement one tool to simulate the transformation, one tool to set the 2.5D direction and location by bending, rotating or stretching.

3.3   Hardware and Material

The hardware system includes a cut machine tool and common flat materials. In our case, we use a laser cutter that will help efficiently convert the digital patterns into flat prototypes. Otherwise, die-cutter, milling cutter, or hand cutter can be used.

This method is suitable for easy-to-cut material with flat and flexible properties which can be easily and cheaply purchased. The candidate materials include everything from natural materials to synthetic materials, such as pp films, paperboard, wood or bamboo board.

4   Experiment

LaserLeast assembles all designs from three basic customizable components that are included in a model library and able to be extended by users. The line shape in one plane can be designed to separate two functional parts with several pieces, which can be bent, rotated or stretched into 2.5D and assembled into 3D with different plug approaches. We conducted two test cases using the line-based workflow and compared with one case using the original process used to prototype a similar 3D shape.

4.1   Test 1: Wavy Line

We employed a wavy line to separate one board into two same pieces with a plug line in every strip top. This case was fabricated using a rotating and bending technique to become 2.5D and final self-plugging with each strip to complete two matching 3D objects (see Fig. 2).

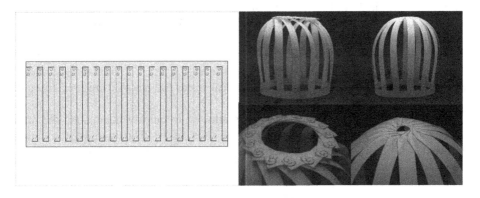

Fig. 2. 3D shape was tested by programmable wavy line design.

4.2   Test 2: Revolving Line

We employed a revolving line to separate one board into two differently shaped pieces with a plug line in every strip top and two connections. This case was fabricated using stretching technique to become 2.5D and used final plugging with connections to complete two different 3D objects (see Fig. 3).

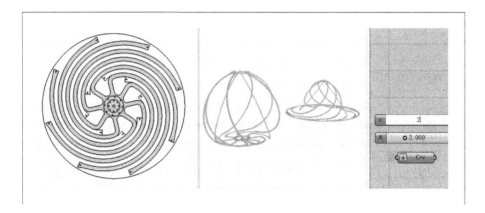

Fig. 3.   3D shape was tested by programmable revolving line design.

4.3   Comparison Results

In order to better position the approach in practice, we further compared two case of LaserLeast with one common subtractive techniques, which have been widely used in the prototyping field of HCI research, and created a new method to solve efficiency, resource, and energy issues and meet new demands. We herein carefully compare the workflow, ease of interaction, fabrication statistics, and final prototypical results using the interlocked slices of Autodesk® 123D™ Make (Fig. 4a) and wavy line case of Laser-Least (Fig. 4b) and revolving line case of LaserLeast (Fig. 4c). The similar model shape was selected for all three methods with identical scales (30 cm x 30 cm x 25 cm) and comparable resolution.

In Autodesk® 123D™ Make, the user is allowed to quickly manipulate the total number and orientation of planar sections with slots. In the 2D pattern, we found that the Autodesk® 123D™ Make system generated regions with multiple shapes with large spare areas, which led to wasted leftover material. Overall, these methods all took less than 10 min to die-cut and less than 10 min to complete the assembly. However, the interlocked slices method achieved 18% material utilization. In the LaserLeast system, wavy line case achieved almost 100% material utilization, and revolving line case achieved 90% material utilization. LaserLeast was in the dominant position in terms of time and material consumption, provided shape composition with aesthetic principle. In addition, the users only need to design line pattern, making the design more ubiquitous use without the modeling expertise.

Approach	Prototype	Pattern	Pattern Area (L × W cm)	Material Utilization
(a) Interlocked Slices		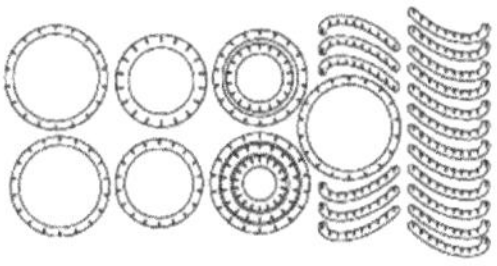	175 × 75	18 %
(b) Wavy Line Case of LaserLeast		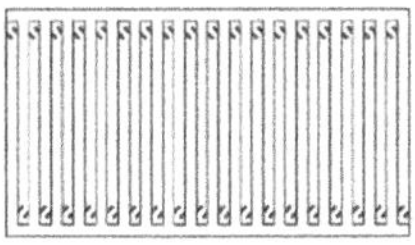	110 × 50	100 %
(c) Revolving Line Case of LaserLeast		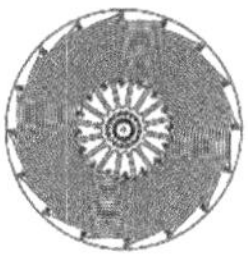	35 × 35	90 %

Fig. 4. Similar shapes were fabricated respectively by (a) interlocked slices, (b) wavy line case of LaserLeast, and (c) revolving line case of LaserLeast.

5 Application

To demonstrate LaserLeast, we now present two application examples to reveal its abilities of optimize- and custom-fabricated objects.

5.1 Optimized Plug-in

According to the optimization problem of cutting path alignment proposed by Laser-Least method, we developed a path generation and re-arrangement plug-in suitable for laser cutting machine. The cutting paths generated by modeling software or vector software can be reassembled in this plug-in. As Fig. 5 shows, the key idea of the plug-in lies in the rearrangement of the vector path of different shapes, through the calculation of the length and curvature of lines, and like a puzzle making the similar parameters of the lines close or together, thus achieving savings in material area and improving material utilization.

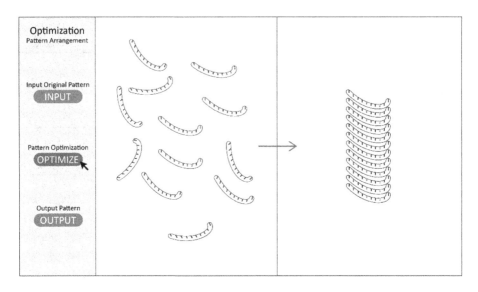

Fig. 5.   Optimized plug-in interface.

5.2   Individual Customized Platform

Through this application, we intend to demonstrate that LaserLeast is a quick method of enabling users participated in individually customizing product during the design and fabrication process.

Based on LaserLeast method, we use the law of revolving line case to achieve a personalized lampshade product design platform, named "MagicLamp". Figure 6 shows

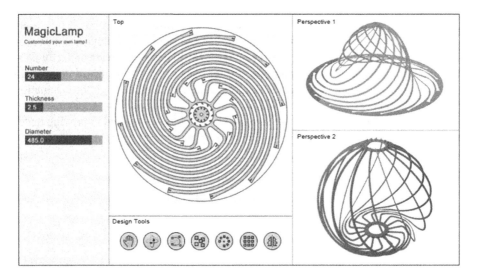

Fig. 6.   User interface of MagicLamp example.

the user interface of this platform, including parametric tools, graphic design, and real-time stereoscopic effect display. Among them, parametric tools are used to support parameter definitions for different thicknesses and attribute materials quickly. Graphic design tools are used for editing line shapes. 3D real-time display interface can be used to assist users timely modification during design process. The user can adjust these tools to build aesthetically desirable units.

On this platform, users can design individual product through the online system anytime, and anywhere. General manufacturing tools, such as laser cutter, can also simplify the original manufacturing system, so that the data of product data can be conveniently connected to the local manufacturing, which achieve optimization of design and manufacturing processes.

MagicLamp was built on the provided revolving line pattern for product design. Parametric tools can be served as the basis for design productivity, enabling users to diversify product form based on the provided pattern. The user can overlap repeatedly, symmetrically or alternately line the units to construct product forms. Figure 7 shows two different designs in the basic pattern from two users.

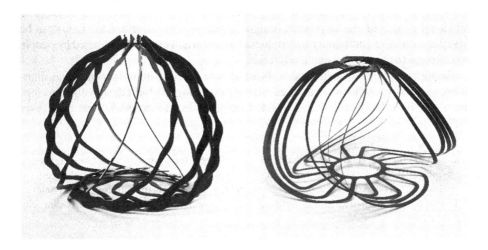

Fig. 7. Multiple results of MagicLamp pattern.

6 Discussion

We introduce a fabrication-aware software platform with two level functions: an improved traditional workflow at the 2D output arrangement stage by gathering two shapes that share one cutting line, and a creative line-based workflow without a 3D modeling stage using three customizable components (line shape, 2.5D method, assembly plug). We then used two test cases to compare with original methods (see Fig. 4).

The figure/ground concept behind LaserLeast offers the following three advantages: (1) Automatic cutting pattern arrangement and line-based design provide a more energy- and resource- saving approach to laser cutting production; (2) Line-based workflow provides an easier and immediate way to produce 3D objects with a laser cutter; and (3) The programming line and customizable components allow increased aesthetical richness and optionality towards a similar shape.

LaserLeast is also subject to limitations: (1) The simulation cannot cover every design and fabrication element and LaserLeast is limited to uncertainty from designed 2D shapes to 3D object shapes whether they are constructed by cutting, bending, and stretching the material. (2) Works only with materials that can be folded and stretched (e.g. hard board, slight wood or Polymethyl methacrylate (PMMA)). (3) Some final products may be limited in pressure capability as a single layer structure.

7   Conclusion and Future Work

Given our current results, the line-based strategy and LaserLeast method will stimulate the creativity of the HCI community to explore green consciousness in laser cutting and individual consciousness in product design. Based on the platform, LaserLeast can be served as a creative community for product innovation and exchange gathered by people from around the world through the Internet.

Future improvements to the method will include function improvement in the simulation, case explorations on line-based strategy including 2D form design, the development of double layer structure, expanded range of usable materials, and more user studies.

Acknowledgements. The authors thank all the reviewers for providing valuable insights and suggestions that have helped in substantially improving this paper, as well as all volunteers for general support. This project is supported by the State Key Program of National Natural Science of China (Grant No. 61332017), National Key Technologies R&D Program (Grant No. 2015BAF14B01).

References

1. Macnab, M.: Design by Nature: Using Universal Forms and Principles in Design. New Riders, Berkeley (2011)
2. Escher, M.C.: Tessellation Work. http://www.mcescher.com/gallery/symmetry/
3. Saul, G., Lau, M., Mitani, J., Igarashi, T.: SketchChair: an all-in-one chair design system for end users. In: Proceedings of TEI 2011, pp. 73–80 (2011)
4. Wibowo, A., Sakamoto, D., Mitani, J., Igarashi, T.: DressUp: a 3D interface for clothing design with a physical mannequin. In: Proceedings of TEI 2012, pp. 99–102 (2012)
5. Savage, V., Zhang, X., Hartmann, B.: Midas: fabricating custom capacitive touch sensors to prototype interactive objects. In: Proceedings of UIST 2012, pp. 579–588 (2012)
6. Davis, F.: A study relating computational textile textural expression to emotion. In: Proceedings of CHI 2015 Extended Abstracts on Human Factors in Computing Systems, pp. 1977–1982 (2015)

7. Mueller, S., Kruck, B., Baudisch, P.: LaserOrigami: laser-cutting 3D objects. In: Proceedings of CHI 2013, pp. 2585–2592 (2013)
8. Umapathi, U., Chen, H.-T., Mueller, S., Wall, L., Seufert, A., Baudisch, P.: LaserStacker: fabricating 3D objects by laser cutting and welding. In: Proceedings of UIST 2015, pp. 575–582 (2015)
9. McKenzie, H.: Greg Payce: Illusions. Ceram. Mon. **60**, 38 (2012)
10. Peek, N., Coleman, J.: Design machines. In: Proceedings of SIGGRAPH 2015: Studio, 2 (2015)
11. Schneegass, S., Sahami Shirazi, A., Döring, T., Schmid, D., Schmidt, A.: NatCut: an interactive tangible editor for physical object fabrication. In: Proceedings of CHI 2014 Extended Abstracts on Human Factors in Computing Systems, pp. 1441–1446 (2014)
12. Beyer, D., Gurevich, S., Mueller, S., Chen, T., Baudisch, T.: Platener: low-fidelity fabrication of 3D objects by substituting 3D print with laser-cut plates. In: Proceedings of CHI 2015, pp. 1799–1806 (2015)
13. Mueller, S., Beyer, D., Mohr, T., Gurevich, S., Teibrich, A., Pfistere, L., Guenther, K., Frohnhofen, J., Chen, H.-T., Baudisch, P.: Low-fidelity fabrication: speeding up design iteration of 3D objects. In: Proceedings of CHI 2015 Extended Abstracts on Human Factors in Computing Systems, pp. 327–330 (2015)
14. Mueller, S., Im, S., Gurevich, S., Teibrich, A., Pfisterer, L., Guimbretière, F.: WirePrint: fast 3D printed previews. In: Proceedings of UIST 2014, pp. 273–280 (2014)
15. Mueller, S., Mohr, T., Guenther, K., Frohnhofen, J., Baudisch, P.: faBrickation: fast 3D printing of functional objects by integrating construction kit building blocks. In: Proceedings of CHI 2014, pp. 3827–3834 (2014)
16. Grasshopper. http://www.grasshopper3d.com/

Ambient Games and Humour

Mobile Augmented Games in Playable Cities: Humorous Interaction with Pokémon Go

Marvin Andujar[1(✉)], Anton Nijholt[2,3], and Juan E. Gilbert[1]

[1] Computer and Information Science and Engineering Department,
University of Florida, Gainesville, USA
{manduja,juan}@ufl.edu
[2] Imagineering Institute, Iskandar, Malaysia
anton@imagineeringinstitute.org
[3] Faculty EEMCS, University of Twente, Enschede, The Netherlands
a.nijholt@utwente.nl

Abstract. Mobile Augmented Reality (AR) games are changing the way players interact with other players and in cities in the real world. The game's content influences players' decision to explore the outside world (whole body movement outside the house) instead of staying inside playing stationary games (not whole body movement required). While users interact with these games in the real world, humorous experiences may occur while players attempt to accomplish a goal. In this paper, we discuss the humor interaction implications that Pokémon Go has in the player's experience in the real world. We also describe how these games can provide humor occurrences based on the theories of humor. We aim to provide a discussion on humorous situations that players experience and contribute design guidelines on incorporating humor in mobile AR games based on what players have experienced.

Keywords: Playable cities · Augmented Reality · Humorous interaction · Pokémon Go · Mobile augmented reality games

1 Introduction

Niantic Inc. in collaboration with Nintendo have released a mobile location-aware Augmented Reality (AR) game, Pokémon Go. This game is a location-based AR game in the real world where the user interacts with the virtual game while physically moving from one location to another. It allows users to meet other players and form a small community based on their interest (community and social networking features are not included in the game). Therefore, this new user-game interaction outside the home is changing the way people interact with mobile games and people and behave in cities. These mobile AR games also bring happy moments where users get into small accidents like falling in a small lake for trying to achieve a goal. A goal can consist of identifying and catching a virtual character at a particular location in the real world. Also, it consists of collecting items to help players get to the next stage of the game and upgrade their levels. Humorous cases are also based on Pokémon spawning in specific locations.

N. Streitz and P. Markopoulos (Eds.): DAPI 2017, LNCS 10291, pp. 575–586, 2017.
DOI: 10.1007/978-3-319-58697-7_43

People sometimes consider the spawning of virtual monsters creepy, but humorous at the same time. Based on online articles and social media postings, players would try almost anything to accomplish their goal. Therefore, it is essential for cities to start discussing regulations and laws to protect players and non-players; especially, when these games start having life events. A life event can consist of players traveling from all over the world to a particular city to catch a rare virtual character (i.e. legendary Pokémon), and they would not be able to accomplish their goal unless they go to the particular city for a specified period on a specific date range.

Mobile AR games need to be adequately studied to deliver the best user experience, induce humorous situations, and to teach users to play within the laws of the given location. Therefore, guidelines on creating such games are needed. Blum et al. conducted a study with 60 players to understand the relationship between presence and game design factors, realism, city context, interaction within the context of AR location aware games through questionnaires, interviews, and video analysis in the wild [2]. This study shows an example of utilizing user experience methods to evaluate these games. These games may introduce humorous situations and enjoyment in smart playable environments. Games such as Pokémon Go are designed with unintended humorous interaction and conditions as discussed by [10]. Therefore, the effectiveness of humorous content also needs to be investigated.

In this paper, we provide a discussion on humorous events caused by playing Pokémon Go. Also, we specify a correlation of the provided humorous occurrences with the theories of humor. Lastly, we discuss design guidelines and characteristics for mobile AR games with humorous interaction in mind.

2 Mobile Augmented Reality Games

The research area of mobile AR games is growing steadily. This growth is because of the advancement of AR technologies (hardware and software) and the improvement of mobile phones processors and their RAM. These improvements allow researchers and industry to design, develop and investigate user-game interaction. Woodard et al. developed an AR game where players can play table tennis where they can see the other player through the webcam. The racket and the ball are both virtual; the players hit the ball with the virtual racket by planning the time and distance of the virtual ball on the camera. The purpose of this work is to investigate the mechanics of interacting with AR virtual objects in a constant environment [17]. Although this work is not based in the real world (outside a building or house), it requires users to use their whole body, which is one of the characteristics of mobile AR games. It also demonstrates player to player interaction during competitive play.

Another game being studied is GeoBoids, which it is an exergame for the whole purpose to motivate people to go outside and exercise. Players run towards a swarm of GeoBoid (known as 3D creatures) and try to capture them. Each GeoBoid varies by its properties like color, shape, flying pattern, and active time during the day or night, and other affinities. The players capture these creatures by executing a swipe gesture on the mobile device that signifies a "point and shoots" interaction [7]. In another exergame, the players move horizontally and vertically on top of an exerpad (a mat similar to the popular game Twister) while holding the phone. The players have to move the laser of the 3D cannon within the phone and physically jump to shoot the virtual aliens or balloons [3]. There are also games specifically for children to be more involved outside the house. The game consists of keeping alive a virtual character by physically finding real trees and interact with them through the game. The players interact with the tree by sending, chopping, and planting the tree, these are accomplished by moving the phone in a particular pattern (the use of gyroscope) [16]. These games show that there is an initiative to investigate various user interactions with mobile games and the physical world for the purpose to make people more physically active. These different investigations are necessary for games to be able to be used in playable cities and accidental and non-accidental humor to occur [11].

3   Pokémon Go

Pokémon Go (Fig. 1) is a mobile AR game that allows players to capture virtual monsters in the real world using their whole body (i.e. walking, use their hands for gestures). Pokémon Go was released in 2016 and developed by Niantic Inc. in collaboration with Nintendo. The game has been able to motivate gamers and older adults (non-gamers) to exercise in the real world while having fun (this is more an outcome than an objective). While users try to catch all the virtual monsters, they encounter them at different locations such as the Mall, restaurants, other people's houses/backyards, close to rivers, beaches, etc. These encounters also vary by distance in meters or kilometers, if a Pokémon is too far away and the player does not have that particular one, s/he may run to try to catch it before it disappears (limited spawn time). When users experience unexpected situations, it may lead towards accidental humorous moments. It also leads towards breaking the city's law that may get the user into trouble, but it can also still be humorous.

Fig. 1. User interface of Pokémon Go (Retrieved from http://techdrake.com/2016/07/pokemon-gos-craze-will-die-down-in-four-months-michael-pachter/)

There are discussions in using Pokémon Go as an example to design future mobile AR games. The idea is to keep the simple user interface and gesture swipe interactions from the game and incorporate their content for different purposes. An area where similar games can be useful is education [4, 5]. Students can go outside and interact with the real world through the phone and learn about zoology, marine biology, and botany [5]. Discussion about humorous interaction in Pokémon Go has not being done, which we do in this paper.

4   Mobile AR Games and Humor Theories: Pokemon Go

There are various theories of humor identified in the literature: incongruity, relief, and superiority/disparagement [1, 10]. Users interaction with AR mobile games can have "accidental humor" varied by these theories. In this section, we discuss how AR location-based games can lead towards accidental humor based on incongruity, relief, or superiority/disparagement, specifically for Pokémon Go.

4.1   Incongruity

In incongruity theory, the object of (comic) amusement is a perceived incongruity through a surprising juxtaposition of events, views or thoughts. In a sequence of events (either in a story or the physical world) an initial interpretation of an event needs to be replaced by a second interpretation. Usually, because of available or suggested context information, the first interpretation is the 'more' stereotypical interpretation. The second interpretation comes into view because of new incoming information that does not contradict earlier information but makes clear that the initial interpretation was based on insufficient and therefore wrongly interpreted information. The two interpretations need to be 'opposing,' not just slight variations to be humorous. This incongruity view is the one that is used to explain jokes, where information is provided sequentially. Incongruity can also emerge when a particular situation allows or asks for two different and opposing views. There is not necessarily a sequence of events, the object, the event or the situation itself allows the two separate interpretations.

There are different kinds of incongruity, the use of context (something that is inappropriate in a particular context), function (use something in a way it was not supposed to be used), or appearance (give an object an unusual appearance that nevertheless has some relation with its function). Other types of incongruity exist as well. They sometimes have been collected in typologies of humor [8]. Interesting are cross-modal incongruities where a view provided by one modality is contrasted by a view obtained from another modality. In incongruity theory understanding the shift from one interpretation to the other is called the resolution of the incongruity.

In Pokémon Go and other AR mobile games, incongruous humor can be more visual than verbal. Figure 2a shows an illustration of a Pokémon appearing in a gay bar. The user tweets the screenshot stating, "OF COURSE a wild Machop spawned at the gay bar last night," this is indicating as a joke that the Pokémon "Machop" can be lesbian/gay. This "joke" can be considered inappropriate to the gay community, but for the heterosexual community, this can be a funny moment because some users may say that this particular virtual creature is gay and this event can be a clarification. Therefore, if the joke is negatively affected by a person, it may be insulting [9]. How would the lesbian/gay community perceive this humor? Is there a difference in perception of this humor between communities at all? These questions should be investigated by utilizing user experience methods to evaluate the use of the gaming content between communities. It is important that this kind of jokes do not necessarily frustrate the gamer but keep them enjoying the gameplay along with their friends [10].

Fig. 2. (a) Pokémon shows up in a gay bar, (Image retrieved from: http://www.telegraph.co.uk/technology/2016/07/11/30-of-the-funniest-tweets-about-pokmon-go/) (b) Pokémon appeared while woman is on labor (Retrieved from http://nerdist.com/19-of-the-funniest-Pokémon-go-finds-fans-have-shared-with-us/)

Another humorous moment and one of the most famous occurrences, occurred when a woman was giving birth, and the husband was catching a Pokémon (Fig. 2b). Some people may consider this joke inappropriate because the "giving birth" moment was possibly not taken seriously while the woman was in pain. Therefore, there can be a perception difference between gender or culture rather than sexual orientation. However, it is humorous how a Pokémon shows up exactly in the room on the bed where the gamer's wife is in labor.

4.2 Relief

Relief theory is the release of frustration that originates from unpleasant life experiences or social and sexual taboos [6]. Mobile AR games elicit positive life experiences and negative life experiences. An example of a negative life experience in Pokémon Go is when players perform a significant amount of physical effort to obtain a 3D character, but fail to capture it because it disappears or escapes. The physical effort can be running for several meters or kilometers. Players become frustrated because they feel their effort was a waste. However, they feel relief when they capture a rare 3D monster in the area or when their friends start providing jokes about his run towards the Pokémon hunting. These events are common while playing the game.

4.3 Superiority/Disparagement

The superiority/disparagement theory refers to when people laugh at the misfortune or inferior of others [13]. We can safely say that this type of humor is very common in human to human interaction. This kind of humor can also be common in player-game interaction, particularly when players compete against other. Superiority humor can happen when a specific player has never been able to defeat another player but was close to accomplishing it. The unbeaten player can recall the occurrence of almost being defeated but never had been.

In Pokémon Go some occurrences can lead towards superiority humor:

- The amount of captured virtual monsters
- The levels and strengths of the captured virtual monsters
- The number of defeated Pokémon gyms
- Their personal level showcased in their virtual character

The occurrences above are achievements that a player can currently accomplish that can lead towards discouraging others based on their inferior achievements but in a humorous way. In games, superiority humor emerges from the competitive mindset that players have while they are playing and after the outcome, they feel relief through humor.

5 Humorous Acts

Nijholt described Humorous acts (HAs) from a telephone conversation and face-to-face conversations perspectives. In telephone conversations, the speaker uses intonation and timing to deliver a humorous act. There are exceptions of paralinguistic sounds on purpose or caused by accident. In face-to-face conversations, HAs can be supported by nonverbal cues. HAs include implicit or explicit references made to the environment that is perceived by the listener in the conversation [9]. Therefore, in this section, we describe similar patterns of HAs when users interact with other users or the environment about Pokémon Go.

5.1 Humorous Acts in User vs. User

In Pokémon Go, users interact with other users by walking around the physical cities and catching Pokémon together by swiping on the mobile device. They also collaborate to defeat another team's gym if they are both on the same team. During these collaborations, there are face-to-face humorous acts while trying to catch a virtual monster or trying to take down a gym. Some of the HAs can consist of one user catching the same Pokémon at the same location as his partner, but stronger. This situation could be judged as an unexpected superior humor. One of the biggest humorous events that happens consistently is the takeover of a gym. For example, when a team takes over another team's gym, then either team can place a new Pokémon on the gym to protect it. However, if there is another (third) team around, they can deposit the Pokémon without the need of beating the gym, because the gym is not protected. When this happens, superiority humor occurs because the team that took over the gym without beating it feel that they have a faster response. It also leads towards frustration from the other team which had to do all the work, but with a little bit of humor.

In Fig. 3, we can see players sitting in different places of cities to catch Pokémon, show their friends and acquaintances their current record. It can be seen that they all sit close to each other even when they do not know each other. When a group of people stays in the same location it is because there is a "lure" (Fig. 4). A lure within the game is placed at a location relatively to a real-world location to attract Pokémon for 30 min. When the activated lure runs out, another player places another one. Therefore, it is a collaboration between players. When many people are attempting to catch the same virtual monster, humorous situations can emerge between verbal and non-verbal cues.

Fig. 3. Players catching Pokémon together at various locations

Fig. 4. Swarms of lures in different locations. Locations are identified by blue boxes and lures are the pink petals surrounding the boxes. (Image retrieved from: http://www.philstar.com/radar/2016/08/11/1612394/are-you-ready-pokemon-go-lure-party-weekend) (Color figure online)

5.2 Humorous Acts in User vs. Environment

There are two types of environments that users interact with when they play the mobile AR games: physical (real world) and virtual (projections from the mobile device). Virtual monsters spawn in different places in the physical environment like the park, restaurants, a person's house, in the middle of the road, and others. When players try to get to those locations there can be causal accidents, where the user falls or almost get hit by an automobile. Although at the moment it happens, tends to be scary, the experience becomes humorous, especially when the user tells the story to their friends over time.

Here are some scenarios that can be considered humorous where players made the decision to do whatever it took to catch Pokémon retrieved from [14]:

- There was a player that broke into a zoo in Ohio, USA overnight to play near a real tiger.
- Two players in San Diego, California, USA fell off a cliff trying to catch a Pokémon. One player was found unconscious, but not severe injured.
- A player catches a Pokémon while his wife gives birth (Fig. 2b).
- A person's house was mistakenly chosen as a Pokémon Gym. Therefore, random players started gathering at that house.
- Pokémon Go gets you cheap beer.

The aforementioned are examples of humorous cases (sometimes dangerous) that players go through in an attempt to catch a Pokémon or take down a gym. These also show that mobile AR games need to incorporate intelligent warnings through machine learning to players to diminish the amount of rule breaking and accidents. Also, there is a need for cities to incorporate new laws and policies to have a safer city and for players still enjoy the game.

Fig. 5. Humorous art of team captains introducing themselves to the professor

5.3   Users and Virtual Avatars

In Pokémon Go, there are human-looking avatars that interact with the player besides the virtual monsters. These virtual humans provide information about how strong a particular Pokémon is when it is captured. Each avatar has a different personality; one is brave (red captain), another intellectual (blue captain), and the last one is funny and clumsy (yellow captain). Based on his clumsiness, users created memes and other types of illustrations of his clumsiness compared to the other characters. These illustrations have been set up for the purpose to provide humor to the Pokémon Go gaming community. These illustrations show that humorous content within games motivates the players to create their humorous representation of those contents to extend the humor. These illustrations can come to mind when the players are hunting virtual monsters in the physical environment and provide further amusement. In Fig. 5, we can see a meme created by a user where each captain introduces himself to the professor that players interact with for different features. The yellow captain was not professional compared to the other two and was juvenile. The professor was not expecting that type of attitude, therefore displayed a surprised expression. Players from the yellow team would end up doing something similar just to imitate their captain. These imitations are humorous and enjoyable to the players.

5.4   User Interaction with Pokémon Go in Humorous Workplaces

Humorous workplaces have physical locations where workers can relax by interacting with humorous smart technologies as humanoids or computers that provide humorous content [1]. According to a poll done by FORBES, employees are playing Pokémon Go during working hours. During gameplay, they build new friendships with coworkers outside their group and obtain more exercise [15]. According to the poll results, nearly 21,000 people spend more than an hour playing the game at work. It shows that Pokémon Go can be an essential experience for workers at companies for them to decrease the probability of disengagement at work. Mobile AR games can be a part of the humorous interaction at work, but new regulations are needed to maintain productivity and make sure coworkers do not encounter conflicts, but enjoy the experience. Specific locations within the workplace should be determined where they can catch Pokémon. Niantic can collaborate with major workplaces, so these virtual monsters can spawn at specific locations within the company, so they would not disturb other employees. Andujar et al. communicates that superiority humor in the workplace can start tensions between coworkers. This type of humor can be the most common when it is obtained from a game. Therefore, if workers are already experiencing inferior comments from peers and also in the game, this may contribute towards depression or disengagement at work [1]. Therefore, it needs to be investigated how these types of humor can be controlled or delivered in a humorous manner and prevent negative experiences and emotions.

6   Design Implications for Location-Aware Mobile AR Games with Humor in Mind

6.1   Humorous Emoticons for Expression

When teams get their gym stolen, there should be humorous images showing comical emotions of getting defeated by another team with sounds. This supports the humorous emotional experience. For example, the mobile game "Clash Royale" contains expression images called "emotes" (Fig. 6). Pokémon Go and other mobile AR games can benefit from incorporating these types of images that help other players express themselves. These images may elicit positive and humorous responses from users.

Fig. 6.   Emotes for users express their feelings towards other players from the mobile game clash royale (Retrieved from https://clashroyale.com/blog/news/emotes)

6.2   Mobile AR Games Characteristics

Location-aware mobile AR games have their positive and negative characteristics of many other types of games. These types of games can lead users to break the law in order to achieve a game play goal. Breaking these rules become humorous events for the users. This is the case because the players feel they are not doing anything to negatively impact the city while playing the game, but it is not legal.

Some characteristics that humorous mobile AR games need to have for the games to be engaging and provide positive user experience:

- Swipe gestures, visual feedback, the use of accelerometer and gyroscope, camera
- Integrated share capability in social media to show funny experiences
- Game elements within the mobile device [2]
  - Environment: world exploration and emotional storyline
  - Interactions: action scenes and moral decisions
  - Characters: human-like behavior and believable characters

Nilsen et al. explored and consolidated the characteristics of AR games in the real world with the use of a computer. The real world and the computer have features that affect the user: physical, mental, social, and emotional [12].

According to Nilsen, the areas of real world and computer are constructed as follows:

- *Physical:* the physical feeling of playing the game, the physical movements and skills a player's use of mouse, and the game's use of physical artifacts.
- *Mental:* problem-solving and deductive thought and reason. Also, decision making with accomplishing game tasks within or outside city regulations.
- *Social:* this is when players play with each other, collaborate, negotiate, compete, and build further relationships.
- *Emotional:* When the game affects the player emotionally (positively or negatively)
- *Humor:* The accidental or planned humor content provided by the developer within the game. Also, the accidental humor that happens when players attempt to accomplish a gaming goal in the real world. Humor was not discussed by Nilsen, this is a novel contribution provided in this paper.

In Table 1, we formulated different characteristics of what a mobile AR game would signify along with humor. This table is motivated and adapted from Nilsen et al., where it was meant for AR games in a computer. Also, humor was not considered in their consolidation. We recommend these characteristics to be taken into consideration when designing, developing, and evaluating mobile AR games with humor in mind.

Table 1. Aspects of real world and mobile of AR mobile games

Characteristics	Real world	Mobile
Physical	- Players use their whole body to accomplish a goal. - The physical world represents the virtual world.	- Players accomplish missions through gestures, touch, voice and the use of pedometer (shake device).
Mental	- Players willing to break city rules to achieve a goal.	- Provide AI opponents, agents, creature avatars.
Social	- Increases face-to-face communication with other players.	- Allows written and audial communication with other players.
Emotional	- Associate the personal feelings of a location along with game play.	- Can stimulate players through sound and mission outcome.
Humor	- Accidental humor when players attempt to achieve a goal.	- Humor occurred from virtual characters.

7 Summary

In this paper, we aimed to provide a discussion of the type of experiences that Pokémon Go exerts on players in the physical world. Humorous situations tend to occur when users interact with the game and with other players and non-players in cities. This unintended humor can be associated with theories of humor: incongruity, superiority/disparagement, or relief. We recommend for these mobile AR games to have humor integrated into the game goals just as games for computers and consoles contain. Humor can improve the user experience and elicit a more positive emotion. We also provided design guidelines and characteristics that researchers and developers should consider for understanding how to deliver a positive and humorous user experience. We hope that this paper also serves as a "jump start" to further investigating humorous interactions with mobile AR games.

References

1. Andujar, M., Nijholt, A., Gilbert, J.E.: Designing a humorous workplace: improving and retaining employee's happiness. In: Chung, W., Shin, C. (eds.) Advances in Affective and Pleasurable Design. AISC, vol. 483, pp. 683–693. Springer, Cham (2017). doi: 10.1007/978-3-319-41661-8_66
2. Blum, L., Wetzel, R., McCall, R., Oppermann, L., Broll, W.: The final TimeWarp: using form and content to support player experience and presence when designing location-aware mobile augmented reality games. In: Proceedings of the Designing Interactive Systems Conference, pp. 711–720. ACM, June 2012
3. Buddharaju, P., Lokanathan, Y.: Mobile exergaming: exergames on the go. In: Proceedings of the International Workshop on Mobile Software Engineering and Systems, pp. 25–26. ACM, May 2016
4. Cochrane, T., Jones, S., Kearney, M., Farley, H., Narayan, V.: Beyond Pokémon Go: mobile AR & VR in education. In: Proceedings of ASCILITE, pp. 136–137 (2016)
5. Dorward, L.J., Mittermeier, J.C., Sandbrook, C., Spooner, F.: Pokémon Go: benefits, costs, and lessons for the conservation movement. Conserv. Lett. **10**, 160–165 (2017)
6. Freud, S.: Jokes and Their Relation to the Unconscious. W.W. Norton, New York (1905)
7. Lindeman, R., Lee, G.: GeoBoids: mobile AR for exergaming. In: Proceedings of the 13th International Conference of the NZ Chapter of the ACM's Special Interest Group on Human-Computer Interaction, p. 100. ACM, July 2012
8. Morreal, J.: Taking Laughter Seriously. State University of New York Press, New York (1983)
9. Nijholt, A.: Conversational agents and the construction of humorous acts. In: Nishida, T. (ed.) Conversational Informatics: an Engineering Approach, Chicester, England, pp. 21–47. Wiley (2007). Chapter 2
10. Nijholt, A.: Towards humor modelling and facilitation in smart environments. In: Advances in Affective and Pleasurable Design, pp. 260–269 (2014)
11. Nijholt, A.: Smart bugs and digital banana peels: accidental humor in smart environments? In: Streitz, N., Markopoulos, P. (eds.) DAPI 2016. LNCS, vol. 9749, pp. 329–340. Springer, Cham (2016). doi:10.1007/978-3-319-39862-4_30
12. Nilsen, T., Linton, S., Looser, J.: Motivations for augmented reality gaming. Proc. FUSE **4**, 86–93 (2004)
13. Raskin, V.: The Primer of Humor Research. Mouton de Gruyter, Berlin (2008)
14. Smith, J.: 19 Ridiculous Pokémon Go Stories (2016). http://www.gottabemobile.com/craziest-pokemon-go-stories-yet
15. Sola, K.: 'Pokémon GO' Poll Shows 69% Of Users Play At Work (2016). http://www.forbes.com/sites/katiesola/2016/07/19/pokemon-go-is-affecting-workplaces-in-three-important-ways/#450105d6e7f
16. Spiesberger, P., Jungwirth, F., Wöss, C., Bachl, S., Harms, J., Grechenig, T.: Woody: a location-based smartphone game to increase children's outdoor activities in urban environments. In: Proceedings of the 14th International Conference on Mobile and Ubiquitous Multimedia, pp. 368–372. ACM, November 2015
17. Woodward, C., Honkamaa, P., Jäppinen, J., Pyökkimies, E.P.: CamBall: augmented networked table tennis played with real rackets. In: Proceedings of the 2004 ACM SIGCHI International Conference on Advances in Computer Entertainment Technology, pp. 275–276. ACM, September 2004

Virtual Reality Games, Therapeutic Play and Digital Healing

Matt Dombrowski[✉] and Jaime Dombrowski

University of Central Florida, Orlando, USA
Mattd@ucf.edu, dr.jdombrowski@gmail.com

Abstract. This paper aims to explore the concept of "digital healing," in which the authors use current virtual reality technology to change the medium in which traditional play therapy practices are delivered. This paper discusses the history of play therapy and the history of virtual reality technology, and how these two concepts can be combined to create digital sand trays. The paper cites current Virtual Reality trends, and explores impacts these current trends can have on other play therapy practices. The paper also explores the author's current research and future implications of this research.

Keywords: Digital healing · Virtual reality · Play therapy · Human computer interaction · Sand tray therapy · Gamification · Video games · Gaming · Digital immersion · Therapeutic play · Augmented reality · Mental health · Digital media · Game design

1 Introduction

How can Digital Media approaches and methodology be utilized to leverage therapeutic healing? This paper aims to explore the concept of "Digital Healing." It will delve into what technology is currently available on the market and how that readily available digital technology can aid therapeutic techniques of a mental health clinician. This paper will dive into virtual worlds, augmented reality and the digitization of a variety of therapeutic treatment techniques. In addition, we will discuss our current research initiative at the University of Central Florida's School of Visual Arts & Design (SVAD) based off of creating digital analogs to sand tray therapy, a therapeutic technique utilized in counseling.

The concept of play therapy has been utilized for generations in efforts to give children a natural way to establish relationships, communicate and problem solve [1]. Therapists use play therapy techniques to help children gain emotional trust with them and heal through use of fantasy in which they are able to explore previous trauma or current life stressors in a safe and non judgmental environment [2]. The idea of taking pre-existing games, such as Candy Land or UNO, and changing the rules to better suit the client are not an uncommon practice for mental health clinicians. The rise of affordable and readily available technology has opened the window to use digital tools in play therapy.

© Springer International Publishing AG 2017
N. Streitz and P. Markopoulos (Eds.): DAPI 2017, LNCS 10291, pp. 587–596, 2017.
DOI: 10.1007/978-3-319-58697-7_44

Digital healing is a concept when therapists use a holistic approach to heal the mind body and soul through the implementation of digital media technology. The mind is able to wander and engage in the same imaginative and creative processes seen in traditional play therapy techniques. Through the healing of the mind, the body is able to cope with more stress and become, in turn, more resilient. With the recent rise and cost reduction of Virtual and augmented reality devices on the commercial market, therapists now have access to previously unattainable tools to aid in their play therapy. Technology ranging from the inexpensive Google Cardboard, to higher priced tools such as the Microsoft Halo lens, allows therapists to engage their clients on a new creative level. The clinician and client now have the ability to share an experience together to help strengthen their therapeutic relationship.

For example, this modality can be applied to the therapeutic technique of sand tray. The sand tray technique was contributed to by H.G. Wells, Margaret Lowenfeld and Dora Kalff. The idea of sand tray is to allow the builder (the client) to develop a world in which they feel connected. They choose items (referred to as miniatures) and put them into the tray (the world) in order to explore their conscious or unconscious thoughts/ feelings. In Jungian theory, the use of creativity would help them find a solution to their problem [3].

With virtual and augmented reality, the client is able to not only create a world they feel connected to but also be immersed in it. They choose items that they can strategically place in their world. Then, they are able to walk around and explore their creation. This allows the client to immerse themselves in their world. The therapist is also able to get a glimpse into world that was created by the client. They are able to see what the client is seeing on the screen and are able to better understand the client's place in their world. While VR and AR tools would not take the place of sand tray therapy, it is based on some of the same principals, and creates an additional tool a therapist can use.

To collect data there will be two groups of participants. Each group will be given a wellness exam before their treatment and after their treatment. The first group will include participants that will use virtual reality to create a digital sand tray. The second group will be the control group and will use traditional sand tray therapy. Each participant will have take part in one-hour therapy sessions over a six week period. After their treatment, each group will be given a post-test to determine which group showed the most progress.

This research is not only relevant now, but will continue to evolve as technology evolves and improves. Future Implications for this research could include providing clients with a way to digitally heal. As the tools and technology improve, so will the clients experience. Future developments will aid the clients abilities interact with their digital environment and be able to feel the weight of the objects chosen and be able to feel the sand run through their hands. It would eliminate some of the limitations of the effectiveness of digital healing versus traditional sand tray therapy in which this is paper is based.

1.1 History of Play Therapy

The first paper that was published on play therapy was in 1921 by Hermione Hug-Hellmuth [1]. Play therapy began to emerge when psychotherapy was shown to be ineffective in treating children, and some adults. Sigmund Freud viewed play as the child's way to communicate and related it to his idea of "free association." He viewed this as the opportunity to see the inner workings of children's minds [4]. Anna Freud continued her father's work viewing play as a vital part of psychoanalysis, rather than a separate modality.

As an extension of play therapy, Dora Klaff worked in conjunction with Carl Jung and Margaret Lowenfeld to derive the concept of sandplay pulling from Eastern ideas [1]. The concepts of sandplay are as follows: conscious and unconscious thoughts are represented in the tray, and the individual has a drive to work towards healing in the tray (Fig. 1). The client will enter the playroom that will contain a sand tray (or multiple trays) and miniatures. The miniatures will range from people, transportation items, animals, furniture, religious artifacts, mystical elements and a variety of other objects. The client will have both calming and bright artifacts, as well as "scary" artifacts (Fig. 2). This gives the client a chance to play out their pleasant memories as well as their traumas. Using the tray as a third/separate entity, the individual is able to take a

Fig. 1. An example of a traditional sand tray from professional development workshop (Source: Jaime Dombrowski)

step back from their experiences, and experience their emotions and feelings through the symbols, which provide the child the opportunity for healing [5].

Fig. 2. Additional example of traditional sand tray from professional workshop (Source: Jaime Dombrowski)

1.2 Virtual Reality History

As graphics have evolved and the ability for consumers to use them more and more, the demand for more immersive technology has also been on the rise. Consumers want a product with no boundaries or constraints, and one that can be created and manipulated based the consumers wishes [6]. The idea of virtual reality was first envisioned by Ivan Sutherland in 1965. Sutherland wanted a technology in which the user could be in a world engaged in the senses and allowed realistic interactions with others [6].

In the first step towards virtual reality, a sensorama was developed in the early 1960s [5]. Morton Heilig developed this multi-sensory simulator. The user would sit at a booth to watch a prerecorded film, hear sound, smell scents, and experience wind and vibrations. For twenty-five cents the user could sit at the booth for 10 min, and experience riding a motorcycle down the streets of New York [7]. The one draw back, was that it wasn't immersive. As a solution, in 1965, Ivan Sutherland proposed the concept of artificial world construction [6]. This concept was made up of interactive graphics, force-feedback, sound, smell and taste. He then went on to develop the Head Mounted Display

(HMD) that utilized head tracking. In 1971, the University of North Carolina created the first prototype of a force-feedback system [6].

Artificial Reality came about in 1975 by Myron Krueger [6]. The idea was that there would be a conceptual environment that had no existence. In 1982, the first flight simulator (Visually Coupled Airborne Systems Simulator) was developed by the US Air Force's Armstrong Medical Research Laboratories. With this, the pilot would have control of the immersive 3-D virtual space by being able to hear and view in real time [8]. Following that, in 1984 a Virtual Visual Environment Display was constructed by NASA Ames [6]. They used off-the-shelf technology for this, including the stereoscopic monochrome HMD. In 1985, the DataGlove was manufactured by the VPL company. This was a device that used a glove as a form of input [9]. Eyephone HMD followed in 1988, which was a head-mounted device. To establish the illusion of depth, this device uses each LCD with a slightly different image. This was the first commercially available virtual reality device.

In 1989, the Fake Space Labs developed BOOM. BOOM is a small box that has two CRT monitors viewed through eye holes [6]. The consumer holds the box to their eyes (similar to binoculars) to move through the virtual world while a mechanical arm measures the position and orientation of the box. The images using the BOOM technology were considered more stable and responded more quickly than their head mounted systems counterparts, as it used mechanical tracking technology [10].

Later in the 1980s, the University of North Carolina developed an application that allowed architectural walkthrough. They used VR devices to improve the quality of HMDs, optical trackers and the Pixel-Plane graphics engine [6]. In 1992, the CAVE was released that featured virtual reality and scientific visualization system. This took a different approach and would project stereoscopic images onto the wall of the room, while the user wore LCD shutter glasses [6]. Augmented Reality became a focus in the early 1990s, in which the aim was to present a virtual world that makes the real world better versus replacing the real world.

There are many terms in which Virtual Reality have been interchanged with: Synthetic Experience, Virtual Worlds, Artificial Worlds or Artificial Reality [6]. All of these names are interchangeable and describe a real-time interactive graphics with three-dimensional models that also use immersion technology and give the user the illusion of participation in a synthetic environment.

2   Current VR Commercial Trends

Virtual Reality is said to be a 30 billion dollar industry by the year 2020 [11]. Piper Jaffray estimates over 500 million VR sets will be sold by the year 2025 [12]. Some experts say that sales of VR headsets will actually surpass sales of smartphones [13]. With this recent boom of readily consumer available VR technology hardware, many people now have access to VR for everyday use. There are a wide variety of consumer VR technologies available to the public. These technologies range from relatively inexpensive wireless headsets to more elaborate desktop computer wired setups. All price points have their advantages and disadvantages.

VR is accessible from a variety of mobile devices. Companies such as Samsung and Google have already thrown their hat into the VR game. Surprisingly, Apple has played no, to a little role in the advancement of VR technology, as of yet. Companies, such as Google, have made mobile VR available cross mobile platform. It has been said that nearly one million people subscribe to the YouTube 360 channel [14]. Companies have also developed their own HMD. The Google Pixel and Samsung Gear allow the viewer to have a hands free interactive 360-degree experience. There are also many additional universal HMD devices for consumers to choose from, non-dependent to their mobile device.

The benefits of these devices are their mobility and availability to everyday consumer. Many of the universal HMD fall under the 100-dollar price-point. One simply needs to insert their smartphone into the HMD to obtain a mobile VR experience.

Mobile VR does not come with its lack of disadvantages. As previously mentioned, there is a strong lack of IOS compatibility and support with VR mobile. In addition, due to the processing limitations of smartphones, many VR experiences lack resolution, and have lower, inconsistent frame rates, which, in turn, can lead the player to feel the effects of motion sickness.

On the other end of the consumer market there are more personal computer based VR setups. Companies such as Oculus, HTC and PlayStation have, respectively, developed their own hardware to enter the VR marketplace.

There is a significant difference in the immersive experience with the computer driven wired VR setups. Due to the processing and graphic capability of a personal computer, these experiences tend to offer faster refresh rate and a more smooth player experience. In addition, various controllers have been developed to interact with these technologies in efforts to blur the lines between the virtual and physical worlds. Dexmo has developed an exoskeleton glove peripheral to mimic the affects of forced feedback in order to simulate virtual touch [15]. In addition, the Manus VR glove, currently in pre-order, will be compatible with the HTC Vive to simulate virtual touch [16].

Wired VR technologies have their fair share of downsides. One of the most noticeable setbacks for the causal VR user is the expensive Price tag. After the consumer purchases a high-end graphics, cutting edge processing computer, third party specialty equipment and the VR unit itself they could see an overall price tag over a few thousand dollars.

VR technology will most likely continue to evolve over its growth during the next few years. With the every growing variety of headsets, the VR developers will have to address a variety of usability and design concerns. To allow for larger consumer scope, HMD developers will have to continue to develop peripherals for those consumers with visual accessibility issues. In addition, the current HMD market is lacking size variety for children.

Even with these current design limitations, there is a positive future for a marriage of VR technology, therapeutic treatment and digital healing.

3   VR Therapy Possibilities

The authors of this paper believe that there are effective ways to merge the technology listed above with the concept of play therapy, specifically, sand tray therapy treatment to encourage digital healing. By utilizing virtual immersion created by the HMD VR headsets, along with the possible inclusion of third party virtual touch peripherals, therapists now can help their clients, not only visualize, but become transported into their play therapy experience.

Therapists can use a combination of readily available mobile HMD in order to allow their client to be fully immersed into their sand tray creation.

In addition, if a therapist was to use the more powerful, wired VR hardware, the client would actually be able to move around freely in their created sand tray environment.

- A variety of questions arise when it comes to validating the effectiveness of VR technology in sand tray play therapy.
- What is the best combination of virtual immersion and sand tray therapy?
- Should the client begin by creating a traditional sand tray that would then be translated into a virtual environment? Perhaps, the client develops a fully immersive VR sand tray from the start of the therapy session? Is a mix of the two methods more effective?
- Does virtual touch play a vital role in virtual sand tray therapy?

4   Research Method/Purpose

Researchers at University of Central Florida's (UCF) School of Visual Arts & Design (SVAD) are partnering with mental health clinicians to study the effectiveness of VR in digital healing through the development of a digital sand tray. Researchers are developing this VR sand tray using the Unity 3D game engine and outputting it to a head mounted device (HMD), such as the HTC VIVE. The research purpose will be to study the possibility of incorporating VR in sand tray therapy. Researchers will start with incorporating VR in a single way (having the client create their world, within the virtual reality sand tray), and will explore other options in the future (have them create their sand tray in the traditional medium and then scan the tray into the virtual world). The act of creating ones physical sand tray is a therapeutic processes in it self. Method 1 has the client entering the VR environment immediately. Their therapist will not be in the virtual space but present in the physical space in efforts to continue a verbal dialog with their client. The client will then proceed to build the sand tray virtually by choosing from a library of pre-digitized miniatures. Method 2 is the traditional approach to sand tray therapy and will not use any virtual reality technology. The goal of this research is to promote digital healing, in which the client is able to heal using digital mediums and their own creativity.

4.1 Design and Sample

Data will be gathered to determine the effectiveness of the inclusion of the digital tool. The study will be conducted at the University of Central Florida. There will be two groups for this study, with each group including a diverse population. The first group will include participants that will be using VR in their session. The second group will be the control group. They will participate in traditional sand tray therapy, without digital interventions. Each group will be given a pre-test and post-test to determine their overall well being before their six week treatment, and after their six week treatment. Each week will consist of one, one-hour session for a total of six sessions over six weeks.

4.2 Intervention

Each group will be given six individual therapy sessions. Each participant will work with the therapist to identify their current mental health issue(s) and what they would like to accomplish over the course of the six-week period. Each participant will get one hour-long session over the course of six weeks. Each participant will be given a wellness assessment before they begin their sessions to determine their overall wellness before beginning treatment. They will also be given this assessment at the end of their six-week session to determine if they made gains in their overall wellness after intervention.

The first group will complete a check-in with their therapist, and then transition immediately into the virtual world. They will choose from the same 200-300 miniatures in the digital world (that will also be available in the physical world), and arrange their sand tray, while actively in the sand tray. The therapist will be able to watch the interactions between the participant and the objects on the TV screen linked to the digital world. They will also be able to process the digital world, verbally, while the participant is in the world.

The second group will be the control group. For this group, the therapist will check in with the client, and then complete their session without the digital element. The participants will pick from the same set of 200–300 miniatures, and create a world using those miniatures in the sand tray. They will then process the world with the therapist and have access to interact with the objects in the physical world.

4.3 Measures

Once all participants have completed their six-week sessions, and completed their pre-test and post-test results will be calculated. The difference in their pre and post tests will be calculated and an average gain for each group will be calculated. The group with the highest gained average will be determined to be the most effective in this study.

5 Conclusion

In conclusion, the authors want to use digital practices to promote healing. The authors will, specifically, model their intervention after the traditional sand tray intervention.

Participants in the study will use current technology to engage in digital healing using their creativity and past experiences. Through this, wellness assessments will be given to participants in order to determine the effectiveness of using digital technology in healing. As current technology becomes less expensive and more prevalent, other markets will need to change their modalities in order to keep up with the changes and be effective in their treatments. This is one step in the direction of making digital practices the new "traditional."

References

1. O'Connor, K.J., Schaefer, C.E., Braverman, L.D.: Handbook of Play Therapy, 2nd edn. Wiley, Hoboken (2016)
2. Schaefer, C., Reid, S. (eds.): Game Play Therapeutic Use of Childhood Games, 2nd edn. Wiley, Hoboken (2000)
3. Green, E.J., Allan, J.: The Handbook of Jungian Play Therapy with Children and Adolescents. John Hopkins University Press, Baltimore (2014)
4. D'Angelo, E.J., Koocher, G.P.: Psychotherapy patients: children. In: Norcross, J.C., VandenBos, G.R., Freedheim, D.K. (eds.) History of Psychotherapy: Continuity and Change, 2nd edn, pp. 430–448. American Psychological Association, Washington, DC (2001)
5. Gil, E.: The Healing Power of Play Working with Abused Children. Guilford, New York (1991)
6. Mazuryk, T., Gervautz, M.: Virtual Reality History, Applications, Technology and Future. https://www.bing.com/cr?
IG=AEAF500E4DE445B2851972364412F53E&CID=2C4DEDF765FF6F1C28E1E7E564
CE6E57&rd=1&h=i6eJ_620zILHgIroOPGdylus8E0fqRYw5vcmtABXWH8&v=1&r=
https%3a%2f%2fwww.cg.tuwien.ac.at%2fresearch%2fpublications
%2f1996%2fmazuryk-1996-VRH%2fTR-186-2-96-06Paper.pdf&p=DevEx,5080.1
Accessed 22 January 2017
7. Heilig, M.: Sensorama. http://www.medienkunstnetz.de/works/sensorama/. Accessed 22 January 2017
8. Lowood, H.E.: Virtual reality (VR). https://www.britannica.com/technology/virtual-reality#ref884320. Accessed 22 January 2017
9. VPL Research Jaron Lanier. http://www.vrs.org.uk/virtual-reality-profiles/vpl-research.html. Accessed 22 January 2017
10. Multimedia From Wagner to Virtual Reality. http://www.w2vr.com/archives/Fisher/07a_Boom.html. Accessed 22 January 2017
11. Sun, L.: 12 Virtual Reality Stats that Will Blow You Away (2016). http://www.fool.com/investing/2016/06/06/12-virtual-reality-stats-that-will-blow-you-away.aspx. Accessed 22 January 2017
12. Thread: 10 Nearly Unbelievable Virtual Reality Statistics & Projections. http://vrtalk.com/forum/showthread.php?2702-10-Nearly-Unbelievable-Virtual-Reality-Statistics-amp-Projections. Accessed 22 January 2017
13. HTC Executive: VR Headset Sales to Surpass Smartphone Sales by 2020 (2016). http://ir.net/news/virtual-reality/124370/vr-headsets-smartphones/. Accessed 22 January 2017
14. Sun, L.: 12 Virtual Reality Stats That Will Blow You Away (2016). http://www.fool.com/investing/2016/06/06/12-virtual-reality-stats-that-will-blow-you-away.aspx. Accessed 22 January 2017

15. Lai, R.: Dexmo exoskeleton glove lets you touch and feel in VR, 24 August 2016. https://www.engadget.com/2016/08/24/dexmo-exoskeleton-glove-force-feedback/. Accessed 22 January 2017

16. Manus VR: The Pinnacle of virtual reality controllers. https://manus-vr.com/. Accessed 22 January 2017

Emergence in Game Design: Theoretical Aspects and Project's Potentialities

Nivia Ferreira[✉], Priscila Trovo, and Sérgio Nesteriuk

Anhembi Morumbi University, São Paulo, Brazil
niviaboz@gmail.com, priscila.a.trovo@gmail.com,
nesteriuk@hotmail.com

Abstract. Games are propitious environments for the appearing of new behavior patterns (emergence). It's necessary to comprehend the nature of these changes taking into account demands and their modifying potential on this process. To support this trajectory, concepts of emergence were presented back from classical sciences to contemporary studies which touch metadesign and game design. This paper aims to investigate the phenomenon of emergence in digital games, encompassing the utilization of projective resources that can increase the interactivity and trigger this process. The research involves literature review, articulation of concepts of complex adaptive system (CAS), emergence incidence in game design and the analysis of three selected objects: Tibia, PokemonGO and The Sims. The perspectives of metadesign usage and artificial intelligence are highlighted as propeller resources of new behaviors. The context, phenomenon and tool relation is discussed concerning: adaptive complex systems, emergence and artificial intelligence. This paper concludes that the usage of methodologies which incorporate metadesign and the gamer as co-designer are more appropriate when dealing with the emergent character of games. Furthermore, the use of artificial intelligences expands the possibilities of interaction in the game, multiplying the amount of active agents in the system.

Keywords: Game design · Emergence · New behavior · Adaptive complex system · Metadesign · Artificial intelligence

1 Introduction

The phenomenon of emergence entails the appearing of new behaviors coming from interactions between basic units of a system, i.e., when two or more parts perform attempts of arrangement and auto-organization, originating an action which is superior to the mere sum of its parts [1]. Although the manifestation of this phenomenon may be observed in different epochs, contexts and fields of knowledge, it became more evident and relevant in contemporaneity with the appreciation of a post-enlightenment thinking based on complexity and interdisciplinarity. We identify the relevance of this research at a moment of game industry ascent [2] and at a time when diversity and complexity of scientific publications in this area increase [3–7].

© Springer International Publishing AG 2017
N. Streitz and P. Markopoulos (Eds.): DAPI 2017, LNCS 10291, pp. 597–611, 2017.
DOI: 10.1007/978-3-319-58697-7_45

We realize this investigation from the perspective of game design, converging the fields of complex adaptive systems, emergencies and artificial intelligences. In this way, we can highlight that elements that previously integrate the system in interaction allow the emergence of something new, modified, uncertain, unexpected, qualitatively differentiated.

This article's aim is to contribute to the development of games by furnishing theoretical aspects to designers and developers in the project of emergences in games, insofar as it's possible to foresee and project them. Therefore, this entails maximizing the experience of emergence since they, per se, belong to the domain of the unforeseen.

We'll investigate the hypothesis that the more a game allows interactions between units of the system, personal or not-personal (NPCs), the more it's capable to adapt and adjust faced with particularities of developed relations. We observe the use of artificial intelligences related to supporting roles – yet not unimportant roles – mediating and promoting interactions with players.

Among the main chains of investigation, the following authors stand out. To contextualize the environment where the phenomenon of emergence occur it becomes important to employ the concepts of complex adaptive systems from the perspective of Holand [8]. As for the appearing of new behaviors and its relation to digital games we utilize Sweetser [9], Salen and Zimmerman [10] and Schell [11] allied to the metadesign conceptions of Vassão [12], Baranauskas, Martins and Valente [13]. To discuss the perspectives of the AI usage in games, we adopt Russel and Norvig [14] and Champandard [15] as main references.

Methodologically, we recognized games as complex adaptive systems and analyzed three of them for identification of patterns of emergence incidence. Lastly, we identified the perspectives of metadesign and artificial intelligence usage in games as project's potentialities. We selected the objects of study following the criteria of adaptive relevance, innovation and emergent contemporaneity, fertility of emergent events, utilizing as examples the games Tibia [16], PokemonGO [17] and The Sims franchise [18].

2   Emergence in Games

To comprehend emergences in games it's necessary to understand the context in which this phenomenon arises. The general systems theory is an analytical approach that seeks to represent the world as a set of fluxes regulated by a variety of feedback processes [19]. This approach is conceived with mathematical content in order to obtain points in common about the system's behavior, allowing, for instance, the reproduction of certain patterns or the simulation of given situations through the manipulation of variables. The complexity demands our possibility of understanding and molding the interaction between things and processes many times of very different nature, under pain of non-capture of what is fundamental in these systems [20].

The work of Avenir Uyemov [21] attempts to mathematically express a system. According to the Russian school [21], system is defined as a set of things (m) of any nature, among which relations R exist, in such a way that the elements of this set end up sharing properties P (Fig. 1).

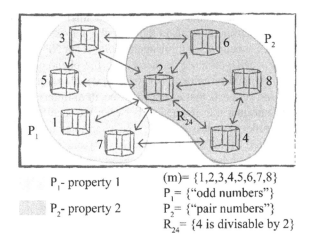

P₁- property 1	(m)= {1,2,3,4,5,6,7,8}
	P_1 = {"odd numbers"}
P₂- property 2	P_2 = {"pair numbers"}
	R_{24} = {4 is divisable by 2}

Fig. 1. Representation of system and its elements.

$$(m)\ S\ =\ _{df}[R(m)]\ P \tag{1}$$

m = an ensemble of agents
S = system
R = set of relations
P = shared properties

Some researchers [8, 22, 23] who deal with complexity prefer to propose in the place of a more closed definition a set of criteria which conceives a given system as a complex system. Some of these criteria are:

- Great number of constituent elements which interact in a non-linear manner;
- Interdependence between the elements of the system;
- Emergent behavior;
- Combined action of cooperation and competition;
- Capacity to store information and transmit it/pass it forward.

All these elements can be identified with clarity in digital games, even though some (genres of) games prioritize or emphasize more or less each of these. We can comprehend "agents" as players and NPCs (Non-Player Characters), "attributes" as rules and mechanics which regulate the experience of playing, "relations" as interactions between agents and "environment" as the game context, always limited by its rules.

Considering that design is the process by which a designer creates a context to be found by a participant and from which the meaning emerges [10], the main facets on which the game designer must focus are: (a) the context (system), which entails spaces, objects, stories and behaviors found in the game; (b) participants, players (agents) who act on the game context in an exploratory or manipulative way and (c) meaning (emergence), interaction and action results during gameplay. Thus, it's possible to understand games as systems [24, 25] for they're an enclosed environment, governed by rules and a stage for interactions among agents. Regarding these interactions, we'll discuss the properties and patterns at different levels in the next chapter – emergence.

In the ambit of games, when two or more agents (players or NPCs) interact with each other and generate new behaviors, we're faced with the phenomenon of emergence. Specifically, in the study field of games, Sweetser [9] develops an investigation about emergence in games and suggests that emergences occur at different levels of depth in the system, making important the distinction between the manifestation of local and global emergences. In order to understand the project variables and the emergent potential in games, we analyzed Tibia [16], PokemonGo [17] and The Sims franchise [18], selected because of their abundance of emergences as we have previously identified.

2.1   Tibia as a Stage for New Behaviors

Local emergences occur when a collective behavior of the system's entities appears in small, localized parts. It is the case in which a group of players (guilds) get together to fight a war in Tibia[1]. This action initiates consequences near the local of the war. High-level players are convoked to take sides, while low-level players feel obliged to get out hunting, altering certain predicted behaviors for a "normal day" just for that local in the game.

Global emergencies occur when the collective behavior of the system's entities relates to the system as whole. We can perceive this when considering that, on one occasion, some Tibia players began to commercialize items in a parallel market[2] and this action started to be so relevant that afterwards the developer company itself [16] decided to incorporate these functions to the game. To Sweetser, [9], a system must be sufficiently abundant, with highly independent entities in order to the global behavior to exist, as happens in a brain, in human being and in societies.

Still trying to comprehend the different emergent manifestations, Sweetser [9] presents three potential emergency orders in games. We can denominate these levels as being of first, second and third order.

Sweetser [9] considers first order emergencies local interactions that have dragged effects or that generate a chain reaction. The player's actions spread throughout the whole game, affecting not only the immediate target, but also the nearest elements. In Tibia, we may consider as first order emergencies the changes in the construction of structures, where players use items in the scenario for users beyond the respawn area[3].

The appearing of second order emergences occur when the players use the basic elements of an environment of the game to make their own strategies and to solve problems in a new way – not always conceived by the game designer. Game characters can equally be able to utilize or combine their basic actions to expose new behaviors

---

[1] Tibia, Massive Multiplayer Online Role-Playing Game (MMORPG), developed by CipSoft. It is one of the oldest games in the genre (1997), counting on a community that surpasses 500.000 players, 40% of these being Brazilian.

[2] Websites and virtual communities in diverse platforms that sold items.

[3] Respawn: programmed reappering of items or enemies in the game that usualy follow a pattern of time and space.

and strategies. These types of emergence are still local effects, for they have a limited range of implications and do not influence the gameplay as a whole. However, they offer to the player the freedom and creativity to change his way of playing.

In Tibia, we also find the use of items beyond their original utility projected by the developers. An activity easily found in the game is the "trap" applied by players in order to confine a character in a square and then attack them, diminishing or even putting an end to their mobility and possibility of escape, blocking a passage. This trap can happen using a parcel, that is, a mailbox that originally serves to send items to others or to yourself. Some players identified its stacking and unsurmountability properties and started to take them inside their backpacks to promote traps. With the amplification of what was possible to do with the item, players had to adapt in order to defend themselves from such tricks[4] or take advantage of them to confine enemies.

Still on the emergence orders, a third order refers to the game as whole, where the phenomenon occurs on a global scale. The game offers flexibility that permits players to find new and exclusive paths, promoting divergence in the narrative, in the game flux, through the interactions between characters or social organizations. Manifestations of third order are abundant in Tibia: the players began to articulate groups, called guilds, with clan-like, family-like or gang-like behaviors. The bonds developed by guild members promote missions to the missions to accelerate the achievement of levels, items and money. Guilds can also be called to wars and situations of revenge, when a character of the group is killed during the game.

Guilds are groups of characters created to gather people who think/play in a similar or complementary manner. They are very popular, since they normally offer a better protection for its members, besides a feeling of belonging. Powerful guilds aggregate players with higher levels and generally have more influence on events and politics than a single lonely player usually has. As in collective sports or teams in general, with the passage of time guilds develop co-working skills and perfect their techniques and game strategies.

Tibia presents an open narrative that allows the player to interact with other players in a different way, making and attributing new utilities to items, having dragged effects[5], tracing unpredictable strategies and generating new behaviors. Piccini [26] recognizes in the narrative of a digital game a complex universe that propitiates to the players the possibility to promote different interpretations and contributions to the construction process of the system value in the game.

Since its conception, Tibia followed the monetization model that would still take years base itself in the gaming market. It allowed fans to play gratuitously, in "freemium" accounts, having the option to pay for additional functions and other benefits later in a premium account. However, a rich parallel market has emerged over the years, where players sold items in "extra-tibia" currencies, paid mercenaries to escort their

---

[4] Events of re-determination of function of items reinforce Flusser's [27] approach on the designer's deceptive nature. In this case, however, players performed the event. (Further ahead, we will consider them as being codesigners.

[5] Dragged effects: the ones that appear in a certain location on the map, but extended and incorporated as culture from the interaction between players.

characters – defending or healing them in missions – hired assassins and other possibilities involving items and actions.

The fact that the designers of Tibia projected it with simple graphics, using the technique of pixel art, 2D, isometric projection with perspective in 135°, supplied the community with the possibility to design new items and to suggest complements to the game's map. It is possible to speculate that this possibility instigated the players' imagination, promoting more engagement and pushing the game's evolution. Players became co-authors and the power to express their desires and making them realized came to fruition with new updates of the game.

Baranauskas [13] sees the player's involvement with the project's development in a positive manner. The author presents the concept of co-design, a shared design process in which the designer acts like a sort of facilitator, planning and allowing the participation of other agents in the creation process. The term co-design has been utilized with the sense of "community design, collaborative design and cooperative design", meaning a set of tools used by designers to engage subjects who are not designers in the creation process and in the development of projects.

Another example of the influence of this player/collaborator in Tibia: characters needing to express their social and affective bonds, such as love relationships and even marriage. The developers accepted this resource and implemented it with the mediation of ceremonies by the NPCs (non-person characters) and with the availability of items to personalize the ceremony.

The fact that Tibia has an open narrative, allowing the engagement of its players in processes of co-design facilitated the adaptive capacity of the game – just like an anthill – surviving to the adversities over time, being a stage of innumerable emergences. The dialogue resources that appear in the log[6] and on the screen permit conversations with several characters and the observation of conversations between other characters in order to get little pieces of information about events, people and places in the game. By permitting this flexible dialogues and tangles, Tibia became a favorable stage for the appearing of emergent narratives.

Although we have presented a summary on the emergences in Tibia, the present analysis did not have the intention to catalog and elect all possible emergences in any games; it would be too pretentious to attempt to predict all these aspects. However, we traced the essence of what promotes this behavior focusing on the case study of Tibia. This choice has to do to its "survival" in the gaming market and the fidelity to its community over more than 20 years, disputing with titles of the same genre that presented better graphics, improved technologies and more resources. We estimate that this occurred thanks to its adaptive potential.

The necessity of considering complex adaptive environments is thought provoking When the game is capable of adapt itself to the adversities, just like the ants of Holland [8], it will potentially acquire more resources for a longer period of time.

After analyzing the potentialities of emergent phenomena in Tibia, it is possible to affirm that the proposal of open, co-design narratives promote more adaptability to the game faced with necessities that appear over time. There is still the necessity and

---

[6] Log: event registration on the chat box.

relevance of investigating other games with this adaptive capacity in depth. This may influence in the game's lifespan, in its engagement level with the player community and in its potentialities.

2.2 PokémonGO

PokémonGo [17] is a game released for mobile devices in the Android and iOS platforms. The game proposes the experience of transiting between the real and the virtual from resources of the augmented reality, in which elements are projected on the screen in real-time by the device's camera [28]. The game encourages the player to explore the surroundings through a system of localization via GPS so as to capture new Pokémon around the map.

PokémonGO allows the connection between players of the community and the formation of teams where the players can meet and explore physical and virtual environments. The game broke download records, reaching Apple Store's[7] top in less than 24 h after its[8]. Some estimate that this success is due to the fact that it belongs to a franchise entailing games, TV cartoons and other successful products.

A question raised by the success of the game is its dissemination that mobilized people of many ages and social classes and revealed the habit of playing in public, since the players were easily recognizable by their movements and eyes on the screen. The relevant factor is that, until then, even millions of people played a game, this culture was restricted to isolated environments and to platforms with less mobility. However, Pokémon reach its height and then had its number of players diminished[9], the reasons for this fall were not identified, but platforms of analysis such as Sensor Tower, AppTopia and SurveyMonkey reveal drop in downloads, engagement and quantity of time playing the game[10].

Furthermore, it is possible to relate the influence of project decisions regarding the game mechanics with the appearing of emergent behaviors. The game was the leading figure in a series of curious events. The mechanics demand players to move to capture new Pokémons or items.

This rule aroused, in a first moment, a wave of people in the streets, walking or running to find Pokémons or new PokéStops, eyes fixed on their cellphones. The inattention of some users caused a series of accidents recorded by newspapers. Afterwards, part of the gamer community began to develop strategies to make the gamer easier, hunting by car. Niantic inserted warnings in the game, speed limits of navigating on the map etc.

---

[7] IOS Platform Application Store.
[8] (Techmundo, 2016) https://www.tecmundo.com.br/pokemon-go/108115-novidade-poke mon-go-numero-1-app-store-24-horas.htm).
[9] Data presented in: http://g1.globo.com/tecnologia/games/noticia/2016/08/pokemon-go-comeca-ter-queda-de-jogadores-e-de-popularidade-nos-eua.html.
[10] Available in: http://www.opovo.com.br/app/maisnoticias/tecnologia/2016/08/24/noticiastec-nologia,3651900/numero-de-jogadores-do-pokemon-go-cai-15-milhoes.shtml.

These attitudes demonstrate a concern and responsibility regarding emergent phenomena. The ways players interact with other agents influence layers of the system following a propagation flux through feedbacks that can transpose the limits of the system. When the agents propose new rules and new utilizations to the elements projected by the developers, then it becomes clear the existence of new roles, players and collaborators.

The incremental innovation presented in PokémonGo, characterized by the incorporation of resources of augmented reality and GPS navigation, triggered a series of emergent phenomena. This resources offer new ways of playing and boost the appearing of new, unpredicted behaviors.

2.3 The Sims Franchise

The Sims franchise, projected by Will Wright, had its first edition released in 2000 and just like Tibia adapted to the wishes of the players, releasing expansions packs and new versions throughout the years. The series is configured as an everyday simulator, in which the player controls one or various avatars capable of working, earning money, building houses, raise pets, marry and many more actions. Some aspects of the mechanics of the game were inspired in Maslow's [29] pyramid to orient the necessities and priorities in the Sims' lives. Therefore, even though every Sim wishes to achieve personal realization, they will have to dedicate themselves to the lower levels of the pyramid (their necessities).

In the first editions of the franchise, the avatars had a limited range of items for customization. This influenced the mobilization of the player community to develop new items that were incorporated to the game packages through manual interventions in the folders. This happened to skin colors, tattoos, clothes, haircuts.

The interventions made by players are known as mods (abbreviation for modifications) and, in many cases, reveal wishes and new necessities of the gamer community. This mods are examples of the multiple roles of the gamer, being able to act as users and co-designers. This characteristic offers to the developers various opportunities to identify the necessities and wishes of users in relation to what was already produced. Mods highlight the agents' restrictions of making some interactions in the system. Thus, the agent alters the system to adapt it to their intention [30]. In some cases, players search for bus or gaps to express their wishes or even the necessity to defy the limits of what have been previously planned.

The Sims franchise was a stage for an emergent phenomenon of appropriation and of generation of transmedia narratives. The gamer community detected the opportunity to record a series of episodes from screenshots of the game and to create the register of narratives that each one produces. The website SimsInMotion[11] registered the 10 best series and soap operas created by players, revealing the engagement of the community with the game's proposal and the game's adaptive potential according to the player's wishes.

---

[11] Access in: http://simsinmotion.com/.

3   Project Resources in Design of Emergences

From analysis of the games and from the propellant resources in the project of the three investigated objects, we highlighted some events and identified points in common in relation to the project resources, present in Table 1.

Table 1. Summary of emergences in Tibia, PokemonGo and The Sims

Practice	Emergence	Type
Co-design	Changing of the scenario through items	Local
	Creation of new items	Global
Open narrative	Appearing of guilds	Global
	Creation of social ties	
	Rents for achieving quests	Local
	Creation of parallel market	Global
	Exploration of new contexts	Local
Augmented reality	Accidents with users	Local
Use of GPS (global positioning system)	Mobilization of the gamer community towards finding and promoting locations with rare items	Global
Use of GPS	Development of apps to circumvent GPS	Local
Open narrative	Utilization of items in an unusual way – example: to use a notebook inside the pool	Local
	Search for ways to cheat, deceive or perform unusual actions in the game – search for bugs. Examples: (a) go inside a pool, delete ladder and cause a suicide. (b) build environments without doors (c) make a male Sim get pregnant by an alien	
Co-design	Production of narratives and soap operas	Local
	Development of new items – clothes, tattoos, skin colors	

Hunicke, LeBlanck and Zubeck [31] also recognize games as systems and propose a formalization, not exactly a methodology, but a way of seeing the game from two perspectives, one being the designer's and the other being the player's (Fig. 2). Comprehending the game as:

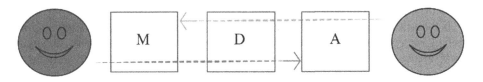

Fig. 2. MDA framework

According to the authors, the player perceives the aesthetic first, followed by dynamics and mechanics, whereas the designer works the other way around. The designer projects first the mechanics and then he constructs the dynamics and aesthetic. MDA is a tool to assist designers to evaluate how choices can affect the whole. In this sense, when thinking about the player's composition of experiences, it becomes necessary to foresee the emergent potential of the game.

This perspective allows the relation with the project methodology of metadesign [12] and Fischer and Giaccardi [32] where the project needs periodical revision in order to absorb the constant changes in users' needs. This methodology is capable to embrace interdisciplinary fields and the inherent complexity of complex adaptive systems and thus the appearing of new behaviors in games should not be considered a problem but as an opportunity to comprehend the user's necessities.

Metadesign is a project framework that considers and supports new forms in which collaborative design can have more space [32]. This proposal brings users closer to the project, making them co-designers and accepting the adaptive process inherent to the project, as observed in Tibia, PokemonGo and The Sims franchise.

The use of the methodology or metadesing resources has its bases on the principle that not all future problems are predictable during the project, when the game is developed. The agents, while playing, will discover mismatches between their expectations and the experience that the game can offer. The moments of crises and mismatches are important because cause new reflections and possible improvements in the project and suggest some potentialities compared to the traditional methodologies [32].

We consider a closed and absolute methodology for game creation impossible, even more when taking into account complexity and emergence. However, it is possible to observe that the approach of the player as co-designer is beneficial and generates shortcuts in the development. For this purpose, we conceive the usage of methodologies that are more flexible to this changing character inherent to games and its active community. In order to continue the research of other ways of potentiate interactions, we point out the use of artificial intelligences and their emergent potential.

4   Artificial Intelligence Usage in Games and New Behaviors

The artificial intelligence is one of the fields explored in the development of games, able to boost and give life to virtual worlds. In spite of hiding itself in deeper layers of development, according to the elemental tetrad [11], the AIs are highly capable of influencing the way a gamer can interact along their journey. One of the most conventional forms of its manifestation in games is the NPCs, whose goal is, in most cases, perform a similar behavior of an avatar controlled by a human.

In this sense, the challenge of developing agents able to interact and learn with inputs from players, responding to stimuli in an individual fashion, enable the personalization of experience, minimize frustration and ensure an experience in flow levels [33] along the game.

Allied to the theory of GameFlow, the usage of artificial intelligences can assist in a field that has not been so explored yet, collecting data from each user, treating them individually and delivering personalized experiences to each one – having the potential to repeat the process in several moments of a same match/play. When this gap is identified, we visualize the implementation of AI techniques in NPCs aiming to use these agents in the game as receptors, interactors and facilitators/deliverers of new behaviors, working actively in the system, as can be observed in Fig. 3.

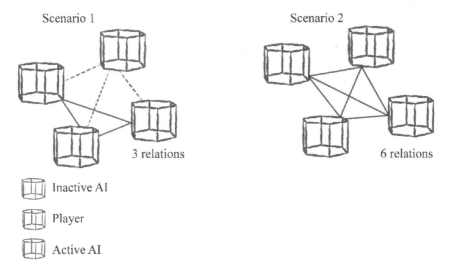

Scenario 1

3 relations

Scenario 2

6 relations

⊞ Inactive AI

⊞ Player

⊞ Active AI

Fig. 3. Scenario 1 – A collection of personal agents and one NPC. Scenario 2 – A collection of personal agents and one NPC endowed with AI.

5   Methods

- Understanding of games as complex adaptive systems and identification of emergences.
- Exploratory case studies where we examined the games Tibia [16], PokemonGo [17] and The Sims franchise [18] which offered parameters for relating project resources and incidence of emergences.
- Articulation of concepts from the theoretical reference and case studies with perspectives of usage of both metadesign and artificial intelligence techniques in game development.

6   Results and Discussions

In this article, we investigate the hypothesis that the more a game allows interactions between system units, personal or not-personal (NPCs), the more it presents the phenomenon of emergence and that characteristic would be linked to its adaptive potential over time, in relation to the wish of players. For this purpose, we investigated the context in which these emergences occur, recognizing games as complex adaptive systems and as stage for appearing of new behaviors. In this perspective, it's still necessary to remark the alternation of roles between agent and agency depending on the observation level and distance at which the entity is situated in relation to the system.

We may conclude that emergences occur and they are not always aspects cherished by game developers, chiefly when not understood. However, these emergences provide a strong adaptive character to the game, revealing in many cases the wishes of players and they can be important sources of information to the developers as how to trace changes in new versions, updates or expansion packs.

We could observe the possibility of conceiving multiple roles to the player, allowing him to be an agent in the game, interacting and generating new behaviors and being an active agent in the conception of new resources, characterizing co-design and metadesign methods. When we observe the characteristics present in Tibia and The Sims, we find that these ample emergent capacities contributed to the games' success and longevity.

From the Tibia gameplay analysis, we observed that the open narrative and co-design resources stand out as responsible for the game's high adaptive level throughout the years and in conformity to the Tibia community necessities. Other resources like the chat box and visualization of other agents' conversations may have influenced this high adaptive potential.

In the case of PokemonGO, the players' interactions generated the emergences while using the incremental innovation of augmented reality + location via GPS. This combination expanded and personalized the game's map for each player, culminating once again in an open narrative. Although the game doesn't offer official resources for dialogues between players the community took action at other platforms, mobilized forums, created apps, arranged meetings and suggested the implementation of new rules, thus generating an environment of collaboration and co-design.

The Sims franchise contributed to the investigation by pointing out desired behaviors from the players, since it is a sort of everyday simulator. The search for opportunities to test the game's limit, to utilize items in an unusual way, revealed wishes of players that could be slowly incorporated by the developers in new package expansions. Another interesting factor was the engagement of the gamer community with the creation of narratives by capturing video clips from the game. This action also transposed the limits of the system and began to compose a universe of transmedia narratives.

The investigation of these three contexts revealed the incidence of some relevant characteristics to the appearing of new behaviors: open narrative and co-design. However, it is possible that this analysis is premature and needs more objects of study and depth for its consolidation. Therefore, it is necessary to investigate a wider range of games as well as to perform counterproof tests in order to certify the actual responsibility of implementing these types of features in games.

Compared to traditional methods, metadesign accepts and promotes the diversity in complex systems. The method proposes detachment from controlling actions and from a single designer authorship. In this case, we assume all members in the system as potential collaborators and co-designers, what indicates a considerably more adapted methodology to the emergent potential of games, since it recognizes this feature and foresees changes after the usage or publication. This scenario is pertinent to the game industry and corroborates with the elements found in the analysis of Tibia, PokemonGO and The Sims franchise, where the gamer community interacted and got involved with the system, modifying it and making it responsible for the interactions, emergences and for alterations in the game mechanics. We can understand the development scenarios, which present fluidity and constant mutations, as metaprojects, chiefly for its dynamic character. This proposal contrasts with conventional methodologies and contributes to the constant reflection on complex, changing scenarios.

We recognize that the use of artificial intelligences make NPCs active in the interactive processes, mediating, promoting and increasing the number of interactions with players. In the field of game design the idea of having one apparently intelligent agent is already enough to provide a fun and personalized experience. However, the use of a correct technique (deterministic or non-deterministic) allied to the theory of GameFlow can contribute to the difficult game adjustments and thus in its adaptive potential in relation to the player's wishes level of aptitude.

7   Conclusions and Future Work

Regarding the methodologies used, we discussed where, when and how we can project emergencies. We also pointed out the necessity of thinking about them already during the project phase, treating the development as a metraproject that is going to be constantly incremented according to the emergence indications revealed by players during game play or even in auxiliary platforms created by the gamer community itself. Collaborative development can be a way of solving complex problems in the field of design, leading users to the sphere of decision-making and contribution to projects. Furthermore, we hope that the present study may contribute to the development of games and future investigations regarding emergences in such contexts.

In relation to future contributions, this investigation opens a range of possibilities on how to analyze in depth each resource and phenomenon to find new patterns of incidence. It also points out the possibility of developing a game with the intention of reaching high levels of emergence, combining all the identified resources or the contrary, to remove all listed resources and verify if it is still possible to find a fertile environment for that reality. Another contribution would be investigating the adaptive capacity of agents endowed with different types of AI, how they develop it and its applications linked to the theory of GameFlow.

In this sense, we estimate that the research had an expiratory character regarding the possibility of promoting emergences in games, pointing out resources in three directions in order to potentiate this phenomenon: the usage of open narratives, co-design and AIs in NPCs. The research opened space for qualitative and quantitative investigation regarding interactions in the system, what deserves better investigation.

References

1. Bunge, M.: Emergencia y convergencia. Gedisa Editorial, Barcelona (2004)
2. Newzoo: Annual Global Games Market Report. NewZoo (2015)
3. Zuanon, R.: Game design and neuroscience cooperation in the challenge-based immersion in mobile devices as tablets and smartphones. In: Streitz, N., Markopoulos, P. (eds.) DAPI 2016. LNCS, vol. 9749, pp. 142–153. Springer, Cham (2016). doi:10.1007/978-3-319-39862-4_14

4. Zuanon, R.: Design-neuroscience: interactions between the creative and cognitive processes of the brain and design. In: Kurosu, M. (ed.) HCI 2014. LNCS, vol. 8510, pp. 167–174. Springer, Cham (2014). doi:10.1007/978-3-319-07233-3_16
5. Zuanon, R.: Designing wearable bio-interfaces: a transdisciplinary articulation between design and neuroscience. In: Stephanidis, C., Antona, M. (eds.) UAHCI 2013. LNCS, vol. 8009, pp. 689–699. Springer, Heidelberg (2013). doi:10.1007/978-3-642-39188-0_74
6. Zuanon, R.: Usign BCI to play games with brain signals: an organic interaction process through NeuroBodyGame wearable computer. In: Huggins, J.E., et al. (eds.) Fifth International Brain-Computer Interface Meeting 2013, pp. 64–65. Graz University of Technology Publishing House, Graz (2013)
7. Zuanon, R.: Bio-interfaces: designing wearable devices to organic interactions. In: Ursyn, A. (ed.) Biologically-Inspired Computing for the Arts: Scientific Data Through Graphics, pp. 1–17. IGI Global, Hershey (2011)
8. Holland, J.: Hidden Order: How Adaptation Builds Complexity. Basic Books, New York (1995)
9. Sweetser, P.: Emergence in Games. Thomson, Boston (2007)
10. Salen, K., Zimmerman, E.: Regras do jogo: fundamentos do design de jogos, vol. 1. Blucher, São Paulo (2012)
11. Schell, J.A.: Arte de Game Design: o Livro Original. Elsevier, Rio de Janeiro (2011)
12. Vassão, C.: Metadesign: ferramentas, estratégias e ética para a complexidade. Blucher, São Paulo (2010)
13. Baranauskas, M.C., Martins, M.C., Valente, J.A.: Codesign de Redes Digitais: Tecnologia e Educação a Serviço da Inclusão Social. Penso, Porto Alegre (2013)
14. Russel, S., Norvig, P.; Inteligência artificial, 3a edn. Campus, Rio de Janeiro (2013)
15. Champandard, A.J.: AI Game Development: Synthetic Creatures with Learning and Reactive Behaviors. New Riders, London (2013)
16. CipSoft: Game Tibia (1997)
17. Niantic: Game PokemonGo (2016)
18. Eletronic Arts: Game The Sims (2000)
19. Bertalanffy, L.V.: Teoria Geral dos Sistemas. Ed. Vozes, São Paulo (2009)
20. Vieira, J.A.: Organização e sistemas. Informática na educação: Teoria e prática 3(1) (2000)
21. Uyemov, A.: Problem of direction of time and the laws of system's development. In: Kubat, L., Zeman, J. (eds.) Entropy and Information in Science and Philosophy, pp. 93–102. Elsevier Scient., Praga (1975)
22. Vassão, C.: Arquitetura livre: Complexidade, Metadesign e Ciência Nômade. Tese de Doutorado. Tese (doutorado em Arquitetura) Universidade de São Paulo (2008)
23. Cardoso, R.: Design para um mundo complexo. Ubu Editora LTDA-ME (2016)
24. Fullerton, T.: Game Design Workshop: A Playcentric Approach to Creating Innovative Games. Paperback, New York (2008)
25. Juul, J.: Half-Real: Video Games Between Real Rules and Fictional Worlds. MIT Press, Cambridge (2005)
26. Piccini, M.: O papel do jogador na construção de sentido em narrativas de jogos digitais: o jogo como forma de expressão do jogador. In SBC - Proceedings of SBGames (2012)
27. Flusser, V.: O mundo codificado: por uma filosofia do design e da comunicação. Cosac Naify, São Paulo (2007)
28. Lucena, M.C.: O Espaço Público e Pokémon Go: um diálogo entre o real e o virtual. Revista Científica ANAP Brasil 9(15) (2016)

29. Ferreira, A., Demutti, C.M., Gimenez, P.E.: A teoria das necessidades de Maslow: a influência do nível educacional sobre a sua percepção no ambiente de trabalho. XIII SEMEAD–Seminários em Administração (2010). ISNN: 2177-3866
30. Champion, E.: Game Mods: Theory and Criticism. Lulu.com, Morrisville (2013)
31. Hunicke, R., Leblanc, M., Zubek, R.: MDA: a formal approach to game design and game research. In: Proceedings of the AAAI Workshop on Challenges in Game AI (2004)
32. Fischer, G., Giaccardi, E.: Meta-design: a framework for the future of end-user development. In: Lieberman, H., Paternò, F., Wulf, V. (eds.) End user development. Human-Computer Interaction Series, vol. 9, pp. 427–457. Springer, Dordrecht (2006). doi: 10.1007/1-4020-5386-X_19
33. Chen, J.: Flow in Games – MFA Thesis. University of Southern California (2008)

Augmented Reality Games for Learning: A Literature Review

Jingya Li[1(✉)], Erik D. van der Spek[1], Loe Feijs[1], Feng Wang[2], and Jun Hu[1,2]

[1] Department of Industrial Design, Eindhoven University of Technology, Den Dolech 2, 5612 AZ Eindhoven, The Netherlands
{Ji.Li,e.d.v.d.spek,L.M.G.Feijs,j.hu}@tue.nl
[2] School of Digital Media, Jiangnan University, Wuxi, China
water6@126.com

Abstract. This study presents a literature review of previous studies of Augmented Reality (AR) games for learning. We classified learner groups, learning subjects, and learning environments mentioned in the literature. From this we conclude that AR games for learning generally have positive effects. We found that the most reported effects for AR learning games were the enhancement of learning performance and the learning experience in terms of fun, interest, and enjoyment. The most commonly used measurements for learning achievements were pre-test and post-test regarding knowledge content, while observations, questionnaires, and interviews were all frequently used to determine motivation. We also found that social interactions were encouraged by AR learning games, especially collaboration among students. The most commonly used game elements included quizzes and goal-setting. Extra instructional materials, 3D models, and face-to-face interactions were most frequently used for AR features. In addition, we came up with five suggestions for the design of AR learning games based on reviewed studies. In conclusion, six interesting findings were discussed in detail in the review, and suggestions for future study were offered to fill the research gaps.

Keywords: Augmented Reality · Education · Learning · Social · Serious games

1 Introduction

Augmented Reality (AR) is the technology that overlaps virtual objects onto the real world objects [1]. It has three main features: the combination of the real world and the virtual world, real-time interaction, and 3D registration [3]. The past few years have witnessed a growing popularity in the research interest for AR since mobile devices such as smartphones and tablets have offered much easier and cheaper access to AR for users than before [1]. Positive effects of AR technology on students' learning were identified in previous studies in the development of skills and knowledge, enhancement of learning experiences, and improvement of collaborative learning [35]. The use of

© Springer International Publishing AG 2017
N. Streitz and P. Markopoulos (Eds.): DAPI 2017, LNCS 10291, pp. 612–626, 2017.
DOI: 10.1007/978-3-319-58697-7_46

AR in education could improve the learning efficiency and provide a more fun experience for students [21].

Serious games can be defined as computer games with educational purposes and see entertainment as an added value. Serious games are gaining increasing importance in education [27], providing an enhanced experience in learning [26]. They were found to be effective with respect to learning and retention [34]. Other frequently reported outcomes included knowledge acquisition and motivational outcomes [9].

AR games refer to the digital games that are played in a real world environment with a virtual layer on top of it [32]. It is possible for players to interact with both the objects in the virtual world and people in the real world, avoiding the social isolation [29]. With the advantages and positive outcomes of AR technology and serious games in the educational field, a growing number of studies focusing on AR games for learning have emerged in the past few years (e.g. studies of EcoMOBILE [11] and study of Mad City Mystery [32]).

1.1 Relevant Literature

The features of AR lead to a variety of positive effects on learning. The interactive 3D models in AR can enhance students' learning experience and collaborative skills; the combination of the real world and the virtual world in AR can support the study of the invisible concept and content; and the rich instructional materials (e.g., text, video, audio, etc.) can attract and immerse students into the learning [35]. In addition to that, some literatures drew attention to the social impacts of AR on students. For instance, the use of AR technology provided more opportunities for students to communicate and collaborate in the real world [20]. The social interactions between students and teachers, students and their parents were also encouraged [33].

Structured literature reviews were found on AR for educational purposes. For example, one systematic review of AR for education investigated 68 AR studies in education and concluded a number of advantages and challenges [1]. In this review, the advantages of AR in educational settings were classified into learner outcomes, pedagogical contributions, interaction, and others. In another review, the definitions, taxonomies, and technologies of AR technology were introduced, and the AR features and their affordances, as well as the solutions for AR challenges, were discovered [35]. Different affordances of location-based AR and image-based AR for science learning were also studied [11]. The review on AR trends in education found the educational field and purposes, target group, advantages, data collection methods, and discussed the trends for AR for educational settings [4].

These literature reviews mainly focused on the advantages and affordances of AR. Moreover, the purposes of using AR were different, such as a practice for lab experiments or an introduction to certain topics [4]. However, the game elements and social factors contained in the AR applications were not addressed enough.

1.2 Purpose of the Study

As can be seen above, numerous studies have been done on the use of AR technology or games in education for students. However, the efficacy of AR learning games as an integrated concept is less well known, let alone what would be successful design strategies for AR learning games. Therefore, the aims of this study is to present a systematic literature review on AR learning games, considering the current state of AR learning games, their effects on students regarding learning outcomes and social interactions, their evaluation techniques, as well as their design principles. To achieve this aim, this study identified and analyzed 26 research articles with the educational use of AR games, published from 2006 to 2016. The research questions are formed as:

RQ1:   What learner groups, subjects, and environments are commonly focused on for AR learning games according to the reviewed studies?

RQ2:   What are the effects of AR learning games on students in terms of learning achievement and motivation and what are the measurements according to the reviewed studies?

RQ3:   What are the effects of social interaction in AR learning games on students according to the reviewed studies?

RQ4:   What kinds of elements or features are commonly used in AR learning games according to the reviewed studies?

RQ5:   What are the suggestions for the design of AR learning games according to the reviewed studies?

2 Method

2.1 Selection Process

In this study, we first searched via Google Scholar. The search terms we used were "augmented reality" combined with "serious games", "learning and games", and "education and games". Additionally, we investigated the references of previous reviews on AR technology in educational field to find relevant studies. We found 63 studies first. Then we examined the selected studies using a set of inclusion and exclusion criteria (see Table 1) and determined whether they were related to the purpose of this study. After the examination, 26 articles were found to be highly relevant to the purpose of this study.

Table 1. Inclusion and exclusion criteria.

Inclusion criteria	Exclusion criteria
Involve AR as primary component	No clear data collection method
Involve game play in the design	Only introduction without evaluation
For educational purposes	For target groups with special needs

2.2   The Data Coding and Analysis Process

The first research question addresses the learner groups, subjects, and environments of AR learning games. The learner groups were divided into kindergarten, primary school students, middle school students, high school students, college students, and not specified in the article. In some studies, more than one learner group was used, then more than one category was applied for the learner group. The subjects of AR learning games were divided by looking for subject-related words in the article. One study might also apply to more than one code for subjects. The environments of using AR learning games were divided into five categories, which were: outdoors, classroom, home, others, and no limits.

The effects and their measurements of AR learning games (RQ2) were coded by reading through the data collection, method, findings, results, discussions, and conclusion sections from the 26 articles. We looked for coding words to identify the effects and measurements. For effects, we used two main categories, learning achievement and motivation. Learning achievement was related to the learning performance, learning effectiveness, and the cognitive load of the knowledge content, while motivation related to a broad view including engagement, interests, fun, satisfaction, and positive attitudes. It should be noted that in some studies, more than one effect could be found, so more than one code might be applied.

As for the effects of social interaction in AR learning games (RQ3), we looked up the coding words: social, collaboration, competition, guide, discussion, communication, reflection, and share from the 26 articles.

To code the elements/features used in AR learning games (RQ4), we read through the design, implementation, and procedure sections from the 26 articles, searching for keywords from the description of the AR games. Sub-categories were classified into two main categories, AR features and game elements.

3   Results and Discussion

3.1   RQ1: What Learner Groups, Subjects, and Environments Are Commonly Focused on for AR Learning Games According to the Reviewed Studies?

Regarding the "learner group", we found that in the past decade, most of the AR learning games focused on primary school students (31%) and middle school students (29%). High school students (20%) followed primary school students and middle school students in popularity (see Fig. 1). Two studies focused on college students (8%). Two studies designed the AR games for college students in the majors of Design [2] and Physics [23]. One potential explanation for this could be that AR learning games can have a positive influence on younger students because they are more evocative and align better to the kind of games they are playing at home [33].

Regarding to the learning "subjects", Science and Biology (38%) were highly focused subjects in the reviewed AR learning games. This might be because the AR technology can provide advantages in reflecting the concept of knowledge in the real world environment, allowing students to observe the objects in real-time. The study of

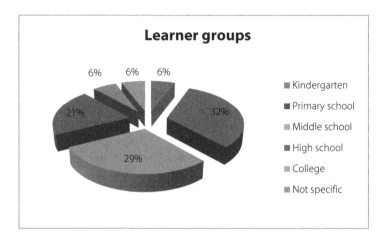

Fig. 1. Learner groups

Physics (12%), History (12%), and Art & Design (12%) were second preferred subjects. The real-time feature of AR enables students to receive feedback or see results immediately, which is favorable for subjects like Art & Design (see Table 2).

Table 2. Subjects of AR learning games.

Subject	Number of papers	Percentage	Sample of research
Science & Biology	10	38%	[6]
Art & Design	3	12%	[2]
Physics	3	12%	[19]
History	3	12%	[32]
Mathematics	2	8%	[9]
Chemistry	2	8%	[33]
Literacy	2	8%	[15]
Others	3	12%	[32]
No specific	2	8%	[12]

We noticed a gap in the subjects of AR learning games. First of all, studies for Literacy (8%), Chemistry (8%) and Mathematics (8%) studying were underrepresented. The uneven situation of subjects should be broken down, which means more attention should be paid to a wider range of subjects [15].

What's more, the existing studies for History learning often made a new game story for students to explore the history of a certain area (e.g. Alien Contact! [11]). The location-based feature of AR technology enhances students' learning experience by allowing them to stand on the historical spots. Other subjects (12%) included culture study [13], 21st century skills [30], and library instruction study [8]. However, we found little focus on the textbook-related content and knowledge, which is also valuable and should be paid attention to.

Regarding to the "environments" to use AR learning games, we saw significant preference from the reviewed studies in using AR learning games outdoors (42%) and in the classrooms (35%). See Table 3. Playing outside is one of the advantages of AR learning games compared to other serious games, which may stimulate interest and excitement in students [6]. On the other hand, it could be difficult for the teacher to control the learning process, and the safety issues should be considered as well. Students might come into dangerous situation, such as car accidents, when they put too much attention to their mobile devices [31]. The AR learning games played in the classroom allowed students to play face-to-face and under the guidance of their teachers. Students could solve problems and collaborate with their classmates [11], and they could immediately get help and feedback from their teachers when they encountered problems or had questions (e.g. AR for preschoolers for Natural Science [7]).

Table 3. Places to use AR learning games.

Subject	Number of papers	Percentage	Sample of research
Classroom	11	42%	[24]
Outdoors	9	35%	[28]
No limits	4	15%	[22]
Home	1	4%	[21]
Others	1	4%	[8]

We found four AR games (15%) with no limits for the environment, and only one AR learning game (4%) was designed specifically for playing at home with the help of parents [2]. Students, especially younger students, spend more time at home than in the classroom, and tend to spend a lot of time playing digital games [25]. Meanwhile, their parents are curious about their learning status. Therefore, it can be effective to design AR learning games that students can play at home. It may encourage them to study more spontaneously and in a more fun way. In addition to that, their safety and communication with parents could also be addressed.

3.2 RQ2: What Are the Effects of AR Learning Games on Students in Terms of Learning Achievement and Motivation and What Are the Measurements According to the Reviewed Studies?

Effects of AR learning games were classified into two main categories in this review, which were learning achievement and motivation (see Table 4).

Regarding to the "learning achievement", half of the reviewed studies reported that AR learning games led to the effective outcomes in achieving learning gains in terms of learning content (e.g. AR for electromagnetism [19] and AR system for library instruction [8]). The positive effects also included the enhancement of learning effi- ciency (15%) and cognitive skills like problem-solving skills, critical thinking skills, multitasking skills and so on (12%). One study (4%) reported that the use of AR learning game could reduce the cognitive load of students [10], while on the contrary,

Table 4. The effects of AR learning games.

Effects	Sub-categories	Numbers of papers	Percentage	Sample research
Learning achievement	Achieve learning gains	13	50%	[18]
	Enhance learning efficiency	4	15%	[10]
	Enhance cognitive skills	3	12%	[30]
	Decrease cognitive load	1	4%	[10]
Motivation	Enhance fun, interest, enjoyment	16	62%	[1]
	Enhance engagement	12	46%	[6]
	Enhance satisfaction	5	19%	[7]
	Enhance willingness to learn	5	19%	[22]
	Provide positive attitude	4	15%	[16]
	Enhance attention	4	15%	[25]
	Enhance confidence	4	15%	[22]

another study showed that students felt frequently overloaded and confused due to the big amount of materials and tasks during the game play [11]. The rest of the reviewed studies (19%) either found AR games were ineffective in the learning achievement or didn't focus on the learning achievement in their studies.

The motivation aspects involved engagement, satisfaction, fun, enjoyment, interest, attention, confidence and positive attitudes of students (e.g. SysteM [15] and AR-based educational game [18]). Previous studies frequently reported that students described the learning experience with AR games as joyful and playful as they had fun playing AR games to learn school knowledge [25]. We found similar result in our review that most of the students (62%) mentioned AR learning games as fun, interesting, or enjoyable (e.g. AR gaming in sustainable design education [2] and mathematical education game based on AR [21]). Nearly half of the studies (46%) also reported that AR learning games engaged them more than traditional learning methods (e.g. AR system for a visual art course [10]). In addition to these two effects, AR learning games were also evaluated to "enhance satisfaction" (19%), "enhance the willingness to learn" (19%), "enhance attention" (15%), "enhance confidence" (15%), and "enhance positive learning attitude" (15%).

Considerably less well studied were the retention effects. Nearly all studies tested the outcomes immediately after the use of the AR games. In addition, most of the students never used AR games before, so a potential novelty effect of a new technology might influence the research results. Therefore, more research should be done focusing on both short-term and long-term impacts on students after learning with AR games.

Different measurements were used to evaluate the effects caused by AR learning games. The review found that the most frequently (38%) used measurement of learning achievement was a pre-test and post-test knowledge test which examines the improvement of knowledge content learning of students before and after the use of AR learning games (e.g. AR technology in marine education [25]). Three studies (12%)

used post-test in their experiments (e.g. AR for preschoolers for Natural Science [7]). From the result we can see that only 50% studies measured learning achievement in terms of the knowledge content, indicating the rest of studies didn't use a proper test or didn't focus on learning at all.

Regarding to the motivation aspect, most of the previous studies (65%) used observation as the main evaluation methods during students' learning and playing process (e.g. AR for enhancing library instruction [8]). The questionnaire also held a high popularity (58%) in the measurement of motivation (e.g. using AR games to teach 21st century skills [30]). Some studies introduced and explained the questionnaire questions in their studies and Keller's ARCS Motivation Model was frequently adopted as the motivation questionnaire (e.g. AR system for a visual art course [10]), whereas other studies didn't explain how they created and evaluated their questionnaire questions to measure the motivation accurately. Interviews as a way to collect qualitative data was also widely used (42%). Pre-survey and post-survey (15%) were used to investigate the changes of attitudes before and after the use of AR games. See Table 5.

Table 5. Measurement methods of effects.

Effect	Method	Number of papers	Percentage	Sample of research
Learning achievement	Pre-test and post-test	10	38%	[25]
	Post-test only	3	12%	[7]
Motivation	Observation	17	65%	[6]
	Questionnaire	15	58%	[33]
	Interview	11	42%	[11]
	Pre-survey and post-survey	4	15%	[30]

3.3   RQ3: What Are the Effects of Social Interaction in AR Learning Games on Students According to the Reviewed Studies?

Collaboration and interaction have emerged to be the main advantages of AR in education [4], since the technology allows users to work or study face-to-face in real life. Based on reviewed studies, we found three main types of social interactions, which were interactions among students, between teachers and students, and between students and parents. See Table 6.

Most of the social interaction effects were found among students and the main effect was to encourage the collaboration (46%). In some AR games, students were required to work in groups to solve a certain task, while the competition (31%) among groups was also promoted. Evidence was also noted in the desire of sharing experiences with classmates (8%). Unlike the rich social interactions among students, the only social interaction between students & teacher (15%) and students & parents (8%) was guidance.

Table 6. Social interactions.

Type	Effect	Number of papers	Percentage	Sample of research
Student-student	Collaboration	12	46%	[5]
	Competition	8	31%	[18]
	Share	2	8%	[10]
Student-teacher	Guide	4	15%	[33]
Student-parents	Guide	2	8%	[15]

Frequently, little attention was paid to the study of how these social interactions affected the learning achievement or motivation in turn. The attitude from classmates, the feedback from teachers, and the help from parents may all have an impact on children's learning outcomes. In addition, AR games should focus more on the interactions between student and teacher, student and parents.

3.4   RQ4: What Kinds of Elements or Features Are Commonly Used in AR Learning Games According to the Reviewed Studies?

AR learning games include AR features and game elements. Different features or elements may have different outcomes regarding to learning achievement and motivation mentioned above. Therefore, this review sought to identify the frequently used AR features and game elements in AR learning games.

Regarding to the "game elements", we found that time limitation was one of the most commonly used elements (46%) in the reviewed studies, which means students have to finish the game in a certain period of time (e.g. AR science game [6]). One reason to explain this might be because the attention span of students is limited, especially for younger students. Teachers might also find the time limitation helpful for them to control the learning progress, or researchers to control for variables in the experiment. The game elements of quiz-based (50%), inquiry-based (35%), and puzzles (30%) were also preferred by the reviewed studies. Students needed to answer questions or finish tasks in the game to continue. Game story (42%) was also another frequently included element in AR learning game design. Students started the game with story or background information, and some of them might play a role (27%) during the game. Another frequently used game element was "collection" (30%). Players tried to look for different information and collect them in order to achieve the goals. The term "goals" was widely used in the reviewed literature, including the aims to get certain points, rewards, or finish a task (50%). Secret missions or hidden content were also included in some games (15%), the process of looking for the hidden mission might stimulate the interest of the students. The feedback element in the game design was mentioned three times (12%), and two board games (8%) were used. See Table 7.

As for the AR features, 38% of reviewed studies used location-based AR, and the rest used image-based AR (62%). These two forms might have different advantages for learning [11]. Since the visualization of knowledge content can promote to the fun experience of AR learning games for students, more than two third of the studies (77%) included extra instructional materials such as text, video, and audio. The 3D models

Table 7. Game elements.

	Game elements	Number of papers	Percentage	Sample of research
Game	Goals	13	50%	[25]
	Quiz-based	13	50%	[10]
	Time limitation	12	46%	[6]
	Game story	11	42%	[8]
	Inquiry-based	9	35%	[32]
	Collection game	8	30%	[5]
	Solve puzzles	8	30%	[13]
	Role play	7	27%	[32]
	Secret mission	4	15%	[18]
	Feedback	3	12%	[15]
	Board game	2	8%	[21]

were also used frequently in AR learning games (54%). Apart from that, some AR learning games (30%) also used physical objects, allowing students to interact in the game by using physical models. Communication in the real world is the main advantage of AR learning games (as opposed to regular videogames), and half of the reviewed studies encouraged face-to-face interactions in their games. AR presentation avatar (15%) and gesture-based input (12%) were also mentioned in previous studies. See Table 8.

Table 8. AR features.

	AR features	Number of papers	Percentage	Sample of research
AR	Location based	10	38%	[25]
	Image based	16	62%	[8]
	Instructional material	20	77%	[5]
	3D model	14	54%	[15]
	Face-to-face	13	50%	[20]
	Physical model	8	30%	[16]
	AR presentation agent	4	15%	[13]
	Gesture-based input	3	12%	[14]

Although we have found the most commonly used game elements and AR features from previous studies, there is still a lack of research on how different AR features and game elements influenced or supported the positive outcomes mentioned above specifically. Questions like which element or feature in the AR game motivated students most during the learning process and why, which element or feature in the AR game helped students learn better during the learning process and why, which element or feature encouraged students to communicate to each other more and why, needed to be answered.

3.5   RQ5: What Are the Suggestions for the Design of AR Learning Games According to the Reviewed Studies?

According to the reviewed studies, we can discern recommendations for the design of AR learning games that potentially lead to positive effects on students. Generally speaking, during the design process, five aspects should be considered, which are learner groups, learning objectives, AR features, game mechanics, and social interactions.

Involve learners in design process
From the reviewed studies, we found that AR learning games might affect different types of learners in different ways. Some students needed to read the text in the game with assistance, while students with higher level of literacy skills could read the text and play by themselves [27]. This study also showed that most of the students hated the idea of a cookie game because they thought it was for little kids to play. To make the students become more willing to play the game, one of the reviewed studies designed different learning contents and story themes for primary school students, middle school students, and high school students respectively [32]. One advantage of AR learning games compared to traditional learning is that it can provide different learning contents to different students [8]. In the study, results showed that different learning types (i.e. field-independent and field-dependent cognitive styles), students responded differently towards the learning material. In another study, students from a higher educational level benefited more from the use of AR learning game than students from a lower educational level [17]. Players in a game could be classified into multiple player types, such as achievers, explorers, socializers, and killers, thus, finding out the player types might be more effective to motivate students [13].

Therefore, when designing an AR learning game, the designers should always involve the target learner groups into the design process, asking for their preferences and feedback for the game concepts, and taking their player types, learning skills and knowledge level into consideration.

Clear learning objectives
We found a variety of effects of AR learning games, from both learning achievement and motivation aspects. It is hard to achieve all of these effects in one game. Therefore, it is important to have specific and clear learning objectives. Some games focused on the improvement of students' knowledge performance (e.g. an innovative AR educational platform using games [13]), some might just want to make students feel more positive about studying (e.g. EcoMOBILE [20]), while some aimed at the development of cognitive skills, such as investigation and inquiry skills (e.g. ARIES [33]). The clear educational objectives are essential for the design of an effective AR learning game. Only when the educational objectives are clear, the proper game elements and AR features can be selected, and effective AR learning games can be designed.

Identify effects of AR features
AR technology makes AR learning games different from other learning games. A study claimed that the use of AR technology could reveal "hidden" objects to explore, which makes students feel special and excited, seeing "invisible" stuffs [5]. Additionally, AR

superimposed materials like text, pictures, video, and audio into a real time environment [13], which could provide students a more comprehensive understanding of the subject, allowing them to "visualize the spatial structure of a complex model by virtually interacting with it" [13].

AR technology compasses various features, and basically divided into location-based AR and image-based AR. While other forms included the use of an AR avatar, physical objects, extra instructional materials (e.g. video, audio, text etc.), and so on. According to our investigation, most of AR learning applications involved more than one feature in their design, but the specific effects of different kinds of AR features were not well studied. For example, does the AR avatar help students engage in the study, or does it distract the students' attention? Identifying the different outcomes and effects of each feature will make the design of AR technology better help students to achieve their goals.

Study the game mechanics

Like AR features, we also found more than ten types of game elements in previous AR learning games. Designers should study the game mechanics and understand how to use different game elements better to improve the learning achievements and motivation. We found some research already took game mechanics into consideration when they designed the AR learning games. For instance, the digital game-based learning theory was used in the design to enhance the effectiveness of marine education and to establish in children fundamental concepts for environmental conservation [8]. In another study we reviewed, design principles for games on science education were also addressed, such as: "ask students to inhabit roles", "activity is organized around challenges", and so on [32]. The use of flow theory was mentioned in another study, including "clear goals", "equilibrium between challenge and personal skill", "merging of action and awareness", "focused attention", "control", "loss of self-consciousness", "time distortion", as well as "self-rewarding" [13]. What's more, gaming mechanics was used to count the scores of the players based on their gaming status [18]. On the other hand, a big amount of studies ignored the game mechanics or didn't mention it in their research. The study of game mechanics can improve the positive advantages of AR learning games.

Encourage social interactions

From this review we can see that the social interactions such as collaboration and competition in the real world were great advantages of AR learning games. AR also enhanced communication skills, encouraging interactions in the classroom between teacher and students, students and students, students and parents, parents and parents and teachers and teachers [7]. However, few previous AR learning games paid attention to the design of the face-to-face social strategy to encourage social interactions in the real world. We found one study included a chat room in the game in order to encourage social behavior [6]. This function allowed students to talk online with the potential to prevent students from talking to each other in the real world. Some other studies allowed users to share information, solve puzzles together, or exchange game items face-to-face in the real world. The designers should keep the social advantage of AR in the AR learning games, trying to design social functions that can lead to better social effects in real life.

4 Conclusion and Future Research

After the review of previous studies of AR learning games, we have six interesting findings. First of all, the subjects and learning content used in previous studies were too narrow. Studies for Science & Biology attracted most of the attention while there were fewer studies focused on the other subjects, such as Literacy and Mathematics. Secondly, most of the current AR learning games was played outdoors or in the classrooms. However, since students spend a lot of time at home and play digital games, it might be more effective to design AR learning games that can be played at home, which may encourage them to study spontaneously and in a more fun way. Thirdly, a notable gap was found in the retention effects. Nearly all studies tested the outcomes immediately after the use of the AR learning games, and more research should be done on both short-term and long-term effects. As for the measurements in previous studies, some commonly used instruments were addressed, while some studies didn't mention how they created and evaluated their instruments. More attention should be paid to the proper measurements for the effects. Fifth, social interaction effects were found by playing AR learning games, especially among students. However, little research focused on how these social interactions affected the learning achievement or motivation in turn. Also, more social effects were found among students than between student and teacher, or student and parents. The AR games that focus more on the interactions between student and teacher, or student and parents may lead to beneficial results for both sides. Last but not least, we found various game elements and AR features were used in the design of the AR learning games. However, there is a lack of systematic research on how different AR features and game elements influenced or supported the effects specifically.

In addition, we came up with five recommendations for the design of AR learning games in order to maximum the positive effects, which are: (1) involve learners in the design process, (2) always have clear learning objectives, (3) design to encourage social interactions, (4) identify effects of AR features, and (5) study the game mechanics in order to select proper elements in the design.

In summary, though the positive effects of the use of AR learning games were widely recognized in the past decade, more research still needed to be done in the future.

Acknowledgements. The author would like to express special thanks to the China Scholarship Council for supporting this PhD study, thank you for the help from Wenting Du and School of Digital Media, Jiangnan University, and thank you for the help from colleagues at Department of Industrial Design, Eindhoven University of Technology.

References

1. Akçayır, M., Akçayır, G.: Advantages and challenges associated with augmented reality for education: a systematic review of the literature. Educ. Res. Rev. 20, 1–11 (2017)
2. Ayer, S.K., Messner, J.I., Anumba, C.J.: Augmented reality gaming in sustainable design education. J. Architectural Eng. 22(1), 04015012 (2016)

3. Azuma, R.: A survey of augmented reality. Presence Teleoperators Virtual Environ. **6**(4), 355–385 (1997)
4. Bacca, J., Baldiris, S., Fabregat, R., Graf, S.: Augmented reality trends in education: a systematic review of research and applications. Educ. Technol. Soc. **17**(4), 133–149 (2014)
5. Boletsis, C., McCallum, S.: The table mystery: an augmented reality collaborative game for chemistry education. In: Ma, M., Oliveira, M.F., Petersen, S., Hauge, J.B. (eds.) SGDA 2013. LNCS, vol. 8101, pp. 86–95. Springer, Heidelberg (2013). doi:10.1007/978-3-642-40790-1_9
6. Bressler, D.M., Bodzin, A.M.: A mixed methods assessment of students' flow experiences during a mobile augmented reality science game. J. Comput. Assist. Learn. **29**(6), 505–517 (2013)
7. Cascales, A., Laguna, I., Pérez López, D., Perona, P., Contero, M.: Augmented reality for preschoolers: an experience around natural sciences educational contents, pp. 103–112 (2012)
8. Chen, C.M., Tsai, Y.N.: Interactive augmented reality system for enhancing library instruction in elementary schools. Comput. Educ. **59**(2), 638–652 (2012)
9. Connolly, T.M., Boyle, E.A., MacArthur, E., Hainey, T., Boyle, J.M.: A systematic literature review of empirical evidence on computer games and serious games. Comput. Educ. **59**(2), 661–686 (2012)
10. Di Serio, Á., Ibáñez, M.B., Kloos, C.D.: Impact of an augmented reality system on students' motivation for a visual art course. Comput. Educ. **68**, 585–596 (2013)
11. Dunleavy, M., Dede, C., Mitchell, R.: Affordances and limitations of immersive participatory augmented reality simulations for teaching and learning. J. Sci. Educ. Technol. **18**(1), 7–22 (2009)
12. El Sayed, N.A.M., Zayed, H.H., Sharawy, M.I.: ARSC: augmented reality student card an augmented reality solution for the education field. Comput. Educ. **56**(4), 1045–1061 (2011)
13. Eleftheria, C.A., Charikleia, P., Iason, C.G., Athanasios, T., Dimitrios, T.: An innovative augmented reality educational platform using gamification to enhance lifelong learning and cultural education. In: 2013 Fourth International Conference on Information, Intelligence, Systems and Applications (IISA 2013), pp. 70–74 (2013)
14. Enyedy, N., Danish, J.A., Delacruz, G., Kumar, M.: Learning physics through play in an augmented reality environment. Int. J. Comput. Support. Collaborative Learn. **7**, 347–378 (2012)
15. Freitas, R., Campos, P.: SMART: a SysteM of Augmented Reality for Teaching 2nd grade students. In: Proceedings of the 22nd British HCI Group Annual Conference on People and Computers: Culture, Creativity, Interaction, vol. 2, pp. 27–30, April 2008
16. Hsiao, K.-F., Chen, N.-S., Huang, S.-Y.: Learning while exercising for science education in augmented reality among adolescents. Interact. Learn. Environ. **20**, 331–349 (2012)
17. Huizenga, J., Admiraal, W., Akkerman, S., Ten Dam, G.: Mobile game-based learning in secondary education: engagement, motivation and learning in a mobile city game: original article. J. Comput. Assist. Learn. **25**(4), 332–344 (2009)
18. Hwang, G.-J., Wu, P.-H., Chen, C.-C., Tu, N.-T.: Effects of an augmented reality-based educational game on students' learning achievements and attitudes in real-world observations. Interact. Learn. Environ. **24**, 1–12 (2015). ISSN: 1049-4820
19. Ibáñez, M.B., Di Serio, Á., Villarán, D., Delgado Kloos, C.: Experimenting with electromagnetism using augmented reality: Impact on flow student experience and educational effectiveness. Comput. Educ. **71**, 1–13 (2014)
20. Kamarainen, A.M., Metcalf, S., Grotzer, T., Browne, A., Mazzuca, D., Tutwiler, M.S., Dede, C.: EcoMOBILE: Integrating augmented reality and probeware with environmental education field trips. Comput. Educ. **68**, 545–556 (2013)

21. Lee, H.S., Lee, J.W.: Mathematical education game based on augmented reality. In: Pan, Z., Zhang, X., Rhalibi, A., Woo, W., Li, Y. (eds.) Edutainment 2008. LNCS, vol. 5093, pp. 442–450. Springer, Heidelberg (2008). doi:10.1007/978-3-540-69736-7_48

22. Lin, H.K., Hsieh, M., Wang, C., Sie, Z., Chang, S.: Establishment and usability evaluation of an interactive AR learning system on conservation of fish. Turk. Online J. Educ. Technol. **10** (4), 181–188 (2011)

23. Lin, T.J., Duh, H.B.L., Li, N., Wang, H.Y., Tsai, C.C.: An investigation of learners' collaborative knowledge construction performances and behavior patterns in an augmented reality simulation system. Comput. Educ. **68**, 314–321 (2013)

24. Liu, W., Cheok, A.D., Lim, C.M.L., Theng, Y.L.: Mixed reality classroom: learning from entertainment. In: DIMEA 2007 Proceedings of the 2nd International Conference on Digital Interactive Media in Entertainment and Arts, pp. 65–72 (2007)

25. Lu, S.-J., Liu, Y.-C.: Integrating augmented reality technology to enhance children's learning in marine education. Environ. Educ. Res. **21**, 1–17 (2014). ISSN: 1350-4622

26. Carvalho, M.B., Bellotti, F., Berta, R., De Gloria, A., Sedano, C.I., Hauge, J.B., Hu, J., Rauterberg, M.: An activity theory-based model for serious games analysis and conceptual design. Comput. Educ. **87**, 166–181 (2015)

27. Carvalho, M.B., Bellotti, F., Berta, R., De Gloria, A., Gazzarata, G., Hu, J., Kickmeier-Rust, M.: A case study on service-oriented architecture for serious games. Entertain. Comput. **6**(1), 1–10 (2015)

28. Perry, J., Klopfer, E., Norton, M., Ave, M.: AR gone wild: two approaches to using augmented reality learning games in Zoos. In: Management, pp. 322–329 (2008)

29. Offermans, S., Hu, J.: Augmented home. In: Anacleto, J.C., Clua, E.W.G., Silva, F.S.C., Fels, S., Yang, H.S. (eds.) ICEC 2013. LNCS, vol. 8215, pp. 30–35. Springer, Heidelberg (2013). doi:10.1007/978-3-642-41106-9_4

30. Schrier, K.: Using augmented reality games to teach 21st century skills. In: International Conference on Computer Graphics and Interactive Techniques, ACM SIGGRAPH 2006 Educators Program (2006)

31. Specht, M., Ternier, S., Greller, W.: Dimensions of mobile augmented reality for learning: a first inventory (2011)

32. Squire, K.D., Jan, M.: Mad city mystery: developing scientific argumentation skills with a place-based augmented reality game on handheld computers. J. Sci. Educ. Technol. **16**(1), 5–29 (2007)

33. Wojciechowski, R., Cellary, W.: Evaluation of learners' attitude toward learning in ARIES augmented reality environments. Comput. Educ. **68**, 570–585 (2013)

34. Wouters, P., van Nimwegen, C., van Oostendorp, H., van der Spek, E.D.: A meta-analysis of the cognitive and motivational effects of serious games. J. Educ. Psychol. **105**(2), 249–265 (2013)

35. Wu, H.K., Lee, S.W.Y., Chang, H.Y., Liang, J.C.: Current status, opportunities and challenges of augmented reality in education. Comput. Educ. **62**, 41–49 (2013)

Humor as an Ostensive Challenge that Displays Mind-Reading Ability

Gary McKeown[✉]

School of Psychology, Queen's University Belfast, Belfast BT7 1NN, UK
g.mckeown@qub.ac.uk

Abstract. Understanding humor in human social interaction is a prerequisite to the creation of engaging interactions between humans and digital assistants, embodied conversational agents and social robots. As these HCI methods become more prevalent and pervasive, more advanced conversational discourse abilities will be required. However, many models of dialogue and human communication used in computer science remain based upon out-dated understanding of the manner in which humans communicate with one another. This paper addresses these issues introducing a view of communication based on Relevance theory and the Analogical Peacock Hypothesis in which humor and humorous interactions are viewed as ostensive challenges inviting the receiver of a communication to engage in greater levels of cognitive processing and effort to resolve the challenge set by a humorous display. The increased effort is rewarded with positive socio-cognitive effects—a humorous payoff and knowledge of the mind-reading abilities of the humor producer.

Keywords: Humor · Mind-reading · Relevance theory · Analogical Peacock Hypothesis · Ostensive challenge

1 Introduction

The use of humor in human communication is perhaps one of the simplest ways to demonstrate a mastery of a given language and a deep understanding of the social and cultural norms within which the humorous communication is taking place. We value displays of humor highly and also often place those who can consistently display wit and conversational humor amongst the most deserving of our social praise and accolades. These factors alone should make humor, and the laughter that often accompanies it, a prime focus for scientific study—unfortunately, they are all too often peripheral within social, cognitive and communication science. In the late 20th century and early 21st century great strides were made in the advancement of natural language processing as a computational endeavour and in the understanding of human language from a computational perspective. However, certain aspects of the intricate use of human language have proven particularly obstinate and resistant to computational modelling. Particularly difficult aspects to model include the understanding of sarcasm, irony,

© Springer International Publishing AG 2017
N. Streitz and P. Markopoulos (Eds.): DAPI 2017, LNCS 10291, pp. 627–639, 2017.
DOI: 10.1007/978-3-319-58697-7_47

metaphor, and humor. Deft use of these aspects of human language show that a communicator understands the nature of the environment in which they find themselves at a deep level—this importantly often involves the incorporation of current contextual information, an awareness of currently salient topics and an awareness of what is likely to be of interest in the minds of the audience to which the humor is oriented. Knowing what is currently relevant and interesting is one of the key challenges in both computational natural language processing and computational modelling of humor; typical current solutions use abstract or out of date toy problem data sets that are unlikely to be current and relevant [1].

McKeown [1,2] has argued that the use of humor and the laughter that relates to humor use are best thought of as mutual displays of the fact that one knows what is happening in the mind of interlocutors. Humor displays mind-reading ability to conversational partners and this creates a desire to socially bond with the humorous person and laughter is, at its core, a social bonding signal.

2   The Shannon and Weaver Model and the Conduit Metaphor

A crucial factor in the computational modelling of humor are the assumptions made concerning the nature of human communication. Usually, a fundamental assumption is to base a conceptualisation of human communication on the commonly used Shannon and Weaver model [3] and some version of what has been termed "the conduit metaphor" [4] or the code model as it is sometimes known [5]. These approaches tend to view communication in general, with human communication as a special case, as a system designed to pass information from one entity or person to another—the main goal of the communication process being the efficient transmission or exchange of information. A schematic diagram of the classic Shannon and Weaver model is displayed in Fig. 1.

In this account—which stems from the mathematical and electronics disciplines from which Shannon and Weaver came—an information source creates a message which is then encoded in some way to create a signal. That signal is sent

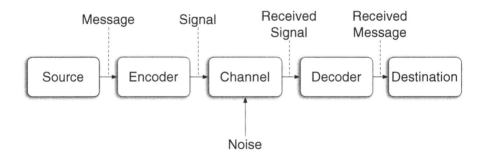

Fig. 1. Shannon and Weaver model of communication [3].

through some communication channel with the possibility of become contaminated by noise. Once in the channel it can be picked up by receivers who may be equipped with the knowledge, motivation and wherewithal to decode the signal and therefore receive the message and the information it contains. This model works very well in the world of electronic signalling and telecommunications—it therefore has had much appeal in the related disciplines of information technology and computer science. However, it has also been widely been adopted in other areas of science where its basic assumptions may not be quite so tenable; it is often taken as a basis for reasoning and thought concerning animal communication and human language and communication. Figure 2 displays a version of the Shannon and Weaver model as it is often adapted and applied to human communication circumstances.

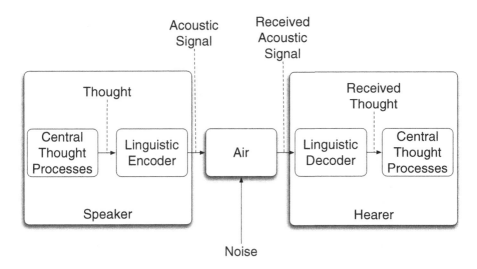

Fig. 2. The Shannon and Weaver model applied to human communication (adapted from Sperber and Wilson, 1995 [5]).

Reddy [4] noted and challenged a similar aspect of the way we think about human communication that is related to the Shannon and Weaver [3] understanding of communication. Reddy suggested that the way that we conceptualise and think about human communication is built upon a strongly held and deeply pervasive metaphor that he termed the conduit metaphor. The central idea is that we talk about and use a narrative about human communication based on a metaphor that suggests we pass information to one another packaged in containers of some form through some general conduit. When we think about how we communicate we use some intuitive form of the Shannon-Weaver formulation moving information from one mind to another; when a container filled with information reaches a receiver they then take it out of the container using some sort of decoding mechanism or linguistic code whereupon they become the possessors of the transmitted information. The english language is replete with uses of the metaphor, some of the examples used by Reddy are: "try to get your thoughts across better," "None of Mary's feelings came through to me with any clarity," "you still haven't given me any idea of what you mean," "you've put each concept into words very carefully," and "trying to pack more thoughts into fewer words". The pervasive nature of this metaphor means it is difficult to escape and retain clarity in communication—and no attempt will be made to do so within this paper. However, it forces us to think about communication in a certain way and constrains us to a certain frame that may not be helpful when we think about the nature of both animal and human communication. It is therefore worth highlighting and making explicit these commonly held underlying assumptions before exploring the nature of human communication, especially in situations in which we seek to create computational models of the necessary processes. As modellers we are too often guilty of accepting assumptions without question when creating models, yet our computational models are completely unaware of these assumptions. Indeed, it is often one of the most useful parts of the computational modelling endeavour that it exposes and makes us aware of assumptions that were difficult to see.

There are many reasons to be doubtful that the Shannon-Weaver formulation or the conduit metaphor that we intuitively use are useful ways to conceptualise both animal and human communication. One of the principle reasons is that many linguistic utterances are highly underdetermined and rely heavily on shared contextual knowledge to ensure correct interpretation. There is much mind-reading that goes on around the process of human communication and one of the most influential theories that explains and clarifies these processes is Relevance theory [5].

3   Relevance Theory and Underdetermined Language

Relevance Theory [5] provides an account for how underdetermined signals function in humans communication. The core realisation is one common to much of linguistic pragmatics—although it is not often stated in these terms—the realisation that there is a lot of mind-reading involved in which a communicator makes an assessment of the knowledge that is already available to the receiver through context and other streams of evidence. This mind-reading is, of course, the scientific view of mind-reading [6], related to perspective-taking, mentalizing, and theory of mind and not the theatrical or telepathic version. Informally, an underdetermined amount of encoded linguistic information is provided in an utterance, after a mind-reading based assessment of the knowledge available to a receiver in a given context. The pre-assessment of the knowledge that is available from the current context in which the communication is taking place—this occurs almost entirely at an unconscious level—allows the communicator to craft an utterance that only contains a minimal amount of information, as much as is required to infer the communicators intended meaning. In other words, the utterance contains only sufficient information that when it is combined with the contextual knowledge available to the receiver, and with any extra non-verbal communication, that all the pieces of evidence taken together produce an inferential interpretation of the meaning communicator is seeking to impart. Rather than it being a matter of encoding the entirety of a message and placing it in a container to be decoded, a careful mind-reading assessment allows the minimal amount of information—the underdetermined linguistic piece of evidence—to be combined with contextual knowledge and non-verbal communication and then assembled within the mind of the receiver to infer intended meaning. As an example, if I were to provide the utterance "John is a soldier," a receiver would take a very different understanding of the utterance if it was provided in the context of a military base or within a school. A further contextual qualification might occur in the school situation if we were in the school play ground where the child may be playing a war-like game or in the presence of the school nurse where the it may mean that John was a child that was sick or had hurt himself and was displaying some stoical qualities while receiving treatment. The linguistic utterance does not change but is interpreted in very different ways dependent on the context in which it is provided. This has important implications for human communication and the cultural knowledge and context that is available and utilised in human communication. This tacit use of background knowledge is not accounted for in the Shannon-Weaver models or at best it is only implied in the encoding and decoding aspects of the model in ways that hide its importance.

4   Cognitive Effect and the Ostensive-Inferential Model

A basic principle of Relevance theory is that an input—an utterance or some information from some external source—is relevant if it has a positive cognitive effect. Wilson and Sperber [7] give the example of a "true conclusion" having a positive cognitive effect as it improves the user's representation of the world. However, according the Analogical Peacock Hypothesis [2], the truth, or verifiable mind-world mappings, are not a core or necessary part of human communication. These mappings between representations and an objective reality have value in problem solving situations and certainly improve representations of the world, yet much of human communication can function without problem without any need for verifiability against evidence from a sensed reality; this becomes obvious when we consider story-telling, myths, legends and religion. What is really important in human communication is information that has some social currency—information that is interesting to others within a chosen social group rather than whether it is true or not. Fantastical or sensational information may have value or positive cognitive effects for an individual irrespective of its veracity. Within Relevance theory, general positive cognitive effects are more likely with relevant material, and, importantly for the current argument, relevant material is also thought to be inversely related to the processing effort required by an input. That is, if an utterance requires greater use of perception, memory or inference it is less likely to be relevant. This core argument of this paper is that in situations of humor this may not be the case. The Relevance theory ideas are based on an assumption that evolutionary selection pressures have led to an inexorable drive towards efficiency creating the "Cognitive Principle of Relevance" that "human cognition tends to be geared to the maximisation of relevance". However, according to the Analogical Peacock Hypothesis much of human communication has developed through sexual selection and entails costly signalling where the need for straightforward efficiency is less obvious and indeed sometimes it could be counterproductive [8]. This means that in situations of creative display as in humor production the goal of being efficient in terms of communication is not necessarily desirable and the cognitive effect of a communication is oriented towards displaying mind-reading abilities rather than the efficient transfer or exchange of information.

Another important aspect of human communication comes from the communicators intentions. A communicator has two kinds of intention when they seek to tell someone something. First, they must first grab someones attention and make them aware that they are about to communicate something and second, they must communicate it. This is part of what is known as the ostensive inferential model in Relevance theory. There is both an intention to inform—the informative intention—and an intention to inform that they wish to communicate something—the communicative intention. The communicative intention is signalled to a receiver by grabbing attention through some sort of ostensive signal [5], this is a signalling of signalhood [9]—it is achieved in many ways, perhaps with a wave or a movement that is slightly incongruous for a situation. Once a receiver becomes aware of an ostensive stimulus or signal then they have knowledge of a communicator's informative intention and this in turn raises expectations of relevance in the utterance that is likely to follow from the communicator.

5   Cognitive Effort and Optimal Relevance

The ostensive-inferential model in combination with the Cognitive Principle of Relevance leads to another general principle, the Communicative Principle of Relevance. This principle suggests that when a message sender makes an ostensive signal indicating that they have an intention to communicate something, they also make the assumption that the receiver will wish to be communicated to. Consequently, they are presuming that the receiver will be interested in the information that they have to say or convey. Therefore, the sender has an expectation that the receiver will engage in the cognitive effort required to infer the meaning the sender wishes to convey; as a result, the receiver will have an expectation that the sender will be maximising the relevance of the utterance—with all the concomitant mind-reading this entails. The Communicative Principle of Relevance states that "every ostensive stimulus conveys a presumption of its own optimal relevance". The idea of optimal relevance suggests that an intention to communicate provides strong evidence to a receiver that a sender thinks that the information they wish to convey is worth a receiver's effort in processing it.

Similarly, given this expectation is being placed in the mind of the receiver, a sender should ensure that they provide a relevant communication if they wish the receiver to understand their communication and if they wish to ensure that they have a reputation as someone worth communicating with in the future.

6 Display and Alignment in the Analogical Peacock Hypothesis

The Analogical Peacock Hypothesis [2] suggests that there are two fundamental kinds of human communication, display and alignment. Display communications are the most fundamental—they concern the display of the mind-reading abilities of the sender. The motivation to display one's mind-reading abilities stems from the evolutionary advantages that are gained through rising up through the ranks of a social hierarchy [10]. The Analogical Peacock Hypothesis combines two evolutionary schools of thought, the social brain hypothesis [11–14], and the use of mental fitness indicators [15,16], to explain this connection between social status and mind-reading display. As our social groups became larger and more sophisticated, those who were better at climbing their social hierarchy would have access to better resources and mating possibilities due to their elevated status; amongst the most important skills required for climbing social hierarchies are the socio-political skills of perspective-taking, mind-reading and theory of mind. The Analogical Peacock Hypothesis argues that at some stage in human evolution these skills became sexually selected, starting an arms race that required ever more intricate ways of displaying these abilities. A first stage involved non-verbal and emotional display, showing knowledge of what was in another individual's mind and their desires through processes of empathy, cooperation, kindness, and gift giving. An evolutionary arms race—typical of sexual selection—amongst those competing to display these skills would require ever more intricate ways to display and ever more discerning abilities to differentiate between those who are skilled displayers. Given enough time the limits of any given signal as a means to differentiate mind-reading and attractiveness in general are likely to be reached. At this point, specific signals are likely to become thresholds that must be reached to retain attractiveness as a potential partner or ally; beyond these thresholds further more intricate means of display would be required in order to discern between high level mind-reading abilities. This would lead to a multi-modal signalling system in which various streams of non-verbal information contributed to the overall signal.

With the arrival of symbolic communication, verbal and analogical styles of display became an option for displaying mind-reading abilities. The original Analogical Peacock Hypothesis paper [2] highlighted the importance of verbal proficiency, intelligence, creativity and humor in this respect; Miller [16] gave a long list of potential mental fitness indicators including culture, music, art and creativity, language in conversation and storytelling, humor (both verbal and nonverbal), and morality such as kindness, honesty, humility, and gift-giving. Many of these indicators are amongst the most sought after qualities in potential mates, commonly found in cross-cultural mate preference studies [17,18]. From the Analogical Peacock Hypothesis point of view one of the most useful tools in signalling mind-reading ability is the creative combination of concepts. Being able to combine concepts in a way that others have not yet thought about displays a strong knowledge of the contents of their mind and shows that one has very strong mind-reading abilities. This creative combination of concepts is a highly typical component of linguistic humor [19,20]. A potential origin for the creative combination of concepts is in human linguistic gossip—a key element of Dunbar's take on the Social Brain Hypothesis [12] and important in the evolution of language [21]. The presentation of information of interest about two members of a social hierarchy involved in some romantic but compromising tryst, for example, provides a salacious or perhaps taboo piece of knowledge that is likely to be of interest, a novel creative combination of sorts. Such news is likely to have been met with surprise, and concomitant jaw-dropping style facial responses, as they are today. More abstract combinations of information and juxtaposition may have arisen through storytelling processes based on fictional gossip style tales leading to humorous combinations. The use of novel salacious gossip is likely to be a form of display of mind-reading. It shows that a sender is aware of what is likely to be interesting to another individual within their shared social hierarchy, and that they have a strong knowledge of what is taboo and permissible behaviour within their culture. This kind of disclosure of information and sharing of social currency is likely to result in a desire for social bonding, although it would not be without risk of social sanction—making it a useful discernment tool in mind-reading ability. Gossip is also a crucial factor in the second main kind of human communication—alignment communications.

The second kind of communication comes about as a result of the first. To be able to display mind-reading abilities one must know what is in the mind of other people. In the modern world this means a lifetime dedicating oneself to learning one's culture and aligning one's mind with those that you are likely to want to impress. The majority of human communication is probably oriented towards alignment. Most of the receiver aspects of human communication are alignment oriented—with a smaller amount based around judging display communications. The distinctions between these types of communications are not strong or clear and people may revert into one or another quickly as opportunities arise and change throughout the dynamics of conversation and social interaction.

The picture presented so far in Relevance theory with the intertwined nature of cognitive effects and effort and the presumption of optimal relevance fits an alignment view of communication more closely than a display view of communication. However it clearly has very strong aspects in which mind-reading is highly important.

7   Humor as an Ostensive Challenge to Increase Cognitive Effort

The core argument being made in this paper is that in the situation in which a humorous exchange is being made a sender is seeking to display their mind-reading ability, and this leads to a special circumstance that is not accounted for in standard Relevance theory. The need to display mind-reading ability means that a sender is doing something more than making a standard underdetermined utterance, in Relevance theoretic terms, or an alignment communication in Analogical Peacock Hypothesis terms. The move to display changes the communicative dynamic. This paper argues that a special kind of ostensive stimulus is required, an *ostensive challenge*, in which the receiver is invited to expend a greater level of cognitive effort than would normally be the case in order to find a not so obviously relevant connection between two or more concepts. In these situations, in which a display communication is being flagged, the presumption of optimal relevance may give way to a principle of obscure and non-salient relevance—an indication that the sender is aware of a relevant connection between these two or more concepts but that it is not easy or simple to make the connection. It then becomes a challenge to the receiver to try and find the connection without being given a clue or punchline by the sender. Upon failure to rise to the challenge the sender may then choose to provide the answer.

There are many kinds of joke or humorous situation that can create an ostensive challenge, however, there are some obvious candidates—some of the most apparent are the earliest joke set-ups that we learn, for instance, the two words "Knock knock..." are famously the start of a joke telling formula. Other highly formulaic examples would be the "I say, I say, I say..." of music hall or vaudeville comedians or a more modern "A [insert joke element] walks into a bar...". There are many smaller and more subtle cues that may be ostensive challenges too, non-verbal facial expressions or changes in tone of voice may serve to highlight the change from an alignment communication to a display communication with an ostensive challenge. These signals of an ostensive challenge highlight the existence of a joke telling or humorous frame but the function remains the same—letting the listener know that they are being challenged to look for an answer that requires an increase in cognitive effort. The challenge being set is that for the concepts offered as a potential combination there exists a relevant conceptual combination—the combination can be found, but finding it will require a greater than typical amount of cognitive effort. If found by the receiver or revealed by the sender there will be a payoff that is worth the extra cognitive effort to find it—a humorous payload.

The ostensive challenge implies that even though the effort is greater the normal level of effort that would be expected in an alignment communication, it will still be worth the cognitive effort to find the connection. If the sender has sufficient mind-reading skills to make a solid inference about the receiver's taste in humor in relation to the quality of joke, and its suitability given the context and mood—the joke or attempt at humor will be funny and make the receiver laugh.

From an Analogical Peacock Hypothesis point of view, the ostensive challenge informs the receiver that a display communication is taking place; the sender is indicating that two or more concepts exist that can be connected in the mind of the receiver, these concepts are typically presented in the joke setup.

It also implies that the sender or joke-teller is aware of the connection but has judged that the receiver is not aware of it. This creates a clear situation in which the sender is letting the receiver know that they are aware of the contents and relational connections between conceptual representations that exist in the receiver's mind—and in an intricate way. The knowledge of the conceptual connection remains within the control of the sender or joke-teller right up until the point of a reveal in the form of a punchline, unless of course the receiver can rise to the challenge and find the connections for themselves.

There is also an additional layer of mind-reading ability on display, one concerning receiver knowledge of humorous taste. The joke-teller is making an assumption that they can tell or are aware of the humorous taste of the receiver. They are also making assumptions about the interaction of humorous taste with current contextual factors such as the social environment and the receiver's mood when the joke is told. That is, an assessment is being made as to whether the receiver will be suitably receptive to the attempt at humor that the joke-telling utterance entails. This involves a number of social risks. Jokes are prepackaged and therefore not original displays of wit, as a result there is a greater onus in any judgement on the assessment of a receiver's receptivity, as the teller usually cannot or does not claim to be a joke's author. Many jokes are met with groans of disapproval rather than laughter if any of the various factors made in the contextual assessment are poorly judged.

8   Positive Socio-cognitive Effects

Encounters that include an ostensive challenge must still have strong positive cognitive effects; perhaps, they may be better termed as positive socio-cognitive effects. These interactions improve the user's representation of the social world. They do not necessarily require mind-world mappings. Nothing in the interaction need refer to an external empirical test of an objective reality—although that may of course be included and may improve the humor by making it a harder to fake signal—the inclusion of context and concurrent facts make quick witted mind-reading ability more obvious [1, 2]. However, mind-world mappings are not necessary. The positive socio-cognitive effect comes from the social evidence that the attempt at humor provides. It allows information concerning the pair of interlocutor's social standing in their present social hierarchy to be adjusted and updated. The sender has taken an opportunity to display, that is, they have seen an opportunity to elevate their social standing with someone with whom they seek to socially bond, and have told them a joke or created a humorous event as part of an affiliative process. These displays are inherently risky, for if they are not performed well and the humor falls flat, the sender will have exposed their desire to socially bond and concurrently displayed an ineffectual ability to adequately mind-read and assess the social mood of the receiver. For the receiver there is a positive socio-cognitive effect in the knowledge that they are viewed as worth the risk of an attempt at an affiliation oriented display. If a receiver provides an honest signal in response, a hard-to-fake genuine laugh, it is a signal that the humor was successful and requires an evaluation or re-evaluation of the relationship—typically this means an elevation of a sender's social standing with respect to the receiver. A display that is not received as humorous but falls flat may be met with a polite low intensity laugh requiring no re-evaluation of social standing, at least not in an upwards direction. A groan or negative comment may indicate that there is value in the social relationship, but that it comes from other dimensions that are not the humorous one, or that sufficient social capital already exists that a current poor performance will be tolerated. An absence of any response at all is likely to mean that there is very little future in the social relationship. Therefore, although the current argument suggests an addition to Relevance theory based thinking concerning humor—one that accommodates the two kinds of communication suggested by the Analogical Peacock Hypothesis—there still remains the overall requirement for positive cognitive effects that make the communicative interchange and social interaction beneficial for both parties.

9 Implications for Computational Models of Humor

The importance of incorporating humor into computational dialogue models of human computer interaction has been made before [22–24], However, due to the intricate nature of human conversational interaction and given the many prevalent and commonly made erroneous assumptions about the nature and function of human communication—some of which are outlined at the start of this paper—there has been little incorporation of humor into dialogues that occur in real-time and that can flow-freely. Most dialogues models are constrained to fixed scenarios or involve tasks such as information provision that are highly functional in nature. Tactics used to incorporate humor in these situations involve the use of canned jokes and self-deprecating humor. This is largely safe ground as it can be pre-prepared and involves little in the way of a need to be aware of contextual knowledge. This approach also requires minimal assessment and knowledge of the minds of an audience or a receiver that any given crafted utterance will be directed towards.

Digital assistants such as Amazon's Alexa, Apple's Siri, Google's "Google Now" feature and Microsoft's Cortana are becoming more prevalent in our daily lives through their presence in our mobile devices and increasingly in our households. To make these interactions less monotonous they will require the use of humor and laughter in a more free flowing way [1]. To achieve this in a convincing manner requires a much stronger assessment and incorporation of the conversational context and receiver knowledge on the part of the sender than is currently occurs. This kind of information is currently available in ways that were not previously accessible and incorporation of mind-reading and contextual knowledge should make interactions much more personable and pleasant. More complete and nuanced models of human communicative interaction are required than simply thinking it is sufficient to provide information. Computational models will require knowledge of social and cultural norms, incorporation of context and assessment of the receiver's goals and desires. They will also need to socially engage at the appropriate level of social distance. This means being very nuanced in the degree to which they target interactions. The use of ostensive challenges will provide a useful tool as these models increase in the level of pervasiveness and intrusion they create in our lives. Providing too much knowledge or mind-reading without the appropriate judgement and etiquette can be perceived as creepy or awkward. Something like an "uncanny valley" of conversational interaction probably exists where too much information can be known about an individual for them to be fully comfortable—an overly informed human gives a "stalker" kind of feeling, a machine will probably feel even worse as it will have implications of the corporate intrusion of privacy. However, the appropriate use of ostensive challenges may permit humor to be tested in ways that will let models learn an individual's sense of humor, what works for certain people and in what circumstances. It may even become a sought after feature in circumstances when a user is bored or requires some elevation in mood. If we are to make genuinely funny and humorous digital companions that are creative in their humor generation rather than simply regurgitating jokes or humorous memes from social media, then delivering humor through the use of ostensive challenges is likely to minimise the degree to which failure to be funny will be detrimental to an overall relationship with a digital assistant.

There are many ethical issues that must be considered concerning the degree to which we wish to have our digital assistants become charming social interactants and companions. Artificial intelligence is not after all artificial sentience; creating the illusion of artificial sentience is an aspect of artificial intelligence that needs to be considered carefully. Adding humor and increasingly appropriate conversational abilities is likely to increase the levels of anthropomorphism we indulge in these algorithms. These systems should require opt-in choices, and much care needs to be taken in not overstepping the mark. These machines are in many ways the equivalent of ventriloquist's dummies and while suspending disbelief for a period of time may be entertaining it is probable that some people will assume that there are actual sentient capabilities within these algorithmically driven entities. Therefore, there is an ethical onus on the producers of such machines to ensure that they are perceived in that way and enjoyed as such, rather than becoming so believable that the attribution of sentience is given where no sentience exists. Creating machines with stronger humor abilities makes that burden of responsibility a stronger obligation.

References

1. McKeown, G.: Laughter and humour as conversational mind-reading displays. In: Streitz, N., Markopoulos, P. (eds.) DAPI 2016. LNCS, vol. 9749, pp. 317–328. Springer, Cham (2016). doi:10.1007/978-3-319-39862-4_29
2. McKeown, G.J.: The analogical peacock hypothesis: the sexual selection of mind-reading and relational cognition in human communication. Rev. Gen. Psychol. **17**(3), 267–287 (2013)

3. Shannon, C., Weaver, W.: A mathematical theory of communication. Bell Syst. Tech. J. **27**, 379–423 (1948)
4. Reddy, M.J.: The conduit metaphor: a case of frame conflict in our language about language. Metaphor Thought **2**, 164–201 (1979)
5. Sperber, D., Wilson, D.: Relevance. Blackwell, Oxford (1986, 1995)
6. Heyes, C.M., Frith, C.D.: The cultural evolution of mind reading. Science **344**(6190), 1243091 (2014)
7. Wilson, D., Sperber, D.: Relevance theory. In: Horn, L., Ward, G. (eds.) Handbook of Pragmatics, pp. 249–290. Blackwell, Oxford (2002)
8. Rosenberg, J., Tunney, R.J.: Human vocabulary use as display. Evol. Psychol. **6**(3), 538–549 (2008)
9. Scott-Phillips, T.C., Kirby, S., Ritchie, G.: Signalling signalhood and the emergence of communication. Cognition **113**(2), 226–233 (2009)
10. Anderson, C., Hildreth, J., Howland, L.: Is the desire for status a fundamental human motive? A review of the empirical literature. Psychol. Bull. **141**(3), 574–601 (2015)
11. Byrne, R.W., Whiten, A.: Machiavellian Intelligence: Social Expertise and the Evolution of Intellect in Monkeys, Apes, and Humans. O.U.P, Oxford (1988)
12. Dunbar, R.I.M.: Grooming, Gossip, and the Evolution of Language. Faber and Faber, London (1996)
13. Dunbar, R.I.M.: The social brain hypothesis. Evol. Anthropol. **6**, 178–190 (1988)
14. Dunbar, R.I.M., Shultz, S.: Evolution in the social brain. Science **317**, 1344–1347 (2007)
15. Miller, G.F.: The Mating Mind. Vintage, London (2001)
16. Miller, G.F.: Mating intelligence: frequently asked questions. In: Geher, G., Miller, G.F. (eds.) Mating Intelligence: Sex, Relationships, and the Mind's Reproductive System. Lawrence Earlbaum Associates, Hillsdale (2007)
17. Buss, D.M., Abbott, M., Angleitner, A., Asherian, A., Biaggio, A., Blanco-Villasenor, A., et al.: International preferences in selecting mates: a study of 37 cultures. J. Cross Cult. Psychol. **21**(1), 5 (1990)
18. Lippa, R.: The preferred traits of mates in a cross-national study of heterosexual and homosexual men and women: An examination of biological and cultural influences. Arch. Sex. Behav. **36**(2), 193–208 (2007)
19. Koestler, A.: The Act of Creation. Penguin, London (1964)
20. Raskin, V., Hempelmann, C.F., Taylor, J.M.: How to understand and assess a theory: the evolution of the SSTH into the GTVH and now into the OSTH. J. Literary Theory **3**(2), 285–311 (2009)
21. Locke, J.L.: Duels and Duets: Why Men and Women Talk so Differently. Cambridge University Press, Cambridge (2011)
22. Morkes, J., Kernal, H.K., Nass, C.: Humor in task-oriented computer-mediated communication and human-computer interaction. In: CHI 1998 Conference Summary, pp. 215–216. ACM, New York (1998)
23. Nijholt, A.: Embodied agents: A new impetus to humor research. In: The April Fools Day Workshop on Computational Humour, Trento, Italy, pp. 101–111 (2002)
24. De Boni, M., Richardson, A., Hurling, R.: Humour, relationship maintenance and personality matching in automated dialogue: a controlled study. Interact. Comput. **20**(3), 342–353 (2008)

Modelling Playful User Interfaces for Hybrid Games

Anna Priscilla de Albuquerque[1(✉)], Felipe Borba Breyer[2], and Judith Kelner[1]

[1] Universidade Federal de Pernambuco, Recife, Brazil
{Apa,jk}@cin.ufpe.br
[2] Instituto Federal de Ensino, Ciência e Tecnologia de Pernambuco, Recife, Brazil
fbb3@cin.ufpe.br

Abstract. Both toy and games industries are investing in hybrid play products. In these scenarios user access the system using toys as input/output, thus, they consist of playful user interfaces. Such systems are complex artifacts since they use real and virtual information. Therefore, they present new challenges to both designers and developers. We supposed both industries could benefit from hybrid design approaches since product concepts. Hence, we applied the model of hybrid gameplay as a practical tool for designing such systems. To achieve it, we included the model in a 16-week class to design hybrid games. In this paper, we detailed model usage in course schedule, and discussed how students experienced it. Besides, we presented student's six working prototypes, including design cycles, and playtesting sessions. After class, we conducted semi-structured interviews with student's representatives. Results revealed model usefulness to describe the system setup and interface elements. Furthermore, according to students, the model vocabulary facilitated communication among team members. Finally, we proposed improvements in model nomenclature based on student's feedback. In addition, we recommend a few topics for a methodological approach to design hybrid games.

Keywords: Hybrid games · Smart toys · Playful user interfaces

1 Introduction

Both toy and games industries are investing in hybrid products as connected toys. These are playful artifacts embedded with electronic components able to connect with other devices. Smart toys can connect with other toys, controllers, smartphones, tablets, and game consoles. Despite electronics, these products use passive technologies as computer vision techniques and touchpoints. Such toys can promote different play experiences, with fixed or open rules. In these, user access the system using toys as input/output (I/O), either in outdoor or indoor environments. Thus, such toys consist of playful user interfaces [1]. We refer to 'playful system' as play activities including hybrid games, connected toys, augmented board games, multimedia applications, interactive story-telling, and open-ended play scenarios. Such systems are complex artifacts since they use real and virtual information. Therefore, they present new challenges to both designers and developers. These challenges include defining what type of data to extract from the environment, how to present this information in the toy's interface, and

© Springer International Publishing AG 2017
N. Streitz and P. Markopoulos (Eds.): DAPI 2017, LNCS 10291, pp. 640–659, 2017.
DOI: 10.1007/978-3-319-58697-7_48

selecting appropriate technologies to collect such data. The relational model for hybrid gameplay [2], works as a tool to describe playful systems. The model can synthesize system setup information in a group of interactive aspects. Our research goal was to turn the model into a practical tool for creating hybrid game concepts. To achieve it, we included the model in a 16-week class to design hybrid games. In this paper, we presented the model and its aspects, then, we detailed its usage in the course schedule, and how students experienced it. Furthermore, we presented student's six working prototypes, including design cycles, and playtesting sessions. After class, we conducted semi-structured interviews with student's representatives, then, we presented data collection procedure, and interview results. Finally, we proposed improvements in model nomenclature based on student's feedback. In addition, we recommended topics for a methodological approach to design hybrid games.

1.1   Design Practices of Hybrid Play Products

Hybrid products available on the market come from traditional toy and games industries, including robotics companies, and independent teams. Hasbro, a toy company, has several products as *Furby*, a stuffed toy robot able to connect to mobile devices. Other, are the *Playmation* connected toys, inspired by *Avengers* franchise. Nintendo, a game company, produces *amiibo* toys; these are character figurines from popular brands, including a set of cards, and plush toys. *Amiibo* toys use near-field communication (NFC) to transfer data to connected game consoles. In 2016, the robot company Sphero, released the wearable *Force Band* along with droid *BB8*, both inspired by *Star Wars* series. Wearing the smart wristband user can control, through gestures, *BB8* movements. Following advances of digital prototyping, small independent teams are releasing new products. These advances include low-cost 3D printing, and electronic components as *Arduino* and *Raspberry* platforms. Moreover, small teams are opting for crowdfunding campaigns to raise resources. For example, *DiDi*, a teddy bear, and *ROXs*, a pervasive game console, have used funding platforms such as *Kickstarter* and *Indiegogo*.

Despite novelty and potential of hybrid interactions, many products have failed on the market. Tyni and Kultima [3], in their study, interviewed professionals of hybrid play products field that worked within 2012 and 2014, accordingly, the hybrid products market experienced an experimental phase. Thus, companies discontinued several products, while still looking for best design practices. Conforming to authors, professionals and companies adopt different trends in their design process. Such trends include toys as a platform for several games, (e.g., *ROXs*, *Tiggly*, and *Osmo*), and games associated with characters and narratives (e.g., *Skylanders*, *Edwin: the duck*, and *Amiibo*). Besides, interviewers claimed that companies make use of disconnect design practices from both toy and game design. Hence, we supposed both industries could benefit from hybrid design approaches since product concepts.

Developing engagement strategies is a problem that affects both *narrative* and *platform* cases. Regarding narrative products, the content design must associate a great *semantic value*. Such content refers to the game or playful activity aspects, including physical features of products. To meet it, larger companies adopt popular franchises such as *Batman* and *Star Wars*. Although, companies discontinued cases as *Mattel*

Apptivity and *Disney Infinity*, despite their products incorporated popular brands. On the other hand, platform cases consist of generic products allowing several play modalities. Thus, such products demand regular content updates to achieve long-term engagement. For example, *ROXs* engagement strategy is allowing custom play modes. Another strategy is developing independent games to a single product, such as *Magikbee* and *Tiggly*. Moreover, many products use artificial intelligence resources to promote spontaneous play interactions and unexpected events (e.g., *Furby*, and *Cozmo*).

A design approach is developing such toys as *meaningful* interface elements. Therefore, we recommend professionals to design playful interface elements as game objects. Then, these may interact with other game objects, either physical or virtual, including the environment, and people. We expect this approach can assist designers of both narrative and platform products since it integrates both interactive and semantic values. For example, in a space themed game, a spaceship toy works as an interface, so, the toy enables player access to game world functions. Besides, viewing toy as a game object, it includes the semantic value of a spaceship. Then, the toy must assimilate game object features, such as power attack, defense, movements, and game stats. Thus, such features when incorporated during development may result in meaningful toys. Hence, we proposed investing in the relationship among interface elements during first design stages.

2   Related Work

In their study, Barba et al. [4] presented results of an experimental class for designing augmented reality (AR) board games. The class was multidisciplinary combining 19 students, from both undergraduate and graduate level. Student's background included fields of arts, design, and technology. All developed projects used game platform *Gizmodo*, a handheld device similar to a portable console. To meet an agile prototyping approach, games used fiducial markers to augment virtual information. Course schedule included four prototyping cycles, exercises with selected technologies, and brainstorming sessions. Authors claimed that first prototypes were alike to existing board games. Yet, following AR technologies practices facilitated students in developing meaningful ideas. In our research, we used a comparable approach, joining students of engineering, computer science, and design. Similarly, several prototypes used computer vision techniques such as color tracking. Otherwise, due student's technology background, we implemented projects using multiple technologies. Hence, our prototypes included electronics such as rumble and servomotors, Bluetooth and Radio Frequency modules, and LEDs. Besides, analogous to Barba et al., our games used visualization and manipulation tasks. However, one of the projects used Kinect along with wearable technology to embodiment facilitation.

Eva Hornecker [5] adapted a tangible interaction framework as a creative method to designing hybrid systems. The proposed method used a card game set during brainstorming sessions. The card set comprised four framework aspects: Tangible Manipulation, Spatial Interaction, Embodied Facilitation, and Expressive Representation. Thus, each group of cards had a color, and each card had a related question, along with representative images and subtitles. The research goal was to use cards to promote discussion among participants, in brainstorming sessions. Hornecker applied the method in 10 sessions with professionals and students. As result, subjects produced games and interactive installations, for both indoor and outdoor environments. Accordingly, the cards enabled groups to discuss the relevance of each framework aspect, facilitating ideas formulation. Similarly, our research adopted a theoretical model as a tool for the creative process. We choose to use the hybrid gameplay model since its descriptive structure enables to name several aspects of playful systems. These, include physical and social interaction, types of I/O technology, and the relationship among interface elements. Taking lessons from Hornecker and the previous study [4], we decided to insert the model as a resource in design stages of conception, ideation, and concept refinement. Furthermore, we opted for a brainstorming method including a sequence of questions. Yet, we used toys as resources rather than a set of cards.

Vissers and Geerts [6] introduced an evaluation method to distinguish tangible objects made from different materials. Authors evaluated five smart dices in augmented board games. Thus, they proposed eight guidelines for smart dice design, considering aspects of shape, material, texture, and its usage. Among these, one guideline related size of objects to player's precaution. For example, users experienced a large dice with caution than a small sized. Similarly, Heijboer and van den Hoven [7] presented a study to analyze the level of abstraction in playful tangibles. The study compared user's perception among adults and children, to differentiate how subjects apprehended object meanings. Such objects were a tangible interface for Totti, a collaborative game. In Totti, objects represented game characters, and each figure related to elements of Nature (e.g., water and fire). Then, each object group had eight abstraction levels, ranging its appearance resembling character's power, to a realistic look. Results revealed a better understanding of second abstraction level in both user groups. Indicating that a few information is enough to assimilate artifacts functional design. Both studies addressed physical aspects related to appearance of objects, and in how users perceive interface elements. Hence, in our study, we explored material aspects of student's prototypes, in addition to computational resources. Especially, on the 3D printed artifacts since students adapted existing toys as interface elements. Thus, students considered both physical and functional design aspects in their projects. For example, to build touchpoint figures, participants tested several materials, such as foil paper, copper wires, magnets, and metal. Moreover, the shape of such objects required allowing direct contact of conductive terminals with user's hands.

3 Research Method

Our research goal was adapting the relational model for hybrid gameplay [2] as a practical tool for designing playful systems. To achieve it, we included the model in a 16-week class to design hybrid games. Hence, the first step of research method was elaborating course structure using the theoretical model. Then, we taught the course in two classes with undergraduate and graduate students. Participants of both classes had experience in fields of Design, Engineering, and Computer Science. Classes took place in

March-July of 2016, at Computer Centre of *Universidade Federal de Pernambuco* (UFPE), Brazil. After class, we conducted semi-structured interviews with student's representatives. The aim was to assess model usefulness in stages of the creative process. Besides, we recognized aspects of the model that required improvements.

3.1   A Relational Model for Hybrid-Gameplay

The relational model describes playful systems relating three entities: *things*, *environment*, and *people* (see Fig. 1). Each relation axis represents a group of interactive aspects between two entities. Besides axes, each entity relates to itself. Things and environment axis shows *what* interface elements do in the interactive environment. While, environment and people axis indicates *where* participants locate in the environment. Then, people and things axis represents *how* they physically interact with interface elements, including what I/O technologies enable such interactions. Finally, the relationships among things and the environment happen in a *physical domain*, while, people's relations occur in a *social domain*.

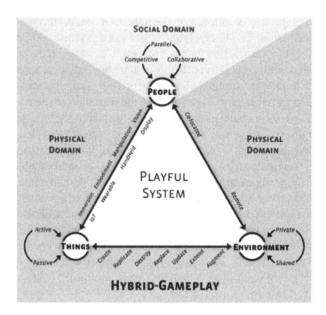

Fig. 1.   Relational Model for Hybrid-gameplay Interaction, current version.

Things are the physical interface elements, so, things are toys and the auxiliary devices enabling interaction. Such devices comprehend things such as computers, tablet, cameras, monitors, and controllers. Then, things communicate with each other using *active* and *passive* technologies. Hence, we name playful things as traditional toys, smart toys, and smart playground. Traditional toys have no embedded technology in their design, yet, smart toys has electronic components. We refer as a smart playground to large installations including multiple connected toys. According to model, things relate to the environment *replicating*, *extending*, *replacing*, *creating*, *destroying*, *updating*, and *augmenting* both real and virtual information in the environment. Showing some mentioned aspects in an example; we start with a physical spaceship connected to a virtual environment. In this scenario, the toy can *replicate* its data in the game environment. Such data may relate to toy appearance and its movement, so, when a user moves the toy, a *replicated* virtual spaceship moves in the environment. Besides, if a user tilts the toy, it can *create* virtual shots, attacking enemies in the environment. Then, while flying across space, the same spaceship may collide with asteroids. Thereby, *destroying* them in the environment. Furthermore, to present feedback of hit damage, the toy may *augment* spaceship health points, flashing a LED displayed on the toy. Thus, as we presented, the interactive aspects simplified concepts in short terms. Therefore, selecting terms, the model described *what* the interface actions in the environment.

Concerning access to information, the environment may be *private* or *shared*. We considered access to both physical interface elements, and other environment elements (e.g., stats, scores, and items). People are *co-located* or *remotely* located in the environment. In addition, they may socially interact through *competition*, *collaboration*, or taking *parallel* actions. People physically interact with things in four perspectives. First, user can *visualize* things, and then, *manipulate* things or part of things. Moreover, they can interact through *embodiment* as moving their body, or use body information (e.g., heart rate). Finally, people can *immerse* in a smart playground, by interacting with its surroundings. Therefore, to enable such interactions, system make use of I/O technologies. These are, *displays*, such as screens, LEDs, or projectors; *handheld devices*, as smartphones, tablets, and smart toys itself; *wearable* technology, including clothing, accessories, and sensors; and through connective technologies of the *Internet of Things (IoT)*.

3.2   Course Schedule

The relational model aims to describe playful system setups of multiple characteristics. Hence, it can describes playful activities with both fixed and open rules, located either indoor or outdoor environments, including on-screen display or none. Therefore, due its synthesis aspect, the model presented as an appropriate tool to define hybrid system concepts. Motivated to put into practice, we inserted the model in a project-based class. We taught the course in two multidisciplinary classes at UFPE campus. The undergraduate class, we called *U1*, joined 23 students from bachelor courses of Computer Engineering, Computer Science, and Design. The second class, we referred as *G2*, reunited 8 students from a graduate program in Computer Science, including both master and doctoral degrees. Students from G2 class had experience in fields of technology, design, and publicity. Besides, participants, from both classes, declared little or no experience in developing hybrid games. So far, a group of students participated in similar projects, such as 2D/3D digital games, AR applications, and Kinect games. In addition, subjects were familiar with game engines, graphic editors, digital prototyping platforms, and 3D modelling software.

The course schedule had 16 weeks, divided in 2 h meetings twice a week. The curriculum comprised initial stages of conception, ideation, selection, concept refinement, and low-fidelity prototyping. After these stages, students produced an initial documentation. Then, we started the prototyping cycles, including playtesting sessions, and a final documentation. Besides, we evaluated the prototypes every two weeks, providing individual guidance for each project. Moreover, we performed complementary lectures and workshops of several design and technology topics. A few students along with specialist guests led these complementary activities. In the first class, we introduced hybrid play products field giving examples from both market and literature. During 2nd week, we presented the model concepts and terms, so, we conducted an exercise. For this coursework, we asked students to previous research 2–3 system examples, and then, described them using the model.

Furthermore, we used Marco et al. [8] approach in the ideation stage. The authors proposed to take inspiration for hybrid games, observing how children play with both traditional and technological toys. Thus, we requested to students bring toys to class. The goal was to use them in a brainstorming session that we named 'Brainstorm Toy'. We adapted Brainstorm Toy from a creative technique called Discussion 66 or Phillips 66 [9]. In these, participants discussed ideas following a sequence of questions; in addition, method proposes rotating subjects in small groups. The goal is to stimulate an exchange of views, to avoid participants to fixate on a single idea. We defined a sequence of questions aiming to extract from toys both physical features and their semantic value. Hence, questions included how people played with toy, what are game genres related to toy thematic, what the physical features of the toy, then how to improve toy features, and how a toy can interact with other toys.

In brainstorming, we divided students into groups of 4–5 participants each. Then, we shared a set of toys among groups. Both opening and closing sessions had 15 min, and rotating sessions last 10 min each. After every rotating session, we exchanged both students and available toys among groups. For the closing session, we reunited initial groups to compile ideas for selection. Thus, we asked students to select 2–3 ideas of their interest, to produce pitch presentations using the model. Hence, subjects used the model to refine game concepts, and to standardize pitch presentations. To assist us in joining final groups, we requested students to inform their skills and abilities in an online sheet. Later, in pitch sessions, participants voted for their three favorite ideas. Despite preference votes, we allocated students in groups based on the list of abilities. Finally, the U1 class composed four groups of 5–6 participants each, and G2 class organized two groups of four students.

At the 4th week, students refined game concepts using paper prototyping. The goal of low-fidelity prototypes was to define core game mechanics and name physical interface elements. Before practice, we reintroduced the model, detailing its individual aspects, and giving examples of each term. Then, we requested students to prototype concepts, following their selected model aspects. We guided each group, and all teams prototyped playable mechanics. In consequence of this stage, students produced the first version of their game design document (GDD). We requested GDDs in two moments, the first document needed to focus on prototyping schedule, including a list of required materials, and individual tasks of each team member. While, the final version covered updates of game balancing, setup changings, and design improvements. We provided to students a template based in a GDD structure proposed by Tim Ryam [10]. Then, the relational model appeared in opening section of document template. The section had to contain a visual representation of prototype model, along with a descriptive text of selected aspects.

The prototypes cycles started at the 5th week, in all stages, we supported students in acquiring or borrowing materials. Participants requested things such as 3D prints, displays, cameras, gaming devices, and electronic components. We evaluated three versions of functional prototypes; also, we guided students on their ongoing work presentations. The students developed their 1st. playable versions implementing features of initial GDDs. We recommended them focusing on physical interface working aspects, and in how integrate selected technologies. For the *alpha* prototypes, we required that games incorporated ending assets, playable gameplay balancing, and the interface in full operation. Then, students used *alpha* prototypes in the public playtesting sessions.

The playtesting sessions occurred in two contexts, a closed test, and a public test. Thus, initial sessions happened in class with students and a few guests. Then, in public sessions, end-users experienced the prototypes. Initial tests aimed to collect technical feedback, and to adjust game setups to avoid complications during public sessions. While, public playtests had a goal to validate game experience with players, also collecting feedback from them. Thereby, we taught lectures on how to conduct user testing, including how to elaborate data collection tools. Hence, each group prepared an approach of data gathering, and we evaluated proposed tools. Such approaches, included pre and post testing questionnaires, semi-structured interviews, and individual or collective evaluations. Afterward, students presented test results in class, thus, each group listed points for future improvement in *beta* versions. Therefore, our last evaluation concerned student's *beta* prototypes along with their updated GDDs. Besides students produced a closing presentation, including a demo video of gameplay prototype.

3.3   Assessing Model Usefulness

One month after classes, we conducted semi-structured interviews with student's representatives of each group. The goal was to assess model usefulness in several stages of the creative process. For selecting participants, we consulted GDDs revision history, so, we identified which of students described their prototypes in documentation. Then, we emailed them to schedule interviews, also asking students to confirm their part or to suggest another representative. We recorded all interviews to transcription; so, we performed free translation from Portuguese to English. Moreover, we used open coding procedure to analyze data on texts, enabling us to point out topics and similar views among participants. Thus, we established an interview script in 11 main questions along with auxiliary questions, or probes, to aid in collecting hidden data. We defined the script aiming to assess how students comprehended and experienced model and its terms. Thereby, we asked questions on what class materials students used to apprehend model terms, and what they think about term's descriptions. Then, we included questions to assess model usefulness, such as how they used model during project stages, how groups communicated using its terms, and if they would recall any terms. Besides, we elaborated questions on other course methods, such as the Brainstorm Toy, paper prototyping, documentation, and playtesting sessions. Our goal was to distinguish model usefulness from other course resources.

4   Results

We divided research results into three sections; first, we presented how students used the model in initial design stages. Then, we showed results on prototyping cycles, followed by student's outcomes of playtesting sessions. Finally, we discussed data from subject's interviews, and presented how their feedback aided us to improve the relational model aspects.

4.1   Modelling Student's Concepts

The initial stages of course schedule were conception, ideation, and documentation. In conception stage, students used the model in a practical exercise of describing existing systems. Overall, subjects produced 50 exercise sheets, so, U1 made 37 sheets, and G2, 13. Then, in exercise, students described 35 single cases, yet, 26 sheets presented 11 repeated systems. Among replicated cases were *Pokemon Go*, *Cubbeto*, *Toymail*, *Amiibo*, *BB8*, and *Cognitoys*. During the brainstorming session, students generated 15 ideas in U1 class, and 10 ideas in G2 class. There, participants described original concepts in a single sentence, or in a sequence of references. For idea selection, students presented 13 pitch ideas in U1 class, and 6 concepts in G2. All presentations consisted of 4–6 slides, introducing an idea using the relational model and its aspects. Hence, students presented what were the things, other setup elements, a few topics and related images, along with a figure of their concept model.

After preferential voting, students selected six game ideas. Students from the U1 class named their four concepts as *Cubica*, *BUD Monster*, *Forecastle*, and *Legends of the World*. Then, G2 students elected two ideas as *Stormstone* and *Undercroft*. Thus, in puzzle battle Cubica, to perform game actions each player uses a Rubik's cube. BUD Monster, a Kinect game, a user wears a haptic glove to experience both tactile and visual feedback from game events. Forecastle is a nautical themed board game where three players had access to dynamic map elements using boat figurines. Legends of the World simulated team battles of several creatures, there, players used character figurines and a card set. Stormstone consisted of a hybrid platform for Role Playing Games (RPG), using metallic figures to interact with a custom game map. In the arcade game Undercroft, to avoid virtual obstacles, a player manipulates an articulated toy on an active board.

Students modelled their six concepts while preparing pitch presentations, and in both initial and final versions of documents. Thus, the initial GDDs had 4–8 pages divided into 5 main sections with several subsections. These were an introduction including concept model, tasks schedule, required materials and components, core game mechanics, and user interface elements. Then, the final version of GDDs had 30–70 pages, these incorporated updates of first GDD sections, along with complementary content. The additional sections referred to arts and design assets, audio content, summary of prototype versions, and user testing reports. In following subsections, we detailed student's models according to records in their final documents. Yet, due to limited pages in paper format, we selected three prototypes to detail. Therefore, to presenting model aspects, we adapted and translated text fragments of student's GDDs. Thereby, results reflected how students experienced the model in classes. Besides, since using the model was an interpretative process, we recognized a few aspects that required adjustments.

Cubica. Cubica (see Fig. 2) is a hybrid puzzle with a turn-based battle system. There, two *co-located* players compete as wizards, guiding mystic creatures using *passive handheld devices*. Then, each player *manipulates* a *private* Rubik's cube, and both players *visualize* virtual game objects through a *shared* on-screen *display*. To activate game actions, players must arrange a single cube's face following required color combos. Thus, a webcam captures the cube's face after players positioning it in a *passive* fixed base. Then, when the system recognizes a valid combo, the cubes *extend* player's in-game actions. Each action is analogous to a single color, so, the system can distinguish the cube faces through its central colored square. The colors and its corresponding actions are: blue to move characters, red to melee attack, orange to ranged attack, white for special attack, green to activate shield, and yellow to energy recharge. Besides color, players need to arrange combos to complete actions. For example, to move a creature, a player selects the face with the blue central square. Then, a user must arrange an adjacent blue square, to indicate movement's direction. Therefore, when players activate valid combos, the cube *creates* game elements on-screen. Players may choose among three creatures of equivalent skills and strengths. Despite the combats, characters can suffer damage through dynamic thorns appearing on the arena.

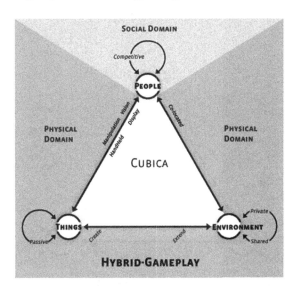

Fig. 2. Student's version of hybrid-gameplay model in *Cubica*

Undercroft. Undercroft (see Fig. 3) is a hybrid arcade game inspired by the *Hole in the Wall* TV game show. The game world is *private*, consisting of a dungeon full of virtual obstacles, as moving walls and traps. Thus, player *visually* access the game through an on-screen *display*, and *manipulating* a *passive* articulated toy. The goal is to *create* poses using the toy that matches with silhouettes of the moving walls. Hence, the player *manipulates* the toy articulating its body, arms, and legs on an *active* board. The articulated toy has magnets located on its foot, enabling it to stand-up on the game board surface. A webcam positioned on game board terminal captures toy's outline in each round. Then, the system identifies through images if the pose was valid. The smart board *extends* all game elements off-screen, so, the game scenario comprises both virtual and real scenarios. To represent virtual elements, the board has a 10 RGB LEDs to *update* game elements proximity. Then, LED colors will vary as a warning sequence, in green to yellow, and red. Besides, the board has a motor mechanism to open a trapdoor, so, if the player loses all health points, the toy falls into the trap. Regarding game elements, the extended moving walls are analogous to elements of Nature, as water, fire, wood, and stone. Moreover, a player can collect *extended* power-ups, so, a user must position any part of the toy inside a range, where the desired item appears. For example, if the item comes from the upper-left corner of the screen, the player may *create* a pose enabling toy's arms to reach it. Therefore, when player catch game element, the player *destroy* it in the environment. Such items can confer either defensive or offensive powers, then, a user can store a single item of each type at a time. To activate them, user press buttons located on the board, therefore, *creating* corresponding game elements on-screen. The four buttons set includes directional arrows, to make the character jump and crouch to avoid traps.

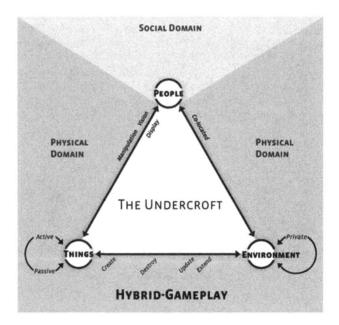

Fig. 3. Student's version of hybrid-gameplay model in *Undercroft*

BUD Monster. BUD Monster (see Fig. 4) is a hybrid Kinect game inspired by Japanese monster movies, or *'kaiju'* genre. In a *private* environment, the player *replaces* a giant marine monster in the game world. So, players access to game through *embodiment* using Kinect technology. Then, to provide *immersion*, the user *wears* a monster glove to *augment* feedback of game actions. The *active* glove communicates to system using Radio Frequency technology, and provides both tactile and visual feedbacks. Thus, the glove *augments* character attacks vibrating a rumble motor, and special attacks flashing three LED displays. The game goal is to destroy the main enemy tower; yet, player must destroy two shield generators first. Then, all three targets locate in different spots of a virtual map *visualized* in an on-screen *display*. Meantime, the player *replaces* the character walking through the map, terrifying citizens, destroying buildings, and attacking army tanks. The number of enemies on-screen relate to destruction level held by the player. Hence, if the monster destroy too many buildings, a giant robot appears from the sky, and user must defeat it. The player *extend* game actions through gestures, these are melee punch, special punch, laser eyes, and monster roar. In the screen, player can *visualize* monster's arms, and it is analogous to user's *wearable*. Besides, during gameplay, player can interact with several characters on dialogue boxes, as the monster boss, the city mayor, TV reporters, and the main enemy. Thus, the game ends when the monster destroys the main tower, or if the NPCs defeat the player.

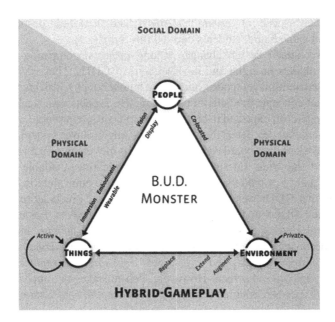

Fig. 4. Student's version of hybrid-gameplay model in *BUD Monster*

Discussion. Students used the relational model in stages of conception, idea selection, and documentation. Starting with conception, while completing exercise sheets, several students requested advice to select model terms. Considering that the students accessed general information of systems through images, videos, and text, they used limited data on both interface and gameplay. Although, in overall, they had selected system aspects consistently. However, analyzing replicated system sheets, we found inconsistency among student's interpretations, especially on things-environment axis. We expected this since it is the model axis containing original terms and concepts. Besides, students had difficulty in selecting aspects of the people-environment axis in single-player systems. Moreover, due people-things axis comprehend its aspects in two columns, several participants made a few mistakes. For example, they selected *'display'* as an I/O technology, without, selecting *'vision'* as a physical interaction. Similarly, happened to *'manipulation'* and *'handheld'*, despite both terms are not inherent, they tend to appear together in several systems.

Participants described and improved their concepts using the model during pitch selection. For this step, students got access to class materials, so, they consulted presentation slides, and we distributed hard copies of model's article [1]. Therefore, students used the model efficiently while describing their ideas. For example, participants better-selected aspects of people-things axis since they could distinguish the terms of two columns. Then, after this stage, students presented no difficulty in selecting both I/O technologies, and physical interactions modalities. In addition, several students started using the center of model's triangle to name things present in their systems. Moreover, we noticed mistakes in things-environment aspects, yet, this time recurrent flaws related to students omitting existing aspects. For example, the concept model of Undercroft presented selected aspects of *'create'*, *'destroy'*, and *'updated'*, despite the system *augment* data on game board, students omitted this term.

We could recognize design changes among projects, comparing how students described their models in initial and final versions of GDDs. Thus, several prototype concepts involved multiplayer modes, and a large number of physical interface elements. Hence, the initial concepts predicted more interactive aspects than final versions. For example, the Undercroft expected to build two smart boards to promote *competitive* and *collaborative* game modes, later, they produced a single-player system. Furthermore, initially, the LEDs on smart board *replicated* the walls movements. In final version, they opted to *extend* the walls through the LEDs, duplicating available gaming area. Regarding the quality of model's description, these were equivalent in both versions. However, the final GDDs were larger documents, and they included projects adjustments, so, during GDDs updates, a few groups made mistakes. For example, BUD Monster team selected aspects of *'replicate'*, *'destroy'*, and *'update'* in initial GDDs. Then, such aspects described their prototype better than the final version. In final GDD, they omitted *'destroy'* aspect, and exchanged *'replicate'* to *'replace'*, despite the monster glove *replicate* on-screen. However, such mistakes not appeared in Cubica since their prototypes had minimal changes from concept to *beta* versions.

4.2   Prototyping Cycles and Playtesting Sessions

Prototype cycles comprised four main stages, including ongoing presentations within each step. The first version was the paper prototypes, in this stage, groups focused on core game mechanics and interface elements of systems. For example, Cubica team defined a grid map, and basic interface aspects, as for how to use the cube to move characters, and release attacks. Other three versions were the working prototypes, then, the 1st playable version required basic interface aspects and its technologies integrated to the core gameplay. In G2 class, the Undercroft presented the active board game, containing LEDs integrated to virtual obstacles, and a 3D printed articulated toy, yet, they did not implemented color detection. Afterward, we required that *alpha* prototypes had an interface in full operation and a playable gameplay balancing. Besides, they had to incorporate finished assets, including animation of virtual elements, graphical user interface, and visual identity. The Stormstone, for example, presented a touch sensitive monitor and metallic figurines of playable characters for both heroes and enemies. Besides, the game had a private terminal, where the RPG master would customize game elements on the map. Then, students used *alpha* prototypes (see Fig. 5) in the public playtesting sessions.

Fig. 5. The *alpha* prototypes: (a) Undercroft, (b) Stormstone, (c) Cubica, (d) BUD Monster, (e) Forecastle, (f) and the Legends of the World.

The public playtesting occurred in two sessions, so, the events received about 25–35 users, in both days. At least, each prototype collected feedback from 10 players. There, users pointed aspects on fun experience, engagement level, game balancing flaws, and interface features. Overall, users evaluated positively all games and according to gathered, their favorite prototypes were the puzzle battle Cubica and the Kinect game BUD Monster. Due technical issues a few prototypes performed partial or adapted functionalities. Both Undercroft and board-game Forecastle that used computer vision techniques for color tracking, found issues on environment lighting. Then, the Undercroft tested their prototype outside the event, and Forecastle exchanged a projector by a monitor. During tests, students gathered feedback from players using different data collection tools. Besides, several groups used a demographic questionnaire to assess player's profile, such as their game preferences. Later, students presented test results in class, so, their presentations showed a list of proposed improvements. We evaluated their presentations and helped them in selecting adjustments for *beta* versions.

Hence, final prototypes, or *beta* versions, were similar to their *alpha* prototypes, nevertheless, including design improvements in consequence of user testing results. Moreover, students produced playtesting reports to incorporate in final GDDs.

Discussion. The paper prototypes were essential to defining basic game design decisions and interface I/O elements. Cubica team, for example, defined both movement and battle systems relating gaming actions to the physical puzzles. Then, these initial decisions grounded mechanics to other game actions in working prototypes. During prototyping cycles, all working versions incorporated improvements, and adjustments followed two main reasons. First, aspects related to planning and development challenges, second, in response to feedbacks of both ongoing presentations and user testing. For example, BUD Monster concepts planned four wearables; these were a pair of gloves and two monster caps, each one representing a character. The idea was enabling users to exchange characters wearing different costumes. However, they implemented a single working glove in time. Concerning development issues, the Forecastle team replaced the projector and physical map with an on-screen display. This, due projector emitted a light that was interfering color tracking of boats on the map. Besides, several prototypes exchange their physical interface materials. Stormstone conductive points used paper foil, magnets, and copper wire. Finally, they replaced 3D prints with metallic figurines and insulation tape. Moreover, modifications promoted by user feedbacks, related to how system presented information in both graphical and tangible interfaces. Such improvements were changing position of visual elements, replacing pictograms of icons, and resizing text content.

Furthermore, the playtesting sessions enabled to assess fun experience promoted by each prototype. Despite functional issues, students of both classes produced playable prototypes. Thereby, their core game mechanics resulted in fun experiences for players, since test reports presented positive evaluations in this topic in all six prototypes. Cubica, BUD Monster, and Forecastle were among best-evaluated games. Thus, students were successful in creating meaningful interface elements that incorporated both interactive and semantic values. Cubica proposed a puzzle battle, where both mechanics and strategies, turned the toy fundamental to interaction. Moreover, the Undercroft team created level design based on physical features of articulated toy. Then, to define virtual wall silhouettes, they had to take pictures of the toy in several poses. Besides, the active board extended game environment, then, it duplicated available gaming area. We supposed such decisions were a consequence of model usage in early stages of development. Hence, to assess model usefulness, we interviewed students, so we presented and discussed its results in the following section.

4.3   Interview's Results

We conducted seven semi-structured interviews with at least one representative student of each group. The interviews lasted 10–15 min, then, during transcription, we attributed codes for participants to ensure anonymity. Therefore, we referred to subjects in this paper using acronyms. According to gather, the model was useful to describe student's prototypes. For example, participant U1A mentioned how model helped their group in determine game characteristics. Similarly, U1C claimed that model assisted in describing their project, since it was easy to visualize game aspects using its terms. Hence, for interviewers, the model facilitated in describing and in better understanding game setup. Thus, as G2G elucidated, "the model helps you to define game setup." Besides, subject G2F commented that through the model was possible to visualize setup complexity, while recognizing the number of selected aspects in the triangle. In addition, subject asserted that the model supported in project planning such as cutting off elements and selecting both feasible and essential aspects. Analogously, U1D said, "initially, we wanted to select every aspect of the model, then, during development, we could know what elements supposed to stay, and which of them we could remove."

According to students, the model helped them during initial stages of development. For example, participant G2F recognized model as a fundamental tool to define hybrid game concepts. Thus, subject U1E declared that model aided in better defining system requirements, before implementing game functions. Besides, subject U1B commented on things-environment axis decisions, "it was good because we had a doubt while choosing extension or replication, then using the model, we could select one of those". Similarly, both U1C and G2G mentioned how the things-environment axis assisted their group in establishing game mechanics. Moreover, students incorporated model vocabulary, so, during interviews, several students used model's terms while commenting on their projects. According to participants, the terms facilitated intergroup communication. For example, U1B claimed, "Since all students knew the vocabulary, made easy to use terms than formulating larger sentences to describe what interface elements would do in the system." Analogously, U1C commented on term *'extend'*, "Just in mentioning the term *'extend'*, someone would ask, where it will *extend*? Will it use a screen? Will it use a projector?" In addition, interviewees claimed that vocabulary helped them to understand other group's projects. For example, U1E said that when visualizing other group's triangle was possible to name what they were developing. The student G2F alleged that terms were useful while talking to other teams, as on comparing how they implemented similar aspects in their projects.

Thus, when we asked on model usage in GDDs, several students mentioned its relevance in the initial documentation. They stated model usefulness to both describe and visualize system aspects. Interviewer G2F thought the model synthesis so useful, that subject suggested us to create similar mechanisms for the entire documentation. Furthermore, students cited other course resources in interviews; these were the Brainstorm Toy, paper prototyping, and playtesting sessions. Then, participants appreciated both brainstorming dynamics and pitch selection. Moreover, they considered paper prototyping a good practice to define initial requirements of their games. Subject U1D commented on the course schedule, "I really liked pitch presentations, as in using toys to generate ideas, also, I've enjoyed paper prototyping practice. The theoretical part was very important, but the practical stages were better. Besides, I found great that happened several playtesting sessions during course schedule." In addition, students asserted on technology and design lectures, distinguishing topics on game engines, computer vision, and concept art.

Implications. Based on interview results, we could recognize points of the model that required adjustments. Overall, students comprehended the three entities and its individual relationships; it is things, people, and the environment. Thereby, participants could distinguish passive from active technologies, access to information, and social interaction modalities. Despite, in their first contact with the model, students presented struggle to understand people-things axis, due it presented aspects displayed in two columns. However, while experiencing the model through the course, they could differentiate physical interactions from types of I/O technologies. For example, subject G2F commented that had difficulty in understanding such aspects since it seemed similar. However, after consulting class materials, the participant stated as "clear" the distinction among groups of aspects. Then, the same process happened with other four subjects. Concerning, people-environment axis, students presented difficulty in locating a person in single-player systems. In consequence, participants felt confused in selecting social interaction aspects of such systems. Interviewer U1B commented that their team implemented a single-player game, and they found issues since model only presented multiplayer aspects.

Regarding things-environment axis, students referred to aspects definitions as "clear", "intuitive", "easy to learn", and "concise". So far, several participants presented issues in selecting model's terms. The aspects that caused more mistakes for students were *'update'*, *'destroy'*, and *'augment'*. For example, subject U1D commented on *'destroy'*, "At first, I did not understand if destroy was related to extinguish an object entirely, or it would apply to a simple game instance. Yet, after seen it implemented in other prototypes, it really helped me to understand its meaning". Several students alleged that examples of aspects in existing systems assisted them in difference model concepts. For example, when G2G referred to the first model exercise, "During exercise, where you showed several examples of existing systems, it helped a lot in understanding the concepts." The, participant U1C claimed, "Yes, the main resource was the examples. Using the examples was easy to know what to do or not, and if our game had an aspect or not". Besides, interviewer U1D mentioned that despite information in the article, the visual material with examples was very elucidative and important. Therefore, according to students, while visualizing existing systems, the aspects presented more clearly.

To address student's issues, we promoted adjustments in all three axes of the model (see Fig. 6). Starting in people-things axis, we replaced term 'immersion' with 'pervasiveness' since the word 'immersion' incorporated multiple aspects on game experience. For example, the BUD Monster team selected 'immersion' in their model, despite their interpretation contrasted the aspect's meaning. Our goal was to select a term to represent systems where people interact with things and its surrounds, such as in smart playgrounds. Hence, we considered the term 'pervasiveness' appropriated to describe the disruptive concept of such systems. Besides, in people-environment axis, we included the term 'single' to describe systems with one player, therefore, representing systems without social interaction among people.

Observing student's prototypes, we noticed that current terms were missing a few interactive aspects. Therefore, we added two new terms in the things-environment axis. Hence, we included 'activate' to represent when things send/receive a single action to the environment. In Undercroft, 'activate' would describe actions where a user presses

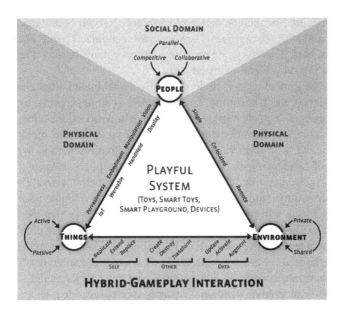

Fig. 6. Hybrid-Gameplay Interaction model update

a button on the game board. Thus, a user would both *activate* power-ups and *activate* character's movement functions. Besides, we inserted 'transform' to represent when things change an existing game object in the environment. Thereby, an interface element may *transform* other game object identity into a new game object. Moreover, 'transform' can refer to changing information of an existing object, such as its position, visual features, and state. We defined such term as a complementary action to both 'create' and 'destroy'. Afterward, we organized all nine interactive aspects into three groups; these are how things are *self*-represented, how things act on *other* game objects, and how things send/receive *data* in the environment. Thus, a physical game object, or interface element, can self-represent in the environment through *replication, extension* or *replacement*. Then, such thing may interact with other game objects *creating, destroying*, or *transforming* their information. Finally, things can send/receive data through an *update*, when things record such data; *activate*, by sending single data to the environment; and *augment*, when system provide data feedback.

5   Conclusion and Future Work

We considered student's outcomes satisfactory since groups have prototyped hybrid game concepts of meaningful interface elements. All six working prototypes promoted fun experiences during playtesting sessions, using either passive or active technologies. The relational model presented as a useful tool to both describe and assimilate hybrid game concepts, in early design stages. Overall, modelling concepts during pitch selection and in initial GDDs had helped students in defining their game setup, as the interactive aspects of interface elements and the environment. Furthermore, the model established a specific vocabulary that aided students in both communications among team members and with other groups. However, we recognized points of the model that required adjustments. Therefore, we proposed improvements based on results of seven semi-structured interviews held with students.

Besides the theoretical model, students positively evaluated other course resources and methods. Hence, the Brainstorm Toy presented as an appropriate tool to generate hybrid game concepts. Yet, we must refine idea selection procedure since, through preferential voting, students discarded concepts of great potential and semantic value. To solve such issue, we would provide an additional evaluation method to analyze interactive aspects of concepts, using model information in pitch selection. Moreover, in paper prototyping, we identified that when groups prototyped interface elements and its interactive aspects, they required little change in working development stages. Thereby, to assure that subjects will prototype such aspects, we suppose that the method could incorporate pre-defined I/O technologies resources including system data flow. Finally, we expect to put in practice the updated model, to both validate improvements and refine model usage in the creative process. Therefore, we will experiment other course formats, such as short duration workshops. Furthermore, we must focus model usage in initial design stages of conception, ideation, concepts modelling, idea selection, and low-fidelity prototyping.

References

1. Nijholt, A.: Playful interfaces: introduction and history. In: Nijholt, A. (ed.) Playful User Interfaces. GMSE, pp. 1–21. Springer, Singapore (2014). doi:10.1007/978-981-4560-96-2_1
2. Albuquerque, A.P., Breyer, F.B., Kelner, J.: A relational model for playful and smart game design. In: Marcus, A. (ed.) DUXU 2016. LNCS, vol. 9747, pp. 252–263. Springer, Cham (2016). doi:10.1007/978-3-319-40355-7_24
3. Tyni, H., Kultima, A.: The emergence of industry of playful hybrids: developer's perspective. In: 20th International Academic Mindtrek Conference, pp. 413–421. ACM, New York (2016). doi:10.1145/2994310.2994358
4. Barba, E., Xu, Y., MacIntyre, B., Tseng, T.: Lessons from a class on handheld augmented reality game design. In: 4th International Conference on Foundations of Digital Games, pp. 2–9. ACM, New York (2009). doi:10.1145/1536513.1536525
5. Hornecker, E.: Creative idea exploration within the structure of a guiding framework: the card brainstorming game. In: 4th International Conference on Tangible, Embedded, and Embodied Interaction, pp. 101–108. ACM, New York (2010). doi:10.1145/1709886.1709905
6. Vissers, J., Geerts, D.: TUIkit: evaluating physical and functional experiences of tangible user interface prototypes. In: 33rd Annual ACM Conference on Human Factors in Computing Systems, pp. 1267–1276. ACM, New York (2015). doi:10.1145/2702123.2702478
7. Heijboer, M., van den Hoven, E.: Keeping up appearances: interpretation of tangible artifact design. In: 5th Nordic Conference on Human-Computer Interaction: Building Bridges, pp. 162–171. ACM, New York (2008). doi:10.1145/1463160.1463178
8. Marco, J., Baldassarri, S., Cerezo, E.: ToyVision: a toolkit to support the creation of innovative board-games with tangible interaction. In: 7th International Conference on Tangible, Embedded and Embodied Interaction, pp. 291–298. ACM, New York (2013). doi: 10.1145/2460625.2460674

9. Denton, D.K.: The Toolbox for the Mind: Finding and Implementing Creative Solutions in the Workplace. ASQ Quality Press, Milwaukee (1999)
10. Ryam, T.: The Anatomy of a Design Document, Part 2: Documentation Guidelines for the Functional and Technical Specifications (1999). http://www.gamasutra.com/features/19991217/ryan_01.htm

Visualizing Incongruity and Resolution: Visual Data Mining Strategies for Modeling Sequential Humor Containing Shifts of Interpretation

Andrew Smigaj[(✉)] and Boris Kovalerchuk

Central Washington University, Ellensburg, USA
{SmigajA,BorisK}@cwu.edu

Abstract. The goal of this paper is to investigate the use of visualization as an approach to modeling humor within text. In particular, we developed algorithmic and automated approaches to visualizing and detecting shifts in interpretation as intelligent agents parse meaning from garden path jokes. Garden path jokes can occur when a reader's initial interpretation of an ambiguous text turns out to be incorrect, leading them down the wrong path to a semantic dead end. Given new information, semantic incongruities arise that require resolution, often triggering a humorous response. This is a work of visual text mining, that is visualizing texts in order to detect patterns and features associated with various text based phenomena such as humor. In this paper we describe three successful approaches to text visualization conducive to identifying distinguishing features given humorous and non humorous texts. These are the use of paired collocated coordinates, heat maps, and two-dimensional Boolean plots. The proposed methodology and tools offer a new approach to testing and generating hypotheses related to theories of humor as well as other phenomena involving incongruity-resolution and shifts in interpretation including non-verbal humor.

Keywords: Computational humor · Natural language understanding · Visual data mining · Incongruity modeling

1 Introduction

While many theories of humor agree that humor often involved the detection of incongruities and their resolution the details remain vague and there is no agreed upon theoretical framework which describes how these incongruities form and are detected by intelligent agents [12]. This paper demonstrates the use of text visualization for modeling humor in text in process known as visual text mining, a subset of visual data mining [4,15]. In particular our approach visualizes shifts in meaning assignment over time as jokes are processed, While this does not fully solve the problem of modeling the specific mechanisms underlying humor, visualization and visual text mining gives us one more data centric tool for detecting features associated with various natural language phenomena Furthermore these approaches

© Springer International Publishing AG 2017
N. Streitz and P. Markopoulos (Eds.): DAPI 2017, LNCS 10291, pp. 660–674, 2017.
DOI: 10.1007/978-3-319-58697-7_49

can be used to model and detect other forms of humor, in particular sequential physical humor, and other phenomena involving shifts of interpretation.

This paper made use of three visualization approaches to model, detect, and classify sequential jokes involving shifts in the interpreted meaning for some ambiguous word. This form of sequential joke has been referred to as a 'garden path' joke to differentiate it from other sequential jokes involving incongruity and resolution which do not involve a shift from on interpretation to the next [1]. The three approaches use a correlation based measure to assign meaning of ambiguous words given the context of the ambiguous word in different parts of a surface level text and relations associated with different meanings of that word as defined in an ontology as a deeper level.

The first visualization shows how meaning correlation scores for two or more opposing meanings are plotted as coordinates using an approach known as collocated paired coordinates [2]. This lets us visually see shifts of meaning associated when given a set of jokes when compared with a set of non jokes. The next visualization uses heat maps to color code the differences of meaning correlation scores given different time steps. The heat maps for the set of jokes is distinguishable from that of non jokes with respect to these meaning correlation differences. Finally the third visualization displays in two dimensions an entire model space consisting of boolean vectors describing meaning correlation over time. The set of jokes and non jokes are plotted on this space allowing us to see the boundary between what is a joke and non joke. To show the power of this approach we compare the results with traditional data mining approaches which result in models describing the same key features. This paper describes all three approaches in detail, including the construction of an informal ontology using web mining to identify semantic relations, and shows how these approaches were used to visualize jokes and non jokes to get experimental results. While improvements can be made the results were encouraging.

The visualization strategies used in this paper can be used to model and detect other forms of humor including sequential physical humor in nonverbal settings. Incongruities and their resolution arise in many other situations involving sensors and analysis where classification occurs. We will briefly discuss the use of the three visualization approaches for modeling and detection physical humor and applications from comedy to any situation where incongruities arise given agents and their sensors.

2   Related Work

Both Computational Humor and Text Visualization as fields have seen extensive activity lately but tend to work on separate topics. Computational Humor deals a lot with the modeling and detection of incongruities within text and many attempts have recently been made attempting to detect or generate jokes using computers [6, 7, 10, 13, 16, 17] but no attempt focused on visualization has been made. On the other hand people working on Text Visualization tend to focus on other topics such as identifying the central topic within a text. To our knowledge this paper is the first attempt to visualize incongruities within text.

3   Incongruity Resolution Theory of Humor and Garden Path Jokes

'Two fish are in a tank. One looks to the other and asks: How do you drive this thing?'

Many predominant theories of verbal humor states that humor is triggered by the detection and resolution of incongruities [12,14]. The dictionary defines 'incongruous' as lacking harmony of parts, discordant, or inconsistent in nature. During the parsing of a text incongruities form when a reader's interpretation of some concept conflicts with other possible interpretations as the text is read. This paper will focus on a particular humor subtype where there is a shift from some interpretation to some opposing other. Dynel calls these jokes "garden path" jokes using the garden path metaphor of being misled [1], while other theorists use the terminology of 'forced reinterpretation' and 'frame shifting' [12]. These jokes are sequential in nature and describe a certain pattern of incongruity and resolution. With a garden path joke a reader establishes some interpretation A as they read the first part of a joke, the setup, but given new evidence included in the second part, the punchline, they must discard this interpretation and establish a new interpretation B. The fishtank joke displays an incongruity; the reader initially interprets the tank to be an aquarium, but given additional information the alternative meaning of a vehicle becomes possible and probable. Incongruities often arise when 'opposing' or 'mutually exclusive' elements simultaneously occur. Different word senses oppose in that when a tank is a vehicle it is not an aquarium. Opposition occurs in many other areas; when it is summer it is not winter, when something is hot it is not cold, and when one is sad they are not happy. To model this we visualize changes of correlation in the context established for mutually exclusive meanings for some ambiguous word and with the context that different parts of text containing that ambiguous word are found in. Similar meanings will have similar contexts according to the distributional hypothesis. Before presenting the visualizations let us discuss the approach used to establish meaning and how we identifying correlation between meaning representations.

4   Establishing Meanings and Meaning Correlations

The sections on estalblishing meaning and meaning correlations are in line with previous work by the authors of this paper [5]. We chose a vector representation of meaning based on the frequency at which words occur in the context of some target word. This is a standard approach taken by a number of researchers in the past for dealing with meaning [8]. These vector of word associations form an informal ontology describing entities and their relations. The material used to build these vectors was retrieved via a web search. Below we consider some ambiguous word A with a number of possible meanings $AM_1...AM_n$ and different parts of some text $P_1...P_m$ containing the ambiguous word A.

4.1 Establishing Vectors of Word Association Frequencies Using a Web Mining Approach

For each meaning AM_x we establish a set of disambiguating keywords $K(AM_x)$ which uniquely identify that meaning. While we hand-chose our keyword sets these can be established using a variety of resources such as wordnet.

Next we use $K(AM_x)$ as a query for a search engine retrieve the top n documents. Let D(q, n) be a search function which retrieves n documents relevant to some query q. The resulting document set for some meaning AM_x is thus designated $D(K(AM_x), n)$.

Finally we compute frequencies of all words occuring within distance j of A given the document set $D(K(AM_x), n)$. We designate this $F(A, j, D(K(AM_x), n)))$ where F is a function that returns a vector of word frequencies. In this paper F uses the term-frequency to inverse document frequency approach (TF-IDF) to establishing word frequencies [11]. $F(A, j, D(K(AM_x), n)))$ represents the meaning for AM_x as a set of word association frequencies or in other words its contexts. These frequencies are ordered by the lexicographic order of the words. Note that we include the frequency of the given word A itself though have experimented with variants which do not include the ambiguous word.

In a similar fashion we established semantics for the ambiguous word A given the different parts $P_1...P_m$ of some text containing A. We denote them as $F(A, j, D(P_1, n))... F(A, j, D(P_m, n))$.

4.2 Calculating Correlation Coefficients

We are interested in how the meaning of A given a search for some phrase Px correlates with the meaning of A given the meaning established for each word sense $AM_1...AM_n$.

We compute the correlation coefficient given the vector of word frequencies associated with A given a search for some part of text P_i, that is $F(A, D(P_i, n))$, and the vector of word frequencies associated with a search for some meaning AM_x, that is $F(A, j, D(K(AM_x), n))$, using some function C which return the correlation. We denote these $C_{iy} = C(F(A, j, D(P_i, n)), F(A, j, D(K(AM_y), n)))$.

All of the jokes in our data set are two part jokes in which two meanings are invoked. Given two meanings of some ambiguous word A and some statement with parts P_1 and P_2 that refer to A, we calculate the following correlation scores:

Given P1 (part one of some text):
$C_{1x} = C(F(A, j, D(P_1, n)), F(A, j, D(K(AM_x), n)))$ is a correlation of meaning AP_1 with meaning AM_x,
$C_{1y} = C(F(A, j, D(P_1, n)), F(A, j, D(K(AM_y), n)))$ is a correlation of meaning AP_1 with meaning AM_y,

Given P2 (part two of some text):
$C_{2x} = C(F(A, j, D(P_2, n)), F(A, D(K(AM_x), n)))$ is a correlation of meaning AP_2 with meaning AM_x,

$C_{2y} = C(F(A, j, D(P_2, n)), F(A, D(K(AM_y), n)))$ is a correlation of meaning AP_2 with meaning AM_y.

4.3 Calculating Correlation Coefficient Differences Given Different Parts of Text

Finally we calculate differences between the correlation coefficients which are useful for joke classification as they describe g correlation movement patterns. For example the difference between C_{1x} and C_{1y} tells us which meaning has greater correlation given P1, the first part of the joke, while the difference between C_{1x} and C_{1y} tells us which meaning has greater correlation given the second part. If $C_{1x} - C_{1y} > 0$ then this meaning x is greater than meaning y given part one. On the other hand the difference between C_{1x} and C_{2x} tells us if a correlation coefficient for some meaning has increased or decreased given part on or part two of some text. If $C_{1x} - C_{2x} > 0$ then the correlation of meaning x has decreased as the text is read in while if $C_{1x} - C_{2x} < 0$ then it has increased.

We calculate the differences between C_{1x}, C_{1y}, C_{2x}, and C_{2y}. The difference $C_{1x} - C_{1y}$ shows which meaning correlates higher given the first part of text, $C_{2x} - C_{2y}$ shows which meaning correlates higher given the second part of text, $C_{1x} - C_{2x}$ shows if meaning X correlates higher in the second part of text compared with the first, and $C_{1y} - C_{2y}$ shows if meaning Y correlates higher in the second part of text compared with the first.

4.4 Building Features from Correlation Coefficient Differences Given Different Time Steps

We then define four Boolean variables $x_1 - x_4$ using these differences:

$x_1 = 1$ If $C_{1x} > C_{1y}$, else $x_1 = 0$

$x_1 = 1$ means the correlation with meaning X is greater than meaning Y given the first part of the text.

$x_2 = 1$ If $C_{1x} > C_{2x}$, else $x_2 = 0$

$x_2 = 1$ means the correlation with meaning X decreased going from part one to part two of the text

$x_3 = 1$ If $C_{1y} < C_{2y}$, else $x_3 = 0$

$x_3 = 1$ means the correlation with meaning Y increased going from par tone to part two of the text

$x_4 = 1$ If $C_{2x} < C_{2y}$, else $x_4 = 0$

$x_4 = 1$ means the correlation with meaning Y is greater than meaning X given the second part of the text.

5   Example

Take a two-part garden path joke J with the parts $P_1 = $ 'fish in tank' and $P_2 = $ 'they drive the tank' that contains the ambiguous word $A = $ 'tank'. Let $tankM_1$

and $tankM_2$ be the two meanings invoked at different points while reading J, that of an aquarium and that of a vehicle.

$P_1=$ "fish in a tank."

$P_2=$ "drives the tank"

$K(tankM_1) = [$ "aquarium", "tank"$]$

$K(tankM_2) = [$ "vehicle", "panzer", "tank"$]$

This is a distilled example of the "fishtank" joke presented in the Sect. 3. In order to concentrate on the issue at hand, i.e. modeling incongruity, we reduced many jokes to simplified form.

We establish vectors for the various meanings of 'tank' using data from searches for $P_1, P_2, K(tankM_x)$ and $K(tankM_y)$ and then calculate the correlation coefficients between these meaning vectors. The meanings for 'tank' found in P_1 and P_2 may or may not be the same as M_1 and M_2. According to the distributional hypothesis, which states that similar meanings will have similar contexts, if they are the same then there should be correlation of context. The correlation of context can be found by comparing the vectors of word associations we extracted via web mining.

Meaning correlation coefficients given P_1:

$$C_{1x} = C(F('tank', j, D('fish\ in\ a\ tank', n)), F('tank', j, D(["aquarium", "tank"], n))) = 0.824$$

$$C_{1y} = C(F('tank', j, D('fish\ in\ a\ tank', n)), F(; tank', j, D(["vehicle", "panzer", "tank"], n))) = 0.333$$

Meaning correlation coefficients given P_2:

$$C_{2x} = C(F('tank', j, D('drives\ the\ tank', n)), F('tank', j, D(["aquarium", "tank"], n))) = 0.389$$

$$C_{2y} = C(F('tank', j, D('drives\ the\ tank', n)), F('tank', j, D(["vehicle", "panzer", "tank"], n))). = 0.573$$

Over the course of a garden path joke there should be a switch in dominant meaning correlation coefficient. Given the first part correlation with meaning X should be greater and given the second part correlation with meaning Y should be greater.

6 Data Set Used in Visualizations

We collected two part jokes of garden path form containing lexical ambiguities and converted them into a simple form by hand as we want to model incongruity rather than focusing on other issues related to parsing text. Algorithmically selecting relevant parts of text P_1 and P_2 from longer texts that contain a lot of additional material is a valid approach but outside the scope of this research. Thus material not relevant to the interpretation of the ambiguous lexical entity was removed. Thus "Two fish are in tank" becomes "a fish in a tank." as the number of fish has little to do with the lexical ambiguity involed in the incongruity we are attempted to model. In order to focus on developing means of visualizing text we let meaning X to be the meaning indicated in the first part of the text and meaning Y to be the secondary meaning.

For each joke we created a non joke of similar form. It contains the same first part but a different non-humorous second part. We strove to change as little as possible, usually only a noun or verb, to preserve the structure of the statement. The following are some examples of jokes and non jokes contained in the data set.

Joke1:

P_1: Two fish are in a tank.

P_2: They drive the tank.

NonJoke1:

P_1: Two fish are in a tank.

P_2: The swim in the tank.

Meaning X search query: 'Aquarium tank'

Meaning Y search query: 'Panzer tank'

Joke2:

P_1: No charge said the bartender..

P_2: To the neutron.

NonJoke2:

P_1: No charge said the bartender.

P_2: To the customer.

Meaning X search query: 'Cost charge'

Meaning Y search query: 'Electron charge.'

7   Visualization Approach 1. Collocated Paired Coordinates

Our first visualization uses a visualization technique known as collocated paired coordinates [2]. Given some ambiguous element with multiple possible meanings, we plot meaning correlation scores established given a part of text and the various meanings as points on a coordinate graph. The Y axis measures the correlation with meaning Y, while the X axis measures the correlation with meaning X. Each part of text in a sequence results in a point and these points are connected with arrows representing time. This allows us to visualize correlation patterns over time. A garden path jokes which involves a shift from one meaning to the next should form a line moving away from one axis and towards another as the meaning correlation score for one meaning lessens and another meaning increases. In our visualization we set the X axis to measure correlation with the meaning invoked by the first part of the text and the Y axis to measure the correlation with second meaning invoked in the second part of text so that the arrows should all move in the same direction as a meaning shift occurs.

Visualization overview:

For P_1 and P_2 we plot the meaning correlation coefficients given two opposing meanings for some ambiguous word with AM_x and AM_y as points:

The X axis represents correlation with some meaning AM_x.

The Y axis represents correlation with some meaning AM_y

1. Plot a point representing the meaning correlations given P_1.
2. Plot a coordinate representing the meaning correlations given P_2.
3. Connect via an arrow indicating time.
4. Color-code green if humorous, red if not, and black if unknown.

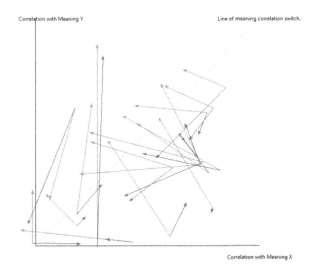

Fig. 1. Collocated paired coordinate plot of meaning context correlation over time. The set of jokes and non jokes plotted as meaning correlation over time using collocated paired coordinates. (Color figure online)

7.1   Discussion

While there are some examples which fail to match the pattern, it is clear that most jokes involve a shift away from correlation with one meaning and towards the second meaning given part two of the joke. Figure 1 shows this as the green arrows, representing jokes, move from one axis to another while the red arrows tend to stay closer to the original meaning as there is no meaning change. An analysis of the handful of cases that do not follow this pattern indicates explainable circumstances such as the web search returning irrelevant documents due to things like a poor choice in keywords or semantic noise. Methods such as dimensionality reduction including latent semantic analysis may help with this. Figure 2 only looks at the meaning correlation coefficients given P_2 which clearly shows that there is higher correlation with meaning Y which opposes some meaning X that was initially established.

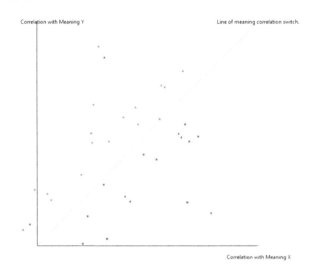

Fig. 2. Second endpoint only. The correlation coefficients given P_2.

8   Visualization 2: Heat Maps

Visualization Overview: In the previous visualization we saw that there is a shift from one meaning correlation being higher to the opposite. To test this intuition we make use of heat maps based on differences in correlation coefficient values given the different meanings and different parts of text. With this approach we can identify potential features that distinguish jokes from non-jokes, assisting in model discovery.

Visualization Algorithm:

1. Organize the correlation coefficient differences as established in Sect. 4.3 in a data frame along with classification of being a joke or not.
2. Color code the correlation score differences based on value.
3. Sort the rows into groups by classification, that is into two groups of joke and non joke.
4. Identify regions of the heat map where there is a distinguishable difference between the joke and non joke sections in terms of color.

8.1   Discussion

While this heat map only uses three colors when color coding correlation coefficients by value, clearly we can identify areas where the joke data set differs from the non joke dataset. Lets look at the column representing the difference between $C_{2x} - C_{2y}$. In Fig. 3 this is the column indicating the difference between correlation with meaning X and meaning Y given the second part of the joke. If this value is less than 0 then meaning Y is greater given P_2, if it is greater

	A	B	C	D
1	name	C1y-C2x	C2x-C2y	class
2	webJoke1	-0.384	-0.012	joke
3	soapJoke1	-0.135	-0.084	joke
4	mouseJoke1	0.039	-0.119	joke
5	terminalJoke1	0.03	-0.129	joke
6	framedJoke1	0.084	-0.138	joke
7	balanceJoke1	-0.2824	-0.1406	joke
8	freeJoke1	0.548	-0.142	joke
9	dogJoke1	0.144	-0.174	joke
10	fishJoke1	-0.056	-0.184	joke
11	chargeJoke1	0.0455	-0.1855	joke
12	chopJoke1	0.096	-0.211	joke
13	potatoJoke1	0.124	-0.256	joke
14	houseJoke1	0.0256	-0.2606	joke
15	bankJoke1	-0.114	-0.375	joke
16	virusJoke1	-0.176	-0.153	joke
17	wavesJoke1	0.158	-0.118	joke
18	catJoke1	-0.283	-0.61	joke
19	webNonjoke1	-0.615	0.639	nonjoke
20	balanceNonJok	-0.635	0.485	nonjoke
21	framedNonjoke	-0.299	0.285	nonjoke
22	dogNonjoke1	-0.139	0.24	nonjoke
23	chopNonJoke1	-0.076	0.224	nonjoke
24	terminalNonjok	-0.08	0.222	nonjoke
25	houseNonjoke	-0.192	0.195	nonjoke
26	potatoNonjoke	-0.03	0.179	nonjoke
27	mouseNonjoke	0.159	0.154	nonjoke
28	soapNonJoke1	-0.318	0.141	nonjoke
29	chargeNonJok	-0.137	0.095	nonjoke
30	fishNonJoke1	-0.146	0.073	nonjoke
31	bankNonjoke1	-0.16	0.027	nonjoke
32	freeNonjoke1	0.645	-0.13	nonjoke
33	catNonjoke1	-0.309	-0.534	nonjoke
34	wavesNonjoke	-0.311	0.128	nonjoke
35	virusNonjoke1	-0.266	0.17	nonJoke

Fig. 3. Heat map for correlation differences. Column A shows that the first meaning has a higher correlation score than the second given the first part of the joke while Column B show that the second meaning Y has a higher correlation than the first meaning X in the second part of the joke.

than 1 then meaning X remains dominant. While we already expected this to happen, the heat map would allow us to automatically identify this value as being a distinguishing feature between classes.

9   Visualization 3: Visualizing a Model Space Using Monotone Boolean Chain Visualizations

In the last viusalization we use a two-dimensional representation of Boolean space based on the plotting of chains of monotonically increasing Boolean vectors [3] to visualize the difference between garden path jokes and non jokes. Vectors are arranged according to their norm, with the all true Boolean vector at one end of the plot and the all false vector at the other. The arrangement of the vectors form chains where monotonicity is preserved, that is as each succeeding vector in the chain is the same as the last except has an additional bit set to one. Each chain describes the change in features. The chains altogether represent a model space based on the Boolean features $x_1...x_4$ derived from the meaning correlation coefficient differences described in Sect. 4.4.

Visualization overview:

1. For each joke/nonjoke establish a vector of Boolean values as described in Sect. 4.4.
2. Establish and visualize a 2D Boolean space representation as described in [3]
3. Plot vectors established each joke or non-joke as a dot on the Boolean plot.
4. Color code the dot as green if humorous, red if not humorous.

Figures 4 and 5 show the resulting visualization using our data set.

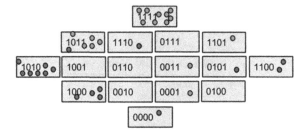

Fig. 4. Monotone boolean plot of jokes and nonjokes. Features from the data set of jokes and non jokes describing differences of correlation given different meanings and time steps plotted as Boolean vectors (Color figure online)

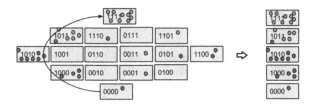

Fig. 5. Single chain. Here one chain of monotonically increasing Boolean vectors is isolated to establish a border between humorous and nonhumorous examples in terms of features. (Color figure online)

9.1   Discussion

Jokes and non jokes can be converted to a vector of Boolean values representing the presence or lack of various features in a such that we can visually distinguish and establish a border between the two classes of humorous and not humorous. By looking at a chains of Boolean vectors that contains examples from each class, each vector containing one additional feature, we can clearly see where non-humorous texts end and humorous ones begin in terms of model features. When looking at chain as shown in Fig. 5 we see that the key difference is the Boolean value which indicates that some second meaning correlated higher than the first given the second part of the text.

10   Comparison with the Results Using a Traditional Decision Tree Based Data Mining Approach

Our analysis of visualizations generated using humorous and non humorous data sets can be compared with the results using traditional data mining approaches. In particular we used a C4.5 decision tree algorithm which resulted in a model indicating the same key features involving changes in meaning correlation as our visualization show.

Resulting C4.5 model:

$If C_{2x} - C_{2y} < 0.0075$ then class= joke (89.4% of 19 examples) $If C_{2x} - C_{2y} >= 0.0075$ then class= nonjoke (100.0% of 15 examples)

The C4.5 decision tree results in one key splitting feature which is the same which we found through the visual data mining process. Given a two part garden path joke involving a lexical ambiguity where some meaning for an ambigous word is implied in the first part of the text, another alternate meaning shows higher correlation given the second.

11   Physical Humor and Humorous Smart Environments

These approaches can be used to detect and classify other forms of humor including physical humor [9]. One situation where these data visualization strategies can be used is in detecting humorous shifts of interpretation given non verbal scenes. There are many non verbal variants of the garden path joke where a viewer is given partial information, makes some assumption, and then given new information resulting in 'forced reinterpretation'. For example consider the image of a lemonade stand. The interpreted 'season' is 'Summer'. Addtional information provided via a 'zoom out' mechanism shows that the lemonade stand is actually in the middle of a snow storm. The viewer must reinterpet the season to be 'Winter'. 'Summer' and 'Winter' are mutually exclusive in that they generally do not exist simultaneously in some given area. A computer vision approach to scene analysis can be used to detect these humorous sequences by identifying instances where scene elements must be reinterpreted given the introduction of new data. Ultimately this approach takes non verbal humor and converts it to verbal humor as most computer vision algorithms take non verbal image data and label it with words such as we find with standard bag of words approaches. This could result in a predictive model but one of the main goal of this session is to build generative models which will generate humor. Let us look at how this might work.

One potential future role for smart environments is to introduce humor for the entertainment of its inhabitants [9]. A smart environment would need the following things to generate sequential humor: a model for variant of sequential humor, an algorithmic approach to using this model, an ontology describing the things which exist in the world and their relations, and finally the methods of introducing new information. First there are many models for sequential humor though many are vague including ours. We hope the results of visual data mining and traditional data mining approaches will help in automating this modeling process resulting in more robust models. Let us look at two of many algorithmic approaches to utilizing this model. The first algorithm is to 'hide and reveal'. With this algoithm the smart environment identifies an incongruity in an environment, hide elements so that one interpretation is likely, and then reveal those elements so that there will be a shift in interpretation. The second algorithm is the 'introduce and reveal' where the smart environment identifies new elements it can introduce to trigger the incongruity resolution process. This will take more extensive computational power as the environment is not just limited to what is already in a scene but all the possibilities of what could be in a scene. Search strategies such as the 'Monte Carlo' search will help when dealing with the massive number of elements a smart environment can introduce. Third the smart environment needs an ontology. This can be something extremely robust and include many types of relations such as causal relations or it could be simpler. A limited ontology might result in less opportunities for humor introduction but will still work. A smart environment does not need to pass a turing test to have a sense of humor. We would like to see smart environments perform their own automated ontology construction such as we do when web mining relations so they each might have a slightly different sense of humor. Finally for sequential humor a smart environment will need a methods of introducing new information. There are many ways of introducing new information which range from very simple to very difficult. Let us look at three of these.

First are the 'pan' and 'zoom' mechanisms where a smart environment can somehow facilitate moving things in and out of view by panning and zooming in or out. In film this may be easy but to actually move items would be hard and to move the platform a user is on even harder. There are some possible intermediate steps such as the use of 'smart windows' with panning and zooming capabilities. For example if an window can adjust its magnification it can zoom in or out, hiding and revealing some detail. Second we have mechanisms based on illumination. Shadows can hide objects and lighting can reveal them. The initial dimmed lighting might show two fish in a tank swimming around but suddenly a light shines on the tanks wheels and barrels. Finally amongst many other techniques for introducing information we have projection based techniques such as the use of film projectors to project images onto surfaces, lighting to project shadows such as when a hanging plant seems like a flying saucer or coat rack a monster, or even something simple like printing off and attaching stickers to objects. For example a smart environment may project the image of wheels onto a fish tank and remove them in a sequence designed to trigger potential shifts in interpretation.

Incongruities and their resolution appear in many other places where classification occurs though. For example in the fruit industry incongruities arise and are resolved many times as day as fruit is sorted in a complex sequential process involving classification at many stages. There is presort, which uses one system to sort fruit but misclassifiees a small percentage. When going through the sizer these are knocked onto belts leading them to cull and peeler bins. Then the sizer classifies but there are still errors so these are caught by hand selection at the tray filler stations. It is a hybrid computer-human sorting operation which allows for fixing mistakes at several stages. In general incongruities can arise and are resolved where classification occurs based on multiple sources of evidence, for example where multiple sensors are used, or where a sensor takes readings at multiple steps in time. These visualization should be able to identity some of these non verbal and non humorous 'mistakes' and their resolution which can be useful for a number of tasks from process control to sensor management.

12   Conclusion

Overall the results from this study show that visualization can be used as a valid strategy for approaching the modeling and detection of humor within text. This paper presented three approaches that were all successful in enabling a person to identify key features that distinguish humorous and non humorous garden path jokes. One future direction is to use these visualization techniques on other joke types to see what they would look like in terms of patterns of meaning correlation over time. These techniques can potentially be used to visualize many other forms of incongruity within texts such shilling within product review sets, paradigm level formation of incongruity and resolution within academic document sets over time, and for other phenomena involving opposing states and patterns of shifting such as the writings of a bipolar patient who might shift from one opposing emotion to the other in a cyclic fashion. They also allow for ploting of many examples at once whic lets us visualize big data in terms of natural language texts. As discussed they can also potentially be used to identify non verbal incongruities and their resolution such as non verbal humor. Overall the results are promosing and these methods will be developed beyond the toy level they are currently at.

References

1. Dynel, M.: Garden paths, red lights and crossroads. Israeli J. Humor Res. **1**(1), 289–320 (2012)
2. Kovalerchuk, B.: Visualization of multidimensional data with collocated paired coordinates and general line coordinates. In: IS&T/SPIE Electronic Imaging, International Society for Optics and Photonics, p. 90170I (2013)
3. Kovalerchuk, B., Delizy, F.: Visual data mining using monotone boolean functions. In: Kovalerchuk, B., Schwing, J. (eds.) Visual and Spatial Analysis, pp. 387–406. Springer, Dordrecht (2004)
4. Kovalerchuk, B., Schwing, J.: Visual and spatial analysis. Advances in Data Mining, Reasoning, and Problem Solving. Springer, Dordrecht (2005)
5. Kovalerchuk, B., Smigaj, A.: Computing with words beyond quantitative words: incongruity modeling. In: 2015 Annual Conference of the North American Fuzzy Information Processing Society (NAFIPS) Held Jointly with 2015 5th World Conference on Soft Computing (WConSC), pp. 1–6, August 2015

6. Labutov, I., Lipson, H.: Humor as circuits in semantic networks. In: Proceedings of the 50th Annual Meeting of the Association for Computational Linguistics: Short Papers-Volume 2, pp. 150–155. Association for Computational Linguistics (2012)
7. Mihalcea, R., Strapparava, C., Pulman, S.: Computational models for incongruity detection in humour. In: Gelbukh, A. (ed.) CICLing 2010. LNCS, vol. 6008, pp. 364–374. Springer, Heidelberg (2010). doi:10.1007/978-3-642-12116-6_30
8. Mikolov, T., Sutskever, I., Chen, K., Corrado, G.S., Dean, J.: Distributed representations of words and phrases and their compositionality. In: Burges, C., Bottou, L., Welling, M., Ghahramani, Z., Weinberger, K. (eds.) Advances in Neural Information Processing Systems 26, pp. 3111–3119. Curran Associates, Inc. (2013)
9. Nijholt, A.: Towards humor modelling and facilitation in smart environments. In: Proceedings of the 5th International Conference on Applied Human Factors and Ergonomics AHFE 2014 (2014)
10. Petrovic, S., Matthews, D.: Unsupervised joke generation from big data. In: ACL (2), pp. 228–232. Citeseer (2013)
11. Rajaraman, A., Ullman, J.D.: Mining of massive datasets. In: Visual Data Mining, pp. 1–17 (2011)
12. Ritchie, G.: Developing the incongruity-resolution theory (1999)
13. Ritchie, G.: The jape riddle generator: technical specification. Institute for Communicating and Collaborative Systems (2003)
14. Schultz, T.R., Horibe, F.: Development of the appreciation of verbal jokes. Dev. Psychol. **10**(1), 13 (1974)
15. Simoff, S.J., Böhlen, M.H., Mazeika, A.: Visual data mining: an introduction and overview. In: Simoff, S.J., Böhlen, M.H., Mazeika, A. (eds.) Visual Data Mining. LNCS, vol. 4404, pp. 1–12. Springer, Heidelberg (2008). doi:10.1007/978-3-540-71080-6_1
16. Taylor, J.M., Mazlack, L.J.: An investigation into computational recognition of children's jokes. In: Proceedings of the National Conference on Artificial Intelligence, vol. 22, p. 1904. AAAI Press, Menlo Park, MIT Press, Cambridge (1999/2007)
17. Valitutti, A., Toivonen, H., Doucet, A., Toivanen, J.M.: "Let everything turn well in your wife": generation of adult humor using lexical constraints. In: ACL (2), pp. 243–248 (2013)

Players' Experience of an Augmented Reality Game, *Pokémon Go*: Inspirations and Implications for Designing Pervasive Health Gamified Applications

Xin Tong[(⊠)], Ankit Gupta, Diane Gromala, and Chris D. Shaw

Simon Fraser University, Surrey, Canada
{tongxint,aga53,gromala,shaw}@sfu.ca

Abstract. *Pokémon Go* is a mobile Augmented Reality (AR) game that blends gameplay with real-life outdoor physical activity. In this game, players locate, catch and interact with virtual creatures called Pokémon. Initial reports and online players' statistics suggest that *Pokémon Go* motivates players to go outside and become more active. This paper describes an online survey we designed and conducted with players from varied locations and different backgrounds. The goal was to gain initial insight about WHY players spend time on this game and WHAT are their primary motivations; WHEN and HOW they play the game; and WHAT potential changes in physical activity *Pokémon Go* may elicit from players. Free-to-play, location-based AR mobile games like *Pokémon Go* are likely to become a new design model for gamified applications that promote physical activity. However, our results imply that in order to sustain motivation and physical activity, the core gameplay and mechanics require thoughtful and engaging design. Further long-term research is needed to understand the benefits and concerns of the game.

Keywords: Augmented reality game · Motive · Physical activity · Play pattern · Implications · Gamified applications

1 Introduction

Admittedly, *Pokémon Go* seems to have caused a wave of popularity among different age groups and cross many types of players. Within the first week of its launch in July, the game attracted over 65 million users [4]. Nevertheless, by August, it only held around 30 million active players. However, very few academic research or papers have explored what caused this phenomenon and what motivated huge amount of players.

A sedentary lifestyle is a contributing factor to chronic disease. Thus, having an active level of physical activity is crucial to. Tools and technologies such as mobile games and some gamification applications have been shown to help people manage their health and wellness. Of particular interest are technologies that are designed for activity tracking and promoting behaviour changes in everyday life, like *Pokémon Go*. *Pokémon Go* is one of the most significant successes in location-based games so far. It has been a common phenomenon that *Pokémon Go* players walk very long distance

© Springer International Publishing AG 2017
N. Streitz and P. Markopoulos (Eds.): DAPI 2017, LNCS 10291, pp. 675–683, 2017.
DOI: 10.1007/978-3-319-58697-7_50

daily to capture certain *Pokémons,* gathered together to wait for the appearance of *Pokémons* at a certain location (*Pokéstop*).

The Human-Computer Interaction (HCI) community has conducted research of location-based gamification applications developed in commercial and academic contexts for many years. *Geocaching* [7] is only one of many examples. However, most of these gamification approaches had limitations, particularly those concerning the potential to change behaviors, such as physical activity. Limitations were attributed to the cost of equipment, the need for players to remain indoors versus outdoors, the inherent "unsocial" nature of games that accommodate or privilege certain groups of players over others, poor long-term adherence and so on [9].

Therefore, for researchers from a health technology perspective, one of the most intriguing aspects of *Pokémon Go* is that people must actually engage in a Physical Activity (PA) (e.g. walking, running, biking) to successfully play the game. Many prior reviews and studies of Active Video Games (AVG, games aimed at promoting Physical Activity) and gamification approaches on mobile platforms have been conducted [3, 5]. Some of these are positive and encouraging whereas others showed a contradictory results. As suggested in [10], *Pokémon Go* shows an early, yet compelling evidences that interventions to promote healthy behaviors should incorporate social dimensions, if they are to be appealing and successful in promoting long-term behavioral change. The article also shows the urgent interests to start creative research projects that measure outcomes from *Pokémon Go* as interventions for facilitating physical activity changes and explore the underlying reasons.

Furthermore, in recent editorial letters and articles in the *Games for Health Journal* [1] and in *Sports and Exercise Medicine* [2], health researchers have begun to pay attention to *Pokémon Go*, and propose potential empirical studies. Relevant questions focus on numerous facets of players' profiles, their motives and play patterns, potential outcomes of playing *Pokémon Go*, and so on. Answers to these questions promise to shed light on gamification approaches and video/mobile games that are designed to facilitate PA. Therefore, in this research, we set out to explore these research questions in order to assess and provide insights regarding the design of gamified applications that intend to increase or to motivate PA.

2   What Is *Pokémon Go*?

Pokémon Go is an Augmented Reality (AR) mobile gaming application that uses GPS location systems to create a map of a player's local environment. Individuals can use their smartphones to track and catch *Pokémons* (virtual monsters) [6]. It was initially released in some countries in July 2016, and has so far expanded to many other countries around the world. *Pokémon Go* was rated the most widely downloaded and used smartphone app in the entire world, surpassing longstanding frontrunners such as *Facebook*, *Twitter* and *Candy Crush* after its release [11].

Pokémon originated from a popular Japanese animé and has since become a huge franchise that includes movies, TV series, comics, toys, themed-products and shops. Therefore, it has huge population of fans. Soon after the associated game *Pokémon Go* was released, it was considered to be one of the most widely downloaded apps in the world.

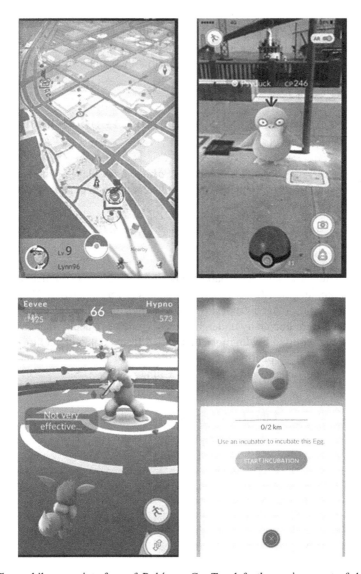

Fig. 1. The mobile game interface of *Pokémon Go*. Top left: the environment of the player's neighborhood with *Pokéstops* and *Pokémon* gyms. Top right: the player is throwing *Pokéballs* to catch *Pokémon*. Bottom left: players are battling each other in the gym. Bottom right: players use distance traveled to hatch Pokémon from an egg. Photo Credits @ Pokémon Go.

In this game, players can go "geocaching" in AR mode with their mobile phones, where the virtual monsters seems to be alive and co-located in the real world. Besides throwing *Pokéballs* to catch the *Pokémons*, players can battle each other with their *Pokémons* in a "gym", hatch eggs by traveling a certain distance, get supplies (like *Pokéballs*) from *Pokéstops*, and so on. (as shown in Fig. 1)

Although a lot of AVG and gamified mobile Apps have been developed and researched for over two decades, few of them have successfully managed to (or have even considered to) engage players in a long-term commitment to facilitate or increase their PA [1]. *Pokémon Go* has a similar fate: the initial interest has not been sustainable and there has been a significant drop off in levels of engagement since its release. Nevertheless, recent data from Microsoft shows that the game can help to increase PA by around 25% [8].

3   Research Methodology: Exploring Players' Motivation and Play Patterns

An online questionnaire designed to explore *Pokémon Go* players' motivation and to identify player patterns was circulated among players through emails, flyers and online websites (such as *Facebook*).

3.1   Participants

Of the forty participants who took part in this study, thirty-two completed the survey. Therefore, incomplete data from the other 8 surveys were removed. The ages of the thirty-two participants ranged from 19-35 (as shown in Table 1), and sixteen were female. Nineteen were university undergraduates, graduates, faculty members and staff. The other thirteen reported holding jobs that varied from cook and chef to UI designer, game developer, cashier, pharmacist, office jobs, and a medical assistant. Most participants were from Canada, and a few from China and the U.S.

Table 1. Participants' age distribution.

Age range	Amount of people
19–24	19
25–29	7
30–34	4
>35	2

Figure 2 shows the number of hours per week players spent on playing *Pokémon Go*, other mobile games, and video games. Most participants devoted more time to playing *Pokémon Go* than other video games or mobile games. Among all frequencies, most *Pokémon Go* players spent more than 10 h per week on the game. For instance, from the table, sixteen people spent 10–20 h playing *Pokémon Go* and ten even spent more than 20 h playing it. However, only seven people were willing to spend more than 10 h to play other mobile games, and three to play video games.

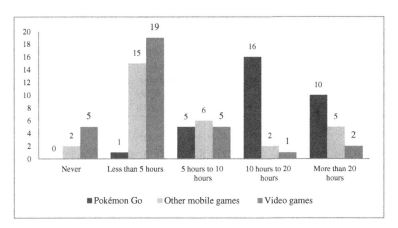

Fig. 2. Participants' weekly hours playing *Pokémon Go*, other mobile games, and PC/console video games.

3.2 Research Instrument and Questionnaire

In the online survey, the participants selected three of the most significant reasons motivating them to play the game, three things they like and dislike most about the game, and three reasons they stopped playing the game (if applicable) from options listed. Table 2 shows some sample answers and options the online survey provided. Moreover, questions regarding *When, Where, and with Whom* were asked. Other questions included: participants' self-reported PA changes, connections with others, chances meeting new people, and time holding cell phones on a 100 Visual Analog Scale. At the end, one open question was asked: what motivates/impresses you most when playing this game?

Table 2. Sample answers participants chose from in the survey questions.

Questions	Optional answers provided
"Three reasons i play *Pokémon Go*"	a. I want to collect the *Pokémons* b. I like the *Pokémon* anime c. People around me are playing and I want to have common topics d. I can have more physical activities e. Nothing particular, just to kill time f. I can meet new people in the gyms/*Pokéstops* g. Other, please specify…
"Three reasons i stop playing *Pokémon Go*"	a. Friends stop playing b. Phone battery, data usage, Internet access or software bugs c. Catch all *Pokémons* d. Cost too much time e. Game gets repetitive f. Hackers g. Other, please specify…
"Three things i like most about *Pokémon Go*"	a. I like the mobile Augmented Reality environment b. I enjoy chasing down *Pokémons* c. Placing the LURE mode and attract *Pokémons* to the *Pokéstops* d. I like hatching eggs using my physical activity data e. I like to collect all the medals, such as Breeder, Ace trainer, etc f. I enjoy the social accessibility of this game, the way I can interact with others g. I like to battle with others in the gyms h. Other, please specify…
"Three things i dislike most about *Pokémon Go*"	a. Embedded players in the gym b. Catching almost the same *Pokémons* c. Simple and Repetitive game mechanis d. Phone battery, data usage, and Internet access or software bugs e. Time-consuming f. Other, please specify…

4   Results

From the results, we have learned the top three ranked motivations, three reasons that stop players from playing, and three game mechanics or features they liked and disliked.

Why play *Pokémon Go*?
Out of all participants, collecting Pokémon ranked first as the players' primary motivation, while the social purpose ranked second, and nostalgia of the *Pokémon* animé ranked third.

Why stop playing *Pokémon Go*?
The main reason players reported that they stopped playing the game was that they caught all *Pokémons*. The second reason participants chose was that the game requires a lot of physical activity and thus too much time and energy.

What do the players like most about *Pokémon Go*?
The three game elements that the subjects liked most were catching *Pokémons* in an AR environment, *Pokéstops* mapped into real-world landmarks, and battling with others in the "gym".

What do the players dislike most about *Pokémon Go*?
The three things subjects disliked most about the game were: the simple *Pokémon-catching* game mechanic (throwing balls); little variation (such as repeated *Pokémons*); and hardware and software problems (bugs, battery, network, etc.).

Regarding when they usually played the game, seven subjects answered "only in transit", sixteen said "leisure time like lunch, or before or after work", and nine reported "any available time". In terms of whom they play *Pokémon Go* with, seventeen reported that they only played with their friends, coworkers or close ones; seven played alone; and eight said both alone and with friends.

These results reveal that the initiative of most players was to catch and collect all *Pokémons*, and that they enjoyed playing the game physically and virtually with others. Most preferred to play the game with people they are familiar with. Although AR was an attractive bonus, the simple game mechanics and repetitive game content led the players to quickly become bored.

For questions related to behavioral changes, most players thought the game kept them physically active (M = 73.13, SD = 19.65), and that playing *Pokémon Go* facilitated their connections with people around them (M = 64.08, SD = 18.16). A downside was that the majority of the participants reported they held their cell phones much longer than before (M = 74.29, SD = 30.79). For chances meeting new people, players held a neutral attitude and desire (M = 34.30, SD = 24.24).

However, many subjects left comments concerning safety and privacy issues, e.g., "*the game collects location data via GPS, so it is easy to track me down,*" "*sex offenders or robbers may take advantage of the Pokéstops,*" and "*there were four Pokéstops around my house that attract people (who) keep coming!*" As P16 reported in the survey, "*There was (the) pitfall of this game that I was catching Pokémons with my friend, standing on the middle of the street, and there was a homeless person that he claimed he got was HIV positive and needed money to buy food. My friend and I were in shock. .. that we worried that person might attack us or something; therefore, it is very important to be aware of your surroundings while playing Pokémon Go.*"

5 Discussion and Conclusion

We can conclude that an AR game with gamification approaches – rewards from *Pokéstops*, collections of *Pokémons*, social interaction (in the gyms) – did encourage players' physical and emotional activity in positive ways. As P28 mentioned in answering the open question, "Pokémon Go *is doing a great educational work by encouraging young generations to go to outdoors and exploring the real world.*"

Although not the primary motivation, *Pokémon Go's* social power should not be underestimated. Players who are friends or co-workers get together to "go hunting" the lovely monsters. Players are not only socially networking, but more importantly, are sharing a common hobby, which may enhance their emotional resonance or sense of belonging. As P05 mentioned, "*I remember once I went to Metrotown with my friend to have a dinner. I saw there were at least 50 people all around the gound where the Pokéstops were, and hoping to catch some Pokémons. I had never ever seen so (many) people outside before the game came out. At that moment, I felt the* Pokémon Go *has changed our daily life. People usually do not go outside. (They) tend to walk more because they want to catch all the Pokémons. Most importantly, I saw people gather together talking when they were at the Pokéstops catching Pokémons.*" Also said by P25, "*When friends point out there is a rare Pokémon nearby, you want to go with them and catch it together.*"

However, there are also a few problematic aspects of this game. In the game, monetary aspects can generate negative effects, as P08 observed, "*it is not fair that people buy lures to catch more Pokémons.*" The simple and limited game features also may reduce the fun, especially over time. This may render long-term motivation unsustainable. Moreover, players have safety and privacy concerns playing the game because of its location-based feature.

The top-ranked motivation to play was attributed to collecting all *Pokémons*, so players may drop out of the game once they fulfill this goal. For example, P01 reported, "*I noticed that a Pikachu was nearby. Usually, I would not go out of my way to catch Pokémon, but since it was rare, I wanted to catch it. I was motivated to walk around the mall to find it.*" But what will happen after P01 catches all *Pokémons* if her/his motivation was to be physically active? In other words, what are the roles of internal motivation, compared to external motivation [5], such as chasing *Pokémons*? Further, if one of the motivations to play *Pokémon Go* is nostalgia, what is the role of nostalgia over time? Similarly, most subjects reported they learned of the game from their friends, installed it, and started to fall in love with the game. To what degree is their "love" for the game attributable to nostalgia, social conformity or cohesion, or sheer novelty (a fad)? Therefore, although this game may act as a catalyst for networking, over time, it may also prove to be a short-term novelty or provoke unintended social and safety problems.

Because this research was conducted from September to October 2016 (a month after the game's launch), a novel effect may have been at play. Other limitations include: (1) it is a global game, but most of the participants were from a few countries mentioned in Sect. 3.1; (2) players self-reported the ratings of their behavioral changes, however, longer term (more than 6-month) observations with concrete data are necessary to assess "change"; (3) a larger participant population will likely elicit more data and greater insights; and (4) the game's popularity may be a short-lived phenomenon.

Overall, benefits reported by players were increased exercise, social connectivity, and outdoor activity. However, players cited concerns about safety, privacy, and time commitment, and some found the game mechanics wanting. Ironically, although players' increased their PA by playing the game, they spent the same amount of time looking at their phones instead of at non-augmented, real-world environments.

Conflict of Interest Statement
The authors declare that there are no conflicts of interest with the *Pokémon Go* App or the company, and this study is for research purpose only.

Acknowledgement. We thank all of the players who participated in this research and we thank Natural Sciences and Engineering Research Council of Canada (NSERC) for funding this study.

References

1. Baranowski, T.: Pokémon Go, go, go, gone? Games Health J. **5**, 293–294 (2016)
2. Williamson, J.W.: Will the 'Pokémon' be heroes in the battle against physical inactivity? Sports Exerc. Med. Open J. **2**(1), 13–14 (2016)
3. Fanning, J., Mullen, S.P., McAuley, E.: Increasing physical activity with mobile devices: a meta-analysis. J. Med. Internet Res. **14**(6), 161 (2012)
4. Serino, M., Cordrey, K., McLaughlin, L., Milanaik, R.L.: Pokémon Go and augmented virtual reality games: a cautionary commentary for parents and pediatricians. Curr. Opin. Pediatr. **28**(5), 673–677 (2016)
5. Tong, X., Gromala, D., Shaw, Chris D., Choo, A.: A field study: evaluating gamification approaches for promoting physical activity with motivational models of behavior changes. In: Kurosu, M. (ed.) HCI 2016. LNCS, vol. 9733, pp. 417–424. Springer, Cham (2016). doi:10.1007/978-3-319-39513-5_39
6. Pokémon GO™. http://www.pokemongo.com/. Accessed 3 Feb 2017
7. Flintham, M., Benford, S., Anastasi, R., Hemmings T., Cabtree, A., Greenhalgh, C., Tandavanitj, N., Adams, M., Row-Farr, J.: Where on-line meets on the streets: experiences with mobile mixed-reality games. In: Proceedings of the SIGCHI Conference on Human Factors in Computing Systems, pp. 569–576 (2003)
8. Althoff, T., White, R.W., Horvitz, E.: Influence of Pokémon go on physical activity: study and implications. J. Internet Res. **18**(12), 315 (2016)
9. LeBlanc, A.G., Chaput, J.-P.: Pokemon Go: a game changer for the physical inactivity crisis? J. Prev. Med. http://www.sciencedirect.com/science/article/pii/S0091743516303656. Accessed 3 Feb 2017
10. Clark, A.M., Clark, M.T.G.: Pokémon Go and research. editorial letter in qualitative, mixed methods research, and the supercomplexity of interventions (2016). doi:10.1177/1609406916667765
11. Lovelace, B., Jr.: Pokemon Go Now the Biggest Mobile Game in US History [WWW Document] CNBC (2016). http://www.cnbc.com/2016/07/13/pokemon-go-now-the-biggest-mobile-game-in-us-history.html. Accessed 3 Feb 2017

Making Fun of Failures Computationally

Alessandro Valitutti$^{(\boxtimes)}$

Dipartimento di Informatica, Università degli Studi di Bari, Bari, Italy
alessandro.valitutti@gmail.com

Abstract. We discuss ideas and propose resources on humor facilitation, as an extension of previous work on this topic. Specifically, we describe a method for achieving humor facilitation as the combination of event detection and generation of funny comments. We focus on user's mistakes as the preferred unexpected and potentially humorous events. Moreover, we implemented an online testbed consisting of a humor facilitator and two interactive environments: a text editor and a video game. The system is meant to provide a tool for empirical evaluation of the proposed framework.

Keywords: Computational humor · Interactive humor · Humor facilitation · Humorous agents · Humorous mistakes

1 Introduction

Fail again. Fail better. — *Samuel Beckett*

In this paper, we discuss ideas and propose resources on humor facilitation. We refer to *humor facilitators* as computer programs capable of detecting potentially humorous events occurring in interactive environments and making them funny through the generation of appropriate comments.

In a previous work on this topic [23], we explored to what extent storytelling could be employed to display a humorous re-interpretation of an unexpected event. The case study showed the effectiveness of an appropriate comic re-interpretation, even though it did not provide a method for performing it from a larger class of interactive situations. One crucial issue is that the humorous re-interpretation of events is a creative process and, as such, knowledge hungry and time-consuming. The required offline process necessary to meet the time constraint would imply a massive effort in knowledge building and indexing. To study a way to overcome these limitations, we focus on user's mistakes as the preferred unexpected and potentially humorous events.

All complex interactive environments are sources of errors. Some action outcomes are to some degree unpredictable (e.g. if and when a required web page will be loaded). In other cases, the complexity of a technological environment contributes to the unpredictability (e.g. undesired autocompletion while typing a web address or a search query). Mistakes are good events for humor. They are unexpected because unwanted and not meant to occur often. In many types of

© Springer International Publishing AG 2017
N. Streitz and P. Markopoulos (Eds.): DAPI 2017, LNCS 10291, pp. 684–695, 2017.
DOI: 10.1007/978-3-319-58697-7_51

interactive programs, the possibility that something might go wrong is part of the design as well as the display of error messages. In other words, modeling the knowledge of user's mistakes is fairly straightforward since part of it is already embedded in the design of the interactive system. In this research, we do not care about mistakes by computer and instead focus on human mistakes as potentially humorous events. The reason is that an artificial agent, to be aware of its errors and to make fun of them, needs to be provided with self-monitoring capabilities not easy to be implemented with state-of-the-art resources. Self-ironic and deceptive agents are beyond the scope of this work.

Another reason for working on human mistakes is that the user can be addressed for being the cause of the undesired event and, thus, be playfully blamed for it. In this way, the humor facilitation can generate comments achieving a form of superiority humor. The user perceives that the computer is making fun of her. However, being mocked by a computer makes the mockery playful.

To have a tool for giving empirical support to the humor facilitation framework, we implemented an online testbed consisting of a humor facilitator and two interactive environments: a text editor and a video game. It is designed to make users perform simple tasks where they are likely to make mistakes. The agent can detect mistakes and, accordingly, gives different types of humorous feedback. The knowledge and linguistic resources underlying event detection and humorous commenting are made available to the research community.

The rest of the paper is organized as follows. In Sect. 2, we give an overview of humorous mistakes, irony, appropriateness, and humor facilitation. Section 3 describes the proposed approach for humor facilitation. We then describe the interactive testbed in Sect. 4. Finally, conclusive remarks and aimed future work are discussed in Sect. 5.

2 Background

2.1 Humorous Mistakes

For years Hofstadter and Moser [9] harvested thousands of examples of linguistic and action mistakes by humans. Started as a hobby, this activity gave them a deeper understanding of the cognitive mechanism underlying the generation of these type of errors. Speech mistakes such as malapropisms or spoonerisms reveal information about personality or cultural background and are often used to intentionally create comical effects [16,25].

Human mistakes are often hilarious, perhaps because they reveal the vulnerable nature of people and, thus, make observers feel entitled to laugh at them. The assumption of superiority theory is that we laugh about the misfortunes of others; it reflects our superiority. This theory can be found in the work of Plato, Aristotle, and Hobbes. Plato suggests that humor is a kind of malice towards those who are considered relatively powerless. Hobbes further explains that humans are in constant competition with each other, looking for the shortcomings of other persons. He views laughter as an expression of a sudden realization that we are better than others.

Superiority humor reflects on Bergson's idea of "mechanical inelasticity". According to it, people making mistakes are comic because their behavior is stereotyped. Their individuality is concealed, and they look *mechanical* and less human [2]. As rephrased by Nijholt, "like a machine, the body continues with what it is doing, it is unstoppable, until its owner is falling and realizing that rather than gazing at the stars he would have been better off with having noticed the banana peel lying on the street in front of him." [14].

Mistakes commonly occur in the usage of technological devices and, in particular, computer applications. In some cases, the mistakes are the consequence of an imperfect automatism build to simplify the execution of some task but introducing new sources of flows. A classical example is the autocompletion and autocorrection features for editing text with a smartphone or other computer devices[1] [22]. Typing text on a touchscreen smartphone or tablet is time consuming. The users tend to speed-up and without checking possible wrong autocorrection, and discover it only after they have already sent the message.

Newbies are more exposed to error making, but sometimes also experts may make silly mistakes, especially if they are tired or under pressure. Other potentially comic events are the effect of bad planning or partial knowledge of the environment. Cavazza et al. focused on this type of mistakes to formalize the corresponding mechanisms of comedy [5].

2.2   Irony

Irony and sarcasm are effective way to address human mistakes. Verbal irony is a rhetorical device in which the intended meaning of statements is different from (and typically opposite of) the literal meaning. Encyclopaedia Britannica defines verbal irony[2] as a "language device [...] in which the real meaning is concealed or contradicted by the literal meanings of the words". In his account of linguistic theories of irony, Wilson [24] emphasizes three frameworks as key steps. The first theoretical framework, coming from classical rhetoric, describes irony as a form of figurative communication. According to this interpretation, ironic meaning is detected by recipients through a process of inference from the literal meaning and its underlying grammatical structure. A limitation of this approach is that it does not give account of the several cases in which the literal content of the utterance is not sufficient to infer the ironic interpretation. An important theoretical change can be ascribed to Grice [7,8], which reframed irony as a pragmatic phenomenon and, as such, it should include the communicative intentions of the writer.

A more recent theoretical description was proposed by Sperber and Wilson [17], according to which an ironic utterance is characterized as "echoic". This term is used to mean that the utterance alludes to some previous remark or a

---

[1] An example website posting funny autocorrection mistakes is retrievable at: www.damnyouautocorrect.com – Retrieved 1 March 2017.

[2] http://www.britannica.com/EBchecked/topic/294609/irony - Retrieved 1 March 2017.

familiar fact, not necessarily expressed by the literal meaning. The intent is to convey a sort of dissociation respect to the fact being echoed. This particular attitude is, thus, the motivation to express a remark in an ironic way.

In the testbed described in Sect. 4, we implemented some of the above concepts for the generation of sarcastic comments as a humorous response to user's mistakes.

2.3 Appropriateness

According to Nijholt [12], appropriateness is what makes jokes or humorous remarks funny in conversational contexts. Appropriateness "does not only refer to the contents of the remark [...], but in particular on an assessment whether or not to produce the humorous utterance". Although this statement refers to the particular case of conversational interaction, we believe that it could be applied to a more general class of interactive humor. Moreover, it suggests the conceptual distinction between the generation of humorous text and its selection and communication on the basis of its appropriateness.

To be recognized as appropriate, a humorous message should satisfy a complex set of conditions, such as:

- **Timing.** The humorous message generated as a response to some event such as user's mistake should be communicated early enough to be perceived as causally-related to the event.
- **Semantic relatedness.** The humorous message should be semantically related to the target event. It should be *about* that event. For example, it could be a witty remark addressing the topic of the current conversation or commenting the event just occurred.
- **Humor genre.** The style of humor characterizing the message should be the most suitable for the current situation. For example, a sarcastic wit could be used to playfully blame someone for doing something wrong. On the other hand, a silly pun might be more effective in helping someone get distracted by something that worries her.
- **Social acceptance.** The message should not be offensive. For instance, it should not contain taboo words [21]. The capability to match this condition is related to the knowledge of the potential recipients.
- **Recipient's cognitive-affective state.** In principle, the message should not distract the recipient if she is performing some task-oriented activity, nor should be delivered if she is in a "negative" mood. In practice, an effective humorous message could be proactively capable of turning a bad mood into a positive one and increase motivation and concentration.

We call *temporal appropriateness* the first condition and *situational appropriateness* the remaining ones.

2.4 Humor Facilitation

A *humorous system* is a computer system capable creating a *humorous effect* (i.e., inducing laughter or other mirth-related responses). Examples of humorous systems are joke or puns generators [3,15,18–21]. This is, of course, extremely challenging to achieve in an interactive context such as a physical environment, whose dynamic behavior is to many degrees unpredictable and difficult to model and control.

To simplify the problem enough to address it with available technological resources, we focus on a particular type of interactive humorous system called *humor facilitator*. Figure 1 shows a taxonomy of interactive humorous systems, identified by the following distinctions:

– **Humorous Environments vs. Humorous Agents.** While in the former ones the humor effect is achieved through the interaction of humans with the environment, in the latter case the humor is provided by one or more autonomous entities capable of interacting with both the environment and its human inhabitants.
– **Comical Agents vs. Facilitators.** We preliminarily introduce the distinction between *actually humorous events* and *potentially humorous events*. An event can be considered *actually humorous* if it typically makes people laugh without any additional intervention. By contrast, an event is *potentially humorous* if it needs some external condition to become actually humorous. Examples of potentially humorous events are unexpected and surprising events. We call *comical agent* a humorous agent entirely responsible for the occurrence of a humorous event. Examples of this type are conversational agents producing knock-knock jokes or punning riddles, or pulling practical jokes. Here the interaction is generally planned in advance and based on the induction of stereotyped behaviors in the human participant. Any unexpected event or different behavior might cause the failure of the humorous script. On the other hand, a *humor facilitator* is defined by the capability to detect a potentially humorous event and make it actually humorous [11,13,23]. For example, it might deliver ironic comments about a situation, ridiculing it and, at the same time, creating a playful context.

There is empirical evidence that surprise is a mediator of humor response (i.e. without it there is no laughter) and playfulness is a moderator of humor (i.e. it makes surprise mirthful) [1]. It is widely accepted that humor is a risky process. A joke can be either hilarious or offensive according to the context or the recipient. Accordingly, the main goal of a humor facilitator should be to perform either mediation or moderation of the humor effect, correspondingly increasing both the probability that an event is perceived as humorous and the intensity of the humor appreciation.

The degree of effort required to a humor facilitator depends on the degree of humorousness of a given type of events, that is the probability of inducing the humor response. In other words, the less an event is potentially humorous, the more effort is needed from the humorous agent. On the other hand, highly

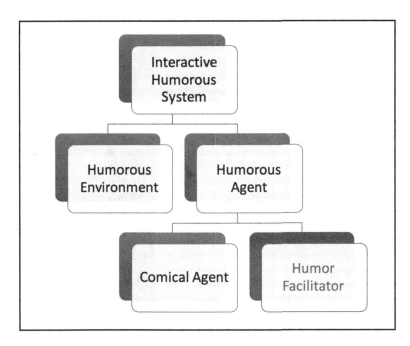

Fig. 1. Taxonomy of interactive humorous systems.

humorous events are rare and, to make them occur more often, a comical agent should intentionally provoke them.

As shown in Fig. 2, we identify three types of events, each associated to a different degree of potential humorousness. The first type consists of *typically funny* (as surprising and affectively charged) *events* (e.g. a baby wearing sunglasses). They make people look funny without the need of additional clues. In this case, the humor facilitation may be limited to just indicating the situation (e.g. through simulated laughter). In some cases, showing a funny event and the context as playful gives people the "permission to laugh". The second type includes *typically surprising but not necessarily funny* events (e.g. scary pranks). They can induce either positive or negative emotions, according to the context or the person's mood. In this case, the facilitation should consist of ways to create a playful context. Finally, the third type includes *not typically funny events* (e.g. signing a formal document). Here, to be effective, the facilitation should entail a higher creative effort to present the event in a funny perspective, as in the photo at the bottom of Fig. 2.

The best type of candidate events for humor facilitation seems the second type (row 2 in Fig. 2). In fact, they have a good degree of potential humorousness but need some additional help to make the context perceived as playful (i.e., they need to be *positively moderated* by the facilitator). Moreover, they occur more frequently than events of type 2. Finally, they do not require the creative effort needed to reframe events of type 3 as funny.

Event Types	Examples	
Typically funny	*Baby wearing sunglasses*	
Typically Surprising but Not Necessarily Funny	*Scary prank*	
Not Necessarily Funny	*Donald Trump signing an official document*	
Re-Framed as Funny	*Donald Trump drawing as a child*	

Fig. 2. Three types of potentially humorous events.

3   Strategy for Humor Facilitation

Figure 3 illustrates the functional structure of a humor facilitator, which is achieved in two steps: (1) detection of a *potentially humorous event* (specifically, a human mistake) and (2) generation of an *appropriate humor-facilitation comment*.

Detection of the Potentially Humorous Event. There are several ways to perform this type of event detection. One possibility is to monitor user's

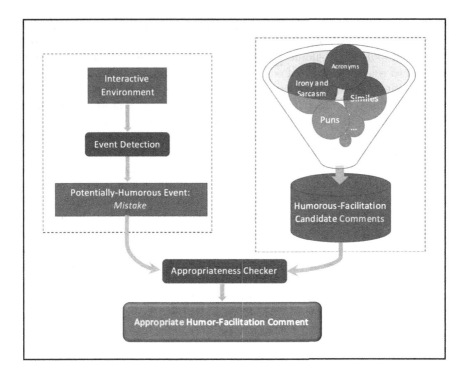

Fig. 3. Main components of the proposed approach to humor facilitation.

behavior. For example, if the user is using an editing software, she might cancel some wrong edit or press the "Undo" key. If the user is interacting with an online community, the mistake might be detected from the comments by other members. A third source of information about possible mistakes is in the design and code of interactive programs and, specifically, in the instructions for the generation of error messages.

Generation of the Appropriate Humor-Facilitation Comment. Once detected the candidate event, the agent selects and communicates the message aimed to achieve the humorous effect. The event is matched against a repository of one-liners (either collected from textual corpora or computer-generated), in order to select the best one according to the conditions of appropriateness listed in Sect. 2.3.

To achieve situational appropriateness, the system should perform measurements of semantic relatedness between the target event and the set of candidate comments. In particular, it could employ distributional-semantics techniques such as Latent Semantic Analysis (LSA) [6] or Latent Dirichlet Allocation [4]. If available, a module for sentiment analysis or opinion mining [10] could be used not only to check not only if the comment is "about" the target event, but also if it expresses the wanted sentiment about it. Finally, if the message satisfies the conditions for appropriateness, it is identified as humorously appropriate and, thus, delivered to the human recipient. If not, the system will continue listening for a new potentially-humorous event. The information about the events is also useful to select the type of comment and the corresponding type of humor (e.g. to decide to what extent aggressive humor should be acceptable). To this aim, the capability to modeling the cognitive and affective state of the human recipient and its social background would be a considerable help.

To satisfy the temporal appropriateness condition, the comment should be delivered within a specific time interval after the event occurrence. The temporal threshold should be fixed in advance and related to the particular type of humorous effect to achieve. In most cases, it should be communicated as soon as possible. Sometimes, by contrast, a delayed remark could be more effective. For example, comments like *"Did you see what just happened?"* or *"Did you really do that?"* (or their equivalent one-liners) might play with the possibility that the human recipient is not aware to have made a mistake or is trying to hide it. However, the best way to achieve an effective timing is to perform, whenever possible, an "offline" check of the appropriateness conditions for a class of potentially occurring events, and a corresponding indexing of the database of humorous comments.

4   Testbed

We implemented the humor-facilitation strategy, described in the previous section, as an interactive web service[3]. This system is made available to researchers that intend to perform empirical studies of the connection between humor facilitation and human response. It is meant to be a modular system to be enriched over time with additional functionalities. The current version consists of two environments and a humor facilitator. In each environment, the user can perform simple tasks and read instruction and comments sent by the agent.

The first environment is an editable text field, where the user can write or modify a document in English. Possible tasks are free writing or answering questions. A second text field is used to show the messages from the agent. Possible user's mistakes are typing wrong English words (in the *free-writing task*) or wrong answers (in the *question-answering* task).

The second environment is a simple video game called *Basketball Shot*. It consists of a ballistic launcher, shown in the left-bottom corner of a canvas. Clicking on it, a ball is launched toward the basket on the opposite side. With the help of a slider, the player can modify the orientation of the launch. The possible user's mistake is, of course, missing the basket. Since the system can calculate the trajectory of the ball while it is on the way, the agent can make comments even before the mistake has occurred.

To increase the probability of mistakes, we use a simple, non-deceptive trick: the task is temporally constrained, and a countdown timer is shown in the corner

---

[3] The system can be accessed at http://valitutti.it/papers/hcii-2017/index.html.

of both environments. The tasks are constrained in such a way they can hardly be achieved before it is game over. In a first version of the system, we introduced subtle forms of deception. Later on, however, we decided to remove this feature, to maintain the focus on humor facilitation. In fact, the deceptive behavior makes the system more recognizable as a comical agent than as a humor facilitator (according to the distinction discussed in Sect. 3).

The generation of humor-facilitation comments is designed according to available resources and two central research questions. The first research question is to what extent the combination of state-of-the-art verbal-humor generation and semantic relatedness are sufficient to increase the humorousness of the event significantly. To achieve situational appropriateness, we require that the outputs of the generator contain at least one word semantically related to the words describing the event. In the specific case of mistakes, their nature suggests generating "valenced comments" expressing an evaluative content. Accordingly, we provided the system with the capability to produce different types of valenced comments: (1) *plain comments* represented by error messages or performance scores, (2) *affectively charged comments* expressing either disdain or solidarity, and (3) *sarcastic comments*, apparently praising the user but actually blaming her (e.g. "*Well done!*", "*I am glad you can accomplish such a difficult task so easily...*", or "*You're as capable as a horse to create French cuisine.*").

5   Conclusions

In this paper, we propose two changes of perspective on interactive humor and, correspondingly, the way to design it. First, we shift the focus from *humorous texts* to *humorous events*. Second, we do not consider *humorousness* as an intrinsic property of events. Rather, we view it as the degree to which an event can be made funny through humor facilitation. In other words, what is meant to be funny is not the event alone, or the agent's comment alone, but the event-comment pair. For this reason, a central role is played by the categorization of events according to a prefixed number of event types (e.g. surprising events, mistakes, emotional events, etc.). Each category should be associated to a corresponding level of potential humorousness and a corresponding type of humor facilitation. We specifically focus on human mistakes as potentially humorous events because they are often sources of hilarity and tend to induce funny comments. Therefore, the most natural corresponding types of humor-facilitation comments employ irony and sarcasm.

As a future work, we aim to extend the knowledge base underlying the generation of humor-facilitation comments to represent not only potentially-humorous events but also potentially funny personality types. They would enable the system to produce sarcastic comments evoking ridiculous traits of people. The distinction between humor facilitator and comical agent is another key aspect of this work. Humor facilitators are intended to react to unpredictable events, while comical agents are supposed to plan and provoke them purposefully. If employed in complex environments, the achievement of humor facilitation seems to be more feasible. Above all, the view behind humor facilitation helps us to believe that funny things are already there. We only need to see them with different eyes.

References

1. Alden, D.L., Mukherjee, A., Hoyer, W.D.: The effects of incongruity, surprise and positive moderators on perceived humor in television advertising. J. Advertising **29**(2), 1–15 (2000)
2. Bergson, H.: Laughter: an Essay on the Meaning of the Comic. Macmillan, London (1911)
3. Binsted, K., Pain, H., Ritchie, G.: Children's evaluation of computer-generated punning riddles. Pragmatics Cogn. **2**(5), 305–354 (1997)
4. Blei, D.M., Ng, A.Y., Jordan, M.I.: Latent dirichlet allocation. J. Mach. Learn. Res. **3**, 993–1022 (2003)
5. Cavazza, M., Charles, F., Mead, S.J.: Generation of humorous situations in cartoons through plan-based formalisations. In: Proceedings of the ACM CHI-2003 Workshop: Humor Modeling in the Interface, University of Twente, Fort Lauderdale, FL (2003)
6. Deerwester, S., Dumais, S.T., Furnas, G.W., Landauer, T.K., Harshman, R.: Indexing by latent semantic analysis. J. Am. Soc. Inf. Sci. **41**(6), 391–407 (1990)
7. Grice, H.P.: Logic and conversation. William James Lectures, pp. 1–143. Harvard University (1967). Reprinted in: Grice, H.P. (1989)
8. Grice, H.P.: Studies in the Way of Words. Harvard University Press, Cambridge (1989)
9. Hofstadter, D., Moser, D.J.: To err is human; to study error-making is cognitive science. Mich. Q. Rev. **28**(2), 185–215 (1989)
10. Munezero, M., Montero, S.C., Sutinen, E., Pajunen, J.: Are they different? affect, feeling, emotion, sentiment, and opinion detection in text. IEEE Trans. Affect. Comput. **5**(2), 101–111 (2014)
11. Nijholt, A.: Conversational agents and the construction of humorous acts. In: Nishida, T. (ed.) Conversational Informatics: an Engineering Approach, chap. 2, pp. 21–47. Wiley, Chicester (2007)
12. Nijholt, A.: Conversational agents, humorous act construction, and social intelligence. In: Proceedings AISB 2005: Social Intelligence and Interaction in Animals, Robots and Agents. Symposium on Conversational Informatics for Supporting Social Intelligence and Interaction. University of Hertfordshire (2005)
13. Nijholt, A.: Towards humor modelling and facilitation in smart environments. In: Ahram, T., Karwowski, W., Marek, T. (eds.) Proceedings of the 5th International Conference on Applied Human Factors and Ergonomics (AHFE 2014), Krakow, Poland, pp. 2992–3006, July 2014
14. Nijholt, A.: Incongruity humor in language and beyond: from bergson to digitally enhanced worlds. In: 14th International Symposium on Social Communication, Santiago de Cuba, Cuba, pp. 594–599, 19–23 January 2015
15. Raskin, V., Attardo, S.: Non-literalness and non-bona-fide in language: approaches to formal and computational treatments of humor. Pragmatics Cogn. **2**(1), 31–69 (1994)
16. Ross, A.: The Language of Humor. Taylor & Francis, Abingdon (1998)

17. Sperber, D., Wilson, D.: Irony and the use-mention distinction. In: Cole, P. (ed.) Radical Pragmatics, pp. 295–318. Academic Press, New York (1981)

18. Stock, O., Strapparava, C.: HAHAcronym: Humorous agents for humorous acronyms. In: Stock, O., Strapparava, C., Nijholt, A. (eds.) Proceedings of the April Fools Day Workshop on Computational Humour (TWLT20), Trento, Italy (2002)

19. Tinholt, H.W., Nijholt, A.: Computational humour: utilizing cross-reference ambiguity for conversational jokes. In: Masulli, F., Mitra, S., Pasi, G. (eds.) WILF 2007. LNCS, vol. 4578, pp. 477–483. Springer, Heidelberg (2007). doi:10.1007/978-3-540-73400-0_60

20. Valitutti, A.: How many jokes are really funny? Towards a new approach to the evaluation of computational humour generators. In: Proceedings of 8th International Workshop on Natural Language Processing and Cognitive Science, Copenhagen (2011)

21. Valitutti, A., Doucet, A., Toivanen, J.M., Toivonen, H.: Computational generation and dissection of lexical replacement humor. Nat. Lang. Eng. 1–23 (2015)

22. Valitutti, A., Toivonen, H., Gross, O., Toivanen, J.M.: Decomposition and distribution of humorous effect in interactive systems. In: Artificial Intelligence of Humor, AAAI Fall Symposium Series, Arlington, Virginia, USA, pp. 96–100, November 2012

23. Valitutti, A., Veale, T.: Infusing humor in unexpected events. In: Proceedings of the 4rd International Conference on Distributed, Ambient and Pervasive Interactions, HCI International, Toronto, Canada, 17–22 July 2016

24. Wilson, D.: The pragmatics of verbal irony: Echo or pretence? Lingua **116**, 1722–1743 (2006)

25. Zwicky, A.: Classical malapropisms and the creation of the mental lexicon. In: Obler, L., Menn, L. (eds.) Exceptional Language and Linguistics, pp. 115–132. Academic Press, Cambridge (1982)

I Read the News Today, Oh Boy

Making Metaphors Topical, Timely and Humorously Personal

Tony Veale[✉], Hanyang Chen, and Guofu Li

School of Computer Science and Informatics, University College Dublin,
Belfield, Dublin 4, Ireland
Tony.Veale@UCD.ie, Hanyang.Chen@ucdconnect.ie

Abstract. Human speakers do not create metaphors in a vacuum. Our rhetorical urges are tempered by a variety of contextual factors, such as *ethos* (does a metaphor reflect my values?), *relevance* (does a metaphor speak to my topic?), *timeliness* (is this a good time to use this metaphor?) and *affect* (does this metaphor stir the desired emotions in my audience?). The 24-h news cycle offers an ideal setting in which to explore automated metaphor generation that is both timely and topical, as not only do journalists rely on pithy metaphors to attract readers, readers often respond to the news with wittily apt, conversation-sparking metaphors of their own. Indeed, as micro-blogging platforms such as Twitter provide digital printing presses for the masses that also allow us to turn our lives and opinions into 140-character headlines, we can use computational techniques to craft personalized metaphors that suit a specific human recipient. In this paper we explore metaphor generation techniques that are shaped for a specific topical context, using approaches to topic modeling such as Latent Dirichlet Allocation, or that reflect the online personality of a specific recipient, as evidenced by their most recent emations or *tweets*. Each approach is instantiated in an autonomous *Twitterbot*, a system that creates and tweets its own content without human curation. We use Twitterbots to study the potential for humour to arise from the timely online interaction of humans and machines.

Keywords: Metaphor · Topicality · Affect · Personality · News · Humour · Twitter

1 Metaphor Mirror on the Wall

We want the news to hold up a mirror to world events, yet we are not so naïve as to expect this mirror to be without bias or distortion. For the news does more than *report*: it shapes our view of events, by telling us where to look, what to see and of times what to *think*. So to readers at one end of the political spectrum, the news emanating from the opposing end can resemble the reflection of a funhouse mirror, leading readers to seek out those providers whose biases and distortions accord with their own. For a balanced view of world events, we can obtain our news from diverse sources, yet jumping between providers of very different orientation or register on the Web can be a jarring source of cognitive dissonance. Nonetheless, to have one's tacit expectations of the news and of

© Springer International Publishing AG 2017
N. Streitz and P. Markopoulos (Eds.): DAPI 2017, LNCS 10291, pp. 696–709, 2017.
DOI: 10.1007/978-3-319-58697-7_52

newsmakers laid bare in this way is also a source of insight that occasionally rises to the level of what Koestler (1964) calls a *bisociation*.

Reporters use metaphor to concisely frame current events from a certain affective perspective. Thus, to say that *"Google's halo has been tarnished"* by recent events is to suggest that many – perhaps the company itself – see Google as a "saint", while to say that *"Oracle's crown has slipped"* is to portray the company as the key player in its field. Such metaphors achieve a subtle coercion, insomuch as they presuppose much more than they are willing to put into words. To *break set* and see beyond any particular framing, we must challenge our received metaphors to invent counter-metaphors (and script oppositions) of our own. This is what it means to engage with the news: not to uncritically treat headlines as bundles of propositions to be added to our individual stores of knowledge, but to imagine how events might look if framed from an opposing perspective. When we debate the news with colleagues and friends, we rely as much on metaphors as on facts to examine our feelings and reach our own conclusions. Lakoff and Johnson (1980) have persuasively championed a conceptual view of metaphor that sees most linguistic metaphors as surface elaborations of deep conceptual schemas such as *Argument is War*, *Life is a Journey*, *Politics is a Game* and *Theories are Buildings*, and it is natural for readers to respond with elaborations of these schemas whenever they underpin the meaning of a headline. Yet the most challenging metaphors are those that use a different conceptual schema, to show that there are multiple sides to the same story, more than a single headline or news source can show. In this paper we set ourselves the task of creating metaphors for incoming headlines on Twitter, so that the news offerings of *@nytimesworld*, *@FOXnews* and *@CNNbrk* can be automatically paired with original metaphors that prompt readers to imagine different, perhaps humorously different, viewpoints on the same story.

Like jokes, metaphors thrive on semantic tension, both in themselves (between *source* and *target* domains) and between the metaphors themselves and their contexts of use. A challenging metaphor should be apt yet surprising, and exhibit what Attardo (2001) calls *relevant inappropriateness* or what Oring (2003) calls *appropriate incongruity*. Ideally, the pairing of metaphor to headline should create what Koestler (1964) calls a *bisociation*, a jarring but meaningful clash of overlapping frames of reference. Pollio (1996) suggests that while persuasive metaphors successfully hide the rift between source and target domains, jokes draw our attention to this rift and revel in its potential to swallow rational thought. We aim for the machine-generated metaphors selected by *@MetaphorMirror*, a Twitterbot that pairs novel metaphors to incoming news headlines, to achieve both of these ends: to appear appropriate to their contexts of use while also hinting at the conflicts of ideas and worldviews that lurk behind the news. Consider the following pairing of metaphor to headline that was tweeted by our Twitterbot *@MetaphorMirror* on the day Fidel Castro died:

The stronger the language of the metaphor, the more humorous the perceived opposition with its target headline. Consider this metaphorical take on the news:

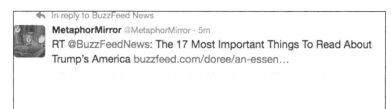

Metaphors such as these can be generated using a hybrid knowledge-driven and data-driven approach that relies on a mix of symbolic and statistical knowledge. In the case above, symbolic knowledge is used to establish and then pithily articulate the overlap between the concepts *Brute*, *Brawler* and *Boor*, while statistical knowledge is needed to map this textual formulation to a headline about the president-elect Donald Trump. Specifically, a robust statistical approach to topic modelling is required to see the non-literal similarities between Mr. Trump specifically – a man whose aggressive and boorish manners are the subject of many newspaper articles, among them those that actually support his agenda – and the stereotypical idea of a brute in a bar brawl. Our goal in this paper is to describe the workings of this hybrid model and to show how the pairing of the topically literal and the metaphorically apt can give rise to script oppositions that are both timely and humorous.

With these goals in mind, the rest of the paper assumes the following structure: Sect. 2 considers the automated generation of metaphors, showing how the creation process must combine rote knowledge with inspiration; Sect. 3 explores the news domain, to model the news as its own conceptual space that can be mapped, via a characterization of topics, onto the space of machine-generated metaphors; Sect. 4 then describes @*MetaphorMirror*, a creative bot that applies this mapping to Twitter news; Sect. 5 presents an empirical evaluation of @*MetaphorMirror*'s pairings of metaphors to headlines; and finally, Sect. 6 shows this approach to topical metaphor generation can be extended to look beyond the content of the major news providers to the emanations of prolific individuals, such as @*realDonaldTrump*. From there we show that our metaphors need not always be keyed to the topics of a news feed, and can instead be formulated to suit the online personalities of individual Twitter users.

2 Metaphors: Shaped by Knowledge and Inspired by Data

The cleverest metaphors are for naught if they cannot be understood by their intended audience, and so it makes good communicative sense to view metaphor generation and interpretation as flip sides of the same process of creative meaning-making. It makes just as much computational sense for us to model automated generation as the flip side of automated interpretation, and to simply apply existing theories of metaphor interpretation *in reverse* so as to allow machines to create novel metaphors of their own. A recent survey by Veale *et al.* (2016) divides computational theories into four interpretation-oriented groupings: the *corrective*, typified by Wilks (1978) and Fass (1991), see metaphor as a semantic anomaly from which an interpretation system must recover a non-anomalous meaning; the *categorial*, typified by Way (1991) and Glucksburg (1998), see metaphor as enlarging one's category system by finding a new place in a new category for an idea exhibitingkey features of that category; the *analogical*, typified by Gentner *et al.* (1989) & Veale and O'Donoghue (2000), who posit that the chasis of a sound metaphor is a structure-mapping analogy between two domains; and the *schematic*, as typified by Lakoff and Johnson (1980), Carbonell (1981) and Hobbs (1981), who see metaphors as surface manifestations of deeper conceptual metaphors which are, in turn, anchored in embodied conceptual schemas for the mind, for emotions, for purposeful action and so on.

Each of these types of approach, though chiefly focused on metaphor interpretation, can in principle be applied to the problem of metaphor generation. For instance, Shutova (2010) presents a statistical approach to metaphor interpretation by paraphrasing, wherein an unconventional metaphorical form is rewritten in more conventional language (e.g. "she *swallowed* her anger" becomes "she *suppressed* her anger"). Though largely corrective, many of the same statistical mechanisms can be applied in reverse to paraphrase normative language using *less* conventional phrasing (e.g., see also Harmon 2015). Veale and Li (2013) present a means of building the kind of dynamic, fine-grained category hierarchy presupposed in the theories of Way and Glucksberg, using information extraction from the web to achieve the necessary scale and diversity. They also demonstrate the utility of their web service, named *Thesaurus Rex*, for understanding *and* generating metaphors via category membership norms. Veale and Li (2011) further show how propositions can be extracted from the *why do* questions that are found in the query logs of popular search engines (or in the query completions offered by these engines), and demonstrate how analogical mapping can be performed over this structured content. Though the most potent schematic structures of Lakoff and Johnson's (1980) conceptual theory have been inventoried in the *Master Metaphor List* (Lakoff 1994), it is also possible to extract commonplace schemas using automated corpus analysis (e.g. see Mason 2004 and, to a lesser extent, Harmon 2015). Veale (2015) uses the Google n-grams (Brants and Franz 2006) to find *is-a* statements with the potential to serve as schemas (such as the 4-gram *"crime* is a *disease")* and uses a mix of property-level knowledge (from Veale and Hao 2007), propositional content (from Veale and Li 2011) and taxonomic structures (from Veale and Li 2013) to filter and instantiate these *pseudo*-schemas in novel but meaningful metaphors.

Reiter and Dale (2006) argue that the generation of complex natural-language artifacts requires two levels of planning: macro-planning (what is it I want to say?) and micro-planning (how do I go about saying it?). While cleaving to this dichotomy, Veale (2015) uses three levels of planning: the *macro*-level (what is the main conceit of the metaphor?); the *macro-micro* (how is this conceit elaborated in a propositional form?); and the micro-level (how is this propositional form to be rendered in English?). As the metaphors in question are to be tweeted by an automated Twitterbot without human curation, the *macro-micro* and *micro* levels explicitly concern themselves with a search for propositions and for linguistic forms that will ultimately yield a pithy remark that can be rendered in 140 characters of less. Veale (2015) describes this search as a language game (a "game of tropes") and describes a Twitterbot named @*Metaphor-Magnet* that employs a wide range of tropes and rhetorical strategies (on the order of 40) to achieve a diversity of outputs that the bot's followers will find interesting and *re*-tweetable.

As @*MetaphorMagnet* uses the Google n-grams to guide its macro-level planning, and uses its various databases of stereotypical properties and behaviours to filter and elaborate its macro plans into workable semantic forms, its designers claim its actions are inspired by data but shaped by knowledge. Consider the following output from @*MetaphorMagnet* (all of whose outputs are visible on Twitter):

> When it comes to the masterpieces they produce,
> some masters can be far from beloved and can be downright lonely.
> Lonely masters produce eerie masterpieces the way
> wolves produce howls. #Master = #Wolf #Masterpiece = #Howl

This double-tweet metaphor is sparked at the macro-level by the Google 2-gram *"eerie masterpieces"*, which prompts the planner to consider juxtaposing *masterpiece* with a known stereotype of *eeriness*. Finding *howl* in its database of stereotypical norms, the system searches the propositional contexts of *masterpiece* and *howl* to find an analogy that can cleanly map one context onto another. A concern for efficiency leads it to use predicate identicality as a matching criterion (Gentner *et al.* 1989), and so the propositions *produce*(masters, masterpieces) and *produce*(wolves, howls) are found to meet this basic requirement for a well-formed analogy. But the analogy is favored for another important reason: as the system believes *masters* are typically *beloved* and *wolves* are typically *lonely*, the antonymy of *lonely* and *beloved* adds a savory dash of semantic tension to the mix. The resulting analogy, which is in part derived from a stereotypical *dis*-analogy, is then tweeted in two parts using the framing device above. The metaphor is inspired by the contingent observation that some masterpieces are *eerie* – this fact is not found in the system's own knowledge – and semantically well-formed due to the careful planning of the *macro-micro* level, yet any pragmatic resonances in the minds of readers are mostly unplanned. Precisely why a masterpiece is eerie in the same way as the howl of a lonely wolf is left to readers to answer. Perhaps each is an expression of a painful longing – to belong? to mate? to be recognized? – but whatever the reason, it is not one that the system feels compelled to share, or even to formulate.

The Google n-grams is also a rich source of pseudo-schemas – copula statements that suggest the equivalence of taxonomically remote ideas – such as *"research* is the *fruit"* (*freq* = 48). The following pair of successive tweets from *@MetaphorMagnet* shows how it can elaborate these "found" objects:

> Remember when research was conducted by prestigious philosophers? #Research = #Fruit
> Now, research is a fruit eaten only by lowly insects. #Philosopher = #Insect

This metaphor employs schematic reasoning in the mold of Lakoff and Johnson (1980) rather than the analogical mode championed by Gentner *et al.* (1989). The system's propositional knowledge informs it that *philosophers* (among others) conduct *research*, while *insects* (among others) eat *fruit*. This pair of propositions is favored over many other candidates because of the antonymy between *prestigious* (a stereotypical property of *philosophers*) and *lowly* (a stereotypical property of *insects*). Crucially then, and especially so for what follows next, the resulting metaphor rests on an incongruity that is made appropriate in a rhetorical setting that serves to yoke two opposing perspectives on its topic, *research*.

3   All the News That's Fit to Fingerprint: A Vector Space Approach

Systems such as *@MetaphorMagnet* generate their outputs in a vacuum, without regard for the context in which their metaphors will later be consumed by readers. There are sound reasons for treating a key generator of content as a black-box; for one, *@MetaphorMagnet* is a 3rd-party system of many moving parts that does not invite the low-level tinkering needed to make it context-sensitive to the news; for another, we want our contextualizing matcher to work with potentially many generators of metaphors in a mostly effortless plug-and-play fashion. Our focus then is on competence rather than performance. We do not view a metaphor generator as the sum of its procedural mechanisms, but as the sum total of the metaphors it is capable of delivering to the *@MetaphorMirror* system. We thus view the matching of contextless metaphors to contextual headlines as a cross-space mapping problem in which elements of one space, the space of headlines, are mapped to apt elements of another, the space of metaphors.

Let us first consider the headline space. News services cater for a diverse readership by segmenting their offerings along thematic lines. The standard topics – *Sport, Politics, Business, Culture*, etc. – are broad umbrella terms under which a great many stories can shelter. Such coarse-grained classifications serve a useful role in the organization of print newspapers and their online incarnations, but they lack sufficient granularity to support a nuanced mapping of arbitrary metaphors to arbitrary headlines. We can, however, use a topic model, such as *Latent Dirichlet Allocation* (Blei *et al.* 2003), to derive a large, fine-grained set of topics from a news corpus that better reflects the intuitive understanding of events that readers bring with them to a news story.

LDA views topics as probabilistic rather than discrete, and generative rather than post-hoc. In constructing a fixed set of tacit and unnamed topics to explain a particular document set – the precise number of topics is specified by the developer – LDA aims to find the best statistical explanation for the observed lexical similarities between texts in the document set. As any given text will exhibit degrees of affinity to n different topics, each topic constitutes a dimension in a vector space in which any text can be represented as an n-dimensional vector with a value for each of all n topics. For our news corpus we choose to build an LDA vector space of $n = 100$ topics. This corpus contains the full text and headlines of 380 thousand news stories from the Web, gathered between 2000 and 2012 from *Bloomberg* (6%), *Economist* (2%), the *Guardian* (12%), the *Huffington Post* (3%), the *Independent* (7%), the *Irish Times* (7%), the *New York Times* (12%), the *Telegraph* (9%), the *Washington Post* (8%), *Reuters* (4%) and *Yahoo News* (30%). To this corpus are added 210,000 news tweets from various sources on Twitter, including @*CNNbrk*, @*FOXnews*, @*WSJ* and @*nytimesworld*, harvested between July 2015 and June 2016. When building the LDA model (using the *gensim* implementation of Řehůřek and Sojka 2010), we used the concatenation of both the lemmatized forms and their POS tags as features of the words in each document for the model.

Let us now consider our metaphor space. As noted above, we employ an extensional rather than an intensional model of this space, and construct it much like our news space: as a large collection of metaphorical micro-texts. These figurative texts are provided by the creators of @*MetaphorMagnet*, who offer large quantities of machine-generated metaphors to other developers for research purposes. This corpus of 22,846,672 metaphors constitutes a wide-ranging sample of @*MetaphorMagnet*'s rhetorical mechanisms and linguistic framings. Once again we use a topic model to capture the tacit themes that recur across these metaphors. However, we do not build a separate topic model for metaphors, but instead build a joint vector space by merging our metaphor corpus with our news corpus. The goal is to accommodate news headlines and metaphors within the very same vector space using the very same topics as dimensions, so that a vector for any given news headline can be directly compared – using a cosine similarity measure – to the vector for any given metaphor. Our choice of the number pf topics is motivated by a desire to achieve an acceptable granularity of themes without encouraging the creation of splinter topics that serve to organize one or another type of content – news or metaphor – but not both together. The success of the joint space depends on the applicability of *all* dimensions to both kinds of content, so instances of each can be meaningfully and incisively compared.

4   *MetaphorMirror* on the Wall, What's the Most Topical Trope of All?

We use LDA to construct a common vector space in which metaphors can sit cheek-by-jowl with news headlines, but we could just as easily have used LSA (or *Latent Semantic Analysis*; see Landauer and Dumais 1997) or Word2Vec (see Mikolov 2013) to construct our joint space. Our requirements of this space are straightforward: every pre-generated metaphor (all 22,846,672 of them) should be pre-assigned an n-dimensional vector of normalized values (where $n = 100$) that reflect a metaphor's affinity to n latent topics or themes; these dimensions should be of equal relevance to metaphors and headlines, to foster the clustering of each kind of content in the same pockets of vector space; and each new headline should be quickly mapped to its own n-dimensional vector in the space as it arrives, so that it can be compared to all metaphors in the same vicinity of the space using a cosine-similarity measure. This is the matching mechanism at the heart of the *@MetaphorMirror* Twitterbot. As headlines arrive from a range of Twitter sources, such as *@CNNbrk*, *@FOXnews*, *@WSJ*, *@Reuters, @nytimesworld*, *@AP* and *@BBCbreaking*, each is reduced to a vector representation (using LDA as our default model) and this vector is compared to that of each metaphor in the space. For efficiency reasons the model *could* insist that each headline must share at least one content word with any metaphor to which it is compared, thus limiting the search for possible comparisons, but the nature of the application is such that an exhaustive search of the metaphor pool is feasible. *@MetaphorMirror* aims to tweet one metaphor/headline pairing per hour on average, and by foregoing the need for literal similarity between metaphor and headline the bot can produce content pairings with no lexical overlap at all.

A metaphor is paired with an incoming headline only if the cosine similarity of the two exceeds a minimum threshold, where the default setting of this threshold is 0.9. If no metaphor is found that exhibits this minimum similarity to the headline, no pairing of metaphor to headline is tweeted. There are other conditions under which the system will not produce a pairing. News organizations often tweet the same headline, or near variants thereof, multiple times in the same day; the system will not attempt to pair a metaphor with a headline that has already produced an earlier successful pairing. Likewise, the system strives to avoid repeating itself, and will not select a pairing involving a metaphor that was tweeted by the system in recent memory. If these concerns for repetition mean that no acceptable metaphor can exceed the threshold for an incoming headline, no pairing is produced or tweeted.

The following pairs a metaphor for demagoguery to a headline from *@FOXnews*:

 In reply to Fox News

MetaphorMirror @MetaphorMirror · 9h
RT @FoxNews: .@newtgingrich says "the country will become enraged" if the violent protests at @realDonaldTrump ...

What is a radical but a crusading demagogue?
What is a demagogue but a cynical radical?

What causes crusading radicals to give up crusades, to incite mobs and to become cynical demagogues?

Notice that the metaphor (which is attached as an image rather than a text string so as not to exceed the 140 character limit on tweets) exhibits no lexical overlap with the arriving headline, yet the LDA topic analysis captures the essential similarity between violent political protest and the actions of a cynical demagogue. Because our vector space is distilled from a wide-ranging corpus of news stories in which stereotypical beliefs influence lexical choice, LDA's latent topics allow these implicit stereotypes to guide the selection of metaphors. For example, the bot tweeted the following metaphor on the death of boxer Muhammad Ali, a graceful fighter who became famous for his mantra "dance like a butterfly": dreams, weightless butterflies that you are, how you charm me with your free illusion. Other stereotypes that guide our appreciation of the news, and of a reporter's choice of words and conceits, also exert an influence on the selection of apt metaphors through the dimensions of the LDA model, as in the choice of the following metaphor for the @*WSJ* headline "*IKEA has big ideas for small spaces*":

Dreams, pleasing gifts that you are, how you comfort me with your cheap appeal.

Inevitably, the system cannot but occasionally reflect the biases of its underlying news corpus. For instance, given this @*WSJ* headline following a mass shooting at an Orlando nightclub, "*RT @Sam Walkers Omar Mateen kept threatening to commit mass murder*", the system finds this to be an apt pairing: Guns, roaring monsters that you are, do not menace me with your evil threat. We consider ways of addressing the bias in the underlying news corpora in our concluding remarks.

Stereotypical associations are central to the bot's aim of tweeting apt metaphors:

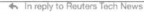

In reply to Reuters Tech News

MetaphorMirror @MetaphorMirror · 56m
RT @Reuters: RT @ReutersTech: Here's what to expect at Apple's WWDC 2016: (Hint: It ... reut.rs/1UO7Vtk

To some visionaries, technology is a detailed specification.

To others, it is a vague dream.

The association between Apple corp and visionaries with a dream may be the stuff of cliché, but it is on shared beliefs that a compelling metaphor is built. Notice how, in seeking to have it both ways, the metaphor portrays two possible sides of the story: the *positive* dream and the *negative* possibility of disappointment. These metaphors are not chosen to tell readers what to think – to be candid, this is beyond the scope *and* the ability of the system – but simply to encourage them to think more.

5   Empirical Evaluation

We view @*MetaphorMirror* as the linguistic and figurative equivalent of a sommelier that responds to news events with an appropriate pairing of metaphor and headline. Just as a good choice of wine can enrich a fine meal, we designed @*MetaphorMirror* to enrich the user's appreciation of the news with a well-chosen metaphor. Sometimes one trusts the sommelier implicitly, other times one sends the wine back in puzzlement or dismay. So to evaluate the capabilities of @*MetaphorMirror* in its capacity as a proposer of topical metaphors in a changing news environment, we use the crowd-sourcing platform *CrowdFlower* to obtain human judgments on the bot's pairing of metaphors to 90 randomly selected news headlines, plucked from the news in early July 2016. We tested the system using vector spaces built from two corpora – the basic news corpus of full stories and headlines (which spans 2000 to 2012) but no news tweets, and the combination of this full-story corpus with a year of news tweets from Twitter. We refer to the first corpus as *fulltext* and the second as *fulltext +tweets*.

In addition to our topic-model approach we evaluated two other vector-based approaches, based on LSA (Landauer and Dumais 1997) and Word2Vec (Mikolov 2013). For the LSA models we again used the *gensim* package of Řehůřek and Sojka (2010) to build 100-dimension compressed vector spaces from each of our two corpora. For the Word2Vec models we used the settings reported in Gatti *et al.* (2015) for their slogan adaptation system – using the average of the embedding of every word in the sentence as the representation of a whole sentence– also using Google News embeddings for our vocabulary (https://code.google.com/archive/p/word2vec). As a baseline we also evaluated wholly random pairings of *@MetaphorMagnet* metaphors to our headlines. It should be noted that this random baseline for metaphor is not the straw man one might expect it to be. Veale (2015) evaluated *@MetaphorMagnet*, by using outputs of another Twitterbot, *@metaphorminute*, as a random baseline. This other bot, from noted Twitterbot creator Darius Kazemi, fills the linguistic template "X is a Y: P and Q" with largely random choices of nouns for X and Y and largely random choices of adjectives for P and Q. When judges on *CrowFlower* were asked to rate the comprehensibility of metaphors from each, Kazemi's bot scored higher than one ought to expect for a random generator, with about 50% of its outputs being rated as moderately to highly comprehensible (compared to 75% for *@MetaphorMagnet*). It seens that framing an idea in the form of a metaphor encourages people to perceive meaning, or the possibility of meaning, where none is actually intended. In the case of our random baseline, we might expect humans who are presented with a metaphor that is grammatically well-formed and semantically coherent to perceive pragmatic resonances with any headline that is paired to it, even if randomly so.

For each pairing of headline and metaphor, and for each condition outlined above, judges were asked to provide ratings for each pairing along three dimensions: *comprehensibility* (of the metaphor and the headline together); *aptness* (of the metaphor to the headline); and *influence* (a self-report of the metaphor's influence on the reader's interpretation and appreciation of the headline). Judges were asked to select values for each dimension from a 5-point (1 to 5) Likert scale. 10 ratings were elicited for each dimension of each pairing under each condition, where the same 90 headlines were paired in each test condition. Table 2 presents the mean values of each dimension under each test condition.

The LDA model derived from a news corpus of *fulltext* stories (to arm the system with stereotypical associations) and a year of recent news tweets (to condition it to recent world events) outperforms the various other settings of the system across all three dimensions. Though Word2Vec shows a slight improvement over both LSA models, the increase in aptness is not very significant. Table 2 provides significance values for the differences of aptness in Table 1, as calculated using a single-sided Welch t-test (only values for significant differences are shown).

Table 1. Mean values (+ std. dev.) of each dimension under each pairing condition

Pairing model	Aptness	Comprehensibility	Influence
LDA (*fulltext + tweets*)	2.95 ± 1.27	3.59 ± 1.05	3.01 ± 1.24
LDA (*fulltext* only)	2.78 ± 1.04	3.54 ± 0.92	2.75 ± 1.03
LSA (*fulltext + tweets*)	2.62 ± 1.10	2.97 ± 1.09	2.44 ± 1.01
LSA (*fulltext* only)	2.40 ± 1.12	2.99 ± 1.15	2.49 ± 1.14
Word2Vec	2.65 ± 0.99	3.38 ± 1.02	2.73 ± 1.00
Random baseline	2.20 ± 1.20	2.54 ± 1.12	2.09 ± 1.24

Table 2. Powers of single-sided Welch t-tests between mean aptness ratings for each test condition. Italic numbers show that the power is less than the threshold $\alpha = 0.05$. Bold numbers show that the power is less than the threshold $\alpha = 0.0001$

	LDA *fulltext only*	Word2Vec *Google news*	LSA *fulltext + tweets*	LSA *fulltext only*	Random *baseline no corpus*
LDA *fulltext + tweets*	*1.8 × 10⁻²*	*3 × 10⁻⁴*	**1.1 × 10⁻⁵**	**4 × 10⁻⁷**	**1×10⁻¹⁵**
LDA *fulltext* only		*4.1 × 10⁻²*	*1.8 × 10⁻²*	**1.6 × 10⁻⁵**	**3×10⁻¹³**
Word2Vec			0.37	*8.0 × 10⁻³*	**3×10⁻¹³**
LSA *fulltext + tweets*				*0.02*	**1 × 10⁻⁷**
LSA *fulltext only*					**1 × 10⁻⁵**

To better understand the distribution of ratings, we placed mean judgments of aptness under all test conditions into four equally-sized bins labeled *Low*, *Average*, *Good* and *Very Good*. Table 3 presents the percentage of headline/metaphor pairings that fall into each bin for human judgments of aptness:

Table 3. Distribution of mean aptness across 4 quality bins for all test conditions

Pairing model	Low	Average	Good	Very good
LDA (*fulltext + tweets*)	1.1%	47.8%	**41.1%**	**10%**
LDA (*fulltext* only)	3.3%	**65.6%**	30%	1.1%
LSA (*fulltext + tweets*)	10%	60%	30%	0%
LSA (*fulltext* only)	17.8%	64.4%	16.7%	1.1%
Word2Vec	10%	57.8%	32.2%	0%
Random baseline	**45.5%**	46.7%	6.7%	1.1%

Again the LDA model, derived from a combination of full text stories and recent news tweets, shows the best distribution of results, suggesting that this serve as our default platform in seeking further increases in aptness. In our concluding remarks we next discuss ways in which LDA can be used in a splintered fashion to address issues of bias in the underlying news corpora on which the model is built.

6 Concluding Thoughts and Future Work

Much research has been conducted on the automated analysis of human personality as expressed through one's lexical choices. Chung and Pennebaker (2008), for example, describe an approach and a resource, named the LIWC (*Linguistic Inquery and Word Count*) for estimating authorly qualities such as anger, depression, anxiety, affability, positivity, arrogance, analyticality, awareness, topicality (or in-the-moment thinking) and social engagement from a person's textual outputs. An online incarnation of this system (at www.analyzewords.com) infers values for these dimensions from the recent tweets of any Twitter account one cares to provide as input. For instance, this tool informs us that @*Oprah* is very upbeat as a Twitter user, while @*realDonaldTrump* is both very upbeat and very angry. Though Twitterbots such as @*MetaphorMagnet* do not pretend to be human – in fact, a key part of their charm for human followers is their combination of overt artificiality *and* meaningfulness to humans – they are nonetheless designed to create and tweet human-quality outputs, and so it is useful to explore what kind of authorly personality they present to the world. The LIWC tool holds no surprises for followers of @*MetaphorMagnet,* however: its personality, based on a sampling of 1,000 words, is deemed to be very angry, very worried, very analytical and very arrogant. While these are interesting qualities for an author to present to readers, the Twitterbot also rates very poorly on the dimension of in-the-moment thinking. So while @*MetaphorMagnet* is capable of generating high-quality metaphors (see e.g. the empirical analysis in Veale 2015) it is also quite incapable of choosing the best time to use them.

The work and the system described in this paper has sought to address this concern about automated metaphor generation in a way that maintains the modular integrity of the generative component. When developers control both the generator and the contextual adapter, as in the system of Gatti *et al.* (2015) which adapts linguistic expressions to recent news content to generate topical slogans, one is free to make the generative component as context-sensitive as the end-application demands. Nonetheless, the ability to generate large portfolios of creative linguistic artifacts in a vacuum, for contextual reuse at a later time, greatly simplies the issue of topical aptness, allowing developers to focus on competence over performance and to plug and play alternate or additional generative components as desired.

@*MetaphorMirror* is an attempt to set automated metaphor generation to a topical metronome. Our initial experimental results are sufficiently encouraging to explore more ambitious ways of using metaphor to influence our understanding of topical events in a biased news environment. In this regard we are excited by the possibilities afforded by parallel vector-space modeling. Though we have here used a monolithic vector space distilled from news harvested from a broad spectrum of news providers, it is practical to build individual vector spaces that marry our stock of pre-generated metaphors to news garnered from providers on different ends of the political spectrum. For instance, it is practicable to build right-leaning and left-leaning vector spaces, and to use these spaces to suggest metaphors for headlines originating from providers of opposing views. In this way, @*MetaphorMirror* can pair news headlines from *CNN,* the *BBC* and the *New York Times* with metaphors suggested by a space of *FOXnews* content, or to pair headlines from *FOXnews* with metaphors suggested by a space of content from *CNN,* the *BBC* and the *New York Times.* As Pollio (1997) argues, we often design our metaphors to appear seamless, so as to paper over the rift between competing points of view. Yet there are times that demand metaphors which alert us to the scale of the rift and to the dangers of ignoring it. These times become more numerous and more demanding as our news media becomes more biased.

References

Attardo, S.: Irony as relevant inappropriateness. J. Pragmat. **32**, 793–826 (2001)

Blei, D.M., Ng, A.Y., Jordan, M.I.: Latent dirichlet allocation. J. Mach. Learn. Res. **3**, 993–1022 (2003)

Brants, T., Franz, A.: Web 1T 5-gram v.1. Linguistic Data Consortium (2006)

Carbonell, J.G.: Metaphor: an inescapable phenomenon in natural language comprehension. Report 2404. Carnegie Mellon Computer Science Department, Pittsburgh (1981)

Chung, C.K., Pennebaker, J.W.: Revealing dimensions of thinking in open-ended self-descriptions: an automated meaning extraction method for natural language. J. Res. Pers. **46**, 96–132 (2008)

Fass, D.: Met*: a method for discriminating metonymy and metaphor by computer. Comput. Linguist. **17**(1), 49–90 (1991)

Gatti, L., Özbal, G., Guerini, M., Stock, O., Strapparava, C.: Slogans are not forever: adapting linguistic expressions to the news. In: Proceedings of IJCAI 2015, the 24th International Conference on Artificial Intelligence, Buenos Aires, Argentina, pp. 2452–2458. AAAI Press (2015)

Gentner, D., Falkenhainer, B., Skorstad, J.: Metaphor: the good, the bad and the ugly. In: Wilks, Y. (ed.) Theoretical Issues in Natural Language Processing. Lawrence Erlbaum Associates, Hillsdale (1989)

Glucksberg, S.: Understanding metaphors. Curr. Dir. Psychol. Sci. **7**, 39–43 (1998)

Harmon, S.: FIGURE8: a novel system for generating and evaluating figurative language. In: Proceedings of the 6th International Conference on Computational Creativity, Park City, Utah, June 2016 (2015)

Hobbs, J.: Metaphor interpretation as selective inferencing. In: Proceedings of the 7th International Joint Conference on Artificial Intelligence, IJCAI 1981, Vancouver, BC, Canada, vol. 1, pp. 85–91 (1981)

Koestler, A.: The Act of Creation. Penguin Books, London (1964)

Lakoff, G., Johnson, M.: Metaphors We Live By. Chicago University Press, Illinois (1980)

Lakoff, G.: The Master Metaphor List. University of California, Berkeley (1994). http://cogsci.berkeley.edu/

Landauer, T.K., Dumais, S.T.: A solution to Plato's problem: the latent semantic analysis theory of acquisition, induction, and representation of knowledge. Psychol. Rev. **104**(2), 211–240 (1997)

Mason, Z.J.: CorMet: a computational, corpus-based conventional metaphor extraction system. Comput. Linguist. **30**(1), 23–44 (2004)

Mikolov, T., Chen, K., Corrado, G., Dean, J.: Efficient estimation of word representations in vector space, January 2013. arXiv:1301.3781 [cs]

Oring, E.: Engaging Humor. University of Illinois Press, Champaign (2003)

Pollio, H.R.: Boundaries in humor and metaphor. In: Mio, J.S., Katz, A.N. (eds.) Metaphor, Implications and Applications, pp. 231–253. Lawrence Erlbaum Associates, Mahwah (1996)

Řehůřek, R., Sojka, P.: Software framework for topic modeling with large corpora. In: Proceedings of the LREC 2010 Workshop on New Challenges for NLP Frameworks, pp. 45–50 (2010)

Reiter, E., Dale, R.: Building Natural Language Generation Systems. Studies in Natural Language Processing. Cambridge University Press, Cambridge (2006)

Shutova, E.: Metaphor identification using verb and noun clustering. In: The Proceedings of the 23rd International Conference on Computational Linguistics, pp. 1001–1010 (2010)

Veale, T., O'Donoghue, D.: Computation and blending. Cogn. Linguist. **11**(3–4), 253–281 (2000)

Veale, T., Hao, Y.: Comprehending and generating apt metaphors: a web-driven, case-based approach to figurative language. In: Proceedings of AAAI 2007, the 22nd AAAI Conference on Artificial Intelligence, Vancouver, Canada (2007)

Veale, T., Li, G.: Creative introspection and knowledge acquisition. In: Proceedings of the 25th AAAI Conference on Artificial Intelligence. AAAI Press, San Francisco (2011)

Veale, T., Li, G.: Creating similarity: lateral thinking for vertical similarity judgments. In: Proceedings of the 51st Annual Meeting of the Association for Computational Linguistics, Sofia, Bulgaria (2013)

Veale, T.: Game of tropes: exploring the placebo effect in computational creativity. In: Proceedings of ICCC-2015, the 6th International Conference on Computational Creativity, Park City, Utah, USA (2015)

Veale, T., Shutova, E., Klebanov, B.B.: Metaphor: a computational perspective. Synth. Lect. Hum. Lang. Technol. **9**(1), 1–160 (2016). Morgan Claypool

Way, E.C.: Knowledge Representation and Metaphor. Studies in Cognitive Systems. Kluwer, Holland (1991)

Wilks, Y.: Making preferences more active. Artif. Intell. **11**, 197–223 (1978)

Author Index